Global
MARKETING
MANAGEMENT

Global
MARKETING
MANAGEMENT

CANADIAN EDITION

Warren J. Keegan
PACE UNIVERSITY

F.H. Rolf Seringhaus
WILFRID LAURIER UNIVERSITY

Prentice Hall Canada Inc., Scarborough, Ontario

Canadian Cataloguing in Publication Data

Keegan, Warren J.
    Global marketing management

Canadian ed.
Includes index.
ISBN 0-13-325804-1

1. Export marketing – Management. 2. International
business enterprises – Management. I. Seringhaus,
F.H. Rolf (Fritz Herman Rolf), 1942–   . II. Title.

HF1416.K44 1996   658.8'48   C95-931321-4

 © 1996 Prentice-Hall Canada Inc., Scarborough, Ontario
A Viacom Company

Prentice-Hall, Inc., Englewood Cliffs, New Jersey
Prentice-Hall International (UK) Limited, London
Prentice-Hall of Australia, Pty. Limited, Sydney
Prentice-Hall Hispanoamericana, S.A., Mexico City
Prentice-Hall of India Private Limited, New Delhi
Prentice-Hall of Japan, Inc., Tokyo
Simon & Schuster Asia Private Limited, Singapore
Editora Prentice-Hall do Brasil, Ltda., Rio de Janeiro

ISBN 0-13-325804-1

Acquisitions Editor: Patrick Ferrier
Developmental Editor: Dawn du Quesnay
Copy Editor: Greg Ioannou
Production Editor: Mary Ann Field
Production Coordinator: Deborah Starks
Permissions/Photo Research: Robyn Craig
Cover Design: Olena Serbyn
Cover Image: Image Bank/Derik Murray
Page Layout: Joan Morrison

Original edition published by Prentice-Hall, Inc.
A Division of Simon & Schuster
Englewood Cliffs, New Jersey
Copyright © 1995, 1989, 1984, 1980, 1974

1 2 3 4 5 RRD 00 99 98 97 96

Printed and bound in U.S.A.

Every reasonable effort has been made to obtain permissions for all articles and data
used in this edition. If errors or omissions have occurred, they will be corrected in future editions provided written notification has been received by the publisher.

Copyright to cases #8 and #12 in this book is held by the University of Western Ontario.

To my Mother, Edla Polson Keegan
and the memory of my Father,
Donald Rayfield Keegan

To Michael and Claire

CONTENTS

Cases 554

Indexes 735

PREFACE

The Canadian Edition of *Global Marketing Management* emerged out of a need to understand the global market place from a Canadian perspective. It puts into practice the principal tenet of the global marketer: benefit from the *similarities* across diverse markets but heed the *differences*. To succeed in the fast-paced, dynamic, complex, interdependent, and competitive global market environment requires the knowledge of concepts, strategies, and the practice of global marketing management. What do we mean by a Canadian perspective of global marketing?

The Canadian student of international or global marketing has too long had to resort to texts reflecting the American view of the world. The Canadian situation, however, differs in many critical respects. Four-fifths of our export trade is with the United States. Our companies, by and large, must pursue niche strategies in global markets. The Canadian corporate landscape has a large share of foreign-owned companies. Such subsidiaries then operate within a larger, global strategic framework. Many smaller companies must balance their global marketing activities between the expanse of the neighbouring U.S. market and the diverse and seemingly limitless market opportunities offshore. This text recognizes Canada's unique situation.

Global marketing has become a challenge that cannot be ignored. World economic integration has advanced under the multilateral framework of GATT and in regional agreements like the North American Free Trade Agreement (NAFTA) and the European Union (EU). NAFTA links Canada, the United States, and Mexico in a program of economic integration and the EU links 15 countries in Western Europe. The member countries of both these regional agreements are actively exploring expanding membership to other countries: central and eastern Europe for the EU, and South American for NAFTA. Various efforts at economic integration are also accelerating in South East Asia, and within the Latin American region.

This book brings a managerial orientation to the challenge of global marketing. It covers small and large companies alike, and takes an analytical approach when necessary. To provide a realistic context, the text is rich in examples from Canada and abroad. Topical Canadian research findings are included to discuss and show current management practice and behaviour. The eighteen chapters of *Global Marketing Management*, Canadian Edition, are structured into six parts: Part I covers a conceptual overview, Part II covers the global marketing environment, Part III discusses targeting global markets, Part IV looks at formulating global marketing strategy, Part V the global marketing mix, and Part VI managing and leading the global marketing effort.

FEATURES

Global Marketing Management, Canadian Edition, includes many outstanding features:

- ▶ global marketing planning is covered early to provide a planning framework for the global marketing management task
- ▶ the challenge posed by cultural diversity of global markets and the need for negotiation skills are emphasized
- ▶ assumptions that the U.S. market is the same as the Canadian market are dispelled and key differences are highlighted
- ▶ important issues of international business law as well as the role of the Canadian and U.S. currency are discussed
- ▶ global segmentation issues are emphasized and their relevance to global marketing decisions demonstrated
- ▶ global strategic partnerships—increasingly significant in global marketing strategy—show how small and large companies can compete through cooperation
- ▶ government support is discussed as an important resource particularly for smaller exporters
- ▶ leadership is discussed as an important part in organizing and controlling the global marketing effort
- ▶ appendices provide in-depth information on global advertising, the role of international trade fairs, export agents and organizations, and leadership in action

▼ Cases

Grouped together at the end of the book for pedagogical flexibility, the cases included in *Global Marketing Management*, Canadian Edition, provide comprehensive and fascinating coverage of global marketing issues. They deal with industrial and consumer goods, small and large companies, and Canadian and international companies, and represent geographic areas such as North America, Latin America, Europe, and Asia and the Pacific Rim.

▼ Supplementary Materials

- ▶ Instructor's Manual with Test Item File
- ▶ *Contemporary Views* (a classroom edition of *The Financial Post* customized for marketing students)

▼ Acknowledgements

Many individuals and organizations freely gave information, advice and the benefit of their experience during the preparation of this book, for which we are very grateful. While those many contributors are acknowledged throughout the text, we wish to thank particularly The Business Council on National Issues, Bank of Canada, Bates Worldwide, Inc., Elsevier Science Ltd., Industry Canada, MacMillan Press Ltd., Political Risk Services Inc., Prospectus Inc., The Laurier Institute, and The University of Western Ontario.

We thank Philip W. Raworth, University of Alberta, for his contribution of the chapter on the Legal and Regulatory Environment, which adds an often neglected but vital dimension to the topic of global marketing. We also wish to express our thanks to Evelyn Bartin, Pierre Casse, Joseph D'Cruz, Joanna Kinsey, George Nowlan, Philip J. Rosson, Alan Rugman, Jacques Schnabel. We would like to thank the following reviewers of this edition: Preet Aulakh, Memorial University of Newfoundland; Joseph de Leon Suarez, Humber College of Applied Arts and Technology; David Litvack, University of Ottawa; and Robert McElhinney, Sheridan College.

For the Canadian cases we are grateful to Paul W. Beamish, Mary Brooks, John R.G. Jenkins, Gayle Duncan, C.B. Johnston, Gordon H. McDougall, Marvin Ryder, Adrian Ryans, Brock Smith, Shari Ann Wortel.

At Prentice Hall we thank Patrick Ferrier, Dawn du Quesnay, and Mary Ann Field for their effective role in bringing this first Canadian edition to the market. Last, but not least, we thank Elsie Grogan for her wordprocessing assistance.

F.H. Rolf Seringhaus
1996

xvi

ONE

Introduction to Global Marketing

Introduction

We live in a global marketplace. As you read this book, you may be sitting in a chair imported from Brazil at a desk imported from Denmark under a lamp from Italy. On your desk you might have a PC clone from Taiwan or perhaps a Macintosh designed in the United States and made in Ireland. Your shoes might have come from Bulgaria, and the coffee you are sipping could be from Latin America or from Africa. In the background you have on your favorite soft-rock radio station playing a Grateful Dead record pressed on a Philips of the Netherlands compact disc. Welcome to the global marketplace: Yesterday's marketing fantasy has become today's reality.

The world has undergone a complete revolution economically from the time only 150 years ago when students sitting at their desks would, perhaps with the exception of the books they were reading, not have any article in their possession that was manufactured more than 100 kilometres from where they lived.

This book is about **global marketing,** which we define as:

the process of focusing the resources (people, money, and physical assets) and objectives of an organization on global market opportunities and threats.

The post-World War II decades have been a period of unparalleled expansion of national enterprises into global markets. Two decades ago, the term *global marketing* did not even exist. Today, global marketing is essential not only for the realization of the full success potential of a business, but even more critically, for the survival of a business. A company that fails to go global is in danger of losing its domestic business to competitors with lower costs, greater experience, better products, and, in a nutshell, more value for the customer.

This book concentrates on the major dimensions of global marketing: the environment of global marketing, global market segmentation and global target marketing, formulating global marketing strategy and plans, the global marketing mix, and managing and leading the global marketing effort. It is assumed that the reader is familiar with marketing as a discipline and with marketing practice in at least one national market environment.

One way to appreciate the market potential for Canadian companies is to recognize that 97 percent of the total world market for all products and services exists outside of the Canadian market. Apart from the limited size of the Canadian home market, the enormity of foreign market opportunities makes it essential for Canadian companies to adopt a global view. The myth that going global is the domain of large companies is dispelled by many small and medium-sized Canadian companies who compete successfully in a global marketplace.

The internationalization of markets is a global phenomenon and makes opportunities abroad a powerful attraction. Increasingly, the motivation for going global is, for many companies, to ensure their survival. In many industries it is clear that the companies that will survive and prosper in this intensely competitive environment are those that embrace a global orientation. Companies that do not face up to the challenges and opportunities of going global will be absorbed by more dynamic enterprises if they are lucky, or will simply disappear in the wake of their more dynamic competitors.

MARKETING: A UNIVERSAL DISCIPLINE

The foundation for a successful global marketing program is a sound understanding of the marketing discipline. Marketing is the process of focusing the resources and objectives of an organization on environmental opportunities and needs. The first and most fundamental fact about marketing is that it is a universal discipline. Marketing is a set of concepts, tools, theories, practices and procedures, and experience. Together these elements constitute a teachable and learnable body of knowledge. Although marketing is universal, marketing practice, of course, varies from country to country. Each person is unique, and each country is unique. This reality of differences means that we cannot always directly apply experience from one country to another. If the customers, competitors, channels of distribution, and available media are different, it may be necessary to change our marketing plan.

▼ The Marketing Concept

During the past three decades the concept of marketing has changed dramatically. The marketing concept has evolved from the original concept, which focused marketing on the product and on making a "better" product where "better" was based on internal standards and values. The objective was profit, and the means to achieving the objective was selling, or persuading the potential customer to exchange his or her money for the company's product. (See Table 1–1.)

The New Concept of Marketing and the Four Ps

The "new" concept of marketing, which appeared about 1960, shifted the focus of marketing from the product to the customer. The objective was still profit, but the means of achieving the objective expanded to include the entire *marketing mix*, or the "four Ps" as they became known: product, price, promotion, and place (channels of distribution).

TABLE 1–1 Marketing Is Everything

	Concept		
	Old	*New*	*Strategic*
Era	Pre–1960	1960–1990	1990–
Focus	Product	Customer	Way of Doing Business
Means	Telling and Selling	Integrated Marketing Mix	Knowledge and Experience
End	Profit	Value	Mutually Beneficial Relationship
Marketing Is . . .	Selling	A Function	Everything

Warren Keegan Associates, Inc., 1994.

The Strategic Concept of Marketing

By 1990 it was clear that the "new" concept of marketing was outdated and that the times demanded a strategic concept. The strategic concept of marketing, a major evolution in the history of marketing thought, shifted the focus of marketing from the customer or the product to the customer in the context of the broader external environment. Knowing everything there is to know about the customer is not enough. To succeed, marketers must know the customer in a context including the competition, government policy and regulation, and the broader economic, social, and political macro forces that shape the evolution of markets.[1] In global marketing this may mean working closely with home-country government trade negotiators and other officials and industry competitors to gain access to a target-country market.

Another revolutionary change in the shift to the strategic concept of marketing is in the marketing objective—from profit to stakeholder benefits. Stakeholders are individuals or groups who have an interest in the activity of a company.[2] They include the employees and management, customers, society, and government, to mention only the most prominent. There is a growing recognition that profits are a reward for performance (defined as satisfying customers in a socially responsible or acceptable way). To compete in today's market, it is necessary to have an employee team committed to continuing innovation and to producing quality products. In other words, marketing must focus on the customer in context and deliver value by creating stakeholder benefits for both customers and employees.

---

[1] For an excellent outline of the importance of political forces in shaping marketing strategy and action, see Philip Kotler, "Megamarketing." *Harvard Business Review* (March–April 1986, pp. 117-124.

[2] Any individual or group with an interest in the activities of a corporation is known as a stakeholder, as opposed to a shareholder who has an equity interest in the corporation and a claim on dividends paid by the corporation. A shareholder is a stakeholder, as are employees, managers, lenders, customers, residents of communities, cities, provinces and countries impacted by the companies' operations, and so on.

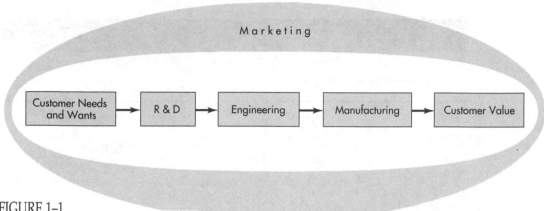

FIGURE 1-1
Value Chain Boundaryless Marketing

Profitability is not forgotten in the strategic concept. Indeed, it is a critical means to the end of creating stakeholder benefits. The means of the strategic marketing concept is strategic management, which integrates marketing with the other management functions. One of the tasks of strategic management is to make a profit, which can be a source of funds for investing in the business and for rewarding shareholders and management. Thus, profit is still a critical objective and measure of marketing success, but it is not an end in itself. The aim of marketing is to create value for stakeholders, and the key stakeholder is the customer. If your customer can get greater value from your competitor because your competitor is willing to accept a lower level of profit reward for investors and management, the customer will choose your competitor, and you will be out of business. The spectacular inroads of the "clones" into IBM's PC market illustrate that even the largest and most powerful companies can be challenged by competitors who are more efficient or who are willing to accept lower profit returns.

Finally, the strategic concept of marketing has shifted the focus of marketing from a microeconomic maximization paradigm to a focus of managing strategic partnerships and positioning the firm between vendors and customers in the value chain with the aim and purpose of creating value for customers.[3] This expanded concept of marketing, which is also referred to as boundaryless marketing, is shown in Figure 1–1.

Marketing, in addition to being a concept and a philosophy, is a set of activities and a business process. The marketing activities are called the four Ps: product, price, place (distribution), and promotion (or communications).[4] These four Ps can be expanded to five Ps by adding probe (research). The marketing management process is the task of focusing the resources and objectives of the organization upon opportunities in the environment. Three basic principles underlie marketing.

---

[3] Frederick E. Webster, Jr., "The Changing Role of Marketing in the Corporation," *Journal of Marketing* (October, 1992), pp. 1–17.

[4] Walter van Waterschoot and Christophe Van de Bulte. "The 4P Classification of the Marketing Mix Revisited," *Journal of Marketing* (October 1992, pp. 83–93 is an excellent review of the strengths and limitations of the 4P classification.

$$V = \frac{B}{P}$$

Where:

V = Value
B = Perceived Benefits
P = Price

Value is enhanced by increasing the numerator or reducing the denominator.

FIGURE 1–2
The Value Equation

▼ The Three Principles of Marketing

The essence of marketing can be summarized in three great principles. The first identifies the purpose and task of marketing, the second the competitive reality of marketing, and the third the principal means for achieving the first two.

Customer Value and the Value Equation

The essence of marketing is creating customer value that is greater than the value created by competitors. The value equation, shown in Figure 1–2, is a guide to this task. As suggested in the equation, value for the customer can be increased by expanding or improving product and or service benefits, by reducing the price, or by a combination of these elements. Companies that use price as a competitive weapon must have a strategic cost advantage in order to create a sustainable competitive advantage. This might come from cheap labor or access to cheap raw materials, or it might come from manufacturing scale or efficiency or more efficient management. Knowledge of the customer combined with innovation and creativity can lead to product improvements and service that matter to customers. If the benefits are strong enough and valued enough by customers, a company does not need to be the low-price competitor in order to win customers.

Competitive or Differential Advantage

The second great principle of marketing is competitive advantage. A competitive advantage is a total offer, vis-à-vis relevant competition, that is more attractive to customers. The advantage could exist in any element of the company's offer: the product, the price, the advertising and point-of-sale promotion, and the distribution of the product. The total offer must be more attractive than that of the competition in order to create a competitive advantage. A company might have a product that is equivalent in quality to that of the competition but no better. If it offers this product at a significantly lower price, and if it can get customers to believe that the quality of the company's product is equal to that of the competition, the price advantage will give the company a competitive advantage. The competitive advantage must exist relative to relevant competitors. If the company is in a local industry, these competitors will be local. In a national industry, they will be national, and in a global industry, they will be global.

Focus

The third marketing principle is focus, or the concentration of attention. Focus is required to succeed in the task of creating customer value at a competitive advantage. All great enterprises, large and small, are successful because they have understood and applied this great principle. IBM succeeded because it was more clearly focused on customer needs and wants than any other company in the emerging data processing industry. One of the reasons that IBM found itself in crisis in the early 1990s was because its competitors had become much more clearly focused on customer needs and wants. Dell and Compaq were giving customers computing power and low prices: IBM was offering the same computing power with higher prices. In earlier days, the IBM name was worth the difference: today, in the maturing computer market, the value of the IBM name is simply not worth much as compared to a name like Compaq or Dell.

A clear focus on customer needs and wants and on the competitive offer is needed to mobilize the effort needed to maintain a differential advantage. This can be accomplished only by focusing or concentrating resources and efforts on customer needs and wants and on how to deliver a product that will meet those needs and wants.

FROM DOMESTIC TO GLOBAL/TRANSNATIONAL MARKETING

In Chapter 2, we present a dynamic typology of the stages of the global/transnational corporation's development. This section outlines the differences between domestic, international, multinational, global, and transnational marketing.

▼ Domestic Marketing

Marketing that is targeted exclusively on the home-country market is called domestic marketing. A company engaged in domestic marketing may be doing this consciously as a strategic choice or it may be unconsciously focusing on the domestic market in order to avoid the challenge of learning how to market outside the home country. A few decades ago, most companies, especially those in countries with large home markets, could be quite successful practicing domestic marketing. Today, there are fewer and fewer industries where a company can prosper, let alone survive, practicing domestic marketing. This book assumes that the reader is familiar with the basic marketing discipline that is required for the successful practice of domestic marketing.

▼ Export Marketing

Export marketing is the first stage of addressing market opportunities outside the home country. The export marketer targets markets outside the home country and relies upon home-country production to supply product for these markets. The focus in this stage is upon leveraging home-country products and experience. A sophisticated export marketer will study target markets and adapt products to meet the specific needs of customers in each country.

▼ International Marketing

The international marketer goes beyond the export marketer and becomes more involved in the marketing environment in the countries in which it is doing business. For example, the international marketer is prepared to source product outside the home country in order to gain greater competitive advantage. The international marketer is less likely to rely upon intermediaries and is more likely to establish direct representation to coordinate the marketing effort in target markets. With its own company subsidiary in a country, the international marketer creates an internal organization that is focused on leveraging a company's products and competencies in the country. The international marketing organization would use the communications campaign developed for the home country.

▼ Multinational Marketing

The international marketing organization begins by focusing on leveraging a company's experience and products. As it focuses upon this task, it becomes aware of the differences and unique circumstances in the country, and establishes a new role for itself: adapting the company's marketing to the unique needs and wants of customers in the country. The multinational marketing organization would develop a unique communications program for its market.

▼ Global/Transnational Marketing

Global/transnational marketing focuses upon leveraging a company's assets, experience, and products globally and upon adapting to what is truly unique and different in each country. It recognizes cultural universals and unique market differences. Instead of an international company approach of applying the communications campaign developed for the home country, or a multinational approach of creating a unique campaign in each country, the global/ transnational company would distinguish between what was global and universal and what was country specific and unique. For example, it might conclude based upon in-depth research that it should develop a global creative platform for a product where sampling was a key success factor in gaining market penetration. The task of each country marketing team in this case would be to develop a unique national sampling plan. The country marketing team would draw upon global creative and combine that with national sampling.

Global marketing does not mean entering every country in the world, nor that a company must be of a certain size. Rather, the decision to enter markets outside the home country depends upon a company's resources appropriate to the objective, and the nature of opportunities and threats. IBM, now a C$75 billion company, began its international expansion more than fifty years ago and operates in over 100 countries. By contrast, Eicon Technology, a C$78 million company founded only ten years ago, has expanded into more than seventy countries through subsidiaries, alliances, and partnerships and occupies a leadership position in its field.

As companies become involved in marketing in two or more countries, the question arises, "Are there differences between domestic and global marketing?"

There are important differences, and at the same time there are basic similarities. First, as we have already pointed out, the basic concepts, activities, and processes of marketing apply as fully to global as they do to domestic marketing. When a company expands its operation to a foreign market, the basic requirements for market success are not relaxed. This seemingly obvious point is overlooked with surprising frequency. Companies enter foreign markets without analyzing both customers and competition, although they would not think of doing this at home. They fail to integrate their total marketing program, although careful attention to integration and fit is standard operating procedure in their home market. They embark upon marketing programs without a clear idea of their ultimate objective or any appraisal of the obstacles that lie in the path of sales and profits.

The differences between domestic and global marketing derive entirely from the differences in national environments within which global marketing is conducted and the differences in the organization and programs of a company operating simultaneously in different national markets. Global marketing can be divided into two basic activities, foreign and international-multinational-global, which are described in the following section.

THE THEORY OF THE CASE

There are three basic theories that the student and practitioner of global marketing should understand. The oldest and most basic is the theory of comparative advantage, which goes back to Adam Smith's *The Wealth of Nations* and the work of David Ricardo. A more recent and equally important theory is the trade or product trade cycle theory discovered by Dr. Raymond Vernon of the Harvard Business School. A third, even more recent theory, which identifies business orientations, was discovered by Dr. Howard Perlmutter of the Wharton School of the University of Pennsylvania.

▼ The Theory of Comparative Advantage

The theory of comparative advantage is a demonstration (under assumptions) that a country can gain from trade *even* if it has an absolute disadvantage in the production of all goods, or, that it can gain from trade *even* if it has an absolute

TABLE 1–2   Comparative Advantage—An Example

1. Production Possibilities of Canada and Greece (1,000 production units)

			BEFORE SPECIALIZATION AND TRADE (IN STANDARD UNITS)			
			CANADA		GREECE	
			Wheat	Apples	Wheat	Apples
Use of Production Units or Production Possibilities						
A	1,000 in wheat,	0 in apples	100	0	20	0
B	750 "	250 in apples	75	8	15	15
C	500 "	500 in apples	50	15	10	30
D	250 "	750 in apples	25	22	5	45
E	0 "	1,000 in apples	0	30	0	60

2. Production and Consumption After Total Specialization and Trade

	CANADA			GREECE		
	Produces	Trades: Imports (+) Exports (−)	Consumes	Produces	Trades: Imports (+) Exports (−)	Consumes
Wheat	100	−30	70	0	+30	30
Apples	0	+40	40	60	−40	20
Trading price	40:30 = 1.3 units apples = 1 unit wheat					
	30:40 = .75 units wheat = 1 unit apples					

advantage in the production of all goods. In other words, if Canada is better (more efficient) in the production of everything than Tanzania, Canada can still gain from specialization and trade. If Tanzania is inferior (less efficient) in the production of everything than Canada, Tanzania can still gain from specialization and trade. How can this be so?

The simplest demonstration of the theory of comparative advantage is a two-country/two-product model, such as the one shown in Table 1-2. In this example, the two countries are Canada and Greece. The two products are wheat and apples, which both produce. There is no money, the products are undifferentiated, and they are produced with production units that are a mixture of land, labor, and capital.

If you take any production mix between the two limits (A) and (E), you will find that the total combined production is less at these production mixes than when there is a concentration of production units on the product in which the country has the greatest comparative advantage. For Canada, this is wheat and for Greece, apples. How do you know that the Canadian comparative advantage is greatest in wheat? To determine the greatest comparative advantage, you must compare the production ratios for the two products. For wheat, Canada has an advantage of 5.0 (100/20). For apples, Greece has an advantage of 2.0 (60/30). In other words, you simply compare what each country can produce under total specialization.

Table 1–2 concludes with a set of questions. Make sure that you are comfortable with the answers. The fourth question raises the matter of price. Since there is no money, you must determine prices on the basis of barter. How much is an apple worth in wheat, and how much is wheat worth in apples?

Does this still seem a little hard to comprehend? A good illustration of comparative advantage is the classic example of the famous impresario, Billy Rose, who was also the world's fastest typist. He faced a decision: "Should I do my own typing or should I pursue a career as a typist?" The answer to both questions was no because even though he had an absolute advantage as a typist over all other typists in the world, his *comparative* advantage was as an impresario. If the objective is to maximize material well-being, both individuals and countries are better off specializing in their area of *comparative* advantage and then trading and exchanging with others in the marketplace.

QUESTIONS

1. Who has the greater advantage in the production of wheat? _____ of apples? _____
2. What is the wheat advantage? _____
3. What is the apple advantage? _____
4. What is the price of wheat in Canada? _____ of apples? _____
5. What is the price of wheat in Greece? _____ of apples? _____
6. What is the maximum price Canada will pay for wheat? _____ for apples? _____
7. What is the maximum price Greece will pay for wheat? _____ for apples? _____
8. Can both countries gain from trade? Why? How?

Limitations of the Theory of Comparative Advantage

Any literate international marketer should be familiar with both the existence and the demonstration of the theory of comparative advantage. However, the theory itself does not relate to the situation faced in the firm. The problem with the theory of international trade, as is so often the case with economic theories, is that reality is far more complex than the limiting assumptions upon which the theory is based. A firm's costs are based not only on factor costs, such as wages and materials, but also on the volume of production. It has been conclusively demonstrated in hundreds of observations of actual cost behavior that there is a relationship between cost and volume that results in a typical decline in costs of 20 to 30 percent with each doubling of accumulated volume in the production of manufactured items.

This empirical observation, which was first suggested by the Boston Consulting Group, is now widely known as experience theory. Thus, even though a firm may be paying higher wages and experiencing other higher-factor costs than it would encounter in other parts of the world, if it has a volume advantage over competitors in lower-cost areas, its net cost position may still be lower.

Another limitation of classical trade theory is that it ignores product and program differentiation. A company's ability to compete in national or international markets is only partly determined by its cost position. Of great importance is the actual product and program differentiation and the effectiveness of the company's customer offering in relation to competitive offerings. For example, the extraordinarily robust and appreciating deutsche mark that has contributed to the rising prices of Mercedes automobiles has not resulted in a displacement of Mercedes from the high-priced segment of the world automobile market. Clearly, demand for the Mercedes and other luxury products is so great that customers are prepared to pay a significant price differential to obtain what they perceive as a unique product.

DRIVING AND RESTRAINING FORCES

The remarkable growth of the global economy over the past 50 years has occurred because the balance of driving and restraining forces has shifted significantly in favor of the driving forces. It is useful to identify these forces to gain an insight into the foundations of the international economy and international markets as they exist today and as they can be expected to develop in the decade ahead.

▼ Driving Forces

These are the forces that are contributing to the growth of international business.

Market Needs

As you will see in Chapter 4, there are cultural universals as well as cultural differences. There is a common element in human nature and in the human psyche that is the underlying basis for the opportunity to create and serve global markets. The word *create* is deliberate. Most global markets do not exist in nature: They must be created by marketing effort. For example, soft drinks, one of the biggest successful global industries, are not needed by anyone and yet today in some countries soft-drink consumption per capita *exceeds* the consumption of water. Marketing has driven this change in behavior.

Advanced global companies have discovered that the same basic segment need can be met with a global approach in selected product markets. Successful global strategies are based on performing a global function or serving a global need. Any industry which addresses these universals is a candidate for globalization. The advertising campaign for a global product may be a global appeal which is adapted to each national culture. For example, De Beers, the South African diamond company, has an advertising campaign to promote the giving of a diamond ring to announce an engagement in Japan, where a diamond is not a traditional engagement custom. The ads are humorous sketches showing a male suitor getting nowhere with flowers, but winning the girl with a diamond. The strategy is logical and sound and has been quite successful because the emotions that surround engagement and marriage are universal and De Beers believes that these universal emotions or needs can be attached to a new want, the diamond.

The advertising campaign for a global product may be a single global execution such as a recent Camel cigarette television commercial showing the macho Camel man repairing a broken bridge across a jungle stream so he can cross in his Jeep and then enjoy a Camel. This campaign ran in every country in the world that permits cigarette ads on TV (except Brazil where they have too many jungles to get excited about the feat), with the only adaptation being the translation of the voice into the target-market language. This type of campaign is possible because there are universal appeals for universal needs. In the case of Camel, the brand is positioned to appeal to a masculine macho image. Marlboro is another enormously successful global brand. Targeted on urban smokers around the world, the brand appeals to the spirit of freedom, independence, and open space symbolized by the cowboy in beautiful, open western settings. The need addressed by Marlboro is universal, and therefore the basic appeal and execution of its advertising and positioning are global.

Technology

Professor Theodore Levitt of the Harvard Business School, perhaps the best-known exponent of global marketing, wrote in his celebrated *Harvard Business Review* article of a "new commercial reality—the emergence of global markets for standardized consumer products on a previously unimagined scale." According to Levitt, "A powerful force drives the world toward a converging commonality, and that force is technology. It has proletarianized communication, transport, and travel. It has made isolated places and impoverished peoples eager for modernity's allurements. Almost everyone, everywhere wants all the things they've heard about, seen, or experienced via the new technologies."[5]

Technology is a universal, uniform, consistent factor across national and cultural boundaries. Any 100 megabyte 486 chip is the same as any other 100–486, no matter where it is made or sold. There are no cultural boundaries limiting the application of technology. Once a technology is developed, it immediately becomes available everywhere in the world. If a company knows how to manage a technology in one country, it has experience that is relevant for the rest of the world. Witness the growth and expansion of international publishing in books, magazines, and newspapers, and now also television and the electronic media.

Cost

Uniformity can drive down research, engineering, design, creative, and production costs across business functions, from engineering and manufacturing to marketing and administration.

The pressure for globalization is intense when new products involve major investments and long periods of development. This is true for pharmaceuticals, where new products typically cost C$50 million to C$100 million to develop over a period of six to ten years. The enormous cost and risk of new-product development must be recovered in the global marketplace, as no single national market is large enough to support investments of this size.

---

[5] Theodore Levitt, "The Globalization of Markets," *Harvard Business Review* (May–June 1983), p.92.

Quality

Global volume generates greater revenue and greater operating margins to support design and manufacturing quality. A global and a local company may each spend 5 percent of sales on research and development, but the global company may have two, three, or even ten times the total revenue of the local. With the same percentage of sales spent on research and development, the global will outspend the local by a factor of two, three, or ten times, as the case may be. The same advantage applies also to manufacturing and marketing. Focusing on one marketing strategy, as opposed to letting each country develop its own, can result in greater marketing effectiveness and efficiency and therefore greater value for the consumer.

Communications and Transportation

The information revolution contributes toward the emergence of global markets. Everybody wants the best, latest, and most modern expression of a product. In regional markets such as Europe, the increasing overlap of advertising across national boundaries and the mobility of consumers have created a pressure on marketers to align product positioning and strategy in adjacent markets. You see this in companies like Nestlé who have a tradition of decentralized country marketing efforts and who operate in markets where local tastes have developed over centuries. Even this combination of local preferences and decentralized marketing is subject to the pressure of overlapping communications and travel. It is increasingly difficult to position the same brand differently in countries where the customers are frequently exposed to brand communications from other markets. When there are overlapping communications, the positioning message and the marketing impact are diluted, and there is a strong pressure to align positioning and brand image.

Leverage

One of the unique advantages of a global company is the opportunity to develop *leverage* or advantages that it has because it operates simultaneously in more than one national market. A global company can develop five types of leverage.

1. *Experience Transfers.* A global company can leverage its experience in any market in the world. It can draw upon strategies, products, advertising appeals, sales management practices, promotional ideas, and so on that have been tested in actual markets and apply them in other comparable markets. There is nothing automatic about this, and it can be misused if the experience transferred is not relevant, but the potential to draw on world experience is a part of the leverage of a global company. An example of a positive experience transfer is RJR-Nabisco's transfer of its successful positioning of Camel in Germany to Spain and then to the world market. An example of negative leverage in experience transfer was Nestlé's application of its European coffee strategy based upon flavor blends to the North American market. The result of this transfer was a decline in market share of 1 percent—a real disaster in the coffee business. Maxwell House, a major competitor, was delighted that Nestlé had applied its European experience to the North American market because the two markets were so different that the experience was not relevant and was misleading.

An example of an experience transfer is a management model. ABB is an example of a company with a management model which it transfers across national boundaries. One of its models is the number of people required in the headquarters of a company. When ABB acquired a Finnish company, it reduced the headquarters staff from 880 to 25 from 1986 to 1989. In Germany, it reduced the headquarters staff from 1,600 to 100 from 1988 to 1989. In Switzerland, headquarters staff was reduced from 4,000 to 200 between 1987 to 1989. When ABB acquired Combustion Engineering (CE) in the United States, in spite of the fact that CE had a justification for every one of the headquarters staff positions, ABB *knew* that the headquarters staff of 800 could be reduced to 25. This is an example of system knowledge transfer.

2. *Systems Transfers.* A global company can refine its planning, analysis, research control, and other systems and apply the refinements worldwide. The leveraging of systems improvements also makes it possible for company staff to communicate with each other.

3. *Scale Economies.* In manufacturing, the global company can take advantage of its greater volume to obtain the traditional single-plant scale advantages and it can also combine into finished products components manufactured in scale efficient plants in different countries.

Just as a national company can achieve economies in staffing by eliminating duplicate staff after an acquisition, a global company can achieve the same economies on a global scale by centralizing functional activities. The larger scale of the global company also creates opportunities to increase the level of competence and quality of corporate staff and expand its role.

4. *Resource Utilization.* A major strength of the global company is its ability to scan the entire world to identify people, money, and materials (or, as economists would put it, land, labor, and capital) that will enable it to compete most effectively in world markets. For a global company, it is no disaster if the value of the "home" currency rises dramatically because for this company there really is no such thing as a home currency. The world is full of currencies, and a global company seeks financial resources on the best available terms and uses them where there is the greatest opportunity to serve a need at a profit.

5. *Global Strategy.* The global company's greatest single advantage is its global strategy. A global strategy is based on scanning the world business environment to identify opportunities, threats, trends, and resources. The global company searches the world for markets that will provide an opportunity to apply its skills and resources to create value for customers that is greater than the value created by its competitors. The global strategy is a design to create a winning offering on a global scale. This takes great discipline, great creativity, and constant effort, but the reward is not just success—it's survival.

▼ Restraining Forces

Market Differences

In every product category, differences are still great enough across national and cultural boundaries to require adaptation of at least some elements of the marketing mix (product, price, advertising and promotion, and channels of distribution). Companies that have ignored these differences and who have tried to implement a global brand strategy without taking differences into account have met with disaster. Global marketing does not work without a strong local team who can adapt the product to local conditions. The list of failures ranges from Christianity to writing instruments. Five centuries of Christian missionary effort in Japan has led to almost no success. The reason is the fact that foreign products do not succeed in Japan unless they are adapted, and Christianity has been offered in an undiluted, unadapted form. Parker Pen recently attempted to implement a top-down global marketing strategy, which ignored local market inputs. The result was a total failure and a sale of the company to the managers of the former U.K. subsidiary.

History

Even in cases where the product itself may be a good candidate for globalization, a brand's history may require a distinct and different marketing strategy and positioning in each country. This is true even for high-potential products such as the image-driven brands. If a brand has an established identity in national markets, it may not be possible to achieve a single global position and strategy.

Management Myopia

In many cases, products and categories are candidates for globalization, but management does not seize the opportunity. A good example of management myopia is any company that does not maintain leadership in creating customer value in an expanding geographical territory. A company that looks backward will not expand geographically.

Organizational Culture

In companies where subsidiary management knows it all, there is no room for vision from the top. In companies where headquarters management knows it all, there is no room for local initiative and in-depth knowledge of local needs and conditions. The successful global companies are marketers who have learned how to integrate global vision and perspective with local market initiative and input. The most striking theme of my interviews with executives of the most advanced global marketing companies was the respect for local initiative and input by headquarters executives and the corresponding respect for headquarters vision by local executives.

National Controls/Barriers to Entry

Every country protects local enterprise and interests by maintaining control over market access and entry. This control ranges from the low-tech tobacco monopoly control of access to tobacco markets to the high-tech national government control of broadcast, equipment, and data transmission markets. Today, tariff barriers have been largely removed in the high-income countries. The significant barriers are the so-called nontariff barriers that make it difficult for foreign companies to gain access to a domestic market. The worldwide movement toward deregulation and privatization, by breaking the link between government and enterprise, is an initiative that will lead to a significant opening up of formerly closed markets. When the telephone company is a state monopoly, it is much easier to require or encourage it to source only from national companies. An independent, private company will be more inclined to look for the best offer, regardless of the nationality of the supplier.

UNDERLYING FORCES
OF INTERNATIONAL BUSINESS

Behind the remarkable growth of the international economy in the post-World War II decades are six basic factors that were not present before the war. It is useful to identify these underlying forces to gain further insight into the foundations of the global economy as it exists today.

▼ Orientations of Management

An orientation is an assumption or belief, often unconscious, about the nature of the world. Dr. Howard Perlmutter of the University of Pennsylvania first observed that there were three basic orientations guiding the work of international executives: ethnocentric, polycentric, and geocentric.[6] This was later expanded to include a regional orientation and became an EPRG schema (ethnocentrism, polycentrism, regiocentrism, geocentrism). This typology, summarized in Figure 1–3, is the basis for the stages of corporate development framework outlined in Chapter 2.

The ethnocentric orientation is an assumption or belief that the home country is superior. Someone with this orientation sees the similarities in markets, and believes that the products and practices that succeed in the home country are superior and, therefore, should be used everywhere. In the ethnocentric company, overseas operations are viewed as being secondary to domestic and primarily as a means of disposing of surplus domestic production. Plans for overseas markets are developed in the home office utilizing policies and procedures identical to those employed at home. There is no systematic marketing research conducted overseas, there are no major modifications to products, and there is no real attention to consumer needs in foreign markets.

The polycentric orientation is the opposite: This is the unconscious belief that each host country is unique and different and that the way to succeed in each country is to adapt to each country's unique differences. In the polycentric stage, subsidiaries are established in overseas markets. Each subsidiary operates independently of the others and establishes its own marketing objectives and plans.

---

[6] Howard Perlmutter, "The Tortuous Evolution of Multinational Corporations," *Columbia Journal of World Business* (January–February 1969).

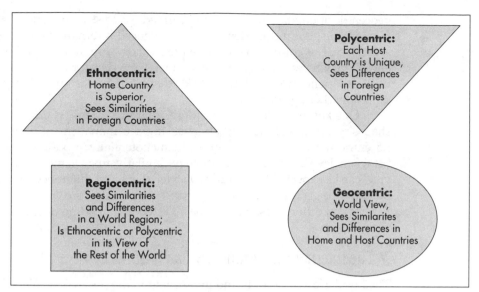

FIGURE 1–3
Orientation of Management and Companies

Marketing is organized on a country-by-country basis, with each country having its own unique marketing policy.

In the regiocentric and geocentric phases, the company views the region or entire world as a market and seeks to develop integrated regional or world market strategies. The geocentric orientation is a synthesis of the ethnocentric and the polycentric orientation. This is the so-called world view that sees similarities and differences in markets and countries, and seeks to create a global strategy that is fully responsive to local needs and wants. The regiocentric or regional orientation is a geocentric orientation that is limited to a region; that is, management will have a world view toward its region, but will regard the rest of the world with either an ethnocentric or a polycentric orientation, or a combination of the two. The ethnocentric company is centralized in its marketing management, the polycentric company is decentralized, and the regiocentric and geocentric companies are integrated.

A crucial difference between the orientations is in the underlying assumption for each orientation. The ethnocentric orientation is based on a belief in home-country superiority. This leads to an extension of home country products, policies, and programs. The underlying assumption of the polycentric approach is that there are so many differences in cultural, economic, and market conditions in each of the countries of the world that it is impossible to attempt to introduce any product, policy, or program from outside or to integrate any country's program in a regional or world context.

The regiocentric and geocentric assumptions hold that it is possible to identify both similarities and differences and to formulate an integrated regional or world marketing strategy on the basis of actual as opposed to imagined similarities and differences. While there can be no question that the geocentric orientation most accurately captures market reality, it does not follow that the geocentric orientation requires an integrated world structure and strategy. To implement the geocentric orientation, experienced international management and a great deal of commitment are required. For companies with limited experience, it may be wiser to adopt a centralized or a decentralized strategy and wait until experience accumulates before attempting to design and implement integrated marketing programs.

One key point to keep in mind is that management orientation not only shapes perception of the world but also impacts management decisions. The ethnocentric manager is likely to ignore many potentially important aspects of a market when devising a marketing strategy. Similarly, management with a polycentric view can be expected to carefully consider all market differences in their decision-making. The geocentric manager pursues a balanced approach, assessing both similarities and differences, that will be reflected in marketing decisions.

▼ The International Monetary Framework

The rapid growth of trade and investment in the post-World War II era has created an increasing need for international liquidity (i.e., money or a means of payment) to facilitate the exchange of goods and services between nations. Until 1969 the world economy relied upon fixed exchange rates and the dollar exchange gold standard with the value of one ounce of gold equal to US$35. Gold and foreign exchange were the basis of international liquidity. Since 1969 exchange rates have been allowed to fluctuate and international liquidity available to nations has been supplemented by the agreement of International Monetary Fund members to accept the SDRs (special drawing rights) in settling reserve transactions. For the first time an international reserve asset is available. The inherent limitations on liquidity expansion through the use of gold and foreign exchange have been overcome. The essential fact concerning the international monetary framework is that for over three decades it has functioned adequately. This evolving structure has every prospect of continuing to function adequately, thus making it possible for companies to finance trade and investment between nations, and to continue their global marketing efforts.

▼ The World Trading System

The post-World War II world trading system was constructed out of a common desire to avoid a return to the restrictive and discriminatory trading practices of the 1920s and the 1930s. There was a commitment to the creation of a liberal world in which there would be a free flow of goods and services between countries. The system that evolved out of this commitment included the General Agreement on Tariffs and Trade (GATT), which provided an institutional framework and a set of four rules and principles for efforts to liberalize trade. The most favored nation (MFN) principle, whereby each country agrees to extend to all countries the most favorable terms that it negotiates with any country is an example of a GATT rule that contributed to the reduction of high tariff levels. Major reductions of tariff levels were accomplished by multilateral negotiations such as the Kennedy Round of the 1960s and the Tokyo Round of the 1970s.

The Tokyo Round's objective was to bring industrial country tariff levels down to roughly 4 percent by 1987. The Uruguay Round of negotiations was concluded at the end of 1993, and further reduced the tariff barriers and addressed the more difficult and contentious problem of non-tariff barriers and as well as the trade in services. On January 1, 1995 the World Trade Organization (WTO) replaced GATT and will conduct future trade negotiations.

One of the complications of the world trading system is that governments tend to encourage and support exporters with subsidies and assistance of various kinds. (One of the most common subsidies is export credit at below-market rates of interest.) This leads to efforts by target market countries to protect their own industry from "unfair" competition.

The major challenge to the trading system in the 1990s is not tariff levels but rather the so-called *nontariff barriers* (NTBs). These include safeguard actions to protect industries, exclusion orders, standards (requiring, for example, that products admitted to the country meet exact specifications that either cannot be met in the case of some natural products or that are very expensive to meet in the case of manufactured products), exclusionary distribution, and administrative delays. (When the French decided that Japanese imports of automobiles were excessive, they simply "applied the rules" and gave each automobile a complete inspection before admitting it to France. Needless to say, this inspection took time, and an enormous backlog of Japanese automobiles accumulated in French ports.) Another nontariff barrier to trade is voluntary restraint or the agreement by the exporting country to limit its exports of product to provide relief to the domestic industry in that country.

Regional Trade Agreements

A regional free-trade agreement (RFTA) is an agreement within a region to expand trade. On the face of it, this would appear to be a good thing. If free trade is a good thing, more of it, even if confined to a single region, should also be a good thing. Instead of using a large organization like the WTO, why not let like-minded groups of countries get together to eliminate trade barriers and in this way spread the good of free trade across the globe? This argument would certainly hold if governments relied upon tariffs to keep out goods and services and if they agreed to keep duties to goods from outside the free-trade area no higher than they were before the RFTA was formed. The problem with this argument is that governments no longer rely upon tariffs to protect industry. Today antidumping rules, *voluntary export restraints* (VERs), and a host of other nontariff barriers are the first line of defense of domestic industry. When RFTA's are formed, this defense can be applied within the RFTA. An expansion of trade between RFTA members may in fact mask a trade diversion between the RFTA and the rest of the world.

In fact, the case for RFTAs is weaker than it looks. A free-trade area will make the world better off in the short term if the amount of trade that it creates exceeds that which it diverts. An RFTA creates trade when low tariffs and other barriers encourage members to buy from each other what they previously made for themselves. This is good. But an RFTA can also divert trade if one member buys from the other what it previously bought from a supplier outside the RFTA.

To prevent RFTAs from diverting trade, you need an outside agency to police new forms of protection—in short, you need the WTO. In other words, FTAs are not an alternative and a strong WTO is needed if they are to succeed.

The second argument in favor of RFTAs is that they will eventually grow and merge. According to Jagdish Bhagwati, one of the world's leading trade experts, it is all too likely that RFTAs will advance trade frontiers more slowly than the WTO because governments will find it hard to resist the protectionist lobbies who will argue that "our market is already big enough." For example, European car makers are using the European Union (EU) to gain protection from Japanese imports. On balance, it is clear that there is no substitute for the WTO as a framework for promoting free trade.[7]

▼ Global Peace

Since 1945 the world has remained free of the major world conflicts that marked the first half of the century. Although postwar geopolitics has been characterized by an abundance of regional and low-intensity conflict, battles continue to be localized and limited to conventional weapons. Although these conditions are not, to be certain, entirely peaceful, they provide a relatively stable foundation for the healthy and rapid growth of the international economy. We live in a paradoxical world where there is bitter regional conflict in many of the middle-income and lower-income countries and regions, and peace in the high-income countries.

Not only is the conflict localized, but it also takes place entirely in the countries outside the advanced country markets, which account for over 80 percent of world market potential. World Wars I and II were high-income country conflicts. Today, war and conflict in the world is within and between countries in the low-income and middle-income categories.

▼ Domestic Economic Growth

Thus, there are two reasons why economic growth has been an underlying force in the expansion of the international economy. First, growth has created market opportunities. The existence of market opportunities has been the major incentive for the international expansion of enterprise. Of course, international enterprise itself contributed to the process of development and the creation of market opportunities in host countries. Second, economic growth has reduced the resistance that might otherwise have developed in response to the entry of foreign firms into domestic economies.

When a country is growing rapidly, receptiveness is encouraged because a growing country means growing markets, therefore, expanding opportunities. Under this condition it is possible for an outside or international company to enter a domestic economy and to establish itself without taking business away from local firms. The growing economy is a classic illustration of the so-called *nonzero-sum game* whereby players can participate and win without doing so at the ex-

---

[7] Jagdish Bhagwati, "Regionalism and Multilateralism: An Overview," Columbia University Discussion Paper No. 603, Department of Economics, Colubmia University, 1992 as reported in "The Trouble with Regionalism" in *The Economist*, June 27, 1992, p.79.

pense of others because their "play" enlarges the total gains to be distributed. Without economic growth, international participation in countries can occur only if global firms are able to take business away from local enterprise. When there is competition between international and domestic enterprise, it is more likely that domestic enterprise will seek governmental intervention to protect its local position if markets are not growing than it is if they are growing. The worldwide recession of the early 1990s created a predictable pressure in most countries to limit access to domestic markets.

▼ Communications and Transportation Technology

The time and cost barriers of distance have fallen tremendously over the past 100 years. Increased speed and capacity and lower cost communications have been a major force facilitating international business expansion. The jet airplane has revolutionized the communications field by making it possible for people to travel around the world in less than 48 hours. One essential characteristic of the effective business enterprise is the face-to-face meeting of those responsible for directing the enterprise. Without the jet airplane, face-to-face contact so essential to business management would not have been possible because the amount of time required to travel the distance involved in international operations would be too great. The jet aircraft has made it possible for executives to be in face-to-face contact at regular intervals throughout the year.

A second major communications development has been the enormous improvement in the ability to transmit data electronically. The cost of transmitting voice, facsimile, television, and data has declined continuously since the end of World War II. The declining cost and increasing availability of transportation and electronic communications have made it possible to manage geographically dispersed operations.

Similarly, transportation technology has been revolutionized. Physical distribution has declined in cost and in the time required for shipment. For example, the cost of shipping automobiles from Japan or Korea by specially designed auto-transport ships to Vancouver can be less than the cost of shipping from Windsor or Oakville plants to either Canadian coast over land.

▼ The Global/Transnational Corporation

The global/transnational corporation, or any business enterprise that pursues global business objectives by relating world resources to world market opportunity, is the organization that has responded to the driving, restraining, and underlying forces in the world. Within the international financial framework and under the umbrella of global peace, the global corporation has taken advantage of the expanding communications technologies to pursue market opportunities and serve needs and wants on a global scale. The global enterprise has both responded to market opportunity and competitive threat by going global and at the same time has been one of the forces driving the world toward greater globalization.

CONCLUSION

Globalization is the single most significant development in marketing in this century. The reality of global markets and global competition is pervasive. Marketing is a universal discipline: This book focuses upon applying the marketing discipline to the opportunities and challenges of global markets. The forces that are driving the world toward greater globalization are greater than the forces that restrain this move. The old theories of international trade focused upon natural resources and crude measures of factor endowments. Newer models focus upon the actual sources of competitive advantage of companies in industries. Ultimately, competitive advantage is based upon understanding what customers need and want and on knowing how to deliver these needs and wants with a competitive advantage. The formula that guides this task is $V = B/P$: value = benefits divided by price. The greater the benefits and the lower the price, the greater the value. The task of the global company is to deliver value to customers located in global markets.

OUTLINE OF THIS BOOK

This book, designed for the student and practitioner of global marketing management, is divided into six parts.

In Part I, we present a conceptual overview of global marketing management and the basic theory of global marketing.

Part II identifies the major dimensions of the environment of global marketing: economic, including the location of income and markets, patterns of trade and investment, stages of market development; social and cultural elements; legal and regulatory dimensions; and the financial framework of global marketing.

Part III addresses the challenge of understanding and targeting global markets. First, we examine global marketing information systems and market research, and then we address the task of evaluating and targeting country markets.

Part IV is concerned with formulating global marketing strategy. First, we identify the major entry and expansion strategies, then we discuss the key dimensions of competitive strategy, and conclude by examining cooperative strategies.

Part V, the core of this book, focuses on the key decision elements of a marketing program: product, price, channel, and communications decisions. This part concludes with a focus on exporting and importing.

In Part VI, we discuss managing and leading the global marketing effort: the structure and organizational alternatives, the control and audit of the global marketing effort. We conclude the book with a look at the future of marketing in a changing global environment.

▼ SUMMARY

Global marketing is the process of focusing the resources and objectives of a company on global marketing opportunities. The driving motives for this are twofold: One is to take advantage of opportunities for growth and expansion and the other is survival. Companies that fail to pursue global oppor-tunities will eventually lose their domestic markets because they will be pushed aside by stronger and more competitive global com-petitors. This book presents the theory and practice of applying the universal discipline of marketing to the global opportunities of world markets.

▼ DISCUSSION QUESTIONS

1. What are the differences among domestic, international, multinational, and global and transnational marketing?

2. What is a stakeholder?

3. Who are the stakeholders of a national company? Of a Canadian-headquartered multinational company? Of a transnational company?

4. Assume that two companies operate in the same twenty countries. The only differ-ence between the companies in their oper-ating strategy is that one is headquartered in Canada and the other is headquartered in Switzerland. What, if any, is the difference between the stakeholders of these two com-panies?

5. At a recent meeting of the American Marketing Association, two marketing schol-ars presented a paper entitled "The Japanese: The World's Champion Marketers." Do you agree? Why or why not?

6. What are the three basic principles of mar-keting? Select a company that you know and assess how well the company is applying these principles.

7. Can a country that has an absolute dis-advantage in the production of everything gain from trade? How?

8. What is the product trade cycle? What are the implications of this cycle for high-income countries? For low-income countries?

TWO

Global Marketing
Planning

Introduction

This chapter outlines an overview of the global marketing planning process. It begins with a conceptual framework for strategy formulation that identifies the steps that must be completed in order to formulate a global marketing strategy.

    International trade, investment, and markets have been the fastest-growing sectors of the world economy since the end of World War II. The dynamic growth of international markets and global marketing has occurred in a context of fundamental underlying forces and concepts. This chapter identifies and explains these forces and concepts and presents a basic conceptual scheme to provide an understanding of the distinctive character of global marketing.

KEY CONCEPTS

There are six key concepts that contribute toward a better understanding of the opportunity and challenge of global marketing. The first and most important is the concept of strategy.

▼ Strategy

Strategy has been defined as the considered response of an organization to the realities of organization stakeholders and the realities of the business environment.

    Table 2–1 presents a conceptual framework for strategy formulation. The framework identifies three strategic dimensions: the external environment of the firm, the organization or the internal environment of the firm, and the values and aspirations of the stakeholders of the firm.

    The strategic planning process requires an assessment of the facts and assumptions concerning the firm's external environment. This assessment can be organized around the macro dimensions of economic, sociocultural, political, and technological factors, and the micro factors of markets, costs, competitors, customers, and government. This assessment should cover the entire world and should ensure that no significant competitor, market, customer, or trend is overlooked. The challenge for the firm in a global market is to insure that the assessment of the environment is global, and not merely national or regional. The global firm must recognize change wherever it occurs and be prepared to respond to opportunity and to threats.

TABLE 2–1   Strategy Formulation—A Conceptual Framework

Stage	Environment	Organization	Stakeholder Values
Strategic dimensions	Economic Sociocultural Political Technological Markets Costs Competitors Customers Government	Human resources/capabilities Marketing Finance Manufacturing Engineering R&D	Size/growth Profitability/return Geographic Social responsibility Aesthetic Style Ethics

1. Strategic process
  a. Identify
  b. Assess
  c. Determine
	Key assumptions, opportunities, threats, trends	Key assumptions, strengths/weaknesses	Relative importance

	Alternatives—What is possible?		Relative importance
2. Determine	{	Objectives and Goals	

3. Identify driving force of the business; distinctive competence.

	Category	Strategic Area
	Products, markets	Products offered, markets served; knowledge of customers. Financial resources/structure new-product development.
	Capabilities	Technology Production capability Method of sale Method of distribution Natural resources
	Results	Size/growth Profitability/return
4. Develop integrated plans and programs for	Control Engineering Finance Human resources	Manufacturing Marketing R&D Social responsibility

5. Plan implementation. Obtain and commit resource to plans and programs. Manage resources.

6. Control. Compare implementation results with plans. Compare environmental, organizational, and value assessment with key assumptions. Recycle to phase 1.

Timing

Evaluate and assess		Forecast, plan, and program	
	Annual operating plan/budget		Guide plan
Past	Present	One year	Medium term	Long term

The line of time
strategy links past, present, and future.

The second strategic dimension is the organization. The strategic process requires the identification of key assumptions about the organization, in particular, its strengths and weaknesses. The third strategic dimension is stakeholder values. Stakeholders are any persons or groups with an interest in the outcome of an organization's activity. They include the shareholders, managers, employees, customers, suppliers, partners, members of the community, state, and country in which the business operates, and so on. As stakeholders often have conflicting values and interests, resolving these conflicting values is a management task that requires political skills and talents.

Stage 1 of the strategy formulation process is the assessment of the opportunities, threats, and trends in the environment; the strengths and weaknesses of the organization; and the desires of the stakeholders, leading to a formulation of what is possible or of the alternatives open to the organization. Stage 2 is the determination of objectives and goals based on the organization's alternatives of what is possible and the relative importance of stakeholder values.

Stage 3 is the identification of the driving force of the business, a critical stage of the process. Each of the identified strategic areas is important, and every successful business must be strong in each of the identified areas. The truly successful business, however, will identify its own particular area of distinctive competence. For example, Eicon Technology Corporation of Montreal, which markets advanced data communications products to connect personal computers to mainframes and geographically remote local area networks (LANs), has made the strategic decision to sell through distributors worldwide rather than its own direct sales organization. It has developed a distinctive competence in training and supporting its distributor network so effectively that it has built a roster of blue chip clients, including Lufthansa, Sandoz, J.P. Morgan, and Renault.[1]

Stage 4 of the process is the preparation of integrated plans and programs in each of the functional areas of the business. The process continues with stages 5 and 6, plan implementation and control, and recycles to stage 1, where the results of the strategy are compared with objectives and goals and with the facts and assumptions about the environment, organization, and stakeholder values. To the extent that the results of the strategy are consistent with objectives, goals, facts, and assumptions, the strategy can be maintained as is. If there are deviations, the strategy must of course be adapted.

Stage 5 is plan implementation. This calls for obtaining and committing resources to the plans and programs.

Stage 6 of the framework—control—overlaps with strategy implementation. In this phase implementation results are compared with plans, and any deviation from plans is reviewed to determine whether this requires an adjustment in the strategy or improvement in the implementation effort. Another aspect of control, and critically important as a part of strategy formulations, is the scanning of the external and internal environments as well as stakeholder values to compare environmental, organizational, and value assessment with key assumptions that were established at the beginning of the strategy formulation process.

---

[1] Mary R. Brooks, Donald J. Patton, and Philip J. Rosson, "The Export Edge," (Ottawa: External Affairs and International Trade Canada, October 24, 1990), p.12.

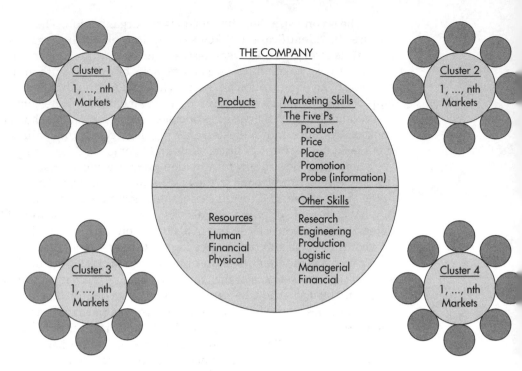

FIGURE 2–1
A Conceptual Framework for Global Marketing: The Company in a World of Clusters of National Market Environments

Timing, shown at the bottom of the framework in Table 2–1, indicates the relationship of the past, present, and future to the strategy formulation process. As indicated in Table 2–1, strategy formulation cuts across the time line. It requires an evaluation and assessment of past events, an assessment and identification of present realities, and an anticipation or forecast of future conditions. Since the past is history, and the future has not yet occurred, the only time period in which we can actually have an impact on the external world is the present. Thus, even though strategy has a profound impact on a company's future, it is implemented in the present. What a manager does on Monday morning is as much a part of the overall strategy of the organization as any thinking about what the organization might be 5, 10, or 15 years from now. Many managers fall into the trap of assuming that there is some magical distinction between future thoughts and present actions. Nothing could be further from the truth. The future is nothing more or less than the outcome of an accumulation of actions in the present.

▼ The Company in the World

Several aspects of global marketing are quite distinct and different from domestic marketing. The first is the context or environment of global marketing. Figure 2–1 suggests the major characteristics of the environment of global marketing. At the center of the diagram is the company, which is defined by four major dimensions: its products, markets served, resources, and skills. The company exists in a world of more than 180 different countries and territories, each of which is in some respects similar to and in other respects different from the other countries. Although each of the countries and territories is in fact unique, both statistical analysis of the major environmental dimensions and managerial judgment agree that it is possible to cluster nationally different market environments to establish groups of countries that result in clear within-group similarities and between-group differences.[2]

▼ Clustering, Segmentation, and Target Marketing

The characteristics of national markets served differ considerably around the globe on many key dimensions. For example, the income per capita of world markets varies from a low of C$38 per capita per annum in Vietnam to a high of $40,970 in Switzerland. At the extremes there is no question that income is a differentiating influence in world markets today. The similarities between the Canadian market and, say, the market in Mali are so small as to be unimportant. Nevertheless, within this wide range of global per capita income, there are clusters of countries at the bottom, in the middle, and at the top that are so similar in income that it becomes a unifying influence rather than a differentiating one.

Another important market characteristic is size. Canada, with a GNP per capita of C$25,024 ranked 12th among industrialized nations in 1992, while the U.S., our neighbor and largest trading partner, ranked 6th with a GNP per capita some 12 percent higher than Canada's. The similarity in GNP per capita masks the very large difference in aggregate between Canada and the U.S. Thus, aggregate size can give a rough indication of a country's consumption capacity (population multiplied by GNP per capita). Similar aggregate size does not necessarily mean similar consumption characteristics. Table 2–2 shows why caution is needed when using these broad indicators.

TABLE 2–2 Consumption Capacity of Selected Countries, 1992

	Pop. (millions)	GNP (per capita)	Consumption Capacity (millions)
Canada	27.4	$ 25,024	$ 685,655
United States of America	255.4	28,081	7,171,860
Switzerland	6.9	43,595	300,809
Mexico	85.0	4,193	356,388
Brazil	153.9	3,347	515,102
China	1,162.0	568	659,900

Source: adapted from "World Development Report 1994," Table 1,. "Basic Indicators," *Bank of Canada Review,* Winter 1993/94, Table A1.

---

[2] See, for example, S. Prakash Sethi, "Comparative Cluster Analysis for World Markets," *Journal of Marketing Research* (August 1971), p. 348, and "Indicators of Market Size for 117 Countries," *Business International* (July 6, 1992) The Economist Intelligence Unit.

Switzerland and Mexico have similar aggregate consumption capacity, as do Canada, China, and Brazil; the income distribution and consumption behaviour, however, across those countries is vastly different. At these extremes, the size of markets is a highly differentiating influence.

For example, the structure, staffing, information, and control systems appropriate for a company's marketing organization to pursue a given market share in Switzerland would be quite different from one needed in the U.S.

A company that is simultaneously marketing in large and small markets must be flexible in its approach to organization, staffing information, and control lest it find itself in the position of enforcing some unified approach to each of these system areas, and as a consequence having organizations, information systems, and control systems that are either inadequate to the size of the market or too elaborate for a smaller market.

Geography is a clustering criterion of great significance. Countries that are close to each other have proximity in common. Thus, we have the North American market, the European market, and the Pacific Basin market.

Language and culture are other market characteristics that differentiate markets. In the media industry, this can be quite significant. The world is divided into language clusters or segments: mandarin, English, Spanish, and so on. Countries can be grouped into these language and culture segments that cut across geography, income, and size.

There are also unique influences that apply to specific industries and products. For example, companies marketing equipment used in the construction and building trades must face the complete welter of codes and regulations that exists, not only internationally but also within a particular national environment in various local political jurisdictions. Consider, for example, the situation faced by a crane manufacturer. In many countries in the world, cranes must have a free-fall capability for instantly releasing their load. This requirement has been established to make the cranes safer. A crane with the capability of a free-fall displacement of its load is difficult to tip over. In other countries, however, there is a requirement that a crane not have a free-fall capacity. The prohibition against free fall is also motivated by a desire to increase the safety of crane operation. The rationale behind the prohibition of free-fall capability is that any crane with this capability is liable to lose its entire load accidentally. In other words, considerations of safety for this particular product have motivated opposite conditions in the area of free fall, and any company that wishes to market this product internationally must be able to respond to these conditions and to offer products that do not have such a capability. One dimension for clustering or segmenting markets is by type of governmental influences including regulation, tariffs, taxes, laws, and codes.

▼ Environmental Sensitivity

A very useful way of looking at products internationally is to place them on a continuum of environmental sensitivity. At one end of the continuum are the environmentally insensitive products, which do not require significant adaptation to the economic and social environments of markets around the world. At the

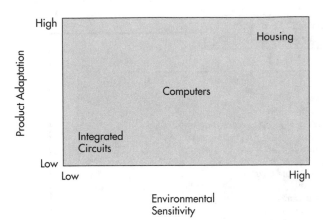

FIGURE 2–2
Environmental Sensitivity–Product
Adaptation Matrix

other end of the continuum are those products that are highly sensitive to differences in economic, sociocultural, physical, and governmental factors in world markets. A company with environmentally insensitive products is going to have to spend relatively less time determining the specific and unique conditions of local markets because the product the company offers is basically universal.

The sensitivity of products can be represented on a scale as in Figure 2–2. At the left of the scale are the environmentally insensitive products. An integrated circuit is an example of an environmentally insensitive product. Moving to the right on the scale is a computer that must be sensitive to the environmental variable of voltage and cycles. In addition, the computer's software documentation must be in the local language. At the far end of the continuum are the products with high environmental sensitivity. Housing falls into this category because it is sensitive to climate and culture, but power generation also falls into this category because it happens that in many countries the local power generation manufacturing companies have a de facto monopoly on national purchases. The greater the environmental sensitivity of a product, the more necessary it is for a company to learn about the way in which its products interact with the specific economic, social and cultural, physical, and prescriptive environmental conditions that exist throughout the world.

▼ Unifying and Differentiating Influences

Figure 2–3 illustrates the application of the concept of unifying and differentiating influences to the task of environmental and market analysis.[3] This concept is based on the fact that in every situation there are both unique and similar aspects. The unique aspects are *differentiating* influences; the similar aspects are the *unifying* influences. If the analysis of a market focuses on only the unique or only the

---

[3] The concept of unifying and differentiating influences was first suggested by John Fayerweather in *International Business Management: A Conceptual Framework* (New York: McGraw-Hill, 1969).

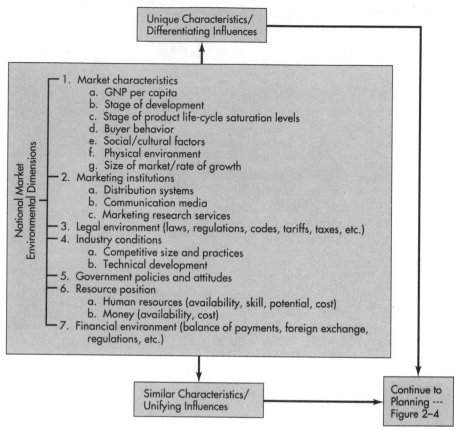

FIGURE 2–3

A Conceptual Framework for Multinational Marketing: Major Dimensions of a National Market Environment, Absolute and Compared with Other Nations

similar aspects, it will be a one-sided analysis that would result in developing a marketing program that is either too standardized or too differentiated. For example, a totally standardized program, based on analysis that recorded only the unifying influences, might establish a single price worldwide for an identical product and not take into account the ability to pay or the competitive situation in the various world markets. This would be simple to design and administer, but it would be costly in terms of lost business and profits that might have been obtained by a more differentiated pricing policy. At the other extreme, if a unique price is calculated for each country, there might be serious transshipment problems as dealers and distributors seek the lowest possible price for their supplies.

Information and conclusions resulting from this scanning feed into the analysis, planning, and control process shown in Figure 2–4, which is concerned with relating opportunities and threats in the world market environment to the basic strengths and weaknesses of the company. The planning process results in the selection of objectives among the alternatives open to the company. Given objectives, companies decide upon an organization appropriate to the company's

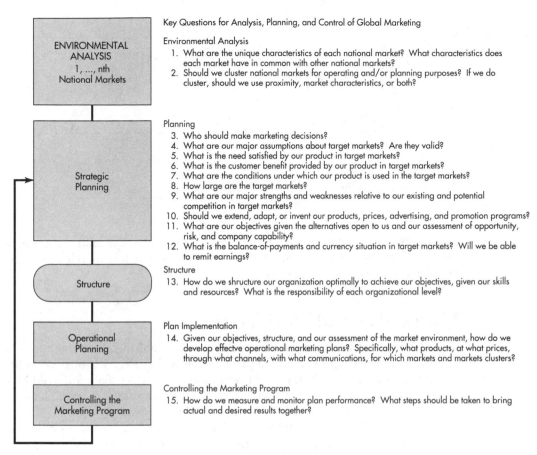

Key Questions for Analysis, Planning, and Control of Global Marketing

Environmental Analysis

1. What are the unique characteristics of each national market? What characteristics does each market have in common with other national markets?
2. Should we cluster national markets for operating and/or planning purposes? If we do cluster, should we use proximity, market characteristics, or both?

Planning

3. Who should make marketing decisions?
4. What are our major assumptions about target markets? Are they valid?
5. What is the need satisfied by our product in target markets?
6. What is the customer benefit provided by our product in target markets?
7. What are the conditions under which our product is used in the target markets?
8. How large are the target markets?
9. What are our major strengths and weaknesses relative to our existing and potential competition in target markets?
10. Should we extend, adapt, or invent our products, prices, advertising, and promotion programs?
11. What are our objectives given the alternatives open to us and our assessment of opportunity, risk, and company capability?
12. What is the balance-of-payments and currency situation in target markets? Will we be able to remit earnings?

Structure

13. How do we shstructure our organization optimally to achieve our objectives, given our skills and resources? What is the responsibility of each organizational level?

Plan Implementation

14. Given our objectives, structure, and our assessment of the market environment, how do we develop effectve operational marketing plans? Specifically, what products, at what prices, through what channels, with what communications, for which markets and markets clusters?

Controlling the Marketing Program

15. How do we measure and monitor plan performance? What steps should be taken to bring actual and desired results together?

FIGURE 2–4
A Conceptual Framework for Multinational Marketing

basic skills and resources. Within the framework of a specified organizational structure, the implementation of decisions about objectives must be accomplished. In marketing this requires the design and specification of products, prices, channels, and communications. Given specified marketing plans, the next step is implementation. The final phase of the global marketing process is control, that is, the measurement and evaluation of performance. The results of this control activity feed back to the planning process and become an important input to the planning cycle.

The process of global marketing requires the marketing manager to answer a number of basic questions to plan and implement a global marketing strategy. The marketing manager must identify opportunities and threats and must know where global markets are located today and where they will be in the future. The remarkable success in recent years of countries such as Singapore, Hong Kong, South Korea, Malaysia, and Thailand is a reminder that opportunity is constantly shifting in the world. The global marketer needs to identify similarities and differences to know what to change and what not to change. To

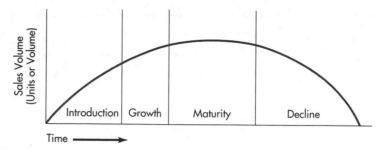

FIGURE 2–5
The Product Life Cycle

do this, an organization must be structured to respond to the unique aspects of country markets and at the same time be capable of transferring relevant experience across national boundaries.

▼ Product Life Cycle/Market Life Cycle

The concept of the PLC (product life cycle) is well established in marketing. The general notion of the PLC is that a product has a characteristic or normal life with a beginning, or birth, and rapid growth (the growth stage), followed by a declining rate of growth, no growth, decline, and eventually, to complete the metaphor, death. This typical PLC is illustrated in Figure 2–5.

Of course, the concept of the PLC does not provide a basis for predicting or forecasting the actual rate of sales growth or the timing of the shifts in rate. In practice, the rate of growth and the timing of change in rate varies across a vast spectrum. Indeed, the whole concept of the PLC is based upon a notion of product that is quite obsolete in today's markets: the notion that a product is launched and that is it. Today, in order to succeed, it is absolutely essential to constantly improve products to increase the value offered to customers. When this is done, the PLC can be extended, as shown in Figure 2–6.

FIGURE 2–6
Extending the Product Life Cycle

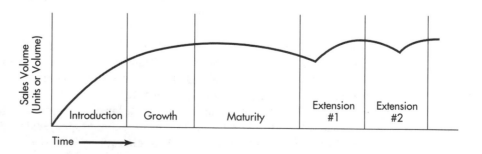

The market life cycle is a related concept. Markets have a beginning, growth stage, maturity, and decline. A company engaged in global marketing will find that not all markets are at the same stage of development. It is important to recognize the stage of market development and match the marketing strategy for the product to that stage. For example, the same product may be at the mature stage in one country and at the growth stage in another. The appropriate marketing strategy for the product will be different for each market. Perhaps greater emphasis will be on price in the mature market, while in the growth-stage market explaining and gaining acceptance will be emphasized. The twin dangers in the global company are that each country will operate in autonomy without the benefit of experience from the rest of the world, or that inappropriate experience will be imposed on the world.

▼ The Product Trade-Cycle Model

The theory of comparative advantage is a pure theory based upon a set of assumptions, which is an abstraction from the complexities of the real world. The theory is a powerful idea and a constant and major influence on the thinking and action of public policymakers in governments around the globe. Nevertheless, it has limiting assumptions. For example, the demonstration of the theory is based on the assumption that the products are undifferentiated (one car is exactly like the next, an orange is an orange is an orange), *and* the complications of prices, money, and exchange rates have been eliminated.

In the real world, products are highly differentiated in the customer's mind and in physical expression. Consumers do not go out to purchase a car, for example, in a market where all cars are the same. The success of international competitors is based on creating value for the customer by differentiating their product. Indeed, one of the important maxims of marketing is that you can differentiate anything. Also, in the real world, exchange rates exist and fluctuate and have a major impact on the cost position of competitors.

In contrast to the pure theory of comparative advantage, the international product life-cycle model discovered by Professor Raymond Vernon of the Harvard Business School is based on empirical actual patterns of trade.[4] As such, it is a valuable complement to the theory of comparative advantage because it helps us understand what is actually happening in the real world of international competition. The model describes the relationship among the product life-cycle, trade, and investment. Vernon's initial work was based on an analysis of U.S. trade in products during the 1950s and 1960s. The international product life-cycle model suggests that many products go through a cycle during which high-income, mass-consumption countries are initially exporters, then lose their export markets, and finally become importers of the product. At the same time other advanced countries shift from the position of importers to exporters later in time, and still later, less developed countries shift from the position

---

[4] Raymond Vernon, "International Investment and International Trade in the Product Cycle," *Quarterly Journal of Economics* (May 1966), pp. 190–207. See also Louis T. Wells, Jr., "A Product Life Cycle for International Trade?" *Journal of Marketing* (July 1968), pp. 1–6; and Sak Onkvisit and John J. Shaw, "An Examination of the International Product Life Cycle and Its Application Within Marketing," *Columbia Journal of World Business* (Fall 1983), pp. 73–79.

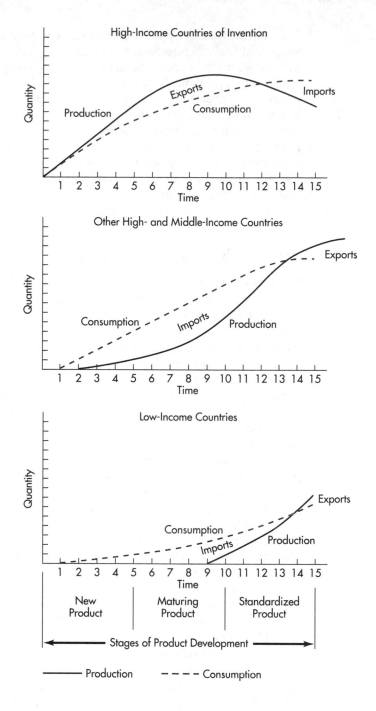

FIGURE 2–7
International Product Life-Cycle

of being importers to being exporters of a product. These shifts correspond to the three stages in the product life-cycle: introduction, growth and maturity, and decline. These stages are represented graphically in Figure 2–7.

The pattern from the point of view of the high-income country is as follows: Phase 1, export strength is exhibited; Phase 2, foreign production begins; Phase 3, foreign production becomes competitive in export markets; and Phase 4, import competition begins. The model suggests that new products are initially introduced in high-income markets. There are two main reasons for this. First, high-income markets offer the greatest potential demand for new products, both consumer and industrial. Second, it is advantageous to locate production facilities close to the product's markets because of the need in the early stages of a product's life to respond quickly and fully to customers in adjusting and adapting the design and performance of the product. Thus, it is typical for products to initially be produced in the market where they will be sold. The first manufacturers of the new product have a virtual monopoly in world markets based on patents, know-how, or a combination of both.

Foreigners who want the new product must order it from companies in the country of invention. In the high-income country of invention and first development, exports for the product begin to grow from a trickle to a steady stream as active export programs are established. In the middle-income foreign countries, entrepreneurs are quick to note the growing markets in the new product and are relatively swift in initiating production to take advantage of lower labor and factor costs in their countries. Their initiative launches the second stage of the cycle, when high- and middle-income-country production supply third-country export markets. As the product reaches maturity, the design, technology, and markets stabilize. Production from low-income countries displaces the high-income production for the product. Frequently the ownership and control of low-income-country production is held by companies who have shifted production from high-income countries to take advantage of lower factor cost in the low-income country.

The final phase of this cycle occurs when the low-income-country manufacturer achieves volume production based on home and export markets and, due to lower factor costs, is able to produce at a lower cost than his or her high-income country counterpart. The low-income-country manufacturer then begins to export to the high-income-country market. The cycle is now complete, and high-income-country companies that once had a virtual monopoly in the product find themselves facing foreign competition in their home market.

The cycle continues as the production capability in the product extends from the other advanced countries to less developed countries of the world that eventually displace the other advanced countries first at home, then in international trade, and finally in the other advanced countries' home market. Textiles are an example of a product that has gone through the complete cycle for the investing country (Britain), other industrialized countries, and finally for less developed countries.

The international product life-cycle is basically a "trickle-down" model of world trade and investment. (See Figure 2–8.) Products are invented and first introduced to the high-income-country markets, then to upper-middle-income countries, and finally to lower-middle- and low-income countries. This was an accurate description of the behavior of investors during the period from 1950 to the early 1970s. And it still describes the behavior of many North American firms who have abandoned efforts

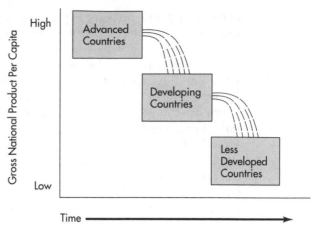

FIGURE 2–8
International Product Life-Cycle—Trickle
Down or Waterfall Approach

to maintain domestic production by shifting production to lower-cost countries or by giving up market share to lower-cost producers in other countries.

The problem with a strategy of seeking low-cost production locations for a product is that it puts the focus of strategy on the wrong dimension. A company that focuses upon getting costs down by moving production to low-income countries can become obsessed with getting costs down and in the process lag its competitors in innovation, in product functionality and features, and in product manufacturability and quality.

Under this assumption, the advanced countries are doomed (or blessed with the opportunity) to constantly discover and introduce new products because they cannot compete with the lower-wage competitors in mature, established products. The cycle is inevitable if the product does not change. Innovations in the product and in the way a product is made enable companies in high-income countries to thrive and prosper in an industry, and in effect, to run an end play around the international trade cycle. Because they constantly innovate, and because they are close to their customers and give their customers what they want, they do not leave an opening for a competitor with low-income-country production.

The international product life-cycle concept has not been as relevant in Canada as in the U.S., because many U.S. firms (often multinationals) had established branch plants here to serve the Canadian market. As growth prospects diminished and the Free Trade Agreement (FTA) altered and reduced the importance of a Canadian production location, subsidiaries were closed, converted to distribution centers, or obtained global product mandates to manufacture products for the world market. A subsidiary with a global product mandate not only has responsibility for production, but also for research design and development, as well as export marketing, albeit in coordination with headquarters.[5]

[5] David Rutenberg, "Global Product Mandating," in K.C. Dhawan, Hamid Etemad, and Richard W. Wright, *International Business: A Canadian Perspective* (Don Mills, Ontario: Addison-Wesley, 1981). Steven Globerman, *Fundamentals of International Business Management* (Englewood Cliffs: Prentice Hall, 1986), pp.346–8.

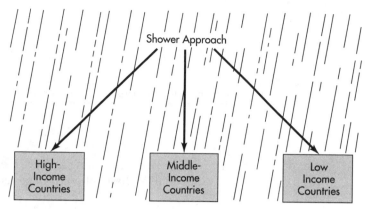

FIGURE 2–9
International Product Life Cycle—Shower Approach

An alternative to the trickle-down approach (or what one writer has called the "waterfall" model[6]) is the "shower" approach. This strategy is to develop a product and simultaneously introduce it in world markets (a shower instead of a trickle). This approach is illustrated in Figure 2–9. The difference between the two approaches begins with assumptions about the nature of world markets. The waterfall strategy, which is obsolete, assumes that markets develop sequentially over time. The shower approach recognizes that we live in a global village and that market opportunities develop simultaneously around the globe.

Nevertheless, there is still an opportunity for competitors to take advantage of lower factor costs in low-income countries to gain an advantage in serving world markets. At the same time, companies with production capacity in high-income countries must always be on the alert for competitive threats that are based on taking advantage of lower-wage rates in low-income countries as a production location for both goods and services. India, for example, is a major production location for software programming. The product is "exported" via satellite signals. You can't see, taste, touch, or feel it, but it is a real export.

THE STAGES OF DEVELOPMENT OF THE TRANSNATIONAL CORPORATION: A DYNAMIC TYPOLOGY

Figure 2–10 identifies five stages in the evolution of the transnational corporation.[7] These stages describe significant differences in the strategy, world view, orien-

---

[6] Kenichi Ohmae, *Triad Power* (New York: The Free Press, 1985), p.21.

[7] For an excellent description of the characteristics of companies at each of the stages, see Christopher A. Bartlett and Sumantra Ghoshal, *Managing Across Borders, The Transnational Solution* (Boston, MA: Harvard Business School Press, 1989).

1. Domestic
2. International
3. Multinational
4. Global
5. Transnational

FIGURE 2–10
Stages of Development of the Transnational Corporation

tation, and practice of companies operating in more than one country. One of the key differences in companies at these different stages is in orientation.

▼ Stage One—Domestic

The stage-one company is domestic in its focus, vision, and operations. Its orientation is ethnocentric. This company focuses upon domestic markets, domestic suppliers, and domestic competitors. The environmental scanning of the stage-one company is limited to the domestic, familiar, home-country environment. The implied motto of a stage-one company is: "If it's not happening in the home country, it's not happening." The world's graveyard of defunct companies is littered with stage-one companies that were sunk by the Titanic syndrome: the belief, often subconscious but frequently a conscious conviction, that they were unsinkable and invincible on their own home turf.

The pure stage-one company is not conscious of its domestic orientation. The company operates domestically because it never considers the alternative of going international. The growing stage-one company will, when it reaches growth limits in its primary market, diversify into new markets, products, and technologies instead of focusing on penetrating international markets.

▼ Stage Two—International

The stage-two company extends marketing, manufacturing, and other activity outside the home country. When a company decides to pursue opportunities outside the home country, it has evolved into the stage-two category. In spite of its pursuit of foreign business opportunities, the stage-two company remains ethnocentric, or home-country oriented, in its basic orientation. The hallmark of the stage-two company is the belief that the home-country ways of doing business, people, practices, values, and products are superior to those found elsewhere in the world. The focus of the stage-two company is on the home-country market.

Because there are few, if any, people in the stage-two company with international experience, it typically relies on an international division structure where people with international interest and experience can be grouped to focus on international opportunities. The marketing strategy of the stage-two company is extension; that is, products, advertising, promotion, pricing, and business practices developed for the home-country market are "extended" into markets around the world.

Almost every company begins its global development as a stage-two international company. Stage two is a natural progression. Given limited resources and experience, companies must focus on what they do best. When a company decides to go international, it makes sense at the beginning to extend as much of the business and marketing mix (product, price, promotion, and place or channels of distribution) as possible so that learning can focus on how to do business in foreign countries.

A fundamental strategic maxim is that it is a mistake to attempt to simultaneously diversify into new customer and new-product/technology markets. The international strategist observes this maxim by holding the marketing mix constant while adding new geographic or country markets. The focus of the international company is on extending the home-country marketing mix and business model.

▼ Stage Three—Multinational

In time, the stage-two company discovers that differences in markets around the world demand an adaptation of its marketing mix in order to succeed. Toyota, for example, discovered the former when it entered the U.S. market in 1957 with its Toyopet. The Toyopet was not a big hit: Critics said they were "overpriced, underpowered, and built like tanks." The car was so unsuited for the U.S. market that unsold models were shipped back to Japan. The market rejection of the Toyopet was chalked up by Toyota as a learning experience and a source of invaluable intelligence about market preferences. The Canadian market was not entered until 1965, when Toyota introduced three models, the 700, a small vehicle with a two cylinder motor; the Crown, a larger car with equipment similar to a North American car; and the Landcruiser, a jeep-like model. Clearly, Toyota used the U.S. experience as a source of invaluable intelligence about market preferences before entering the Canadian market. There is, for the emerging global company, no such thing as failure, only learning experiences and successes in the constantly evolving strategy and experience of the company.

When a company decides to respond to market differences, it evolves into a stage-three multinational that pursues a multidomestic strategy. The focus of the stage-three company is multinational or in strategic terms, *multidomestic*. (That is, this company formulates a unique strategy for each country in which it conducts business.) The orientation of this company shifts from ethnocentric to polycentric.

A polycentric orientation is the assumption that markets and ways of doing business around the world are so unique that the only way to succeed internationally is to adapt to the different aspects of each national market. Like the stage-two international, the stage-three multinational, polycentric company is also predictable. In stage-three companies, each foreign subsidiary is managed as if it were an independent city state. The subsidiaries are part of an area structure in which each country is part of a regional organization that reports to world headquarters. The stage-three marketing strategy is an adaptation of the domestic marketing mix to meet foreign preferences and practices.

A classic example of a stage-three multidomestic company was Philips of the Netherlands in the 1960s. Philips, at that time, was a pure stage-three company. It relied upon relatively autonomous national organizations (called NOs in Philips parlance) in each country. Each NO developed its own strategy. This approach worked quite well for Philips until the company faced competition from Matsushita and other Japanese companies that had adopted global strategies. The difference in competitive advantage between Philips and its Japanese competition was dramatic. Matsushita, for example, adopted a global strategy that focused its resources on serving a world market for home entertainment products.

In television receivers, Matsushita offered European customers two models based upon a single chassis. Philips, in contrast, offered European customers seven different models based on four different chassis. If the customers had demanded this variety, it would have made Philips a stronger competitor. Unfortunately for Philips, their product offering was not based upon customer demand. Customers wanted value in the form of quality, features, design, and price. Philips's offering of greater variety in the technical design was based not upon what customers were asking for, but rather on Philips's structure and strategy. Each major country organization had its own engineering and manufacturing group and, therefore, each major country came up with its own design and did its own manufacturing. This stage-three approach to product design and manufacturing was attractive to the Philips NOs, which enjoyed a high degree of autonomy. However, it was not attractive to Philips customers, who were looking for value. They were getting more value from Matsushita's global strategy than from the multinational strategy of Philips. Why? Matsushita's global strategy concentrated resources on creating value for consumers: Philips's multinational strategy squandered resources in a duplication of effort that led to greater product variety at a cost which was passed on to consumers with no corresponding consumer benefit.

Since the Matsushita strategy offered greater value to the customer, Philips lost market share. To meet the Japanese challenge, Philips decided to adopt a global strategy. The first step in this direction was to create what Philips called *industry main groups* in the Netherlands. These groups were responsible for developing a global strategy for R&D, marketing, and manufacturing.

The decline of the multinational corporation is based upon this type of confrontation a thousand times over, and the judge in this competition is the customer. Because the global strategy creates more customer value, it has been winning this contest.

▼ Stage Four—Global

The stage-four company makes a major strategic departure from the stage-three multinational. The global company will have either a global marketing strategy or a global sourcing strategy, but not both. It will either focus on global markets and source from the home or a single country to supply these markets, or it will focus on the domestic market and source from the world to supply its domestic channels. Examples of the stage-four global company are Harley Davidson and Benetton. Harley is an example of a global marketing company. Harley designs and manufactures super heavyweight motorcycles in the United States and targets world markets. The key engineering and manufacturing assets are all located in the home country (the United States). The only Harley investment outside the home country is in marketing. Benetton creates fashion and sportswear through state-of-the-art communications, highly automated design, production, and distribution technology for its worldwide customers. Each of these companies is operating globally, but neither of them is seeking to globalize all of the key organization functions.

The stage-four global company strategy is a winning strategy if a company can create competitive advantage by limiting its globalization of the value chain. Harley Davidson gains competitive advantage because it is American designed and made, just as BMW and Mercedes have traded on their German design and manufacture. Benetton is a global fashion company whose network strategy includes over 7,000 franchised retail stores in over 110 countries, who are serviced by some eighty representative offices whose 800 staff interface with its retail stores.[8] It sources from over 350 contract manufacturers, maintains a close relationship with suppliers and retailers to ensure continuous product innovation and strict merchandising standards. Its competitive advantage is perception and speed to remove much of the "fashion risk."[9]

Should Harley start manufacturing motorcycles in Mexico? Should Benetton centralize its production locations? The answer to these questions is that it all depends. In the case of Harley, since the company's competitive advantage is based, among other things, on its "made in the USA" image, shifting production outside the United States does not seem advisable at this point in time. For Benetton, the issue may be more difficult. Regional production centers may present an opportunity for greater cost efficiency and could extend Benetton's basic competence into what are now contract manufacturers. On the other hand, the present system is fast and continuously modernized, and its network strategy and management is successful, which make it advisable to retain the status quo.

▼ Stage Five—Transnational

The stage-five transnational corporation is much more than a company with sales, investments, and operations in many countries. This company, which is increasingly dominating markets and industries around the world, is an integrated world enterprise that links global resources with global markets at a profit. There is, to be sure, no "pure" transnational company example, but there are a growing number of companies that exhibit many, and in some cases most, of the following characteristics of the global corporation.

The stage-five company is geocentric in its orientation: It recognizes similarities and differences and adopts a world view. This is the company that thinks globally and acts locally. It adopts a global strategy allowing it to minimize adaptation in countries to that which will actually add value to the country customer. This company does not adapt for the sake of adaptation. It only adapts to add value to its offer.

The key assets of the transnational are dispersed, interdependent, and specialized. Take R&D, for example. R&D in the transnational is dispersed to more than one country. The R&D activities in each country are specialized and integrated in a global R&D plan. The same is true of manufacturing. Key assets are

---

[8] The Benetton Group, "United Colors of Benetton," company information, 1994.

[9] L. Bruce, "The Bright New World of Benetton," *International Management* (1987), 42:11, pp.24–35.

dispersed, interdependent, and specialized. Caterpillar is a good example. Cat manufactures in many countries and assembles in many countries. Components from specialized production facilities in different countries are shipped to assembly locations for assembly and then shipped to customers in world markets. If Cat were a multinational company, each country would manufacture all components in country, assemble in country, and ship only to in-country customers.

Knowledge in the transnational is created by all functions at all locations and is jointly developed and shared globally. In a transnational, experience and knowledge are shared globally. If this is done effectively, this is a source of great power and competitive advantage for the transnational. At Colgate, for example, the French subsidiary has developed great expertise and knowledge of dishwashing by using video camera research of consumers washing dishes. This knowledge has been shared with all Colgate operating companies in a video entitled *Dishwashing in France*. No one expects this video to get a Palme d'Or or an Academy Award, but then Colgate is not in the movie business. It is in, among other things, the household cleaning business.

Scanning or Information Acquisition. The stage-five company scans the world for opportunity and threat. This is a critical dimension of the transnational company and a dimension of performance that any company can achieve. Indeed, every company, regardless of the geographic scope of its current operations and regardless of its geographic aspirations should be aware of what is happening in its industry and in markets globally. Knowledge about market and competitive developments and about economic, cultural, political, and technological trends is strategically important for both offensive and defensive reasons. Even if a company has, let us assume, wisely decided to concentrate on serving domestic markets with domestic manufacturing and sourcing, global scanning is vital to insure that any significant development in the world that might impact the company or its employees is noted and reflected in company strategy.

In contrast, the scanning of companies in stages one, two, and three is limited to its area of operations.

Vision and Aspirations. The transnational company is not content to think in terms of operating in a single national or even a single regional environment. It accepts the truth behind the motto: "Grow or die!" Its aspiration is global: global markets, global customers, and the ability to stand head to head against other global competitors.

The implications of this element are of critical importance for the CEO. It is not necessary for every executive and employee of a global company to have global vision. Indeed, the "troops" and even senior business managers may be appropriately focused upon the domestic market. However, if the CEO does not have global vision, its presence in the lower ranks of the company will not really make much of a difference.

Without global vision, a company will not seek and find the opportunities that will enable it to become global. Before action comes aspiration.

So, if a company is going to become global it must first aspire to be global. Before action is the plan, and before the plan is the aspiration, and before the aspiration is inspiration.

Geographic Scope. What a company does with the information generated by a strategic global scanning and environmental assessment depends upon its strategy alternatives. The best strategy is to concentrate the forces to ensure that real customer value and competitive superiority are achieved in each target market. Clearly, not every company should operate globally. Indeed, many should limit the geographic scope of their operations to a single country or even to a single region within a country.

An apparent paradox here is the notion of a global strategy for a company that operates in a single country. However, the global strategy that we are describing is not a simple formula. Having a global strategy does not mean that you must or should do business in a certain number of countries, or even in more than one country. Having a global strategy means that you scan globally for information about opportunities and threats and for information about resources that you might acquire in order to better serve your customers. Then each company must decide what its strategy will be. For example, if your business franchise is in distribution, a global strategy may not be appropriate. However, even if a company decides that its geographic scope should be limited to one country, global scanning is important in order to make sure that all potential opportunities and threats in the world, and not just in the home country, are tracked.

Operating Style. In a transnational company, key functions such as finance, research and development, new-product development, product management, and purchasing are integrated on a global basis. At Colgate, for example, all R&D is part of a global effort. There is no such thing as U.S. or Canadian or French or British or Japanese R&D at Colgate. Technology is universal, and the customer base served with the applied technologies is global. Therefore, R&D is part of a single Colgate program that is dispersed geographically but integrated functionally. This integrated approach replaces the decentralized, bottom-up approach of the international company.

Marketing. A basic marketing issue faced by every company is whether to extend the marketing mix "as is," that is, to take whatever is offered in the home country and offer that same product, price, advertisement, and so on to the foreign market, or to adapt the home-country mix to local differences, or to create a new marketing mix for a global market. The stage-two company extends its marketing mix. The stage-three company adapts its marketing mix. In contrast, the stage-four company extends, adapts, and creates a marketing mix.

There is confusion on this point. Some people have assumed that the global/transnational corporation limits itself exclusively to the creation of products for the world market. This assumption is often made by those who want to set up a debate so they can assert that the global corporation is a myth, that any company that does not adapt to local differences is doomed, and so on.

Clearly, any corporation in today's highly differentiated world must adapt to local significant differences, and in spite of all of the differences in the world there are enough similarities to create opportunity for companies that concentrate on extending their product to world markets. The global corporation extends, adapts, and creates global products from scratch or by extending existing brands as appropriate.

Adaptation. The global corporation adapts products and the marketing mix where appropriate. Mercedes-Benz has positioned itself as a superluxury car in North America and in much of the world outside Europe. In Germany and its neighboring countries, Mercedes is both a luxury car and a basic automobile. The Mercedes is, for example, the standard taxi of Germany. This niche is reserved for Ford, Chevrolet, and Plymouth in North America.

Extension. Some products require no adaptation or change whatsoever. BIC's line of pens, butane lighters, and razors, for example, is identical worldwide. They serve their customers' basic need to draw lines, make flames, and cut hair. The only changes BIC makes in its products are in the packaging in order to take advantage of local supplier materials and market preferences concerning quantity. Nevertheless, BIC finds that success in a market depends critically on the marketing skill and talent of the local manager who must adapt BIC's pricing, promotion, and channel strategy to the competitive and market conditions in his or her country.

Creation via Extension. An example of the creation of a global brand by extending a national brand is RJR-Nabisco's Camel cigarette brand. This product was a local brand in many countries when the company decided to try to develop it as a world brand. The strongest Camel position was in Germany. On a country-by-country basis, RJR-Nabisco was able to extend the positioning of Camel in Germany to other European countries and then to the world.

Creation. Creation is the development of a new product for an identified market. In the case of the global corporation, this market may be global, and the creation may be a global brand if it is a consumer product. An excellent example of a global brand is the Sony Walkman. The Walkman is personal portable sound. The original idea for this product was suggested to Mr. Morita, the chairperson of Sony, by a golfing partner. Mr. Morita believed that the demand for personal portable sound was global and decided to introduce the Walkman as a global product instead of using the country-by-country approach of earlier eras.

In some industries, such as pharmaceuticals, the only justification for the enormous expenditures and long development and testing times for new products is a global market. A single-country market, even if it is very large, is not big enough to pay back the cost of developing a new product.

Scorekeeping. The transnational company measures its market and competitive performance on a national and a global basis. Many companies say they are companies with a global strategy and then describe their competitive position in the home market or vis-à-vis industry competitors in the home country. This is an almost certain indication that the company's real strategy is international or multinational. General Motors, for example, is not a global corporation. Its focus is on its share of the Canadian and U.S. market and its market position vis-à-vis Chrysler and Ford. The global measure would be market share and competitive position in the worldwide automotive industry, including, of course, the major Japanese and European competitors.

Human Resource Policy. The transnational corporation does not have a national bias in the selection and assignment of people. Its rule is simple: Pick the best person for the job. The same rule applies to the development of human resources. The best people, regardless of nationality, are developed for key positions everywhere in the world. This is in contrast to the international company, which reserves top positions worldwide for home-country nationals, and to the multinational company, which reserves top jobs in each host country for host-country nationals.

Purchasing. The transnational company purchases its product from the best source worldwide. This does not necessarily mean going to the lowest-wage or even to the lowest-cost country. The best source may be a factory located in a high-wage advanced country that achieves world low-cost producer status on the basis of automation and efficiency, or it may be from a home or host country that is not the lowest-cost source but which values the company's contribution to the country's welfare by creating jobs.

Preferred Form of Partnership. The history of joint ventures by stage-two and stage-three companies is one of relatively high instability. International and multinational companies enter into joint ventures with foreign partners to take advantage of combined resources and experience in addressing business opportunities. These are typically created to address a single-country opportunity, often the home country of one of the partners.

Today, the transnational corporation is careful to screen potential alliances to ensure that they fit the company's global strategic plan. These alliances, or global strategic partnerships (GSPs), are distinguished from stage-two and stage-three joint ventures because they are part of a global strategic design and not a single-country effort. The lesson from experience with partnerships is clear: Partners should do their best to form compatible and complementary marriages that bring the necessary resources and energy to a project. Partners should also be realistic and recognize that not all marriages succeed. A prenuptial agreement is an excellent idea because it paves the way for a relatively simple separation should the two parties find it difficult or impossible to work with each other. For example, Rupert Murdoch's News Corporation's partnership with Hachette, to launch new *Elle* and *Premiere* magazines in North America and in the United Kingdom, provided that if the partners could not agree on an issue of importance, they would dissolve their relationship with a buyout, with the flip of a coin deciding who buys and who sells.

▼ The Stages Compared

Tables 2–3 and 2–4 illustrate how a company changes as it moves across the stages of development. Notice that the international and domestic company have the same orientation: ethnocentric. Both are home-country oriented. Whenever you find a company doing business in many countries that is still focused upon home country customers, practices, and competition, you have an

TABLE 2–3 Stages of Development I

Stage and Company	1 Domestic	2 International	3 Multinational	4 Global	5 Transnational
Strategy Model	Domestic N.A.	International Coordinated Federation	Multidomestic Decentralized Federation	Global Centralized Hub	Global Integrated Network
View of World	Home Country	Extension Markets	National Markets	Global Markets or Resources	Global Markets and Resources
Orientation	Ethnocentric	Ethnocentric	Polycentric	Mixed	Geocentric

ethnocentric company. This changes as a company moves toward stage five, and becomes a geocentric world view in the stage-five company. A company's view of the world changes as it develops: The international company sees extension market opportunities, the multinational company sees a world of national markets, the global company sees world resources or world markets, and the transnational sees global markets and resources and similarities and differences in each country in the world.

As summarized in Table 2–4, the role of the country unit changes dramatically as a company develops. The country unit in the international company is responsible for adapting and leveraging competencies. In the multinational this responsibility extends to exploiting local opportunities. In the global company, the country unit is responsible for marketing or sourcing, and in the transnational it is responsible for making a contribution to the worldwide success of the company by its country operations, and by sharing its experience with the entire organization.

TABLE 2–4 Stages of Development II

Organization Characteristics

Stage and Company	1 Domestic	2 International	3 Multinational	4 Global	5 Transnational
Key Assets	Located in home country	Core centralized, others dispersed	Decentralized and self-sufficient	All in home country except marketing or sourcing	Dispersed, interdependent, and specialized
Role of Country Units	Single country	Adapting and leveraging competencies	Exploiting local opportunities	Marketing or sourcing	Contributions to company worldwide
Knowledge	Home country	Created at center and transferred	Retained within operating units	Marketing developed jointly and shared	All functions developed jointly and shared

STRENGTHS AT EACH LEVEL

International
Ability to exploit the parent company's knowledge and capabilities through worldwide diffusion of products

Multinational
Flexible ability to respond to national differences

Global
Cost advantage through centralized operations

Transnational
Combines the strengths of each of the preceding stages in an integrated network, which leverages worldwide learning and experience

FIGURE 2–11
Stages of Development III, Strengths at Each Level

As shown in Figure 2–11, each of the stages has strengths and advantages. The international exploits the parents' capabilities on a global scale, the multinational adapts to national differences, the global realizes cost advantages, and the transnational combines the strengths of each of the previous stages into an integrated network, which leverages worldwide assets, learning, and experience.

The transnational corporation is the winning model for the 1990s and the next century. The successful transnationals have three basic capabilities and advantages. The first is global efficiency. They deliver the greatest value to their customers at the lowest cost by leveraging their resources and assets. For example, one of the costs of a product is engineering design. A transnational will leverage its engineering resources by using the minimum number of model variations consistent with customer needs and wants. The multinational company will duplicate engineering effort without regard to customer needs simply because it is organized on the assumption that there are differences between national markets. The transnational does not assume. If there are differences, it responds. If there are no differences, it leverages its efforts.

The second advantage of the transnational is its ability to stimulate worldwide innovation and learning, and to transfer this innovation and learning throughout the organization. A world-class transnational will encourage innovation throughout the world and will make sure that any relevant innovation is transferred to the world organization. Motorola is an example of an emerging transnational that does this. The company estimates that it is saving over C$2.7 billion annually from quality programs that have emphasized teamwork. The company has an annual competition where teams from all over the world compete for recognition and awards. In 1993, 24 teams from six countries in Europe, North America, and Asia competed in what the company calls the Total Customer Satisfaction Team.

Competition. The competition involves traveling to Chicago in January and presenting to a top-management judging panel.[10]

[10] "At Motorola, Quality is a Team Sport," *The New York Times,* January 21, 1993, p. D-1.

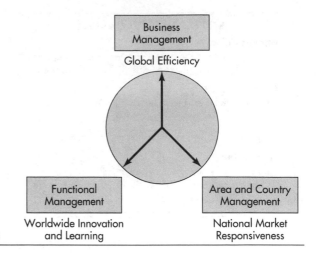

FIGURE 2–12
Transnational Multiple Strategic Capabilities

The third advantage of the transnational is that like the multinational, it is responsive to national markets and customer needs and wants. The difference between the transnational and the multinational is that the multinational focuses exclusively on differences in a country, while the transnational focuses upon differences and similarities and seeks ways of creating value for customers at the lowest cost. These advantages are summarized in Figure 2–12.

▼ An Emerging Transnational Company: The News Corporation

Murdoch's News Corporation Ltd. is an excellent example of an emerging transnational corporation. It now spans three continents and is expanding from its strong base in newspaper and magazine and database print products to establish a position as a major television broadcaster in Australia, the United States, and Europe as a programming producer. Some observers believe Murdoch has demonstrated vision and an ability to see around corners. He recognized that print's share of advertising revenue is declining, which led him to establish a major position in television broadcasting and in the production of broadcast products for television stations. His acquisitions have tapped world financial markets, and have been supported by the cross-subsidization of investments (cash from the United Kingdom has been poured into the United States to finance the acquisition of television stations and of 20th Century Fox) and by the transfer of experienced executives across national boundaries.

REQUIREMENTS FOR A SUCCESSFUL GLOBAL MARKETING PLAN

The successful global plan is an integrated set of effective national marketing plans. Each national marketing plan should be based upon three foundations:

1. Knowledge of the market and the marketing environment—especially of customers, competitors, and the government.
2. Knowledge of the product—the formal product, its technology, and its core benefit.
3. Knowledge of the marketing function and discipline.

A global/transnational company must decide how it will obtain these three key types of knowledge on a global basis. It must also decide how it will assign responsibility for formulating a marketing plan. If plan formulation is assigned to national subsidiaries, the global headquarters must ensure that the subsidiary planners are fully informed on the technical and engineering characteristics of the product as well as up to date in their functional skills. One of the ways of doing this is to involve headquarters marketing staff specialists in the planning process so that they can ensure that the highest standard of product and functional knowledge is associated with the local marketing staff's market knowledge.

Thus, the global/transnational plan is neither the product of the subsidiary nor the product of headquarters. It is neither "top down" nor "bottom up" but rather an interactive product that combines inputs from both the global and the local perspective. This balance is essential if the plan is to approximate the objective of global optimization as opposed to national suboptimization.

The global/transnational plan should be initiated by a global overview that assesses the broad nature of opportunity and threat on a global basis and breaks down this assessment on a country-by-country basis with an indication of sales and earnings targets for each country. These targets are proposed by headquarters as guidance to each national organization for the formulation of country plans. Guidance at this stage of the process should be guidance, and not a directive. The national organization should come up with its own target, and compare that to the target suggested by world headquarters. If there is a difference between the country target and the national organization target, this should openly challenge headquarters, and the challenge should produce a dialogue that searches for the realistic target. After receiving guidance from headquarters, country units need to develop programs that will achieve the targets specified by the guidance. After preparing their plans, headquarters and subsidiaries come together to negotiate an agreement. Headquarters is seeking top performance from each company unit and the integration of its global plan. If a country unit is a supplier for home-country and third-country markets, production schedules and transfer prices must be agreed upon. If a country unit is to market a product produced elsewhere in the company, the sales and delivery plans must be coordinated.

▼ What Kind of Global Plan?

Standardized

A standardized global marketing plan offers a number of advantages. First, there are significant cost savings if standardization is practiced. A company that limits the number of models and variants of its product can achieve longer production runs and greater economies of scale. This is elementary and has been demonstrated in actual practice thousands of times over. Henry Ford was probably the first industrialist to demonstrate the potential of mass production for achieving scale economies and creating a national market. Similarly, the Italian appliance industry during the 1960s achieved remarkable cost reduction through standardization and long production runs and in the process took a leadership position in Europe. Of course, cost savings can be achieved not only in production but also in packaging, in distribution, and in the creation of advertising materials. There are other benefits of standardization. In an increasingly mobile world a standardized product is the same in every national market and is therefore uniform for increasing numbers of customers who travel across national boundaries. There are pressures today to standardize products so that the customer can develop standardized programs in its operations. Another benefit of standardization is that it extends successful products and good ideas into all markets. There are, however, a number of obstacles to standardization. Market characteristics may be so different in so many major ways that it is impossible to offer a standardized product. There was, for example, simply no significant market in Europe (or in Japan, or in many other countries) for the standard, full-size North American car. It was too large to fit in the streets, it consumed too much gasoline, and the licensing fees—usually based on the size of engine—were too expensive. All in all, it did not appeal to buyers outside of North America. Automobile manufacturers who wish to compete in more than a very minor segment of the world market must adapt their product or develop products to suit market preferences in the rest of the world.

In cases where the same product can be sold, other elements of the marketing mix can be obstacles to standardization because of environmental differences in company position. For example, consider the company whose market-share position is quite different from market to market. Although other characteristics in markets may be relatively similar, different market-share positions make standardization of promotional and pricing decisions extremely difficult. Where the local position is commanding, an advertising message that expands the total market for the product category will benefit the dominant company. But the same company may have a minor position in an adjoining market where its advertising strategy should be to obtain a share of the market for its particular product.

Decentralized

Many companies have followed a decentralized planning approach either because of poor results using the standardized approach or after noting the many differences from country to country in market environments. This approach has received perhaps more support in marketing than any other functional area. An executive of a major international company expressed this view as follows. "Marketing is conspicuous by its absence from the functions which can be planned at the corporate headquarters level. It is in this phase of overseas business activity that the variations in social patterns and the subtlety of local conditions have the most pronounced effect on basic business strategy and tactics. For this reason, the responsibility for marketing planning must be carried out by those overseas executives who are most familiar with the local environment."

A common feature of both the standardized and the decentralized approaches is the absence of responsibility for analysis and planning at the headquarters level for multicountry marketing programs. In the standardized case such activities are assumed to be unnecessary. Once the marketing problem is solved for the home country, it is solved for the world. In the decentralized company the need for analysis and planning to respond to local conditions is recognized, but it is assumed that knowledgeable efforts can only be attempted at the country level and that there is no opportunity for effective supranational participation in these activities.

Interactive

A third approach to formulating a global marketing plan is the interactive, or integrated, approach. This is superior to either the standardized or the local plan because it draws on the strengths of each of these approaches in planning to formulate a synthesis. Under the interactive marketing planning approach, subsidiaries are responsible for identifying the unique characteristics of their market and ensuring that the marketing plan responds to local characteristics.

Headquarters, both global and regional, is responsible for establishing a broad strategic framework for planning in such matters as deciding on major goals and objectives and on where to allocate resources. In addition, headquarters must coordinate and rationalize the product design, advertising, pricing, and distribution activities of each subsidiary operation. Headquarters must constantly be alert to the trade-off of concentrating staff activities at headquarters locations in an attempt to achieve a high level of performance versus the advantages of decentralizing staff activities and assigning people directly to subsidiaries.

Each decision must stand on its own merit, but there are significant opportunities for the improvement of performance and cost saving by concentrating certain activities at one location. For example, many companies have successfully centralized the preparation of advertising appeals at world or regional headquarters. Another activity that can be done in one location is product design. Information and design criteria need to come from the world, but the design itself can be done by one design team in a single location.

▼ Planning Practices

Sorenson and Weichmann, in a survey of 100 senior executives in 27 leading multinationals in consumer packaged-goods industries, found that on their

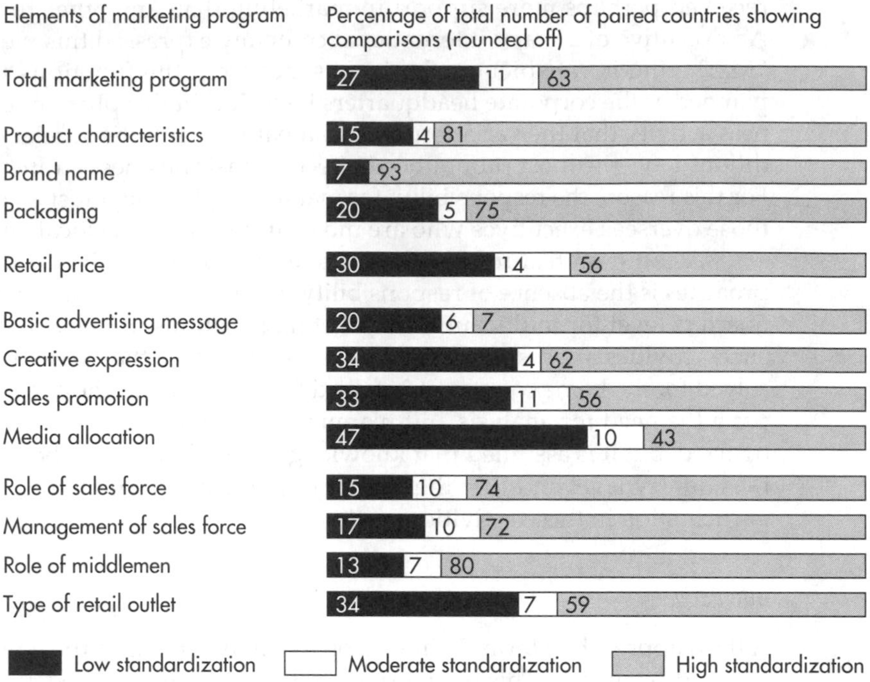

Elements of marketing program | Percentage of total number of paired countries showing comparisons (rounded off)

Elements of marketing program	Low standardization	Moderate standardization	High standardization
Total marketing program	27	11	63
Product characteristics	15	4	81
Brand name	7		93
Packaging	20	5	75
Retail price	30	14	56
Basic advertising message	20	6	7
Creative expression	34	4	62
Sales promotion	33	11	56
Media allocation	47	10	43
Role of sales force	15	10	74
Management of sales force	17	10	72
Role of middlemen	13	7	80
Type of retail outlet	34	7	59

■ Low standardization ☐ Moderate standardization ▨ High standardization

FIGURE 2–13

Index of Standardization of Marketing Decisions Among European Subsidiaries of Selected Multinational Enterprises

Source: Reprinted by permission of *Harvard Business Review*. An excerpt from "How Multinationals View Marketing Standardizations" by Ralph Z. Sorenson & Ulrich E. Wiechmann, issue May–June 1975. Copyright © 1975 by the President and Fellows of Harvard College; all rights reserved.

index, 63 percent of the total marketing programs were judged to be highly standardized.[11] The degree of standardization for the other elements of the marketing mix in the Sorenson and Weichmann study is shown in Figure 2–13. The highest degree of standardization observed was in product physical characteristics, brand names, and packaging. In addition to advantages of longer production runs, executives mentioned the advantages of better international legal and trademark protection and the intangible advantages of having a worldwide as opposed to a merely national brand franchise. This is increasingly valuable as consumers become more mobile.

In contrast to product decisions, pricing decisions are much less standardized. Manufacturing costs, competitors' prices, taxes, company market position, tariffs and duties, and so on vary from country to country, making it extremely difficult to standardize prices.

---

[11] Ralph Z. Sorenson and Ulrich Weichmann. "How Multinationals View Marketing Standardization." *Harvard Business Review* (May–June 1975), pp. 38 ff.

In advertising and promotion, Sorenson and Weichmann found that almost three-quarters of the advertising messages had been highly standardized but that the frequency of standardization for media allocation was much lower. The explanation for this difference is the fact that advertising media availability varies considerably among countries.

The major finding, however, of the Sorenson and Weichmann study is that the real competitive advantage of the transnational company comes not from the extent to which it is able to standardize marketing programs but rather the extent to which it is able to standardize the marketing process. To the successful transnational, it is not really important whether marketing programs are internationally standardized or differentiated; what is important is that the process by which these programs are developed is standardized. A standardized process provides a disciplined framework for analyzing marketing problems and opportunities. It also provides a framework for the cross-pollination of experience, ideas, and judgments from one market to another. Sorenson and Weichmann quote a headquarters executive:

> A total standardization of all the elements of the marketing mix is hardly thinkable. On the other hand, the intellectual method used for approaching a marketing problem, for analyzing that problem, and for synthesizing information in order to arrive at a decision, can absolutely be standardized on an international basis.

> It is desirable that marketing decisions be as decentralized as possible toward the field of economic battle. Nevertheless, if decision-making is done in each country according to the same intellectual process, it can be more easily understood by headquarters management: a standard process eliminating guesses in the subjective side of marketing permits one to arrive more easily at the standardization of certain elements of the marketing mix.[12]

Customizing Global Marketing

Clearly, global marketing has pitfalls but it can also yield impressive advantages. The standardization of marketing mix elements and effective coordination and transfer of experience can exploit the company's products and ideas, minimize cost, and maximize the quality of the company's total offering.

It is a fundamental mistake to view global marketing as an either/or proposition. To apply the concept of global marketing and make it work, flexibility is absolutely essential. Managers must tailor their approach to fit their own products and markets and make their plan work.

Quelch and Hoff identified four dimensions of global marketing: business functions, products, marketing mix elements, and countries.[13] They then compared the approach of Nestlé and Coca-Cola in adaptation versus standardization in each of these dimensions. Their findings are shown in Figures 2–14 and 2–15.

It is clear from these findings that Coca-Cola has proceeded much farther toward standardization than Nestlé. To conclude, however, that Coca-Cola is

---

[12] Sorensen and Weichmann, ibid., p. 40.

[13] J. A. Quelch and E. J. Hoff, "Customizing Global Marketing," *Harvard Business Review* (May–June 1986), pp. 59–68.

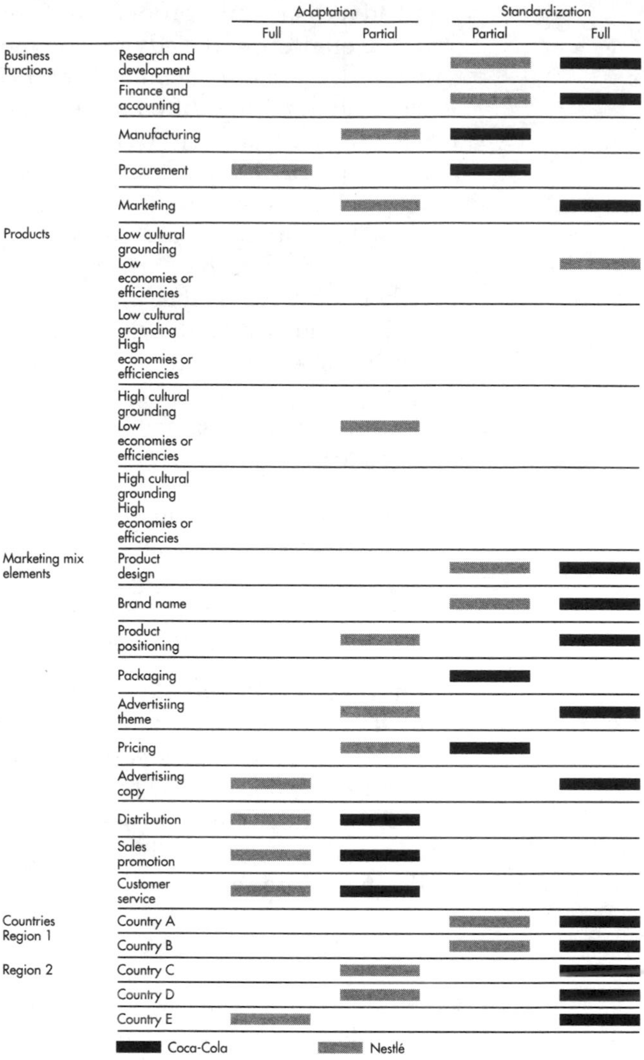

		Adaptation		Standardization	
		Full	Partial	Partial	Full
Business functions	Research and development			Nestlé	Coca-Cola
	Finance and accounting			Nestlé	Coca-Cola
	Manufacturing		Nestlé	Coca-Cola	
	Procurement	Nestlé		Coca-Cola	
	Marketing		Nestlé		Coca-Cola
Products	Low cultural grounding / Low economies or efficiencies				Nestlé
	Low cultural grounding / High economies or efficiencies				
	High cultural grounding / Low economies or efficiencies		Nestlé		
	High cultural grounding / High economies or efficiencies				
Marketing mix elements	Product design			Nestlé	Coca-Cola
	Brand name			Nestlé	Coca-Cola
	Product positioning		Nestlé		Coca-Cola
	Packaging			Coca-Cola	
	Advertisiing theme		Nestlé		Coca-Cola
	Pricing		Nestlé	Coca-Cola	
	Advertisiing copy	Nestlé			Coca-Cola
	Distribution	Nestlé	Coca-Cola		
	Sales promotion	Nestlé	Coca-Cola		
	Customer service	Nestlé	Coca-Cola		
Countries Region 1	Country A			Nestlé	Coca-Cola
	Country B			Nestlé	Coca-Cola
Region 2	Country C		Nestlé		Coca-Cola
	Country D		Nestlé		Coca-Cola
	Country E	Nestlé			Coca-Cola

Legend: ■ Coca-Cola   ▨ Nestlé

FIGURE 2–14

Global Marketing Planning Matrix: How Far to Go

Source: Reprinted by permission of *Harvard Business Review*. An excerpt from "Customizing Global Marketing" by John A. Quelch & Edward J. Hoff, issue May–June 1986. Copyright © 1986 by the President and Fellows of Harvard College; all rights reserved.

a global marketer and that Nestlé is not would be simplistic and would miss the point that each company must address its own unique product, market, and organizational circumstances in determining the extent and degree to which it can proceed along the path of standardization. Figure 2–15 shows a global marketing planning matrix, which is a framework for guiding a company in getting from where it is to where it would like to be. It is important to recognize that even in the case of Coca-Cola, which directs most of the elements of the marketing mix from its Atlanta headquarters, there is great emphasis on the role and importance of country marketing management to ensure that critical elements of the marketing program are adapted to local market and competitive con-

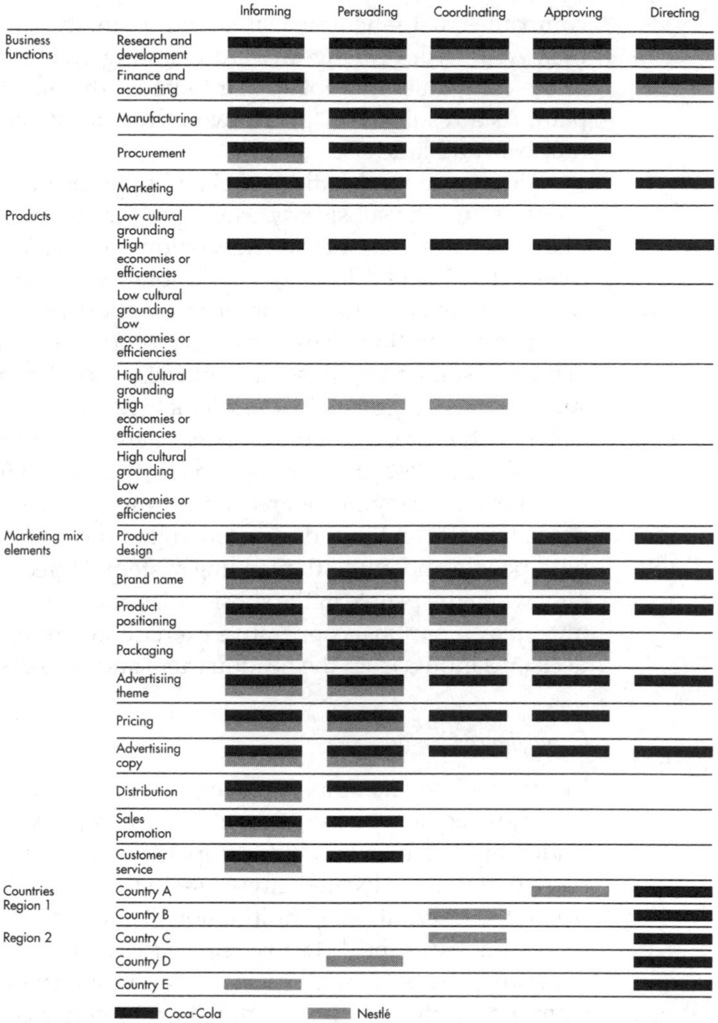

Global Planning Matrix with columns: Informing, Persuading, Coordinating, Approving, Directing

		Informing	Persuading	Coordinating	Approving	Directing
Business functions	Research and development					
	Finance and accounting					
	Manufacturing					
	Procurement					
	Marketing					
Products	Low cultural grounding High economies or efficiencies					
	Low cultural grounding Low economies or efficiencies					
	High cultural grounding High economies or efficiencies					
	High cultural grounding Low economies or efficiencies					
Marketing mix elements	Product design					
	Brand name					
	Product positioning					
	Packaging					
	Advertisiing theme					
	Pricing					
	Advertisiing copy					
	Distribution					
	Sales promotion					
	Customer service					
Countries Region 1	Country A					
	Country B					
Region 2	Country C					
	Country D					
	Country E					

Coca-Cola   Nestlé

FIGURE 2–15
Global Planning Matrix: How to Get There

Source: Reprinted by permission of *Harvard Business Review.* An excerpt from "Customizing Global Marketing" by John A. Quelch & Edward J. Hoff, issue May–June 1986. Copyright © 1986 by the President and Fellows of Harvard College; all rights reserved.

ditions and effective execution. A proactive headquarters organization and a proactive global strategy do not alone guarantee success. To succeed a company must have a strong country marketing team to ensure responsiveness to the national market and effective execution.

The Annual Operating Plan

Hulbert and Brandt found that the annual operating plan (AOP) was the keystone for virtually all firms in their sample.[14] The exception was several Japanese

---

[14] James M. Hulbert and William K. Brandt, *Managing the Multinational Subsidiary* (New York: Holt, Rinehart and Winston, 1980).

companies that relied on a six-month planning cycle. Most companies combine their AOP with a rolling-forward planning system that covers a five-year period. Many companies did not appear to know the difference between a budget and a plan. As a result their "plans" were two- to fifteen-page documents filled with numbers and little else.

There are two locations of planning problems in the local company: the headquarters and the subsidiary. Headquarters problems include poor definition of planning roles and unclear expectations. The AOP is a cooperative effort, and a clear definition of roles and responsibilities is necessary to ensure that it is done well. Another headquarters problem is a short-run perspective and an insensitivity to foreign conditions. The subsidiary problems with planning include a cultural bias against planning in some countries, a local market myopia that arises when subsidiary management dedicates itself to furthering the growth and profit of the subsidiary at the expense of the broader interests of the worldwide company.

The purpose of planning is to create a design for action. It should be a major force for increasing the degree of integration and coordination in the global company. Hulbert and Brandt concluded that most of the problems with planning lie with people and not with planning systems. Effective global planning is possible only when the people in the subsidiaries and the headquarters recognize that each must play a part in a cooperative exercise that must be based on information and decisions inputs from the headquarters and the subsidiary.

Competence Centers

In a transnational company, a competence center is an organizational unit that is designated as the business unit in the company with a responsibility for global leadership of a business. The competence center is an operating unit of the company that may be located anywhere in the world. This is in contrast to the practice in the international, multinational, and global companies of identifying the home country as the de facto competence center for the world. In the transnational company, units from all over the world compete with each other for the assignment or designation as global competence centers. The mission of a competence center is to provide leadership in the formulation and implementation of a global business strategy for a business. The competence center should be the organization that is most competent to lead a company in a business or function. Its role is to provide leadership for a global business, and to manage its business in the country in which it operates.

An example of the application of this concept is the case of a an American, global auto parts company, which decided to enter the auto tune-up service business with a franchise business model. This idea originated in a regional headquarters of the company and was tested in a major Latin American country. The business was a big success in Latin America. After reviewing this success, top management of the company decided that the market for tune-up service represented a major opportunity for the company and designated the company's Latin American regional headquarters as the worldwide competence center for the business.

The competence center assumes the role of worldwide product division headquarters for the business. At some point in time and experience, the competence center may be organizationally and physically relocated to strengthen its ability to lead and coordinate the business worldwide. Initially, however, the competence center is an existing team of experts in a country that understands a business and takes on responsibility for the globalization of the business from its existing location.

The basic concept underlying the competence center is that competence in a global company is globally dispersed. It opens up the paths to leadership in a business. The top strategy positions are no longer automatically reserved for the headquarters. It can be a part of a global plan to develop product X in country Y and then to transfer country Y's experience directly to other markets without channeling it through a single, unitary world headquarters. With competence centers, the function of world headquarters is distributed to many locations

▼ SUMMARY

There are a number of key concepts that aid marketers in realizing global market potential including the concept of strategy, which identifies the three key elements of strategy: the environment, the organization, and the values of stakeholders in the organization. The foundation of strategy is an understanding of opportunities and threats in the environment, of strengths and weaknesses in the organization, and of values of organization stakeholders. In addition to the concept of strategy, the chapter identifies other key concepts such as clustering, environmental sensitivity, unifying and differentiating influences, and the trade-cycle model.

Companies that decide to expand beyond their home country change. The chapter outlines a five-stage typology of development of a company from domestic to transnational. The most advanced stage of development is the transnational, which is a company that thinks global and acts local. Each of the stages of development has advantages, and the transnational combines all of the advantages of each of the previous stages. Companies are not pure types: actual companies are almost always a mixture of the different stages of development. Each company's path of development is unique. Some have moved through all of the stages in an orderly progression and others have leapfrogged stages in the typology to develop as global or transnational companies.

▼ DISCUSSION QUESTIONS

1. What are the major dimensions of the strategy formulation conceptual framework? Do these dimensions apply to the past, the present, or the future?

2. What is the meaning of the term *environmentally sensitive?* Cite an example of an environmentally sensitive product.

3. Which type of product provides a greater opportunity for the global company: the low or high environmentally sensitive product?

4. If you were the marketing manager of a luxury watch company, how would you cluster or segment world markets? What criteria would you use to segment the world? Why?

5. What is the product trade-cycle model? What is the link between this model and the product life-cycle?

6. What happens to the location of production of a product when it becomes mature? Why?

7. What are the stages of development of the transnational corporation? Why does an organization move from one stage to the next? Can an organization skip stages in its development?

▼ BIBLIOGRAPHY

Books

AHARONI, YAIR, *The Foreign Investment Decision Process*. Boston: Division of Research, Graduate School of Business Administration, Harvard University, 1966.

BRACELET, CHRISTOPHER A., AND SUMATRA GHOSHAL, *Managing Across Borders, The Transnational Solution*. Boston, MA: Harvard Business School Press, 1989.

DANIELS, JOHN D., AND LEE H. RADEBAUGH, *International Business: Environments and Operations (5th ed.)*, Reading, MA: Addison-Wesley, 1989.

HIEBING, ROMAN G., JR., AND SCOTT W. COOPER, *The Successful Marketing Plan*. Chicago: NTC Business Books, 1990.

OHMAE, KENICHI, *The Borderless World: Power and Strategy in the Interlinked Economy*. New York: Harper Business, 1990.

OHMAE, KENICHI, *Triad Power: The Coming Shape of Global Competition*. New York: The Free Press, 1985.

Articles

BARNEVIK, PERCY (interviewed by William Taylor), "The Logic of Global Business: An Interview with ABB's Percy Barnevik," *Harvard Business Review*, 69, no. 2 (March–April 1991), 90-105.

HOY, HAROLD J., AND JOHN J. SHAW, "The United States Comparative Advantage and Its Relationship to the Product Life Cycle Theory and the World Gross National Product Market Share," *Columbia Journal of World Business* (Spring 1981), pp. 40–50.

ONKVISIT, SAK, AND JOHN J. SHAW, "An Examination of the International Product Life Cycle and Its Application Within Marketing," *Columbia Journal of World Business* (Fall 1983), pp. 73–79.

PERLMUTTER, HOWARD V., "The Torturous Evolution of Multinational Corporations," *Columbia Journal of World Business* (January–February 1969).

————, "Social Architectural Problems of the Multinational Firm," *Quarterly Journal of AIESEC International*, 3, no. 3 (August 1967).

SIMMONDS, KENNETH, "Multinational? Well, Not Quite," *Columbia Journal of World Business* (Fall 1966), pp. 115–122.

WIND, YORAM, SUSAN P. DOUGLAS, AND HOWARD V. PERLMUTTER, "Guidelines for Developing International Marketing Strategy." *Journal of Marketing*, 37 (April 1973), 14–23.

THREE

Economic
Environment

Introduction

A major characteristic of the global marketers' world is the diversity of marketing environments in which they conduct their operations. The economic dimensions of this world market environment are of vital importance. This chapter examines the characteristics of the world economic environment from a marketing perspective.

The global marketer is fortunate in having a substantial body of data available that charts the nature of the environment on a country-by-country basis. Each country has national accounts data indicating estimates of gross national product, gross domestic product, consumption, investment, government expenditures, and price levels. Also available on a global basis are demographic data indicating the number of people, their distribution by age category, and rates of population growth. National accounts and demographic data do not exhaust the types of economic data available. A single source, *The Statistical Yearbook of the United Nations*, contains global data on agriculture, mining, manufacturing, construction, energy production and consumption, internal and external trade, railroad and air transport, wages and prices, health, housing, education, communication (mail, telegraph, and telephone), and mass communications by book, film, radio, and television. These data are available for all high-income countries. The less developed a country is, the scarcer is the availability of economic data. In the low-income countries of the world, one cannot be certain of obtaining anything more than basic national accounts, demographic, and external trade data. Nevertheless, in considering the world's economic environment, the marketer's problem is not one of an absence of data but rather of an abundance. This chapter will identify the most salient characteristics of the economic environment to provide the framework for further consideration of the elements of a global marketing program.

THE WORLD ECONOMY—AN OVERVIEW

The world economy has undergone revolutionary changes during the past 50 years.[1] Perhaps the greatest and most profound change is the emergence of global markets and global competitors who have steadily displaced local competitors. The integration of the world economy has increased from less than 10

---

[1] See Peter F. Drucker, "The Changed World Economy," *Foreign Affairs* (Spring 1986) and various issues of *The Economist*, for example, "The European Community," *The Economist*, July 11, 1992, or "When China Wakes," *The Economist*, November 28, 1992.

percent at the turn of this century to approximately 50 percent today. Even as recently as 25 years ago, the world was far less integrated than it is today. There were many companies, many products, and great differentiation. Take automobiles, for example. In 1960, the European Renault, Citroen, Peugeot, Morris, Volvo, and others were radically different than the American Chevrolet, Ford, or Plymouth, or the Japanese Toyota or Nissan. These were different cars for different markets. Today, the world car is a reality for Toyota, Nissan, and Honda. Indigenous North American car makers have yet to succeed with a world car, although Ford, with its European model Mondeo, is going that way.[2] The changes continue. Within the past decade, there have been five major changes:

- ► Capital movements rather than trade have become the driving force of the world economy.
- ► Production has become "uncoupled" from employment.
- ► Primary products have become "uncoupled" from the industrial economy.
- ► The world economy is in control. The macroeconomics of the nation-state no longer control economic outcomes.
- ► The 75-year "contest" between capitalism and socialism is over. The clear success of the capitalist system over the communist centrally controlled model has led to the collapse of communism as a model for the organization of economic activity and as an ideology.

These remarkable changes are contrary to much of the received doctrine of economic theory, and they are of great significance and importance to government and business practitioners. Practitioners cannot wait until there is a new theory—the likelihood of success is much greater when actions are based on the new reality of the changed world economy. The first change is the increased volume of capital movements. World trade is greater than ever before. Trade in goods and so-called *invisibles* (services) is running at roughly C$7.2 trillion per year. Global foreign exchange transactions run more than $1 trillion per day, which is $270 trillion per year, or some 38 times the volume of world trade in goods and services.[3] There is an inescapable conclusion in these data: Capital movements far exceed the volume of trade finance. The value of a country's currency is no longer determined by the state of its trade accounts alone, as it was in the past. Rather, capital movements and trade together shape the value of a currency.

The second change is that although employment in manufacturing remains steady or has declined, production continues to grow. The pattern in agriculture where fewer and fewer produce more and more continues. In Canada, manufacturing accounts for about one-quarter of GNP. This is true of all the other major industrial economies as well. Manufacturing is not in decline—it is

---

[2] "The World Car: Enter the McFord," *The Economist* (July 23, 1994).

[3] "Financial Indicators," *The Economist* (July 16, 1994), p. 97; and "Central Bank Survey of Foreign Exchange Market Activity in April 1992," *Bank for International Settlements*, Monetary and Economic Department, Basle (March 1993), Table 1, p. 6.

employment in manufacturing that is in decline. Countries like the United Kingdom, which have tried to hold onto blue-collar employment in manufacturing, have lost both production and jobs for their efforts, a bitter fruit indeed.

The third change is the "uncoupling" of the primary products economy from the industrial economy. Commodity prices have collapsed to levels that are as low as during the Great Depression. There is a major depression in the primary products economy, and it seems as if it has had almost no impact on the industrial economy, in contrast to the past when a sharp drop in raw material prices would bring on a worldwide depression in the industrial economy.

The fourth major change is the emergence of the world economy as the dominant economic unit. Companies and countries that recognize this fact have the greatest chance of success. Those who do not recognize this fact will suffer decline and bankruptcy or overthrowal. MIT economist Lester Thurow asserts in his recent study that global competition is no longer niche but head to head.[4] In niche competition, every player provides something different and, as a result, everybody wins. In direct (head-to-head) competition, somebody must lose.

The last change is the end of the "cold war." In a very real sense, communism as an economic and political system has been overthrown by the success of the capitalist market system. The overwhelmingly superior performance of the capitalist enterprise, market allocation system has led the countries that have adopted socialism to renounce their ideology and their attempt to manage their economies with a single central plan.

The real secret of the success of Germany and Japan is their focus on the world economy and world markets; the first priority of their governments and businesses has been their competitive position in the world. Canada, in contrast, has focused on the domestic and the U.S. economies and much less on her global competitive position.

Changes in global competition are bringing countries into more direct confrontation with their main economic rivals than was the case in the past. Yesterday's global forces were founded on exports of products and services not available to competing nations. Natural resources and agricultural products still account for 20 percent of Canada's exports.

ECONOMIC SYSTEMS

There are three types of economic systems: capitalist, socialist, and mixed. These classifications are based on the method of resource allocation in the system, which is *market allocation, command* or *central plan allocation,* and *mixed allocation,* respectively. There are no pure examples of market or central plan allocation systems. All actual systems are mixed allocation.

---

[4] Lester Thurow, *Head to Head: The Coming Economic Battle Among Japan, Europe, and America* (New York: William Morrow and Company, Inc., 1992).

▼ Market Allocation

A market allocation system is one which relies upon the customer or consumer to allocate resources. Consumer choice or purchase under a market system decides what will be produced by whom. The market system is economic democracy—money gives you the right to vote for the goods of your choice. Consumers and customers write the economic plan of market allocation systems with their purchase decisions and purchase intentions. Canada, the United States, Europe, and Japan, which account for three-quarters of gross world product, are examples of predominately market allocation systems. The clear superiority of the market allocation system in delivering the goods and services that people need and want has led to its expansion to the former socialist bloc.

▼ Command Allocation

In a command allocation system, resource allocation decisions (i.e., which products to make and how to make them) are made by government planners. The number of automobiles, shoes, shirts, motorcycles, television sets, and the size, color, quality, features, and so on of every product are determined by government planners. Under the command system, consumers are free to spend their money on what is available, but the decisions about what is produced and, therefore, what is available are made by the state planners. The former Soviet Union and China were leading examples of countries relying upon command allocation. The new independent republics have been undergoing the arduous shift to a market allocation system, while in China this process is relatively selective and controlled. Cuba and North Korea are the last remaining predominantly command allocation economic systems.

▼ Mixed System

There are no pure market or command allocation systems. All market systems have a command sector and command systems have a market sector. All capitalist market systems are "mixed" (i.e., they have elements of market and command allocation). The command allocation of the market economy is the proportion of gross domestic product that is taxed and spent by government. This proportion for the 24 OECD (Organization for Economic Cooperation and Development) member countries ranges from 32 percent of gross domestic product in the United States to 64 percent in Sweden. Canada's share of 42 percent is similar to that of many other Western European countries.[5] In Sweden, therefore, where 64 percent of all expenditures are controlled by government, the economic system is more command than market as contrasted with the United States where the system is more market than command. One of the profound changes that is taking place in the world today is the move toward *privatization,* which is another way of describing the move within a mixed economy toward greater reliance upon the market.

---

[5] *OECD Economic Outlook,* no. 50 (December 1991), (Paris: OECD, 1991), p. 206.

TABLE 3–1   Productivity and Investment in the World Economy, 1971–1990 (1980 $ thousand)

	1971–75	1976–80	1981–85	1986–90
Gross Product Per Worker				
Developed market economies	20.2	22.2	23.0	25.8
Eastern Europe and USSR	6.0	7.3	8.2	9.2
Developing Countries	1.5	1.7	1.8	1.9
Africa	1.8	2.0	1.8	1.8
Asia, excluding West Asia	0.6	0.8	0.9	1.2
Latin America and Caribbean	5.4	6.0	5.9	5.8
World	5.5	6.0	6.2	6.6
Investment per Worker				
Developed market economies	5.1	5.2	5.1	6.2
Eastern Europe and USSR	1.9	2.3	2.3	2.4
Developing Countries	0.3	0.4	0.5	0.5
Africa	0.4	0.5	0.4	0.3
Asia, excluding West Asia	0.2	0.2	0.3	0.4
Latin America and Caribbean	1.2	1.5	1.1	0.9
World	1.4	1.5	1.5	1.6

Source: World Economic Survey 1992; United Nations

Just as the market economies have command sectors, command economies have market sectors where production and prices are set by forces of supply and demand. Farmers in most socialist countries, for example, are permitted to offer part of their production in a free market. China has given considerable freedom to business and individuals in the Guangdong Providence to operate within a market system.

There is a growing consensus about the effectiveness of a market system in delivering value and deregulation. This has led voters and governments to support initiatives to move toward the privatization of services that had been part of government-owned or regulated industries.

▼ Productivity Around the Globe

There is a close relationship between growth of labor productivity, as measured by the growth on output produced per person in the labor force, and the share of investment in GNP. But productivity is not determined exclusively by investment. It depends, in particular, on the technology embodied in the investment, management and labor skills, education, level of unemployment, and so on.

From the first half of the 1970s to the latter half of the 1980s, gross output per worker rose only about 20 percent in the world as a whole (see Table 3–1). Most of the increase took place in the developed market economies, where investment per worker has been far higher than in the rest of the world. It is interesting to note that investment per worker in the former socialist bloc countries that are now in transition to market economies was never as much as half the level of the developed market economies.

TABLE 3–2	Stages of Market Development					
Income Group by Per Capita GNP	1992 GNP ($billion)	1992 GNP per Capita ($)	% of World GNP	1992 Population (million)	Number of Countries
High-Income Countries GNP per Capita >$14,500	20,674	25,260	79.9	818.44	27
Upper-Middle-Income Countries GNP per Capita >$2,500 but <$14,500	2,983	3,272	11.5	912.03	55
Lower-Middle-Income Countries GNP per Capita >$500 but <$2,500	1,592	807	6.2	1,974.37	55
Low-Income Countries GNP per Capita <$500	639	370	2.5	1,724.17	42

Productivity growth in the developing countries displayed a pattern that has been repeated for almost all macroeconomics indicators: Latin America and the Caribbean experienced a measure of productivity growth in the 1970s and stagnation thereafter; Africa has enjoyed virtually no growth in average productivity in the entire period, and Asia's productivity has doubled, despite a very low starting point. Not surprisingly, investment per worker barely rose at all in the developing countries, and in Africa and Latin America it actually declined. In these countries, in particular, it is crucial that investment spending be raised in a significant and sustained manner.

MARKET DEVELOPMENT

▼ Stages of Market Development

Global country markets are at different stages of development. GNP per capita is a useful demographic segmentation base. Using this base, we have divided global markets into five categories. Although the income definition for each of the stages is arbitrary, countries in the five categories have similar characteristics so the stages provide a useful basis for global market segmentation and target marketing. The categories are shown in Table 3–2.

Low-Income Countries

Low-income countries, also known as "third world" or preindustrial countries, are those with 1992 incomes of less than C$500 per capita. The characteristics shared by countries at this income level are:

1. Limited industrialization and a high percentage of the population engaged in agriculture and subsistence farming.

2. High birth rates.
3. Low literacy rates.
4. Heavy reliance on foreign aid.
5. Political instability and unrest.
6. Concentrated in Africa south of the Sahara.

These countries are limited markets for all products, and are not significant locations for competitive threats.

Lower-Middle-Income Countries

Lower-middle-income countries, also known as less developed countries (LDCs), are those with a 1992 GNP per capita of more than C$500 and less than C$2,500. These countries are at the early stages of industrialization. Factories are erected to supply a growing domestic market with such items as clothing, batteries, tires, building materials, and packaged foods. These countries are also locations for the production of standardized or mature products such as clothing for export markets.

Consumer markets in these countries are expanding. They represent an increasing competitive threat as they mobilize their relatively cheap and often highly motivated labor to target markets in the rest of the world. In mature and standardized labor intensive products, they have a major competitive advantage.

Upper-Middle-Income Countries

Upper-middle-income countries, also known as industrializing countries, are those with 1992 GNP per capita between C$2,500 and C$14,500. In these countries, the percentage of population engaged in agriculture drops sharply as people move from the agricultural to the industrial sector and the degree of urbanization increases. Many of the countries in this stage are rapidly industrializing. They have rising wages and high rates of literacy and advanced education, but they still have significantly lower wage costs than the advanced countries. With the capability of the advanced countries and lower wage rates, they frequently become formidable competitors and experience rapid economic growth led by exports.

High-Income Countries

High-income countries, also known as advanced, industrialized, postindustrial, or First World countries, are those with a 1992 GNP per capita above C$14,500. With the exception of a few oil-rich nations, the countries in this category reached their present income level through a process of sustained economic growth.

The term *postindustrial countries* was first advanced by Daniel Bell of Harvard. Bell suggests that the main difference between the industrial and the postindustrial society is that the sources of innovation in a postindustrial society are derived increasingly from the codification of theoretical knowledge rather than from "random" inventions. Other characteristics, summarized in Table 3–3, are the importance of the service sector (more than 50 percent of GNP); the crucial importance of information processing and exchange; and the ascendancy of knowledge over capital as the key strategic resource, of intellectual technology over machine

TABLE 3–3 The Postindustrial Society: A Comparative Schema

MODES (Mode of Production)	PREINDUSTRIAL (Extractive)	INDUSTRIAL (Fabrication)	POSTINDUSTRIAL (Processing, Recycling Services)		
			Tertiary	Quaternary	Quinary
Economic sector	Primary Agriculture Mining Fishing Timber Oil and gas	Secondary Goods producing Manufacturing Durables Nondurables Heavy construction	Transportation Utilities	Trade Finance Insurance Real estate	Health Research Education Government Recreation
Transforming resource	Natural power Wind, water, draft animals, human muscle	Created energy Electricity—oil, gas, coal Nuclear power	Information Computer and data transmission systems		
Strategic resource	Raw materials	Financial capital	Knowledge		
Technology	Craft	Machine technology	Intellectual technology		
Skill base	Artisan, manual worker, farmer	Engineer, semiskilled worker	Scientist, technical, and professional occupations		
Methodology	Common sense, trial and error, experience	Empiricism, experimentation	Abstract theory: models, simulations, decision theory, systems analysis		
Time perspective	Orientation to the past	Ad hoc adaptiveness, experimentation	Future orientation, forecasting, and planning		
Design	Game against nature	Game against fabricated nature	Game between persons		
Axial principle	Traditionalism	Economic growth	Codification of theoretical knowledge		

Source: Physics Today (February 1976), p. 47.

technology, of scientists and professionals over engineers and semiskilled workers, and of theory and models over empiricism.

▶ Other aspects of the postindustrial society are an orientation toward the future and the importance of interpersonal and intragroup relationships in the functioning of society.

▶ Canada, the United States, Sweden, and Japan are examples of postindustrial or advanced societies. Japan is a particularly interesting case of a postindustrial society.

The Japanese in many respects are uniquely suited in their basic cultural orientation to adapt to the basic requirements of a postindustrial society. Cooperation and harmonious interaction, for example, are important keystones of the Japanese culture. This is in marked contrast to Britain, which has experienced difficulty in emerging from the industrial stage of development largely because of the inability of labor and management to find mutually acceptable ways of adapting to the adjustments required by technological, organizational, and managerial modernization.

The Japan Computer Usage Development Institute prepared a document in the early 1970s called "The Plan for Information Society—A National Goal Toward Year 2000," which is a good example of a conscious statement of the qualities and goals of a postindustrial society. The introduction to the report states:

> During almost a century, since the Imperial Restoration, Japan endeavored to build a modernized industrial society, and has almost reached this goal. However, Japan is now confronting multitudes of social and economic problems that include pollution problems, excessively dense population problems in urban areas, economic depression resulting from industrial and economic structures, increases in aged population, etc.

> In the advanced countries, de-industrialization is now under way, and the world is generally and steadily shifting from the industrialized society to the information society. Therefore, this committee proposes the establishment of a new national target, "Realization of the Information Society."

> The ultimate goal of the information society is the realization of a "society that brings about a general flourishing state of human intellectual creativity." Intellectual creativity may be defined as a process of exploring into future possibilities by fully employing information and knowledge with the aim of materializing such possibilities.

Product and market opportunities in the postindustrial society are more heavily dependent upon new products and innovations than in industrial societies. All the basic products are already owned. Household saturation levels are extremely high, and a marketer seeking to expand his or her business must either expand the share of existing markets, which is always difficult, or create a new market. This market condition is an incentive for new-product development and is an important driver for creativity and innovation in the postindustrial society.

TABLE 3–4 Stages of Market Development

Country Income Segmentation
High Income (Advanced Countries) + C$14,500
Upper Middle Income (NICs) + C$2,500
Lower Middle Income (DCs) + C$500
Low Income (LDCs) < C$500
Basket Cases (BCs)

Basket Cases

A basket case is a country with economic, social, and political problems that are so serious they make the country unattractive for investment and operations. Some basket cases are low-income, no-growth countries that lurch from one disaster to the next. Others are formerly growing and successful countries divided by political divisions that lead to civil strife, declining income, and often considerable danger to residents if there is outright civil war. Basket cases caused by a civil war are dangerous territory. Most companies find it prudent to avoid these countries during active conflict.

The republics of the former Soviet Union present an interesting situation where income is declining and there is considerable economic hardship. The potential for disruption is certainly high. Are these republics basket cases or are they attractive opportunities with good potential for moving into the high-income category? These countries present an interesting risk-reward trade-off, and a challenge to every company to decide whether or not to take the risk. Table 3-4 summarizes the stages of market development.

▼ The Location of Income

In charting a plan for multinational market expansion, the single most valuable economic variable for most products is income. For some products, particularly those that have a very low unit cost, population is a more valuable predictor of market potential than income. Cigarettes are an excellent example of this type of product. Nevertheless, for the vast range of industrial and consumer products in international markets today, the single most valuable and important indicator of potential is income.

Income is not an accurate or a precise measure of potential; it is only an approximate indicator. For example, Canada's per capita GNP is approximately eight times that of Brazil. This figure is of initial interest to a manufacturer of light sockets and light bulbs and suggests a Canadian market eight times larger on a per capita basis. However, the average number of light sockets per home in Brazil is five versus 25 in Canada, a difference of 5 times. When market potential is estimated on the basis of the number of Brazilian homes, the size of the Brazilian market can be estimated more precisely. With additional data on the average utilization of light bulbs in Brazilian households, the light-bulb marketer with data on the number of homes could identify the exact potential in Brazil. Without the household data, the marketer could estimate roughly on the basis of total GNP.

Gross national product and other measures of national income converted to Canadian dollars or any similar economic measures should ideally be calculated on the basis of purchasing power parities (i.e., what the currency will buy in the country of issue) or through direct real product comparisons. This would provide an actual comparison of the standards of living in the countries of the world. Since these data are not available in regular statistical reports, throughout this book we use instead conversion of local currency measured at the average Canadian dollar foreign exchange spot rate. The reader must remember that exchange rates equate, at best, the prices of internationally traded goods and services. They often bear little relationship to the prices of those goods and services not entering the international trade, which form the bulk of the national product in most countries. Agricultural output and services, in particular, are generally priced lower in relation to industrial output in developing countries than in industrial countries. Furthermore, agriculture typically accounts for the largest share of output in developing countries. Thus, the use of exchange rates tends to exaggerate differences in real income between less developed and more developed countries.

The United Nations' International Comparison Project (ICP) developed a sophisticated method for measuring total expenditure, which has been used to derive more reliable and directly comparable estimates of per capita income. The World Bank has published a comparison of ICP findings with its own Atlas figures based on exchange rate conversion. Table 3–5 compares World Bank GNP data based on exchange-rate conversion of local currency GNP with the ICP's more sophisticated measure. India's real income, for example, is three times greater than that indicated by the exchange comparison. The ICP income figure is 1.5 times greater than that indicated by the exchange comparison. In short, the use of exchange rates tends to distort real income or standard-of-living measures. Nevertheless, the use of exchange rates does provide a rough

TABLE 3–5 Per Capita Currency Conversion Method (Atlas GNP) Compared with International Comparison Project Method (ICP-GDP), 1987, 1988 (indices U.S. = 100)

Country	GDP ICP (1988)	GNP Atlas (1987)
India	4.3	4.6
Kenya	4.9	6.1
Indonesia	9.3	10.5
Colombia	19.5	23.8
Hungary	30.2	30.4
Spain	40.4	50.5
Germany	68.7	80.7
Switzerland	88.1	95.8
Canada	88.7	91.0
United States	100.0	100.0

Source: Prepared by authors, based on data from World Development Report, 1994, Table 30, pp. 220–1, Robert Summers and Alan Heston (1991), "The Penn World Table (Mark 5): An Expanded Set of International Comparisons, 1950–1988," *The Quarterly Journal of Economics*, Vol. CVI, May, Issue 2, pp. 327–368.

TABLE 3–6 Global Income and Population, 1992

Market	GNP C $ (billion)	GNP Per Capita C $	% of World GNP	Population (million)	% of World Population
World (Total)	25,890	4,718	100	5,487	100
Triad (Total)	20,026	25,528	77	784	14
U.S. and Canada	7,707	27,235	30	283	5
Japan	4,113	32,905	16	125	2
Western Europe	8,206	21,794	32	376	7
Other High Income	648	19,091	3	34	1
Upper Middle Income	2,983	3,272	12	912	17
Lower Middle Income	1,593	807	6	1,974	36
Low Income and Unavailable Data	640	370	2	1,782	32

measure of income levels and has the merit of being an easily obtainable figure. Beyond the exchange distortion, there is the distortion of money itself as an indicator of the welfare and standard of living of a people. A visit to a mud house in Tanzania will reveal many of the things that money can buy: radios, an iron bed frame, a corrugated metal roof, factory-made beer, bicycles, shoes, snapshots, soft drinks, and razor blades. But Tanzania's per capita income of C$130 does not reflect the fact that instead of utility bills, Tanzanians have the local well and the sun. Instead of nursing homes, tradition and custom ensure that elderly are cared for by their relatives. Instead of expensive doctors and hospitals, there is the witch doctor and healer. Much of the wealth of the rich industrialized countries is really only a free good or service in a poor country that has been "monetized." Thus, poor countries' demand for goods and services is not revealed in per capita income analysis.

With these qualifications in mind, the reader is referred to Tables 3–6 and 3–7, which show the location of world income and population by region in 1992. The striking fact revealed by these tables is the concentration of income in the triad, the United States and Canada, the European Union (EU), and Japan, which accounted for 77 percent of global income but only 14 percent of the world's population in 1992.

The concentration of wealth in a handful of large industrialized countries is the most striking characteristic of the global economic environment. This characteristic appears again if one examines the world regions and again if one examines the distribution of wealth and income within countries. The United States is, of course, a colossus in North America, as is the former Soviet Union in Eastern Europe. In 1992 these countries accounted for 91 percent and 70 percent, respectively, of their region's GDP (gross domestic product). In Western Europe, France, West Germany, and the United Kingdom accounted for almost 65 percent of that region's GDP. In Asia, Japan accounted for 73 percent of the region's GDP! In Latin America, Argentina, Brazil, and Mexico accounted for 73 percent of LAFTA (Latin America Free-Trade Area) GDP.

The top ten countries in 1992 are all located in the triad with the exception of China (see Figure 3–1). No one knows what the future will bring, but extrapolation of the growth of the period between 1980 to 1990 to the year 2020 produces

TABLE 3–7   Global Income and Population, 1992

Global Income and Population	1992 GNP (C$billion)	1992 GNP per Capita ($C)	% of World GNP	1992 Population (million)	% of World Population
Country Summary					
World Total	25,980	4,718	100.0	5,486.98	100.0
High Income	20,674	25,607	79.9	818.44	14.9
Triad Total	20,026	25,528	77.3	784.49	14.3
U.S. and Canada	7,707	27,235	29.8	283.01	5.2
Japan	4,113	32,905	15.9	124.99	2.3
European Economic Area	8,206	21,794	31.7	376.49	6.9
Other High Income	648	19,091	2.5	33.95	0.6
Upper Middle Income	2,983	3,272	11.5	912.03	16.6
Lower Middle Income	1,595	807	6.2	1,974.37	36.0
Low Income and Unavailable Data	640	307	2.5	1,782.13	32.5
Expansion of Markets Above*					
High-Income Countries	20,674	25,607	79.9	818.44	14.9
GNP per Capita > C$14,500					
United States	7,008	27,376	27.1	255.99	4.7
Canada	700	25,897	2.7	27.02	0.5
Japan	4,113	32,905	15.9	124.99	2.3
EC	7,070	21,407	27.3	330.26	6.0
Belgium	192	19,149	0.7	10.04	0.2
Denmark	143	27,800	0.6	5.19	0.1
France	1,388	24,390	5.4	56.91	1.0
Germany	1,984	25,770	7.7	77.00	1.4
Italy	1,230	21,269	4.7	57.82	1.1
Luxembourg	14	37,665	0.1	0.38	0.0
Netherlands	325	21,531	1.3	15.08	0.3
Portugal	65	6,190	0.3	10.50	0.2
Spain	551	13,912	2.1	39.64	0.7
United Kingdom	1,177	20,403	4.5	57.71	1.1
EFTA	1,019	31,274	3.9	32.58	0.6
Austria	185	24,180	0.7	5.02	0.1
Finland	168	33,546	0.7	5.02	0.1
Iceland	7	26,162	0.0	0.26	0.0
Norway	126	29,459	0.5	4.28	0.1
Sweden	255	29,646	1.0	8.60	0.2
Switzerland	277	41,047	1.1	6.76	0.1
Asia	138	15,874	0.5	8.73	0.2
Hong Kong	92	15,520	0.4	5.94	0.1
Singapore	46	16,629	0.2	2.79	0.1
Caribbean	4	20,264	0.0	0.17	0.0
Bermuda	2	29,440	0.0	0.06	0.0
Virgin Islands, U.S.	2	15,463	0.0	0.11	0.0
Oceania	427	20,377	1.7	20.98	0.4
Australia	374	21,340	1.4	17.52	0.3
New Zealand	54	15,507	0.2	3.46	0.1
Oil Producing Countries	78	19,305	0.3	4.07	0.1
Kuwait (est.)	43	18,288	0.2	2.33	0.0
United Arab Emirates	36	20,670	0.1	1.74	0.0

TABLE 3–7   Global Income and Population, 1992 *(Continued)*

Global Income and Population	1992 GNP (C$ billion)	1992 GNP per Capita (C$)	% of World GNP	1992 Population (million)	% of World Population
Upper-Middle-Income Countries	2,983	3,272	11.5	912.01	16.6
GNP per Capita > C$2,500 but < C$14,500					
Eastern Europe	785	2,222	3.0	353.40	6.4
Hungary	37	3,551	0.1	10.51	0.2
Former USSR	574	1,952	2.2	293.95	5.4
Former Yugoslavia	88	3,633	0.3	24.13	0.4
Middle America	292	3,137	1.1	93.17	1.7
Mexico	265	2,955	1.0	89.64	1.6
South America	678	3,159	2.6	214.64	3.9
Argentina	91	2,756	0.4	33.20	0.6
Brazil	513	3,272	2.0	156.88	2.9
Venezuela	62	2,971	0.2	20.86	0.4
Oil Producing Countries	371	3,332	1.4	111.48	2.0
Iran	177	2,907	0.7	60.98	1.1
Saudi Arabia	82	4,995	0.3	16.37	0.3
Africa	127	3,034	0.5	41.99	0.8
Asia	617	7,357	2.4	83.89	1.5
Caribbean	19	5,633	0.1	3.31	0.1
Western Europe	5	9.376	0.0	0.58	0.0
Middle East	83	9,238	0.3	8.99	0.2
Oceania	4	7,652	0.0	0.56	0.0
Lower-Middle-Income Countries					
GNP per Capita > C$500 but < C$2,500					
Eastern Europe	135	2,072	0.5	65.32	1.2
Poland	81	2,097	0.3	38.50	0.7
South America	140	1,487	0.5	93.93	1.7
Chile	33	2,390	0.1	13.63	0.2
Oceania	7	1,163	0.0	5.75	0.1
Fiji	2	2,121	0.0	0.77	0.0
Oil Producing Countries	41	2,023	0.2	20.30	0.4
Iraq	41	2,023	0.2	20.30	0.4
Africa	150	929	0.6	161.64	2.9
Asia	617	7,357	2.4	83.89	1.5
Caribbean	12	1,196	0.0	10.04	0.2
Middle America	36	1,209	0.1	30.20	0.6
Middle East	153	1,735	0.6	88.17	1.6
Low-Income Countries	640	370	2.5	1,724.17	31.4
GNP per Capita < C$500					
Asia	504	398	1.9	1,264.78	23.1
Bangladesh	29	246	0.1	119.08	2.2
India	396	447	1.5	885.16	16.6
Africa	132	293	0.5	451.6	8.2
Caribbean	3	427	0.0	6.7	0.1
Oceania.	0.2	224	0.0	1.0	0.0

* "Expansion of Markets" secton does not show all countries for a particular region.

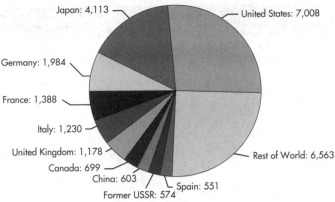

FIGURE 3–1
World GNP Top 10—1992 (in Billions)

interesting results, shown in Figure 3–2. The United States and Japan remain in the first and second positions, but China and South Korea overtake Germany; the former Soviet Union is no longer on the list, and India appears on the list for the first time. No one knows, of course, what the future will bring, but these extrapolation results do suggest that China, with its combination of high real income growth and relatively low population growth is a strong candidate to become a leading world economic power.

An examination of the distribution of wealth within countries again reveals patterns of income concentration, particularly in the less developed countries outside the communist bloc. Adelman and Morris found that the average share of GNP accruing to the poorest 20 percent of the population in less developed countries included in their study was 5.6 percent as compared with 56 percent going to the top 20 percent. The income of the bottom 20 percent was about one-fourth of what it would have been had income been distributed uniformly throughout the population. Their study suggests that the relationship between the share of in-

FIGURE 3–2
World GNP Top 10—2020 (in Billions)

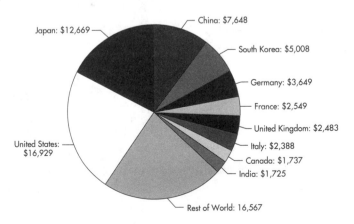

come at the lowest 20 percent and economic development varies with the level of development. Economic development is associated with increases in the share of the bottom 20 percent only after relatively high levels of socioeconomic development have been attained. At the early stages of the development process, economic development works to the *relative* disadvantage of the lowest income groups. Brazil, for example, has become one of the world's most unequal societies, with the top 20 percent of the country's population earning 65 percent of national income; the bottom 20 percent earns less than 3 percent. This is the most extreme income inequality that the World Bank has measured—far worse than in Bangladesh.[6]

Adelman and Morris found that countries with a higher share of national income accruing to the poorest 20 percent were characterized by low or moderate degrees of dualism in their economies and by the pursuit of agriculturally oriented foreign trade policies. Countries in which the smallest portion of national income (2 percent) accrued to the lowest 20 percent were characterized by sharp dualism in their economies, which were centered on foreign finance and foreign-managed exploitation of natural resources.

Today a different type of inequality has impressed itself on the conscience of the world—the vast and growing gap between the rich and the poor nations. There are several crucial questions concerning the present economic distance between these nations: When did it evolve? How large is it? What were the dimensions of time and space that brought it about? Can it be bridged in the foreseeable future?

At the beginning of the industrial revolution over 200 years ago, the economic landscape of the world was relatively flat in contrast to the present uneven world where there are very high mountains and very low plains. Even as late as 1860 more than half the population of northwestern Europe and North America was engaged in agriculture—not much different from the share of the population engaged in agriculture in the preindustrial countries at present. Yields per hectare of land, share of industries in total output, and illiteracy ratios were only marginally different. The peoples of Western Europe, for example, did not have the means to be much better off economically than the rest of the world. World output of pig iron in 1850 was only 4.6 million tons, and half of it was produced in Great Britain. The most advanced countries were still in the last days of the Iron Age. Even by 1870, world output of steel was no more than 700,000 tons—less than one-fifth of India's output in 1961.

Empirical evidence about the income levels in industrialized countries supports this picture. Professor S. S. Kuznets has, by applying known rates of growth, extrapolated backward the per capita income of the industrial countries in the early 1950s. The data in Table 3–8 show the years when such regression (extrapolation backward) yields a per capita income of US$200 in comparable 1952–1954 prices.

A weighted average and straight-line extrapolation suggest that the average per capita income in industrial countries as a group was about US$170 in 1850, or only 70 percent higher than that of the preindustrial countries in the early 1960s. If the United Kingdom and the United States are excluded, the average income in the rest of this group would have been US$150 in 1850.

Although these estimates make no allowance for free sunshine and the lower requirements for survival in the warmer climates, it seems clear that the economic landscape of the 1850s was relatively flat. The actual conditions of life for the masses in the

---

[6] Jim Rohwer. *The Economist*, 321, no. 7736, December 7, 1991, S6–S7.

TABLE 3–8	Year When Country Achieved a Per Capita Income of $200 in 1952–54 **Prices**		
United States	1832	Sweden	1889
United Kingdom	1837	Russia	1889
Canada	1846	Italy	1909
France	1852	Mexico	1950
Germany	1886	Japan	1955

Source: Simon Kuznets, Six Lectures on Economic Growth. "Lecture II: The Meaning and Measurement of Economic Growth", Glencoe, IL., The Free Press of Glencoe, 1959, pp. 12–28, Table 3.

richest and the poorest countries were not significantly different. This is in sharp contrast to the conditions today where the gap between the living standard of the majority in the high-income countries is vastly different than that of the majority in the low-income countries. This growing gap between the richest and the poorest countries is a tremendous incentive to people in poor countries to move to a high-income country to seek economic opportunity and a higher standard of living.

Since 1850 the distribution of population between the industrial and the preindustrial countries has not altered significantly. But between 1850 and 1992, the industrial countries' share of world income increased from 39 to 75 percent. The annual compound rates of growth during this period, which have so profoundly altered the world's distribution of income, were 2.7 percent in total output, and 1.8 percent in per capita output. The magnitude of change as compared with the previous 6,000 years of our civilized existence is enormous; over one-third of the real income and about two-thirds of the industrial output produced by people throughout recorded history were generated in the industrialized countries in the last century. The significance of these growth figures is that relatively small average annual rates of growth have transformed the economic geography of the world. What the industrial countries have done is to systematize economic growth or, put another way, they have established a process of continuous, gradual change. Patel has calculated that India, one of the poorest countries in the world, could reach U.S. income levels by growing at an average rate of 5 to 6 percent in real terms for 40 to 50 years. This is no more than the lifetime of an average Indian, and about half the lifetime of an average American. To point out the possible does not of course make it a probable event, but it does underline the fact that economic distance created by sustained growth can also be removed by sustained growth, as Japan has so dramatically demonstrated in recent years.

The world has changed enormously from biblical times when Saint Matthew observed, "For ye have the poor always with you." Today, much more than was true 2,000 years ago, wealth and income are concentrated regionally, nationally, and within nations. The implications of this reality are crucial for the global marketer. A company that decides to diversify geographically can accomplish this objective by establishing operations in a handful of national markets.

▼ The Location of Population

We have already noted the concentration of 77 percent of world income in the triad (the United States and Canada, the EU, and Japan). In 1992, the ten most populous countries in the world accounted for 57 percent of world income, and the five largest account for 37 percent (see Table 3–9). The concentration of income in the high-income and high-population countries means that a

TABLE 3–9 The Ten Most Populous Countries: 1992 with Projection to 2020

Global Income and Population	1992 Population (million)	% of World Population	Population Growth Rate (%) 1980–90	Projected Population 2020	1992 GNP (C$billion)	Per Capita Income (C$)	% of World GNP	
WORLD TOTAL	5,486.98	100.00		9,404.09	11,463.37		100.00	
1. China	1,167.96	21.29	1.5	1,772.06	602.53	515	2.56	
2. India	885.56	16.14	2.1	1,584.68	395.74	446	1.68	
3. Former USSR	293.95	5.36	0.9	377.77	573.94	1952	2.44	
4. United States	255.99	4.67	1.0	338.23	7,008.05	27,376	29.76	
5. Indonesia	188.92	3.44	2.0	328.91	138.10	731	0.59	5 largest: 37.03
6. Brazil	156.88	2.86	2.2	288.53	513.32	3272	2.18	
7. Nigeria	125.64	2.29	3.4	320.40	37.95	302	0.16	
8. Japan	124.99	2.28	0.6	147.78	4112.79	32,905	17.47	
9. Pakistan	121.31	2.21	3.3	301.11	58.22	479	0.25	
10. Bangladesh	119.08	2.17	2.6	244.32	29.33	246	0.12	10 largest: 57.21

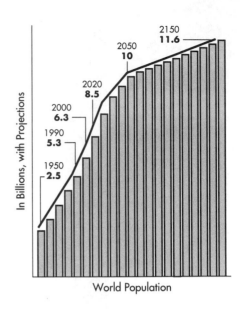

FIGURE 3-3
World Population
Source: Copyright 1992, Time, Inc. Reprinted by permission.

company can be global (in the sense that its income is derived from a number of countries at different stages of development instead of being concentrated in a single national market that is at one stage of development) and at the same time be operating in ten or fewer countries.

For products whose price is low enough, population is a more important variable than income in determining market potential. Although population is not as concentrated as income, in terms of size of nations, there is a pattern of considerable concentration. The ten most populous countries in the world account for roughly two-thirds of the world's population today.

People have inhabited the earth for over 2.5 million years. The number of human beings has been small during most of this period. In Christ's lifetime there were approximately 300 million people on earth, or roughly one-third of the number of people on mainland China today. World population increased tremendously during the eighteenth and nineteenth centuries. By 1850 world population had reached 1 billion. Between 1850 and 1925 it had increased to 2 billion, and from 1925 to 1960 it had increased to 3 billion. World population is now approximately 5.3 billion. At the present rate of growth by the middle of the next century world population will reach at least 7.9 billion and could be as high as 12 billion, with a probable level of 10 billion.[7] (see Figure 3-3).

There is a negative correlation between country population growth rate and income level. The higher the population growth rate, the lower the income level. According to a recent United Nations report, 97 percent of the world's population growth is likely to come from developing and undeveloped countries.[8]

---

[7] "The Battle of the Bulge", *The Economist* (September 3, 1994), p.23.

[8] Cited in an article by James Cook, "The Ghosts of Christmas Yet to Come," *Forbes,* June 22, 1992, pp. 92–95.

One avenue of hope to reduce the population growth rate lies in education. A recent study shows that as adult female literacy increases, the number of births per woman declines dramatically.[9]

▼ Marketing and Economic Development

An important concern in marketing is whether or not it has any relevance to the process of economic development. Some people believe that marketing is a field that is relevant only to the conditions that apply in wealthy, industrialized countries where the major problem is one of directing society's resources into ever-changing output or production to satisfy a dynamic marketplace. In the less developed country, it is argued, the major problem is the allocation of scarce resources into obvious production needs. The important focus in the less developed countries is on production and how to increase output, not on customer needs and wants.

It can also be argued that the marketing process of focusing an organization's resources on environmental opportunities is a process of universal relevance. The role of marketing in the low-income country is the same as the role in the high-income country, that is, to identify people's needs and wants, and to focus the efforts of organizations to respond to these needs and wants. For example, less developed countries have a need for washing and cleaning. Because of the low-income levels, this washing is done by hand. It is not feasible for less developed countries to engage in the production and sale of automatic, electrically operated washing machines because the expense and the complexity of these devices far exceed the economic and productive capabilities of these societies. The application of the marketing process under these conditions should lead to the development of a washing device that is appropriate to the economic capability of the society. The possibilities for the development of an inexpensive hand-operated washing machine are considerable.

The economics literature places a great deal of emphasis on the role of marketing in economic development when marketing is defined as distribution. In his book *West African Trade*, P. T. Bauer considered the question concerning the number of traders and their productivity.[10] The number and variety of traders in West Africa had been much criticized by both official and unofficial observers. Traders were condemned as wasteful and were said to be responsible for wide distributive margins both in the sale of merchandise and in the purchase of produce. Bauer examined these criticisms and concluded that they stemmed from a misunderstanding. He argued that the West African system economized in capital and used resources that were largely redundant, such as labor, and therefore that it was a productive system by rational economic criteria.

A simple example illustrates Bauer's point. A trader buys a package of cigarettes for 1 shilling and resells them one at a time for 2 cents each, or for a total of 2 shillings. Has this person exploited society to the extent of 1 shilling, or has the trader provided a useful service? In a society where consumers can afford to smoke only one cigarette at a time, the trader has provided a useful service in

---

[9] "The Battle of the Bulge", *The Economist* (September 3, 1994), p.23.

[10] Peter T. Bauer, *West African Trade* (London: Routledge and K. Paul, 1963).

substituting labor for capital. In this case, capital would be the accumulation of an inventory of cigarettes by a consumer. The first obstacle to this accumulation, which is the possession of a shilling, is paramount. However, even if these consumers were able to accumulate a shilling, their standard of living would not allow them to smoke the 20 cigarettes fast enough to be consumed in a fresh condition. Thus, even if consumers were able to save and accumulate a shilling, they would end up with a package of stale cigarettes. The trader in this case, by breaking bulk, serves the useful function of making available a product in a quantity that consumers can afford and in a condition that is attractive. As income levels rise, the purchaser will smoke more frequently and will be able to buy an entire package of cigarettes. In the process the amount of local resources consumed by distribution will decline and the standard of living will have risen. Meanwhile, in the less developed condition where labor is redundant and cheap and where capital is scarce, the availability of this distribution function is a useful one and a rational application of society's resources.

Another function of distribution in economic development, which Peter Drucker identifies, is the important business experience provided by distribution.[11] Both Bauer and Drucker argue that experience in the distributive sector is valuable because it generates a pool of entrepreneurial talent in a society where alternatives for such training are scarce. Adam Smith in *The Wealth of Nations* observed, "The habits besides, of order, economy, and attention, to which mercantile business naturally forms a merchant, render him much fitter to execute with profit and success, any project of improvement."

CONSUMPTION PATTERNS

▼ Engel's Law

Income is the single most important variable affecting market potential for most products. How does income affect consumption? Every marketer is aware of the relationship between income level and consumption patterns and, therefore, frequently uses income segmentation in defining a market. The nature of income elasticity (the relationship between demand changes and changes in income) for food was first observed and formulated by the nineteenth-century Prussian statistician, Ernst Engel. Engel discovered a uniform condition in European countries that he surveyed: When income grew above a certain minimum, expenditures on food as a percentage of total income decreased, although the absolute amount of food expenditures was maintained or increased. This pattern of expenditures on necessities is referred to as Engel's law and has been confirmed by empirical budget studies. One survey, published by the United Nations Food and Agricultural Organization in Rome, recorded the elasticity of demand for food along with per capita income in dollars. This survey revealed that low-income countries have an income elasticity of demand for food of 0.9, whereas in high-income countries the income elasticity of demand for food is 0.16. This means that 90 cents out of

---

[11] Peter Drucker, "Marketing and Economic Development," *Journal of Marketing* (January 1958), pp. 252–259.

every additional dollar in income in low-income countries is spent on food, as compared with 16 cents for high-income countries. By and large there is an inverse correlation between GNP per capita and income elasticity of demand for food. As incomes rise, the elasticity of demand for food declines.

▼ Product Saturation Levels

In general, product saturation levels, or the percentage of potential buyers or households owning a particular product, increase as national income per capita increases. However, in markets where income is sufficient to enable consumers to buy a particular product, other factors must be considered. For example, the sale of air conditioners is explained by income *and* climate. People of average income level in a low-income country cannot afford an air conditioner no matter how hot it is. High-income people in a northern climate can easily afford an air conditioner but have no need for one.

According to a market survey on the ownership of appliances in OECD countries, the ownership of electric vacuum cleaners ranged from a high of 99 percent in the Netherlands to a low of 39 percent in Greece. The differences in ownership of this appliance in these countries are explained only partially by income. A more important factor in understanding ownership levels is the type of floor covering used in the homes. Almost every home in the Netherlands contains rugs, whereas in Greece floors are usually tile and the use of rugs is uncommon. This helps to illustrate the importance of need in determining sales potential for a product.[12]

Income is a major determinant of ownership of consumer durable goods. The effect of rising incomes in Japanese households is dramatic. For products that are major labor-saving tools, such as washing machines and refrigerators, rising incomes increase ownership to more than 95 percent. The average Japanese household owns a refrigerator and washing machine. Over 95 percent have color televisions and vacuum cleaners and keep warm in winter using kerosene stoves and keep cool in summer using electric fans. Even though well supplied with consumer durables, Japan is more energy efficient than other nations. Appliances tend to be smaller, fit the size of the home, and use less power. Ownership of central heating, a major energy consumer, is very low. Although air conditioner sales show high rates of growth, total ownership remains relatively low. Energy consumption has been increasing as more families purchase cars and add to their stock of appliances. To reduce their household energy bills, many consumers are replacing present durables with larger and more efficient models.

BALANCE OF PAYMENTS

The balance of payments is a record of all of the economic transactions between residents of a country and the rest of the world. The Canadian balance of payments for the period from 1984 to 1993 is shown in Table 3–10.

---

[12] *The Economist Book of Vital World Statistics* (London: Hutchinson Business Books Limited, 1990) p. 233.

The balance of payments is divided into a so-called *current* and *capital* account. The current account is a record of all of the recurring merchandise and service trade and private gifts and public aid transactions between countries. The capital account records all of the direct investment (investments that involve control, which for balance-of-payments reporting purposes is defined as any investment that involves 20 percent or more of the equity of a company), portfolio investment (investments that involve less than 20 percent of the equity of a company), and other short- and long-term capital flows. The changes in reserves and the so-called net errors and omissions are the accounts that make the balance of payments balance. In general, a country accumulates reserves when it is in surplus above the line (i.e., the net of the current and capital account transactions) and it gives up reserves when it is in deficit above the line.

The important fact to recognize about the overall balance of payments is that it is always in balance. Imbalances occur in subsets of the overall balance. For example, a commonly reported balance is the balance on merchandise trade or, in short, the trade balance (line 3 in Table 3–10).

As you can see in Tables 3–10 and 3–11, since 1984 Canada has had a surplus on its merchandise trade balance. Canada's trade surplus has been more than offset with an outflow of capital (Table 3–10, lines 6 and 7) so that the Current Account balance was unfavorable. The trade and capital flows between Canada and individual countries vary considerably. Canada's Current Account with the United States, for example, has been favorable between 1984 and 1988, unfavorable (i.e., a negative balance) from them to 1992, and favorable again in 1993. The main reasons were fluctuations in the merchandise and services flows, while capital outflows (for interest payments, etc.) remained quite stable around the C$10 billion mark over the period (Table 3–11).

Our trade with Japan, on the other hand, has generally shown an unfavorable balance since 1985. The Current Account, however, shows a trend of an increasingly unfavorable balance largely due to outflows of Canadian capital to Japan.

TRADE PATTERNS

Since the end of World War II, world merchandise trade has grown faster than world production. In 1989, high-income countries were responsible for more than 80 percent of world merchandise trade exports or imports. The structure of world trade is summarized in Table 3–12. The importance of the triad countries (the United States and Canada, Western Europe, and Japan) is quite pronounced: They accounted for 65 percent of world exports and 64 percent of world imports.

▼ Merchandise Trade

Table 3–13 shows trade patterns for the world. In 1992, the value of world trade was approximately C$4.3 trillion, with 78 percent of world exports generated by industrialized countries, and 22 percent by developing countries. The EU accounted

TABLE 3-10 Canadian Balance of Payments, 1984–1993 (Current C$ Billion)

Current Account	1984	1985	1986	1987	1988	1989	1990	1991	1992	1993
1. Merchandise Exports	111.33	119.06	120.31	126.31	137.77	141.51	146.09	141.09	156.56	181.02
2. Merchandise Imports	91.49	102.66	110.37	115.11	128.86	135.45	136.64	136.10	147.58	169.31
3. Merchandise Trade Balance	19.84	16.40	9.94	11.23	8.91	6.06	9.45	4.99	8.98	11.71
4. Services Receipts	14.70	15.85	17.80	19.07	21.53	22.38	23.23	24.02	25.38	27.24
5. Services Payments	19.13	20.71	22.99	25.38	27.52	30.62	34.58	36.06	38.16	39.79
6. Services Balance	-4.43	-4.86	-5.19	-6.31	-5.99	-8.24	-11.35	-12.04	-12.78	-12.55
7. Non-Equity Transfers	-13.48	-14.33	-24.03	-16.44	-18.71	-21.49	-23.91	-21.92	-24.20	-24.68
8. Net Current Account	1.68	-3.09	-11.39	-11.60	-15.49	-23.39	-25.94	-29.03	-27.68	-25.21
Capital Account										
9. Direct Investment	-2.94	-3.90	-5.65	-9.37	-6.50	-5.45	-4.90	-6.20	-4.50	-9.24
10. Portfolio Investment	-2.07	-1.32	-2.24	-1.94	-2.98	-4.01	-2.19	-6.90	-6.77	-12.75
11. Investment Inflow	15.05	12.07	24.85	30.27	35.82	34.40	37.11	44.44	27.78	51.58
12. Net Capital Account	4.48	9.39	14.08	14.75	16.07	22.76	27.36	33.51	23.83	32.20

Source: Based on data from *Bank of Canada Review,* Spring 1994, Tables 31, 32.

TABLE 3–11 Canadian Merchandise Trade, Services and Current Account Balances with United States and Japan, 1984–1993 (Current C$ Billion)

	1984	1985	1986	1987	1988	1989	1990	1991	1992	1993
UNITED STATES										
Merchandise Trade Balance	18.92	20.38	16.89	17.62	13.83	11.31	15.95	12.98	16.77	21.79
Services Balance	-3.46	-3.41	-3.41	-4.67	-4.66	-6.83	-9.39	-10.51	-10.86	-10.15
Current Account Balance	6.72	8.27	4.87	5.67	.97	-3.80	-3.36	-5.27	-2.82	2.27
JAPAN										
Merchandise Trade Balance	.23	-.46	-1.75	-.73	.31	.28	-.40	-1.74	-1.60	-.42
Services Balance	.35	.49	.47	.50	.64	.85	.76	.79	.76	.88
Current Account Balance	-.18	-1.69	-3.92	-4.08	-3.30	-3.62	-4.56	-5.64	-5.90	-4.61

Source: Based on data from *Canada's Balance of International Payments, Fourth Quarter, 1993*, Statistics Canada, Ottawa, Tables 21, 22c.

for 40 percent, the United States and Canada accounted for 15 percent, and Japan accounted for 9 percent. In 1990, 60 percent of the EU's exports and 51 percent of its imports were intra-EC (see Table 3–14, EEC line). If the EU were considered a single country, its share of world exports would be 16 percent, or about four times that of Canada, and substantially more than U.S. exports. Trade growth outside industrialized countries has been slow. Industrialized nations have increased their share of world trade by trading more among themselves, and less with the rest of the world (see Figure 3–4).

The top 20 exporting and importing countries of the world are shown in Table 3–15. With the exception of Korea and China, all are high-income countries.

Table 3–16 shows export volume in the period from 1984 to 1990 for the world's 24 leading exporters. Portugal's outstanding performance during this period is a result of that country's success in taking advantage of its entry into the EU. The positive relationship between export growth and economic growth is quite striking. The reason for the relationship is that export growth reflects the ability of a country's companies to penetrate foreign markets. This ability requires a competitive advantage and the ability to project this advantage into a competitive market. The ability to compete is a reflection of overall organizational skill and competence including the ability to "read" markets and to make and deliver products that offer competitive value to customers. This ability is the engine that creates wealth and economic growth.

TABLE 3–12 Value of World Merchandise Trade and its Structure, 1992 (C$ Billion, Percent)

	Exports 1992	Imports 1992	Average Annual Growth Rate (%)	
			Exports 1980–92	Imports 1980–92
World	4,319,910	4,574,532	4.9	4.9
High Income Countries	3,397,617	3,571,684	4.9	5.8
Middle Income Countries	708,143	780,902	3.7	2.2
Low Income Countries	214,150	221,946	6.9	2.7

EXPORTS (percentage share of merchandise exports):

	Fuels, Minerals, Metals	Other Primary Commodities	Machinery & Transport Equipment	Other Manufactures
High Income Countries	7	11	43	39
Middle Income Countries	32	19	18	31
Low Income Countries	21	17	9	53
World	12	13	37	39

IMPORTS (percentage share of merchandise imports):

	Fuels, Minerals, Metals	Other Primary Commodities	Machinery & Transport Equipment	Other Manufactures
High Income Countries	9	6	35	51
Middle Income Countries	10	6	38	46
Low Income Countries	9	9	34	49
World	9	6	35	50

Source: World Development Report 1994, Tables 13, 14, 15.

Table 3-17 shows Canadian exports and imports for 1984 to 1993. Notice that Canada has been in a trade surplus with the world during this period except for 1989, but also that the trade surplus has been declining for most of the period.

Table 3-18 shows Canada's merchandise trade by major area for the period from 1984 to 1993. The United States dominates Canada's trade. Our next largest single trading partner is Japan, while the EEC (now European Union) is the largest trading bloc—outside of NAFTA. It is also noteworthy that Canada has had a trade deficit with the EEC for many years.

TABLE 3–13 Exports and Imports of the World to and from the Areas Listed (in Millions of U.S. Dollars)

	Exports (F.O.B.)			Imports (C.I.F.)		
	1988	*1989*	*1990*	*1988*	*1989*	*1990*
Areas						
IFS World Total (US$ Bi)	2,699.3	2,913.8	3,325.0	2,774.8	3,009.4	3,455.0
DOTS World Total	2,693.4	2,912.8	3,339.6	2,773.8	3,002.2	3,450.6
Industrial Countries (US$ Bi)	1,958	2,118	2,449	2,016.1	2,160.9	2,500.1
Developing Countries	689,839	744,726	835,509	746,592	832,674	935,954
Africa	64,507	65,103	73,846	66,131	74,466	86,196
Asia	342,136	381,836	433,172	362,822	403,131	456,448
Europe*	80,139	83,095	95,105	84,684	85,714	86,086
Middle East	99,008	100,572	105,801	103,082	124,568	150,387
Western Hemisphere†	104,048	114,120	127,585	129,874	144,794	156,837
USSR & selected other countries n.i.e.‡	81,676	86,095	73,905	78,319	78,997	68,476
Memorandum Items						
EEC (US$ Bi)	1,043	1,125	1,357	1,058	1,122	1,359
Triad** (US$ Bi)	1,740	1,881	2,182	1,780	1,909	2,208
Oil Exporting Countries	96,543	98,488	108,864	132,497	160,121	195,419
Nonoil Developing Countries	593,296	646,238	726,646	614,095	672,553	750,535
Annual Percent Change						
World	14.4	8.1	14.7	14.6	8.2	14.9
Industrial Countries	13.2	8.2	15.7	14.9	7.2	15.7
Developing Countries	18.1	8.0	12.2	14.1	11.5	12.4
Africa	12.1	0.9	13.4	5.9	12.6	15.8
Asia	29.0	11.6	13.4	22.5	11.1	13.2
Europe	5.7	3.7	14.5	11.4	1.2	0.4
Middle East	7.4	1.6	5.2	−3.1	20.8	20.7
Western Hemisphere	11.4	9.7	11.8	15.1	11.5	8.3
USSR & selected other countries n.i.e.	14.8	5.4	−14.1	8.5	0.9	−13.2

† Latin America, Greenland, Netherland Antilles, and other not spec.
* Defined as: Albania, Bulgaria, Cuba, East Germany, the Mongolian Republic, North Korea, Czechoslovakia, and the USSR, which are not included in the world trade table published in the IFS.
**Canada, the U.S., Europe, and Japan.
‡ in the absence of a more suitable term that would conveniently cover the countries included in the third category (Europe), they are referred to as USSR and selected other countries n.i.e.
Source: DOTS = Direction of Trade Statistics and IFS = International Financial Statistics

TABLE 3–14 Exports and Imports of Areas Listed to and from EEC (in Millions of U.S. Dollars)

	Exports (F.O.B.)			Imports (C.I.F.)		
	1988	*1989*	*1990*	*1988*	*1989*	*1990*
Areas						
DOTS World Total (US$ Bi)	1,043	1,125	1,357	1,058	1,122	1,359
Industrial Countries	870,291	935,656	1,127,092	872,049	924,953	1,114,827
Developing Countries	156,330	171,756	208,439	168,130	176,892	218,973
Africa	28,440	31,080	39,581	34,620	37,313	43,896
Asia	53,847	58,339	70,292	51,661	57,350	66,750
Europe*	23,821	24,528	28,188	24,042	25,093	35,805
Middle East	25,119	31,253	40,936	37,309	37,185	48,152
Western Hemisphere†	25,103	26,555	29,442	20,499	19,951	24,370
USSR & selected other countries n.i.e.	16,542	17,933	21,645	18,039	20,274	24,979
Memorandum Items						
EEC	633,078	678,827	828,655	624,493	667,606	820,202
Oil Exporting Countries	31,728	38,234	49,665	36,694	36,644	47,442
Nonoil Developing Countries	124,602	133,522	158,775	131,436	140,248	171,531

† Latin America, Greenland, Netherland Antilles, and other not spec.
* Europe is defined as: Albania, Bulgaria, Cuba, and East Germany.

Source: DOTS = Direction of Trade Statistics

FIGURE 3–4

Merchandise Exports To The EC, 1991
Source: Copyright © 1992, The Economist Newspaper Group, Inc. Reprinted by permission.

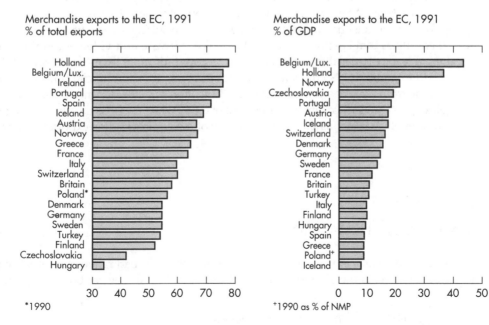

Merchandise exports to the EC, 1991
% of total exports

Holland
Belgium/Lux.
Ireland
Portugal
Spain
Iceland
Austria
Norway
Greece
France
Italy
Switzerland
Britain
Poland*
Denmark
Germany
Sweden
Turkey
Finland
Czechoslovakia
Hungary

30 40 50 60 70 80
*1990

Merchandise exports to the EC, 1991
% of GDP

Belgium/Lux.
Holland
Norway
Czechoslovakia
Portugal
Austria
Iceland
Switzerland
Denmark
Germany
Sweden
France
Britain
Turkey
Italy
Finland
Hungary
Spain
Greece
Poland⁺
Iceland

0 10 20 30 40 50
⁺1990 as % of NMP

TABLE 3–15 Twenty Leading Exporters and Importers in World Merchandise Trade, 1993 (Billions of C$ and % of World)

EXPORTS (F.O.B.)			IMPORTS (C.I.F.)		
1. United States	$599.7	12.6%	1. United States	$777.7	15.9%
2. Germany	466.9	9.9	2. Germany	421.7	8.7
3. Japan	465.6	9.8	3. Japan	310.8	6.3
4. France	269.5	5.7	4. United Kingdom	270.8	5.5
5. United Kingdom	236.0	5.0	5. France	259.2	5.3
6. Italy	216.6	4.6	6. Italy	189.6	4.5
7. Canada	187.0	3.9	7. Hong Kong	179.2	3.7
8. Hong Kong	174.1	3.7	8. Canada	179.2	3.7
9. Netherlands	172.8	3.6	9. Netherlands	162.5	3.3
10. Belgium-Luxembourg	149.6	3.1	10. Belgium-Luxembourg	152.1	3.1
11. China-P.R.	118.6	2.5	11. China-P.R.	134.1	2.7
12. Taiwan	109.6	2.3	12. Singapore	109.6	2.2
13. South Korea	105.7	2.2	13. South Korea	108.3	2.2
14. Singapore	95.4	2.0	14. Spain	105.7	2.2
15. Switzerland	81.2	1.7	15. Taiwan	99.3	2.0
16. Spain	81.2	1.7	16. Mexico	83.8	1.7
17. Mexico	67.0	1.4	17. Switzerland	78.6	1.6
18. Sweden	64.4	1.4	18. Austria	63.2	1.3
19. Malaysia	60.6	1.3	19. Malaysia	59.3	1.2
20. Australia	55.4	1.2	20. Australia	58.0	1.2
World	4,755.4	100.0	World	4,896.0	100.0

Source: Adapted from GATT Focus, July 1994, p. 2.

▼ Services Trade

Probably the fastest growing sector of world trade is trade in services. Unfortunately, the statistics and data on trade in services are not as comprehensive as those for merchandise trade. Many countries (especially low-income countries) are deficient in enforcing international copyrights and patent laws resulting in a loss of service income to countries that create service products like software and video entertainment. Invisible exports, as they are often called, account for more than 40 percent of total world exports. In 1993 the total of service exports, non-commercial transfers, and income from overseas assets reached C$ 3.1 trillion. Canada depends least on invisible exports, which account for 4.4 percent of GDP, while the US is the world's biggest exporter of invisibles, as shown in Table 3-19 of the world's leading exporters and importers of services.[13]

NATIONAL CONTROLS OF INTERNATIONAL TRANSFERS

The nation-states of the world exercise control over a broad range of international transfers. Items transferred include not only goods and services but also money,

---

[13] "Invisible Exports," *The Economist*, (July 16, 1994) p. 97.

TABLE 3–16   Growth of Leading Exporters, 1984–90 (average annual percent change)

Countries	Growth of Export Volume†
1 Portugal	214.7
2 Hong Kong	190.1
3 Saudi Arabia	187.0
4 China, People's Rep.‡	179.7
5 Switzerland	149.8
6 Germany D.R.	138.3
7 Spain	134.2
8 Chile	133.4
9 Italy	128.5
10 Belgium-Luxembourg	126.7
11 France	121.8
12 Singapore	119.2
13 Germany, F.R.*	110.0
14 Korea Rep.	106.6
15 Netherlands	99.8
16 United Kingdom	97.2
17 Sweden	93.9
18 United States	80.4
19 Japan	69.5
20 Argentina	52.4
21 Canada	45.4
22 Mexico	23.0
23 USSR	21.6
24 Brazil	19.5

† Data from DOTS
‡ of which Taiwan, province of China, is responsible for 34.4 percent.
* Data cover the former area of Federal Republic of Germany through June 1990 and the area of united Germany beginning with July 1990.

Data Source: DOTS Table prepared by author

people, technology, and rights. All these elements are important aspects of the multinational marketing mix, particularly goods, money, and people.

There are several motives for controlling international transfers. A major motive is to accomplish economic goals. The earliest economic goal of controls over international transfers was to generate a government revenue source. Today, with the exception of low-income countries, the revenue motive is not a principal factor guiding national policy in this area. More common motives today are protection of local industry and fostering the development of local enterprise. The three motives work together. A country can increase national revenues by increasing tariffs and duties on transfers of goods and at the same time can provide protection for local infant industries or for local enterprise that has political influence.

Employment is a major economic goal influencing controls over international transfers. When the free play of economic forces results in heavy competitive pressure, which in turn creates domestic unemployment, political forces activated by management, as well as workers in affected industries, are often capable of bringing pressure to control international transfers. The controls may be in the form of higher tariffs or import quotas that place an absolute quantity limit on the quantity by weight, value, or volume of goods that may enter the country.

TABLE 3–17 Canadian Exports and Imports of Merchandise, 1984–1993 C$ (1986 Constant Dollars)

Year	Merchandise Trade Balance	EXPORTS				IMPORTS			
		Total[1]	Food	Natural Resource Materials	Manufactured Goods	Total[1]	Food	Natural Resource Materials	Manufactured Goods
1984	15.60	108.12	11.27	44.10	52.17	92.52	7.11	21.49	65.70
1985	12.97	115.07	10.20	47.16	56.10	102.10	7.24	23.84	71.21
1986	9.94	120.31	11.57	49.92	56.86	110.37	7.60	25.50	76.27
1987	7.49	124.71	13.06	54.34	57.17	117.22	7.98	24.54	80.74
1988	2.47	136.28	12.76	59.12	63.62	133.81	8.00	31.24	92.29
1989	-3.30	137.79	11.30	58.78	66.88	141.09	8.73	33.25	96.23
1990	3.78	144.79	13.04	59.31	69.91	141.01	9.27	33.68	94.73
1991	1.57	146.21	10.38	61.27	67.85	144.64	9.58	32.23	98.25
1992	4.90	158.79	14.97	64.19	76.42	153.89	10.39	34.40	104.60
1993	5.08	174.90	14.46	67.09	90.06	169.82	11.35	37.22	116.58

[1] includes other categories besides the three major categories listed.

Source: Based on data from *Bank of Canada Review*, Spring 1994, Tables J5, J6.

TABLE 3–18 Canadian Exports and Imports of Merchandise by Major Trading Area, 1984–1993 (C$ billions) (1986 Constant)

Year	EXPORTS				IMPORTS			
	U.S.	EEC	Japan	Others	U.S.	EEC	Japan	Others
1984	84.81	7.09	5.71	13.70	65.89	8.52	5.47	11.59
1985	93.79	6.94	5.59	12.73	73.40	10.57	6.06	12.62
1986	93.32	8.01	5.81	13.16	76.42	12.60	7.57	13.76
1987	96.60	9.29	6.76	13.67	78.98	13.81	7.49	14.82
1988	102.64	10.90	8.33	15.89	88.79	15.34	7.96	16.76
1989	105.47	11.77	8.60	15.66	94.10	14.58	8.29	18.46
1990	109.73	12.03	7.84	16.48	93.77	15.11	8.25	19.50
1991	106.72	11.43	6.94	15.99	93.73	14.09	8.68	19.58
1992	121.16	11.37	7.23	16.79	104.39	13.45	8.83	20.90
1993	145.33	10.79	7.94	16.95	123.53	13.73	8.36	23.68

Source: Based on data from *Bank of Canada Review*, Spring 1994, Table J3.

TABLE 3–19 Twenty Leading Exporters and Importers in World Trade in Commercial Services, 1992 (Billions of C$ and % of World)

EXPORTS			IMPORTS		
1. United States	$196.1	16.2%	1. Germany	$135.2	11.3%
2. France	123.6	10.2	2. United States	130.1	10.9
3. Italy	78.7	6.5	3. Japan	117.9	9.9
4. Germany	77.8	6.4	4. France	101.7	8.5
5. United Kingdom	66.5	5.5	5. Italy	81.2	6.8
6. Japan	59.9	5.0	6. United Kingdom	56.7	4.8
7. Spain	43.7	3.6	7. Netherlands	43.1	3.0
8. Netherlands	43.6	3.6	8. Belgium-Luxembourg	39.8	3.3
9. Belgium-Luxembourg	42.2	3.5	9. Canada	32.8	2.8
10. Austria	36.2	3.0	10. Spain	26.7	2.2
11. Switzerland	23.0	1.9	11. Austria	23.9	2.0
12. Singapore	21.9	1.8	12. Taiwan	23.1	1.9
13. Hong Kong	20.5	1.7	13. Sweden	22.9	1.9
14. Sweden	19.2	1.6	14. Switzerland	20.7	1.7
15. Canada	19.2	1.6	15. Saudi Arabia	17.8	1.5
16. Denmark	17.8	1.5	16. Norway	17.7	1.5
17. Norway	16.1	1.3	17. South Korea	17.6	1.5
18. Mexico	16.1	1.3	18. Australia	16.5	1.4
19. South Korea	15.4	1.3	19. Hong Kong	14.4	1.2
20. Taiwan	12.8	1.1	20. Mexico	14.0	1.2
World	1,208.3	100.0	World	1,293.8	100.0

Source: Adapted from GATT Focus, July 1994, p. 2.

Economic and political goals and different value systems are the prime reasons for controls on international transfers. The barriers that existed between Canada and South Africa or those that continue to exist between the United States and Cuba, for example, exist because of major differences between the values and objectives of two respective countries. Many of the barriers based upon different political systems have come down with the end of the cold war and the division of the world into East and West. Barriers based upon different value systems and domestic rigidity continue. The farmers of the world, for example, are committed to getting as much protection as possible from their government whether they be Japanese, European, or Canadian. Because of the political influence of the farm lobby in every country, controls on trade in agricultural products continue to distort economic efficiency in spite of the efforts of trade negotiators to open up agricultural markets.

Every country is free to impose controls on transfers and thereby protect domestic producers. The price of this protection can be very high. There are two costs to consider. The first is the cost to consumers whether they be household or business buyers. Any limitation of the access to markets of foreign producers raises the price and cost to domestic consumers and lowers their standard of living and their competitiveness if they are a company consumer. The second cost is the impact on the competitiveness of domestic companies. If companies are protected from competition, they may be less stimulated to create and sustain world-class competitive advantage. One of the greatest stimuli to competitiveness is the open market. When a company faces world competition, it must figure out how to serve a niche market better than any company in the world, or it must figure out how to compete in face-to-face competition.

An example of how competitiveness has benefited consumers is the Canadian automotive industry. Anyone who has experience with North American automobiles prior to 1985 can remember the bad old days when the industry turned out cars of poor quality when compared to imports. The dramatic increase in the quality of North American designed and produced automobiles is a direct result of the stimulus of foreign competition. When the automobile companies figured out that they were not going to be able to obtain trade protection from foreign competitors, their only option was to innovate and to build and market automobiles that could begin to compete.

▼ Why Identify Control Motives?

The identification of motives for controlling international transfers is important because this is the first step in the formation of a behavioral model of nation-states in the economic policy area. Admittedly, any behavioral model of a nation will be an extremely rough approximation of the reality it attempts to describe. Nevertheless, moves by nations have as great an impact on the success of international marketing programs as do moves of individual competitors. It is essential that the international marketing planner account for and attempt to forecast possible moves by nation-states that would affect marketing programs being designed.

The current Japanese situation is a good example of how motives influence national controls over international transfers. The Japanese have established a worldwide reputation for the stringency of their barriers to direct entry into the Japanese economy and market. It has been difficult for foreign companies to establish successful direct operations in Japan. In many industries, the Japanese restricted any form of foreign entry until their own industry established a strong base both in Japan and in the international economy.

The major controlling factor that has forced the Japanese to admit foreign companies into the Japanese economy has been the fact that Japan has a major stake in foreign markets. Because the Japanese are committed to their position in world markets, they must be responsive to the concerns of the national governments who control access to these markets. In a real sense, then, Japan is a hostage to its own world market position. Concurrently, the Japanese position has led to a substantial balance-of-payments surplus and the accumulation of large reserves that have created further pressure for allowing greater access to the Japanese markets both of imported goods and of direct operations by foreign companies.

The hostage framework applies to advanced countries because all advanced countries today are involved in symmetrical relationships with other advanced countries. They are at the same time both importers and exporters of manufactured goods, both recipients of direct investments and foreign operations, and both direct investors and foreign operators.

The relationships between advanced countries and less developed countries, on the other hand, are not nearly so symmetrical. In general, less developed countries export raw materials to the advanced countries and import manufactures from them. Moreover, the flow of direct investment and foreign operations is one way—from the advanced countries to the less developed countries.

As a result, the companies from advanced countries have an economic stake in the less developed countries that is not reciprocated. This lack of symmetry in the relationship between advanced countries and less developed countries creates a less stable economic and political environment in the underdeveloped country because there is no hostage motive controlling pressures to restrict or constrain the operations of foreign investors and foreign-based exporters. It is the marketing planner's responsibility to establish a matrix of economic, social, political, cultural, and security motives to estimate the general level of environmental conditions that will exist in the less developed country over the company's planning horizon. In general, if a country is economically successful, as defined by sustained real growth and the absence of excessive balance-of-payments pressures, the business environment will typically remain favorable. Usually, if a country gets into difficulty, pressures will develop and take different forms. These pressures can affect companies' access to foreign exchange, repatriation of capital (profits or dividends), import/export mechanisms, access to local industries, and more. Another form of response to local frustration may be the requirement that foreign companies localize management and ownership.

THE GLOBAL ENVIRONMENT

Global warming, deforestation, dissipation of the ozone layer, and biodiversity are just a few of the critical issues of the 1990s.[14] The second Earth Summit, the United Nations Conference on Environment and Development in Rio de Janeiro, brought up an agenda that posed questions about the future of our children, of the world's resources, and about how to most efficiently manage these resources so as to perpetuate world growth and prosperity.[15] The meeting gathered more than 100 world leaders and 30,000 other participants in what was considered the largest event of its category ever. The central premise of the Earth Summit was that environmental problems can no longer be solved at the national level. Some of the striking arguments raised at the summit, using the United States as a basis for contrast, were:

EARTH ALERTS

▶ The United States has 5 percent of the world's population, uses 25 percent of the world's energy, emits 22 percent of all CO_2 produced, and accounts for 25 percent of the world's GNP; whereas,

▶ India has 16 percent of the world's population, uses 3 percent of the world's energy, emits 3 percent of all CO_2 produced, and accounts for 1 percent of the world's GNP.

▶ In the past decade, levels of stratospheric ozone, which shields living things from harmful ultraviolet radiation, have declined 4 percent to 8 percent in the northern and southern hemispheres.

---

[14] "Hot Stuff," *The Economist*, July 11, 1992.

[15] The first Earth Summit was held 20 years ago in Stockholm. See Philip Elmer-Dewitt, "Summit to Save the Earth," *Time*, June 1, 1992.

- Because of drought, desertification, erosion, and population growth, per capita grain production in Africa has dropped 28 percent since 1967.
- In communities near Russia's Aral Sea, widespread use of agricultural pesticides has been linked to esophageal-cancer rates seven times as great as the national average.

EARTH SAVERS

- If the United States increased average automobile-fuel economy from 8.5l to 5.9l per 100km, the country could ultimately save 380 million litres of oil a day (about the amount now imported) and could prevent 440 million tons of carbon dioxide (7 percent of current CO_2 emissions) from entering the atmosphere each year.
- By switching from incandescent to compact fluorescent lighting, the United States could conceivably conserve 147 billion kwh of energy annually (equal to the output of 37 giant power plants) and thus save about US$11 billion a year on utility bills.

Environmental concern is going beyond the stage of talk and discussion. New regulations are being implemented, and consumers are expressing their concern about this issue in their purchasing behavior. Companies can position themselves on the leading edge of response to these concerns by making certain that they operate and comply with regulations in the world's most demanding countries. By doing this, they ensure that they are capable of meeting the world's highest standard. This leaves them well prepared to respond to any upgrade of standards in any of the other countries in which they operate. It also puts them in a position, if they choose to do so, to provide leadership in raising standards of environmental protection.

▼ SUMMARY

The economic environment is a major determinant of market potential and opportunity. Since the single most important indicator of market potential is income, the first step in determining the potential of a country or region is to identify the total and, even more significantly, the per capita income. In general, as people's incomes rise, they spend less on necessities and more on discretionary purchases. One of the ways of determining market potential for a product is to evaluate product saturation levels in the light of income levels. In general, it is appropriate to compare the saturation levels of countries or of consumer segments with similar income levels. Countries and markets go through typical stages of market development. Although development is on a continuum, it is possible to identify distinct stages and formulate general estimates about the type of demand that will be found in a country or market at a particular stage of development. In advanced countries, for example, more than half the gross national product is accounted for by services as opposed to goods, and the market for services reflects this mix in the value of GNP. In a preindustrial country, the market for services and goods is very small because, by definition, the country has very low income levels.

▼ DISCUSSION QUESTIONS

1. Where is world income located? What are the stages of national market development, and what percentage of world income is found in each of the stages?

2. What is the pattern of income distribution in the world today? How do developing countries' markets compare with high-income-country markets in the proportion of income going to the bottom and the top 20 percent of the population?

3. A manufacturer of long-range radios is assessing the world market potential for his products. He asks you if he should consider developing countries as potential markets. How would you advise him?

4. Are income and standard of living the same thing? What is meant by the term *standard of living*?

5. The saturation level of kerosene heaters in Japan was 92.2 percent in 1978. The founder of Kerosan noticed this high saturation level and concluded that there was a huge untapped market for kerosene heaters in North America and Western Europe, where saturation levels were less than 1 percent. Is this scientific marketing or wishful thinking? Explain.

6. What happens to consumption patterns as incomes rise? What are the implications of this for marketers in a low- or lower-middle-income country which has a high rate of growth?

▼ BIBLIOGRAPHY

Books

GALBRAITH, JOHN KENNETH, *The Nature of Mass Poverty*. Cambridge, MA: Harvard University Press, 1979.

GILDER, GEORGE F., *Microcosm: The Quantum Revolution in Economics and Technology*. New York: Simon and Schuster, 1989.

ISAAK, ROBERT A., *International Political Economy*. Englewood Cliffs, NJ: Prentice-Hall, Inc., 1991.

JAFFE, EUGENE D., *Grouping: A Strategy for International Marketing*. New York: American Management Association, 1974.

KENNEDY, PAUL, *The Rise and Fall of Great Powers*. New York: Random House, 1987.

KRAVIS, IRVING B., et al., *A System of International Comparisons of Gross Product and Purchasing Power*. Washington, DC: International Bank for Reconstruction and Development, 1975.

PORTER, MICHAEL E., *The Competitive Advantage of Nations*. New York: The Free Press, 1990.

SHAPIRO, ALAN C., *Multinational Finance Management*, 3rd ed. Boston: Allyn and Bacon, 1989.

THUROW, LESTER, *Head to Head: The Coming Economic Battle Among Japan, Europe, and America*. New York: William Morrow and Company, Inc., 1992.

Articles

DRUCKER, PETER, "Marketing and Economic Development," *Journal of Marketing* (January 1958), pp. 252–259.

LEWIS, ARTHUR W., "The Slowing Down of the Engine of Growth," *American Economic Review* (September 1980), pp. 555–564.

PROWSE, MICHAEL, "Is America in Decline?" *Harvard Business Review* (July–August 1992), pp. 36–37. Michael Prowse is a Washington-based columnist for the *Financial Times of London*.

"The European Community," *The Economist*, July 11, 1992, pp. 5–30.

FOUR

Social and Cultural Environments

CHAPTER OUTLINE

Introduction

This chapter focuses on the social and cultural forces that shape and affect individual behavior in the world market environment. Every person in the world reflects the interaction of his or her own unique personality with the collective forces of the culture and milieu in which he or she has developed and experienced life. The approach of this chapter reflects the book's conceptual orientation, which is based on the assumption that individuals and cultures of the world are characterized by both differences and similarities.

The task of the global marketer is to recognize both the similarities and the differences and incorporate this perception into the marketing planning process so that strategies, products, and marketing programs are adapted to significant and important differences. At the same time, the global marketer must also perceive relevant similarities and avoid unnecessary and costly adaptations to marketing strategies and programs. The objective of this chapter is to provide an analytical approach to understanding cultural dynamics in the marketplace.

The popular definition of culture is, "What I've got and you haven't." "My taste in clothing, music, food, and so forth is cultured, and yours, of course, is not." This popular definition confuses taste and culture. For the anthropologist, culture is "the ways of living built up by a group of human beings that are transmitted from one generation to another." Culture includes both conscious and unconscious values, ideas, attitudes, and symbols that shape human behavior *and that are transmitted from one generation to the next.* In this sense, culture does not refer to the instinctive responses of people, nor does it include one-time solutions to unique problems, or passing fads and styles. Culture is passed on from one generation to the next.

From a marketing perspective culture in the preceding sense is obviously important. However, as a marketer it is important to respond to *all* ways of living and values, ideas and attitudes whether or not they are passed on from one generation to the next.

BASIC ASPECTS OF CULTURE

Anthropologists agree on three characteristics of culture: (1) It is not innate, but learned. (2) The various facets of culture are interrelated—touch a culture in one place and everything else is affected. (3) It is shared by the members of a group and defines the boundaries between different groups.[1]

Because culture has such an important influence on customer behavior, it is useful to outline some of the major assumptions concerning the nature of culture. The following assumptions are drawn from recent anthropological literature and have fairly general acceptance among anthropologists.

Culture consists of learned responses to recurring situations. The earlier these responses are learned, the more difficult they are to change. Many aspects of culture influence the marketing environment. Taste, for example, is a learned response that is highly variable from culture to culture and has a major impact on the market environment. Preference for such things as colors and styles is culturally influenced. For example, ". . . green is a highly regarded color in Moslem countries, but has negative connotations in Southwest Asia, where it is associated with disease, while white, usually associated with purity and cleanliness in the West, signifies death in Asian countries. Red, a popular color in most parts of the world, is poorly received in some African countries."[2] Attitudes toward whole classes of products can be a function of culture. For example, in Canada and the United States, there is a high cultural predisposition to be interested and intrigued by product innovations that have a "gadgety" quality. Thus, the electric knife, the electric toothbrush, the Water-Pik (a dental appliance that cleans teeth and gums with a pulsating stream of water under high pressure), and a host of appliances find a ready and very quick market here even though many of these products are often purchased, used for a period of time, and then quietly put away and never used again. There is unquestionably a smaller predisposition to purchase such products in other developed-country markets such as Europe.

A reasonable hypothesis is that this difference is partially a result of cultural differences. Nevertheless, because incomes in other industrial-country markets and Canada are different, the influence of income on behavior and attitudes is also at work. Indeed, the basic question that must be answered by marketers seeking to understand or predict behavior is: "To what extent do cultural factors influence behavior independent of income levels?" The profusion of automobiles, convenience foods, disposable packages, and other articles in the trial markets of Canada, the United States, Europe, and Japan suggests that many or perhaps even most consumer products have universal appeal and will be purchased in any country, regardless of cultural differences, when consumer disposable income reaches a high enough level.

▼ The Search for Cultural Universals

For the international marketer the search for cultural universals provides a valuable orientation. A universal is a mode of behavior existing in all cul-

---

[1] Edward T. Hall, *Beyond Culture* (Garden City, NY: Anchor Press/Doubleday, 1977), p. 16.

[2] Richard R. Still and John S. Hill, "Multinational Product Planning: A Meta Market Analysis," *International Marketing Review* (Spring 1985), p. 60.

tures. To the extent that aspects of the cultural environment are universal as opposed to unique, it is possible for the international marketer to standardize such aspects of his or her marketing program as product design and communications, which are two of the major elements of a marketing program. Fortunately for the international marketer, much of the apparent cultural diversity in the world turns out to be different ways of accomplishing the same thing.

A partial list of cultural universals was developed by George P. Murdock and includes the following:

> Age grading, athletic sports, bodily adornment, calendar, cleanliness training, community organization, cooking, co-operative labor, cosmology, courtship, dancing, decorative art, divination, division of labor, dream interpretation, education, ethics, etiquette, family feasting, fire making, folklore, food taboos, inheritance rules, joking, kin groups, kinship, language, law, magic, marriage, mealtime, medicine, modesty concerning natural functions, mourning music, nomenclature, obstetrics, penal sanctions, personal names, population policy, postnatal care, pregnancy usage, property rights, propitiation of supernatural beings, puberty customs, religious rituals, residence rules, sexual restrictions, soul concepts, status differentiation, superstition, surgery, tool making, trade, visiting, weaning, and weather control.[3]

Let us consider music as an example of how these universals apply to marketing decision making. Music as an art form is part of all cultures; thus, the musical song-type commercial is universally feasible. Although music is culturally universal, its style is not internationally uniform. Therefore, the type of music that is appropriate in one part of the world may not be acceptable or effective in another part. A campaign might utilize a bossa nova rhythm or "cha-cha-cha" beat for Latin America, a rock rhythm for North America, a "high life" for Africa, and so on. In this way the universal forms can be adapted to cultural styles in each region.

With increasing travel and communications many of the national attitudes toward style in clothing, color, music, and food and drink are becoming international and even universal. This internationalization of culture has been significantly accelerated by multinational companies that have recognized an opportunity to extend their product/communications strategies into international markets. With their expansion into international markets, companies such as Coca-Cola, Pepsi-Cola, Levi Straus, McDonald's, IBM, and Apple are proving that cross-cultural acceptance can overcome cultural distinctiveness. As Professor Levitt points out in his celebrated article on the globalization of markets,

> Ancient differences in national tastes or modes of doing business disappear. The commonalty of preference leads inescapably to the standardization of products, manufacturing, and the institutions of trade and

---

[3] George P. Murdock, "The Common Denominator of Culture," in *The Science of Man in the World Crisis*, ed. Ralph Linton (New York: Columbia University Press, 1945), p. 145.

commerce. Small nation-based markets transmogrify and expand. Success in world competition turns on efficiency in production, distribution, marketing, and management, and inevitably becomes focused on price.[4]

▼ The Anthropologist's Standpoint

As Ruth Benedict points out in her classic *The Chrysanthemum and the Sword*, no matter how bizarre one's act or opinion, the way a person thinks, feels, and acts has some relation to his or her experience. Successful international marketers must adopt this assumption if they are to understand the dynamics of a foreign market.

Any systematic study of a foreign market requires a combination of toughmindedness and generosity. The appreciation of another way of life cannot develop when one is defensive about one's own way of life; it is necessary to be secure in one's own convictions and traditions. In addition, generosity is required if one is to appreciate the integrity and value of other ways of life and points of view. The international marketer needs to develop an objective standpoint that recognizes diversity, seeks to understand its origins, and avoids the pitfalls of both rejection and identification. There are many paths to the same end in life—the international marketer knows this and rejoices in life's rich diversity.

▼ Communication

The ability to communicate in one's own language is, as everyone knows, not an easy task. Whenever languages change, there is an additional communications challenge. This is especially so when the language and the culture are different. For example, "yes" and "no" are used in an entirely different way in Japanese than in western languages. This has caused much confusion and misunderstanding. In English, the answer "yes" or "no" to a question is based on whether the answer is affirmative or negative. In Japanese, this is not so. The answer "yes" or "no" may refer to whether or not the answer affirms or negates the question. For example, in Japanese if you were asked, "Don't you like meat?" you would answer "yes" if your answer is negative. You might say, for example, "Yes, I don't like meat."

Perhaps the most challenging form of communication is nonverbal rather than verbal communications. The West tends to be verbal, and the East more nonverbal. The American anthropologist W. Caudill conducted a study to compare American and Japanese mothers' attitudes toward child rearing. One of the most significant differences that he found was that American mothers talked to their babies even before they reached the babbling stage, whereas Japanese mothers seldom talked to theirs. There is a greater expectation in the East that people will pick up nonverbal cues and understand intuitively without being told.[5] Many business and government executives have learned to their chagrin that when Japanese executives said yes to a proposal, what they really meant was "yes, I hear you," not "yes, I agree."

---

[4] Theodore Levitt, "The Globalization of Markets," *Harvard Business Review* (May–June 1983), pp. 93–94.

[5] Tsune Shirai, "What Is an 'International Mind'?" *PHP* (June 1980), p. 25.

ANALYTICAL APPROACHES
TO CULTURAL FACTORS

▼ Introduction

The reason cultural factors are a challenge to global marketers is that they are hidden from view. Culture is learned behavior passed on from generation to generation and is difficult for the inexperienced or untrained outsider to fathom. Unless we learn how to let go of our cultural assumptions, we will be limited in our understanding of the meaning and significance of the statements and behaviors of the people from a different culture whom we are trying to do business with.

For example, if you come from a culture that encourages responsibility and initiative, you could experience misunderstandings with a client or boss from a culture that encourages people to remain in personal control of all activities. Your boss would expect to be kept advised in detail of what you were doing when you might be taking the initiative assuming that your boss would appreciate your willingness to take responsibility.

To transcend cultural myopia, it is important to know that there are cultural differences and that they can be learned and incorporated into your experience base. There are several basic facts that will accelerate your ability to learn about other cultures:

1. The beginning of wisdom is to accept that we will never fully understand ourselves or others—people are far too complex to be "understood." As Carl Jung pointed out, "There are no misunderstandings in nature . . . misunderstandings are found only in the realm of what we call 'understanding.' "[6]

2. Our perceptual systems are extremely limited. We "see" almost nothing. Our nervous systems are organized on the principle of negative feedback (i.e., our nervous system operates so smoothly that the only time our control system is brought into play is when input signals deviate from what we expect).

3. We spend most of our energy managing perceptual inputs.

4. When we experience or perceive bizarre behavior, there is something behind this behavior (i.e., a cultural system of beliefs and values that we do not understand).

5. If we want to be effective in a foreign culture, we must attempt to understand beliefs, motives, and values. This requires an open attitude, one that transcends our own culture.

▼ The Need Hierarchy

In the search for cultural universals, an extremely useful theory of human motivation was developed by the late A. H. Maslow.[7]

---

[6] C. G. Jung, *Critique of Psychoanalysis*, Bollingen Series XX (Princeton, NJ: Princeton University Press, 1975), par. 776, p. 228.

[7] A. H. Maslow, "A Theory of Human Motivation," in *Readings in Managerial Psychology*, eds. Harold J. Levitt and Louis R. Pondy (Chicago: University of Chicago Press, 1964), pp. 6–24.

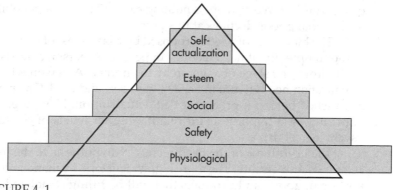

FIGURE 4–1
Maslow's Hierarchy of Needs

Maslow hypothesized that people's desires can be arranged into a hierarchy of needs of relative potency. As soon as the "lower" needs are filled, other and higher needs emerge immediately to dominate the individual. When these higher needs are in turn satisfied, new and still higher needs emerge. Figure 4–1 illustrates the hierarchy identifying the major needs formulated by Maslow.

Physiological needs are at the bottom of the hierarchy because they are most fundamental. They include food, water, air, protection from the elements, comfort, sex, and so on. For the person who is extremely hungry, no other interest except food exists. The individual thinks only about food, wants only food, and has little interest in writing poetry, reading a good book, or acquiring a new automobile or anything other than satisfying an overwhelming need for food. Once these physiological needs are gratified, a new set of needs emerges that Maslow categorizes as safety needs. Safety, in general, refers to a feeling of well-being and a sense that danger is not present in the environment. A person whose physiological and safety needs are satisfied will feel the need for friendships and love relationships and will strive to gratify these needs, which Maslow called social needs.

Once these "lower" needs have been satisfied, two higher needs emerge. First is a need for esteem. This is the desire for self-respect, self-esteem, and the esteem of others and is a powerful drive creating demand for status-improving goods. The status symbol exists across the spectrum of stages of development. In developing East Africa women who owned bras always wore them with straps exposed to show the world that they owned a bra. In Canada a more expensive automobile was for decades a standard form of status improvement.

The final stage in the need hierarchy is self-actualization. When all the needs for sex, safety, security, friendship, and the esteem of others are satisfied, discontent and restlessness will develop unless one is doing what one is fitted for. A musician must make music, an artist must paint, a poet must write, a builder must build, and so on. As Albert Einstein said when asked how he withstood the acclaim he received for his accomplishments and the peril of corruption by praise, "One is tempted to stop and listen to it. The only thing is to turn away and go on working. Work, there is nothing else."[8] There is a possibility that demand for material goods declines at this point.

The hierarchy of needs proposed by Maslow is, of course, a simplification of the complexity of need feelings in people. A person's needs do not progress neatly from one stage of a hierarchy to another. A person who is fulfilling self-actualization needs is also in need of love, sex, and food. One may be restless and dissatisfied before approaching self-actualization. Nevertheless, the hierarchy does suggest a hypothesis for relating higher levels of consumption to basic psychological drives.

The usefulness of the need hierarchy hypothesis to the international marketer is its universality. The more highly developed a market, the greater the proportion of goods and products that will be filling social and esteem needs as opposed to physiological. As countries continue to develop, it appears that self-actualization needs begin to affect consumer behavior. In Canada or the United States, for example, the automobile is no longer a universal status symbol, and many younger consumers are turning away from material possessions. In Los Angeles, for example, a company called Rent-A-Wreck has discovered a thriving market among affluent Hollywood residents who are reacting to what they consider to be a low-brow esteem for expensive cars and who assert their cultural values by driving "wrecks." As countries progress through the stages of economic development, more and more members of a society are operating at the level of esteem needs and higher, having satisfied physiological, safety, and social needs.[9]

Although there are abundant sources of stereotypes that suggest enormous differences in the basic nature of different nationalities and races, increasing evidence is accumulating to dispute these stereotypes. In a study of 25 overseas operations of a large manufacturing company, Sirota and Greenwood found considerable similarity in the work goals of employees:

> The implications of our study may be considered at a number of different levels.
>
> Perhaps most relevant to the managers of international organizations is the considerable similarity we have found in the goals of employees around the world. This finding has an extremely important policy implication: since the goals of employees are similar internationally, corporate policy decisions, to the extent that they are based on assumptions about employee goals, can also be international in scope.
>
> It is not only Americans who want money, or Frenchmen who want autonomy, or Germans who want their work skills utilized and improved. A management whose policies and practices reflect these stereotypes (for example, providing few advancement opportunities in some countries or using certain countries as dumping grounds for routine, unchallenging work) should

---

[8] Ronald W. Clark, *Einstein: The Life and Times* (New York: World, 1971).

[9] An anomaly of modern times is the emergence of a need for safety in many regions of the world. Indeed, the high incidence of crime in some developed countries may leave their residents with a lower level of satisfaction of this need than in many so-called "poor" countries.

be prepared to suffer the consequences of managing a frustrated and un-committed work force.

In this respect, it would be interesting to determine how much of the difficulty experienced in managing employees in other countries is due not to cultural differences at all but, rather, to the automatic and psychologically self-serving assumption of differences that, in reality, may be minor or even nonexistent.[10]

▼ The Self-Reference Criterion

A way of systematically reducing the extent to which our perception of market needs is blocked by our own cultural experience was developed by James Lee. Lee terms the unconscious reference to one's own cultural values the *self-reference criterion*, or SRC. He addresses this problem and proposes a systematic four-step framework for eliminating this form of myopia.[11]

1. Define the problem or goal in terms of home-country cultural traits, habits, and norms.
2. Define the problems or goal in terms of the foreign cultural traits, habits, and norms.
3. Isolate the SRC influence in the problem and examine it carefully to see how it complicates the problem.
4. Redefine the problem without the SRC influence and solve for the foreign market situation.

Lee provides the following example of an application of this analytical approach. An automobile manufacturer withdrew its assembly operation from Karachi under government pressure to manufacture automobiles or to sell out. Taking this pressure as the beginning of a product design problem, how might the company have proceeded at the time of its entry into the Pakistani market?

Step 1. Define the business problem or goal in terms of domestic cultural traits, habits, or norms. Western countries are characterized by transportation needs geared to speed, promptness, comfort, and style. Advanced country highways demanded a cruising speed of 95 to 110 kilometres per hour, and 80- to 100-octane gasoline was available. Manufacturing techniques were very sophisticated; foreign exchange was not a businessperson's problem.

Step 2. Define the business problem or goal in terms of the foreign cultural traits, habits, or norms. Make no value judgments. Pakistan was a culture characterized by a strong desire to be mobile but with a low

---

[10] David Sirota and Michael J. Greenwood, "Understand Your Overseas Workforce," *Harvard Business Review* (January–February 1971), p. 60.

[11] James A. Lee, "Cultural Analysis in Overseas Operations," *Harvard Business Review* (March–April 1966), pp. 106–114.

technological skill level. There was extreme pressure on foreign exchange. Consumer credit was a future hope.

Step 3.   Isolate the SRC influence in the problem and examine it carefully to see how it complicates the problem. The significant differences between steps 1 and 2 suggest strongly that the needs upon which the advanced country model were originally based did not exist in Pakistan and that a modification of these models was needed by the market.

Step 4.   Redefine the problem without the SRC influence and solve for the foreign market situation. This would require the design of a car to fit Pakistan's cultural and economic specifications. Lee maintains that such a car would be made of angle, channel, and strap iron. The capital investment in Pakistan would be about $100,000 in hard currency and in the equivalent amount in the local currency for each 1,000 units of annual capacity. The car would sell for approximately $2,000, would have a cruising speed of 40 miles an hour, and would travel 80 miles on a gallon of low-octane gasoline.

▼ Diffusion Theory

Since the late 1930s hundreds of studies have been directed toward achieving and understanding the process through which an individual adopts a new idea.[12] In his book *Diffusion of Innovations*, Everett Rogers reports on 506 diffusion studies that suggest some remarkably similar findings. This enormous body of research has suggested concepts and patterns that are extremely useful to international marketers because they are involved in introducing innovations in the form of their products into markets.

An innovation is something new or different, either in an absolute sense or in a situational sense. In an absolute sense, once a product has been introduced anywhere in the world, it is no longer an innovation because it is no longer new to the world. However, a product introduced in one market may be an innovation in another market because it is a new and different product for the new market. Thus, in international marketing, companies are in the position of marketing products that may be simultaneously new-product innovations in some markets and mature, postmature, or declining products in other markets. Thus, the findings from studies of the diffusion of innovations have great relevance to the various circumstances in which international marketers finds themselves.

The Adoption Process

One of the basic elements of the theory of the diffusion of innovations is the concept of an adoption process, the mental process through which an individual passes from the time of his or her first knowledge of an innovation to the time of adoption or purchase of the innovation. Research suggests that an individual

---

[12] This section draws from Everett M. Rogers, *Diffusion of Innovations*, 3rd Edition (New York: Free Press, 1983).

passes through five different stages in proceeding from first knowledge of a product to the final adoption or purchase of that product. These stages are as follows:

1. *Awareness.* At this stage the customer becomes aware for the first time of the product or innovation. Studies have shown that at this stage impersonal sources of information such as advertising are most important. Frequently one of the major objectives of advertising in international marketing is to create product awareness where the product is an innovation in the new market.

2. *Interest.* During this stage the customer knows of the product and, because of an interest in the product, seeks additional information. In the information gathering, the customer has shifted from a viewing position to a monitoring position. The customer will incorporate any information on the product in question if information on it should come into his or her possession. Additionally, because of an interest in the product, the customer will engage in research activities to acquire additional information.

3. *Evaluation.* In this stage the individual mentally applies the product or innovation to the present and anticipated future situation and decides whether or not to try the product.

4. *Trial.* After learning of the product, obtaining information about it, and mentally deciding whether or not to try the product, the customer's next stage is trial or actual purchase depending on the cost of the product. If the product is expensive, then a customer will not purchase it without trial, although the trial may be mental or theoretical rather than actual. A good example of an actual trial that does not involve purchase would be the automobile demonstration ride. For the inexpensive product, trial often involves purchase, but can also involve a free sample. In inexpensive products, adoption is defined as repeat purchase as opposed to a single purchase that is defined as trial.

5. *Adoption.* In this stage the individual either purchases the more expensive product that has been tried without purchase or continues to purchase (repeat purchase) the less expensive product, such as a razor blade. As a person moves from the evaluation to the trial to the adoption stage, studies show that personal sources of information are more important than impersonal sources. It is during these stages that the representative and, perhaps even more important, word of mouth come into play as major persuasive forces affecting the decision to buy.

Characteristics of Innovation

One of the major factors affecting the rate of adoption of an innovation is the characteristics of the innovation itself. Rogers suggests five characteristics that have a major influence on the rate of adoption of an innovation. They are as follows:

1. *Relative advantage.* How does a new product compare with existing products or methods in the eyes of customers? The perceived relative advantage of a new product versus existing products is a major influence on the rate of adoption. An example of a product with a high perceived relative advantage is the transistor

radio vis-à-vis the tube-type radio. If a product has a substantial relative advantage vis-à-vis the competition, it is at a great advantage in the market.

2. *Compatibility.*   This is the extent to which a product is consistent with existing values and past experiences of adopters. The history of product failures in international marketing is replete with examples that were caused by the lack of compatibility of the new products in the target market. The fluffy frosted cake mixes were introduced by U.S. companies into the United Kingdom where cake was eaten at tea time with the fingers rather than as a dessert with a fork. The result was lack of sales and failure. The Renault Dauphine was introduced into Canada and the United States in 1959 to a market that subjected automobiles to driving conditions far more rigorous than those encountered in France. The result was product breakdowns and failure. The Jolly Green Giant attempted to market corn in Europe where the prevailing attitude at the time was that corn is a grain that is fed to hogs and not to people. The result was a lack of sales and severe losses on investments in European corn production. These products did not succeed in international markets because of the lack of compatibility with existing values and patterns of behavior.

3. *Complexity.*   This is the degree to which an innovation or new product is difficult to understand and use. If a product has a high coefficient of complexity, then this is a factor that can slow down the rate of adoption, particularly in developing country markets with low rates of literacy.

4. *Divisibility.*   This is the degree or extent to which a product may be tried and used on a limited basis. In the international market, wide discrepancies in income levels result in major differences in acceptable levels of divisibility. Hellmann's mayonnaise, a product of CPC International, was simply not selling in U.S.-size jars in Latin America. The company then placed the mayonnaise in small plastic packets and immediately sales developed. The plastic packets were within the food budgets of the local consumers, and they required no refrigeration, another plus.

5. *Communicability.*   This is the degree to which results of an innovation or the value of a product may be communicated to a potential market.

The major dimensions of the product that determine the rate of its adoption or penetration of international markets are its relative advantage vis-à-vis other products, its compatibility with existing values and patterns of behavior, and the price of the product relative to the price of competing or substitute products. A fourth major factor is the availability of the product. Finally, the communicability and the effectiveness of communications concerning the product are a major influence affecting the rate of adoption.

Adopter Categories

Adopter categories are classifications of individuals within a market on the basis of their innovativeness. The hundreds of studies of the diffusion of innovation demonstrate that adoption is a social phenomenon and, therefore, is characterized by the normal distributions as shown in Figure 4–2.

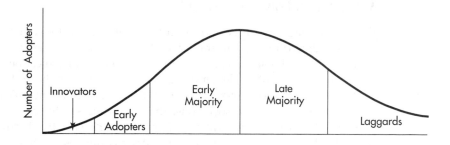

FIGURE 4–2
Adopter Categories

Five categories have been assigned to the segments of this normal distribution. The first 2.5 percent of people to purchase a product are defined as innovators. The next 13.5 percent are defined as early adopters, the next 34 percent as the early majority, the next 34 percent as the late majority, and the final 16 percent as laggards. Studies show that innovators tend to be venturesome, more cosmopolitan in their social relationships, and wealthier than those who adopt later. Early adopters are the most influential people in their communities, even more than the innovators. Thus, the early adopters are a critical group in the adoption process, and they have a great influence on the majority, who make up the bulk of the adopters of any product. Several characteristics of early adopters stand out. First, they tend to be younger, have higher social status, and are in a more favorable financial position than later adopters. They must be responsive to mass-media information sources and must learn about innovations from these sources because they cannot simply copy the behavior of earlier adopters.

One of the major reasons for the normal distribution of adopter categories is the so-called *interaction effect*. This is the process through which individuals in a social system who have adopted an innovation influence those who have not yet adopted. Adoption of a new idea or product is the result of human interaction. If the first adopter of an innovation or new product discusses it with two other people, and each of these two adopters passes the new idea along to two other people, and so on, the resulting distribution follows a binomial expansion. This mathematical function follows a normal shape when plotted.

From the point of view of the marketing manager, steps taken to persuade innovators and early adopters to purchase a product are critical. These innovators must make the first move and are the basis for the eventual penetration of a product into a new market because the majority copy their behavior.

▼ High- and Low-Context Cultures

Edward T. Hall has suggested the concept of high and low context as a way of understanding different cultural orientations.[13] In a low-context culture, messages are explicit; words carry most of the information in communication (see Figure 4–3). In a high-context culture, less information is contained in the verbal part of a message, since much more information is in the context of communication, which includes the background, associations, and basic values of the communicators. Who you are—that is, your values and position or place in society—is crucial in the high-context culture, such as in Japan or the Arab countries. In these cultures, a bank loan is more likely to be based upon who you are than upon formal analysis of pro forma profit and loss statements and balance sheets. In a low-context culture, deals are made with much less information about the character and background and values of the participants and much more reliance upon the words and numbers in the loan application. Examples of low-context cultures would be Canadians or Americans or, perhaps even more distinctly, the Swiss-Germans.

In general, high-context cultures get along with much less legal paperwork than is deemed essential in low-context cultures such as Canada. In a high-context culture, a person's word is his or her bond. There is less need to anticipate contingencies and provide for external legal sanctions in a culture that emphasizes obligations and trust as important values. In these cultures, shared feelings of obligation and honor take the place of impersonal legal sanctions, thus, the importance of long and protracted negotiations that never seem to get to the point. Part of the purpose of negotiating for a person from a high-context culture is to get to know the potential partner.

FIGURE 4–3
Messages and Context
Source: Adapted from Edward T. Hall, *Beyond Culture* (Garden City, NY: Anchor Press/Doubleday, 1976).

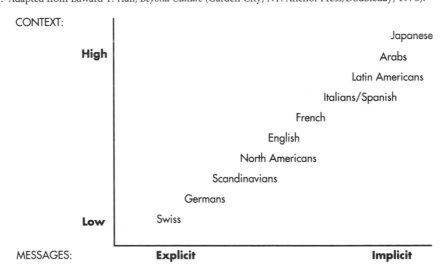

---

[13] See Edward T. Hall, *Beyond Culture* (Garden City, NY: Anchor Press/Doubleday, 1976) and "How Cultures Collide," *Psychology Today* (July 1976) pp. 66–97.

TABLE 4–1 High- and Low-Context Cultures

Factors/ Dimensions	High Context	Low Context
Lawyers	Less important	Very important
A person's word	Is his or her bond	Is not to be relied upon; "get it in writing"
Responsibility for organizational error	Taken by highest level	Pushed to lowest level
Space	People breathe on each other	People carry a bubble of private space with them and resent intrusions
Time	Polychronic—everything in life must be dealt with in terms of its own time	Monochronic—time is money Linear—one thing at a time
Negotiations	Are lengthy—a major purpose is to allow the parties to get to know each other	Proceed quickly
Competitive bidding	Infrequent	Common
Country/regional examples	Japan, Middle East	Canada, United States, Northern Europe

For example, insisting on competitive bidding can cause complications in low-context cultures. In a high-context culture, the job is given to the person who will do the best work and whom you can trust and control. In a low-context culture, one tries to make the specifications so precise that a builder is forced by the threat of legal sanction to do a good job. According to Hall, a builder in Japan is likely to say, "What has that piece of paper got to do with the situation? If we can't trust each other enough to go ahead without it, why bother?"

Although countries can be classified as high or low context in their overall tendency, there are of course exceptions to the general tendency. These exceptions are found in subcultures. Canada, for example, is a low-context culture with subcultures that operate in the high-context mode.

Table 4–1 summarizes some of the ways in which high- and low-context cultures differ.

▼ Perception

The vital, critical skill of the global marketer is perception, or the ability to see what is so in a culture. Although this skill is as valuable at home as it is abroad, it is of particular importance to the global marketer because of the widespread tendency to rely on the self-reference criterion (SRC). The self-reference criterion is the unconscious tendency to draw on memory and assumptions about people instead of perceptions of how they actually behave and think.[14]

The SRC is a powerful negative force in global business and one of the major causes of failure and misunderstanding. To avoid the SRC, you must

---

[14] See discussion of SRC earlier in this chapter.

suspend your experience and be prepared to acquire new knowledge about human behavior and motivation.

The complexities of intercultural communications, perceiving another culture's motivations and behaviors, are such that it would be easy to become paranoid about the hazards of doing business across cultures. Actually, the main obstacle is attitude, as we have learned from our experience with the Japanese culture. If you are sincere and truly want to learn about a culture, you will find that people respond to your sincerity and interest and will help you acquire the knowledge you need to be effective. If you are arrogant and insincere and believe that you are right and "they" are wrong, you can expect a full measure of trouble and misunderstanding. The best antidote to the problem of misperceiving a situation is constant vigilance and an awareness that there are many opportunities to err. This should create an attitude of openness to see what is so. Every global marketer should strive to suspend judgment and simply perceive and take in the facts.

NEGOTIATIONS: CROSS-CULTURAL CHALLENGES

Abroad, the international marketer faces counterparts from diverse cultural backgrounds. Business practices vary immensely across the globe. They are, for the most part, evolved from cultural characteristics and local commerce. For the international marketer, business negotiations and understanding buyers and their decision-making, on one hand, present a major challenge; on the other hand, they present one of the best opportunities to apply knowledge and understanding of cross-cultural differences.

Cultural ethnocentrism at negotiations creates problems because it often reflects perceived stereotypes and a lack of sensitivity towards other cultures. The framework of cultural context suggested by Hall and discussed earlier in this chapter helps in understanding why this is so and how cross-cultural negotiations might be handled appropropriately.

Donald Hendon has conducted seminars on cross-cultural negotiations in many countries and suggests eight characteristics an ideal international negotiator should possess.[15] Such a negotiator

1. Should understand the decision-making process of the country and work effectively within it
2. Is flexible to handle effectively even the most delicate issues, such as bribery, and manage these within the local context
3. Has a keen sensitivity in an intercultural situation; is able to empathize with local counterparts, anticipate and respond appropriately to emotional and social needs
4. Can communicate and relate effectively with local counterparts; is a perceptive observer of subtle communication clues in the verbal and non-verbal behavior of the hosts

---

[15] Donald W. Hendon and Rebecca Angeles Hendon, *World-Class Negotiating – Dealmaking in the Global Marketplace* (New York: John Wiley & Sons, Inc., 1990) pp.35–45, with permission.

TABLE 4–2 Negotiating Style Contrasts: North Americans, Arabs, and Russians

	North Americans	Arabs	Russians
Primary Negotiating Style and Process	Factual: Appeals made to logic	Affective: Appeals made to emotions	Axiomatic: Appeals made to ideals
Conflict: Opponent's Arguments Countered with ...	Objective facts	Subjective feelings	Asserted ideals
Making Concessions	Small concessions made early to establish a relationship	Concessions made throughout as part of the bargaining process	Few, if any, small concessions made
Response to Opponent's Concessions	Usually reciprocate opponent's concessions	Almost always reciprocate opponent's concessions	Opponent's concessions viewed as weakness and almost never reciprocated
Relationship	Short term	Long term	No continuing relationship
Authority	Broad	Broad	Limited
Initial Position	Moderate	Extreme	Extreme
Deadline	Very important	Casual	Ignored

Source: Reprinted from *International Journal of Intercultural Relations, 1:3,* E.S. Glenn, D. Witmeyer, and K.A. Stevenson, "Cultural Styles of Persuasion", pp. 52–66. Copyright 1984 wth kind permission from Elsevier Science Ltd., The Boulevard, Bradford Lane, Kidlington 0X5 1GB, UK.

5. Has personal stability, a sense of inner security and the ability to handle stress on-the-job
6. Uses humor, with good taste and discrimination, to "break the ice" and enhance the pleasant ambience of the negotiations
7. Can tolerate ambiguity and is patient, even in situations of great pressure
8. Becomes involved with the counterpart's organization, actively seeking allies and extending his/her network of influence

These demanding and challenging requirements are often lacking in international marketers. The difference between successful and unsuccessful negotiations is often based on the negotiator's inter-cultural competence rather than the object product or service.

There are distinct differences between negotiating styles, as we can see in Table 4-2, contrasting North American, Arab, and Russian styles.

It is also helpful to view cultural differences from the perspective of affinity zones[16], such as Latin America, North America, Western Europe, and so on. Figure 4-4 shows the idea of cultural affinity zones for Europe.

Cultural affinity zones do not describe political boundaries. Rather they are based on criteria at the interface of culture and marketing, such as language, religion, family life patterns, work relations, and consumption patterns. This is the case between Norway and Sweden, Spain and Portugal, or Austria and Germany, to name a few examples. Two zones, Scandinavia and the Mediterranean countries,

---

[16] The concept of cultural affinity zones is described by J.C. Usunier and P. Sissmann, "L'interculturel au service du marketing", *Harvard L'Expansion* (Spring 1986) 40; pp.80–92.

are quite separate, while the middle zones of central European countries serve as a bridge.[17]

A similar idea is contained in the concept that the many nations of Latin America can be seen as five regions based on the demographics of sociology and culture. Stereotypical thinking about Latin America and its 450 million inhabitants is as inappropriate as regarding the 370 million West Europeans as alike. Latin American countries are grouped as:[18]

FIGURE 4–4
Europe's Cultural Affinity Zones

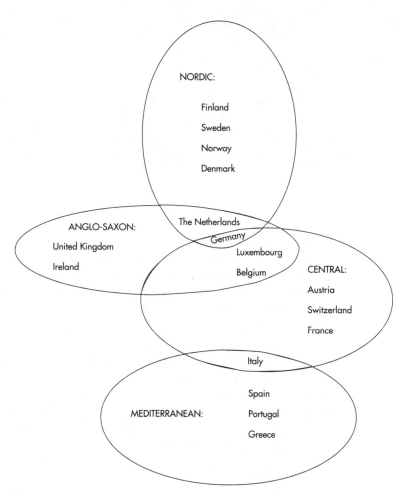

[17] Jean-Claude Usunier, *International Marketing — A Cultural Approach* (Hertfordshire: Prentice-Hall International (UK), 1993), pp. 207-8.

[18] Marlene L. Rossman, "Understanding the Five Nations of Latin America", *Marketing News* (October 11, 1985).

- Mexico – Spanish-speaking, bridging North and Central America
- Brazil – Portugese-speaking
- Caribbean Latin America – includes Puerto Rico, Dominican Republic, Panama, Honduras, coastal Venezuela, Caracas, and coastal cities of Colombia
- European Latin America – includes Argentina, Chile, Uruguay, most of Colombia, Southern Brazil, Costa Rica, and Lima, Peru
- Indian Latin America – includes Bolivia, Paraguay, Ecuador, Peru (except Lima), Guatemala, and El Salvador

The United States poses cultural challenges for Canadian international marketers. Its demography alone suggests the need for tailored approaches. For example, the Hispanic population is nearly as large as Canada's total population and over 50 percent live in California and Texas. While there are also various sub-segments – those of Cuban origin, of Mexican or Latin American origin – Hispanics represent a "foreign consumer market with special needs" in the United States.[19] While there are many similarities between Canadian and American managers[20], it is also clear that just as there are regional differences in consumer demographics, business behavior differs across regions in the United States and must be responded to if the international marketer is to succeed.

The suggestion here is that the marketer can define markets on socio-cultural dimensions.

Table 4-3 summarizes and compares characteristics of business behavior found in Japan, North America, and Latin America. There are some stark differences between Canadians, Japanese, and Latin Americans. Most of the differences between Canadians and Japanese, which are high context for example, occur because in Japan personal relationship and trust — without show of emotions — rather than legal contracts form the basis for business. In Latin America, which also falls into the explicit, high context range, personal relationships are also important; however, everyday life is permeated overtly with emotions.[21] It would be wrong to suggest that all Latin Americans are alike, but their cultural and behavioral similarities are greater amongst themselves than those between Canada and Chile, Brazil, or Argentina, for example.

Western Europe falls into the medium to low context, more explicit, range of Hall's classification. Within Western Europe, Nordic countries, Germany, and Switzerland emphasize objectivity, contract, and efficiency in their dealings. This tendency clearly diminishes to lesser transparency of dealings in the Mediterranean countries. The French tend to be somewhat legalistic, however, capable of "bending" the rules and using facts more casually if it suits their purpose.[22]

---

[19] Alfredo Corchado "Hispanic Supermarkets Are Blossoming", Wall Street Journal, January 23, 1989, B1.

[20] Geert Hofstede, Culture's Consequences: International Differences in Work-related Values, (Beverly Hills: Sage Publications, 1980).

[21] This section draws on A.Coskun Samli, Richard Still and John S. Hill, International Marketing – Planning and Practice (New York, MacMillan Publishing Company, 1993) pp.330-40.

[22] *The Economist Guide*—France, (1990) p. 72-3.

TABLE 4–3 Japanese, North American, and Latin American Business Behavior

Japanese	North American	Latin American
Emotional sensitivity highly valued	Emotional sensitivity not highly valued	Emotional sensitivity valued
Hiding of emotions	Dealing straightforwardly or impersonally	Emotionally passionate
Subtle power plays; conciliation	Litigation not as much as conciliation	Great power plays; use of weakness
Loyal to employer. Employer takes care of its employees	Lack of commitment to employer. Breaking of ties by either if necessary	Loyalty to employer (who is often family)
Group decision-making consensus	Teamwork provides input to a decision maker	Decisions come down from one individual
Face-saving crucial. Decisions often made on basis of saving someone from embarrassment	Decisions made on a cost benefit basis. Face-saving does not always matter	Face-saving crucial in decision making to preserve honor, dignity
Decision makers openly influenced by special interests	Decision makers influenced by special interests but often not considered ethical	Execution of special interests of decision maker expected, condoned
Not argumentative. Quiet when right	Argumentative when right or wrong, but impersonal	Argumentative when right or wrong; passionate
What is down in writing must be accurate, valid	Great importance given to documentation as evidential proof	Impatient with documenttion as obstacle to understanding general principles
Step-by-step approach to decision making	Methodically organized decision making	Impulsive, spontaneous decision making
Good of group is the ultimate aim	Profit motive or good of individual ultimate aim	What is good for the group is good for the individual
Cultivate a good emotional social setting for decision making. Get to know decision makers	Decision making impersonal. Avoid involvements, conflict of interest	Personalism necessary for good decision making

Source: Reprinted from Pierre Casse, Training for the Multicultural Manager: A Practical and Cross-Cultural Approach to the Management of People, (Washington, D.C., 1982). Used with permission.

Italians with their emotional, outgoing personality are masters at "changing the cards on the table," which can make it difficult for the foreigner to know where negotiations stand. Their concept of contract does not stem from the Anglo-Saxon tradition that the formal document backs up the parties' intent; rather, the document itself is the contract and establishing "intentions" is of limited importance and consequence.[23]

Other regions of the world, of course, are posing challenges to the Canadian international marketer. The emerging South-East Asian countries and the formerly-communist Eastern European countries are two notable, important regions. In some of the South-East Asian countries, some business practices were fashioned by earlier colonial days, such as the processing of contracts through notaries, a Dutch convention. In Indonesia, Malaysia, and Singapore, the legal systems are based on English law.[24]

---

[23] *The Economist Business Travellers Guides — Italy*, (New York: Prentice Hall, 1989) p. 77.

[24] *The Economist Guide — South-East Asia*, Indonesia, p.76.

One overriding item is the high-context nature of the South-East Asian countries. Principles such as the relative lack of rhetoric, flexibility of time, the absence of overtly displayed emotions, face-saving through avoiding confrontation and masking true feelings, or response, decision or agreement by consensus are typical Asian characteristics found throughout the region (except in Philippine society, which was significantly influenced by the Spanish and later by American presence and defies a simple description).[25]

Among the Eastern European countries, diversity is as much a key word as in South-East Asia. Historical and cultural roots differ greatly between many of these countries and they are emerging after the demise of communist control and philosophy. In Russia, and some other states, remnants of the centralized, bureaucratic committee method of business negotiation survive. The Western businessman may find it difficult to determine who is in charge, who owns what, and who has the authority to negotiate or to sign a contract.[26] Countries like the Czech Republic, Poland, and Hungary are making great strides towards a market-based economy and are embracing Western business practices.

It would be sheer folly for a foreigner to deal in high context cultures without careful and comprehensive preparation. This includes awareness of racial factors, the status of women, the building of relationships, the role of time, the importance of the group versus the individual, the mixing or separation of business, and entertainment.

▼ Learning from the Mistakes of Others—A Case Example: Marketing an Industrial Product in Latin America

Much has been written about specific cultural differences in various regions of the world. The cultural variety of the world is so great that it is neither feasible nor prudent to attempt to capture these differences in a single volume. The following actual case suggests, however, the way in which cultural differences influenced the marketing of an industrial product in Latin America.

A Latin American republic had decided to modernize one of its communication networks at a cost of several million dollars. Because of its reputation for quality, the government approached American company "Y."

The company, having been sounded out informally, considered the size of the order and decided to bypass its regular Latin American representative and send instead its sales manager. The following describes what took place.

> The sales manager arrived and checked into the leading hotel. He immediately had some difficulty pinning down just who it was he had to see about his business. After several days without results, he called at the American Embassy where he found that the commercial attaché had the up-to-the-minute information he needed. The commercial attaché listened to his story. Realizing that the sales manager had already made a number of mistakes, but figuring that the Latins were used to American

---

[25] ibid., Philippines, p. 149.

[26] Chrystia Freeland, "The Rough Etiquette of Russian Deal-making", *Financial Times*, April 16-17, 1994, p. I.

blundering the attaché reasoned that all was not lost. He informed the sales manager that the Minister of Communications was the key man and that whoever got the nod from him would get the contract. He also briefed the sales manager on methods of conducting business in Latin America and offered some pointers about dealing with the minister.

The attaché's advice ran somewhat as follows:

1. You don't do business here the way you do in the States; it is necessary to spend much more time. You have to get to know your man and vice versa.

2. You must meet with him several times before you talk business. I will tell you at what point you can bring up the subject. Take your cues from me. (Our American sales manager at this point made a few observations to himself about "cookie pushers" and wondered how many payrolls had been met by the commercial attaché.)

3. Take that price list and put it in your pocket. Don't get it out until I tell you to. Down here price is only one of the many things taken into account before closing a deal. In the United States, your past experience will prompt you to act according to a certain set of principles, but many of these principles will not work here. Every time you feel the urge to act or to say something, look at me. Suppress the urge and take your cues from me. This is very important.

4. Down here people like to do business with men who are somebody. In order to be somebody, it is well to have written a book, to have lectured at a university, or to have developed your intellect in some way. The man you are going to see is a poet. He has published several volumes of poetry. Like many Latin Americans, he prizes poetry highly. You will find that he will spend a good deal of business time quoting his poetry to you, and he will take great pleasure in this.

5. You will also note that the people here are very proud of their past and of their Spanish blood, but they are also exceedingly proud of their liberation from Spain and their independence. The fact that they are a democracy, that they are free, and also that they are no longer a colony is very, very important to them. They are warm and friendly and enthusiastic if they like you. If they don't, they are cold and withdrawn.

6. And another thing, time down here means something different. It works in a different way. You know how it is back in the States when a certain type blurts out whatever is on his mind without waiting to see if the situation is right. He is considered an impatient bore and somewhat egocentric. Well, down here you have to wait much, much longer, and I really mean much, much longer, before you can begin to talk about the reason for your visit.

7. There is another point I want to caution you about. At home, the man who sells takes the initiative. Here, they tell you when they are ready to do business. But most of all, don't discuss price until you are asked and don't rush things.

The Pitch. The next day the commercial attaché introduced the sales manager to the Minister of Communications. First, there was a long wait in the outer office while people kept coming in and out. The sales manager looked at his watch, fidgeted, and finally asked whether the minister was really expecting him. The reply he received was scarcely reassuring, "Oh yes, he is expecting you but several things have come up that require his attention. Besides, one gets used to waiting down here." The sales manager irritably replied, "But doesn't he know I flew all the way down here from the United States to see him, and I have spent over a week already of my valuable time trying to find him?" "Yes, I know," was the answer, "but things just move much more slowly here."

At the end of about thirty minutes, the minister emerged from the office, greeted the commercial attaché with a double abrazo, throwing his arms around him and patting him on the back as though they were long-lost brothers. Now, turning and smiling, the minister extended his hand to the sales manager, who, by this time, was feeling rather miffed because he had been kept in the outer office so long.

After what seemed to be an all too short chat, the minister rose, suggesting a well-known cafe where they might meet for dinner the next evening. The sales manager expected, of course, that, considering the nature of their business and the size of the order, he might be taken to the minister's home, not realizing that the Latin home is reserved for family and very close friends.

Until now, nothing at all had been said about the reason for the sales manager's visit, a fact which bothered him somewhat. The whole setup seemed wrong; nor did he like the idea of wasting another day in town. He told the home office before he left that he would be gone for a week or ten days at most, and made a mental note that he would clean this order up in three days and enjoy a few days in Acapulco or Mexico City. Now the week had already gone and he would be lucky if he made it home in ten days.

Voicing his misgivings to the commercial attaché, he wanted to know if the minister really meant business, and if he did, why could they not get together and talk about it? The commercial attaché by now was beginning to show the strain of constantly having to reassure the sales manager. Nevertheless, he tried again: "What you don't realize is that part of the time we were waiting, the minister was rearranging a very tight schedule so that he could spend tomorrow night with you. You see, down here they don't delegate responsibility the way we do in the States. They exercise much tighter control than we do. As a consequence, this man spends up to 15 hours a day at his desk. It may not look like it to you, but I assure you he really means business. He wants to give your company the order; if you play your cards right, you will get it."

The next evening provided more of the same. Much conversation about food and music, about many people the sales manager had never heard of. They went to a night club, where the sales manager brightened up and began to think that perhaps he and the minister might have something in common after all. It bothered him, however, that the principal reason for his visit was not even alluded to tangentially. But every time he started to talk about electronics, the commercial attaché would nudge him and proceed to change the subject.

The next meeting was for morning coffee at a café. By now the sales manager was having difficulty hiding his impatience. To make matters worse the minister had a mannerism that he did not like. When they talked he was likely to put his hand on him; he would take hold of his arm and get so close that he almost "spat" in his face. As a consequence, the sales manager was kept busy trying to dodge and back up.

Following coffee, there was a walk in a nearby park. The minister expounded on the shrubs, the birds, and the beauties of nature, and at one spot he stopped to point at a statue and said: "There is a statue of the world's greatest hero, the liberator of mankind!" At this point, the worst happened, for the sales manager asked who the statue was of and, being given the name of a famous Latin American patriot, said, "I never heard of him," and walked on.

The Failure. It is quite clear from this that the sales manager did not get the order, which went to a Swedish concern. The American, moreover, was never able to see the minister again. Why did the minister feel the way he did? His reasoning went somewhat as follows:

"I like the American's equipment and it makes sense to deal with North Americans who are near us and whose price is right. But I could never be friends with this man. He is not my kind of human being and we have nothing in common. He is not simpático. If I can't be friends and he is not simpático, I can't depend on him to treat me right. I tried everything, every conceivable situation, and only once did we seem to understand each other. If we could be friends, he would feel obligated to me and this obligation would give me some control. Without control, how do I know he will deliver what he says he will at the price he quotes?"

Of course, what the minister did not know was that the price was quite firm, and that quality control was a matter of company policy. He did not realize that the sales manager was a member of an organization, and that the man is always subordinate to the organization in the United States. Next year maybe the sales manager would not even be representing the company, but would be replaced. Further, if he wanted someone to depend on, his best bet would be to hire a good American lawyer to represent him and write a binding contract.

In this instance, both sides suffered. The American felt he was being slighted and put off, and did not see how there could possibly be any connection between poetry and doing business or why it should all take so long. He interpreted the delay as a form of polite brush-off. Even if things had gone differently and there had been a contract, it is doubtful that the minister would have trusted the contract as much as he would a man whom he considered his friend. Throughout Latin America, the law is made livable and contracts workable by having friends and relatives operating from the inside. Lacking a friend, someone who would look out for his interests, the minister did not want to take a chance. He stated this simply and directly.[27]

PRODUCTS

Cultural factors are important influences on the marketing of products and must be recognized in formulating an international marketing plan. For industrial products, the impact of culture manifests itself in a different way than for consumer products. For example, different conventions regarding specifications are important. Safety standards and product calibrations vary across countries, although the ISO 9000 standards are rapidly gaining acceptance as a global standard. Product certification and approval procedures differ and can be quite time-consuming and costly to obtain. The bureaucracy involved in this process is one aspect of the cultural influences affecting international marketing.

Consumer products, on the other hand, are probably more sensitive to cultural differences. Observation and studies agree that independent of social class and income, culture is a significant influence on consumption behavior, media usage, and durable goods ownership. Among consumer products, food is probably the most sensitive of all. Campbell's reportedly lost over $10 million trying to change the wet soup habits of the German consumer from dehydrated soup to a canned soup concentrate.

A major cultural factor in food marketing is the attitude and practice of homemakers toward food preparation. Campbell Soup discovered in a study conducted in Italy that Italian homemakers were spending approximately 4.5 hours per day in food preparation in contrast to the less than 60 minutes a day spent in food preparation by North American homemakers.

Indeed Campbell's discovered how strong the feeling against convenience food in Italy was by asking a random sample of Italian homemakers the following question: "Would you want your son to marry a canned soup user?" The response to this question was sobering. Of the respondents, 99.6 percent answered, "No!" Rising incomes will affect Italian attitudes toward time and convenience and will have a major effect on the market for convenience foods. Meanwhile, the habits and customs of people continue to affect food markets independently of income levels.

Thirst is a universal physiological need. What people drink, however, is very much culturally determined. The market for coffee presents an interesting demonstration of the effect of culture on drinking habits. In the United Kingdom instant

---

[27] Edward T. Hall, "The Silent Language in Overseas Business," *Harvard Business Review* (May–June 1960), pp. 93-96. ©1960 by the President and Fellows of Harvard College; all rights reserved.

coffee has 90 percent of the total coffee market as compared with only 15 percent in Sweden. The other countries in the Atlantic community fall between these two extreme points. Instant coffee's large share of the British market can be traced to the fact that in hot beverage consumption, Britain has been a tea-drinking market. Only in recent times have the British been persuaded to take up coffee drinking. Instant coffee is more like tea than regular coffee in its preparation, and so it was natural that when the British did begin to drink coffee they should adopt instant rather than regular coffee. Another reason for the popularity of instant coffee in Britain is the practice of drinking coffee with a large quantity of milk, so that the coffee flavor is masked. Differences in the coffee flavor are thus hidden, so that a "better cup" of coffee is not really important. Sweden, on the other hand, is a coffee-drinking country. Coffee is the leading hot beverage. The product tends to be consumed without large quantities of milk and, therefore, the coffee flavor is not masked.

Data on consumption patterns of soft drinks in Western Europe and Canada demonstrate, however, that there are conspicuous differences in the demand for soft drinks. The average Canadian drinks about four times as many soft drinks as the average Frenchman, or 1.6 times as many as the average German. The British drink the most soft drinks in Europe and consumption has reached nearly 80 percent of Canadian consumption. In general, the average European's consumption of soft drinks is only about 40 percent of the 146.9 litres per capita Canadians consume in a year.[28] This helps to explain why Cott Corporation, a producer of private label soft drinks, has targeted Europe as a major source of growth. The U.K. provides a solid, if highly competitive, entry base for the European soft drink market. Cott's agreements with Cadbury Beverages Ltd. gives the company access to bottling plants in Spain, Portugal, Belgium, France, and Germany, in addition to its own bottling plant in Britain.[29] Market-expansion plans for the diverse market environments throughout Europe were foreshadowed by the private label brand Classic Cola which Cott Corp. began producing for the giant J. Sainbury chain in the U.K. in 1994.[30]

The differences in soft drink consumption are associated with much higher per capita consumption of other kinds of beverages in Europe. For example, the French and Italians prefer mineral water to soft drinks. German per capita consumption of beer is much higher than in Canada. Wine consumption in France and Italy is about eight times that in Canada. Why is there such a difference between the popularity of soft drinks between Western Europe and Canada? The following factors are responsible for the differences:

$$C = f(A, B, C, D, E, F, G)$$

C = consumption of soft drinks

WHERE

f = function of
A = influences of other beverages' relative prices, quality, and taste

---

[28] *European Marketing Data and Statistics 1994* (London: *Euromotinor*, 1994), Table 1407, p. 358.

[29] Eric Reguly, "Cott Eyes European Growth," *The Financial Post*, May 24, 1994, pp.1, 3

[30] "Cott Expanding Cola Wars", *The Globe and Mail*, June 2, 1994, p. B2.

B = advertising expenditure and effectiveness, all beverage categories
C = availability of products in distribution channels
D = cultural elements, tradition, custom, habit
E = availability of raw materials (particularly of water)
F = climatic conditions, temperature, and relative humidity
G = income levels

Culture is an important element in determining the demand for soft drinks. But it is important to recognize that it is only one of seven factors and, therefore, is an influencing rather than a determining factor. If aggressive marketing programs (including lower prices, more intensive distribution, and heavy advertising) were placed behind soft drinks, the consumption of this product would increase more rapidly than it would otherwise. However, it is also clear that any effort to increase the consumption of soft drinks in Western Europe would be pitted against cultural tradition and custom and the competition of widely available alternative beverages. Culture in this case is a restraining force, but because culture is changing so rapidly, there are many opportunities to accelerate changes that favor a company's product.

The world's champion consumers of alcoholic beverages are the French, closely followed by the Spanish, Swiss, Hungarians, Belgians, Germans, and Portuguese. The differences, shown in Table 4-4, only tell part of the story. For example, if we examine the share of income spent on alcoholic beverages, a different aspect of consumer behavior emerges, namely, how important a component alcohol is in the context of personal consumption. Using such a measure, the U.K., Hungary and Bulgaria lead the list.

The penetration of the U.S. beverage market by bottled water is an excellent example of the impact of a creative strategy on a firmly entrenched cultural tradition. The U.S. culture, until recently, did not include drinking bottled water. The general attitude in the United States was, "Why pay for something that is free?" Perrier, the French bottled water firm, decided to take a shot at the U.S. market by hiring Bruce Nevin, an experienced American marketing executive, and giving him a free hand to formulate a creative strategy.

Nevin decided to reposition Perrier from an expensive imported bottled water (which no red-blooded sane American would touch) to a competitively priced lo-cal beverage in the soft-drink market. To back up this positioning, Nevin launched a major consumer advertising campaign, lowered prices, and moved the product from the gourmet section of the supermarket to the soft-drink section. That marketing strategy involved the significant adjustment or adaptation of three of the four Ps: price, promotion, and place. Only the product was left unchanged.

The Perrier campaign showed how culturally based behavior can be changed by creative marketing strategy. Others have also benefited from the fact that the U.S. market undoubtedly was ready for bottled water. Evian, another French company, has succeeded in the market for spring water — unflavored and uncarbonated table water. In the premium, branded spring-water market, Evian holds a 50 percent market share. The Canadian brand Naya has developed a strong market presence in the U.S. and is second with a 10 percent share. The suc-

TABLE 4–4 Top 20 Countries in Consumption of Alcoholic Beverages	
Country	Alcohol Consumption[1] (Litre per capita) 1988
France	13.0
Spain	12.7
Switzerland	11.0
Hungary	10.7
Belgium	10.7
Germany (West)	10.6
Portugal	10.5
Italy	10.0
Austria	9.9
Denmark	9.6
Bulgaria	8.9
Australia	8.8
Czech/Slovak Republics	8.6
Netherlands	8.3
New Zealand	8.3
Canada	8.0
U.K.	7.7
U.S.A.	7.6
Romania	7.6
Poland	7.2

[1]Calculated to 100% alcohol.

Source: Data based on: *The Economist,* "Book of Vital World Statistics" (London: Hutchinson Business Books, 1990.)

Euromonitor, "International Marketing Data and Statistics" (London: Euromonitor, 1983, 1984)

World Bank, "World Development Report, 1994" (New York: Oxford University Press, 1994).

cess of Nora Beverages' Naya water benefited significantly from its use of "direct store" distributors in contrast with the traditional grocery brokers.[31]

Eating habits are changing all over the world in response to rising incomes. The basic trends in a country with rising incomes are toward the increasing consumption of packaged, convenience foods that save time for the homemaker and add variety to menus. This is the basic and unmistakable trend, but companies have discovered that specific discrete changes are not always easy to accomplish. In the early 1960s General Mills decided to be one of the first companies to profit from the increasing sales of dry breakfast cereals in Japan. By the time General Mills had organized to move into this market, the cereal boom had leveled off. General Mills discovered that not enough Japanese families were willing to order the extra milk that dry cereals require. And even when they did increase the quantities of milk they purchased, they preferred to drink the extra amount without cereal.

---

[31] Michael Slater "Riding the Wave," *Report on Business Magazine* (April 1993), p. 67.

NATIONALISM

Nationalism is a term that describes the powerful influence of collective forces that are unleashed by the social, economic, and cultural group that we call a nation. The world today is swept by the forces and passions of nationalism and the currents seem to be running in two directions.

Among the advanced countries, there is an unmistakable tendency and direction toward the affirmation of a world community and interdependence. Indeed, in Sweden, one of the most advanced social democracies in Europe, there is even a conscious expression of the national goal of strengthening the sense of community within the nation and affirming through international cooperation and support the role of Sweden in the world community. Although these goals may not be as clearly articulated in other industrial nations, the implicit national objectives are clear. When difficulties develop in the economic relations between industrialized countries, negotiations since the end of World War II have always led to a resolution of the problem. This occurs because the negotiations take place within the framework of a shared commitment to cooperation and interdependence.

The interdependence of the industrialized or advanced countries is based upon a perception of mutual advantage. Although industries that are exposed to strong foreign competition will often strongly disagree with national free-trade and open-market policies, the business community recognizes that the nation gains more than it gives up in participating in the international economy. Moreover, each advanced country is exposed to overseas risk because it has its own investors and assets abroad. If it should decide to discriminate against foreign investors, the home countries of the foreign investors can always retaliate against its overseas investors. This is in effect a mutual hostage situation where each side is restrained by its asset and business interest exposure. This mutual dependency does not exist between advanced and less developed countries. For example, when Venezuela expropriated multinational oil companies in the mid-1970s, there were no equivalent assets in the companies' domicile countries to retaliate against.[32] Indeed, Venezuela is an example of the roller coaster ride foreign companies have to cope with and its oscillation between stability and volatility is still characterized as a market that is "not for the faint-hearted."[33]

As a consequence, investors in companies operating in less developed countries must be prepared to justify on a continuing basis the contribution they are making to the perceived welfare of the less developed state. Since most companies are unable to demonstrate a continuing unique advantage over local enterprise, this typically requires a very flexible attitude and willingness to adjust the terms and conditions of participation in the developing country. Only enterprises that have a unique advantage technologically or in some other way are able to resist efforts on the part of less developed states to appropriate equity and management participation in their operations.

---

[32] J.S.Kobrin and B.J. Punnett, "The Nationalization of Oil Production 1918–1980" in *Risk in the Political Economy of Resource Development*, D.W. Pearce, H. Siebert and I. Walter, eds. (London: MacMillan Press, 1984).

[33] John Shiry, "Venezuela Not for the Faint-Hearted", *The Financial Post*, October 5, 1994, p.15.

CROSS-CULTURAL COMPLICATIONS
AND SUGGESTED SOLUTIONS

Business is conducted in an ever-changing environment, a blend of economic, political, cultural, and personal realities and events. Different understandings of the respective obligations of the parties to a commercial transaction will often occur even when the parties belong to the same low-context society and the transaction is embodied in a legal document, which can seldom anticipate all contingencies. Further negotiation between parties who have contracted with each other is often needed, and practical considerations will usually be given greater weight than strict legal interpretation because only legal counsel really wins when there is business litigation.

Business relationships between parties of different cultures and/or nationalities are subject to additional challenges. Parties from different countries may have trouble coming to contract terms because of differences in the laws governing their respective activities and problems of enforcement across international boundaries. No matter what is stated in a contract, it is usually extremely difficult and costly to sue a party for breach of contract except on his or her home turf, which may be an insurmountable advantage for the home-country participant.

When a party from a high-context culture takes part in a business understanding, the factors discussed in the preceding two paragraphs may be even further complicated by very different beliefs about the significance of formal business understandings and the ongoing obligations of all parties. Hall's anecdote about the American sales manager in Latin America describes a basic implicit disagreement about what is important for a business relationship. The sales manager sincerely believed that a well-written contract was all that would be required for his firm to comply fully with its obligations. The minister failed to understand this. But the sales manager failed to understand that in many parts of the world, things can be accomplished only if personal ties exist. (Personal ties will also sometimes be important for getting things done in the low-context environments.)

Natural and human-induced catastrophes, political problems, foreign exchange inconvertibility, widely fluctuating exchange rates, depressions, and changes in national economic priorities and tariff schedules dominate the business environment in many of the countries outside the triad markets. One cannot predict precisely how the most carefully laid plans will go awry, only that they will. The marketing executive dealing with a foreign market must build mutually felt trust and empathy with business contacts because these feelings will be required to sustain an enduring relationship. Appointing a host national as foreign sales representative will not eliminate the issue. The "rep" must act as the company's surrogate and, therefore, adhere to company philosophy while building the personal relationships necessary to achieve the company's business objectives. The corporation that moves around its international staff or otherwise impedes the formation of personal relationships between its people and host nationals of what might be called high-context subcultures diminishes its chances to overcome business crises.

In 1986, Mexico imposed severe foreign exchange restrictions. Companies that had sold products or services to Mexican parties with selling terms other than "confirmed irrevocable international letter of credit" learned they would have to wait for very long periods of time before receiving payment in a "hard" currency such as U.S. dollars. Mexican companies dependent on certain critical foreign supplies (essential ingredients, spare parts, and so on) were subjected to a rationed supply of the foreign exchange for new orders. In this situation personal relationships superseded contractual obligations. Perhaps administrators needed to be convinced that a certain transaction deserved a priority allocation of foreign exchange. Perhaps the foreign seller decided to accept payment in Mexican products (barter) or in pesos that had to be invested in Mexico. Perhaps a foreign seller needed the best guarantees obtainable in a difficult situation that his or her clients would fulfill their obligations as soon as they could find ways to do so. All these matters have become almost routine problems in international business. Although there are standard approaches, most solutions emerge from taking creative advantage of opportunities available through personal links.

The greatest importance must be assigned to contacts and business associates who can be fully trusted and whose culture-influenced perceptions are understood and predictable. Indian society is at least as ethnically and culturally diverse as that in Europe, and business practices are probably even more varied than in Europe.

Personal relationships are an essential ingredient for the international businessperson, as well as thorough preparation and a willingness to at least consider the merits of accommodating to the host culture's ways of doing business and thus are important attributes.

▼ Training in Cross-Cultural Competency

Sensitization to other ways of thinking, feeling, and acting is the goal of any program aiming to train managers to be able to deal effectively with people (customers, suppliers, clients, bosses, and employees), customs, and ideas from other countries and regions. Managers must learn to question their own beliefs, to overcome the SRC, and to adapt the way they communicate, solve problems, and even make decisions. Multicultural managers must learn to question and to reevaluate their feelings concerning such rudimentary management issues as leadership, motivation, and teamwork; this means an examination of some extremely fundamental and personal systems of belief. Finally, managers must learn to overcome stereotypes they hold regarding individuals from differing regions, countries, races, and religions.

A recent study by Ashridge Management College reflects the growing importance of intercultural competence in management: among the key characteristics an international manager should possess, sensitivity to different cultures and language skills ranked among the top five. Of great interest is the finding that among the five most important training programs organizations provide to management slated for international responsibilities are cross-cultural training and language training. Although these results are from Western Europe, where

Box 4–1
How to Be More International

- ▶ Global thinking and expertise:
  - – Broaden your understanding of the global business environment by reading extensively. In addition to books and articles, newspapers and magazines with an international focus should make up this regular reading list, in particular:

    > *The Economist*
    > *Financial Times*
    > *International Management*
    > *Far Eastern Economic Review*
    > *World Trade*
    > *EuroBusiness*
    > *International Business*
    > *International Herald Tribune*
    > *Le Monde*
    > *Die Welt*
    > *Frankfurter Allgemeine*
    > *La Stampa*

  - – Make yourself a global expert on your own industry. Understand its world standard of competition and find out what global competition is doing. Use commercial intelligence services to monitor industry trade journals at home and abroad. Go to seminars, conferences, and study tours to remain up-to-date.
  - – Seek out the best industry practices and consider adopting them in your company. See for yourself, travel, attend trade shows and exhibitions; there is no substitute for direct experience.
- ▶ Global linkages:
  - – Understand your company's informal networks around the globe and pursue cross-border links wherever possible. Management development programs offer excellent opportunities.
- ▶ – Tap into networks outside your company. Contacts made at conferences or seminars and through alumni associations are often useful.
- ▶ Global leadership and values:
  - – Learn anything you can about cultural differences and how they impact communication management style, business practices, negotiation, and team-working. There is no need to be a complete expert on the countries where you do business, but you must know enough about the local environment to modify your approach.
  - – Understand your own cultural roots, motivation, and ehtical standpoint.
  - – Acquire or improve your knowledge of other languages.
  - – Take focused courses in international business and management topics.

Source: Based on Kevin Barham and David Oates, *The International Manager* (London: Business Books Limited and The Economist Books Ltd. 1991) pp. 181–2.

management has historically had to function in a multicultural setting to a much greater extent than our managers, the message for Canadian companies is clear.[34]

One approach to accomplish sensitization is the use of workshops, incorporating case studies, role playing, and other exercises designed to permit participants to confront a relevant situation, contemplate what their own thoughts and actions would be in such a situation, and analyze and learn from the results. They must be able to understand and evaluate their motivations and their approaches to their own work. Often role playing will bring out thoughts and feelings which otherwise might go unexamined or even unacknowledged. A variety of other less familiar techniques have been used for cross-cultural training; what all these techniques have in common is that they are designed to teach members of one culture ways of interacting effectively in another culture.

The aspiring international marketing manager should seek personal development in three broad areas: global thinking and expertise, global linkages, and global leadership and values. Box–offers a brief checklist of the objectives for each of these three areas.

▼ SUMMARY

Culture has both a pervasive and changing influence on each national market environment. International marketers must recognize the influence of culture and must be prepared to either respond to it or change it. International marketers have played an important and even a leading role in influencing the rate of cultural change around the world. This is particularly true of food, but it includes virtually every industry, particularly in consumer products. Soap and detergent manufacturers have changed washing habits, the electronics industry has changed entertainment patterns, clothing marketers have changed styles, and so on.

In industrial products culture does affect product characteristics and demand but is more important as an influence on the marketing process, particularly in the way business is done. International marketers have learned to rely upon people who know and understand local customs and attitudes for marketing expertise. Often, but not always, these are local nationals.

▼ DISCUSSION QUESTIONS

1. Marketing is a universal discipline. There is no such thing as American marketing, French marketing, Japanese marketing, and so on. Do you agree or disagree? Why or why not?

2. It is a mistake to label the United States a low-context culture. There are many aspects of the U.S. business world that are extremely high context. Do you agree or disagree?

3. The world is becoming more and more monocultural. Today you can get Japanese noodles in the United States and McDonald's hamburgers in Japan. Cultural factors are simply not as important as they were 50, even 10, years ago. Discuss.

---

[34] Kevin Barham and David Oates, *The International Manager* (London: Business Books Limited and The Economist Books Ltd., 1991), pp.69, 166.

▼ BIBLIOGRAPHY

Books

ABEGGLEN, JAMES C., AND GEORGE STALK, JR., *Kaisha, The Japanese Corporation*. New York: Basic Books, Inc., 1985.

ADLER, NANCY J., *International Dimensions of Organizational Behavior*. Boston: Kent Publishing Co., 1986.

BENEDICT, RUTH, *The Chrysanthemum and the Sword*. Rutland, VT: Charles E. Tuttle, 1972.

_____, *Patterns of Culture*. Boston: Houghton Mifflin, 1959.

BLACK, J. STEWART, HAL B. GREGERSEN, AND MARK E. MENDENHALL, *Global Assignments: Successfully Expatriating and Repatriating International Managers*. San Francisco: Jossey-Bass, 1992.

COLLINS, ROBERT J., AND JANE WALMSLEY, *Japanthink, Ameri-think: An Irreverent Guide to Understanding the Cultural Differences Between Us*. New York: Penguin Books, 1992.

DE TOCQUEVILLE, ALEXIS, *Democracy In America*. New York: New American Library, 1956.

ENGEL, J. F., R. D. BLACKWELL, AND D. T. KOLLAT, *Consumer Behavior*. New York: Holt, Rinehart and Winston, 1978.

FIELDS, GEORGE, *From Bonsai to Levis*. New *Journal of Advertising Research*, 33, no. 4 (July/August 1993), 40–48.

———, *Gucci on the Ginza*. Tokyo and New York: Kodansha International, 1989.

HAGEN, E., *On the Theory of Social Change*. Homewood, Ill.: Dorsey Press, 1962.

HALL, EDWARD T., *Beyond Culture*. Garden City, N.Y.: Anchor Press Doubleday, 1976.

———, AND MILDRED REED HALL, *Understanding Cultural Differences*. Yarmouth, ME: Intercultural Press, 1990.

HAMADA, TOMOKO, *American Enterprise in Japan*. Albany, NY: State University of New York Press, 1991.

_____, AND ANN JORDAN, *Cross-Cultural Management and Organizational Culture*. Williamsburg, VA: Dept. of Anthropology, College of William and Mary, 1990.

HARRIS, PHILIP R., AND ROBERT T. MORAN, *Managing Cultural Differences*. Houston: Gulf Publishing Co., 1986.

JOYNT, PAT, AND MALCOLM WARNER, *Managing in Different Cultures*. New York: Columbia University Press, 1985.

KANG, T. W., *Gaishi: The Foreign Company in Japan*. New York: Basic Books, 1990.

MCCLELLAND, D., *The Achieving Society*. New York: Van Nostrand, 1961.

MORAN, ROBERT T., AND WILLIAM G. STRIPP, *Dynamics of Successful International Business Negotiation*. Houston: Gulf Publishing Co., 1991.

OSGOOD, CHARLES EGERTON, WILLIAM H. MAY, AND MURRAY S. MIRON, *Cross-Cultural Universals of Affecting Meaning*. Urbana: University of Illinois Press, 1975.

REISCHAUER, EDWIN O., *The Japanese*. Cambridge, MA: The Belknap Press of Harvard University Press, 1977.

TAKAMIYA, SUSUMU, AND KEITH E. THURLEY, *Japan's Emerging Multinationals: An International Comparison of Policies and Practices*. Tokyo: University of Tokyo Press, 1985.

YAMADA, HARU, *American and Japanese Business Discourse: A Comparison of Interactional Styles*. Norwood, NJ: Ablex Publishing, 1992.

Articles

CLARK, TERRY, "International Marketing and National Character: A Review and Proposal for an Integrative Theory," *Journal of Marketing*, 54, no. 4 (October 1990), 66–79.

DULEK, RONALD E., JOHN S. FIELDEN, AND JOHN S. HILL, "International Communications: An Executive Primer," *Business Horizons*, 34, no. 1 (January/February 1991), 20–25.

FORD, JOHN B., AND EARL D. HONEYCUTT, JR., "Japanese National Culture as a Basis for Understanding Japanese Business Practices," *Business Horizons*, 35, no. 6 (November/December 1992), 27–34.

GUPTARA, PRABHU, "Multicultural Aspects of Managing Multinationals," *Management Japan*, 26, no. 1 (Spring 1993), 7–14.

HAMPDEN-TURNER, CHARLES, TOM PETERS, AND JAY JAIKUMAR, "The Boundaries of Business: Commentaries from the Experts," *Harvard Business Review*, 69, no. 5 (September/October 1991), 93–101.

HERBIG, PAUL A., AND HUGH E. KRAMER, "Do's and Don'ts of Cross-Cultural Negotiations," *Industrial Marketing Management*, 21, no. 4 (November 1992) 287–298.

HILL, DAVID, "Negotiating with the Japanese: Tips for the Uninitiated—Learning from the Successes (and Mistakes) of Others," *East Asian Executive Reports*, 15, no. 12 (December 15, 1993), 8, 14.

JACOBS, LAURENCE, CHARLES KEOWN, REGINAL WORTHLEY, AND KYUNG-IL GHYMN, "Cross-Cultural Colour Comparisons—Global Marketers Beware!" *International Marketing Review*, 8, no. 3 (1991), 21–30.

KVINT, VLADIMIR, "Don't Give Up on Russia," *Harvard Business Review*, 72, no. 2 (March/April 1994), 62–74.

LIN, CAROLYN A., "Cultural Differences in Message Strategies: A Comparison Between American and Japanese Commercials," *Journal of Advertising Research*, 33, no. 4 (July/August 1993), 40–48.

MINTU, ALMA T., AND ROGER J. CALANTONE, "A Comparative Approach to International Marketing Negotiation," *Journal of Applied Business Research*, 7, no. 4 (Fall 1991), 90–97.

MIRACLE, GORDEN E., KYU YEOL CHANG, AND CHARLES R. TAYLOR, "Culture and Advertising Executions: A Comparison of Selected Characteristics of Korean and U.S. Television Commercials," *International Marketing Review*, 9, no. 4 (1992), 5–17.

REARDON, KATHLEEN KELLEY, AND ROBERT E. SPEKMAN, "Starting Out Right: Negotiating Lessons for Domestic and Cross-Cultural Business Alliances," *Business Horizons*, 37, no. 1 (January/February 1994), 71–79.

SCHNEIDER, SUSAN C., AND ARNOUD DE MEYER, "Interpreting and Responding to Strategic Issues: The Impact of National Culture," *Strategic Management Journal*, 12, no. 4 (May 1991), 307–320.

STENING, BRUCE W., AND MITCHELL R. HAMMER, "Cultural Baggage and the Adaption of Expatriate American and Japanese Managers," *Management International Review*, 32, no. 1 (First Quarter 1992), 77–89.

SUGIURA, HIDEO, "How Honda Localizes Its Global Strategy," *Sloan Management Review*, 32, no. 1 (Fall 1990), 77–82.

TUNG, ROSALIE L., "Handshakes Across the Sea: Cross-Cultural Negotiating for Business Success," *Organizational Dynamics*, 19, no. 3 (Winter 1991), 30–40.

"Understand and Heed Cultural Differences," *Business America*, 112, no. 2 (1991), 26–27.

USUNIER, JEAN-CLAUDE G., "Business Time Perceptions and National Cultures: A Comparative Survey," *Management International Review*, 31, no. 3 (Third Quarter 1991), 197–217.York: Mentor, New American Library, 1983, 1985.

FIVE

Legal and
Regulatory
Environment

Introduction

Like all business activity, international marketing management takes place within a legal framework. Because of its global nature, this framework is a complex mosaic of national and international, private and public, and global and sub-global laws and practices, or rules. Thus, international marketers face many sets of rules. They will discover that simply finding out what the rule is, or whose law prevails, in a given situation is a difficult task. The most apt term to describe this amalgam of rules is international business law.

   International business law as an input into global marketing management is undervalued as it is usually restricted to the operational side.[1] Lawyers are used almost exclusively to implement marketing strategy by formulating contracts, registering intellectual property rights, incorporating companies, and so forth. Yet, legal considerations are also crucial to the formulation of global marketing strategies, whether they relate to product, market entry, promotion, or pricing. For example, one cannot set a low introductory price for goods in a new foreign market without considering the effect of that country's anti-dumping rules, or determine the viability of exporting as a market entry mode in ignorance of the trade regime of the importing nation.

   In this chapter, we discuss both the operational and the strategic importance of international business law. Because of the growth in cross-border trade in services and the distinct problems involved in such trade, the chapter ends with a specific section on services. The aim is not to provide a compendium of law but to familiarize marketing managers with the major legal issues that may confront them as they plan and implement their global strategies. First, however, we look at the sources and scope of international business law.

INTERNATIONAL BUSINESS LAW: SOURCES AND SCOPE

▼ National Rules

Their International Character

Despite their domestic character, the national rules of the 150-odd nations that engage in international trade are one of the most important components of interna-

---

[1] Philip Raworth, *Legal Guide to International Business Transactions* (Toronto: Carswell, 1991), in particular pp. 1-5.

tional business law. This importance derives from two factors. First, international rules cover only a small part of business activity with the rest being regulated exclusively by individual nations. Second, the international rules themselves must in most cases be implemented by national laws.

Thus, national rules both reflect and complement the international rules, which justifies their inclusion as part of international business law. However, no one can be expected to know the rules of over a hundred nations. What the international marketing manager should know, however, is the basic character of a country's legal system and whether individual national rules are consistent with applicable international rules.

The Types of Legal Systems[2]

The major split in legal systems is between those areas under English influence that follow common law, and those under the influence of Roman law and the Napoleonic Code that have a civil law system. Within Canada, this means that English Canada has a common law system and Quebec a civil law system. Abroad, England, Wales, Ireland, the former Dominions and most of the United States are common law, while the rest of the world, including Scotland, is civil law.

It is said that the major distinction between the two systems is that in common law the general principles of law applicable to a situation are established from previous judicial decisions, whereas civil law is based on first principles that are set out in a code and adapted to the case at hand. It should, however, be noted that common law jurisdictions frequently codify the principles that it has extrapolated from precedents. Two major examples are the 19th century imperial Sale of Goods Act, which was adopted in all the common law provinces of Canada, and the Uniform Commercial Code, which is recognized by 49 of the United States. It is also the case that an increasing proportion of law in both the common law and civil law systems derives from legislation, which is of necessity code law.

Thus, the traditional distinction between these two legal systems is not entirely satisfactory, and international marketers may in any case be hard-pressed to ascertain the significance of such legal niceties. For them it is probably more significant that the civil law judicial system is divided into civil, commercial, and criminal law, which means that commercial law has its own administrative structure and courts. Also, as we shall see later in the section on contractual issues, civil law tends to be less arcane than common law but also less flexible.

A third type of legal system is that based on Islam. This system derives from the Koran and contains certain principles, such as the stricture against interest, that mark it off from both civil and common law. Thus, it behooves the international marketer to be very careful when dealing with Islamic countries. Generally speaking, however, the national laws that apply to international trading are more secular than those that regulate purely domestic activity.

The Relationship Between National and International Rules

The relationship between national and international rules is both complementary and adversarial. As we mentioned above, national rules are needed both to

---

[2] Carolyn Hotchkiss, *International Law of Business* (New York: McGraw-Hill, 1994) pp. 47-98.

implement international rules and to regulate those many matters for which there are no international rules. Conflict between the two sets of rules occurs where national implementation is imperfect or non-existent with the result that a benefit is denied to foreign traders or an obstacle is erected against them. No direct remedial action is possible by the foreign trader in this situation as only nations can bring an action against other nations for such breaches of their international obligations. All individuals can do is to inform their governments and incite them to take the necessary steps against the offending nation.

▼ International Rules

The Public Law of International Business (International Economic Law)

Nature and Enforceability. The public law of international business is that area of public international law that governs the economic relations between nations. It can thus properly be termed international economic law. Like other areas of international law, it consists of rules that nations consider binding upon themselves and which apply to private parties regardless of their wishes. Breaches of the rules, however, can only be remedied by action at nation-to-nation level. Generally speaking, there is no adequate international judicial and administrative framework to enforce international law so that, in practice, it applies only to the extent that nations are willing to relinquish their rights. However, economic self-interest renders enforcement more effective in the area of international economic law.[3] Retaliatory trade actions, for example, underpin the dispute settlement procedures of the World Trade Organization (WTO) and the regional trade treaties, while the need to preserve the good will of the International Monetary Fund (IMF) helps that body enforce its exchange rules.

A partial exception to this unenforceability is the law of the European Union (EU), some rules of which apply directly in the member states without the need for national implementation.[4] In addition, the Court of Justice of the EU can require member states to implement other Union laws, and failure to do so can result in a fine. However, there is no central administrative machinery in the EU for the enforcement of the judgment or fine, or for preventing member states from thwarting the application of direct Union rules. Nevertheless, it is probably more appropriate to treat the law of the EU as federal rather than international law.[5] The EU now comprises Austria, Belgium, Denmark, Eire, Finland, France, Germany, Greece, Italy, Luxembourg, Netherlands, Portugal, Spain, Sweden, and the United Kingdom.

---

[3] Jackson, "Governmental Dispute in International Trade Relations: A Proposal in the Context of GATT," *Journal of World Trade Law* (1979) 13, p. 1; Robert P. Parker, "Dispute Settlement in the GATT and the Canada-US Free Trade," *Journal of World Trade Law* (1989) 23, p. 83.

[4] Philip Raworth, *The Legislative Process in the European Community*, Deventer: Kluwer (1993) pp. 9-14.

[5] Philip Raworth, "Too Little, Too Late? Maastricht and the Goal of a European Federation", *Archiv des Voelkerrechts* (1994) 32:1, p.24.

Instruments and Scope of International Economic Law. The major international instruments that constitute the international economic rules are the following[6]:

▶ The 1994 Agreement Establishing the WTO (WTO Agreement), which incorporates and expands the 1947 General Agreement on Tariffs and Trade (GATT) and extends coverage to services via the General Agreement on Services (GATS), intellectual property protection via the Agreement on Trade-Related Aspects of Intellectual Property Rights (TRIPS), and investment via the Agreement on Trade-Related Investment Measures (TRIMS)

▶ The various instruments concluded under the auspices of the United Nations such as the Generalized System of Preferences (GSoP) and those establishing the International Centre for the Settlement of Investment Disputes (ICSID) and the Multilateral Investment Guarantee Agency (MIGA)

▶ The 1944 Articles of Agreement of the IMF, as amended by the 1976 Jamaica Agreement

▶ The various agreements concluded under the auspices of the Organization for Economic Cooperation and Development (OECD), in particular the codes liberalizing capital movements and invisible operations and those dealing with taxation and foreign direct investment. These OECD agreements are really guidelines rather than binding rules, but members are expected to follow them

▶ The various intellectual property conventions that are administered by the World Intellectual Property Organization (WIPO), in particular the 1883 Paris Convention (patents, trade names, trademarks, industrial designs, and geographical indications), the 1886 Berne Convention and 1961 Rome Convention (copyright), and the 1989 Washington Treaty (integrated circuits). There are also a number of agreements providing for international applications for intellectual property protection, namely the 1970 Patent Cooperation Treaty, the 1925 Hague Agreement (industrial designs), and the 1891 Madrid Agreement and 1973 Trademark Registration Treaty (trademarks)

▶ The various regional economic integration treaties, in particular those establishing the EU (formerly the European Economic Community (EEC) or "Common Market"), the North American Free Trade Association (NAFTA), and the Southern Cone Common Market (Mercosur)

▶ The general rules of public international law. These rules apply mostly indirectly in that they oblige nations to respect their international obligations. Directly, only the doctrines of "act of state" and "sovereign immunity" are relevant to international business

The WTO Agreement, the UN-brokered agreements on the GSoP, ICSID and MIGA , the WIPO agreements, and the IMF articles are global in scope as all nations are entitled to take part even though some, including China and Russia, do not always participate. The OECD agreements are subglobal as only certain

---

[6] These instruments can be found in the *United Nations Treaty Series* (UNTS), the *U.S. Treaties and Other International Agreements* (TIAS), the *Canadian Treaty Series* (CTS), *International Legal Materials* (ILM), or directly in publications from the international agency involved. EU legislation is published in the *Official Journal of the Communities* (OJ, series L). GATT/WTO documents can be found in the *Basic Instruments and Selected Documents* (BISD).

nations are allowed in the organization. Membership belongs mainly to the rich developed world, although Mexico and Turkey are also members and Chile, South Korea and the Czech Republic may soon join. Regional agreements are also, of course, subglobal.

International economic law regulates three areas: trade in goods and services (WTO, GSoP, GATS, TRIPS, NAFTA, EU, Mercosur), monetary exchange and convertibility (IMF, OECD, EU) and capital flows and investment (OECD, ICSID, MIGA, TRIMS, NAFTA, EU, Act of State doctrine). There now follows a brief overview of each area.

Trade Rules. Initially, trade was regulated by GATT, which only applies to goods. GATT aims at lowering tariffs and eliminating or greatly reducing the use of non-tariff barriers (NTBs) to restrict trade. NTBs comprise all obstacles that are not tariffs. The most common are quantitative restrictions ("quotas"), abuse of standards, contingent protection (anti-dumping and countervail actions) and emergency action, onerous customs procedures and subsidies. The WTO Agreement incorporates and strengthens the GATT rules, particularly with respect to the agricultural and textile sectors, prohibits the circumvention of GATT by the use of voluntary export restraints, adds some rules on preshipment inspection and, most significantly, brings intellectual property protection and services within the international trade rules for the first time.[7]

The rules on services have to deal with quite different issues than those that pertain to trade in goods, as services are intangible and the restrictions on trading them are aimed at the providers and recipients rather than at the services themselves. Typical restrictions are prohibitions on the provision of services, legal and fiscal disincentives against using foreign providers, the requirement of local qualifications and registrations, immigration and exchange controls, and local presence requirements.

WTO rules permit the establishment of regional trading blocs that provide for even freer trade between bloc members. Thus, within the bloc the members are treated preferentially. This creates a potential problem of trade diversion for countries outside the bloc. One unfortunate example of this is the elimination of trade in aluminum between the United Kingdom and Canada in favor of French aluminum after the United Kingdom joined the EEC. On the other hand, foreign firms established within the bloc can usually take advantage of the preferential arrangements.

Regional trading blocs, discussed in more detail in Chapter 8, proliferated in the 1960s and 70s in all areas of the world. However, they have only been successful in the developed world. Examples are the EU and the European Free Trade Association (EFTA) and the agreements between Eire and the United Kingdom (now superseded by the two countries' membership in the EU), New Zealand and Australia, and Canada and the United States. NAFTA represents a new development with the inclusion of a developing country (Mexico) into the Canada–United States arrangement.

---

[7]See the commentary on the agreements making up the new WTO Agreement in Philip M. Raworth and Linda C. Reif, *The Practitioner's Deskbook Series: The Law of the WTO*, New York: Oceana Publications, 1995.

The major reason for the failure of regional integration between developing countries was clearly that they all followed protectionist policies, which mesh uneasily with lowering trade barriers with your neighbors. Also, the countries tended to trade more with developed than other developing countries. All of this is now changing, and it is possible that third-world regional arrangements may be more effective in the future. One possible candidate is Mercosur, which embraces Argentina, Brazil, Uruguay and Paraguay and which is the successor of such illustrious failures as the Latin American Free Trade Association, the Andean Pact, and the Latin American Integration Association. However, there is a question mark over the future of Mercosur, as it may well succumb to an extension of NAFTA just as EFTA was swallowed up by the EEC. Chile is already negotiating for entry into NAFTA, and Argentina is a future candidate.

A final word on the EU is in order. This regional grouping, which started out as a common market, will eventually be transformed by the 1992 Treaty of Maastricht into an economic and monetary union. This betokens a much greater integration than any other regional agreement envisages, and it commits its members to a form of loose federation. In many ways, it is appropriate to regard the EU as an embryonic nation and, as was stated above, its law as federal rather than regional in nature.

International Monetary Rules. At the 1944 Bretton Woods conference, the IMF was given responsibility for managing the monetary system. Stability was secured by fixed exchanges rates based on the U.S. dollar and parity changes (devaluations and revaluations) were only allowed with IMF approval. However, fixed exchange rates did not survive the removal of the U.S. dollar from its gold standard on 15 August 1971, and the major currencies have floated ever since. This practice was officially validated by the 1976 Jamaica Agreement. The result has been to weaken the role of the IMF in assuring monetary stability, which has become increasingly a matter for consultation and cooperation within the OECD. The IMF retains its authority over exchange controls on the purchase of foreign currency for trade in goods and ancillary services (shipping, insurance and banking). They may only be introduced with the authorization of the Fund. Similarly, a nation must maintain a freely convertible currency by re-purchasing its currency held by foreign central banks in the absence of IMF authorization to the contrary.

The OECD has a 1973 Code of Liberalization of Current Invisible Transactions. It prohibits controls on payment for the receipt of foreign services and requires the free international flow of dividends, rents, royalties, interest, and profits. In addition, The EU establishes an area where there are no exchange controls at all. The individual national currencies are loosely bound by parities (except the British, Italian, Swedish, Finnish, and Greek currencies, which are outside the Exchange Rate Mechanism), and it is intended that they will coalesce to form a single European currency, the ECU, by the end of the century. This is what is meant by monetary union.

Capital and Investment Rules. No international rules guarantee the right to invest or move capital internationally. However, the 1982 OECD Code of Liberalization of Capital Movements prohibits controls among OECD members on the international purchase and sale of securities and land, foreign direct investment and disinvestment, and the physical exportation of currency. The OECD Code on Invisible Operations is also relevant in so far as it provides for the free flow of the proceeds of foreign activities, such as dividends, profits, and interest payments. In addition, the OECD has put forward a model tax treaty that deals with the problem of double taxation. In 1976 the OECD issued a Declaration on International Investment, which falls short of requiring member countries to accept foreign direct investment but which obliges them to treat foreign companies in the same way as national companies ("national treatment").

TRIMS sets out global rules that prevent countries from restricting foreign companies' access to foreign inputs. The NAFTA and EU rules eliminate any discriminatory performance requirements on foreign companies from within the bloc. They also provide the regional partners with a right to invest in each other. There are EU directives on double taxation of companies operating in different members of the Union.

Disputes between an investor and a host government are not normally justiciable in the investor's home country, as the act of state doctrine does not allow a domestic court to pronounce on the actions of foreign governments within their territory. However, such disputes may be brought before ICSID. It is also possible to acquire insurance under MIGA.

The Private Law of International Business (International Commercial Law)

Nature and Enforceability. The private law of international business consists of the rules that parties choose to have applied to an international transaction or relationship and that they can enforce against each other in national courts or international arbitration tribunals. Sometimes, as with the ICC Uniform Customs and Practice for Documentary Credits and the 1980 U.N. Convention on the International Sale of Goods, these rules apply unless the parties specifically exclude them. This body of law can be termed *international commercial law*. The only principle of public international law that applies to this private area is that of sovereign immunity, which precludes actions for breach of contract against governments.

Much of international commercial law has evolved from private commercial practice among merchants, the so-called *lex mercatoria*.[8] However, much of the "common" law is now codified and new codes are constantly being adopted. Codification is done by private bodies, such as the International Chamber of Commerce (ICC), by official bodies such as the United Nations Commission on International Trade Law (UNCITRAL) and the International Institute for the Unification of Private Law (UNIDROIT) and by government action through conventions and the UN, such as the 1958 New York Convention on Foreign Arbitral awards.

Instruments and Scope of International Commercial Law. International commercial law concerns in particular contractual matters (terms, choice of law and

---

[8] See Harold J. Berman and Colin Kaufman, "The Law of International Commercial Transactions (Lex Mercatoria)," *Harvard International Law Journal*, 1978, 19, p. 221.

Box 5–1
Major Instruments in International Commercial Law

▶ In *contractual matters:*
1955 Hague Convention on the Law Applicable to International Sale of Goods
1958 New York Convention on the Recognition and Enforcement of Foreign Arbitral Awards
1958 Hague Convention on Jurisdiction of Contractual Forum in Case of International Sale of Goods
1964 Hague Convention on the International Sale of Goods
1964 Hague Convention on the Formation of Contracts for the International Sale of Goods
1965 Hague Convention on Choice of Court
1968 EEC Convention on Jurisdiction and the Enforcement of Judgments in Civil and Commercial Matter
1971 Hague Convention on the Recognition and Enforcement of Foreign Judgments in Civil and Commercial Matters
1974 Hague Convention on the Limitation Period in the International Sale of Goods
1975 ICC Rules of Arbitration and Conciliation
1976 UNICITRAL Arbitration Rules
1978 ICC Uniform Rules for Contract Guarantees
1980 UNCITRAL Conciliation Rules
1980 UN Convention on Contracts for the International Sale of Goods
1980 EEC Convention on the Law Applicable to Contracts
1983 UNIDROIT Convention on Agency in the International Sale of Goods
1985 UNCITRAL Model Law on International Commercial Arbitration
1985 Hague Convention on the Law Applicable to Contracts for the International Sale of Goods
1986 CPR Model Procedure for Settlement of Transnational Business Disputes,
1990 ICC International Commercial Terms (Incoterms)
▶ In *transport:*
1924 Hague
1968 Hague-Visby and 1978 Hamburg Rules for International Carriage of Goods by Sea
1929 and 1955 Warsaw Conventions on International Air Carriage
1956 Convention on the Contract for the International Carriage of Goods by Road
1970 Convention on the Carriage of Goods by Rail
1975 ICC Rules for a Combined Transport Document
1981 UN Convention on International Multimodal Transport of Goods
▶ In *insurance:*
1990 ICC Incoterms
▶ In *payment matters:*
1978 ICC Uniform Rules for Collections
1983 ICC Uniform Customs and Practices for Documentary Credits
1986 ICC Standard Form for issuing Documentary Credits

adjudication), transport, insurance and payment. Some of the major instruments that complement the "common law" rules are shown in Box 5–1.[9]

In summary, international business law covers a very large field. As an abstract body of law, it is rather forbidding, and the international marketing manager may have difficulty discerning its direct applicability to the everyday business of marketing. The two sections that follow attempt to dispel the mystery by explaining how the various rules of international business law affect in practical terms the operation and implementation of global marketing strategies.

STRATEGIC IMPORTANCE OF INTERNATIONAL BUSINESS LAW FOR GLOBAL MARKETING MANAGEMENT

▼ Product

Two types of decision have to be made with respect to product. Where a target market has already been selected, the viability of a particular product for this market must be considered. Otherwise it is a question of choosing a target market for a particular product.

In both instances, the national rules of the target market are a crucial input. They concern above all standards-related measures. These measures consist of the following: *technical regulations,* which lay down product characteristics with which compliance is compulsory; *standards,* which are non-binding documents drawn up by a recognized body that set out product characteristics; and *conformity assessment procedures,* which are any procedure that determines compliance with a technical regulation or standard. Although standards are not legally binding, they acquire a compulsory nature where their use is mandated by insurance companies or in contracts. Requirements in the agricultural sector are called sanitary and phytosanitary measures. The rules are very similar to those for standards-related measures.

Standards-related measures are one of the most significant barriers to foreign market entry because of the cost, time, and expertise involved in making goods to new specifications. In addition, the conformity assessment procedure offers additional opportunity for making life difficult for the foreign manufacturer. A classic example is the French decision in the early 1980s to have all video recorders from Japan inspected at an inadequately staffed centre situated at Dijon, well away from the port of entry. The result was to reduce drastically the number of Japanese video recorders on the French market. However, the picture is not always negative; it may be that the intrinsic quality of a product gives it an advantage over its rivals in a strictly regulated market. What really matters is whether the legal framework *fits* the exporter.

---

[9] These instruments are mainly found in *International Legal Materials* (ILM) and in publications of the international agency involved.

NAFTA and the WTO Agreement on Technical Barriers to Trade both offer some protection against unreasonable national rules.[10] Both require domestic and foreign products to be treated equally, which particularly applies to the conduct of conformity assessment procedures as it gives the foreign manufacturer the right to establish compliance by self-testing where this possibility is available to domestic producers. There are also provisions on the acceptance by the importing country of test data from the exporting country, and the agreements encourage a system under which products would be tested exclusively in the exporting country. The WTO Agreement specifically prohibits the siting of facilities in a manner that causes inconvenience to foreign traders.[11]

Both NAFTA and the WTO Agreement also seek to curtail the protectionist potential of standards. They mandate the use of international standards where they are available and stipulate that technical regulations must fulfill a legitimate objective, such as health, safety, performance, or environmental protection. Nations are encouraged (and required under NAFTA) to accept other nations' technical regulations as equivalent to their own where they are satisfied that the latter adequately fulfill the objectives of their own regulations. Countries must also set up at least one inquiry point to answer questions from foreign traders on its standards-related measures.

Within the EU, the member states are obliged to accept goods from other member states that meet the harmonized EU requirements or, where these do not yet exist, have been legally put on the market.[12] At the same time, individual member states may maintain their stricter national technical regulations with respect to domestic products and *goods coming from outside the EU.* However, once non-EU goods have been put into free circulation in one member state, they may be shipped freely to any other member state. This situation has considerable strategic importance for foreign traders. First, it means that it is wise to choose as the port of entry into the EU a country that has the least onerous national rules. Second, it means that it is now possible to circumvent the strict standards of a country like Germany by transshipping the goods through a laxer member state like the United Kingdom. This possibility would exist in other regional blocs provided there is the same level of internal liberalization. At present this is not the case.

Other national rules also impinge on the viability of a product in a particular market. Important among these are consumer protection laws. Onerous requirements concerning warranties and after-sales service must be factored into the cost of a product and could undermine its competitiveness. Product liability laws must also be taken into consideration, particularly where they provide for strict liability as in the EU or where national practice is to award ludicrously large damages as in the United States. Here also, there is a significant hidden cost element.

---

[10] The following discussion refers to NAFTA, arts. 904-908, and WTO *Agreement on Technical Barriers to Trade*, arts. 2-9.

[11] Arts. 5.2.6

[12] E.C. Treaty, art. 100a. See also *Rewe-Zentrale AG v. Bundesmonopolverwaltung fuer Branntwein,* 120/78, [1979] ECR 649.

Further considerations that can diminish the attractiveness of a product in a particular market are price controls and the level of indirect taxation. The former are perhaps less common and can be circumvented to some extent by a shrewd pricing policy. Indirect taxation can pose a greater problem. In international trade, goods are exported free from the indirect taxes imposed in the country of exportation but are then subject to the indirect taxes of the importing country. Sometimes the latter are considerably higher, which reduces the attractiveness of the product in the importing country. Greek cigarettes are an example; they bear little indirect tax in Greece but are taxed at a very high level when exported to Denmark. The situation has changed somewhat as there is now a modicum of harmonization of indirect taxation in the EU.

A final point concerns third party rights. Before a product is exported to a particular market, there must be certainty that the product does not infringe on any protected rights, such as a patent or trade name, in the importing country and that the manufacturer, where it is a licensee, has the right to export to that market. In the former case, goods may be seized and impounded at the border where there is an infringement of local intellectual property rights.

▼ Market Entry

There are many different ways for a Canadian company to enter a foreign market and we discuss these in detail in Chapters 9 and 11. For our puposes here, the legal issues of the main entry forms of exporting, licensing, and investment are discussed. The first is by manufacturing the goods in Canada and exporting them. The goods may be sent directly to the ultimate consumer or indirectly via a distributor. Agents may be used to find customers in the case of direct exporting. Contract entry is where the goods are manufactured locally by a foreign company on behalf of the Canadian company. This may be a contract manufacturing agreement under which the foreign company manufactures the goods but leaves their sale in the target market up to the Canadian company. More common is the licensing or franchising agreement under which the goods are both manufactured and sold by the foreign company. In this chapter we shall concentrate on the licensing arrangement within the contract entry mode. Finally, the Canadian company may set up its own facilities and both manufacture and sell its goods in the target market. This is investment entry.

The problem facing the global marketing manager is, however, more complex than just choosing a mode of market entry. Unless goods are exported from Canada, it will also be necessary to decide where to establish the foreign facilities or licensee and which markets, if any, to serve by exports from this foreign centre. In this chapter, we do not attempt to separate out these complex issues but to list and explain the legal issues that impact upon the decision-making process. This impact will, however, vary depending upon the particular company situation. In the case of high tariffs, for example, the company may dispose of means to reduce the cost of manufacture and thus preserve exporting as a feasible entry mode. More likely, it will have to consider local production to circumvent the tariffs, but whether this is done by contract or investment entry will depend upon

Box 5–2
The Impact of Legal Issues on Market Entry

In favor of export entry
Exchange controls
Non-convertibility of currency
Lax intellectual property laws
Problems with foreign direct investment
Problems with corporate tax laws
High withholding taxes on royalties
Royalty payment problems
Problems with licensing laws, including competition laws
Problems with joint ventures, including competition laws
Strict employment laws
Intense and volatile local laws

Against export entry
High tariffs and non-tariff barriers
Standards-related problems
Problems with distributorship laws, including competition laws
Problems with agency laws, including competition laws
Strict after-sales service requirements
Government procurement requirements

In favor of licensing
High tariffs and non-tariff barriers
Standards-related problems
Problems with distributorship laws, including competition laws
Problems with agency laws, including competition laws
Strict after-sales service requirements
Government procurement requirements
Problems with foreign direct investment
Problems with corporate tax laws
Taking advantage of regional rules
Strict employment laws
Intense and volatile local laws

Against licensing
High withholding taxes
Royalty payment problems
Problems with licensing laws, including competition laws
Exchange controls
Non-convertibility of currency
Lax intellectual property laws

In favor of investment entry
High tariffs and non-tariff barriers
Standards-related problems
Problems with distributorship laws, including competition laws

Problems with agency laws, including competition laws
Problems with licensing laws, including competition laws
Strict after-sales service requirements
Government procurement requirements
High withholding taxes on royalties
Royalty payment problems
Advantageous corporate tax laws
Taking advantage of regional rules
Lax employment laws
Lax intellectual property laws

Against investment entry
Exchange controls
Non-convertibility of currency
Problems with foreign direct investment
Problems with corporate tax laws
Strict employment laws
Problems with joint ventures, including competition laws
Intense and volatile local laws

many other business and legal factors. Box 5–2 lists the various factors that operate within the target market and indicates only whether, on the whole, they favor a particular entry mode or not.

▼ The Legal Issues

Convertibility and Exchange Controls. The exchange regime in a target country affects all modes of doing international business, as we will discuss in Chapter 6. For example, exporters of goods and services require payment for their products, licensors need to receive royalties from their licensees and foreign facilities abroad are expected to send profits or dividends back home.

The first aspect of an exchange regime to be considered is the national exchange rate rules. Currencies may float, be pegged to another currency, or crawl. The crawl is in reality a peg that is adjusted at given intervals according to certain established economic criteria. The international rules governing exchange rate regimes are very lax. Under the Articles of the IMF, a country may use whichever of the three systems it likes as long as it informs the IMF of its choice.[13]

The impact on market entry decisions of the exchange rate system in place in a given country is minor. Theoretically, the more rigid the system, the more stable the currency, but in reality economic factors and the financial markets determine a currency's stability rather than the legal rules under which it operates.

Much more significant from a market entry standpoint are the national rules on exchangeability of a currency. If a currency is not exchangeable at *all* for

---

[13] Art. IV:2

foreign currency, it is non-convertible. The Articles of the IMF require convertibility from its members, but many developing countries have been authorized to disregard this requirement.[14]

Non-convertible currencies are unacceptable tender in international business unless you have use for money that only has value in the target country. This may be the case with investors who can use their local currency profits to sustain and expand their operations. An example is MacDonalds in Russia. However, even here the investor is presumably counting on the currency becoming convertible eventually so that the profits can be returned to the home company. Licensors and exporters, who require usable proceeds, cannot accept payment in a non-convertible currency. This eliminates licensing as an entry mode unless the licensee is able to pay the royalty in a freely exchangeable currency (a "hard" currency) and the licensor is satisfied that this is a durable arrangement. Exporters are in an easier position, as they can simply ensure that payment is made in a hard currency before the goods are shipped. Thus, non-convertibility favors export but is unfavorable for licensing and, generally speaking, investment entry.

Some currencies, though officially convertible, are subject to controls on their exchangeability by *non-residents*. These are often referred to as "soft" currencies. Exchange controls on *residents* differ from non-resident controls in that they do not affect the currency's status outside the country. Anyone, resident and non-resident alike, is at liberty to exchange the currency freely once outside the national boundaries. This is why resident controls are usually complemented by prohibitions on physical exportation and payment to foreigners in local currency. Exchange controls on residents can exist even with respect to a hard currency. Quite strict controls were retained on the British pound until 1979, and Italian and French residents only acquired the right to exchange their currencies freely in 1990.

IMF rules prohibit all exchange controls but only in the case of payment for goods, and even here derogations may be granted.[15] The OECD Code of Liberalization of Current Invisible Transactions prohibits exchange controls with respect to trade in services and the flow of royalties, dividends and profits.[16] The OECD Code of Liberalization of Capital Movements requires access to foreign currency for the purpose of investment abroad and freedom to exchange the proceeds of disinvestment.[17] However, the OECD Codes are subject to many exceptions[18] and, in any case, only apply to the OECD countries, which, for the most part, no longer maintain exchange controls. NAFTA also requires that all proceeds resulting from a Canadian investment in Mexico or the United States must be freely exchangeable.[19] This affects dividends, profits, royalties from a subsidiary, and disinvestment proceeds.

The impact of non-resident controls depends somewhat on their nature. If, for example, they limit the amount of national currency that may be ex-

---

[14] Art. VIII:4
[15] Art. VIII:2, 3.
[16] Arts. 1, 2.
[17] Arts. 1, 2.
[18] The exceptions are the same in the two codes: arts. 2b (reservations), 3 (public order and security), and 7 (economic and financial emergencies).
[19] Art. 1109.

changed following disinvestment, this will affect only investment entry. If, on the other hand, they impose a general limitation on the amount of national currency that non-resident individuals or banks may exchange, this will also affect licensing.

Exporters can deal in similar fashion with resident exchange controls. They are a greater problem in the case of licensing and investment entry, however, as royalties, profits and dividends are generated in the local currency. Thus, the controls cannot be circumvented. They remain a disincentive to these modes of market entry unless a durable arrangement is made for access to hard currency.

Intellectual Property Laws. Companies rightfully wish to protect themselves against others stealing their ideas or profiting from their reputation. This can be done by way of various devices, such as patents, registered trademarks and industrial designs, and copyright. However, intellectual property protection is a national matter. There are no international patents, for example. What is more, not all countries protect intellectual property or make such protection available to foreigners. This means that patents, trademarks, industrial designs, or copyright that are protected in one country may not be protected in another.

Various international conventions dealing with intellectual property partially address the problem. The most important are the Paris Convention, which deals with industrial property (patents, trademarks, trade names, industrial designs), the Berne and Rome Conventions, which deal with copyright, and the Washington Treaty, which is concerned with integrated circuits. Signatories must make national protection devices available to nationals from other signatory states. In addition, the Paris Convention provides that if you file in a signatory country within a certain time of the home filing, you will be afforded the date of the first filing for priority purposes.[20] You also do not forfeit your right to protection because of any prior acts.

The drawback to these international conventions is that they do not always specify the nature of the protection that must be afforded, and that most developing countries are not signatories. TRIPS is intended to overcome this by strengthening the rules of the existing conventions and putting their application on a world-wide basis. Thus, all members of the WTO must apply the rules of the Paris, Berne, and Washington agreements.[21] They must also comply with new requirements that provide for a uniform level of intellectual property protection throughout the world.[22] Developing countries are granted between five and ten years to comply with TRIPS.[23]

Intellectual property protection is particularly important when a company is making its knowledge available to a licensee. Without the ability to establish a proprietary interest, licensing would be the equivalent of giving one's technology away. Thus, the absence or inadequacy of a country's intellectual property laws speaks strongly against licensing as a market entry mode. In this

---

[20] Art. 4.

[21] TRIPS, arts. 2, 9, 35.

[22] *Inter alia*, TRIPS sets the minimum length of protection at 50 years for copyright (art. 12), indefinite for trademarks (art. 18), 10 years for industrial designs (art. 26), 20 years for patents (art. 33), and 10 years for lay-out designs (art. 38).

[23] Arts. 65, 66.

situation, complete control over the technology must be maintained, which means using export or investment entry.

Problems with Foreign Direct Investment

Prohibition on Foreign Direct Investment. Some countries prohibit foreigners from ownership in local companies. Such prohibition rests normally on ideology or extreme nationalism. With the disappearance of the Soviet Union and many other Communist regimes, outright prohibition of foreign direct investment is now rare. However, a large number of countries, including the United States and other developed nations, prohibit foreign direct investment in certain economic sectors.

There is no global right to invest abroad. Nor does the 1976 OECD Declaration on International Investment give such a right within the developed countries; it merely stipulates that foreign investments between OECD countries must be treated in a non-discriminatory way once they are allowed.[24] Regional agreements like NAFTA and the EU give an actual right to invest, but even here it is subject to general rules against private ownership in a particular sector.[25] In addition, certain sectors are exempt altogether from the NAFTA obligation, such as the petroleum industry in Mexico. The United States has negotiated bilateral treaties with a range of countries giving its companies a right to invest in them, but Canada has not followed suit.

The strategic effect of prohibitions on foreign direct investment is very obvious. It quite simply excludes the investment entry mode.

Mandatory Local Equity. Many developing countries require a certain percentage of domestic companies to be owned by local nationals. Often this translates into majority local ownership. No global rules regulate this question. Nor is it mentioned in the 1976 OECD Declaration, although mandatory local equity is probably a requirement that discriminates against foreign companies. However, mandatory local equity is unusual in OECD countries. The only exception is Mexico, but here the NAFTA applies and it prohibits outright local ownership requirements for investors from Canada and the United States.[26]

Majority local ownership implies a loss of control, while even minority local ownership can create problems. For example, if the subsidiary is to act in the interests of all its shareholders, this may prevent it from fulfilling its role within the global conglomerate. IBM's decision to leave India rather than reduce its equity by 60 percent was based on its belief that it would lose more in shared control than it would gain from continued operations under the new rules. Other companies reached different conclusions. Colgate Palmolive became an Indian company and maintained its dominant position in a growing market. Ciba-Geigy used the local equity rules to raise additional funds for growth and diversification and more than doubled its sales. This underlines what was said earlier, namely that not all companies will reach the same con-

---

[24] Art. 2. In fact, Article II:4 of the Declaration specifically confirms the right to resrict foreign direct investment.

[25] See NAFTA, arts. 1101, 1102.

[26] Art. 1102:4.

clusion based on the same legal situation in the target country. Nevertheless, local equity requirements generally speak against investment entry.

Interference with the Company's Activities. Host governments dispose of an array of means for making life difficult for foreign companies. First, they can intervene in its decision-making process. A common form of intervention is to require a local majority on the Board of Directors.[27] This is a relatively benign requirement within the North American corporate scene as the real power lies elsewhere. In any case, a local compliant lawyer can always be found to fill the position! Thus, it is permitted under NAFTA. More serious are the requirement for local appointments among management and direct government interference. Such measures are not permitted under NAFTA[28] and they will fall afoul of the OECD Declaration where they are discriminatory. There are no global rules, however, and such interference is still a relatively common problem in developing countries.

Host governments can also simply discriminate against foreign companies. Access to local capital markets, customers, distributors and advertising outlets can be limited, as can the company's product line. Discriminatory tariffs can be placed on the company's imports and discriminatory taxes on its profits. It can be denied the full benefit of national intellectual property laws. New global rules will prohibit some of these discriminatory measures. Thus, the new TRIMS agreement guarantees the company's right to import goods freely[29] while the TRIPS agreement will give a right to adequate protection of its intellectual property. Both the OECD Declaration and NAFTA prohibit all discriminatory measures,[30] which provides Canadian investors with an effective protection, albeit limited to its OECD and North American partners.

Performance requirements are another favorite ploy that is used against foreign companies. It may be prohibited from exporting, although more frequently it is forced to export either by an absolute requirement or by relating its right to sell locally to the quantity of its exports. It may be constrained to use domestic products or inputs by way of local content or local use rules and/or restrictions on imports. Mandatory transfer of technology is also quite common. To the extent that performance requirements are normally discriminatory, they infringe the OECD Declaration.[31] This does not help much, as such requirements tend to be imposed most frequently by developing countries. Some global protection is now available under TRIMS, which prohibits exports bans and domestic use rules.[32] However, it does not apply to forced exports or technology transfers. NAFTA outlaws all performance requirements between Mexico, the United States, and Canada.[33]

Finally, interference in the activities of foreign companies was particularly common in developing countries. In India, for example, following enactment

---

[27] This is required, for example, under the federal Canadian Business Corporations Act, s. 114(2).

[28] Art. 1107:2.

[29] TRIMS, Annex.

[30] OECD Declaration, art. 2; NAFTA, art. 1102.

[31] Art. 2.

[32] Annex.

[33] Art. 1106.

of the 1974 Foreign Exchange Reserve Act, foreign companies had to submit to a host of regulations. These included limiting production to the original product line, limitations on importing equipment, limitations on the compensation of expatriate executives to the drastically lower level of nationals and sometimes even limits on compensation to Indians, unrealistic export commitments, and strict transfer of technology requirements. Many of these rules were later copied in whole or in part by Malaysia, Indonesia, the Philippines, Nigeria, Brazil, and many other developing countries. However, in the late 1980s, after a "lost decade" in Latin America of debt crisis and no growth, countries like Argentina and Mexico began to reverse these restrictive and discriminatory laws in order to attract foreign investment. The demise of Communism and the disappointments of socialist experiments in the third world have led to a general extension of this liberalizing trend. A few countries, like Malaysia, may buck the trend, but it is true to say that the interference is now much less. Where it still exists, it is clearly a disincentive to investment entry. American writers refer to it as "creeping expropriation," which is perhaps a little over-dramatic and reflects that quaint American belief that the right to private property connotes a right to act in relation to it without any external constraints.

Expropriation. The most drastic measure that can be taken against foreign investors is to expropriate their property and operations. No global rules prohibit expropriation or determine how it should be done. Indeed, opinion is divided. The developed nations, who provide most of the foreign investment, hold to the 1962 UN Resolution on Permanent Sovereignty,[34] according to which expropriation must be for a public purpose and compensation must be given that is adequate and prompt. The developing countries hold to the 1974 UN Charter of Economic Rights and Duties,[35] under which expropriation and compensation are left to the discretion of the expropriating country. The United States and some European countries have signed bilateral investment treaties with certain developing countries that follow the 1962 approach. Canada has not followed suit. The OECD Declaration and NAFTA also prescribe this approach for the OECD and North American countries, respectively.[36]

One point for Canadian investors to note is that Canadian courts apply the act of state doctrine in its entirety. This doctrine holds that the court of one country is not competent to judge the validity of acts done by the government of another country within its own borders.[37] In the United States, the 1964 Foreign Assistance Act[38] obliges U.S. courts not to apply this doctrine where the foreign act in question is a violation of international law. Thus, where an expropriation contravenes the principles of the 1962 Resolution, U.S. investors could probably attack the expropriating country's assets in the United States. No equivalent statute exists in Canada to temper the rigor of the act of state doctrine.

Two international conventions offer some help in expropriation cases. One provides for the International Centre for the Settlement of Investment Disputes

---

[34] UNGA Resolution 1803 (XVII) of December, 1962, art. I:4.

[35] UNGA Resolution 3281 (XXIX) of 12 December, 1974, art. 2(2)(c).

[36] OECD Declaration, art. 2; NAFTA, art. 1110.

[37] See *Luther v. Sagor*, [1921] 3 KB 532 (English Court of Appeal).

[38] USCS para.2370(e).

(ICSID), which is a neutral body for the adjudication of expropriation and compensation disputes, set up in 1965. The parties involved must submit to ICSID's jurisdiction[39] and abide by its decision, which is final and binding.[40] NAFTA makes submission to ICSID mandatory for disputes involving Mexico, Canada, and the United States.[41]

Another convention from 1985 sets up the Multilateral Investment Guarantee Agency (MIGA) to protect foreign investors against expropriation. It issues guarantees against expropriation, but does not protect investors in volatile countries where protection is most necessary.

The danger of expropriation or even a record of such behavior in the past is a powerful disincentive to investment entry. However, the incidence of expropriations is widely exaggerated by the business community, especially among those without international experience. In the case of U.S. companies, the total value of major expropriations over the years 1917 to 1965 was less then 5 percent of total U.S. foreign direct investment. This includes expropriations by Communist regimes, which constituted a major proportion of all expropriations. Canadian investors have suffered even less.

Corporate Law Problems. Occasionally, the corporate law of a particular country can have an unfavorable impact on an investment entry decision. It may require the investor to assume a corporate form that causes it difficulties; it may mandate workers' councils, as a recent EU directive does,[42] that bring about an unacceptable level of employee involvement in the company's activities; it may pose limitations on the votes that a single shareholder may cast, thus undermining the ability to control a subsidiary. Financial disclosures rules may also be unacceptable, particularly where they require information on the whole corporate group. Smaller companies may be deterred by the complexity and cost of incorporating a foreign subsidiary. Formalities, requirements, and fees are frequently much more onerous abroad than in Canada, particularly in civil law jurisdictions. Many countries, for example, stipulate a minimum amount of subscribed capital, which can be as high as C$50,000.

Problems with Licensing, Distribution, and Agency Laws, Including Competition Laws

General Rules. By and large, the common law leaves the format of licensing, distributor, and agency agreements up to the parties. In some civil law jurisdictions and above all in developing countries, rules are imposed. Maximum or minimum terms ranging from ten to thirty years often apply to these agreements. The licensor's or exporter's liability for product defects may be mandatory in some countries. Termination of all three types of agreement sometimes requires a high level of compensation. Agents may also be protected by employment laws that require longer holidays, more generous social benefits, and better conditions of work than is usual in Canada. The rules on dismissal and

---

[39] ICSID Convention, art. 25(1).

[40] ICSID Convention, arts. 53, 54.

[41] Art. 1122.

[42] Council Directive 94/95, OJ L268/94

redundancy may also be stricter. Such common arrangements as sub-licensing, agreements with subsidiaries, export restrictions on licensees and distributors, cross-licensing, and confidentiality clauses to protect know-how may not be allowed or may be subjected to special approval. Compulsory grant-backs of improvements made by a licensee are usually illegal, and even buy-backs may be either proscribed or the compensation payable to the licensee made subject to review. Rarely permitted under any circumstances are no-challenge clauses, under which a licensee agrees not to contest the validity of the licensor's rights. All such rules are national in origin and are not subject to any international regulation. Where they are particularly onerous for the foreign party, they may impose a change in market entry strategy.

Competition Laws. One of the main issues with respect to licensing and distributorships relates to certain restrictive arrangements that may violate national or, in the case of the EU,[43] regional competition laws. Usually, licenses, agencies, and distributorships are given for particular countries or territories. The licensee, agent, or distributor is not allowed to work other markets and in return is protected against encroachments at home. National rules may not allow such arrangements, particularly where they entail a prohibition on exporting. In the EU, for example, absolute protection of a licensee's territory is limited to five years, after which time the parallel importation of products that have been legally marketed and purchased in another member state must be allowed.[44] This means that one licensee can fill orders that come from other member states within the EU ("passive sales") although active solicitation of customers outside the licensed territory remains prohibited ("active sales"). In the case of distributors, passive sales cannot be prohibited even for an initial five years.[45] Agency agreements, on the other hand, are less controlled in most countries, and it is quite usual to restrict and protect agents' territories.

Customer limitations are rarely allowed for distributors and licensees, but limitations on the use for which licensees may manufacture products are quite common. Clauses dealing with the licensee's and distributor's purchasing obligations require care. Tie-ins, collection buying, and even exclusive purchasing arrangements may not be permitted. There is also a general reticence over clauses requiring the licensee to take additional non-protected material in order to obtain the license. Price-fixing is almost universally prohibited for distributors and licensees, while restrictions on the right of agents, licensees, and distributors to deal in competitive products as well as restrictive covenants are normally acceptable only as long as they are reasonable and seek only to protect the other party's legitimate interests.

There are no international rules on competition laws. At most, there are some procedural rules but these are destined to facilitate the enforcement of national rules.[46] As violations of national or EU competition law can be very costly, it is essential to make sure that agreements do not infringe on them. Where the restrictions affect a company's global strategy, this may well speak against licensing or setting

---

[43] EC Treaty, arts. 85–90.

[44] Commission Regulation 2349/84, OJL 219/84, art. 1(6). See also *Centrafarm BV v. Winthrop BV*, 16/74, [1974] ECR 1183 (European Court of Justice).

[45] Commission Regulation 1983/83, OJL 173/83, art.1.

[46] See for example OECD Revised Recommendation Concerning Cooperation between Member Countries on Restrictive Business Practices Affecting International Trade (1986) 25 ILM 1629.

up a distributorship in that country. Agency agreements are much less affected by national competition laws.

Problems with Royalties. Apart from exchange restrictions, which we discussed earlier, a country may restrict the payment of royalties from licensees in other, more direct ways. The amount payable may be calculated as a percentage of the licensee's sales or it may be set annually by other criteria. Alternatively, the host country may place a ceiling on the amount that may be remitted. Royalty payments that continue beyond the term of the protection granted under the law of the licensee's state as well as payment for know-how are often not allowed. These restrictions tend to be stricter where the licensee is a subsidiary. Indeed some countries do not permit the payment of royalties at all to foreign parent companies. NAFTA is the only international instrument that regulates these problems for Canadian licensors, but it only applies to royalties from subsidiaries in Mexico and the United States.[47] Also, it is not clear that it would invalidate any of the above rules where they also apply between local parents and subsidiaries. Clearly, difficulties in getting paid speak strongly against licensing.

Problems with Joint Ventures, Including Competition Laws

General Rules. National rules requiring majority local equity, interference in the joint venture's activities, the danger of expropriation, and corporate law problems can also affect joint ventures and can make this form of investment entry unattractive. In addition, other national provisions may cause problems by their regulation of such matters as the grounds for terminating the joint venture, the compensation payable to the local party upon termination, minimum foreign financial contributions, minimum profit distribution to the local party, the accounting practices to be used by the joint venture, and the method for evaluating contributions in kind.

Competition Laws. Joint ventures are prone to fall afoul of national competition laws as they are by their very nature restrictive of competition where the partners are competitors. Although certain joint activities (such as research and development) are now widely accepted, joint production, sales, and distribution agreements are problematic unless great care is taken to avoid price-fixing or market-sharing. Where the joint venture agreement eliminates all meaningful competition in a market, there is a danger of abuse of a dominant position. It is necessary to preserve competition between the partners and the joint venture company to the extent that this is possible without undermining the efficacy of the joint venture. Agreement by partners not to compete after the end of the joint venture may not be allowed.

Tariffs and Non-Tariff Barriers

Goods entering a country may be subject to both tariffs and all manner of non-tariff measures, of which we will look here at quantitative restrictions, customs matters, abuse of contingent protection devices, and standards-related measures. The WTO Agreement, however, provides quite strict global rules that govern national trade rules, while trade relations between Mexico, Canada, and the United States are also regulated by NAFTA.

---

[47] See art. 1109.

Tariffs have always existed in international trade, and as long as they are not excessive, it is possible for exporters and importers to live with them. In general, they are not now a major barrier to trade in goods. This was not always the case, as between the two world wars high tariffs practically stifled international trade. GATT was responsible for reducing them since 1947 to an average of less than 10 percent. Under the WTO Agreement, tariffs are further reduced across the board by an average of 40 percent. Under NAFTA, tariffs between Canada and the United States will be completely eliminated by January 1, 1998, and by January 1, 2008, between Mexico and Canada.[48]

Nevertheless, tariffs cannot be disregarded in planning a global marketing strategy. In the first place, all countries exempt certain goods from the WTO-imposed tariff levels. A few goods are even exempt from the NAFTA provisions on tariff elimination. Secondly, the effect of tariffs is accentuated by preferential treatment that other countries may give to non-Canadian goods. Thus, Canada has difficulty finding markets for its newsprint and lumber products in the EU because its rivals in Scandinavia pay no tariffs at all. Similar disadvantages can occur when dealing with other regional blocs, such as the Mercosur countries of South America. The GSoP provides for reduced tariffs for developing countries, which can also divert trade in their direction. Where a target market has high tariffs or provides the opportunity for trade diversion to competitors from other countries, exporting may have to be replaced by another mode of market entry.

Quantitative Restrictions. Quantitative restrictions are the most impenetrable barrier to exports. Theoretically, they are prohibited under GATT, but they are circumvented in two ways. First, the exception granted for agricultural quotas has been interpreted so widely as practically to eliminate free trade in agriculture. Second, many countries have prevailed upon their trading partners voluntarily to limit their exports. These so-called voluntary export restraints (VERs) are none other than quotas in disguise. Canada has been both the victim and perpetrator of VERs.

The WTO Agreement tightens up the rules on quotas and the Agreement on Safeguards decrees VERs are to be eliminated by July 1 1999.[49] NAFTA contains no additional general provisions on quotas but does eliminate completely some agricultural quotas, such as those on meat and cereal exports from Canada to the United States.

Quantitative restrictions have a very definite impact on global marketing strategy. It is impossible to use export entry into a market from which one's products are excluded.

Customs Matters. International rules deal with the more obvious abuses in customs procedures. GATT theoretically prohibits excessive fees and formalities,[50] while the WTO Customs Valuation Code prohibits the arbitrary valuation of imported goods.[51] NAFTA abolishes the customs user fees maintained by both

---

[48] Chapter 3 of the NAFTA Agreement sets out the tariff rules for the three NAFTA partners.
[49] Art. 11.
[50] Art. VIII.
[51] Arts. 1-8.

Mexico and the United States.[52] Generally speaking, however, customs matters have limited strategic importance as they rarely lead to a change in market entry strategy.

Abuse of Contingent Protection. Anti-dumping and countervailing duties are intended as a corrective measure to protect domestic industry against injury from dumped (i.e., underpriced) or subsidized imports. These so-called "contingent protection" devices, however, can easily be abused. The margin of dumping or the subsidy may be calculated according to questionable criteria, injury to domestic industry may be assumed without sufficient proof or unfairly imputed to the offending imports, and duties may be imposed where only a minor proportion of domestic industry is affected or involved.[53]

The WTO Anti-Dumping and Subsidies Codes strengthen the existing GATT rules in order to deal with these abuses. NAFTA provides for a bilateral panel to review national decisions imposing anti-dumping or countervailing duties.[54] It rules whether the national decision-making body has correctly applied national law, which, it should be emphasized, must be consistent with the new WTO rules.

Abuse of contingent protection by foreign countries will not only raise the price of the Canadian import by the amount of the duty, it will also involve the Canadian exporter in a long and expensive foreign law suit. This is thus a significant and costly barrier to export entry, particularly into the United States where domestic producers easily resort to legal procedures against foreign imports.

Taxation

Corporate Tax Problems. Two problems facing companies whose operations extend to one or more foreign countries are the level and manner of taxation of corporate profits in the country where they are made and the issue of double taxation.

Double taxation is a normal cost of investment entry that must be factored into any market entry calculations and may speak against this form of entry. The problem is less acute, however, where there is a bilateral tax treaty with the foreign country in question. High corporate and withholding taxes and unfair taxation of branches, on the other hand, can be avoided by setting up operations elsewhere. Thus, they tend to determine where rather than whether investment entry is to take place. Low corporate taxation, low or non-existent withholding taxes, and tax incentives in the form of reductions or exemptions are the other side of the coin and favor investment entry.

Withholding taxes on royalties. Royalties from foreign countries are normally subject to withholding taxes unless a bilateral treaty provides for taxation solely by the licensor's country.[55] Clearly, high withholding taxes on royalties are a

---

[52] Art. 310.

[53] See Alan M. Rugman & Andrew Anderson, *Administered Protection in America*, New York: Methuen; London: Croom-Helm, 1987; Philip Raworth, "Legal Barriers to Government Export Promotion," in F.H.Rolf Seringhaus and Philip J. Rosson *Government Export Promotion: A Gloal Perspective*, London: Routledge Publishers, 1990.

[54] NAFTA Agreement, chapter 19.

[55] OECD Model Tax Treaty, art. 12 (1).

disincentive to the use of licensing and it is important to ascertain whether a bilateral tax treaty limits the withholding tax on royalties.

Taking Advantage of Regional Arrangements. The preferential treatment that members of blocs accord each other is generally available to any enterprise operating within the bloc. Thus, a foreign licensor working with Canadian technology or a subsidiary of a Canadian parent can take advantage of the trade liberalization within the EU or Mercosur, to name but two regional blocs. In addition, the EU has a number of trade agreements with third countries, to which a Canadian company can acquire access if it operates through a licensee or an establishment in the EU. Exporting from Canada will secure none of these benefits.

Problems with Pricing

Anti-Dumping and Countervail Action. There are various reasons for exporting goods at a price below the domestic price. They range from the perfectly acceptable strategies of using low prices to gain a foothold in a new market or passing on the benefit of government subsidies to consumers to the more dubious practices of liquidating excess goods or eliminating competitors in the target market. WTO rules do not distinguish between these reasons.[56] Thus, importing countries are entitled to take action against all underpriced imports as long as they cause injury to a major proportion of domestic industry in the importing country. As noted earlier, the new WTO agreements on countervail and anti-dumping actions re-affirm this injury requirement.[57]

Where the low price is made possible by government subsidies, the importing country can levy a countervailing duty in the amount of the subsidy. The WTO Subsidies Agreement now defines what a subsidy is,[58] which should act as a restraint on the tendency of U.S. courts to find a subsidy in almost any Canadian public expenditure that is not replicated in the United States. The Agreement also contains a list of non-actionable subsidies, but it is very limited.

Where no subsidy is involved, the importing country may impose an anti-dumping duty. This may not exceed the amount by which the export price is higher than the domestic price in the exporting country, the so-called "margin of dumping." However, additional damages may be awarded where the dumping is predatory, (i.e., intended to eliminate local competition). The WTO Anti-Dumping Code contains rules to make sure that the margin of dumping is calculated fairly.[59] Prices must be compared at the same level of trade (normally ex-factory) and in respect of sales made at the same time and in the same quantities. The same rate of exchange must be used to render the two prices into the domestic currency of the importing country. This last rule should help Canadian exporters to the United States, where courts have on occasion manufactured a margin of dumping by using different exchange conversion dates.

Exporters should be very careful when pricing their goods below the domestic ex-factory selling price or when accepting subsidies on their exported goods.

---

[56] See GATT, art. VI:1; WTO Anti-Dumping Code, art. 2.

[57] WTO Anti-Dumping Code, art. 5:2; WTO Subsidies Code, art. 11:2.

[58] Arts. 1, 2.

[59] Art. 2.

Not only will this advantage be vitiated by contingent duties, but the costs of the ensuing law suit and any damages that are awarded for predatory dumping could be catastrophic.

Competition Laws. Many countries, especially the United States and the EU, maintain strict competition rules against any form of price manipulation. The most common practices are price-fixing, price differentials, and unfair pricing. As the fines for breach of local competition laws can be very high, it is wise to make sure that one's pricing policy does not contravene them. In some countries, those responsible may even go to prison.

Price-fixing can take place through vertical resale price arrangements between different levels of the marketing chain or through horizontal price agreements between competitors. This practice is nearly always prohibited where there are local competition laws.

Price differentials are rather more subtle, and many companies indulge in them without realizing that they may be illegal. In essence, they reflect an understandable desire to adapt prices to a particular market. Thus, one might charge a higher price in Germany that one does in Portugal. Such a policy may be acceptable as long as customers retain the right to purchase in the lower-price territory; it becomes more dubious, and illegal in the EU, where the price differential is enforced by a prohibition on cross-territorial sales.

Unfair pricing covers a multitude of sins from price discrimination between customers that is not justified by commercial reasons and price-gouging to the use of low prices to eliminate competition. Here again, local competition law may prohibit one or other or all of these practices.

Transfer Pricing and Price Controls. While we discuss transfer pricing in Chapter 13 in the context of pricing decisions, it should be mentioned here that this practice occurs when goods are sold between different parts of a company. Most frequently, transfer pricing occurs on an international level. Thus, goods may be exported at a low price in order to reduce the level of import duties or to ensure that the profits are made in an importing country where corporate taxes are lower. Alternatively, export prices may be inflated in order to transfer profits to Canada or circumvent ceilings on the payment of dividends.

Although widespread, transfer pricing can be problematic. National tax authorities, including Revenue Canada, often treat amounts transferred out of the country as hidden taxable income.[60] The company will thus be penalized for tax evasion as well as having to pay tax on the hidden income. In some jurisdictions, transfer pricing is a criminal offence. In many cases, it is disallowed as a non-arm's-length transaction when discovered.

Price controls reduce the freedom of a company to raise prices. In non-market economies, the initial selling price may even be dictated. This is obviously the more confining approach, particularly as the set price is probably also unmovable. Controls on price raises, such as those introduced by the Canadian government in the mid-1970s, make the choice of initial price all the more important. It must be as high as possible without becoming a deterrent to purchasers. Price controls will not, however, affect exporters where they do not apply to goods from abroad.

---

[60] Income Tax Act, ss. 91(1), 95(2).

Other Problems

Intense and Volatile Local Laws. In addition to the content of local laws, one must also consider their intensity and volatility. Over-regulation tends to increase costs and frustrate innovation. Volatility creates a climate of uncertainty, particularly when it includes making laws effective retroactively. This is definitely an unfavorable factor for investment entry while favoring exporting. It does not positively affect licensing, but, where local production is necessary, it encourages licensing over investment entry.

Employment Laws. One of the ironies of the recent NAFTA negotiations was the insistence of the U.S. on minimum employment standards. While general conditions of employment in North America exceed those in developing countries, they compare poorly with Western European norms.[61] Only health and safety rules and non-discrimination provisions compare favorably. With the exception of the United Kingdom, which is closer to the North American model, European countries thus reserve unpleasant surprises for the North American employer. Unless a company is able to adapt and exploit other competitive advantages that continental Europe has to offer, investment entry in Western Europe favors the United Kingdom.

After-Sales Service Requirements. After-sales service may be imposed by law or expected by customers. National rules and attitudes differ widely from the lax legal requirements and long-suffering customers of some Canadian provinces to the stricter legal regime of the EU and the notoriously high expectations of the Japanese consumer. There are no international rules governing after-sales service.

Strict after-sales service requirements necessitate a presence in the target market. In the case of the exporter, this can be provided by the distributor or a separate service company. However, the exporter will probably have to train and supervise the foreign service operation if an adequate standard is to be maintained. As a result, it may be easier for the company to produce the goods abroad itself or license the whole operation.

Government Procurement Requirements. Governments have a natural tendency to want to support national or regional industry when making purchases for governmental use. In many instances, this preference for purchasing national or local products is mandated by law. Both the WTO Agreement and some regional agreements limit this freedom to discriminate against foreign products.

Under the WTO Agreement on Government Procurement, governments cannot discriminate against foreign suppliers with respect to contracts for supplies of goods and some services that meet a 130,000 SDR threshold. Unfortunately, this Agreement only applies to named national entities and excludes contracts in the public utilities sector.[62] Moreover, it is difficult to enforce and only a limited number of countries (including Canada, Japan, the U.S. and the EU) are signatories to it. NAFTA offers Canadian companies a much

---

[61] Permitted working hours are longer, the employer's share of social charges is smaller, minimum wages are lower, holidays as well as sick and maternity leaves are shorter, and workers' involvement in the company's affairs is rarer.

[62] Art. 1.

greater and surer access to the government procurement markets of Mexico and the United States.[63] It includes all goods and services, and the threshold amounts are considerably lower. In addition, it contains meaningful enforcement procedures. At present, the NAFTA provisions only apply to named federal entities but it is intended to extend its application to state and provincial entities. One drawback is the number of sectors that Mexico has been allowed to exempt. The EU also has regional government procurement rules, but, at least in the public utilities sector not covered by the WTO Agreement, it requires member states to give a preference to goods with over 50 percent EU content.[64]

As a general rule, it is wiser for Canadian companies to produce goods locally, either through investment entry or licensing, where the customer is a foreign government outside the NAFTA region. Even where the WTO Government Procurement Agreement applies, it has not proved very effective in opening up opportunities.

LEGAL ASPECTS OF THE IMPLEMENATION OF A GLOBAL MARKETING STRATEGY

The legal side of the implementation of a global marketing strategy is best left to lawyers. Nevertheless, it is wise for the marketing manager to be familiar with the more common issues that are likely to arise, as they can have a substantial impact on time and cost. Here, we look at some of these issues.

▼ Competition Law: Scope and Application

Competition law exists to combat restrictive business practices. These may take place by agreement between certain parties or may be the unilateral acts of a major player in a particular market.

Restrictive agreements are either horizontal or vertical. Horizontal agreements are between parties at the same level in the marketing chain, for example, between two or more competing manufacturers, distributors, or licensees. A joint venture is a horizontal agreement. Vertical agreements are between parties at different levels in the marketing chain, for example, between a manufacturer and distributor or a licensee and licensor. Both types of agreement are common in international business and are in themselves perfectly legal. However, they may become illegal under national (or EU) competition law where they degenerate into restrictive practices, such as price-fixing, exclusive purchasing, market allocation, production limitation, territorial exclusivity, or any other scheme that limits competition in the marketplace.

A supplier is considered to have a dominant position in a market when its share is particularly significant, a figure that can vary between 30 percent and 60 percent. Dominance in itself is not illegal under competition law but it may

---

[63] NAFTA Agreement, chapter 10.
[64] Council Directive 93/38, OJL 199/93, art. 36(3).

become so when there is abuse. Examples of abuse of dominant position are unfair pricing, unjustified discrimination between customers, market segmentation, and imposing restrictive vertical agreements.

Normally, the law of the country where the restrictive practice is implemented governs. In the case of the EU, this means the national law of a member state unless the practice has a European dimension, in which case Union law applies. There are two exceptions to this normal rule, however. Canadian competition law applies to foreign practices where they have a direct effect in Canada by reducing the real value of Canadian exports, restricting export activity among Canadian businesses or limiting competition in the supply of export services.[65] The U.S. is more diligent in the extraterritorial application of its competition law and may apply it to foreign activities that have any substantial impact in the United States even where this impact is secondary (i.e., not directly related to the restriction of competition).[66] Thus, a strategy by a Canadian company that restricts the activity of a U.S. subsidiary in Africa, for example, may be justiciable before a U.S. court if it is shown to reduce the income of the U.S. shareholders.

Restrictive practices may be heavily penalized by fines and damages as well as by the nullification of the practice in question. Imprisonment is possible, as for example in Canada, but this ultimate sanction is rarely imposed. In order to enforce their competition laws against Canadian enterprises, foreign authorities need, of course, to carry out their investigations and execute the eventual court judgment in Canada. Under the 1986 OECD Recommendation on Cooperation between Member Countries on Restrictive Practices and the 1984 Canada-U.S. Memorandum of Understanding, the gathering of information in Canada requires notification and consultation with the Canadian authorities. It is normally permitted unless the federal Attorney General considers that it is against Canada's interests.[67] Foreign competition judgments are enforceable in the same way as any other foreign judgment as long as they do not impose criminal sanctions or conflict with Canadian public policy.[68]

It is necessary to proceed very carefully in matters that touch upon competition law. Some countries have procedures that allow you to clear a particular practice in advance. Alternatively, you may be able to apply for an exemption. The EU has a number of block exemptions for such arrangements as joint R & D, licensing, distribution agreements, exclusive purchasing agreements, and insurance agreements. These apply automatically to a practice as long as it conforms strictly to the conditions set out in the legislation.

---

[65] Competition Act, s.45.

[66] U.S. courts now often decline to intervene in such cases on the basis of international comity – see *Timberlane Lumber Co. v Bank of America*, 549 F. 2d. 597 at 611-615 (U.S. Court of Appeal, 9th Circuit). See also James M. Grippando "Declining to Exercise Extraterritorial Antitrust Jurisdiction on Grounds of International Comity," *Virginia Journal of International Law*, 1983, 23, p.395.

[67] Foreign Extraterritorial Measures Act, ss. 3,5.

[68] ibid. 2.8.

TABLE 5-1 Countries Involved in Intellectual Property Piracy

	Software	Music	Pharmaceuticals	Films	Books
On Priority Watch List:					
China	✓	✓		✓	✓
Japan	✓			✓	
South Korea	✓	✓	✓	✓	✓
India	✓	✓	✓	✓	✓
Saudi Arabia	✓	✓		✓	
Turkey	✓	✓	✓	✓	
Thailand	✓	✓	✓	✓	✓
Argentina	✓	✓	✓	✓	✓
On Watch List:					
Italy	✓	✓		✓	
Spain	✓		✓	✓	
Poland	✓	✓		✓	✓
Indonesia		✓	✓	✓	✓
Taiwan	✓		✓	✓	✓
United Arab Emirates	✓	✓	✓		
Australia	✓	✓	✓	✓	
Venezuela	✓	✓		✓	✓
Philippines		✓		✓	✓
Greece	✓	✓		✓	
Egypt	✓		✓	✓	✓
Pakistan		✓		✓	✓
Cyprus				✓	✓
Peru	✓	✓			✓
El Salvador		✓		✓	
Guatemala		✓		✓	✓

Source: Adapted from Dave Savona, "Waging War on Pirates," *International Business*, January 1995, p. 44.

▼ Intellectual Property Protection

Intellectual property piracy is costing U.S. multinationals alone more than C$50 billion in lost annual revenues. Among the products most vulnerable are films, music, software, pharmaceuticals, and books. Piracy in software has reached alarming levels: 35 percent of software in use in the United States is pirated, relatively modest when compared to 57 percent in Germany, 80 percent in Japan, and an estimated 100 percent in many Asian nations. In the U.S., the trade department has posted a list of the key offenders of intellectual property rights (see Table 5-1).[69] Protection of intellectual property is therefore a major concern for global marketers.

Industrial Property. There are two major problems with respect to the protection of industrial property, which includes patents, trademarks, trade names, and industrial designs. The first is the cost and time involved in making all the applications for protection, and the other is that of securing adequate protection in foreign countries.

There are international agreements that provide for a single application for protection between the signatory states, which constitute a union for cooperation

---

[69] Dave Savona, "Waging War on Pirates," *International Business*, January 1995, pp. 42-47.

in the filing, searching, and examination of applications. The agreements are the 1970 Patent Cooperation Treaty, the 1925/1867 Hague Agreement on the International Deposit of Industrial Designs, and the 1891/1967 Madrid Agreement on the International Registration of Marks or 1973 Trademark Registration Treaty. Unfortunately, Canada has only signed up to the PCT, which means that individual applications for industrial designs and trademarks will have to be filed in whichever country protection is sought. Trade names are treated differently, as the Paris Convention, to which Canada adheres and which will eventually apply on a world-wide basis by virtue of TRIPS, provides that they are protected everywhere without the need for any local registration.[70] The 1973 European Patent Convention enables a patent applicant to file a single application covering all of the Western European states as well as Turkey[71] and thus achieve the advantage that the application will be subject to only one grant procedure. However, the procedure does not result in the existence of one single unitary patent but rather leads to a bundle of national patents governed by national law. A single unitary patent is planned for the fifteen member states of the EU,[72] and one can already obtain a single trademark that is valid throughout the Union.[73]

Obtaining legal protection in another country also poses problems. The protection may simply not be available, or it may have been forfeited by prior acts such as use or filing for registration in Canada. Priority is also a problem, as it is quite feasible for third parties to acquire rights in one country on the basis of your information filed as part of application in Canada or elsewhere. The Paris Convention and TRIPS, however, take care of these problems, as we have seen earlier, as long as filings for registration are undertaken in all potential target countries within the time limits laid down by the Paris Convention. Time, therefore, is of the essence.

Copyright. Copyright is the proprietary right existing in literary, artistic, and scientific works. Under the Berne Convention copyright protection is automatically extended in all signatory states to the unpublished work of a national of a signatory state and to a work that is first published in a signatory state.[74] No registration is necessary even where the national law requires it. Under TRIPS, the Berne Convention will eventually be applied worldwide, and its protection is extended to computer programs and compilations of data as well the related rights of performers, producers of sound recordings, and broadcasters.[75] Until recently, the United States applied only the provisions of the Universal Copyright Convention, which requires works to bear the symbol © accompanied by the name of the copyright proprietor and the year of publication.[76] It now adheres to the Berne Convention and TRIPS, so there is no absolute need to comply with the UCC format.

---

[70] Art. 8.

[71] The signatory states are Austria, Belgium, Denmark, Germany, Finland, France, Greece, Ireland, Italy, Liechtenstein, Luxembourg, Monaco, Netherlands, Norway, Portugal, Spain, Sweden, Switzerland, Turkey, United Kingdom, Yugoslavia.

[72] Convention for the European Patent for the Common Market, OJL 17/76.

[73] Council Regulation 40/94, OJL 11/94.

[74] Arts. 4, 5, 6.

[75] TRIPS, arts. 9-14.

[76] Art. III:1.

Know-How. Know-how comprises information that is not generally known and that has commercial value attributable to its secrecy. It normally concerns the manner in which to use technology or run a business. In most countries it cannot be protected by registration, and so the proprietor of such information must resort to contractual guarantees. There is thus no protection against third persons who discover the secret by themselves. Under TRIPS, members of the WTO are obliged to make it possible for know-how to be protected through private agreements.[77]

▼ Sales Agreement and INCO Terms

Export of goods or services requires an international sales agreement, whether it be directly with the end-user, with the distributor, or with the supplier's subsidiary in the target market. The agreement is often an extraordinarily complex document that regulates the sale, transportation, and insurance of the goods. Individual sales agreements with distributors or with the subsidiary are normally less comprehensive, as the basic terms have often been set down in advance in a distributorship or intra-firm agreement,

Apart from terms concerning the subject matter of the contract, the bulk of the international sales agreement is to do with transportation, insurance, documentation, transfer of risk, and the payment mechanism. As far as transportation is concerned, it is necessary to stipulate the place, date, and mode of transport as well as who is to pay for it. The amount of the insurance, the risks to be covered, and the party responsible for payment must also be stated.

Developing countries may require a preshipment inspection (PSI) certificate (called a Clean Report of Findings) that verifies the quality, quantity, and price of the imported goods. PSI activities have caused problems and there is now a WTO Agreement on PSI that protects exporters from such abuses as divulgence of confidential information, discrimination, delays, and unfair treatment.[78]

Transportation, insurance, documentation and risk are often regulated in an international sales contract by recourse to the Incoterms, which are standard clauses defining the responsibilities of the buyer and seller in these matters. The Incoterms were first formulated in 1936, but the latest revision dates from 1990. They are divided into four groups and apply to different modes of transport, as shown in Box 5–3.

The most commonly used Incoterms are those from Groups F and C. Table 5–2 gives a summary of the responsibilities of the two parties under these terms.

The transfer of risk between buyer and seller is another matter of importance. The risk passes from seller to buyer: For FCA delivery is into the custody of carrier named by buyer; for FAS delivery is alongside named vessel at named port; for FOB delivery on board named vessel at named port; for CFR/CIF once goods pass ship's rail; for CPT/CIP once goods pass into custody of first international carrier.

---

[77] Art. 39.

[78] WTO Agreement on Preshipment Inspection, art.2.

Box 5-3
Incoterms and Transport Modes

Group E — the seller makes the goods available at own works, warehouse or store
Ex Works (Delivery at a named place): mode of transport is irrelevant.

Group F — seller must deliver the goods to a point of departure within the exporting country
FCA (Free (named) carrier at a named place): usable for any mode of transport, but particularly common in rail and air transport.

FAS (Free alongside named ship at a named port of shipment): used only in transport by sea or waterway.

FOB (Free on board named ship at a named port of shipment): used only in transport by sea or waterway.

Group C — seller must deliver the goods to a point of destination outside the exporting country but without assuming the risk of loss or damage
CFR (Cost and freight to a named port of destination): used only in transport by sea or waterway.

CPT (Carriage paid to a named place of destination): usable for any mode of transport.

CIF (Cost, insurance and freight to a named port of destination): used only in transport by sea or waterway.

CIP (Carriage and insurance paid to a named place of destination): usable for any mode of transport.

Group D — seller must deliver the goods to a point of destination outside the exporting country at own risk of loss or damage
DAF (Delivered at frontier at a named place): usable for any mode of transport.

DES (Delivered ex ship at a named port of destination): used only in transport by sea or waterway.

DEQ (Delivered ex quay at a named port of destination): used only in transport by sea or waterway.

DDU (Delivery duty unpaid at a named place of destination): usable for any mode of transport.

DDP (Delivery duty paid at a named place of destination): usable for any mode of transport.

These Incoterms are normally incorporated by reference into the sales agreement, but one should be sure before doing so that the term used corresponds to one's contractual intentions. It is also wise to include the year, as the 1990 terms differ from earlier versions. Unfortunately, the Uniform Commercial Code terms are used widely in the United States, and these differ from the 1990

TABLE 5–2 Responsibilities of Parties Under Inco Terms

	RESPONSIBILITY OF:	
	Seller	**Buyer**
Packing	All of F and C terms	
Export Dues	All others of F and C terms	FAS
Export Documents & Costs	All others of F and C terms	FAS (with seller's cooperation)
Pre-Shipment Inspection		All of F and C terms
Freight (arrange)	C terms	F terms
Freight (costs)	C terms	F terms
Import Dues		All of F and C terms
Import Document		All of F and C terms (with seller's cooperation)
Insurance (arrange)	CIF and CIP	All others of F and C terms
Insurance (costs)	CIF and CIP	All others of F and C terms

Incoterms. For example, it is possible to have the term FOB (cost and freight to a named destination) under the UCC, an arrangement that would be rendered by CFR or CPT under the Incoterms. It should, however, be noted that the term CFR is sometimes still found in the former style of CF or C&F.

▼ Bribery and Corruption

When companies operate abroad, they face a continuum of choices concerning company ethics. At one extreme, they can refuse to make any compromises with local customs and eschew all forms of extra-contractual payment. At the other extreme, they can abandon any attempt to maintain company ethics and follow local custom in distributing whatever extra-contractual payments are necessary to bring business to a successful conclusion. Between these extremes, companies may select varying degrees of extension of home country ethics. One approach is to make a distinction between payments made in order to secure special and un-justified favors and those made to ensure that officials perform their actual functions. In other words, a bribe to a member of a foreign government in order to secure an order for aircraft is not the same as a bribe to a customs official to secure the clearance of one's goods within a reasonable period.

Bribes to local officials are not illegal under Canadian law but are the subject of international disapproval. The United Nations has drawn up a Draft International Agreement on Illicit Payments that calls for states to make such bribery punishable by appropriate criminal penalties.[80] One country that has heeded this call is the United States. In 1977, it passed the Foreign Corrupt Practices Act (FCPA), which makes it a crime for U.S. corporations to offer bribes in order to obtain or retain business in a foreign country. The FCPA excludes "grease" payments to low-level officials to avoid red tape and expedite normal procedures, such as customs clearance or obtaining permits. A number of persons and corporations have been convicted under the FCPA, and jail sentences in the range of one to five years as well as fines in excess of US$1 million have

---

[80] Art. 1..

been imposed. Opinion is divided as to whether the FCPA has had a negative impact on the export performance of U.S. industry.

SERVICES AND INTERNATIONAL BUSINESS LAW

Trade in goods is trade in objects for their own sake and for the value of the object alone. Trade in services is the transfer of the benefit of an act, either alone or in connection with an object. Intangible services are such acts as entertainment, banking transactions, meals, accommodation, and professional advice. Once the act is over, there is nothing tangible left to which one can point as the object of the transaction. Tangible services are those that are communicated via an object, like entertainment via a video cassette or professional advice via a report, and those that are built into the object, like changing a muffler, duplicating a key, or constructing a power station. In the first instance, the consideration is paid almost entirely for the service that is transmitted via the object; in the second instance, the consideration for the object is higher by the value of the service incorporated.

For the most part, tangible services are traded and encounter the same problems as goods. In this section, therefore, we deal with intangible services, which are traded in one of five ways, as shown in Box 5–4.

Box 5–4
Trading Intangible Services

1. The recipient can come to the provider's home base, as when a person comes to hear a concert in another country or seeks the advice of a local lawyer.
2. The provider can provide the service to the recipient from the home base via telecommunications, as when legal advice is given over the telephone or a concert is enjoyed via television in another country.
3. The provider can provide the service to the recipient in the latter's country on a temporary basis and then return home, as when an entertainer gives a concert abroad or a lawyer pleads a case before a foreign bar.
4. The provider can establish a permanent base in a foreign country from which the recipients are serviced, as when a law firm or bank sets up an office in another country.
5. A local entity can be given a franchise to provide the service under license, which is a common practice in the case of consumer services like restaurants, hotels, etc.

▼ Obstacles to the International Trade in Intangible Services

Prohibition. Prohibitions on the provision of services by foreigners are quite common. They may take the form of a prohibition on offering or receiving the service. Citizenship requirements, lack of access to what is needed to provide the service, or a legal requirement for the recipient to use a domestic provider can also act as prohibitions.

NAFTA eliminates such prohibitions between Mexico, the United States, and Canada, albeit with a number of excepted areas.[81] Prohibitions cannot apply to services that have been listed in a nation's schedule appended to GATS.[82]

Prohibitions will definitely preclude mode 3 (see Box 5–4), but it should be possible to provide the service from home under modes 1 and 2 unless the prohibition operates upon the recipient. Provision of services from a subsidiary in the host country should be possible as long as it is considered a domestic operation. There should be no problems with franchise entry.

Restricted Market Access. There are numerous ways in which access to the market can be restricted for a foreign provider. Quantitative restrictions may limit the foreign provider's number of operations or outlets or volume of business. There may be obstacles placed on the inflow of goods needed for the service to be performed. Access to public telecommunications networks or securities markets or anything else that is absolutely necessary for the provision of the service can be limited. A requirement of a local presence or substantial local capital can also have a restrictive effect.

NAFTA bans most such restrictions within the service sectors to which it applies, but it only provides for future commitments on the abolition of quantitative restrictions.[83] Market access must be guaranteed according to the commitment in a country's GATS schedule.[84] If a service sector is included in a national schedule, there are no quantitative restrictions allowed unless the schedule explicitly so states.

The types of obstacles that restrict market access would probably not affect entry modes 1 and 2 except where they relate to the need for a local presence or capital. They will definitely affect mode 3, and it is possible that even a foreign-owned subsidiary would be subject to some of these restrictions. On the other hand, a franchise operation by a local national would be exempt from market restrictions.

Discrimination. Among the numerous ways to discriminate against foreign providers are higher taxation by disallowing certain deductions that are available to nationals, or by providing subsidies to local providers, or easier access to networks, infrastructure, and advertising. NAFTA requires national treatment of providers between Mexico, the United States, and Canada.[85] GATS also

---

[81] Arts. 1202, 1204.

[82] Art. XVI.

[83] Arts. 1202, 1205, 1207.

[84] Art. XVI.

[85] Art. 1202.

stipulates national treatment in the case of services that are included in a country's schedule.[86]

Discrimination could certainly affect a service provider operating from the home base under modes 1 and 2. It could equally affect mode 3 and possibly mode 4 unless the permanent establishment is considered a domestic operation. Once again, a local franchise operation would not suffer from any discrimination.

Exchange Controls. Exchange controls on the payment of foreign services are not a matter for the IMF. As mentioned earlier, they are prohibited by the OECD, and now also under NAFTA[87] and for scheduled services under GATS.[88] The remittance of dividends, profits, and royalties can also be affected where they originate from a subsidiary or franchise in the host country. Such controls also fall within the scope of NAFTA[89] and the OECD Code, but they are probably not covered by GATS.

Exchange controls have the potential to affect all modes of service entry negatively. Provision of services from a home base under modes 1 and 2 is affected by controls on the provider's access to foreign currency, while inability or difficulty in converting local currency into hard currency affects the provision of services in the host country under modes 3 to 5.

Problems with the Movement of Persons. A common way of providing services is for the provider to enter the host country on a temporary basis. There are, however, many obstacles to such a mode of provision. The foreign provider may need to have local qualifications (which may take years to obtain), register in a local body, and comply with local standards. As such requirements can easily be defended on the basis of public policy, they are validated by both NAFTA and GATS as long as they are not unreasonable or clearly protectionist in nature. However, under GATS, there is provision for countries to place commitments on these matters in their schedule, such as mutual recognition of foreign qualifications or the waiver of local registration requirements.

The foreign provider also needs to be able to enter, reside, and work in the host country on a temporary basis. This need conflicts with the strict regulation of immigration that is practiced by many countries. However, under NAFTA, the three rights of entry, residence and work are granted as long as the provider meets the general immigration requirements of the host country. There are no equivalent provisions in GATS, but the WTO members are supposed to negotiate some commitments by mid-1995 that would be put in their schedules. However, it is unlikely that this timetable will be kept. Clearly, these obstacles relate exclusively to the provision of services under mode 3.

Foreign Direct Investment and Franchising. The rules here are no different than in the case of facilities that are set up for trade in goods. Franchising is similar to licensing except that a whole business system is transferred. Thus, problems with franchising tend to mirror those encountered in licensing and discussed

---

[86] Art. XVII.

[87] Art. 1202:1(b).

[88] This would appear to follow from the footnote to Article XVI.

[89] Art. 1109.

elsewhere. The NAFTA right to FDI extends to services, but there is no express right in GATS to provide services from a permanent establishment in the recipient's country. Neither agreement deals directly with franchising.

Where there are problems or prohibitions with respect to foreign direct investment, this relates exclusively to the provision of services under mode 4. Problems with franchising only affect entry mode 5.

▼ Implementation

Where services are provided from a home base under modes 1 and 2, there is not much legal work that is needed in addition to that required by any service transaction. Temporary entrance in the host country necessitates the regular entry, residency permits, and work permits. This applies within NAFTA as well. There is also the question of qualifications, registration, and standards, as well as customs procedures. There is little point in making the journey if any one of these requirements cannot be met. In the case of foreign direct investment and franchising, implementation entails much the same legal points as in the case of goods.

▼ SUMMARY

This chapter sets out the scope of international business law and its application to both the strategy and implementation of global marketing management. Hopefully, it has helped the reader understand that the legal environment is not just a matter to be left to lawyers and postponed to the very end of the transaction. Law is as important as an input into marketing strategy decisions as it is in the form of implementing procedures. The global marketing manager should seek a better acquaintance with the international legal environment. This chapter is intended to serve as an introduction to — and inspiration for — such a quest.

▼ DISCUSSION QUESTIONS

1. What are the two main systems of national law?

2. What makes up international business law?

3. What are the major issues with respect to standards-related measures?

4. In which different ways do exchange controls and high tariffs impact on market entry decisions?

5. Discuss how national competition laws can affect the format of a licensing agreement.

6. Outline the problems that intellectual property protection poses in international business and how these can be resolved.

7. Describe the major obstacles to the international trade in intangible services and how they impact on the various service entry modes.

▼ BIBLIOGRAPHY

Books

CARBONNEAU,THOMAS E., *Resolving Transnational Disputes Through International Arbitration*. Charlottesville: University of Virginia Press, 1984.

CASTEL, JEAN-GABRIEL, ARMAND L.C. DE MESTRAL AND WILLIAM C. GRAHAM, *The Canadian Law and Practice of International Trade*. Toronto: Emond-Montgomery Press, 1991.

CHRISTOU, RICHARD, *International Agency, Distribution and Licensing Agreements*. London: Longmans, 1986.

DELAUME, GEORGES R., *Law and Practice of Transnational Contracts*. New York: Oceana Publications, 1988.

FEKETEKUTY, GEZA, *International Trade in Services*. New York: Oceana Publications, 1988.

GOODE, ROYSTON M., *Commercial Law*. Hammondsworth: Penguin Books, 1982.

GOVERNMENT OF CANADA, North American Free Trade Agreement. Ottawa: Minister of Supply and Services, 1993.

HOLBEIN, JAMES R. AND DONALD J, MUSCH, *The Practitioner's Deskbook Series: NAFTA*. New York: Oceana Publications, 1994.

HOLTZMANN, HOWARD M. AND JOSEPH E. NEUHAUS, *A Guide to the UNCITRAL Model Law on International Arbitration*. Deventer: Kluwer, 1989.

HONNOLD, JOHN, *Uniform Law for International Sales under the 1980 United Nations Convention*. 2nd. Ed. Deventer: Kluwer, 1991.

LITKA, MICHAEL P., *The International Dimensions of the Legal Environment of Business*. Boston: PWS-Kent, 1988.

RAWORTH, PHILIP M., *The Legal Guide to International Business Transactions*. Toronto: Carswell, 1991.

RAWORTH, PHILIP M. AND LINDA C. REIF, *The Practitioner's Deskbook Series: The Law of the WTO*. New York: Oceana Publications, 1995.

Articles

BERMAN, HAROLD J. AND COLIN KAUFMAN, "The Law of International Commercial Transactions (Lex Mercatoria)," *Harvard International Law Journal*, 1978, 19.

GOTTLIEB, RICHARD S. DEBA P. STEGER AND DAVID H. PEARSON, "Current and Possible Future International Rules Relating to Trade Adjustment Policies — Subsidies, Safeguards, Trade Adjustment Assistance: A View from Canada," *Canada-US Law Journal*, 1988, 14.

HARNIK, HANS, "Recognition and Enforcement of Foreign Arbitral Award," *American Journal of Comparative Law*, 1983, 31.

MORTON, COLLEEN S., "The Impact of the Free Trade Agreement on the Flow of Services Between Canada and the United States", *Canada-US Law Journal*, 1990, 16.

RAWORTH, PHILIP M., "Economic Integration, the GATT and Canada-US Free Trade," *Ottawa Law Review*, 1986, 18.

REIF, LINDA C., "Conciliation as a Mechanism for the Resolution of International Commercial and Business Disputes," *Fordham International Law Journal*, 1990-91, 14.

SIX

Foreign Exchange and Financial Decisions

Introduction

When comparing global and domestic marketing, apparent differences are often matters of degree rather than kind. For example, cultural differences exist among nations, but similar differences also exist within nations. Indeed, it can be argued that the differences among people *within* a country or culture are greater than the differences *between* countries and cultures. Similarly, the basic *function* of money in global marketing is no different than its function in domestic marketing. Money facilitates the specialization of production and exchange of goods and services.

Indeed, without money, international business would be reduced to a pure barter system. Foreign exchange makes it possible to do business across the boundary of a national currency. *However, foreign exchange is an aspect of global marketing that involves certain financial decisions, activities, and risks that are completely different than those facing a domestic marketer.* When business is conducted in a single country, with domestic customers and suppliers paying in the domestic currency, there is no exchange risk.[1] All prices, payments, receipts, assets, and liabilities are in the national currency. However, when a company operates outside the home country, it must deal in foreign exchange. This thrusts the company into the turbulent world of exchange risk, which impacts financial resources and decisions, and even more importantly, pricing strategy. The global marketer is exposed to exchange risk whenever business involves payments or receipts in foreign currencies or the ownership of assets in foreign countries.

For Canadian marketers, our exchange rate with off-shore countries is not a simple reflection of bi-lateral trade and competitiveness, rather the Canadian dollar is valued "through" the U.S. dollar. In other words, foreign currencies are valued against the US$ and the C$'s value relative to the US$ then generates the respective foreign currency exchange rate for our dollar. The US$ is still a powerful international currency and some 61 percent of the world's foreign-exchange reserves and more than one-half of global private financial wealth is held in US$.[2]

---

[1] A notable exception is the risk of financial loss due to fluctuations in the price of agricultural products—corn, wheat, and other commodities—faced by grain dealers in domestic markets. Commodities dealers utilize some of the same types of tools as global marketers (e.g., options and futures discussed later in Chapter 7) to manage this risk.

[2] "Will the buck stop here?", *The Economist* (November 12, 1994) p.88.

TABLE 6–1 U.S. Dollars Required to Buy Canadian Dollars, 1984–1993 (Average annual noon spot rates)	
1985	.7325
1986	.7197
1987	.7541
1988	.8124
1989	.8445
1990	.8570
1991	.8728
1992	.8276
1993	.7753

Source: *Bank of Canada Review* (Winter 1994)
Table I1, p. 592.

This is an important difference for Canadian companies compared to those in any other industrialized country. Our exchange rate with off-shore countries is effectively trilateral.

Customers, the ultimate judges of the success of a company's marketing effort, are seeking value. Value is a function of the relationship between the package of measurable and intangible benefits that customers get from a product and the price of the product. Price is, in part, a function of cost, and foreign exchange rates are an important determinant of a global company's cost position. Table 6–1 shows how the value of a Canadian dollar in terms of U.S. dollars has fluctuated over the ten years to 1993.

From 1980 to 1987, the Canadian dollar had steadily lost value against the U.S. dollar (Table 6–1). Between 1988 and 1991, a marked recovery occurred; however, since then a steady and dramatic decline reduced the value of the Canadian dollar once more. The exchange-risk roller coaster for Canadian business is captured in Table 6–2, which shows major currencies in units of C$.

A low value of the Canadian dollar improves the price competitiveness of Canadian goods in foreign markets and thus helps exports. At the same time, prices of goods imported into Canada—whether wine from France or CD players from Japan—become more expensive. Over the past ten years, the C$ has generally declined in value against the yen, the deutsche mark, and the French franc with a favorable effect on exports, but also putting upward pressure on prices of products imported into Canada. Clearly, foreign exchange rates directly impact the quality and effectiveness of a company's marketing effort, especially in the area of pricing.

While Chapter 3 described the economic environment *within* the countries and regions of the world, this chapter explores the environment comprising the financial agreements, factors, and forces that affect trade relations and marketing opportunities *between* countries. Here, we outline the history and dimensions of the arrangements and forces—formal as well as informal, official as well as private— that make up the global financial system. Global marketers must be familiar with these arrangements and forces, and understand currency risk and exposure, in order to formulate global sourcing and financial strategies. These, in turn, will support global marketing strategies. The driving force and energy of the successful

TABLE 6-2 Canadian Dollar Against Major Currencies, 1984–1993 (Average annual noon spot rates)

	British £	German DM	French Fr	Japanese ¥
1984	1.7300	.4564	.1487	.00546
1985	1.7701	.4677	.1533	.00577
1986	2.0388	.6425	.2010	.00830
1987	2.1725	.7384	.2208	.00919
1988	2.1929	.7028	.2072	.00961
1989	1.9415	.6304	.1858	.00861
1990	2.0808	.7234	.2147	.00809
1991	2.0275	.6934	.2039	.00852
1992	2.1302	.7757	.2288	.00955
1993	1.9372	.7804	.2279	.01165

Source: Bank of Canada Review (Winter 1994) Table I1, p. S92.

company must be marketing, because it is marketing that is focused upon creating value for customers. Managers at global companies must carefully monitor and manage their companies' financial environment—especially foreign exchange—if marketing objectives are to be achieved.

A BRIEF HISTORY OF THE INTERNATIONAL FINANCIAL SYSTEM[3]

▼ 1944–1971

At Bretton Woods, New Hampshire, in 1944, finance ministers and other representatives of the Allied powers met to create an international financial framework that would encourage and support postwar reconstruction and economic growth. In addition to providing for currency convertibility, the architects of the postwar system intended to stimulate trade and investment via orderly adjustment of currency values as a means of maintaining ongoing equilibrium in exchange rate values. A central figure at Bretton Woods was British economist John Maynard Keynes, who advocated the creation of the single international currency, the bancor. The value of world currencies would be established relative to this new international reserve asset, the supply of which would expand in tandem with global economic development. Keynes envisioned the bancor as replacing gold (supplies of which were relatively fixed) and supplementing each nation's individual currency.

Lord Keynes's specific recommendation concerning the bancor was not adopted; the world was apparently not yet ready for "paper gold." There would indeed be a new international reserve asset, but it would consist of gold and various currencies. However, Lord Keynes's broader vision of the creation of a world lending organization

---

[3] A firsthand account of the events described in this section is provided in Paul Volcker and Toyoo Gyohten, *Changing Fortunes: The World's Money and the Threat to American Leadership* (New York: Times Books, 1992).

TABLE 6–3   The Old International Monetary System, 1944–1971

1. Fixed or "pegged" exchange rates. All currencies were "pegged" to the U.S. dollar.
2. Country commitments to maintain fixed or "pegged" exchange within ± 1 percent of the fixed rate.
3. Valuation of the U.S. dollar for official transactions at $35 = one troy ounce of gold. The U.S. government committed to exchange official dollars for gold at a price of $35.00 = one troy ounce of gold. "Official" dollars, that is, dollars held by the central bank of IMF members, could be exchanged for gold at this price. Under this system, the dollar was literally better than gold because you could earn interest on dollar holdings and exchange dollars for gold at any time. If you held gold, you had storage costs and, of course, earned no interest.
4. Official reserves of gold, U.S. dollars, and the IMF position (the latter being a small technical element).
5. Control of adjustment in fixed exchange values by prescribed IMF procedures. In practice, there were infrequent, large devaluations under this system as opposed to smaller percentage adjustments through revaluations as well as devaluations.

was realized. Two new institutions composed the cornerstone for the new financial system that emerged from Bretton Woods. The International Bank for Reconstruction and Development (or IBRD, also known as the World Bank, with headquarters in Washington, DC), was chartered to promote economic development and reconstruction by making loans to war-torn countries. The International Monetary Fund (IMF) was chartered to oversee the management of the international financial system and make currency adjustments.

The main elements of the system, summarized in Table 6–3, were fixed or pegged rates for all currencies, tight bands of fluctuation around the pegged rates, a dollar that was both defined in terms of its gold value and exchangeable for gold, and controlled adjustment of fixed exchange values.

As we discussed in the previous chapter, fixed exchange rates vis-à-vis the U.S. dollar collapsed in 1971 since an accumulation of dollars in exporting countries, and official reserves held by central banks around the world far exceeded the U.S. supply of gold (which, as Keynes had warned, was relatively fixed). The U.S. could no longer honor its commitment to redeem official dollars for gold. The unilateral withdrawl of the U.S. from its promise to redeem official dollars for gold signaled the collapse of the old system of reserve currencies, and the world moved to a new system: the foreign exchange market.[4]

special drawing rights: reserve assets created by the IMF to increase liquidity for international business. Countries can use SDRs to compensate for balance-of-payments deficits.

---

[4] For an excellent discussion, see Andrew Kreiger, *The Money Bazaar: Inside the Trillion-Dollar World of Currency Trading* (New York: Times Books, 1992), Chs. 6 and 8.

▼ Today's System:
Managed Dirty Float with SDRs

The old fixed exchange system has been replaced with a *managed dirty float with SDRs*. What does this mean? *Float* refers to the system of floating or fluctuating exchange rates. In today's system currencies are "up for auction," with rates floating or adjusting in the foreign exchange market subject to all the forces of supply and demand. In other words, the buying and selling activities of currency traders determine a specific currency's value on a given day. *Dirty* refers to the fact that governments participate in the foreign exchange market in an effort to influence exchange rates. The term *dirty* is an allusion to the fact that governments are in the market to influence exchange rates rather than to make money. *Managed* refers to the specific use of fiscal and monetary policy by governments to influence exchange rates.

Special drawing rights (SDRs) were created by the IMF to supplement the dollar and gold as reserves. SDRs are owned reserve assets allocated by the IMF to member countries according to a formula that takes into account share of gross world product, share of world trade, and other factors. SDRs create liquidity and, in so doing, facilitate trade among nations. Participants in the IMF with a balance-of-payments need can use SDRs to obtain currency from other participants designated by the fund. The value of one SDR represents a weighted average of five currencies: the U.S. dollar, the German mark, the French franc, the Japanese yen, and the British pound. In fact, some countries such as Burma, Jordan, and Libya, for example, pursue an exchange rate policy of pegging the value of their currencies to SDRs. The effect of a declining C$ over the past decade had a corresponding effect on SDRs in C$ from 1.327 in 1984 to 1.801 in 1993.

As of June 1992 quotas totaling 91.6 billion SDRs (equivalent to US$135 billion) had been allocated to IMF members; 26.7 billion SDRs have actually been lent. Besides mandating the use of SDRs to help countries deal with balance-of-payments deficits, the IMF also permits a variety of additional uses among participants including settlement of financial obligations, swaps, donations, and security for performance of financial obligations. From 1985 to 1986 there were 46 such transfers totaling SDR 111 million.

Today, 165 countries, including many from the former communist bloc, are IMF members; as of July 1992, nine of the 15 republics of the former Soviet Union had joined. The fund oversees the operation of the international monetary system; exercises surveillance over the exchange rate policies of members; monitors developments in the field of international liquidity and manages the SDR system; provides temporary balance-of-payments assistance to members in external difficulties; and performs a variety of other functions including technical assistance designed to promote effective cooperation in international financial relations.

---

foreign exchange: any currency that is purcased or sold in the foreign exchange market.

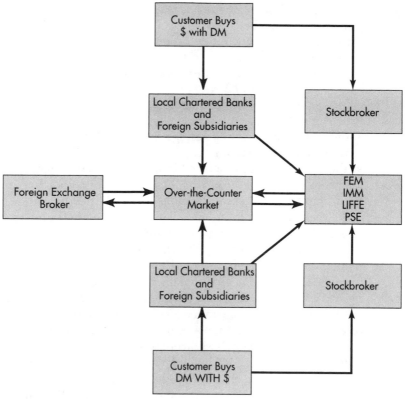

FIGURE 6–1

Structure of Foreign Exchange Markets

NOTE: The Foreign Exchnage Market (FEM) in Montreal and the International Money Market (IMM) in Chicago trade foreign exchange futures and DM futures options. The London International Financial Futures Exchange (LIFFE) trades foreign exchange futures. The Philadelphia Stock Exchange (PSE) trades foreign currency options.

Source: Adapted from *Federal Reserve Bank of St. Louis* (March 1984), p. 9.

FOREIGN EXCHANGE

What is foreign exchange? Is the Canadian dollar foreign exchange? Is the French franc foreign exchange? The answer, of course, is that it depends. If the Canadian dollar is used in Canada, it is not foreign exchange. If it is traded for another currency, it becomes, in that transaction, foreign exchange. Similarly, the French franc in France, or for that matter anywhere else in the world, is still a French franc when it is held by a French resident or citizen. It becomes foreign exchange when it is traded for any other currency and is held by a non-French person or institution.

What is the foreign exchange market? All the people and institutions who buy and sell currency are the foreign exchange market. If you sell dollars to a Russian on the street in Moscow, you have created a retail foreign exchange market right on the spot of the transaction. This is a real foreign exchange market, but it is retail and represents a minute percentage of the total annual trade in foreign exchange. The real foreign exchange market in terms of volume is a wholesale market between banks and institutional traders of foreign exchange. This market is conducted by professional traders at trading desks who are in contact with each other via telephone and on-line real-time monitors that track transactions and bid and offer prices for various currencies.

The principal players in the foreign exchange market are the Canadian chartered banks, who account for nearly two-thirds of all the foreign exchange turnover in Canada.[5] Other players include brokerage houses with "over the counter" transactions, the Foreign Exchange Market in Montreal (FEM) for futures and options exchange contracts, as well as other international traders such as the International Monetary Market (IMM) in Chicago, the London Financial Futures Exchange (LIFFE), and the Philadelphia Stock Exchange (PSE). The relationship among these institutions is shown in Figure 6–1.

The *spot market* is for immediate delivery or, in the interbank market, for delivery within two business days of the transaction. The market for future delivery is called the *forward market*. The volume of trading in the foreign exchange market is enormous. According to most estimates, global turnover in the market exceeds C$900 billion a day, making it the world's largest financial market. These figures are so huge it is hard to get a handle on them. For example, in any two weeks, foreign exchange traders do as much business as importers and exporters of goods and services do in a year.[6] The three major markets and their average daily turnover in April 1989 were: London (C$210 billion), New York (C$150 billion) and Tokyo (C$140 billion). Each market has its own focus: London is $/£ (30 percent), New York is $/DM (34 percent), and Tokyo is $/¥ (82 percent).[7]

Thus, the foreign exchange market consists literally of a buyer's and a seller's market where currencies are traded for both spot and future delivery on a continuous basis. As such, this market represents one example of a true market where prices are based on the combination of forces of supply and demand that come into play at the moment of any transaction. A currency in this market is worth what people are willing to pay for it and what they are willing to sell it for.

▼ Foreign Exchange Market Dynamics

Figure 6–2 shows a supply curve of Canadian dollars and two demand schedules for dollars by holders of German deutsche marks. In the example, demand moves from D_1 to D_2, with a resultant increase in the price of dollars from 1.00 to 2.00 deutsche marks. In this example, we assume that the supply of dollars is constant and that for various reasons the demand for dollars by holders of deutsche

---

[5] "Central Bank Survey of Foreign Exchange Market Activity in April 1992," *Bank of International Settlements*, Monetary and Economic Department, Basle (March 1993) Table. VI, p. 21

[6] George Anders, "Answers to Commonly Asked Questions About Currency Trading in a Wild Week," *The Wall Street Journal*, September 17, 1992, p. A7.

[7] "The Currency Carousel," *The Economist* (August 23, 1986) p. 64, "The Economist Survey: Financial Centers," *The Economist* (June 27, 1992) p. 4.

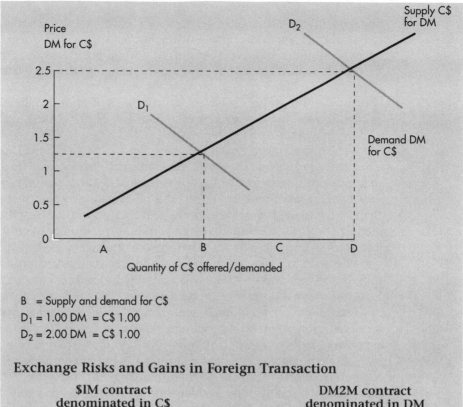

B = Supply and demand for C$
D_1 = 1.00 DM = C$ 1.00
D_2 = 2.00 DM = C$ 1.00

Exchange Risks and Gains in Foreign Transaction

	$1M contract denominated in C$			DM2M contract denominated in DM	
DM/C$ Exchange Rate DM	*Canada Seller receives*	*Germany Buyer pays in C$*		*Canada Seller receives*	*Germany Buyer pays in*
2.00	$1 mill.	DM.500 mill.		$1 mill.	DM2mill.
1.50	1 mill.	.666 mill.		1.3 mill.	2 mill.
1.00	1 mill.	1.00 mill.		2 mill.	2 mill.

FIGURE 6–2
The Foreign Exchange Market (DM=deutsche marks)

marks increases from quantity *B* to quantity *D*. Such an increase in demand could result from a multiplicity of factors, for example, a major shift in German consumer preferences from domestic and other foreign sports equipment to equipment imported from Canada, or a desire on the part of German investors to shift their assets and wealth from Germany to Canada because of concerns about the political stability and future security of investments in Germany, or a response by German investors to high interest rates in Canada, or a belief by holders of DMs that the dollar will gain in strength and the DM will lose in value, or a host of other factors. If the net effect of such factors is an increase in demand for dollars, all other things being equal, the price of the dollar will rise. This is known as a revaluation of the dollar and a devaluation of the deutsche mark.

The price of one currency in any other currency is the result of the forces of supply and demand expressed in the foreign exchange market. The foreign exchange market itself consists of traders operating principally by telephone engaging in transactions to meet customer requirements with their counterparts in banks and foreign exchange trading houses around the world. These foreign exchange traders are operating during normal business hours in every world time zone, with the result that foreign exchange trading activity is being conducted on a 24-hour basis every day of the year. When traders in Europe conclude their work at the end of a business day, the basis of prices for their trading on the following working day will be established in North America, then Australia and Japan while they are sleeping.

The purchases and sales in the foreign exchange market represent supply and demand of each of the world's traded currencies deriving from actual trade in goods and services, as well as short- and long-term capital flows and speculative purchases and sales. To the extent that a country sells more than it buys, there will be a greater demand for its currency and a tendency for it to appreciate in value. If the foreign exchange market were influenced only by purchases and sales to support actual trade in goods and services, it would be a rather simple matter to forecast foreign exchange rates. Unfortunately, there are many other forces and motives that affect buying and selling currencies. Short- and long-term capital flows and speculative purchases and sales are a major source of supply and demand for foreign exchange. Short-term capital is sensitive to interest rates, long-term capital to return expectations, and both are sensitive to perceptions of risk.

Governments intervene regularly in the foreign exchange market to either support or depress the price of their own or other currencies. Government intervention is normally aimed at dampening the fluctuations in foreign exchange rates or attempting to influence over the short and medium term the actual exchange rate. For example, many governments are reluctant to see the value of their currency appreciate because their exporters fear the effects that rising exchange value will have on their price competitiveness in foreign markets. In response to this basic domestic pressure, governments engage in extensive trading to stem the rise in their own currency value.

While government efforts in the long run will not prevail against fundamental economic or political factors, they can have a definite effect on exchange values in the short and medium run.

▼ Forecasting Foreign Exchange Rates

Foreign exchange rate forecasting is one of the most hazardous tasks imaginable. The reason for the difficulty in forecasting foreign exchange rates is simple: There are a multitude of factors and forces which determine rates, and many of these factors and forces are not quantifiable. Any forecast of exchange rates is necessarily a combination of economic analysis and judgment.

> **purchasing power parity:** an economic principle stating that a change in the relationship between price levels in two different countries will require an adjustment in the currency exhange rate to offset the price-level difference.

Purchasing Power Parity

One of the most important and durable of all the economic fundamentals that must be considered in forecasting foreign exchange rates is purchasing power parity (PPP). This venerable concept holds that from an equilibrium exchange rate, a change in the relationship between domestic and foreign price levels will require an adjustment in the currency exchange rate to offset the price level difference. According to this principle, if inflation causes price levels to go up in country *A* while prices remain the same in country *B*, then the currency in country *A* should be devalued relative to the currency in country *B*. In plain English, PPP means that, if country *A* experiences inflation while country *B* does not, one unit of currency *A* will no longer buy the goods and services in equivalent amounts in country *B* unless the currency in country *B* is revalued (i.e., increases in value) by the same amount as the rate of inflation in country *A*.

The lower or higher a country's rate of inflation as compared to the world's rate, the greater will be the purchasing power parity effect. If prices in local currency rise faster or more slowly than prices in the rest of the world, an equal adjustment of the exchange value of the currency in the opposite direction will restore equilibrium to correct relative price levels. For example, if a Mercedes 220 costs DM51,000 and the exchange rate is DM1.50 = C\$1, the Mercedes 220 will cost C\$34,000. If there is a zero rate of inflation in Germany and a 20 percent rate of inflation in Canada, an exchange rate of DM 1.25 = C\$1 would restore equilibrium. This is because inflation would result in the Mercedes 220 costing C\$40,800 (C\$34,000 × 120 percent—the Canadian rate of inflation), and at the new exchange rate, C\$40,800 is still equal to DM51,000 (40,800 × 1.25 = 51,000). Since the Canadian money supply would have expanded by 20 percent, the new exchange value of the deutsche mark would insure that 1.2 units of the depreciated dollar would buy the same amount of goods that 1 unit of the pre-inflationary dollar could purchase, for example, the Mercedes that left the factory in Germany with a sticker price of DM51,000.

To take another example, assume that the rate of exchange between Germany and Canada is DM1.50 = C\$1. Assume that the rate of inflation in Canada is 10 percent per year, and that the rate of inflation in Germany is zero. According to PPP, the exchange rate after one year ($t + 1$) would be DM1.35 = C\$1 or DM1.50 = C\$1.10. To a German, what could be purchased in Canada at t for DM1.50 would cost DM1.65 *if there were no adjustment in the exchange rate.* An appreciation of the deutsche mark in the foreign exchange market by 10 percent would exactly offset the Canadian 10 percent rate of inflation so that the latter would have no effect on the deutsche mark's purchasing power in Canada. Similarly, in t a Canadian could purchase DM1.50 worth of goods in Germany for \$1.00. One year later, at $t + 1$, DM1.50 would cost a Canadian or a holder of dollars C\$1.10. A German seller of a DM1.50 product will receive C\$1.10, which exactly offsets the effect of Canadian inflation. The purchasing power of C\$1.10 in $t + 1$ = the purchasing power of C\$1.00 at t. The exchange rate offsets the impact of differential inflation rates to maintain a purchasing power constant for each currency.

A similar approach to purchasing power parity compares world prices for a single well-known product: McDonald's Big Mac hamburger. The so-called

TABLE 6–4 Big Mac Hamburger Index Selected Countries, April 1994 Purchasing Power Parity

Country	Price in Local Currency	Implied PPP of the Dollar	Canadian Equivalent	Actual C$ Exchange Rate	Over/Under C$ Valuation
Canada	C$ 2.86	-	2.86	-	-
France	FFr 18.5	6.46	4.41	4.19	+ 54%
Germany	DM 4.60	1.60	3.73	1.23	+ 30%
Italy	Lite 4.550	1590	3.85	1180	+ 34%
Japan	¥ 391	136	5.22	74.8	+ 82%
Chile	peso 948	331	3.19	297	+ 11%
Czech Republic	Kys 50	17.48	2.37	21.07	- 7%
Brazil	Cr $1500	524	2.23	672	- 12%
Russia	rble 2900	1013	2.27	1274	- 11%
Malaysia	M$ 3.77	1.31	1.40	2.69	- 51%

Source: Adapted from "Big Mac Currencies", *The Economist,* April 9th, 1994, p. 88 and "Financial Indicators" and "Emerging Market Indicators", *The Economist,* April 9th, 1994, pp. 115–116.

Big Mac index is a "quick and dirty" way of determining which of the world's currencies are too weak or strong. The underlying assumption is that the price of a Big Mac in any world currency should, after being converted to dollars, equal the price of a Big Mac in Canada. Any country where the Big Mac price (converted to C$) is higher than the Canadian price would have an overvalued currency; conversely any country where the price is lower than the Canadian price would have an undervalued currency.

Table 6–4 shows the Big Mac index for selected countries in April, 1994. The first column of figures shows the price of a Big Mac in the local currency. The second column shows the implied PPP of the Canadian dollar, obtained by dividing the local currency price by the dollar price. Thus, for example, in Germany a Big Mac costs DM4.60, yielding a Big Mac PPP of 1.60 (4.60 ÷ 2.86 = 1.60). Note that the DM/C$ exchange rate at the time was only 1.23 to 1, meaning that C$2.86 would be the equivalent of DM3.73, not enough to buy a Big Mac in Frankfurt. Thus, we can see that the C$ is undervalued against the DM by about 30 percent. In other words, based on the Canadian price for a Big Mac, the DM/C$ exchange rate ought to be 1.60 to 1, not 1.23 to 1. As you can see from the table, the C$ appears most undervalued against the Japanese yen and the French franc and overvalued against the Malaysian dollar.

When countries are judged according to PPP, which is often done compared to the U.S., as shown in Table 6–5, Canada ranks as the second most properous nation in the world. Note that Canada does not make the top ten list if standard of living is measured in terms of per capita GDP—it is in 11th place with $18,834.

If foreign exchange transactions were concluded solely to provide exchange for purchases of goods and services (i.e., the current account of the balance of payments) and if rates of inflation were easily predictable, PPP would be a reliable and useful predictor of the foreign exchange rate. To forecast exchange rates, one would need only to forecast differential rates of price inflation. Unfortunately, the

TABLE 6–5 Purchasing Power and Per Capita GDP with PPP Compared

Purchasing Power (US = 100)		Per Capita GDP (US $)	
1. United States	100.0	1. Switzerland	$27,748
2. Canada	92.5	2. Bermuda	23,793
3. Switzerland	87.0	3. Iceland	23,640
4. Norway	84.4	4. Japan	23,325
5. Iceland	79.0	5. Norway	21,724
6. Luxembourg	79.0	6. Finland	21,156
7. Kuwait	78.6	7. Sweden	22,155
8. Sweden	76.9	8. Denmark	20,988
9. Denmark	74.2	9. United States	19,815
10. West Germany	73.8	10. West Germany	19,815

Data Source: The Economist's Book of Vital World Statistics, 1990, pp. 40–41.

current account of the balance of payments is not the sole measure of demand and supply of foreign exchange, and rates of inflation are not easy to predict.

An example from the U.S. shows the risk in anticipating exchange rates. Between 1980 and 1985, in spite of growing deficits on the current account of the balance of payments, the U.S. dollar continued to soar in value in foreign exchange markets. This was contrary to PPP theory, and foreign exchange traders who based their purchases on PPP suffered major losses. During this period, it was a case of the dog's tail (capital movements) wagging the dog (current account of the balance of payments). According to PPP, the dog is the current account of the balance of payments, and the capital account is the tail.

Factors Influencing Currency Value in Foreign Exchange Markets

There are a host of factors that impact the foreign exchange rate of currency. In addition to PPP, they include economic factors related to a country's fiscal, monetary, and economic policies. Economic policy and performance that create a rate of economic growth that is higher than the world average will over the long run increase the exchange value of a country's currency. The best examples of currencies reflecting this fact are the Japanese yen and the German mark. Although it is not yet apparent, this fundamental economic law will be reflected in the exchange value of the Korean won, the Taiwan dollar, and the currency of any other country that is growing in real terms faster than the world's average rate of growth.

Another important economic factor is interest rate as compared to world averages. If the real rate of interest in a country (real interest is the nominal rate of interest minus the rate of inflation) is higher than the interest rate in comparable countries, this will attract capital, create demand for the country's currency, and will put upward pressure on the currency value in the foreign exchange market. This was exactly the case in the fall of 1992, when the strength of the German mark led to chaos in the currency trading world.

Another economic factor is the importance of a currency in the world financial system. A key currency, such as the U.S. dollar, is less subject to eco-

TABLE 6–6 Factors Influencing Currency Value in Foreign Exchange Markets

Economic Factors

1. Balance of payments.
2. Nominal and real interest rates.
3. Domestic inflation.
4. Monetary and fiscal policies.
5. Estimate of international competitiveness, present and future.
6. Foreign exchange reserves.
7. Attractiveness of country currency and assets, both financial and real.
8. Government controls and incentives.
9. Importance of currency in world finance and trade.

Political Factors

10. Philosophies of political party and leaders.
11. Proximity of elections or change in leadership.

Expectational or Psychological Factors

12. Expectations and opinions of analysts, traders, bankers, economists, and businesspeople.
13. Forward exchange market prices.

The Bottom Line

The bottom line for all of the preceding factors is that foreign exchange rates are determined by transactions reflecting the sum total of all of the motives, reasons, and beliefs behind currency supply and demand. The intersection of the supply and the demand is the foreign exchange rate.

nomic laws, such as purchasing power parity, because it is held by individuals, companies, and countries for many purposes. The willingness to hold the dollar creates a demand source that impacts its exchange market value.

Political factors are important determinants of currency value. These include the country's political situation, especially the philosophy of the party in power and the proximity of elections.

In the short run, perhaps the most important factors impacting currency value are expectative or psychological factors, or what analysts and traders *believe* is going to happen. This is a psychological/speculative factor because it really amounts to what analysts and traders believe other analysts and traders believe is going to happen. This is why most traders of foreign exchange do not pay a great deal of attention to the so-called fundamentals. They believe that all information about the value of a commodity can be read on the screen or tape.

Notwithstanding the short-run factors and the attitudes of traders that influence exchange rates, the fundamentals cannot be avoided. A country's ability to purchase foreign goods and services is based on its ability to earn foreign exchange. If that ability is limited, its ability to maintain its exchange value will be limited. Table 6–6 is a partial list of factors that impact foreign exchange rates.

TABLE 6–7 Balance Sheet of MyCorp International-France, June 30, 1994

Cash	FFr1,000,000	Debt	FFr5,000,000
Accounts receivable	3,000,000	Equity	6,000,000
Plant and equipment	5,000,000		
Inventory	2,000,000		
	FFr11,000,000		FFr11,000,000

Dollar translation on June 30, 1994 FFr4 = $1

Cash	$250,000	Debt	$1,250,000
Accounts receivable	750,000	Equity	1,500,000
Plant and equipment	1,250,000		
Inventory	500,000		
	$2,750,000		$2,750,000

Dollar translation on July 1, 1994 FFr5 = $1

Cash	$200,000	Debt	$1,000,000
Accounts receivable	600,000	Equity	1,200,000
Plant and equipment	1,000,000	Currency	
Inventory	400,000	Equity	
	$2,200,000		$2,200,000

Source: Adapted from Michael Melvin, *International Money and Finance,* 2nd ed. (New York: Harper & Row, 1989), pp. 100–101. Reprinted by permission of HarperCollins Publishers, Inc.

BUSINESS IMPLICATIONS OF EXCHANGE RATE FLUCTUATIONS[8]

▼ Exchange Rate Exposure

Exchange rate exposure (sometimes called exchange risk exposure) refers to the degree to which a company is affected by exchange rate changes. There are two categories of exposure: translation (also known as accounting exposure), and economic exposure.

Translation/Accounting Exposure

The measure of the degree to which exchange rate fluctuations affect a company's book value and earnings when financial statements of global operations are consolidated and stated in the company's home currency is known as translation exposure. Translation exposure is relevant for companies with subsidiary or joint-venture operations in foreign markets and occurs because of an accounting fundamental: Balance sheet accounts (i.e., assets and liabilities) must balance. Owner's equity is the key to keeping liabilities in balance with assets. If the foreign currency has weakened between the date reflected on the foreign balance sheet and the date the foreign balance sheet is consolidated with home-country financial documents, the value of every item listed as an asset on the for-

---

[8]This section draws heavily on Chapters 8, 9, 10, 11 in Alan C. Shapiro, *Multinational Financial Management,* 3rd ed. (Boston: Allyn and Bacon, 1989).

eign balance sheet will decrease; owner's equity must decrease as well to keep the accounts in balance. This means a decrease in the book value of the company in terms of home-country financial statements. Of course, the converse is also true: If the foreign currency strengthens relative to the home-country currency, owner's equity, and thus book value, will increase.

Table 6–7 shows the situation for a hypothetical Canadian company and its French subsidiary when the foreign currency weakens against the dollar. The Canadian financial statements show assets and liabilities balancing at $2,750,000 when the French statements are translated at an exchange rate of FFr4 = $1 on June 30, 1994. However, if the French franc weakens on July 1, the Canadian financial statements will have to reflect the adjustment; the new figure of $2,200,000 reflects the drop in book value due to exchange rate fluctuations.

Foreign currency translations by Canadian firms must adhere to generally accepted accounting principles. The Canadian Institute of Chartered Accountants (CICA) issued a standard, known as Section 1650, which requires that all foreign-country balance sheets accounts be translated at the currency exchange rates prevailing at the date reflected on the home-country balance sheet.

It is important to remember that translation exposure simply reflects accounting reports of the value of foreign operations. Book value, however, does not really say anything about a company's future cash flows. Cash flow issues that stem from fluctuating currencies have a direct influence on company investment decisions, as well as decisions regarding markets and production.

▼ Operating Exposure

The degree to which exchange rate fluctuations affect a company's market value as measured by its stock price (recall that translation exposure impacts a company's book value rather than its market value) is known as operating or economic exposure. Operating exposure is the impact of currency fluctuations on the present value, hence, the purchasing power of a company's expected future cash flows. The change in value depends upon the impact of exchange rate changes on sales, costs, and prices. Operating exposure can be further divided into two categories: transaction exposure and real operating exposure.

Transaction Exposure

Transaction exposure measures changes in the value of existing financial obligations as a result of exchange rate change. Companies with substantial sales revenues from foreign operations and markets may be affected by exchange rate movements. For example, during a period of an appreciating Canadian dollar, companies would seek to protect themselves against lower sales revenues through foreign exchange trading (see next section). Table 6-8 lists selected companies with over US$1 billion annual sales that also derive one-third or more of those sales outside the home country. Obviously, currency exposure is a critical issue for Nestlé, with nearly 99 percent of annual sales taking place outside Switzerland. Smaller companies are equally sensitive to foreign exchange rates and need not only be aware of the exposure but also take action to protect their sales revenue from foreign markets.

TABLE 6–8 Selected Companies With One-Third or More of Sales Outside the Home Country

Company	Home Country	Total Sales (US$ billion)	% of Sales Outside Home Country
Nestlé	Switzerland	32.9	98.8
Philips	Netherlands	30.0	94.0
Unilever	Great Britain/ Netherlands	35.3	75.0
Canon	Japan	9.4	69.0
Sony	Japan	16.3	66.0
Gilette	United States	3.8	65.0
Colgate	United States	5.0	64.0
Falconbridge	Canada	1.5	62.0
Cominco	Canada	1.1	61.0
IBM	United States	62.7	59.0
3M	United States	12.0	46.0
Coca Cola	United Stated	9.0	45.0
Inco	Canada	2.5	45.0
Noranda	Canada	6.8	41.0
Magna	Canada	1.9	40.0
Bombardier	Canada	2.5	35.0

Source: Company reports and *Report on Business Magazine,* April 1993.

Real operating exposure arises when currency fluctuations, together with price changes, can alter a company's future revenues and costs. In this sense, the firms that face operating exposures include not only those that have overseas operations but also those whose manufacturing plan calls for sourcing goods abroad. Economic exposure arises whenever companies commit to setting up new-product development centers and distribution systems, getting foreign supply, or installing foreign production facilities.

In dealing with the economic exposure introduced by currency fluctuation, the key issue is the company's ability to use price as a strategic tool for maintaining its profit margins. Can the company adjust its product prices in various markets given a rise or fall of foreign exchange rates? The ability to adjust the selling prices depends on the price elasticity of the demand for the company's products or services. The less price sensitive the demand, the greater the price flexibility a company has in responding to exchange rate changes. Price elasticity, in turn, depends on the degree of competition and the location of the competitors.

MANAGING EXCHANGE RATE EXPOSURE

As we saw earlier in this chapter, it is very difficult to accurately forecast the movement of exchange rates. Over the years, the search for other ways of managing cash flows to eliminate or reduce exchange rate risks has resulted in the development of numerous techniques. Such techniques fall into two categories: techniques that are used to reduce the transactions and translation exposures, and the techniques that are used to reduce the real operating exposure.

▼ Tools for Managing Transaction Exposure

Hedging

Hedging exchange rate exposure involves establishing an offsetting currency position such that the loss or gain of one currency position is offset by a corresponding gain or loss in some other currency. A basic rule of thumb is this: If you predict that the value of the foreign currency will weaken against the home currency, a hedge to protect against potential transaction losses is the way to go. Conversely, if you expect the foreign currency to appreciate or strengthen against the home currency, then you can expect a gain, rather than a loss, on foreign transactions when converting them into the home currency. Given this situation, you may decide not to hedge at all.

External hedging methods for managing both transaction and translation exposure involve an outside institution, namely, the foreign currency market. Specific hedging tools include forward contracts and currency options. Internal hedging methods include price-adjustment clauses, borrowing or lending in foreign currencies, and offsetting purchases and sales in a foreign currency.

Forward Market Hedge

The forward market is a mechanism for buying and selling currencies at a pre-set prices for future delivery. If it is known that a certain amount of foreign currency is going to be paid out or received at some future date, a company can insure itself against exchange loss by buying or selling forward. With a forward contract, the company can lock in a specific fixed exchange rate for a future date and thus immunize itself from the loss (or gain) caused by the exchange rate fluctuation. By consulting any published source (such as the *Globe and Mail*'s or *The Financial Post*'s foreign exchange section), you can determine exchange rates on any given day. In addition to spot prices, one, two, three, six, and twelve months forward rates are quoted for the major currencies.

In the first half of the 1980s, the Canadian dollar rose in value against the world's currencies. Consider, for example, the case of a Canadian exporter selling to a customer in Germany under a DM-denominated contract. At the beginning of 1983, the deutsche mark/Canadian dollar exchange rate was DM1.9447/C$1. If the Canadian exporter anticipated receiving DM10 million by the end of 1983, the dollar value of the deal would have been C$5.142 million (DM10 million/C$1.9447). However, by the end of 1983 the dollar had strengthened against the mark, to DM2.2050/C$1. Thus, those DM10 million were only worth C$4.535 million, and the exporter would have faced a C$607,000. transaction loss.

The exporter could have turned to the forward market at the beginning of 1983 to hedge the dollar value of the German receivables due at year's end. The company could have locked in at a twelve-months rate of DM2.0127/C$1, a rate that reflected the predictions of many forecasters that the dollar would appreciate in 1983 (which, in fact, it did do). Note that, at the prevailing forward rate in January 1983, our exporter would have done well, covering nearly three-quarters of the potential losses from a weaker mark by hedging. The exporter would have received C$4.968 million for the DM10 million, a price that was actually C$433,000 more than the dollar amount originally expected at the actual 1983 year-end exchange rate.

Often, the Canadian exporter would also look at the forward rates for the foreign currency in terms of both, the C$ and the US$, the Canadian/U.S. spot rate of the day, and the US$ forward rate in C$. Thus, the cross-rates of C$ and US$ may influence whether to purchase forward contracts in C$ or US$.

Foreign Currency Options

Companies use the forward market when the currency exposure is known in advance, for example, when a firm contract of sale exists. In some situations, however, companies are not certain about the future foreign currency cash inflow or outflow and, thus, techniques such as forward contracts are inappropriate. Consider the risk exposure of a U.S. company that bids for a foreign project but won't know if the project will be granted until sometime later. The company needs to protect the dollar value of the contract by hedging the *potential* foreign currency cash inflow that will be generated if the company turns out to be the winning bidder.

A foreign currency *option* is an alternative for such situations. A *put option* gives the buyer the right, not the obligation, to sell a specified number of foreign currency units to the option seller at a fixed price, up to the option's expiration date. (Conversely, a *call option* is the right, but not the obligation, to buy the foreign currency). In the example of bidding the foreign project, the company can take out a put to sell the foreign currency for the home-country currency at a set price in the future. In other words, the company locks in the value of the contract in the home-country currency. Thus, if the project is awarded, the future foreign currency cash inflow has been hedged by means of the put option. If the project is *not* awarded, the company can trade the put option in the option market without exercising it; remember, options are rights, not obligations. The only money the company stands to lose is the difference between what it paid for the option and what it received upon selling it.

Companies may choose to manage foreign exchange exposure in either one or both directions. Gennum Corporation, which markets its integrated circuits globally, derives 88 percent of its revenues outside of Canada, and 41 percent outside of North America.[9] The company invoices all of its off-shore sales in Canadian dollars and so effectively eliminates any foreign exchange exposure of its revenues. Other companies use different approaches. For example, Avon, the direct-sales cosmetics company, has mapped out two strategies. The first calls for using forward contracts to cover not only the amount to be expatriated from the United Kingdom, Japan, Germany, and other markets, but also a certain portion of profits forecast for the coming year. The second strategy calls for hedging half of the exposure in the forward market and half with options.

Risk Shifting. Financial officers of global firms can avoid transaction exposure altogether by demanding a particular currency as the payment for its foreign sales (for example, Gennum Corporation, which demands C$ as the payment currency for its off-shore sales). This, however, does not eliminate currency risk; it simply shifts the risk to the customer. In common practice, companies prefer

---

[9]Annual Report, Gennum Corporation, (Burlington, 1993) p.15.

to invoice exports (receivables) in strong currencies and imports (payables) in weak currencies. However, in today's highly competitive world market, this practice may reduce a company's competitive advantage vis-à-vis a competitor who is willing to carry transaction exposure in order to gain competitive advantage.

Exposure Netting. Exposure netting is a portfolio approach to hedging, which involves offsetting the currency exposure with offsetting exposures in the same or different currency. Exposure netting involves one of three possibilities. First, a firm can offset a long position in a currency with a short position in that same currency. For example, one operating unit of the company may have more yen than it needs (i.e., it is "long" in yen), while another unit may have payables denominated in yen (i.e., it is "short" in yen). The company can save the expenses associated with buying pounds through a bank by shifting funds internally. Second, if the exchange rate movements of the two currencies are positively correlated, then a long position in one currency can be offset with a short position in the other. Finally, if the currency movements are negatively correlated, then two short (or long) positions can be used to offset each other.

▼ Managing Translation Exposure

The forward contract and exposure netting methods described previously can also be used to hedge translation exposure. In addition, companies can use the method of adjusting fund flows among the affiliates to hedge the translation exposures. The essential idea behind the fund adjustment is to increase hard-currency assets (likely to appreciate) and decrease soft-currency liabilities (likely to depreciate), at the same time decreasing the hard-currency liability and increasing the soft-currency liability. For example, if a local currency appears likely to devaluate, companies can reduce their exchange rate loss by reducing the level of local currency cash, tighten credit terms to decrease accounts receivable, increase local currency borrowing, delay accounts payable, and so on. Following is a list of actions which can be taken by a company in the case of local currency depreciation.

- ► Sell local currency forward.
- ► Reduce levels of local currency cash and marketable securities.
- ► Tighten credit (reduce local currency receivables).
- ► Delay collection of hard-currency receivables.
- ► Increase imports of hard-currency goods.
- ► Borrow locally.
- ► Adjust transfer prices on the sale of goods between affiliates.
- ► Delay payment of accounts payable.
- ► Speed up dividend and fee remittances to parent and other subsidiaries.
- ► Speed up payment of intersubsidiary accounts payable.
- ► Delay collection of intersubsidiary accounts payable.
- ► Invoice exports in foreign currency and imports in local currency.

    The opposite can be done if the local currency is expected to appreciate.

▼ Managing Economic Exposure

Economic exposure to exchange rate risk is based on the sensitivity of company's projected currency inflows and outflows over a specified time period to the combination of exchange rate changes and inflation. Economic exposure exists not only on those known incomes and expenses (such as maturing receivables and payables; confirmed orders and purchases; principal and interest of corporate debts, and dividend payments), but also with those that are expected on the basis of the company's future worldwide capital investment, sales, and sourcing plans for material and labor.

Pricing Strategy

In factoring exchange rate changes into companies' pricing strategies, two key questions to answer are: (1) Should market share or profit maximization be emphasized; and (2) how frequently should prices be adjusted?

Market Share versus Profit Margin. Following an appreciation of the home currency or, equivalently, a depreciation of foreign currency, companies may have to consider increasing the foreign currency prices of their products sold overseas to recover some the profit losses due to exchange rate shifts. But in those same countries where currencies have depreciated, overseas producers in the same industry will now have a competitive cost advantage. They can use that advantage to expand market share by maintaining, or increasing only slightly, their local currency prices. Thus, it is unlikely that the exporting company will be able to raise its product prices by the full extent of the foreign currency devaluation. When overseas competitors hold the line on prices, the exporter will be forced to absorb a percentage of the reduction in home currency revenues to maintain the market share.

This was exactly the situation faced by Japanese automobile manufacturers in the North American market. In 1985, the U.S. dollar, and the Canadian dollar began a decline against the yen and other currencies. By late 1986, the yen had appreciated nearly 50 percent and the price advantage, enjoyed by Japanese imports because of the strong dollar, had disappeared. Japanese car makers, such as Toyota, Honda, and Nissan coped with this challenge by raising their North American prices about 15 percent, lowering manufacturing costs, and absorbing the remaining currency exposure in lower profits.[10] This would have been an opportunity for the Big Three to hold the line on prices and thus increase their market share. Instead, Ford, GM, and Chrysler raised their prices in step with their Japanese competitors and thus opted for higher corporate profits rather than higher market share. The Japanese share of the car market continued to increase rather than decrease as a result of the exchange rate.

In the situation of home currency devaluation, an exporter can gain a competitive price advantage on the world market by reducing prices and expanding market share (penetration pricing). Note that companies do not have to reduce export prices by the full amount of the devaluation of home currency. For that matter, they don't have to reduce export prices at all; another option is increasing

---

[10] Paul Ingrassia and Damon Darlin, "Tokyo's Troubles: Japanese Auto Makers Find the Going Tough Because of Yen's Climb," *The Wall Street Journal*, December 15, 1986, p. 1.

unit profitability (price skimming). The factors that influence the decisions include the persistence of the exchange rate changes, economies of scale, the cost structure of expanding output, price elasticity of product demand, and the likelihood of attracting competition if high unit profiability is obvious.

Indeed, the price cushion generated by the lower home market currency may allow the exporter to use price as a strategic variable. A lower product price in the host market may increase sales volume. Extra profits can be invested in expanding sales staff and dealer promotion in an effort to gain wider distribution.

Frequency of Price Adjustments. The frequency of price adjustments depends on the length of time that the real foreign exchange rate change is expected to persist. A general rule of thumb is that movements in the exchange rate toward equilibrium of purchase power parity are likely to be longer lasting than the movements away from the equilibrium.

While companies can adjust the prices in response to the exchange rate changes, the ability and willingness to adjust prices are two different things. Many companies view the stability of prices over a period of time as a good way to maintain loyalty of their distributors and customers. For companies that are selling through catalogs, it is essential to keep prices stable because of the long lead time required to prepare and distribute catalogs.

Advance planning in adjusting prices is particularly important if price controls are expected to follow a currency devaluation. One way to deal with price controls without risking loss of market share is to raise list prices but continue selling at existing prices, or selling at a discount of raised list prices. Price control can be avoided by eliminating part or all of the discount. Another way of avoiding price controls is to develop alternative products, which are only slightly different from existing product, and sell them at the higher prices. For example, a product Model 86B could be replaced with the Model 88TX. The two products could be functionally identical, but with a different name, catalog number, and designation, and the newer model could be priced differently than its predecessor.

Never before in history has the financial environment of business offered so many opportunities, financial resources, techniques, and instruments to support and sustain creative marketing strategies. The world's financial markets have demonstrated there is a virtually infinite supply of financial resources to support creative business strategy. It is important to remember that the core of a company's business strategy is its marketing strategy. In today's financial environment, a company with a sound marketing plan should be able get the financial resources needed to implement the plan.

▼ SUMMARY

The international financial system is continually evolving. Today's system is based on floating exchange rates where exchange values are established by the market forces of supply and demand. The factors that determine the ultimate levels of supply and demand for exchange are numerous, interrelated, and in a word, complex. Forecasting foreign exchange value is extremely difficult in the present financial environment.

The implications of fluctuating exchange rates for companies who do not wish to expose themselves to exchange risk can in effect sell the risk (or purchase cover for the risk) by using various hedging techniques.

The financial resources of the world are truly an example of the principle of infinite supply. Any company with a sound marketing strategy and plan should be able to obtain the financial resources needed to implement them.

▼ DISCUSSION QUESTIONS

1. You are exporting to country X. Assume that you have an operating profit on sales of 30 percent. If the exchange rate for country X's currency appreciates, what, if anything, would you do to your export prices in your home currency? If you do nothing, your prices will rise in country X. If you reduce your prices by the percentage amount of the devaluation of your currency, your prices in country X will remain unchanged. Prepare a brief memo outlining your position and the assumptions underlying your position.

2. What causes foreign exchange rates to change? Are exchange rates predictable? Why? Why not?

3. If over the course of a year prices rise 100 percent in Argentina and 1 percent in Germany, what would you expect to happen to the value of the deutsche mark and the peso, all other things being equal? Why?

4. In your own words, what does purchasing power parity (PPP) mean? Why is the concept of PPP useful?

▼ BIBLIOGRAPHY

Books

EITEMAN, DAVID K., ARTHUR I. STONEHILL, AND MICHAEL H. MOFFETT, *Multinational Business Finance*. 6th ed. Reading, MA: Addison-Wesley Publishing Company, 1992.

RODRIGUEZ, RITA M., AND E. EUGENE CARTER, *International Financial Management*. 3rd ed. Englewood Cliffs, NJ: Prentice-Hall, Inc., 1984.

SHAPIRO, ALAN C., *Multinational Financial Management*. 3rd ed. Englewood Cliffs, NJ: Prentice Hall, Inc., 1989.

SMITH, ROY C., AND INGO WALTER, *Global Financial Services*. New York: Harper & Row, 1990.

Articles

LESSARD, DONALD, "Finance and Global Competition," Unpublished working paper prepared for Colloquium on Competition in Global Industries, Harvard Business School, Boston, April 1984.

SEVEN

Global Marketing
Information
Systems
and Research

Introduction

Information, or useful data, is the raw material of executive action. The global marketer is faced with a dual problem in acquiring the information needed for decision making. In the advanced countries the amount of information available far exceeds the absorptive capacity of an individual or an organization. The problem is superabundance, not scarcity. While advanced countries all over the world are enduring an information explosion, there is relatively little information available on the marketing characteristics of less developed countries and the former communist states in Eastern Europe. Thus, the global marketer is faced with the problem of information abundance and information scarcity. Information has the pragmatic role of reducing uncertainty. Generally, global marketing management directs the thrust of a firm's activity in response to market opportunities. The necessary decisions result from the interaction of knowledge and information at the management level. It is important to understand that the "right" information increases knowledge.[1] The global marketer must know where to go to obtain information, the subject areas that should be covered, and the different ways that information can be acquired. Information acquired must be processed in an efficient and useful way. The process of information acquisition is known as *scanning*. The section that follows presents a scanning model for multinational marketing. The chapter continues with an outline of how to conduct global marketing research and concludes with a discussion of the management of the marketing information collection system and the marketing research effort.

ELEMENTS OF A GLOBAL INFORMATION SYSTEM

▼ Information Subject Agenda

A subject agenda, or list of subjects for which information is desired, is a basic element of a global marketing information system. Because each company's subject agenda should be developed and tailored to the specific needs and objectives of the company, it is not possible to suggest an ideal or standard agenda.

---

[1] F.H. Rolf Seringhaus, "Export Knowledge and its Role in Strategy and Performance", *Finnish Journal of Business Economics*, (1991) 40:1, p.4.

TABLE 7–1 Thirty-One Categories for a Global Business Intelligence System

Category	Coverage
I. Market Information	
1. Market potential	Information indicating potential demand for products, including the status and prospects of existing company products in existing markets.
2. Consumer/customer attitudes and behavior	Information and attitudes, behavior, and needs of consumers and customers of existing and potential company products. Also included in this category are attitudes of investors toward a company's investment merit.
3. Channels of distribution	Availability, effectiveness, attitudes, and preferences of channel agents.
4. Communications media	Media availability, effectiveness, and cost.
5. Market sources	Availability, quality, and cost.
6. New products	Nontechnical information concerning new products for a company (this includes products that are already marketed by other companies).
II. Competitive Information	
7. Competitive business strategy and plans	Goals, objectives. Definition of business; the "design" and rationale of the company.
8. Competitive functional strategies, plans, and programs	Marketing: Target markets, product, price, place, promotion. Strategy and plan; finance, manufacturing, R&D, and human resource strategy, plans, and programs.
9. Competitive operations	Detailed intelligence on competitor operations. Production, shipments, employee transfers, morale, etc.
III. Foreign Exchange	
10. Balance of payments.	Government reports.
11. Nominal and real interest rates.	Expert estimation.
12. Inflation rate compared to weighted trading partner average.	PPP theory.
13. Estimate of international competitiveness.	Expert judgment.
14. Attractiveness of country currency and assets to global investors.	Currency demand.
15. Government policy re: country competitiveness.	Expert assessment.
16. Country monetary and fiscal policy.	Expert assessment.
17. Spot and forward market activity.	Market reports.
18. Expectations and opinions of analysts, traders, bankers, economists, businesspeople.	General assessment.
IV. Prescriptive Information	
19. Foreign taxes	Information concerning decisions, intentions, and attitudes of foreign authorities regarding taxes upon earnings, dividends, and interest.
20. Other foreign prescriptions and laws	All information concerning local, regional, or international authority guidelines, rulings, laws, decrees other than foreign exchange and tax matters affecting the operations, assets, or investments of a company.
21. Home-country prescriptions	Home-country incentives, controls, regulations, restraints, etc. affecting a company.
V. Resource Information	
22. Human resources	Availability of individuals and groups, employment candidates, sources, strikes, etc.
23. Money	Availability and cost of money for company uses.

TABLE 7–1 (Cont.)

Category	Coverage
24. Raw material	Availability and cost.
25. Acquisitions and mergers	Leads or other information concerning potential acquisitions, mergers, or joint ventures.
	VI. General Conditions
26. Economic factors	Macroeconomic information dealing with broad factors, such as capital movements, rates of growth, economic structure, and economic geography.
27. Social factors	Social structure of society, customs, attitudes, and preferences.
28. Political factors	"Investment climate," meaning of elections, political change.
29. Scientific technological factors	Major developments and trends.
30. Management and administrative practices	Management and administrative practices and procedures concerning such matters as employee compensation, report procedure.
31. Other information	Information not assignable to another category.

Therefore, any framework such as that proposed in Table 7–1 is only a starting point in the construction of a specific agenda for any particular organization.

The general framework suggested in Table 7–1 consists of six broad information areas with 31 information categories. The framework satisfies two essential criteria. First, it is exhaustive. It accepts all the subject areas of information encountered, whether a company has limited foreign market involvement or has global operations. Second, the categories in the framework are mutually exclusive. Any kind of information encompassed by the framework can be correctly placed in one and only one category.

Prescriptive information covers the rules for action in the foreign market. This category incorporates information from guidelines to regulations, rulings, and laws by public and private groups and authorities.

▼ Scanning Modes: Surveillance and Search

Once the subject agenda has been determined, the next step in formulating a systematic information-gathering system in the organization is the actual collection of information. There are two important modes or orientations in information collection or scanning: surveillance and search.

In *surveillance* the scanner is oriented toward acquiring relevant information that is contained in messages that cross his or her scanning attention field. In *search* the scanner is deliberately seeking information, either informally or by means of an organized research project. The two orientations and their components are briefly described in Table 7–2.

The significance of determining scanning mode is the measure it offers (1) of the extent that a scanner actively seeks out information, as contrasted to the more passive acquisition of information, and (2) of the scanner's attention state at the time of acquiring information.

TABLE 7-2	Scanning Modes

Modes	Coverage
Surveillance Orientation	
Viewing	General exposure to external information where the viewer has no specific purpose in mind other than exploration.
Monitoring	Focused attention, not involving active search, to a clearly defined area or type of external information.
Search Orientation	
Investigation	A relatively limited and informal seeking out of specific information.
Research	A formally organized effort to acquire specific information, usually for a specific purpose.

Scanning is a vital activity in staying abreast of technological, political, economic, social, and legal developments in the global business environment. Many companies use some form of scanning.[2] Smaller companies use business and trade publications to remain informed, while larger firms may set up more formal systems.

Another aspect to consider is the firm's level of foreign market experience. Firms new to foreign markets need to acquire and learn a great deal more, and thus have needs for different information, than firms with substantial foreign market experience. As foreign market experience accumulates so does the knowledge of information sources and the ability to evaluate their content.

One study found (see Table 7-3) that the bulk of information acquired by headquarters executives of major U.S. multinational firms is gained through surveillance as opposed to search (73 percent versus 27 percent). However, viewing (general exposure), the least oriented of the surveillance modes, generated only 13 percent of important external information acquired, where monitoring generated 60 percent.[3]

TABLE 7-3 Relative Importance of Scanning Modes in Acquiring Global Information		
		Percent of Information Acquired
Surveillance		73
Viewing	13	
Monitoring	60	
Search		27
Investigation	23	
Research	4	
Total		100

---

[2] Ram Subramanian, Nirmala Fernandes, and Earl Harper, "Environmental Scanning in U.S. Companies: Their Nature and their Relationship to Performance," *Management International Review* (1993) 33:3, p.274.

[3] Warren J. Keegan, "Scanning the International Business Environment: A Study of the Informational Acquisition Process," Doctoral Dissertation, Harvard Business School, 1967.

This paucity of information generated by viewing is the result of two factors. One is the extent to which management is exposed to information that is not included in a clearly defined subject agenda. The other is management's receptiveness to information outside of this agenda. Both factors operate to limit the relative importance of viewing as a scanning mode. Every manager limits his or her exposure to information that will not have a high probability of being relevant to the job or company. This is a rational and necessary response to the basic human mental limitations. A person can handle only a minute fraction of the data available to him or her. Because exposure absorbs limited mental resources, exposure must be selective.

Nevertheless, receptiveness by the organization as a whole to information not explicitly recognized as important is vital. The effective scanning system must ensure that the organization is viewing areas where developments that could be important to the company might occur. Innovations in information technology have increased the speed with which information is transmitted while simultaneously shortening the life of its usefulness to the firm. Strides in technology have also placed new demands on the global firm in terms of shrinking reaction times to information acquired. In some instances, the creation of a full-time scanning unit having explicit responsibility for acquiring and disseminating information on subjects of importance to the organization may be required.

SOURCES OF INFORMATION

▼ Human Sources

As can be seen in Table 7–4, people are the most important source of information for headquarters executives of global companies.[4] The most important human source of external information is company executives based abroad in company subsidiaries, affiliates, and branches. The importance of executives abroad as a source of information about the world environment is one of the most striking features of the modern global company. The general view of headquarters executives is that company executives overseas are the people who know best what is going on in their areas. Typical comments of headquarters management are:

> Our principal sources are internal. We have a very well informed and able overseas establishment. The local people have a double advantage.

TABLE 7–4	Sources of Information (in percent)	
Location of Sources		**Types of Sources**	

Location of Sources		Types of Sources	
Inside organization	34%	People	67%
Outside organization	66	Documentary	27
		Physical phenomena	6

---

[4] Ibid.

They know the local scene and they know our business. Therefore, they are an excellent source. They know what we are interested in learning, and because of their local knowledge they are able to effectively cover available information from all sources.

The presence of an information network abroad in the form of company people is a major strength of the global company. It may also be a weakness in the scanning posture of a company that has only partially extended the limits of its geographical operations because inside sources abroad tend to scan only information about their own countries or region. Although there may be more attractive opportunities outside existing areas of operation, the chances of their being noticed by inside sources in a domestic company are very low because the horizons of domestic executives tend to end at national borders. In his book on foreign trade, Kindleberger identifies the impact of horizons upon trade patterns:

> A man may be perfectly rational, but only within a limited horizon. As a consumer, he will normally restrict his expenditures to those goods offered to given ambit. Over his horizon there may be brilliant opportunities to improve his welfare as a consumer or his income as a producer, but unless he is made aware of them, they will avail him nothing.[5]

Distributors, consumers, customers, suppliers, and government officials are also important information sources. Information from these sources is largely obtained by country operating personnel as opposed to headquarters staff. Other sources are friends, acquaintances, professional colleagues, freelance university consultants, and candidates for employment, particularly if they have worked for competitors. As shown in Table 7–5, personal human sources of information far exceed impersonal sources in importance.[6] Of the human sources utilized by respondents, 86 percent are personal. Interestingly, when human sources inside and outside the company are compared, 97 percent of sources inside the company are personal. The comparison suggests that lack of acquaintanceship is a barrier to the flow of information in an organization, thus underlining the importance of travel and contact.

Significantly, three-quarters of the information acquired from human sources is gained in face-to-face conversation. Why is face-to-face communication so important? There are many factors involved. Some information is too sensitive to transmit in any other way. Political information from government sources, for example, could be damaging to the source if it were known that the source was transmitting certain information. In such cases word of mouth is the most secure way of transmitting information. Information that includes estimates of future developments or even appraisals of the significance of current happenings is often considered too uncertain to commit to writing. One executive in commenting upon this point said:

---

[5] Charles P. Kindleberger, *Foreign Trade and the National Economy* (New Haven, CT: Yale University Press, 1962), p. 16.

[6] A *personal* source is either a friend or an acquaintance and an *impersonal* source is a person not known by the recipient. Normally, a person becomes a personal source after a face to face meeting.

TABLE 7–5 Comparison of Personal and Impersonal Human Sources (in percent)

Source Relationship	Inside Sources	Outside Sources	All Human Sources
Personal sources	97%	80%	86%
Impersonal sources	3	20	14
Total	100%	100%	100%
Number of instances	$\Delta = 33$	$N = 60$	$N = 93$

People are reluctant to commit themselves in writing to highly "iffy" things. They are not cowards or overly cautious; they simply know that you are bound to be wrong in trying to predict the future, and they prefer to not have their names associated with documents that will someday look foolish.

Other information does not have to be passed on immediately to be of value. For example, a division president said:

Information of relevance to my job [strategic planning] is not the kind of information which must be received immediately. Timeliness is not essential; what is more important is that I eventually get the information.

The great importance of face-to-face communication lies in the dynamics of personal interaction. Personal contact provides an occasion for executives to get together for a long enough time to permit communication in some depth. Face-to-face discussion also exposes highly significant forms of communication, such as the tone of voice, the expression of a person's eyes, movements, and many other forms of communication that cannot be expressed in writing. One executive expressed the value of face-to-face contact in these terms:

If you really want to find out about an area, you must see people personally. There is no comparison between written reports and actually sitting down with a man and talking. A personal meeting is worth four thousand written reports.

The greatest technological contribution to face-to-face communication of information has been the jet aircraft, which has made it possible for executives in a far-flung organization to maintain personal contact with one another. A measure of the importance of travel in international operations is provided by the size of travel budgets. The average travel budget of international executives (area directors, department heads, and key executives) is in excess of $30,000 annually. It is not unusual to find executives whose travel budgets exceed $100,000 annually.

▼ Documentary Sources

Of all the changes in recent years affecting the availability of information, perhaps none is more apparent than the outpouring of documentary information. The outpouring has created a major problem, the so-called information explosion. The problem is particularly acute for international marketers who must be informed about numerous national markets.

Although executives are overwhelmed with documentary information, only a handful of companies employ a formal system for monitoring documentary information. The absence of formal monitoring systems has resulted in a considerable amount of duplication. A typical form of duplication is the common practice of an entire management group reading one publication covering a particular subject area when several excellent publications covering the same area are available.

The best way to identify unnecessary duplication is to carry out an audit of reading activity by asking each person involved to list the publications he or she reads regularly. A consolidation of the lists will reveal the reading attention of the group. In a surprisingly large number of instances, the reading attention of the group will be limited to a handful of publications to the exclusion of other publications of considerable merit. An elaboration of this procedure could involve consultation with experts outside the company regarding the availability and quality of publications in relevant fields.

External documentary sources are a valuable source of information for part of every company's international information requirement, and they are also a particularly valuable source of information for the student who typically does not have the human and written sources available to a long-time professional working in the field.

▼ Perception of Information and Media

In addition to information from human and documentary sources, sensory perception helps the global marketer by providing the context and background information through observing a situation. This helps to register the full extent of the information in the recipient's mind. For example, a Canadian food exporter only appreciated the different type and size of a retail outlet such as the French *hypermarche*, examples of which are Auchan and Carrefours, after actually visiting and walking past the more than sixty check-out aisles of such an outlet.

Of course, in global marketing, direct perception requires travel. The importance of the need to travel is well recognized. In a study of Canadian exporters, personal travel to foreign markets was rated as the single most important method of acquiring information.[7]

The medium is the channel through which information is transmitted. Any marketing information system is based on three basic media: the human voice for transmitting words and numbers, printed words and numbers, and direct perception through the senses of sight, hearing, smell, taste, and touch. Each of

---

[7] F.H. Rolf Seringhaus, "A Comparison of Export Marketing Behavior of Canadian and Austrian High-Tech Firms," *Journal of International Marketing* (1993) 1:4, p.59.

TABLE 7–6   Global Marketing Information: Perception and Media

Perception	Media/Technology
Sensation (five senses)	Electronic
Sight	Telephone
Reading text	Telex
Viewing images	Facsimile (fax)
Direct perception	Electronic mail
Hearing	Television
Smell	Radio
Taste	Cable
Touch	Print
Intuition (sixth sense)	Letters
Holistic perception	Reports/memos
	Magazines
	Newspapers
	Books
	Transportation
	Land
	Sea
	Air

these basic information system media has been extended in recent years by important innovations in electronic and travel technologies. Of particular importance to the marketing information system have been the impressive developments in telephone, telex, satellite communication networks for voice and data, and transportation via jet aircraft. The basic media of a global marketing information system are summarized in Table 7–6.

The telephone and facsimile are important media for the transmission of information internationally. In one study 67 percent of all important international information acquired by international executives was from human sources, and 81 percent of this information was transmitted by voice.[8] Moreover, of the human information transmitted by voice, 94 percent was communicated in face-to-face conversation. This finding underlines the importance of the jet aircraft as a communications device because a large proportion of the important information transmitted in international marketing is accomplished by people who have come together in a face-to-face situation as a result of such high-speed travel. It also underscores the growing tendency of global firms to seek more efficient and cost-effective methods of transferring information among its worldwide locations.

Colgate-Palmolive Co. recently succeeded in standardizing its disparate and frequently incompatible electronic mail systems at locations around the globe. The process was tedious but Colgate realized that employee productivity would increase if it had a corporatewide messaging system. The result is that employees in 165 countries now exchange messages and files easily, with electronic mail traffic almost doubling over the three years since the system was fully implemented. Evidently, an undertaking of this magnitude must have had the full support of senior management inside and outside the marketing

---

[8] Keegan, "Scanning the International Business Environment."

function and must have been an integral part of strategic planning. These issues will be taken up again later in this chapter.

MARKETING RESEARCH

Information is a critical ingredient in formulating and implementing a successful marketing strategy. Marketing research is the gathering of information in the search scanning mode. There are two modes of search:

Investigation—a relatively limited and informal seeking out of specific information.

Research—a formally organized effort to acquire specific information for a specific purpose.

There are two ways to conduct marketing research. One is to design and implement a study with in-house staff. The other is to use an outside firm specializing in international marketing research. Regardless of whether the study is conducted in or out of house (or using a combination of both), a company has an ongoing need for information, and thus market research, in order to understand its foreign market environment, its buyers, its markets, and growth opportunities. Table 7–7 profiles the relative strengths and weaknesses of international market research activity in Canadian exporters. As awareness of the need for research is demonstrated, it is also apparent that companies make choices with respect to the emphasis on such market research.[9]

It is not our intention to repeat a detailed procedure or process of market research here—many excellent market research texts are available—but instead to draw your attention to several key factors and issues. We need to ask, "Why is international market research different?" The answer is multifaceted. First, different cultures and markets have different norms, values, societal structure, and decision-making. Assumptions we hold may not apply, nor may our concepts of the role of time or money be transferable. Second, there are new parameters, for example tariffs and duties, foreign currencies, documentation, different practices, and behaviors of conducting business in foreign markets. Third, a broader definition of competition is often required to undertand foreign markets in terms of competitors, buying preferences, and market opportunities.

These are challenges for the international marketer and they have a direct impact on the information gathering and market research function of the company.

▼ Comparability of International Data

International statistics are subject to more than the usual number of caveats and qualifications concerning comparability. An absence of standard data-gather-

---

[9] F.H. Rolf Seringhaus "Export Knowledge and its Role in Strategy and Performance," *The Finnish Journal of Business Economics* (1991) 40:1, pp.12,14.

TABLE 7–7 Strengths and Weaknesses in Export Research of Canadian Companies

Export Marketing Activity	Export Market Research Area	Research Capability: Strong	Medium	Weak
Understanding Market Environment:	- Competition - Product demand potential	✔	✔	
Understanding Buyers:	- Customer preferences - Buying behaviour and decision - Market segmentation	✔		✔ ✔
Marketing Planning & Information Development:	- Transport costs, methods - Product pricing - Product adaptation - Distribution options - Standardizing marketing - Market tests of product - Promotion mix or methods - Product image tests	✔	✔ ✔ ✔	 ✔ ✔ ✔ ✔
Market Entry, Development and Expansion:	- Search for new export markets - Evaluation of export marketing - Export market entry options	✔ ✔		 ✔

Source: F.H. Rolf Seringhaus (1991), "Export Knowledge and Its Role in Strategy and Performance", The Finnish Journal of Business Economics, 40:1, p. 14.

ing techniques is the basis for some of the lack of comparability in international statistics. In Germany, for example, consumer expenditures are estimated largely on the basis of turnover tax receipts, whereas in the United Kingdom consumer expenditures are estimated on the basis of data supplied not only by tax receipts but also from household surveys and production sources.

As Table 7-8 shows, the pervasiveness of communications media varies greatly across countries as well. Such comparisons are not only indicators of the relative quality of country data, but also, more importantly, of the relative accessibility of consumers through common media.

Even with standard data-gathering techniques, definitional differences would still remain internationally. In some cases, these differences are minor; in others, they are quite significant. Germany, for example, classifies the purchase of a television set as an expenditure for recreation and entertainment, whereas the same expenditure falls into the classification of furniture, furnishings, and household equipment in Canada.

Survey data are subject to perhaps even more comparability problems. When PepsiCo International, a typical user of international research, reviewed its data it found a considerable lack of comparability in a number of major areas. Table 7–9 shows how age categories were developed in seven countries surveyed by PepsiCo.

TABLE 7–8   Communications Media in Selected Countries

	Population (millions)- Mid 1992[a]	Daily Newspapers (circ. per 1000) 1988[b][d]	TV Sets (% Households) 1990/91[c]	Radios (% Households) 1990/91[c]	Telephones (# of people per telephone) 1986/88[b]	Domestic Mail (letters per capita) 1988
North America:						
Canada	27.4	225	96	100	1.3	161
U.S.	255.4	259	97	100	1.3	645
Mexico	85.0	127	29		10.4	5
Western Europe:						
Germany	80.6	344[1]	97[1]	99[1]	1.6[1]	225
France	57.4	193	94	98	1.6	321
UK	57.8	421	98	90	1.9	231
Italy	57.8	99	98	92	1.5	92
Spain	39.1	75	98	95	4.1	100
Austria	7.9	358	96	95	1.9	323
Sweden	8.7	534	97	93	1.0	208
Finland	5.0	543	94	96	1.4	n.a.
Eastern Europe:						
Czech/Slovak Republics	15.6	332	95	75	2.6	92
Hungary	10.3	262	21	40	16.2	149
Bulgaria	8.5	316	93	95	4.5	58
Poland	38.4	200	70	79	8.5	37
Russia	149.0 218[2]	442[2]	45[2]	96[2]		10.3[2]
Africa:						
Nigeria	101.9	9[3]	8[4]	59[3]	366.7	8
Ghana	15.8	42[3]	n.a.	41[3]	178.8	4
South Africa	39.8	45	n.a.	70[3]	6.9	49[5]
Asia-Pacific:						
Japan	124.5	566	99	98[3]	1.8	163
India	883.6	28	26	14[3]	191.0	16
Thailand	58.0	15	36	71[3]	52.6	8
Indonesia	184.3	16	38	20[3]	n.a.	2
China	1,162.2	n.a.	32	n.a.	149.8	5
Australia	17.5	264	97	n.a.	1.8	188
Latin America:						
Brazil	153.9	48	48	n.a.	11.3	24
Argentina	33.1	n.a.	66	n.a.	9.7	n.a.
Colombia	33.4	48[6]	50	n.a.	13.0	4
Chile	13.6	67	n.a.	n.a.	15.5	14
Venezuela	20.2	186[7]	60	n.a.	11.3	15

[a] World Bank, "World Development Report" New York:Oxford University Press, 1994).

[b] *The Economist*, "Book of Vital World Statistics" (London: Hutchinson Business Books, 1990).

[c] Euromonitor, "International Marketing Data and Statistics 1993", and "European Marketing Data and Statistics, 1994", London, Eurominitor, 1993, 1994.

[d] UCLA Latin American Centre Publications, "Statistical Abstract of Latin America", 1993.

1) West Germany; 2) Former USSR; 3) 1978, 4) 1980; 5) 1977; 6) 1979; 7) 1984.

TABLE 7–9 Age Classification from Consumer Surveys, Major Markets

Mexico	Venezuela	Argentina	Germany	Spain	Italy	Philippines
14–18	10–14	14–18	14–19	15–24	13–20	14–18
19–25	15–24	19–24	20–29	25–34	21–25	19–25
26–35	25–34	25–34	30–39	35–44	26–35	26–35
36–45	35–44	35–44	40–49	45–54	36–45	36–50
46+	45+	45–65	50+	55–64	46–60	
				65+		

Source: PepsiCo International.

While flexibility may have the advantage of providing groupings for local analysis that are more pertinent (14 to 19, for example, might be a more pertinent youth classification in one country, whereas 14 to 24 might be a more useful definition of the same segment in another country), PepsiCo's headquarters marketing research group pointed out that if data were reported to the company's headquarters in standard five-year intervals, it would be possible to compare findings in one country with those in another. Without this standardization, such comparability was not possible. The company's headquarters marketing research group recommended, therefore, that standard five-year intervals be required in all reporting to headquarters, but that any other intervals that were deemed useful for local purposes be perfectly allowable. PepsiCo also found that local market definitions of consumption differed so greatly that it was unable to make intermarket comparisons of brand-share figures. Representative definitions of consumption are shown in Table 7–10.

One important qualification about comparability in multicountry survey work is that comparability does not necessarily result from sameness of method. A survey asking the same question and using the same methods will not necessarily yield results that are comparable from country to country. For example, if the data were recorded by household, the definition of household in each of these countries could vary. The point is that comparability of results has to be established directly; it does not simply follow from the sameness of method. Establishing that results will be comparable depends upon either knowing that

TABLE 7–10 Definition of Consumption Used by PepsiCo Market Researcher

Mexico	Count of number of occasions product was consumed on day prior to interview.
Venezuela	Count of number of occasions product was consumed on day prior to interview.
Argentina	Count of number of drinks consumed on day prior to interview.
Germany	Count of number of respondents consuming "daily or almost daily."
Spain	Count of number of drinks consumed "at least once a week."
Italy	Count of number of respondents consuming product on day prior to interview.
Philippines	Count of number of glasses of product consumed on day prior to interview.

methods will produce identical measurements or knowing how to correct any bi-ases that may exist.

▼ Assessing Market Opportunity

The vice presidents of finance and marketing of a shoe company were traveling around the world to estimate the market potential for their products. They arrived in a very poor developing country and both immediately noticed that no one in this country was wearing shoes. The vice president of finance said, "We might as well get back on the plane. There is no market for shoes in this country." The vice president of marketing replied, "What an opportunity! Everyone in this country is a potential customer!"

This story underlines the difference between existing and potential markets. The existing market for shoes in the country was zero. The potential market was zero in the eyes of the vice president of finance but it was enormous in the eyes of the vice president of marketing.

There are three basic categories of demand and therefore of market opportunity: existing demand, latent demand, and incipient demand. *Existing markets* are, as the term suggests, those in which customer needs are being served by existing suppliers. At least in theory, the size of existing markets can be measured. The task of measurement is one of devising a method for identifying the rate of purchase or consumption of the product.

Latent demand is demand which would be expressed if product were offered to customers at an acceptable price. Latent demand is the demand for any new product which succeeds. Before the product is offered, demand is zero. After the offer, there is existing demand. Personal computers are an example of a product for which there was enormous latent demand. The PC revolution sparked by Apple is an outstanding example of tapping a latent market.

Incipient demand is demand that will emerge if present trends continue. If you offer a product to meet incipient demand before the trends have had their impact, you will have no market response. After the trends have had a chance to unfold, the incipient demand will become latent demand. An outstanding example of incipient demand is the impact of rising income on demand for consumer durables, automobiles, and so on. You can be absolutely certain that as income per capita rises in a country, the demand for automobiles will also rise. Therefore, if you can predict a country's future rate of income growth, you can also predict the growth rate of its automobile market. Table 7–11 summarizes the different types of demand.

Assessing a market opportunity requires a measure of both the overall size of a market and the competitive conditions in the market. It is the combination of total size and competitive conditions that determines sales opportunity and profit. In global marketing, companies focusing on existing markets must first estimate the size of these markets and then assess their overall competitiveness as compared with their competitors by measuring product appeal, price, distribution, advertising, and promotional coverage and effectiveness. Cameras are a good case in point. Before 1960, German companies dominated the 35mm camera market with their range finder design. Enter the Japanese. The Japanese offered a su-

TABLE 7–11   Three Categories of Demand

	Existing	Latent	Incipient
Definition	Customer needs are being served by existing products/suppliers.	Customer needs are not being served by existing products/suppliers.	Customer needs do not exist now but will emerge in future if present trends continue.
Characteristics	Can be precisely measured or estimated.	Cannot be precisely measured or estimated. Will materialize if the marketing mix combination that meets the need is offered. Examples include market for instant pictures tapped by Polaroid in 1947; market for personal computers in 1976, or fast-food franchises in the former Soviet Union.	If trends continue, will become a latent market. Is not an existing market; would not respond if product were offered.

The author is indebted to H. Igor Ansoff for suggesting the terms *existing, latent,* and *incipient demand.*

perior design (they were the first to develop the single-lens reflex design in the 35mm camera). While the overall quality and design of Japanese cameras were high, prices were relatively low, distribution was intensive, and communications were at least as good as those of the competition (mainly German companies). The results of this Japanese tour de force were dramatic. In 1960 Germany exported $42 million and Japan $16 million. By 1970 Japanese exports had increased from approximately 40 percent to 270 percent of German exports during this period. The Japanese have continued to innovate in this area and today they virtually monopolize the market.

A second market objective in international marketing is to identify and exploit latent markets. These markets present a very different challenge from those presented by existing markets, where the main challenge is the competition. The major challenge in successfully exploiting latent markets is the identification of market opportunity. Initial success will not be competitiveness, but rather ability to identify opportunity and launch a marketing program to supply the latent demand. Of course, if there are other companies producing the same or equivalent products, it is important to assess the likelihood and expected timing of competitive entry into latent markets. An example of a latent market is the demand for small refrigerators in North America for the vacation trailer or caravan. European and Japanese companies were producing small refrigerators for the household market and their smallest models were well suited to the needs of the North American camper. The same type of market developed for the subcompact car. People wanted small inexpensive transportation, but the Big Three car companies would not offer a North America made product to fill this need. Foreign companies exploited an existing latent market and positioned themselves in an emerging incipient market. Because of their leadership in exploiting this market, foreign manufacturers held 33 percent of the Canadian market in 1993.

The British and Japanese motorcycle industries provide an example of different approaches to market demand. The British industry was well established before World War I and had attained a leading position in world markets. In 1968, 6,455 motorcycles were imported into Canada from Britain compared to 12,162 from Japan. From 1969 onwards British motorcycles began a steady decline in Canada (and in the U.S.) while Japanese motorcycle sales increased rapidly. By 1972 British imports were 3,112 and Japanese imports had reached 91,336. The reason was that the Japanese, in short time of four years, opened up entirely new markets with products that attracted an entirely new segment of the population to motorcycle riding. Japanese machines were cheaper and more reliable than the British machines. The combination of product design, quality, price, and aggressive advertising and promotion resulted in a 440 percent increase in market size, which was almost entirely captured by the Japanese. In 1968 the British industry held a 32 percent share of the Canadian market for motorcycles. By 1982, the British share of this market was a mere 0.1 percent. Today, the British industry is defunct.

Incipient international markets are those that will emerge as a consequence of known conditions and trends. Internationally these are important for planning purposes. In advanced countries, because of high wages, there is a ready market for any product that saves labor and thereby reduces costs. Because domestic labor is scarce and incomes are high, there is also a ready market for household labor-saving devices. The same pressures or forces operate throughout the world. Companies marketing labor-saving products can predict with reasonable accuracy when demand will emerge in a country as wages and incomes rise and can plan to deploy their resources to tap these markets as they emerge.

▼ Special Problems
in International Marketing Research

The objectives just outlined are not unique to international marketing. However, international market researchers do face special problems and conditions that differentiate their task from that of the domestic market researcher. First, instead of analyzing a single national market, the international market researcher must analyze many national markets. Each national market has unique characteristics that must be recognized in analysis. And for many countries, the availability of data is limited. This limitation is particularly true of less developed countries where statistical and research services are relatively primitive.

The small markets around the world pose a special problem for the international researcher. The relatively low-profit potential in smaller markets permits only a modest marketing research expenditure. Therefore, the international researcher must devise techniques and methods that relate the expenditures on research to the profit potential of markets. The smaller markets put a premium on discovering economic and demographic relationships that permit demand estimation from a minimum of information and on inexpensive survey research that sacrifices some elegance to achieve results within the constraints of the smaller market research budget.

Another frequently encountered problem in developing countries is that data may be inflated or deflated for political expediency. For example, a Middle Eastern country revised its balance of trade in a chemical product by adding 1,000 tons to its consumption statistics. It did this to encourage foreign investors to install domestic production facilities. Consumer research is inhibited by a greater reluctance on the part of people to talk to strangers, greater difficulty in locating people, and an absence of telephones. Both industrial and consumer research services are less developed, although the cost of these services is much lower in a high-wage country.

▼ Five Rules for International Research

Experience suggests that there are five rules that, if followed, will contribute to the preparation of research reports that will be effective management tools.

1. Before you begin your research, ask yourself these questions:
   a. What information do I need? What will I do with the information when I get it?
   b. Where can I get this information? Is it available in files, in a library, or on line from a database?
   c. Why do I need this information?
   d. When do I need the information?
   e. What is this information worth to me in dollars (or yen, and so on)?
   f. What would be the cost of not getting the information?
2. Start with desk research. Use the available information in your own files, libraries, on-line databases, trade associations, and so on. Refer to the information appendix of this chapter for guidance on information sources. Quite often, the information you are looking for is in your own files or in an easily obtainable public source.
3. Identify the type of information that is available from overseas sources. Just because the information is or is not available at home does not mean that it is or is not available abroad. The general rule is the more developed the country, the greater the information available.
4. Know where to look. If you do not know, go to someone who does. Your embassy or commercial attaché may be able to offer help.
5. Do not assume that the information you get is comparable or accurate. Check everything. Use common sense and logic to evaluate the comparability and accuracy of the information obtained from overseas sources.

▼ Survey Research

When data are not available through published statistics or reports, direct collection is necessary. One of the most important means of collecting market data is the survey. Survey research involves interviewing a target group, for example, potential customers, to obtain the desired information. Normally a questionnaire is essential to ensure a successful survey. This questionnaire is the basis of the interview, which may be conducted face to face, over the telephone, or via mail.

Direct market research through a survey requires that the data generated is comparable from one country to another, thus the concept of equivalence requires a brief discussion.

Conceptual equivalence deals with the question whether the concept of interest (e.g., fast food or elementary schooling) is interpreted and understood in the same way across different markets. Market researchers must pay close attention to this issue, as these two examples illustrate. The problem of functional equivalence is shown by bicycle use: in Canada, bicycles are mainly used for recreation but in the Netherlands, they are used mostly for personal transportation. Definitional equivalence can be a problem through consumer perception or officially through classification by government agencies: a person of the same chronological age can be at a different stage of the life or family cycle in different countries. It may not be possible to standardize age groups across countries and have the same definitional equivalence.[10]

Similarly, when the market researcher develops a questionnaire, it is instrument equivalence as opposed to measure equivalence that is important. First, language should be considered carefully and the meaning of a question, rather than a literal translation, should be given in the foreign language. Backtranslation—a question is translated by one translater into the foreign language and then translated back into the source language by a different translator—will allow the market researcher to assess whether the meaning intended was indeed conveyed. Measurement scales are another area of concern and caution should be used when employing such standard measures as Likert or semantic differential scales in other cultures.[11]

The following is not intended to be a complete guide to questionnaires but, rather, a summary of design with particular reference to conditions in developing countries.

A good questionnaire has three main characteristics:

1. It is simple.
2. It is easy for respondents to answer and for the interviewer to record.
3. It keeps the interview to the point and obtains desired information.

To achieve this, the following principles should be observed:

1. *Single-element questions.* An apparently simple question may have many elements. Questions should focus on a single element.
2. *Expected replies.* Wherever possible, expected replies should be listed on the questionnaire where the interviewer can check the answer. This eliminates a difficult coding task of trying to decide what people meant by replies that are written out on the questionnaire.

---

[10] Sak Onkvisit and John J.Shaw, *International Marketing*, 2nd Edition, (New York: MacMillan Publishing Company), pp.393-4.

[11] Ibid., p. 396–7.

3. *Ambiguity in questions.* Carelessly worded questions can be ambiguous, as can questions with words that are not understood by respondents. Therefore, questionnaires must be carefully stated in language that even the least educated respondents will understand.

4. *Leading questions.* Leading questions suggest answers and should be avoided. For example, "Do you prefer brand X because of its high quality?" is an assertion that provides its own answer.

5. *Personal and embarrassing questions.* This is a difficult area to deal with. One rule is to rely upon local managers and experts who are familiar with local customs and mores. It is important to ensure, however, that the local adviser is not excessively conservative in his or her judgments about what can be asked. Therefore, the use of several judges is advisable to ensure that a single bias is not determining the questionnaire design.

6. *Pretesting.* A pretest is invaluable in determining whether or not a questionnaire accomplishes what is desired. No matter how much thought and effort go into questionnaire design, there are always unanticipated problems or ambiguities that are often identified in a pretest.

▼ Sampling

Sampling is the selection of a subset or group from a population that is representative of the entire population. The two basic sampling methods in use today are probabilistic and nonprobabilistic sampling. In a probabilistic sample, each unit chosen has a known chance of being included in the sample. In a random sample, which is one type of probabilistic sample, each unit has an *equal* chance of being selected. The results of a probabilistic sample can be projected to the entire population with statistical reliability.

The results of a nonprobabilistic sample cannot be projected with statistical reliability. For example, a quota sample is the selection of the proportions that are known to exist in the universe. Since the units that are selected in a quota sample do not have an equal or even a known chance of being selected, the results of a quota sample cannot be projected with any statistical reliability to the universe. However, if there are no reasons to expect that the quota is significantly different from the universe, then it is assumed that the sample will be representative of other characteristics. Thus, only the random or probabilistic sample produces results of statistically measurable accuracy. This is the major advantage of a probability sample. The disadvantage of a probability sample is the difficulty of selecting elements from the universe on a random or probability basis. The quota sample does not require selection on a probability basis and is, therefore, much easier to implement. Its main disadvantage is the possible bias that may exist in the sample because of inaccurate prior assumptions concerning population or because of unknown bias in selection of cases by field workers.

Three key characteristics of a probability sample determine the sample size:

1. The permissible sampling error that can be allowed, *e*.
2. The desired confidence in the sample results. In a statistical sense the confidence is expressed in terms of the number of chances in 100 tries that the

results obtained could be due to chance. Confidence is usually desired at the 99 percent level and is expressed as three standard errors, t.

3. The amount of variation in the characteristic being measured. This is known as the standard deviation, s.

The formula for sample size is:

$$n = \frac{(t^2)(s^2)}{e^2}$$

WHERE

n = sample size

t = confidence limit expressed in standard errors (three standard errors = 99 percent confidence)

s = standard deviation

e = error limit

The important characteristic of this formula from the point of view of international marketers is that the sample size, n, is not a function of the size of the universe. Thus, a probability sample in Thailand requires the same sample size as one in Canada if the standard deviation in the two populations is the same. This is one of the basic reasons for scale economies of marketing research in larger markets.

A quota sample is designed by taking known characteristics of the universe and including respondents in the sample in the same proportion as they occur in the known characteristic universe. For example, population may be divided in six categories according to income as follows:

Percent of population	10%	15%	25%	25%	15%	10%
Earnings per month	0–10	10–20	20–40	40–60	60–70	70–100

If it is assumed that income is the characteristic that adequately differentiates the population for study purposes, then a quota sample would include respondents of different income levels in the same proportion as they occurred in the population, that is, 15 percent with monthly earnings from 10–20, and so on.

ANALYTICAL TECHNIQUES FOR RESEARCHING INTERNATIONAL MARKETS

▼ Demand Pattern Analysis

Industrial growth patterns provide an insight into market demand.[12] Production patterns, because they generally reveal consumption patterns, are helpful in assessing market opportunities. Additionally, trends in manufacturing production indicate potential markets for inputs to the manufacturing process.

---

[12] This section is adapted from Reed Moyer, "International Market Analysis," *Journal of Marketing Research* (November 1968).

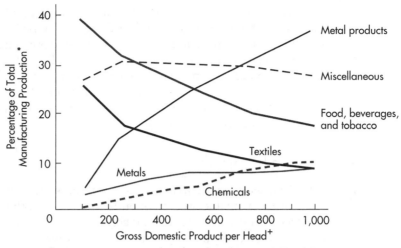

*Base on time series analysis for selected years, 1899–1957, for 7 to 10 countries depending on commodity.

+Dollars at 1955 prices.

FIGURE 7-1
Typical Patterns of Growth in Manufacturing Industries

Figure 7–1 illustrates patterns of growth in large industry categories. It relates the percentage of total manufacturing production accounted for by major industrial groups to gross domestic product per capita. At the early stages of growth in a country, when per capita incomes are low, manufacturing centers on necessities: food, beverages, textiles, and light manufacturing. As incomes grow, these industries decline relatively and are replaced in importance by heavy industries.

▼ Income Elasticity Measurements

Income elasticity describes the relationship between demand for a good and changes in income. Symbolically, it can be expressed as

$$\frac{\Delta Q_A / Q_A}{\Delta Y / Y} = \text{Income elasticity of demand for product } A$$

where Q represents the quantity demanded and Y represents income. When the elasticity coefficient is <1, it is said to be inelastic. If a 10 percent increase in Y results in a 20 percent increase in the quantity A demanded or consumed, the income elasticity coefficient is 2.0. In this relationship A is said to be income elastic because the coefficient is 1. If a 10 percent increase in Y results in only a 5 percent increase in quantity A demanded or consumed, the income elasticity coefficient is 0.5. Since it is less than 1, the coefficient of elasticity is said to be inelastic.

Income elasticity studies covering both consumer and industrial products show that necessities such as food and clothing tend to be income inelastic; that is, expenditures on products in this category increase but at a slower percentage rate than do increases in income. This is the corollary of Engel's law, which states that as incomes rise, smaller proportions of total income are spent on basic necessities such as food and clothing. Demand for durable consumer goods such as furniture, appliances, and metals tends to be income elastic, increasing relatively faster than increases in income.

▼ Estimation by Analogy

Estimating market size with available data presents challenging analytic tasks. When data are unavailable, as is frequently the case in both less developed and industrialized countries, resourceful techniques are required. One resourceful technique is estimation by analogy. There are two ways to use this technique. One way is to make cross-sectional comparisons, and the other is to displace a time series in time. The first method, cross-sectional comparisons, amounts simply to positing the assumption that there is an analogy between the relationship of a factor and demand for a particular product or commodity in two countries. This can best be explained as follows:

Let

X_A = demand for product X in country A
Y_A = factor that correlates with demand for product X in country A, data from country A
X_B = demand for product X in country B
Y_B = factor that correlates with demand for product X in country A, data from country B

If we assume that

$$\frac{X_A}{Y_A} = \frac{X_B}{Y_B}$$

and if X_A, Y_A, and Y_B are known, we can solve for X_B as follows:

$$\frac{X_{A1}}{Y_{A1}} = \frac{X_{B2}}{Y_{B2}}$$

Basically, estimation by analogy amounts to the use of a single-factor index with a correlation value obtained from one country applied to a target market. This is a very simple method of analysis, but in many cases it is an extremely useful, rough estimating device whenever data are available in at least one potentially analogous market for product sales of consumption and a single correlation factor. Some researchers have been quite creative in identifying analogous products. A major U.S. chemical company, for example, found that soup consumption was the only reliable index forecasting chemical sales in Asia.

Displacing time is a useful method of market analysis when data are available for two markets at different levels of development. This method is based on the assumption that an analogy between markets exists in different time periods or put another way, that the markets in question are going through the same stages of market development. The method amounts to assuming that the demand level for product X in country A in time period 1 was at the same stage as demand in time period 2 in country B. This can be illustrated as follows:

Let

X_{A1} = demand for product X in country A during time period 1
Y_{A1} = factor associated with demand for product X in country A during time period 1
X_{B2} = demand for product X in country B during time period 2
Y_{B2} = factor or factors correlating with demand for product X in country A and data from country B for time period 2

Assume that

$$X_{B2} = \frac{(X_{A1})(Y_{B2})}{Y_{A1}}$$

If X_{A1}, Y_{A1}, and Y_{B2} are known, we can solve for X_{B2} as follows:

$$X_{B2} = \frac{(X_{A1})(Y_{B2})}{Y_{A1}}$$

The use of the method of displacing time involves arriving at an estimate of when two markets were at similar stages of development. One might assume on the basis of analyzing factors associated with demand that the market for product X in Mexico in 1986 was comparable to the markets for the same product in Canada in 1946. If this assumption were valid, by obtaining data on the factors associated with demand for product X in Canada in 1946 and in Mexico in 1986, as well as actual Canadian demand in 1946, one could solve for the unknown, that is, potential demand for product X in Mexico in 1986.

Any technique as simple as estimation by analogy is subject to substantial limitations. The following factors should be kept in mind in using this technique.

1. Are the two countries for which the analogy is posited really similar either in cross section or in displaced time? To answer this question, the analyst must understand the similarities and differences in the cultural systems in the two countries if a consumer product is under investigation and in the technological systems if an industrial product is being considered.

2. Have technical and social developments resulted in a situation where demand for a particular product or commodity will leapfrog previous patterns, skipping entire growth patterns that occurred in more developed countries? For example, it is clear that washing machine sales in Western Europe leapfrogged the pattern of sales in North America. In Canada the consumer went from hand-washing machine methods to nonautomatic washing machines and then, when they were finally available and reliable, to semiautomatic and fully automatic machines. In Western Europe many consumers have skipped the entire progres-

sion from nonautomatic to semiautomatic machines and have moved from hand washing to fully automatic equipment. Thus, it is clear that the simple analogy between the growth in sales for nonautomatic, semiautomatic, and automatic machines does not exist between North America and Western Europe. Nevertheless, the analyst might conclude that one could lump together the nonautomatic and semiautomatic equipment in the Canadian market and use this growth pattern as the basis for estimation by analogy of potential demand in Western Europe.

3. The distinction between potential demand for a product based on underlying factors, and actual sales based on the combination of potential demand, and the offering conditions of a product should be kept clearly in mind. If there are differences among the availability, price, quality, and other factors associated with the product in two markets, potential demand in a target market will not develop into actual sales of a product because the offer conditions are not comparable.

▼ Comparative Analysis

Comparative analysis of market potential and marketing performance is one of the unique opportunities in international marketing analysis. While this approach is used extensively in multinational firms, it is equally useful in smaller companies active in several foreign markets. Such analysis reveals how much of a company's experience in one market is applicable to another. For example, a recent study of Canadian exporters showed that companies who had successfully entered a foreign market could not expect to repeat such success when entering a different foreign market without careful market research to provide guidance on the competitive setting in that market.[13]

Most comparative market research is focused on one or more of these questions:

- ▶ Who are the marketers?
    Provides a comparison of marketing institutions available.
- ▶ What do marketers do?
    Shows which functions they perform and how they compare.
- ▶ How are marketers interacting?
    Determines their level of competition and cooperation.
- ▶ What is government's role?
    Shows the type and level of government involvement.
- ▶ What are the key dimensions?
    Contrasts existing quality and quantity relationships.
- ▶ What do marketers contribute?
    Shows how effective and efficient their performance is.
- ▶ How does the environment affect markets?
    Shows what role ecological issues play.[14]

---

[13] F.H. Rolf Seringhaus, "Do Experienced Exporters have Market Entry Problems?" *The Finnish Journal of Business Economics* (1987) 36:4, p. 386.

[14] Adapted from Coskun Samli, Richard Still, and John S. Hill, *International Marketing* (New York: MacMillan Publishing Company) pp. 377–8.

▼ Cluster Analysis

The objective of cluster analysis is to group variables into clusters that maximize within-group similarities and between-group differences. This objective is well suited to international marketing research because the national markets of the world are made up of similarities as well as differences that are clustered within regions and across income levels or stages of economic development. A number of computer programs are available for cluster analysis.

▼ Multiple-Factor Indexes

A multiple-factor index measures potential demand indirectly by using as proxies variables that either intuition or statistical analysis suggests can be closely correlated with the potential demand for the product under review.

Gross indicators such as GNP, net national income, or total population are useful in constructing an index, but wherever possible the analyst should restrict the use of factors to variables that are closely related to product demand. For example, an analyst interested in the potential demand for small electrical appliances might conclude on the basis of cross-national analysis and the time series analysis within single countries that personal disposable income was the best proxy measure of expenditures on small appliances. If the analyst is attempting to measure demand for coffee-making appliances of all types, an essential additional proxy would be the number of coffee drinkers in the country and the type of coffee preferred.

Ordinarily, market indexes are constructed not to measure total potential but to rank submarkets or to assign potential shares of the total market to each submarket. An index of this kind can be used to establish sales quotas or evaluate sales performance. A Brazilian index assigns a potential to the state of Sao Paulo of 30 percent of the nation's total. If sales of the company's product fall below 30 percent, and the product sales are related to the three-factor index, management would have reason to question the performance in that submarket. Obviously, such a tool must be used with great care. Full investigation may show that the sales performance in Sao Paulo is satisfactory but that the index is an inaccurate measure of potential.

▼ Regression Analysis

Regression analysis can be a powerful tool for predicting demand in international markets. If the researcher elects to use multiple regression tactics, which is the use of independent or predictor variables to estimate a dependent variable, there are computer programs available today that follow a stepwise procedure. The procedure selects the independent variable that accounts for the most variance in the dependent variable, and then the variable that accounts for most of the remaining variance, and so on until the user decides to stop. Using these tactics the analyst can select from a set of potential predictor variables those variables that explain the greatest amount of variance in the independent variable under investigation.

TABLE 7–12 Regression of Amount of Product in Use per 1,000 Population on Gross National Product

Product	Number of Observations	Regression Equation	Unadjusted^2
Autos	37	$-21,071 + .101x$	.759
Radio sets	42	$8.325 + .275x$	.784
Television sets	31	$-16.501 + .074x$	.503
Refrigerators	24	$-21,330 + .102x$	.743
Washing machines	22	$-15.623 + .094x$	.736

Source: Reed Moyer, "International Market Analysis," *Journal of Marketing Research* (November 1968).

Table 7–12 summarizes regression results that relate consumption of various commodities to a single macroeconomic indicator, GNP per capita. A linear simple regression model of the form $Y = A + BX$ was used, where Y is the amount of product in use per thousand population and X is GNP per capita. As can be seen from the unadjusted R^2, in Table 7–12, this single microeconomic variable explains from 50 to 78 percent of the variation in the dependent variables.

The results in Table 7–12 can be interpreted as follows. An increase in $100 per capita GNP will result on the average in an increase of ten automobiles, ten refrigerators, nine washing machines, seven television sets, and twenty-seven radio sets per thousand population.

The variance in the dependent variable under investigation could be reduced by adding variables that are related to demand. For example, in the case of automobiles, in addition to looking at income, data could be obtained on the road system availability, on the price of automobiles, on the availability of public transportation, on the cost of keeping and operating an automobile, and on other relevant factors that could affect the sale of automobiles. With these additional variables, it is possible to follow a stepwise progression analysis strategy and select that combination of variables that explains the greatest amount of variance in automobile sales consistent with an acceptable level of statistical significance.

Many products do not lend themselves to simple single-variable regression analysis. Moyer, for example, found a very poor fit for a regression of cement consumption per capita on gross disposable product per capita. Fortunately, however, the consumption of many products can be estimated reasonably accurately by a knowledge only of income for GNP per capita in the market under investigation.

To use regression to estimate demand, analysts must first compute the regression using those predictor variables that are expected to explain variation in the dependent variable. If the unexplained variation is reasonably low, the analyst may use the results of these calculations to estimate current demand in countries for which no demand data are available. Getting the estimate of demand requires that the data on the predictive or independent variable be available. Assume, for example, that we want to estimate the ownership of refrigerators in country X where data on ownership are unavailable. Through regression analysis of 24 countries we have the equation $Y = -21.330 + 102X$, $R^2 = 0.743$, which is statistically significant at the 0.01 level where Y equals refrigerators in use per thousand population and X equals GNP per capita. GNP per capita in country X is $1,000. Using this equation we calculate the number of refrigerators in use to be 80.67 per thousand population. If we expect GNP per capita in country X to grow to, say, $1,300 during the next five years, and if our regression equation is valid over this range of incomes, using the same equation the number of refrigerators per thousand population in five years in country X will be roughly 111.

HEADQUARTERS CONTROL OF GLOBAL MARKETING RESEARCH

An important issue for international marketing management is where to locate control of the company's research capability. When research on foreign markets is required by a company that has no foreign subsidiaries, the key question is: do the expertise and resources required exist in-house? For companies with foreign affiliates or partners, the question of who is to participate in and control the research is more relevant.

The level and length of a company's foreign market experience, as mentioned earlier, also influence the approach to international market research. Those new to foreign markets learn and accumulate experience along the way and proceed from fairly general to increasingly comprehensive market research. Indeed, the greater the international marketing skill, the more foreign-market research-active the company becomes.[15] Nevertheless, a company's international market research tends to be less rigorous and less formal compared to domestic market research.[16]

The global company with an extensive foreign market presence thus can use resident expertise of a subsidiary and, depending on the automony arrangements, maintain control over the market research process. In practice, this means that the global company will, whenever possible, conduct research that is comparable. Comparable data based on experience in other parts of the world provide more possibilities for insight into market dynamics.

Research needs and practice vary widely across companies; however, comparability requires that scales, questions, and research methodology be standardized. To achieve this, the company must inject a level of control and review of marketing research at the global level. The person responsible for worldwide marketing research must respond to local conditions as he or she searches for a research program that may be implemented on a global basis. It is most likely that the marketing director will end up with a number of programs tailored to clusters of countries that exhibit within-group similarities. The agenda of a coordinated worldwide research program might look like that in Table 7–13.

---

[15] F.H. Rolf Seringhaus "Export Knowledge and its Role in Strategy and Performance," *The Finnish Journal of Business Economics* (1991) 40:1, pp.7.

[16] S.Tamer Cavusgil, "International Marketing Research: Insights into Company Practices," *Research in Marketing* (1984) 7, p. 267.

TABLE 7–13 Worldwide Marketing Research Plan

Research Objective	Country Cluster *A*	Country Cluster *B*	Country Cluster *C*
Identify market potential			X
Appraise competitive intentions		X	X
Evaluate product appeal	X	X	X
Study market response to price	X		
Appraise distribution channels	X	X	X

The headquarters manager of worldwide research should not simply "direct" the efforts of country research managers. It is his or her job to ensure that the corporation achieves maximum results worldwide from the total allocation of its research resources. To achieve this, the manager will need to ensure that each country is aware of research being carried out in the rest of the world and that each country is involved in influencing the design of its own country as well as the overall research program. Although each subsidiary will influence the country and the overall program, the manager of worldwide research must be responsible for the overall research design and program. It is his or her job to take inputs from the entire world and produce a coordinated research strategy that generates the information needed by managers to achieve global sales and profit objectives.

▼ The Management of the Marketing Information System

Organizing, implementing, and monitoring a global marketing research strategy and program is no easy task. It is not simply a marketing issue; it is actually an organizational imperative. The global organization is faced with the following needs:

An efficient method or system to scan and digest published sources and technical journals in the domestic country and then expand this to other countries.

Daily scanning, translating, digesting, abstracting, and electronic input of information into a market intelligence system. Despite the advances in global information, its translation and electronic input is mostly manual. This will continue for the next few years, particularly in developing countries.

Expanding information coverage to other regions of the world.

The theory and techniques used for accomplishing these and other information-gathering tasks were described earlier in this chapter. It is critical, however, that these tasks are coordinated in a way that is coherent with, and contributes to, the overall strategic direction of the organization. It is incumbent upon the marketing information system and research function to provide relevant information in a timely, cost-efficient, and actionable manner.

Over the past few years, we have seen dramatic changes in worldwide political and economic events. With the eruption of the Gulf crisis and war, the demise of communism, and the liberation of several Eastern European countries, the demand for access to credible worldwide business and political information has increased. Today's economic environments require worldwide news information on a daily basis that is less than a week old. Within Canada, several large corporations have developed a corporate or market intelligence system that meets the challenges presented by the overabundance (and frequent scarcity of certain types) of information. In firms such as these, senior management has made a commitment to this type of system. This is crucial. It keeps management throughout the organization abreast of industry, markets, competition, and products on a global basis. Typically, the strategic planning or market research departments staff these systems. They distribute information to senior management and to managers throughout the organization.

But despite the wealth of evidence that "information" and information technology are rapidly transforming almost all phases of economic and business activity, relatively little formal attention has been paid to the effects of the transformation on marketing theory and practice. This implies two important consequences: (1) the emergence of knowledge or information itself as an asset in its own right, often with significant marketplace value, and (2) the blurring of current boundaries and the (potentially radical) redefinitions of traditional conceptual categories—between the firm and the outside world as well as within the firm itself.

▼ The Marketing Information System as a Strategic Asset

The boundary between the firm and the outside world is dissolving and marketing has historically been responsible for managing many of the relationships across that boundary. The boundary between marketing and other functions is also dissolving, leading to the conclusion that the traditional notion of marketing as a distinct functional area within the firm is becoming obsolete. The process of marketing decision making is also changing. This is due largely to the changing role of information from a support tool to information as a wealth-generating, strategic asset.

Some firms are experimenting with "flatter" organizational structures, that is, less hierarchical, less centralized decision-making structures. These types of organization facilitate the exchange and flow of information between otherwise noncommunicative departments. The more information intensive the firm, the greater the degree to which marketing is involved in activities traditionally associated with other functional areas and vice versa. In such firms there is parallel processing of information.

Information intensity in the firm impacts market attractiveness, competitive position, and organizational structure. The greater the information intensity of a firm, the more the traditional product market boundaries shift such that the firm increasingly faces new sources of competition from firms in historically noncompetitive industries, particularly if those firms are also information intensive.

The emergence of the *superindustry* combining telecommunications, computers, financial services, and retailing into what is essentially an information industry is perhaps the most obvious and dramatic example of the phenomenon. Firms as diverse as Bell Canada, Northern Telecom, IBM, and various financial institutions now find that they are in direct competition, often with essentially the same products, not as a result of diversification, but of the rather natural extension and redefinition of their traditional product lines and marketing activities. This development reflects the fact that many of the firms' products have evolved to the point where significant portions of their value added are no longer based on their historically unique product features but rather on the information exchanged as part of customer transactions—much of which cuts across traditional product lines.

The greater the information intensity of a firm, the more its management tends to define its industry (and, hence, its competitors) in terms of market or customer characteristics, as opposed to product characteristics. Indeed, for the newly competing firms, what gives strategic continuity to the emerging businesses in which they participate is the apparent belief that the basis for differential advantage does not lie in products but in the relationships cultivated with a particular set of consumers or markets.

▼ An Integrated Approach to Information Collection[17]

Organized intelligence is the coordinated organization activity of keeping under surveillance whatever parts of the entire environment the organization decides to monitor in order to bring about a systematic collection and analysis of competitive intelligence to serve the needs of the organization as a whole. Organizing for intelligence requires more than gathering and disseminating good intelligence. Many companies that simply assign an analyst to the task of gathering, analyzing, and disseminating intelligence encounter problems in getting managers to use the output, in gaining credibility for the output and its function, and in establishing the relevance of the output for users.

The role of organized competitive intelligence in shaping strategy will depend on its ability to supplement rather than replace the informal activities of employees, especially those of top management. One obstacle to a fully integrated marketing information system (fully integrated comprising both formal and informal information-gathering techniques) is that monitoring activities are not usually fully integrated with the decision-making process. Without the information being put to use, the monitoring effort will invariably fail to make a given company more competitive. The influential work by Michael Porter on competitive strategy coupled with increasing global competitive pressures and loss of market dominance for many American companies has helped bring environmental scanning into a new focus. The emphasis has been on competitive intelligence rather than on broader environmental scanning. When considering the possibility of establishing an organized intelligence system, a company may want to review the questions listed in Table 7–14.

---

[17] This section is adapted from Benjamin Gilad, "The Role of Organized Competitive Intelligence in Corporate Strategy," *The Columbia Journal of World Business,* 24, no. 4 (1989), 29–36. Copyright 1989. Reprinted with permission.

TABLE 7–14   When Does a Company Need Organized Intelligence?

1. Are top executives well informed about the competitive conditions in the market, or do they typically grumble about lack of sufficient knowledge?
2. Do proposals and presentations by middle management show an intimate knowledge of competitors and other industry players? Do these managers seem to know more than what has been published in trade literature?
3. Do managers in one department/division know of intelligence activities in other units? Do they share intelligence regularly?
4. How many times during the last six months was management surprised by developments in the marketplace? How many decisions yielded less than satisfactory results and what percentage was caused by lack of an accurate assessment of competitive response?
5. Has competitive pressure increased in the industry in question? Does management feel comfortable about its state of familiarity with foreign competitors?
6. How much does the company spend on on-line databases? How many users know about the availability of the system and how to access it?
7. Do users of information suffer from overload of data but underload of good analysis and estimates of implications to the company?

▼ SUMMARY

One of the most basic ingredients of a successful marketing strategy is information. The global marketer must scan the world for information about opportunities and threats. The two equally important modes of scanning are surveillance by keeping in touch with an area of information, and search by actively seeking out information. Both are important and require conscious attention to design and management. This chapter outlines a conceptual framework for organizing the scanning activity of individuals and organizations.

▼ DISCUSSION QUESTIONS

1. What is the major source of information for headquarters executives of global companies?

2. What are the different modes of information acquisition? Which is the most important for gathering strategic information?

3. What determines the horizons of managers? Why do some managers seem to see farther and more clearly than others?

4. Assume that you have been asked by the president of your organization to come up with a systematic approach to scanning. The president does not want to be surprised by major market or competitive developments. What would you recommend?

5. What is the difference between latent and existing demand?

6. What are some examples of countries that might lend themselves to the use of lead-lag analysis?

7. What is the rationale for the use of the technique of estimation by analogy?

8. Suppose you were the marketing director of a global organization. What arguments would you present to other senior managers to enlist their cooperation in coordinating information collection and exchange efforts? How would you convince them that marketing intelligence should be considered a strategic asset?

▼ BIBLIOGRAPHY

Books

DOUGLAS, SUSAN P., AND C. SAMUEL CRAIG, *International Marketing Research*. Englewood Cliffs, NJ: Prentice-Hall, 1983.

HEATH, DANIEL, AND OXFORD ANALYTICA, *America in Perspective: Major Trends in the United States Through the 1990s*. Boston: Houghton Mifflin, 1986.

JAFFE, EUGENE D., *Grouping: A Strategy for International Marketing*. New York: AMA, 1974.

KELLY, JOHN M., *How To Check Out Your Competition: A Complete Plan For Investigating Your Market*. New York: Wiley, 1987.

KIPLINGER, AUSTIN H., AND KNIGHT A. KIPLINGER, *America in the Global 90's: The Shape of the Future—How You Can Profit From It*. Washington, DC: Kiplinger Books, 1989.

KRAVIS, IRVING B., ZOLTAN KENESSEY, ALAN HESTON, AND ROBERT SUMMERS, *A System of International Comparisons of Gross Product and Purchasing Power*. Baltimore: Johns Hopkins University Press, 1975.

KRUGMAN, PAUL R., *The Age of Diminished Expectations: U.S. Economic Policy In The 1990s*. Cambridge, MA: MIT Press, 1990.

WEEKLY, JAMES K., AND MARK K. CARY, *Information for International Marketing: An Annotated Guide to Sources*. New York: Greenwood Press, 1986.

Articles

ADLER, LEE, "Managing Marketing Research in the Diversified Multinational Corporation," in *Marketing in Turbulent Times and Marketing: The Challenges and Opportunities—Combined Proceedings*, ed. Edward M. Mazze. Chicago: American Marketing Association, 1975, 305–308.

CAVUSGIL, S. TAMER, "Qualitative Insights into Company Experiences in International Marketing Research," *Journal of Business and Industrial Marketing* (Summer 1987), 41–54.

DAVENPORT, THOMAS H., MICHAEL HAMMER, AND TAUNO J. METSISTO, "How Executives Can Shape Their Company's Information Systems," *Harvard Business Review*, 67, no. 2 (March/April 1989), 130–134.

DAVIDSON, LAWRENCE S., "Knowing the Unknowable," *Business Horizons*, 32, no. 5 (September/October 1989), 2–8.

DOUGLAS, SUSAN P., C. SAMUEL CRAIG, AND WARREN J. KEEGAN, "Approaches to Assessing International Marketing Opportunities for Small- and Medium-sized Companies," *Columbia Journal of World Business* (Fall 1982), 2–30.

GILAD, BENJAMIN, "The Role of Organized Competitive Intelligence in Corporate Strategy," *Columbia Journal of World Business* (Winter 1989), 29–35.

GLAZER, RASHI, "Marketing in an Information-Intensive Environment: Strategic Implications of Knowledge as an Asset," *Journal of Marketing* (October 1991), 1–19.

GREEN, ROBERT, AND ERIC LANGEARD, "A Cross-National Comparison of Consumer Habits and Innovator Characteristics," *Journal of Marketing* (July 1975), 34–41.

LINDBERG, BERTIL C., "International Comparison of Growth in Demand for a New Durable Consumer Product," *Journal of Marketing Research* (August 1982), 364–371.

MOYER, REED, "International Market Analysis," *Journal of Marketing Research* (November 1968).

SETHI, S. PRAKASH, "Comparative Cluster Analysis for World Markets," *Journal of Marketing Research*, 8 (August 1971), 350.

SHARER, KEVIN, "Top Management's Intelligence Needs: An Executive's View of Competitive Intelligence," *Competitive Intelligence Review* (Spring 1991), 3–5.

STANAT, RUTH, "Tracking Your Global Competition," *Competitive Intelligence Review* (Spring 1991), 17–19.

Vogel, R. H., "Uses of Managerial Perceptions in Clustering Countries," *Journal of International Business Studies* (Spring 1976), 91–100.

Wasilewski, Nikolai, "Dimensions of Environmental Scanning Systems in Multinational Enterprises," Pace University, Working Papers No. 3, May 1993.

EIGHT

Global Segmentation and Regional Market Characteristics

Introduction

Before a company pursues market expansion opportunities by entering new geographic markets, management must first analyze the global environment. The company exists in a world of more than 200 countries and territories, each of which differs from all the others in some respects. At the same time, there will be ways in which various countries, and the people who live in them, resemble each other as well. Global market segmentation may be defined as the process of identifying groups or sets of potential customers at either the national or subnational level who are likely to exhibit similar buying behavior.[1]

After marketers have identified segments, the next step is **targeting,** that is, evaluating the segments and focusing marketing efforts on a country or group of people that has significant potential to respond. Targeting reflects the reality that a company should identify those consumers that it can reach most effectively and efficiently. Finally, companies must plan a way to reach their chosen target market(s) by determining the best **positioning** for their product offerings. Positioning means finding a way to fix the product in the minds of potential buyers in the target market by devising the appropriate marketing mix.

GLOBAL MARKET SEGMENTATION

Interest in global market segmentation dates back to the earliest traders. In the late 1960s, one observer suggested that the European market could be divided into three broad categories—international sophisticate, semisophisticate, and provincial—solely on the basis of consumers' presumed receptivity to a common advertising approach.[2] Another writer suggested that certain themes such as the desire to be beautiful, the desire to be free of pain and healthy, and the love of mother and child were universal and could be used in advertising around the globe.[3]

---

[1] See Salah S. Hassan and Lea Prevel Katsanis, "Identification of Global Consumer Segments: A Behavioral Framework," *Journal of International Consumer Marketing*, 3, no. 2 (1992), p. 17 for a similar definition.

[2] John K. Ryans, Jr., "Is It Too Soon to Put a Tiger in Every Tank?" *Columbia Journal of World Business* (March–April 1969), p. 73.

[3] Arther C. Fatt, "The Danger of 'Local' International Advertising," *Journal of Marketing* (January 1967).

In the 1980s, Ted Levitt noted that consumers in different countries increasingly seek variety, and that the same new segments are likely to show up in multiple national markets. Thus, ethnic or regional foods such as sushi, Greek salad, or hamburgers might be in demand anywhere in the world. Levitt's thesis was that such "pluralization of consumption" or "segment simultaneity" allows marketers to pursue a segment on a global scale.

Global market segments, that is groups of buyers who share a small set of key characteristics or attributes and, consequently, a desire for a product, exist. Examples can be found in the luxury product classes; Chanel handbags or Rolex watches are product examples this global segment buys.

Today, advertising agencies and global companies are likely to segment world markets according to several key criteria: demographics (including national income and size of population), psychographics (values, attitudes, and lifestyles), behavioral characteristics, and benefits sought. It is also possible to cluster different national markets using key dimensions of their business and market environments—for example, government regulation—to establish groupings.

▼ Demographic Segmentation

Demographic segmentation is based on measurable characteristics of populations such as age, gender, income, education, and occupation. A number of global demographic trends, such as fewer married couples, fewer children, changing roles of women, and higher incomes and living standards, are driving the emergence of global segments.[4]

For most consumer and industrial products, national income is the single most important segmentation variable and indicator of market potential. Per capita income varies widely in world markets, from a low of C$72 in Mozambique to a high of C$43,600 in Switzerland. A traditional approach to demographic segmentation involved clustering countries into segments of high, middle, and low income; companies simply targeted those with the highest income levels.

The Canadian market, with a per capita GNP of C$25,000, over C$680 billion total GNP in 1992, and a population of more than 27 million people is the seventh largest economy in terms of consumption capacity (see Chapter 2 for more discussion). By comparison, other industrialized countries with a similar per capita income can be much larger, for example the U.S., or much smaller, Belgium, in terms of total annual income.

Patterns of prosperity no longer conform to national borders. For example D'Arcy Masius Benton & Bowles created the concept of the "golden circles's of Europe." It shows that within a 250-mile ring around Cologne, Germany, live Western Europe's wealthiest consumers.[5]

---

[4] Teresa J. Domzal and Lynette Unger, "Emerging Positioning Strategies in Global Marketing," *The Journal of Consumer Marketing*, 4, no. 4 (Fall 1987), 26–27.

[5] "The Myth of the Euroconsumer," *The Economist* (Nov. 4, 1989) p.79.

About 75 percent of the world's GNP is located in the triad—North America, Japan, and Western Europe. Thus, by segmenting in terms of the single demographic variable of income, a company could reach the most affluent markets by targeting three areas: the European Union (EU), North America, and Japan.

Many global companies also realize that for products whose price is low enough—for example, cigarettes, soft drinks, ball point pens, and transistor radios—population is a more important segmentation variable than income. Thus, China and India, with respective populations of 1.2 billion and 900 million, represent attractive target markets for all companies with low-priced consumer products. One marketing challenge in a country like China where average per capita GNP is only C$570 is to successfully serve the existing mass market for low-price consumer products.

It is important to recognize that the preceding income figures quoted for China and India are average figures. There are also high-income segments in each of these countries that are quite large and fast growing. Marketers should never be blinded by averages. It is also important to point out that the preceding average income figures do not reflect the standard of living in these countries. In order to really understand the standard of living in a country, it is necessary to determine the purchasing power of the local currency. In all cases for low-income countries, the purchasing power of the local currency in the low- income country is much higher than that implied by the exchange value of the low-income-country currency. In other words, the C$570 per capita income average for China is 3,590 Chinese renminbi (6.3 renminbi = C$1.00) and 3,590 renminbi will buy much more in China than C$570 will buy in Canada.

A more contemporary approach to demographic segmentation involves variables besides national income, such as age. One example of the importance of demographics in global segmentation is the global teenager market—young people between the ages of 12 and 19.[6]

The global telecommunications revolution and frequent travel are two critical driving forces behind the emergence of this segment.[7] Teens' exposure to and interest in fashion, music, and a youthful lifestyle are homogenizing influences on a global scale. The result is that teenagers in Toronto, Paris, Hong Kong, London, Rome, Tokyo, New York, Berlin, and Stockholm share experiences that influence their remarkably consistent consumption behavior.

Young consumers may not yet have conformed to cultural norms—indeed, they may be rebelling against them. This fact, combined with shared universal needs, desires, and fantasies (for name brands, novelty, entertainment, trendy and image-oriented products) make it possible to reach the global teen segment with the persuasive power of unified marketing programs of companies such as Coca-Cola, Benetton, Sony, Swatch, and PepsiCo Inc. Global media such as MTV provide a perfect vehicle for reaching this 1.3-billion-person, multi-billion-dollar purchasing power segment. Satellites such as AsiaSatI are beaming Western programming and commercials to tens of millions of viewers in China, India, and scores of other countries.

---

[6] Marcus W. Brauchli, "Star Struck: A Satellite TV System Is Quickly Moving Asia into the Global Village," *The Wall Street Journal*, May 10, 1993, pp. A1, A8

[7] This section draws heavily on Salah S. Hassan and Roger D. Blackwell, *Global Marketing – Perspectives and Cases*, (Fort Worth: Dryden Press, 1994) pp. 67–71.

TABLE 8-1 The Global Teenager Segment: Selected Characteristics

Dimensions	Attributes
shared values	growth, change, future, learning, play
benefits sought	novelty, trendy image, fashion statement, name brands
demographics	aged 12–19, well-traveled, high media exposure
communication media	teen magazines, MTV, radio, video, peers, role models
distribution channels	general retailers with name brands
price range	affordable

Source: Adapted from S.Hassan and K. Katsanis, "Identification of Global Consumer Segments: A Behavioural Framework", *Journal of International Consumer Marketing*, (1990) 3:2, pp. 11-28.

Clearly, the teenager segment comprises several microsegments such as pre-adolescents, female/male teens, and adolescents. Table 8–1 highlights some of the shared values of the global teenager segment.

Another global segment is the so-called elite: older, more affluent consumers who are well traveled and have the money to spend on prestigious products with an image of exclusivity. This segment's needs are spread over various product categories: durable goods (prestigious automobiles such as Mercedes Benz); nondurables (upscale beverages such as Perrier mineral water or Chivas Regal scotch); and financial services (American Express Gold and Platinum cards).

Technological change in telecommunications makes it easier to reach the global elite segment. Global telemarketing with International 800 (or similar) services is a viable option today as Bell Canada, via "Canada Direct", offers such services in more than 34 countries. An increased reliance on catalog marketing by upscale retailers such as Harrods, Laura Ashley, and Ferragamo has also yielded impressive results.

▼ Psychographic Segmentation

Psychographic segmentation is the process of grouping people in terms of their attitudes, values, and lifestyles. Data are obtained by means of questionnaires that require respondents to indicate the extent to which they agree or disagree with a series of statements. Psychographics are primarily associated with SRI International, a market research organization in the U.S., as well as Canada Lifestyles Inc. in Canada. SRI's original VALS and updated VALS 2 analyses of U.S. consumers are widely known.

One early application of psychographics outside of North America focused on value orientations of consumers in the United Kingdom, France, and Germany. Although the study was limited in scope, the researcher concluded that "the underlying values structures in each country appeared to bear sufficient similarity to warrant a common overall communications strategy."[8] Psychographic analyses of the Japanese market have been conducted by SRI International; broader-

---

[8] Alfred S. Boote, "Psychographic Segmentation in Europe," *Journal of Advertising Research*, 22, no. 6 (December 1982–January 1983), 25.

scope studies have been undertaken by several global advertising agencies, including Bates Worldwide Inc., D'arcy Massius Benton & Bowles (DMBB), and Young & Rubicam (Y&R).[9] These analyses have given marketers a detailed understanding of such segments as the global teenager and global elite discussed earlier. International marketers can enlist this expertise either through Canadian agencies or international offices of global advertising agencies.

Bates Worldwide's GLOBAL SCAN™

GLOBAL SCAN™[10] is an ambitious study that encompasses eighteen countries, mostly located in the triad. To achieve the goal of identifying attitudes that could help explain and predict purchase behavior for different product categories, the researchers studied consumer attitudes and values, as well as media viewership/readership, buying patterns, and product use. The survey attempts to identify both country-specific and global attitudinal attributes.

Some sample statements, of the hundreds used with respondents, are:[11]

- ▶ My greatest achievements are still ahead
- ▶ Everything is changing too fast today
- ▶ I work hard and I play hard
- ▶ I am often asked by my friends for my opinions on new trends
- ▶ I think of myself as a sophisticated person
- ▶ I try to eat natural foods most of the time
- ▶ I feel that I am too much in debt today
- ▶ Advertising doesn't tell people the truth about products

Combining the results from the 18 countries yielded a segmentation study known as Target Scan, a description of five global psychographic segments that can be used as target profiles, or as brand-specific targets. The relative size of these target profiles for ten countries are compared in Figure 8–1. Bates Worldwide has labeled the segments as strivers, achievers, pressured, traditionals, and adapters. Bates gives the following main characteristics of these lifestyle segments:[12]

Strivers. People who have busy schedules and demanding lives. They push themselves hard to obtain the success they anticipate in the future. They are burdened with the stress and time pressure of not having made it yet. They are likely to be starting families—yet another demand on them. Snack and convenience foods fit into their fast-paced lifestyles, and they are major consumers of many of the products we advertise.

Achievers. Prototypical baby boomers, leaning to the upscale and professional/managerial, who have already achieved much of what the strivers

---

[9] The following discussion is adapted from Rebecca Piirto, *Beyond Mind Games: The Marketing Power of Psychographics* (Ithaca, New York: American Demographics Books, 1991).

[10] GLOBAL SCAN™ is the property of Bates Worldwide, Inc.

[11] "Global Items," Bates Worldwide Inc. (New York: personal communication, January 1995).

[12] "Description of lifestyle segments," Bates Worldwide Inc. (New York) used with permission.

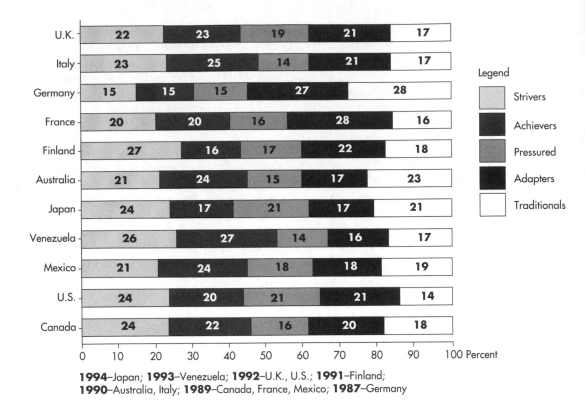

FIGURE 8–1
Global Lifestyle Segments (Selected Countries)
Source: GLOBAL SCAN™ Lifestyle Segments, Bates Worldwide, Inc. Used with permission.

are still working hard to attain. Health, nutrition, and fitness are important to them. They are stylish and they lead mass-market opinion. They go for quality and sophistication, and are interested in technology.

Pressured. A group with somewhat more women than men that is caught in a relatively lowly station in life. They feel the pressures of living from many directions at once: from their role as women, from economics, from broken families, from ageing, and so on. This pressure obliterates any joy from their lives. While they say that nutrition is important to them, they also splurge. Convenience products fit well in their lives.

Adapters. An older group who are contented with themselves, yet open to change. They are making a comfortable adjustment to the 1990s. They accept modern, mainstream values, without rejecting their own traditional views. They represent a good market for travel and continuing education.

Traditionals. A conservative group, these people are unwilling to accept the changes around them. They stick to the tried and true, the old-fashioned ways of thinking, eating and running their lives. There are three key attitudes that define this group: the man is the boss, the woman stays at home, and the pet is an animal. Clearly, everything has its place.

While GLOBAL SCAN™ is a helpful tool for identifying consumer similarities across national boundaries, it can also help to highlight differences *between* segments in different countries. For example, in Canada the 8 million baby boomers help swell the ranks of strivers and achievers to close to half the population. In Germany, on the other hand, the striver segment is older and comprises a smaller share of the population. GLOBAL SCAN™ has also pinpointed important differences between Canadians and Americans, who are often considered to belong to the same geographic segment of North America. Bates highlights some key differences between Canadians (English-speaking) and Americans, for the strivers segment, this way:

> Canadians are not as pessimistic about society's materialism, and feel more optimistic that the rewards will eventually be worth the effort. They are pushing harder to succeed, work much harder, yet feel less pressure and better adjusted; they find work more fulfilling, are prouder of their work place, and are more inclined to put career before family. Canadians are greater risk takers and are more eager for change. They are more optimistic about their ability to get ahead and are more likely to want financial advice; more Canadians want luxury goods others cannot have, and seek status and performance in their cars. Convenience foods of all kinds play a big part in their lives.[13]

Similarly, GLOBAL SCAN™ revealed marked differences between the circumstances that strivers find themselves in in different countries. These differences translate into different preferences. While Canadians see cars as a symbol of status and performance, Americans buy cars that are fun, stylish, and that present good value; Japanese strivers consider cars to be an extension of their homes and will accessorize them with lavish features—curtains or high-end stereo systems, for example. This means that different advertising appeals and product positioning would be necessary when targeting strivers in these three countries.

D'arcy Massius Benton & Bowles's Euroconsumer Study

DMBB's research team compiled a fifteen-country study titled "The Euroconsumer: Marketing Myth or Cultural Certainty?" The researchers identified four lifestyle groups: successful idealists, affluent materialists, comfortable belongers, and disaffected survivors. The first two groups represent the elite, the latter two represent mainstream European consumers.

---

[13] *Global Scan Presentation Canada*, Bates Worldwide Inc. (October 17, 1989) with permission.

Successful Idealists. Comprising from 5 to 20 percent of the population, this segment consists of persons who have achieved professional and material success while maintaining commitment to abstract or socially responsible ideals.

Affluent Materialists. These status-conscious "up-and-comers," many of whom are business professionals, use conspicuous consumption to communicate their success to others.

Comfortable Belongers. Comprising one-quarter to one-half of a country's population, this group, like Global Scan's adapters and traditionals, is conservative and most comfortable with the familiar. Belongers are content with the comfort of home, family, friends, and community.

Disaffected Survivors. Lacking power and affluence, this segment harbors little hope for upward mobility and tends to be either resentful or resigned. This segment is concentrated in urban neighborhoods of high crime such as found in inner-city areas. Despite disaffected survivors' lack of societal status, their attitudes nevertheless tend to affect the rest of society.

Y&R's Cross-Cultural Consumer Characterizations (4Cs)

4Cs is a twenty-country psychographic segmentation study focusing on goals, motivations, and values that help to determine consumer choice. The research is based on the assumption that "there are underlying psychological processes involved in human behavior that are culture-free and so basic that they can be found all over the globe."[14] Three overall groupings can be further subdivided into a total of seven segments: constrained (resigned poor and struggling poor), middle majority (mainstreamers, aspirers, and succeeders), and innovators (transitionals and reformers). The goals, motivation, and values of these segments range from "survival," "given up," and "subsistence" (resigned poor) to "social betterment," "social conscience," and "social altruism" (reformers). Figure 8–2 shows some of the attitudinal, work, lifestyle, and purchase behavior characteristics of the seven groups.

Combining the 4Cs data for a particular country with other data permits Y&R to predict product and category purchase behavior for the various segments. Yet, as was noted earlier in the discussion of Global Scan, marketers at global companies that are Y&R clients are cautioned not to assume they can develop one strategy or one commercial to be used to reach a particular segment across cultures. As a Y&R staffer notes, "As you get closer to the executional level, you need to be acutely sensitive to cultural differences. But at the origin, it's of enormous benefit to be able to think about people who share common values across cultures."[15]

▼ Behavior Segmentation

Behavior segmentation focuses on whether or not people buy and use a product, as well as how often, and how much they use it. Consumers can be categorized in terms of **usage rates**—for example, heavy, medium, light, and nonuser.

---

[14] Ibid., p. 161.
[15] Ibid., p. 165.

Consumers can also be segmented according to *user status*—potential users, nonusers, ex-users, regulars, first-timers, and users of competitors' products.

In 1993 Tambrands Inc., marketers of Tampax brand tampons, launched a C$25 million global advertising effort in North America, Eastern and Western Europe, Latin America, and the Pacific Rim. The campaign had two strategic purposes directly related to usage rates and user status. One spot was designed to show women new times and ways to use tampons; it included advice from gynecologists that tampons can safely be worn overnight, a creative appeal reflecting

FIGURE 8–2
Y&R's 4Cs

Resigned Poor

Attitudes	Work	Lifestyle	Purchase Behavior
Unhappy	Labor	Shut-in	Staples
Distrustful	Unskilled	Television	Price

Struggling Poor

Attitudes	Work	Lifestyle	Purchase Behavior
Unhappy	Labor	Sports	Price
Dissatisfied	Craftspeople	Television	Discount stores

Mainstreamers

Attitudes	Work	Lifestyle	Purchase Behavior
Happy	Craftspeople	Family	Habit
Belong	Teaching	Gardening	Brand loyal

Aspirers

Attitudes	Work	Lifestyle	Purchase Behavior
Unhappy	Sales	Trendy sports	Conspicuous consumption
Ambitious	White collar	Fashion magazines	Credit

Succeeders

Attitudes	Work	Lifestyle	Purchase Behavior
Happy	Managerial	Travel	Luxury
Industrious	Professional	Dining out	Quality

Transitionals

Attitudes	Work	Lifestyle	Purchase Behavior
Rebellious	Student	Arts/crafts	Impulse
Liberal	Health field	Special-interest magazines	Unique products

Reformers

Attitudes	Work	Lifestyle	Purchase Behavior
Inner growth	Professional	Reading	Ecology
Improve world	Entrepreneur	Cultural events	Homemade/grown

Box 8–1
On Subculture Segmentation of Consumers in the U.S.

The African-American Market
▶ Generally as diverse a white consumers. Some distinctions are that they are more likely to try new products, particularly clothing, while staying brand loyal when they have found something they like. Spending power is on the rise. This subgroup is, on average, six years younger than whites. The African-American middle class is increasingly targeted in recognition of that community's increasing buying power and importance.

The Hispanic-American Market
▶ A more distinct subculture than African-Americans because more than two-thirds speak Spanish at home. They tend to be more traditional and conservative than most other groups. The dominant role of the man is acknowledged. They exhibit brand loyalty and faith in the quality of nationally advertised products. Advertising has a stronger influence on this group than others. This market has grown four times faster than the general population and attracts increasing attention from companies.

The Asian-American Market
▶ This is the most highly educated and affluent subgroup. They possess a strong ethnic identity and great cultural diversity. The Chinese represent the largest group, followed by Filipinos, Japanese, Vietnamese, and Koreans. The high rate of immigration shows this group growing fourteen times faster than the general population. General campaigns are not effective and have created difficulty in targeting these diverse groups.

Source: Adapted from Henry Assael, *Marketing Principles and Strategy* (Fort Worth: Dryden Press, 1993) pp.118–120.

research showing that two-thirds of tampon users don't use them at night. Other creative executions featured stylish women who scoff at sanitary pads, which Tambrands doesn't make. This message may be particularly effective in reaching nonusers in overseas markets, where tampon use is not as high as in Canada and the U.S.[16]

The failure of some Canadian retailers who expanded into the U.S. shows both the danger in assuming that Canadian and U.S. consumers behave alike, and in treating segmentation of the market lightly. Lessons learned from these failures suggest that, compared with Canadian consumers, Americans:[17]

▶ are more price sensitive

▶ demand more service, quality and convenience

---

[16] Laura Bird, "Tambrands Plans Global Ad Campaign," *The Wall Street Journal*, June 22, 1993, p. B8

[17] Henry Lane and Donald F. Hunter, "How To Survive In U.S. Retail Markets," *Business Quarterly* (Winter 1990) pp. 62-3.

- ▶ prefer stores with deep product offerings rather than a generalized product mix
- ▶ are sophisticated comparative shoppers
- ▶ have different and rapidly changing tastes

▼ Benefit Segmentation

Global benefit segmentation focuses on the numerator of the value equation—the B in $V = B/P$. This approach can achieve excellent results by virtue of marketers' superior understanding of the problem a product solves or the benefit it offers, regardless of geography. For example, Nestlé discovered that cat owners' attitudes toward feeding their pets are the same everywhere. In response, a pan-European campaign was created for Friskies Dry Cat Food. The appeal was that dry cat food better suits a cat's universally recognized independent nature.

GLOBAL TARGETING

As discussed in the introduction to this chapter, segmenting is the process by which marketers identify groups of consumers with similar wants and needs. **Targeting** is the act of evaluating and comparing the identified groups and then selecting one or more of them as the prospect(s) with the highest potential. A marketing mix is then devised that will provide the organization with the best return on sales while simultaneously creating the maximum amount of value to consumers.

▼ Criteria for Targeting

The three basic criteria for assessing opportunity in global target markets are the same as in single-country targeting: current size of the market segment and anticipated growth potential; competition; and the compatibility of the target with the company's overall objectives and the feasibility of successfully reaching it.

Current Segment Size and Growth Potential. Is the market segment currently large enough that it presents a company with the opportunity to make a profit? If it is not large enough or profitable enough today, does it have high growth potential so that it is attractive in terms of a company's long-term strategy? Indeed, one of the advantages of targeting a market segment globally is that while the segment in a single-country market might be too small, even a narrow segment can be served profitably with a standardized product if the segment exists in several countries.[18] As noted previously, the billion-plus members of the global "MTV Generation" constitute a huge market that, by virtue of its size, is extremely attractive. A good example of the need for conservatism in estimating the size and growth for market segments is China. Box 8–2 shows that segments need to be clearly defined.

---

[18] Michael E. Porter, "The Strategic Role of International Marketing," *The Journal of Consumer Marketing*, 3, no. 2 (Spring 1986), 21.

Potential Competition. A market or market segment characterized by strong competition may be a segment to avoid. Fuji, however, entered the Kodak-dominated North American color film market nearly two decades ago. Its strategy of pricing below Kodak and offering several film products to the "advanced amateur" segment, which Kodak has neglected, quickly gave Fuji a hold in the market. Kodak's distribution clout in the supermarket and drugstore chains, as well as its responsiveness to market needs, has prevented Fuji from expanding its market share much beyond 10 percent. Because of this, Fuji concentrated on Europe, where it has increased its market share from 10 to 25 percent over the past

---

Box 8–2
China's Potential Consumer Market

The Chinese market with its 1.2 billion population is a magnet to foreign companies. All major global consumer brands, including Cadbury's chocolate; Pizza Hut; Kraft's Maxwell House coffee; Knorr bouillon cubes; McDonald's; Kentucky Fried Chicken; Marlboro and Lucky Strike cigarettes; Carlsberg, Foster's, and San Miguel beers; Estee Lauder cosmetics; Louis Vuitton handbags; and Unilever's Omo and Procter & Gamble's Ariel detergents are vying for a foothold to serve the Chinese market.

The reality is that only about one-sixth of the population, those individuals with an income of C$1,300 or more, are considered *economically active*. A vast difference in income exists between the 20 percent of Chinese who live in urban areas from the 80 percent in rural China. The average urban household has an annual income of C$660, compared with less than one-fourth of that in rural households.

Retail sales of basic packaged goods, such as cosmetics, toothpaste, and washing powder are expected to expand quickly. Sales of more expensive products, like jewellery, compact disks, household appliances, jeans, cameras, and furniture, should grow between 20 and 25 percent annually over the next decade:

Three consumer segments exist, according to DRI/McGraw-Hill:

▶ *Imported luxury goods* segment of 5 million people buy products, such as designer watches, cosmetics, spirits; the wealthiest 1 percent live in urban areas, and 0.2 percent in rural areas.

▶ *Imported middle class goods* segment of 20 million people buy products such as jeans, sports footwear; the top 2.5 percent live in urban areas, and 1 percent in rural areas.

▶ *Locally made middle class goods* segment of 65 million people buy products such as inexpensive appliances, consumer goods; the top 10 percent are in urban areas, and 4 percent in rural areas.

Source: Based on "How Not to Sell 1.2 Billion Tubes of Toothpaste," *The Economist* (December 3, 1994) pp.75-6.

decade, a considerable threat to Kodak, which holds about 40 percent of the film market. Kodak, on the other hand has invested heavily in the world's second-largest market for photographic supplies, Japan, where it has achieved a 10 percent share of the market.[19]

Compatibility and Feasibility. If a global target market is large enough, and if strong competitors are either absent or not deemed to represent insurmountable obstacles, then the final consideration is whether a company can and should target that market. To be sure, reaching global market segments requires considerable resources—for advertising, distribution and other marketing expenditures. Another question is whether the pursuit of a particular segment is compatible with the company's overall goals and established sources of competitive advantage.

▼ Selecting a Global Target Market Strategy

After evaluating the identified segments in terms of the three preceding criteria, marketers must next decide on the appropriate targeting strategy. There are three basic categories of target marketing strategies: undifferentiated marketing, concentrated marketing, and differentiated marketing.

Undifferentiated Global Marketing. Undifferentiated global marketing is analogous to mass marketing in a single country. Strictly speaking, it involves creating the same marketing mix—product, price, distribution, and communications—for a broad mass market of potential buyers. The appeal of undifferentiated global marketing is clear: Standardized products mean lower production costs. The same is true of standardized global communications. Undifferentiated global marketing is a strategy that calls for extensive distribution in the maximum number of retail outlets.

Executives at Revlon International recently adopted the strategy of undifferentiated target marketing when they announced their intention of making Revlon a global name. President Paul Block announced that "All Revlon North American advertising for all products, whether they are cosmetics, skincare, haircare, or Almay, will now be used worldwide."[20] The global theme is keyed to a "Shake That Body" campaign. Revlon's strategy calls for developing the huge consumer markets that are emerging in Eastern Europe, including Hungary and the former Soviet republics.

Concentrated Global Marketing. The second global targeting strategy involves devising a marketing mix to reach a single segment of the global market. In cosmetics, this approach has been used successfully by House of Lauder, Chanel, and other cosmetics houses that target the upscale, prestige segment of the market.

---

[19] Clare Ansberry, "Uphill Battle: Eastman Kodak Co. Has Arduous Struggle to Regain Lost Edge", *The Wall Street Journal*, April 2, 1987, pp. 1,12.

[20] Pat Sloan, "Revlon Eyes Global Image; Picks Y & R," *Advertising Age*, January 1, 1993, p. 1.

Differentiated Global Marketing. The third target marketing strategy represents a more ambitious approach than concentrated target marketing. It entails targeting two or more distinct market segments with multiple marketing mix offerings. This strategy allows an organization to achieve wider market coverage. Unilever NV and Cosmair Inc. are examples of companies pursuing a differentiated global marketing strategy by targeting both ends of the perfume market. Unilever markets Calvin Klein and Elizabeth Taylor's Passion, both targeted at the luxury market; Wind Song and Brut are its mass-market brands. Cosmair sells Trésor and Giorgio Armani Gio to the upper end of the market and Gloria Vanderbilt to the lower end. Mass marketer Procter & Gamble, known for its Old Spice and Incognito brands, also embarked upon this strategy with its 1991 acquisition of Revlon's EuroCos, marketers of Hugo Boss for men and Laura Biagiotti's Roma perfume. Now P&G is launching a new prestige fragrance, Venezia, in Canada, the United States, and nine European countries.[21]

GLOBAL PRODUCT POSITIONING

After the global market has been segmented and one or more segments have been targeted, it is essential to plan a way to reach the target(s). To achieve this task, marketers use **positioning,** a process whereby a company establishes an image for its product in the minds of consumers relative to the image of competitors' product offerings. In today's global market environment, many companies find it increasingly important to have a unified global positioning strategy.

Can global positioning work for all products? One study suggests that global positioning is most effective for product categories that approach either end of a "high-touch/high-tech" continuum.[22] Both ends of the continuum are characterized by high levels of customer involvement and by a shared "language" among consumers.

▼ High-Tech Positioning

Personal computers, video and stereo equipment, and automobiles are examples of product categories where high-tech positioning has proven effective. Such products are frequently purchased on the basis of concrete product features, although image may also be important. Buyers typically already possess or wish to acquire considerable technical information. High-tech products may be divided into three categories: technical products, special-interest products, and demonstrable products.

---

[21] Gabriella Stern, "Procter Senses Opportunity in Posh Perfume," *The Wall Street Journal,* July 9, 1993, pp. B1, B5.
[22] The following discussion is adapted from Domzal and Unger, "Emerging and Positioning Strategies in Global Marketing," pp. 27–37.

Technical Products. Computers, chemicals, tires, and financial services are just a sample of the product categories whose buyers have specialized needs, require a great deal of product information and who share a common "language." Computer buyers in Russia and Canada are equally knowledgeable about "486 microprocessors, 80-meg hard drives, and 8 meg of RAM." Marketing communications for high-tech products should be informative and emphasize features.

Special-Interest Products. While less technical and more leisure or recreation oriented, special-interest products also are characterized by a shared experience and high involvement among users. Again, the common language and symbols associated with such products can transcend language and cultural barriers. Fuji bicycles, Adidas sports equipment, and Canon cameras are examples of successful global special-interest products.

Products that Demonstrate Well. Products that "speak for themselves" in advertising of features and benefits can also travel well. The Polaroid instant camera is an example of a highly demonstratable and very successful global product.

▼ High-Touch Positioning

Marketing of high-touch products requires less emphasis on specialized information and more emphasis on image. Like high-tech products, however, high-touch categories are highly involving for consumers. Buyers of high-touch products also share a common language and set of symbols relating to themes of wealth, materialism, and romance. The three categories of high-touch products are products that solve a common problem, global village products, and products with a universal theme.

Products that Solve a Common Problem. At the other end of the price spectrum from high-tech, products in this category provide benefits linked to "life's little moments." Ads that show friends talking over a cup of coffee in a café or quenching thirst with a soft drink during a day at the beach put the product at the center of everyday life and communicate the benefit offered in a way that is understood worldwide.

Global Village Products. Chanel fragrances, designer fashions, mineral water, and pizza are all examples of products whose positioning is strongly cosmopolitan in nature. Fragrances and fashions have traveled as a result of growing worldwide interest in high-quality, highly visible, high-price products that often enhance social status. However, the lower-priced food products just mentioned show that the global village category encompasses a broad price spectrum.[23]

In global markets, products may have a global appeal by virtue of their country of origin. The "Canadian-ness" of Bauer sports equipment, and the "American-ness" of Harley-Davidson enhances their appeal to cosmopolitans around the world. In consumer electronics, Sony is a name synonymous with vaunted Japanese quality; in automobiles, Mercedes is the embodiment of legendary German engineering.

---

[23] Ibid., p. 31.

Products that Use Universal Themes. As noted earlier, some advertising themes and product appeals are thought to be basic enough that they are truly transnational. Additional themes are materialism (keyed to images of well-being or status), heroism (themes include rugged individuals or self-sacrifice), play (leisure/recreation), and procreation (images of courtship and romance).

It should be noted that some products can be positioned in more than one way, within either the high-tech or high-touch poles of the continuum. A sophisticated camera, for example, could simultaneously be classified as technical and special interest. Other products may be positioned in a "bi-polar" fashion, that is, as both high-tech and high-touch. For example, Bang & Olaafson consumer electronics, by virtue of their design elegance, are perceived as both high-tech and high-touch.

REGIONAL MARKET CHARACTERISTICS: COOPERATIVE TRADE ARRANGEMENTS

It is not necessary to be an expert on every country in the world to manage a global marketing program. Obviously, in-depth market and country knowledge must be applied to the country marketing effort by members of the business team, but team members may be local agents, representatives, or employees. The critical skill of the global marketer is working with his or her team. The purpose of this section is to give you a better understanding of world market characteristics so you can work effectively with the marketing team in serving customers in the different countries of the world.

This section, which is organized around world regions, presents a broad overview of the markets of the world. The first half of the section outlines economic cooperation and preferential trade arrangements. The second half describes the characteristics of the major regional markets of the world and concludes with an in-depth study of one country market.

▼ Economic Cooperation and Preferential Trade Arrangements

Since World War II there has been a tremendous interest in economic cooperation. The enthusiasm for economic cooperation has been stimulated by the success of the European Union. There are many degrees of economic cooperation, ranging from the agreement of two or more nations to reductions of barriers to trade, to the full-scale economic integration of two or more national economies. In the nineteenth century, the German Zollverein and the British imperial preference system were the two most important agreements leading to the reduction of internal tariff barriers in Germany and international barriers in the British Empire.

The best-known preferential arrangement of this century was the British Commonwealth preference system, known as the imperial preference system before World War II. This system was very important for Canada's trade with the United Kingdom, Australia, New Zealand, India, and certain other former British colonies in Africa, Asia, and the Middle East. The decision by the United Kingdom to join the European Economic Community resulted in the demise of this system. This development illustrates the constantly evolving nature of international economic cooperation.

GATT

The General Agreement on Tariffs and Trade (GATT) is a binding contract between 103 governments whose objective is to promote trade among members. GATT members include developing nations (constituting over two-thirds of membership), all of the Organization for Economic Cooperation and Development (OECD), central and eastern European countries, plus twenty-nine observer countries who apply GATT rules on a defacto basis. GATT negotiators opened the world to merchandise trade, and tariffs fell from an average of 40 percent in 1945 to 5 percent today. Tariff reductions resulted in a tremendous growth in trade. Between 1945 and 1975, the volume of trade expanded by roughly 500 percent.[24] With tariffs on goods greatly reduced, attention has turned to other impediments to trade. In recent years, the basic technique of protectionism has shifted from tariffs to subsidies and market sharing. Market sharing goes against one of the basic tenants of GATT—nondiscrimination (i.e., a country is not allowed to set different tariffs on the same good imported from different countries).

Since 1986, the GATT has been conducting the largest trade negotiations ever. In these negotiations the Uruguay Round discussions are focused on nontariff measures that restrict or distort trade, agricultural trade policy, trade in services, protection of intellectual property, and reductions in restrictions on foreign investment.[25] The key to this round has been the subsidy- and quota-ridden trade in food, which has developed outside the multilateral framework. Affluent countries protect and subsidize farm production. The surplus output is later sold at artificially low prices. According to the OECD, the cost to rich-country taxpayers and consumers is more than C$240 billion a year. Poor countries, which now include those in Eastern Europe, are denied their natural path out of poverty—food exports.[26]

Free Trade Area

A free trade area (FTA) is a group of countries that has agreed to abolish all internal barriers to trade among its members. Country members of a free trade area can and do maintain independent trade policies vis-à-vis the third countries. To avoid trade diversion in favor of low-tariff members (for example, importing goods in the member country with the lowest tariff for shipment to countries

---

[24] *The Economist*, "GATT's Last Gasp," December 1, 1990, p. 16.

[25] Joseph A. McKinney, "How Multilateral Trade Talks Affect the U.S.," *Baylor Business Review* (Fall 1991), pp. 24–25.

[26] *The Economist*, "Free Trade's Fading Champion," April 11, 1992, p. 65.

within the area with higher external tariffs), a system of certificates of origin is used and customs inspectors police the borders between members. Examples of FTAs are the European Free Trade Area formed in 1960 and the Canada-U.S. Free Trade Area, which formally began in 1989.[27]

Customs Union

The customs union is the logical evolution of the free trade area. In addition to eliminating the internal barriers to trade, members of a customs union agree to the establishment of common external barriers. The European Economic Community (EEC and later EC) from 1957 to 1992 has included a customs union, along with other agreements.

Economic Union

An economic union builds upon the elimination of the internal tariff barriers and the establishment of common external barriers. It seeks to coordinate economic and social policy within the union to allow free flow of capital and labor from country to country. Thus, an economic union is a common marketplace not only for goods but also for services and capital. The full evolution of an economic union would involve the creation of a unified central bank, the use of a single currency, and common policies on agriculture, social services and welfare, regional development, transport, taxation, competition, and mergers. A fully developed economic union requires extensive political unity, which makes it similar to a nation. The further integration of nations that were members of fully developed economic unions would be the formation of a central government that would bring together independent political states into a single political framework. The European Community is approaching its target of completing most of the steps required to create a full economic union. Much remains to be done including the creation of a single currency, which is now targeted for implementation before year-end 1999.

▼ Regional Economic Cooperation

In addition to the multilateral initiative of GATT, countries in each of the world's regions are seeking to lower barriers to trade within their regions. The following section describes the major regional economic cooperation agreements.

Andean Group

This group, officially known as the Acuerdo de Cartagena (from the Cartagena Agreement which established it in 1969) and also known as the Grupo Andino (Andean Group) or the Pacto Andino (Andean Pact), aims to accelerate the harmonious development of its member states through economic and social integration. The members of the group are Bolivia, Colombia, Ecuador, Peru, and

---

[27] Michael Parkin and Robin Bade, Economics-Canada in the Global Environment (Don Mills: Addison-Wesley Publishers Ltd, 1991) pp. 636-7.

Venezuela. The organization consists of a commission, a council, a junta (a technical body responsible for the agreement's implementation), a parliament, a court of justice, a reserve fund, and a development corporation.

ANCOM's main goals include the following:[28]

- ▶ The development of member countries through economic and social integration and cooperation.
- ▶ The elimination of interregional trade barriers through gradual tariff reductions and a common external tariff.
- ▶ The approval of a common approach to foreign investment.
- ▶ The creation of Andean multinational enterprises.
- ▶ The conclusion of basic agreements for industrial programs.

In 1992 the Andean Pact became Latin America's first operating subregional free trade zone, with a total of 97 million consumers. Under the pact, all foreign exchange, financial and fiscal incentives, and trade subsidies were to be abolished by December 1992. A high-level commission will be appointed to look into any unfair trade practices among countries. Member nations plan to unify their customs systems by 1995. Until then, common external tariffs (CETs) will be in effect at different levels depending on the products involved. However, the CET does not apply to agricultural products, which are governed by a separate Common Agricultural Policy pact.

The Andean Pact is a much smaller entity than the Southern Cone Common Market (MERCOSUR) and nearly insignificant in relation to the free trade area that has come into being under the North American Free Trade Agreement (NAFTA).[29]

Association of South East Asian Nations (ASEAN)

The Association of South East Asian Nations is an organization for economic, political, social, and cultural cooperation among its six member countries: Brunei, Indonesia, Malaysia, the Philippines, Singapore, and Thailand. ASEAN was established in 1967 with the signing of the Bangkok Declaration.

The ASEAN group has 340 million people and a GNP of C$595 billion in 1994. The group's per capita GNPs range from C$24,100 in Singapore to C$1,000 for Indonesia. ASEAN is the sixth largest trading partner to the United States. Two-way trade between the United States and ASEAN totaled C$48 billion in 1993.[30]

There is a growing realization among ASEAN officials that broad common goals and perceptions are not enough to keep the association alive. A constant problem is the strict need for consensus among all six members before

---

[28] *Business International-ILT Latin America* (July 1991).

[29] *Business International*, 39, no. 1 (January 13, 1992), 11.

[30] George Paine, "U.S.-ASEAN Dialogue in Bangkok Will Review Economic Issues," *Business America* (May 21, 1990), pp. 2–3 and Statistics Canada, Catalogue 65-001 (1994).

proceeding with any form of cooperative effort. Although the six countries of ASEAN are geographically close, they are divided in most other respects. One of the reasons the association has remained in existence is because it does almost nothing. In mid-1987 the president of the Philippines was urging the association to become a real political and economic force and proceed with real economic integration.

An ASEAN economic treaty is being actively discussed. If adopted such a treaty would radically alter the customary mode of ASEAN cooperation. Instead of moving along at a slow and often erratic pace, unencumbered by targets or deadlines, a new treaty would impose obligations on member states. Under the treaty, a series of targets might be involved, culminating in the declaration of a free trade area by 2000.[31]

The ASEAN countries are also members of the larger Asia-Pacific Economic Co-operation forum (APEC), which was founded in 1989. APEC members, in addition to the ASEAN countries, include Australia, Canada, Chile, China, Hong Kong, Japan, Mexico, New Zealand, Papua New Guinea, South Korea, Taiwan, and the United States. Its long-term goal is free trade. Because of the inclusion of trading giants like Canada, Japan, and the U.S., the interpretation of any APEC trade statistics requires caution. While APEC accounted for some 46 percent of global exports in 1993, 70 percent of these exports went to other APEC countries, but 43 percent went to other South-East Asian countries. Thus the ASEAN group features prominently within APEC.[32]

Caribbean Community and Common Market (CARICOM)

The Caribbean Community and Common Market was formed in 1973 as a movement toward unity in the Caribbean. It replaced the Caribbean Free Trade Association (CARIFTA) founded in 1965. The members are Antigua and Barbuda, Bahamas, Barbados, Belize, Dominica, Grenada, Guyana, Jamaica, Montserrat, Saint Christopher and Nevis, Saint Lucia, Saint Vincent and the Grenadines, and Trinidad and Tobago.[33]

Although the name sounds impressive, the population of the entire 13-member Caribbean Community is 6 million, fewer than the population of each of the three large, non-CARIFTA Caribbean nations—Haiti, Cuba, and the Dominican Republic. Even if one adds these islands, the total population amounts to about 32 million.[34]

The Caribbean Community's main activity is economic integration by means of a Caribbean Common Market. During the 1980s, the economic difficulties of member states hindered the development of interregional trade. Another problem was the difficulty of applying the CARICOM Rules of Origin,

---

[31] Michael Vatiloptos, "Sense of Purpose—New Challenges Lead Member States to Examine Role," *Far Eastern Economic Review,* (June 20, 1991) 152:25, pp. 24–25.

[32] "APEC – The Opening of Asia," *Economist* (November 12, 1994) pp.23-6.

[33] *The Europa World Yearbook 1991,* vol. 1 (London: Europa Publications Limited, 1991) p. 108.

[34] Robert Pastor and Richard Fletcher, "The Caribbean in the 21st Century," *Foreign Affairs,* (Summer 1991) 7:3, 100.

which attempt to verify that imported goods genuinely come from within the community.[35] As a result, CARICOM has been largely stagnant since it was founded, but at a July 1991 meeting the group agreed to speed integration, and targeted a single-market economy by January 1, 1993.[36]

The CARICOM bloc of English-speaking Caribbean states has a special arrangement under the Caribbean Basin Initiative (CBI), for duty-free access to the United States market.

Central American Common Market (CACM)

Central America is trying to revive its common market, which was set up in the 1960s. It collapsed in 1969 when war broke out between Honduras and El Salvador after a riot at a soccer match involving the two countries. The five members, El Salvador, Honduras, Guatemala, Nicaragua, and Costa Rica, decided in July 1991 to reestablish the common market by 1994.[37]

The Secretariat for Central American Economic Integration (SIECA), headquartered in Guatemala City, is composed of ministers responsible for economic integration and regional development. SIECA is charged with helping to coordinate the movement toward a Central American common market. It has been serving as secretariat for a group of customs experts whose aim is to create a Uniform Customs Duty.[38] External tariffs on the isthmus are to fall to a range of 5 to 20 percent.[39]

Cooperation Council for the Arab States of the Gulf (GCC)

The organization, generally known as the Gulf Cooperation Council, was established in 1981 by six Arab states: Bahrain, Kuwait, Oman, Qatar, Saudi Arabia, and United Arab Emirates.

The organization provides a means of realizing coordination, integration, and cooperation in all economic, social, and cultural affairs. Gulf finance ministers drew up an economic cooperation agreement covering investment, petroleum, the abolition of customs duties, harmonization of banking regulations, and financial and monetary coordination. The GCC formed committees to coordinate trade development in the region, industrial strategy, agricultural policy, and uniform petroleum policies and prices.[40]

The Gulf Cooperation Council is one of three newer regional organizations. In 1989, two other organizations were established. Morocco, Algeria, Mauritania, Tunisia, and Libya banded together in the Arab Maghreb Union (AMU), while Egypt, Iraq, Jordan, and North Yemen created the Arab

---

[35] *Europa Yearbook 1991*, p. 108.

[36] *Business Latin America, Business International* (January 13, 1992), p. 12.

[37] "Free-Trade Free-For-All," *The Economist*, (January 4, 1992) p. 57.

[38] "More Than a Dream: Regional Economic Integration in Central America," *ABOARD*, a 1991 interview with the assistant secretary-general of SEICA, p. 69.

[39] *Financial Times* (February 11, 1992) p. 4.

[40] *The Europa Yearbook 1991*, p. 123.

Cooperation Council (ACC). Many Arabs see their new regional groups (the GCC, ACC, and AMU) as embryonic economic communities, which will foster the development of inter-Arab trade and investment. The newer organizations are more promising than the Arab League, which consists of 21 member states and has a constitution that requires unanimous decisions.[41]

Economic Community of West African States (ECOWAS)

The Treaty of Lagos establishing ECOWAS was signed in May 1975 by sixteen states with the object of promoting trade, cooperation, and self-reliance in West Africa. The members are: Benin, Burkina Faso, Cape Verde, The Gambia, Ghana, Guinea, Guinea-Bissau, Ivory Coast, Liberia, Mali, Mauritania, Niger, Nigeria, Senegal, Sierra Leone, and Togo.

In 1980 the member countries agreed to establish a free trade area for unprocessed agricultural products and handicrafts. Tariffs on industrial goods were also to be abolished; however, there were implementation delays. By January 1990, tariffs on twenty-five items manufactured in ECOWAS member states had been eliminated. The organization installed a computer system to process customs and trade statistics and to calculate the loss of revenue resulting from the liberalization of intercommunity trade. In June 1990, ECOWAS adopted measures that would create a single monetary zone in the region by 1994.[42]

The European Union (EU)

The European Union (formerly known as the European Community) was established by the Treaty of Rome in January 1958. The six original members were Belgium, France, Holland, Italy, Luxembourg, and West Germany. In 1973, Britain, Denmark, and Ireland were admitted, followed by Greece in 1981, Spain and Portugal in 1986, and Austria, Finland, and Sweden in 1995. In 1987, the then twelve EU member countries gave themselves until the end of 1992 to create a genuine single market in goods, services, and capital.

Since the end of 1992, people have been able to move freely across national borders inside the EU. The twelve-nation EU represents 345 million people, a combined gross national product of C$7.2 trillion, and a 39 percent share of world exports. Figure 8–3 presents the European Community's exports by destination.

The EU has agreed to create a single European currency and bank. This is known as economic and monetary union (EMU). The implementation of this agreement raises the issue of the extent to which countries sharing a currency need to coordinate taxes and budgets. There is concern in Germany that the deutsche mark, an important foundation of Germany's economic success, will be replaced by a less stable European currency.

The member governments have also agreed in principle to a European political union. This would not create a single European government, but it would mean more power for the European Parliament, more majority voting in the

---

[41] "A Survey of the Arab World," *The Economist*, (May 12,1990) pp. 3, 19.

[42] *The Europa World Yearbook, 1991*, pp. 133–134.

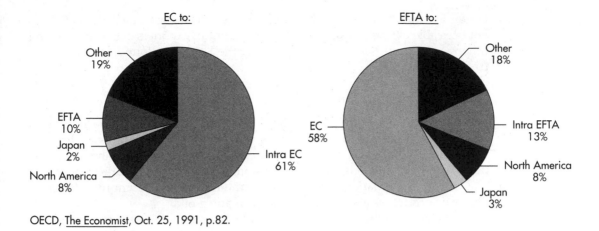

EC to:

Other 19%
EFTA 10%
Japan 2%
North America 8%
Intra EC 61%

EFTA to:

Other 18%
Intra EFTA 13%
North America 8%
Japan 3%
EC 58%

OECD, <u>The Economist</u>, Oct. 25, 1991, p.82.

FIGURE 8–3
European Exports 1990
By Destination—% of Total
(*Data Sources:* Copyright © 1991, The Economist Newspaper Group, Inc. Reprinted with permission.)

Council of Ministers (the 12-member intergovernmental group that really runs the EU), and more say for the EU on foreign policy and defense.[43]

Some recent historic agreements include the following:

The Maastricht Treaty. A December 1991 EC summit resulted in a timetable for the final stages of economic and monetary union. Between now and the end of 1996, the 15 member countries will bring their economies in line with the standards required to introduce fixed exchange rates and a single currency. This will happen in January 1997 if a simple majority is ready; otherwise, it will start automatically in January 1999. The Maastricht negotiators were more hesitant in moving toward political union. The treaty created a procedural labyrinth for foreign policy decisions and social legislation, as well as for research and industrial policy.

European Economic Area. (EEA). In October 1991, the EC and the European Free Trade Association (EFTA) reached agreement on the creation of a European Economic Area, which aims to achieve the free movement of goods, services, capital, and labor between the two blocs beginning January 1993. Under the EEA, the EFTA countries will adopt all the EC's single-market legislation.

European Agreements. In December 1991, Czechoslovakia, Hungary, and Poland became associate members of the EC through what are known as "European Agreements." This new arrangement will lead to a gradual elimination of tariffs and quantitative restrictions on bilateral trade in industrial goods.

Completing the single-market program by year-end 1992 was a major EU program. The Council of Ministers adopted 282 pieces of legislation and regu-

---

[43] "The European Revolution," *The Econimist,* (November 9, 1991), pp. 59–60.

lations to achieve this goal. EU enlargement is a major issue. Finally, the EU has not been able to reach an agreement with other farm exporters over subsidies and other agricultural issues that were part of the Uruguay Round of multilateral trade talks.[44]

European Free Trade Association (EFTA)

The European Free Trade Association (EFTA) was established by the Stockholm convention of 1959. As of 1995, the four remaining EFTA countries are Iceland, Liechtenstein, Norway, and Switzerland. EFTA's objective is to bring about free trade in industrial goods and an expansion of trade in agricultural goods.

EFTA's population is 10 percent of the European Community. Its gross domestic product is about half that of Germany alone.

In October 1991 after fourteen months of negotiations, the twelve EC nations and the then seven EFTA members agreed to set up a European Economic Area (EEA) in 1993. If the proposal is ratified by the European Parliament and by all nineteen countries, the EEA will be the world's largest bloc, with 377 million consumers, almost one-third of world GNP (32 percent) and 46 percent of world trade. The EEA will be a free trade area, not a customs union with common external tariffs. EFTA members will maintain border controls with the EC, denying them the benefit of the single market. Many EFTA countries see the European Economic Area as a first step toward full membership in the European Community.

Total inter-EFTA exports in 1990 were $29 billion as compared to exports to the European Community of $130 billion, $18 billion to the United States and Canada, $7 billion to Japan, and $40 billion to the rest of the world.[45]

North American Free Trade Area (NAFTA)

In 1988 Canada and the United States signed a free trade agreement (Canada-U.S. Free Trade Agreement or FTA), which was enlarged in 1993 to include Mexico in a North American Free Trade Area (NAFTA). NAFTA created a free trade area with a 1992 population of 373 million and a gross national product of C$8 trillion.

All three governments will promote economic growth through expanded trade and investment. The benefits of continental free trade will enable all three countries to meet the economic challenges of the decades to come. The staged elimination of barriers to the flow of goods, services, and investment, coupled with strong intellectual property rights protection (patents, trademarks, and copyrights) will benefit businesses, workers, farmers, and consumers.

The United States is Canada's largest trading partner and some 80 percent of the merchandise exported goes to the U.S. The combined three-way trade with the U.S. and Mexico is approaching C$300 billion.

Organization for International Economic Cooperation (OIEC)

The Council for Mutual Economic Assistance (COMECON, CMEA) was established in 1949 on a Soviet initiative with Bulgaria, Czechoslovakia, Hungary,

---

[44] *Business International*, (January 13, 1992), pp.3–4.

[45] "European Economic Area: A Short Shelf-Life," *The Economist*, (October 26, 1991), pp. 60–61; "Lest a Fortress Arise," pp. 81–82.

Poland, and Romania as the other founding members. The German Democratic Republic, Mongolia, Cuba, and Vietnam joined later and Yugoslavia had associate status. Its purpose was to create a common market among its members and to promote the coordination and integration of their economies.

With the transition in Eastern Europe from command to market economies and the start of trade in convertible currency, the member governments decided to disband COMECON in January 1991. A successor body called the Organization for International Economic Cooperation (OIEC) was created on an interim basis to wind down the remnants of COMECON. The OIEC has an advisory and consultative role, although it will deal with questions of tariffs and quotas, and the development of relations with other organizations, including the European Community. East European members are committed to market principles and integration in the world economy.[46]

Southern Cone Common Market (MERCOSUR)

Argentina, Brazil, Paraguay, and Uruguay, with a combined population of 198 million and a gross domestic product of C$620 billion, agreed in March 1991 to form the Southern Cone Common Market (MERCOSUR) for goods, services, capital, and labour by 1995. The four nations plan to dismantle nontariff barriers and implement a common external tariff. Their aim is free trade of no less than 80 percent of goods by the year 2005.[47] Their accord also commits them to pursue common trade, agriculture, transport, and communications policies.

Much depends on the successful outcome of this experiment in regional cooperation. If Brazil and Argentina can work well together, hopes for an integrated Latin America will rise significantly. Brazil has the largest population and economy (in terms of both gross domestic product and exports) and reserves of natural resources. Argentina has the third largest economy and fourth largest population in Central and South America. A major impediment to integration is the lack of discipline and responsibility in the economic and political spheres, which is reflected by the volatility of their currencies.[48]

South African Development Coordination Conference (SADCC)

SADCC was set up in 1980 by the region's black-ruled states to promote trade and cooperation. The ten members are Angola, Botswana, Lesotho, Malawi, Mozambique, Namibia, Swaziland, Tanzania, Zambia, and Zimbabwe. The real block to trade has been SADCC's poverty. The group's combined GNP of $30 billion is half of Greece's and a third of South Africa's.[49]

---

[46] Brian Hunter, ed., *The Statesman's Year-Book, 1991–92* (New York: St. Martin's Press, 1992), p. 50.

[47] NAFTA is not alone," *The Economist* (June 18, 1994) p. 47.

[48] *Business International,* (January 13, 1992), p. 11.

[49] "Across the Border," *The Economist* (November 3, 1990), pp. 22–23 (Survey of South Africa).

REGIONAL MARKET CHARACTERISTICS: GEOGRAPHIC CLUSTERS

There are innumerable ways of dividing the countries of the world into different regional markets. In effect, defining regional markets is an exercise in clustering countries where, it is hoped, both within-cluster similarities and between-cluster differences will be maximized. Clustering can be accomplished with the use of mathematical programs that determine the spatial relationship of objects (countries), defined by variables (market measures), or by judgmental analysis on the basis of both explicit and implicit criteria. In the section that follows, national markets are clustered judgmentally on this basis of geographic proximity. A brief survey of each region is presented. Japan is examined in greater detail as an example of a more in-depth analysis. Some global statistics precede the market surveys in order to give an overview of the relative size and growth rates of each of the world regions.

▼ World Statistics by Region

As can be seen in Figure 8–4, 87 percent of the world's wealth is concentrated in Western Europe, North America, and the Asia/Pacific region. These regions also enjoyed the fastest growth between 1980 and 1990 (see Figure 8–5). Eastern Europe, Latin America, the Middle East, and Africa have much smaller economies and experienced slower growth.

The disparity in wealth is illustrated in Figure 8–6. The 1992 per capita GNP in North America was C$27,200 as compared with C$930 in Africa. Japan's per capita income was approximately C$32,900, whereas it was only C$2,300 for the entire Asia/Pacific region, which includes China and India. Per capita in-

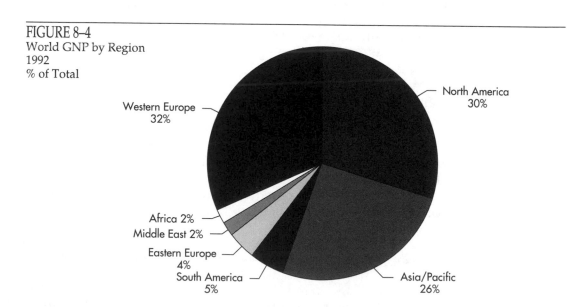

FIGURE 8–4
World GNP by Region
1992
% of Total

North America
30%

Western Europe
32%

Africa 2%

Middle East 2%

Eastern Europe
4%

South America
5%

Asia/Pacific
26%

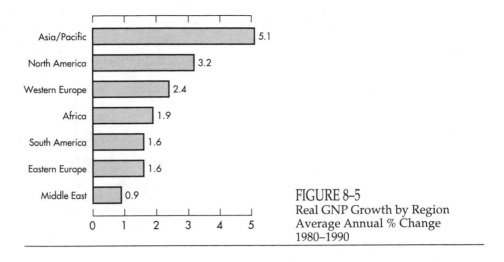

FIGURE 8-5
Real GNP Growth by Region
Average Annual % Change
1980–1990

come in the Asia/Pacific region, Western Europe, and North America has grown faster than elsewhere in the world (see Figure 8–7).[50]

▼ Western Europe

Western Europe, covering less area than Australia, generated nearly 32 percent of global income in 1992. The region has twenty-three countries (fifteen EU and four EFTA countries, Channel Islands, Gibraltar, Greenland, and Malta) and a total population of approximately 377 million. Populations range from 260,000 in Iceland to 77 million in Germany.

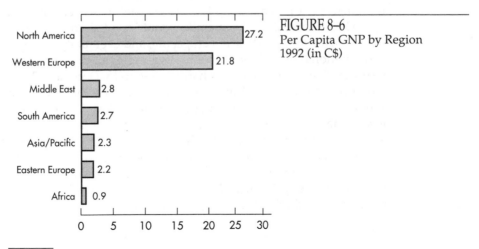

FIGURE 8-6
Per Capita GNP by Region
1992 (in C$)

[50] *Business International* (January 13, 1992), pp. 6–7.

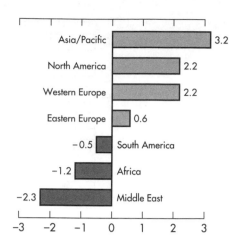

FIGURE 8–7
Real Growth in GNP Per Capita
Average Annual % Change
1980–1990

The countries of Western Europe are among the most prosperous in the world although their income is unevenly distributed. The average per capita annual income in Portugal is C$6,200 as compared with C$41,000 in Switzerland. Even though there are differences in income and obvious differences in language and culture, the once varied societies of Western Europe have grown remarkably alike. Where they still do differ in family and work patterns, they tend to be moving in the same direction.

In Western Europe, the proportion of women between 25 and 34 in the labor force has doubled in the past thirty to forty years. A growing number of adults now prefer just one child or none. A Europe of tiny families will age fast. In the world as a whole, half the people are under 24 years old. By contrast, half the EU's citizens are over 34. Young Europeans of both sexes have more education than their grandparents. The biggest job growth has been in services.[51]

The objective of the EU member countries is to harmonize national laws and regulations so that goods, services, people, and eventually money can flow freely across national boundaries. As a motivating goal, the community set a target of substantially completing this harmonization by December 31, 1992. The EU is attempting to shake up Europe's cartel mentality by handing down rules of competition patterned after American antitrust law. The EU is encouraging the development of a communitywide labor pool, and improvements to highway and rail networks are now being coordinated. European Monetary System (EMS) is already operating with a European Currency Unit (ECU) as its basis. The ECU exists on paper and in computers, based on a basket of "weighted" currencies. Some companies price their EU supplies and products in the ECU, thereby saving the time and cost of exchange transactions.[52]

---

[51] "The New Europeans," *The Economist,* (November 16, 1991), pp. 65–66.

[52] *International Business* (January 1992), pp. 49–50.

Box 8–3 shows the number of European, Canadian, American, and Japanese companies by industry that are on the *Fortune* Global 500 list.

▼ Eastern Europe

Eastern Europe includes the Balkan countries (Albania, Bosnia-Hercegovina, Bulgaria, Croatia, Macedonia, Montenegro, Romania, Slovenia, and Yugoslavia), the Baltic states (Estonia, Latvia, and Lithuania), the Commonwealth of Independent States (the former Soviet Union), the Czech and Slovak Federal Republic, Hungary, and Poland. Extraordinary political and economic reforms swept Eastern Europe focusing attention on a new market of 430 million people. The East Bloc accounted for 6.9 percent of world gross domestic product in 1990 and per capita GNP was C$4,275. With wage rates much lower than those in Spain, Portugal, and Greece, Eastern Europe represents not only an important market but also a low-cost manufacturing opportunity.

Marketing is undoubtedly a key to achieving the economic development of Eastern European countries. Due to the number of barriers that exist, it may take several decades for marketing to reach a level of sophistication comparable to Western Europe. The people must "unlearn" the past ways of life and then learn about democracy and capitalism. The countries need to develop their infrastructures and a legal and contractual framework to do business. A convertible currency is needed in order to transfer economic power from the government to consumers and customers. A business culture needs to be developed as well as a mechanism for forecasting demand.[53]

Consumer products require minimal adaptation for sales in Eastern European markets. Many East Bloc consumers are familiar with western brand names and view them as being of higher quality than domestic products.

The distribution infrastructure in Eastern Europe is weak. In most countries, the initial sales of Western consumer products will be restricted to major cities. Wholesalers are underdeveloped. Insufficient and unattractive retail space, the absence of self-service, and the three-line system (to select, pay for, and pick up merchandise) make shopping time consuming and frustrating.[54]

A fledgling marketing research industry is now emerging in Budapest, Prague, Warsaw, and Moscow. Because of the dearth of consumer information, consumer surveys are a necessary first step. Unlike blasé Western consumers, people in Eastern Europe are more than willing to answer questions. After years of directives from the top, people are flattered to be asked their opinions.[55]

▼ North America

The North American market is a distinctive world regional market. The United States and Canada represent a concentration of wealth and income in a closely linked economic and political environment that presents unique marketing characteristics. The United States, with 250 million people, had a per capita GNP of U. S. $22,700 in 1992. The U.S. market offers the combination of high per capita income, large population, vast space, and plentiful natural resources. High product ownership levels are associated with a high income and relatively high receptivity to innovations and new ideas both in consumer and industrial products. The U.S. has more global industry leaders than any other single country in the world. As Box 8–3 shows, only Japan rivals the U.S. in the number of global companies.

The U.S. market is as large as all of Western Europe, and is twice as large as the Japanese market. Another distinctive feature is that because of its size, there is, compared to other countries, more of an arm's-length relationship between business and government. This can provide greater opportunities for competing in the U.S.

Canada, with one-tenth of the population of its southern neighbor, and a 1992 GNP per capita of C$25,800, is uniquely dependent on the U.S. market. The

[53] Dr. Allan C. Reddy, "The Role of Marketing in the Economic Development of Eastern European Countries," *Journal of Applied Business Research*, 7, no. 3 (Summer 1991), 104, 106–107.

[54] John A. Quelch, Erich Joachimsthaler, and Jose Luis Nueno, "After the Wall: Marketing Guidelines for Eastern Europe," *Sloan Management Review* (Winter 1991), pp. 90–91.

[55] Lourdes Lee Valeriano, "Western Firms Poll Eastern Europeans to Discern Tastes of Nascent Consumers," *The Wall Street Journal*, April 27, 1992, pp. B1–B2.

value of the trade in goods and services between Canada and the U.S. was more than C$330 billion in 1993, making it the world's largest bilateral trading relationship. Some 80 percent of Canadian exports are destined for the American market. The role and importance of Canadian companies in the world is understated in summaries such as *Fortune*'s Global 500 listing in Box 8–3 because of the pervasive foreign ownership and control in Canadian industry. Many companies with a significant stake in the economy and foreign trade are foreign-owned. Many of these firms operate as autonomous profit centers within companies' global structures, in the area of global competition and often with global product mandates.[56] An example is Digital Equipment Canada (U.S.-owned), which exports 49 percent of its C$1.2 billion and has a global mandate: it sells PCs in North and South America, point-of-sale terminals globally, and servers globally except in Europe.[57]

U.S. investment dominates the foreign ownership element in Canadian business and many of these companies, such as General Electric and IBM, use the Canadian subsidiaries as major global suppliers of some of their products.

▼ Asia / Pacific

The twenty-three-country Pacific Rim region is a colossus, with 60 percent of the world's population. The region accounted for 23 percent of global income in 1990. Seventy-six percent of the region's income was concentrated in Japan, which has only 4 percent of the region's population. The four economic "tigers" of East Asia—South Korea, Taiwan, Singapore, and Hong Kong—have forged the fastest industrial revolutions the world has ever seen. Behind them are another four countries which are getting close to the point of industrial take-off—Thailand, Malaysia, Indonesia, and China. China with a population of 1.2 billion potential consumers is a country no marketer can afford to ignore.

Japan

Population density and geographic isolation are the two crucial and immutable factors that cannot be discounted when discussing Japan as a world market. It is interesting that while Japan's territory occupies 0.28 percent of the world total, and its population makes up only 2.3 percent of the world total, Japan generates 15.9 percent of the world's GNP. Japan's per capita GNP is C$32,900 compared with China's C$480.

Seventy-two percent of Japan's land area is mountainous, the residential area represents only 3 percent, and the industrial area is merely 1.4 percent. As a result, land prices are high. Another unique characteristic is that Japan is becoming acutely short of workers due to the steady decline in the birthrate since 1974. To cope with the labor shortage, more women and older people are being recruited.[58]

---

[56] Allan M. Rugman and Joseph R. D'Cruz, *New Visions for Canadian Business: Strategies for Competing in the Global Economy* (Toronto: Kodak Canada Inc., 1990) p. 21.

[57] "The Financial Post 500," *The Financial Post Magazine*, 1994, p. 104; and Suan Kendall "Manufacturing Excellence Earns Digital's Canadian Plant a Global Mandate," *The Globe and Mail*, Advertising Supplement, December 13, 1994, p.FS5

[58] Steven Butler, "The Vanishing Workers," *Financial Times* (December 16, 1991), p.1 (survey).

Mastering the Japanese market takes flexibility, ambition, and a long-term commitment. Japan has changed from being a closed market to one that's just tough. There are barriers in Japan in terms of attitudes, not laws. The key is to master certain basics for doing business in Japan. There must be a commitment to top-quality products and services. It is also essential to understand the culture. Products and marketing must be tailored to local tastes. Countless visits and socializing with distributors are necessary to build trust. Marketers must be willing to forgo profits for several years. They must also master the *keiretsu* (pronounced "kay-rhet-sue") system of tightly knit corporate alliances.[59]

Almost all of Japan's familiar companies belong to some kind of *keiretsu*. *Keiretsu* are critical to the country's special brand of capitalism, a system that pulls together an alliance of industry, government, capital, and high technology. Although *keiretsu* companies constitute less than 0.1 percent of all companies in Japan, they account for 78 percent of the value of all shares on the Tokyo Stock Exchange.[60] The *keiretsu* relationships are not agreements among competitors (cartels), but among customers and suppliers contributing at different levels to the manufacture of a single product. Toyota, for example, buys parts from *keiretsu* partners that are incorporated into the finished vehicle. Such relationships, if all parties remain loyal, give outside suppliers no opportunity to break in.[61]

Negotiating in Japan. According to an American consultant born in Japan, there are ten elements that form the core of her counsel to Western companies with little or no Japanese experience:

1. Find out everything you can about the people you plan to meet. Know the *keiretsu* that you will be dealing with.

2. Never expect a quick deal. Be prepared for many meetings during which relationships can build slowly.

3. Be ready and willing to take part in the small talk that precedes any real discussion of business.

4. Avoid confrontation. This is liable to lead to a loss of face for one side or the other and can end negotiations.

5. Do not be deceived by what may appear as a lack of emotion among the Japanese. Japanese are both emotional and sensitive; however, they contain their emotions.

6. The Japanese do not offer opinions easily. You should not inquire whether the Japanese with whom you are dealing agree or disagree. They will not give their opinion but rather the answer they think you expect.

7. A nod of the head in Japan does not mean "yes." A nod is likely to mean no more than "I hear you" or "I take your point."

8. A call to more meetings is a good sign. An invitation to further meetings means the Japanese are beginning to trust you.

---

[59] Aimee Stern, "How to Make It in Japan," *International Business* (November 1991), pp. 35, 37.
[60] Carla Rapoport, "Why Japan Keeps on Winning," *Fortune,* (July 15, 1991), p. 76.
[61] Donald I. Baker and Donald B. Ayer, "A Misguided Assault on Keiretsu," *The New York Times,* March 22, 1992, p. F13.

TABLE 8–2 Comparisons and Contrasts in Culture, Tradition, and Behavior Between Japan and Canada

	Japan	Canada
Myth / Hero Emphasis	Group	Individual/Idealistic
Attitude	Self-denial, Dependence	Self-expression, Independence, Conciliation
Emphasis	Obligations	Rights
Style	Cooperation	Competition
Assumptions	Interdependence	Independence
View of Self	Organization Man	Individual with a Skill
Cultural Attitude 1	We Are Unique	Shared Values
Cultural Attitude 2	Willing to Borrow / Adopt / Adapt	Import, Adopt, Invent
Organizational Goal 1 (Jobs / Employment)	Share of Market	Profitability, Financial Success
Organizational Goal 2	World Markets	North American Markets
Organizational Goal 3	Quality, Customer Value	Production, Financial Return
Worker Identification	Company	Craft, Function
Management	Generalist	Specialist
Trust In	Feeling	Thinking
Governmental Business Relations	Emphasis On Cooperation	Emphasis On Separation and Cooperation
Financial Structure (Debt:Equity)	80:20	40:60
Key Stakeholders	Employees	Shareholders
Key Values and Goals	Perfection, Harmony, Consensus	Peace, Order, Good Government

Note: The authors are indebted to Chikara Higashi, member of the Japanese Diet and President, Recia, Tokyo, for assistance in preparing this table.

9. Only rarely is there a single identifiable decision maker in Japanese business. You may be dealing with one person in a series of meetings, but that person will still want to go away to talk with colleagues, both junior and senior.

10. Consensus should not be undervalued. When it is reached things will move very fast.[62]

Table 8–2 summarizes the major contrasts in Canadian and Japanese cultural values and orientation. At the top of the table is the overall orientation of the two societies. Each recognizes the importance of both the individual and the collective, but a fundamental difference between the two countries is the fact that Canada emphasizes the importance of the individual, while Japan emphasizes the importance of the collective.

In Japan there is an affirmative attitude towards dependence, while in Canada, independence and conciliation are emphasized.[63] In Canada, as in the U.S., we prefer authoritarian decision-making, whereas the Japanese culture values participative decision-making more highly. Canadian culture emphasizes competition; Japan, however, values and celebrates cooperation. The

---

[62] James Bredin, "Japan Needs to Be Understood," *Industry Week,* April 20, 1992, pp. 24, 26.

[63] Doi, *The Anatomy of Dependence,* (Tokyo: Kodanssha International, 1973).

Japanese also have a definite preference for compromise; while this trait is valued in Canada, our preference is for confrontation.

Canadian decision-making is quick but often implementation is protracted, whereas the Japanese are very slow due to the concensus process in decision-making but very quick and steady in implementation. Our style tends to be more direct in contrast with the Japanese indirect style. Canadian decision-making is more short-term oriented than in Japan, where the more interactive and participatory style of decision-making—because it is so deliberate and incorporates so many inputs—is necessarily more long-term.

▼ Oceania

Australia and New Zealand are island economies in the Asian region that were originally settled by Europeans. The combined population is 21 million, or 0.4 percent of the world total. The income level in both countries is relatively high. Per capita GNP for Australia, in 1992, was C\$21,300, and C\$15,500 in New Zealand. The region accounts for 1.7 percent of global income. The real rate of growth in Australia, which has been stimulated by the enormous mineral resources of the continent, has exceeded 4 percent per year.[64]

Australia has a population of 17.5 million. Its mid-sized economy (C\$370 billion in 1992) is very dependent on trading conditions in world markets for its major exports of low value-added agricultural and mineral products. In 1989, the ratio of Australia's imports to GNP was about 18 percent, while the ratio of exports to GNP was 13.1 percent. Asia is Australia's largest market, taking 55 percent of Australia's exports in 1990 compared with just 26 percent in 1960.[65]

The domestic marketing environment in Australia is serviced by product and marketing mix strategies comparable to advanced Western and Japanese markets. A major challenge facing all marketers in Australia is the spread out location of the eight major markets across a vast continent. This presents distribution and communication considerations, which tend to increase national marketing costs.

New Zealand is a small, developed country with a population of 3.5 million and a land area approximately the size of Japan or the United Kingdom. Only 40 years ago the country had the world's third highest standard of living as measured by per capita GNP. New Zealand now stands at number twenty-four, passed in the last decade by Hong Kong and Singapore. The principal cause of the decline in the relative wealth of New Zealand was the country's failure to respond quickly enough to the decline in prices for agricultural commodities, which make up 62 percent of its exports.

Australia and New Zealand have a special relationship; however, there is no apparent desire in either country to merge governments. Although both countries cooperate closely in many areas, there are also many differences in outlook, culture, and character. Citizens of each country do move freely into the other. There are no barriers or border restrictions on trade between the two countries.[66]

---

[64] *Business International,* July 8, 1991, p. 230.

[65] "We're Number 18 and Trying Harder," *The Economist,* April 4, 1992, p. 4 (survey).

[66] "A Glimmer of Recovery" and "The Australian Connection," *Financial Times,* July 9, 1991, pp. 11, 14.

▼ Latin America

Latin America, with 4.6 percent of the world's wealth and 8.2 percent of its population, is a developing region with an average per capita income of $3,200 in 1992. The region includes the Caribbean, Central America, and South America. Latin America is home to 452 million people—a population greater than Western Europe or Eastern Europe. The allure of the Latin American market has been its considerable size and huge resource base.

After a decade of no growth, crippling inflation, rising foreign debt, protectionism, and bloated government payrolls, the countries of Latin America have shown a startling change. Balanced budgets are in as well as privatization. All of the countries of Latin America, except for Cuba and Haiti, now have democratically elected governments. The free market, open economies, and deregulation have begun to replace the policies of the past.[67] Mexico, Venezuela, and Chile are enjoying exciting growth. Also improving are Argentina, Colombia, Bolivia, and Ecuador. Brazil, Uruguay, and Peru have lagged behind.

Latin America is rapidly moving to eliminate barriers to trade and investment. In many countries, tariffs that sometimes reached 100 percent or more have been lowered to 10 percent to 20 percent. In recent years, Latin American countries have also focused on developing subregional common markets. These initiatives are seen as precursors to freer trade with NAFTA, which would create a hemispheric free trade area.[68]

Much of Latin America and Eastern Europe is seeking to emulate Chile's export-driven success. Chile boasts an impressive record in privatization and it pioneered debt-for-equity swaps as a way of retiring part of its foreign debt. Some say the Chilean experience was the key to the change in economic thinking in Latin America.[69]

The Mexican economy grew at an average rate, net of population growth, of −0.9 percent per year during the 1980s. This net growth rate has increased to about 4.0 percent in the 1990s. Inflation has dropped from 160 percent a year to less than 20 percent. Since the mid-1980s more than three-quarters of Mexico's state-owned companies have been privatized. Ninety million consumers, 40 percent under age 40, have more to spend than they have had in a decade.

Companies that want to manufacture in Mexico can set up a wholly owned subsidiary, a joint venture, or a maquiladora program. The maquiladora works best for companies aiming to export most of their goods back to Canada or the United States. It allows manufacturing, assembly, or processing plants to import materials, components, and equipment duty-free; in return they use Mexican labor. When the completed product is exported, say, to Canada, the maquiladora pays duty only on the value added in Mexico.[70]

---

[67] Nathaniel C. Nash, "A New Discipline Brings Change to Latin America," *The New York Times*, November 13, 1991, pp. 1A, 5D.

[68] Alan Reynolds, "Sunshine in the South," *Forbes* (September 16, 1991), p. 205.

[69] Leslie Crawford, "Chilean 'Miracle-Makers' for Hire," *Financial Times*, (April 2, 1992), p. 5.

[70] Nancy J. Perry, "What's Powering Mexico's Success," *Fortune* (February 10, 1992), pp. 109, 114–115.

Canadian companies have been using the maquiladora option for a number of years. Subsidiaries of Ideal Equipment Ltd. of Montreal were set up in 1978, as well as Custom Trim Ltd. of Waterloo, in 1984; Dominion Group Inc. of Toronto, in 1987; and Noma Industries Ltd. of Toronto in 1990, to name a few.[71]

Latin American reforms show a broad shift away from the policy of protectionism toward recognition of the benefits of market forces and the advantages of participating fully in the global economy. Multinational corporations are watching developments closely. They are encouraged by import liberalization, the prospects for lower tariffs within subregional trading groups, and the potential for establishing more efficient regional production.[72]

▼ Middle East

The Middle East includes fifteen countries: Bahrain, Egypt, Iran, Iraq, Israel, Jordan, Kuwait, Lebanon, Oman, Qatar, Saudi Arabia, Syria, United Arab Emirates, and the two Republics of Yemen. The region accounted for 2.1 percent of 1992 world GNP. The Middle East has a total population of approximately 197 million and an average per capita GNP of C$1,700.

The majority of the population is Arab followed by a large percentage of Persians and a small percentage of Israelis. Persians and Arabs share the same religion, beliefs, and Islamic traditions, making the population 95 percent Muslim and 5 percent Christian and Jewish. Despite this apparent homogeneity, heterogeneity exists within each country and within religious groups.

Business in the Middle East is driven by the price of oil. Seven of the countries have high oil revenue: Bahrain, Iraq, Iran, Kuwait, Oman, Qatar, and Saudi Arabia hold more than 75 percent of the free world oil reserves. Oil revenues have widened the gap between poor and rich nations in the Middle East, and the disparities contribute to political and social instability in the area.

The Middle East does not have a single societal type with a typical belief, behavior, and tradition; each capital and major city in the Middle East has a variety of social groups differentiated by their religion, social classes, educational fields, degrees of wealth, and so forth. In general, however, Middle Easterners are warm, friendly, and clannish. Tribal pride and generosity toward guests are basic beliefs. Decision making is by consensus, and seniority has more weight than educational expertise. Life of the individual centers on the family. Authority is acquired by aging, and power is related to family size and seniority. In business relations, Middle Easterners prefer to act through trusted third parties and they also prefer oral communications. A recent change in the region was the falling apart of pan-Arabism during the Persian Gulf War. Some interpret this change as part of a new opportunity for the region. Pan-Arabism, a form of nationalism and loyalty that transcended borders, was an anti-Western dogma that helped trap the Arabs in the past. To defeat Iraq, the Gulf Arabs and their

[71] *Mexico - Canada: Partnering for Success* (Ottawa: Prospectus Publications Ltd.) p. 43.

[72] *Business International* (January 13, 1992), p.11.

allies broke many of their unwritten rules including accepting help from the United States, Israel's friend. By the end of 1991, Arabs and Israelis were engaged in direct peace negotiations.[73] The Palestinian dilemma has long had serious repercussions in the region.

Saudi Arabia remains the most important market in this region. The country is a monarchy with 16 million people. Saudi Arabia has 25 percent of the world's known oil reserves.

Connection is a key word in conducting business. Well-connected people find their progress is made much faster. Bargaining is a Middle Eastern art, and the visiting businessperson must be prepared for some old-fashioned haggling. Establishing a personal rapport, mutual trust, and respect are essentially the most important factors leading to a successful business relationship. Decisions are usually not made by correspondence or telephone. The Arab businessperson does business with the individual, not with the company. Most social customs are based on the Arab male-dominated society. Women are usually not part of the business or entertainment scene for traditional Muslim Arabs.

There are some important conversation subjects that one would be wise to avoid, most of which are considered an invasion of privacy:

1. Avoid bringing up subjects of business before getting to know your Arab host. This is considered rude.
2. Avoid any questions or comments on a man's wife or female children. This is taboo.
3. Avoid pursuing the subjects of politics or religion.
4. Avoid any discussion of Israel.[74]

▼ Africa

The African continent is an enormous land mass. It is not really possible to treat Africa as a single economic unit. The continent is divided into three distinct areas: the Republic of South Africa, North Africa, and Black Africa located between the Sahara Desert in the north and the Zambezi River in the south. The market is large with 687 million people. Africa, with 1.9 percent of the world's wealth and 12.5 percent of its population, is a developing region with an average per capita GNP of about C$900.

The Republic of South Africa has a GNP per person of C$3,200. South Africa suffers from the same problems as the rest of the continent: slow growth, big families, and low investment. The gold mines, which generate half of South Africa's exports, are winding down. Unemployment is close to 50 percent. Sanctions, official and unofficial, restricted South African growth. With the elimination of apartheid and the removal of sanctions in 1992, trade and tourism should improve. Foreign banks are expected to start lending again.[75]

---

[73] "A New Arab Order," *The Economist,* (September 28, 1991), pp. 4–5 (survey).

[74] Philip R. Harris and Robert T. Moran, *Managing Cultural Differences* (Houston: Gulf Publishing Company, 1987), pp. 466–477.

[75] "Businessman's Burden," *The Economist* (November 3, 1990), p.14 (Survey of South Africa).

In North Africa the 78 million Arabs are differentiated politically and economically. They are richer and more developed, with many of the states benefiting from large oil resources. The Arab states have been independent for a longer period than have the Black African nations.

Nigeria is the largest nation of Africa with a population of 126 million in 1992 and a GNP of C$38 million. The stability of Nigeria's general economic situation is highly dependent on the international oil market. Per capita income in 1992 was C$340.

The challenge to marketing in the low-income markets of Africa is not to stimulate demand for products but to identify the most important needs of the society and develop products that fit these needs. There is much opportunity for creativity in developing unique products that fit the needs of the people of the developing countries rather than merely giving copies of products that have been developed for richer countries and, therefore, may not be the most suitable product for the poorer country.

MARKETING IN LESS DEVELOPED COUNTRIES

The shortage of goods and services is the central problem of developing countries and the most pressing need is to expand production. Marketing is a discipline that guides the process of identifying and fulfilling the needs and wants of people. Clearly, marketing is needed in less developed countries.

Long-term opportunities can be nurtured in less developed countries. Greater competitive pressures will force firms to reevaluate their strategies and look for new markets in less developed countries. Even some fast-growing, less developed countries are initiating business in countries that lag behind them. Emerging markets can be lost through indifference and preemptive foreign competition. In deciding whether to enter a less developed country:

- ▶ Look beyond per capita GNP. The per capita figures may hide the existence of a sizable middle class in that market. India, for example, has a huge middle-class market that is hidden by the country's average statistics.

- ▶ Consider less developed countries collectively rather than singly. One market may not be appealing; however, there may be broader possibilities with neighboring countries.

- ▶ Remember that not all LDCs are the same. Some have good prospects for stability, growth, and development, others are falling apart, and still others may look promising but may be high-risk situations.

- ▶ Weigh the benefits and costs of being the first firm to offer a product or service in a less developed country. Governments of less developed countries often award special treatment to companies that set up operations, including tax subsidies and infant industry protection. Entering a successful LDC is an opportunity to get in on the ground floor of a significant market opportunity.

► Set realistic deadlines for results. Due to different legal, political, or social forces, events may move slowly.[76]

Despite the serious economic difficulties now facing less developed countries in Southeast Asia, Latin America, Africa, and Eastern Europe, many of these nations will evolve into attractive markets. The important role of marketing in the less developed countries is to focus resources in organizations on creating and delivering products that best serve the needs of the people. Basic marketing concepts can and should be applied to design a product that fits the needs and ability to buy in the market of the less developed country. These concepts must also be applied to educate the taste and preferences of the people to accept these products. Marketing in the dynamic sense can relate resources to opportunity and satisfy needs on the consumer's terms.

▼ SUMMARY

The global environment must be analyzed before a company pursues expansion into new geographic markets. Through global market **segmentation,** the similarities and differences of potential buying customers can be identified and grouped. Demographics, psychographics, behavioral characteristics, and benefits sought are common attributes used to segment world markets. After marketers have identified segments, the next step is **targeting.** In this step the identified groups are evaluated and compared; from them the prospect or prospects with the greatest potential are selected. The groups are evaluated on the basis of factors such as segment size and growth potential, competition, and compatibility and feasibility. After evaluating the identified segments, marketers must decide on an appropriate targeting strategy. The three basic categories of global target marketing strategies are undifferentiated marketing, concentrated marketing, and differentiated marketing.

Finally, companies must plan a way to reach their chosen target market(s) by determining the best **positioning** for their product offerings. Here marketers devise an appropriate marketing mix to fix the product in the mind of the potential buyers in the target market.

One of the ways of dealing with the complexity of a world with nearly 200 national markets is to focus upon world regions. Each country in the world is sovereign and unique, but there are similarities among countries in the same region that make a regional approach to marketing planning useful. In this chapter, we examine countries in geographic regions. In other chapters, we examine countries and markets organized by stage of development as indicated by average per capita income. It is important to have a broad overview of the nature of world regions so that there will not be any serious oversights in developing the marketing plan.

---

[76] Donald G. Halper and H. Chang Moon, "Striving for First-Rate Markets in Third-World Natiions, "*Managerment Review*" (May 1990), pp. 20–21.

▼ DISCUSSION QUESTIONS

1. What are the four main approaches to segmenting markets and how do they contribute to understanding target markets?

2. How can a targeting strategy and product/service positioning assist a consumer goods company to succeed in the Chinese market.

3. Discuss how regional trade arrangements are likely to influence a company's global marketing strategy.

4. Why is it important for the global marketing manager to be aware of differences in culture, tradition, and behavior between Canada and Japan?

▼ BIBLIOGRAPHY

Books

HASSAN, SALAH S., AND ROGER D. BLACKWELL, *Global Marketing.* Orlando, FL: The Dryden Press, 1994.

Articles

GREEN, PAUL E., AND ABBA M. KRIEGER, "Segmenting Markets with Conjoint Analysis," *Journal of Marketing,* 55, no. 4 (October 1991), 20–31.

MORWITZ, VICKI G., AND DAVID SCHMITTLEIN, "Using Segmentation to Improve Sales Forecasts Based on Purchase Intent: Which 'Intenders' Actually Buy?" *Journal of Marketing Research,* 29, no. 4 (November 1992), 391–405.

WOLFE, BONNIE HEINEMAN, "Finding the International Niche: A "How to" for American Small Business," *Business Horizons,* 34, no. 2, 13–17.

NINE

Strategy Alternatives for Global Market Entry and Expansion

Introduction

Every firm, at every point in its history, faces a broad range of strategy alternatives. In far too many cases, companies fail to appreciate the range of alternatives open to them and, therefore, employ only one strategy—often to their grave disadvantage. The same companies also fail to consider the strategy alternatives open to their competitors and leave themselves vulnerable to the dreaded "Titanic" syndrome, or the thud in the night that comes without warning and sinks the ship.

Some companies are making the decision to "go global" for the first time; other companies seek to expand their share of world markets. Companies in either situation must address issues of marketing management before deciding to enter or expand global markets via exporting, licensing, joint ventures, or ownership. The relative preferences of Canadian companies for each strategy alternative are shown in Table 9–1.

GLOBAL ENTRY AND EXPANSION: MARKETING MANAGEMENT ISSUES

Global entry or expansion strategy must begin with marketing. In Chapter 8, we discussed market segmentation and targeting. The following questions must be asked when planning market entry: How much do we know about the markets? How much control do we want to have over the marketing of our products? How much risk and uncertainty are we prepared to handle? Which markets should be targeted in which sequence? Which countries, and which segments in target countries? The next step for marketers is to establish clear objectives for volume, share of market, sales, and profits; they must then decide how to implement the marketing effort. Should this be done through direct marketing operations in the target market or through agents or representatives? If we use agents, how much support do they require, how much support should we give them, and how should we communicate with them? Specifically, how do we ensure that we will get accurate and timely market feedback from our agents, and how can we ensure that all of the information they need to represent us effectively is transferred to them?

Entry into foreign markets presents a host of barriers companies need to understand and overcome. These barriers will have some influence on the

TABLE 9–1 How Canadian Companies Enter Foreign Markets	
Exporting	67%
Licensing	3%
Joint venture	5%
Wholly-owned subsidiary	25%

Source: Adapted from Nicolas Papadopoulos and Derek Janzen, "Country and Method of Entry Selection for International Expansion: International Distributive Arrangements Revisited," *Dimensions of International Business*, No. 11 (Spring 1994) pp.46–7.

choice of entry strategy. (See Table 9–1.) It is fair to say that nearly all companies venturing into foreign markets need to overcome entry barriers. For example, such barriers may be either informational or operational/resource-based. Information on foreign markets or customers is seldom readily available, yet it is crucial for the company's planning and marketing effort. Similarly, many companies are uncertain about how to operate in a foreign market, whether to deal directly with customers or through intermediaries. Then there is the task of finding an agent.

Canadian companies have indicated the following major problems in exporting to foreign markets: Governmental barriers (such as customs and tariffs), different competitive practices, selecting a reliable distributor, inadequate transportation systems, and various non-tariff barriers such as documentation and red tape.[1]

The list of barriers can be easily extended; however, the level of a company's knowledge and skill in dealing with these is what matters. When access to distribution is a problem, perhaps a partnership with a local company would be the preferred entry method. When the regulatory setting requires minimum local content, perhaps a manufacturing joint venture or subsidiary is needed. When the political climate is unstable, exporting may be preferable to direct investment.

A recent study confirmed that Canadian companies prefer investment as an entry strategy for markets that are "hot," contractual arrangements for those that are "moderate," and exporting for markets that are "cold."[2]

The level of political and economic risk associated with a country should also be of prime concern to management when looking at global market entry and expansion. For example, we want to know about civil unrest and political turmoil, about the security of investment or the market's stability, about economic

---

[1] E. Kaynak and L. Stevenson, "Profile Analysis of Nova Scotia Exporters," Proceedings, ASAC (1982) pp.98–108.

[2] Papadopoulos and Jansen, op. cit, p.46.

TABLE 9–2 Political and Economic Risk, Selected Countries

Country	Turmoil¹⁾	Financial Transfer	Investment	Exports	Real GDP — Average Growth	Real GDP — (%)	Inflation (%)	Current Acct. Balance ($billions)
ALGERIA	18 mos. very high	C+²⁾	C	D+	1990-94	1.6	26.7	-.20
	5 yrs. very high	C-	D	D	1995	4.0	35.0	-.30
ARGENTINA	18 mos. moderate	B-	B	B-	1996-2000	3.0	25.0	.0
	5 yrs. moderate	B-	A-	B	1990-94	5.7	504.9	-3.69
					1995	4.5	4.0	-8.00
MEXICO	18 mos. low	B	A-	B+	1996-2000	5.0	7.0	-5.00
	5 yrs. low	B-	A	B-	1989-93	2.9	18.9	-14.22
					1994	2.0	8.0	-20.00
INDONESIA	18 mos. moderate	B-	A-	B-	1995-99	3.8	5.0	-18.00
	5 yrs. low	B	B	B-	1990-94	6.8	9.4	-3.37
					1995	7.0	8.0	-3.00
FRANCE	18 mos. low	A+	A	A+	1996-2000	7.2	9.0	-3.30
	5 yrs. low	A+	A-	A	1990-94	1.0	2.6	+2.56
					1995	2.9	1.5	+22.00
JAPAN	18 mos. low	A	A	A	1996-2000	3.0	2.5	+5.00
	5 yrs. low	A+	A+	A+	1990-94	2.6	2.1	+95.56
					1995	3.0	2.0	+100.00
RUSSIA	18 mos. moderate	B-	C-	B-	1996-2000	3.2	2.5	+.50
	5 yrs. moderate	B-	C	C	1989-93	-8.3	470.0	-1.75
					1994	-15.0	1000.0	-6.00
SOUTH AFRICA	18 mos. high	B	B	B	1995-1999	1.5	200.0	-5.00
	5 yrs. moderate	B	B+	B	1990-94	.1	12.3	+1.26
					1995	4.0	8.5	-1.00
					1996-2000	5.0	10.0	-1.00

¹⁾ risk ratings from low to very high; ²⁾ A+ equals least, D- equals most risk

Source: Based on Political Risk Letter, "Political and Economic Forecast Table," *Political Risk Services,* Vol. XVI, No. 9, September 1, 1994, pp.6–10, with permission.

indicators, and so on. Table 9–2 highlights such critical, commercially available information for selected countries.

Thus, forecasts of political and economic risk complement other sources of information that global marketing management considers when weighing the pros and cons of foreign market entry and expansion.

We need to consider another issue here: Do companies move through different stages of foreign market involvement? In other words, do exporters ultimately set up a manufacturing subsidiary? We can safely say that there is no prescribed sequence of foreign market entry and involvement companies follow. Why? Companies seek the arrangement to carry on business in a foreign market that is most effective for them. This means that they might be exporting to one market, have a sales/service subsidiary in another, and a joint-venture partnership to manufacture in yet another market.

Newbridge Networks of Kanata, Ontario, which makes a wide range of equipment solutions for digital networks, entered the United Kingdom in 1986 by setting up a sales office. The internationalization of the telecommunications industry pointed to a large market potential for its products. By 1988 a production subsidiary was built which doubled in size in 1990.[3]

Some companies will expand and intensify their foreign market activities and evolve into a global network of subsidiaries. Others remain exporters, although this does not prevent them from seeking and developing new markets.

Molson Breweries' recent deal to export Molson Ice to China is an example of adapting market entry strategy to a complex market situation. China's highly fragmented beer market—it has over 800 domestic brewers—holds enormous potential and is sought after, as the creation of joint ventures with other foreign brewers suggests. Molson Breweries is testing the market through exports before deciding on investing in a joint venture.[4]

What matters is the goal of the company: For example the majority of companies that became MNEs (Multinational Enterprises) set up subsidiaries because they encountered difficulties in distributing their products.

EXPORTING

Exporting is the most traditional and well-established form of operating internationally. A company may engage in *direct exporting*, that is, sales between the company and a second-country distributor or customer that functions as the importer. A company engaging in *indirect exporting* sells through an intermediary located in the home country.

About two-thirds of Canadian companies doing business in foreign markets use exporting. About one-quarter of Canadian exporters export to their foreign subsidiaries. Thus, the combination of exporting and distribution or

---

[3] QDM Ltd, *Link '92: The Experience of Successful Canadian Companies in Europe*, report prepared for External Affairs and International Trade Canada (Ottawa: November 1991) p.30.

[4] Marina Strauss, "Molson looks to long-term gains in China," *The Globe and Mail, Report on Business*, October 6, 1994, B3.

- market or project analysis and selection; intelligence gathering
- matching resources (personnel, technology, products) with market objectives
- assessment of market entry modes and needed support assistance
- selection of product-promotion techniques, channels of distribution and servicing
- monitoring and adjustments

Source: Adapted from P. Verzariu, *Countertrade, Barter and Offsets* (New York: McGraw-Hill, 1985) Table 10, p.141.

marketing subsidiary can create effective forward market access. A relatively small but important share of exporters use intermediaries. That is, they export indirectly, usually through trading houses. As Table 9–3 shows, exporting through a trading house means that the Canadian company trades convenience for knowledge and learning. In other words, the trading house undertakes all market research and development activities.

Because exporting requires no investment in manufacturing operations abroad, it is often identified as a low-cost alternative.

Minimal expenditures are required to obtain an export license, contact a freight forwarder, arrange financing, and so on. However, if it is done effectively and well, exporting requires significant investments in marketing. This investment begins with intensive market study leading to the development of a country marketing strategy. The hallmarks of this strategy may be products adapted to customer needs and preferences in the market (or left unchanged if appropriate) and price, distribution, and communication policies that are an integrated part of the country marketing strategy.

One advantage of exporting is that it allows manufacturing operations to be concentrated in a single location, which may lead to scale economies. Many companies in a variety of industries have concluded that concentrated manufacturing operations give them cost and quality advantages over the alternative of decentralized manufacturing. Of course, this approach has a potential downside: Managers at factories located far from export customers may not be responsive to customer needs and wants.

Part of the export versus local manufacture decision is an exercise in cost analysis and forecasting, which can be facilitated by advanced management science techniques in linear programming. Indeed, a number of companies have developed sourcing models that take into account all cost factors and compute the lowest-cost source for supplying markets. Another part of the export versus local manufacture decision is estimating political risk and conditions affecting access to target markets. For example, many companies have decided to invest in foreign market manufacturing facilities even though they could more cheaply supply target markets from home-country manufacturing operations because their access to the target markets is blocked by formal or informal trade barriers or the threat of such barriers. Local manufacturing, then, can be a strategy for obtaining or retaining market access.

The decision to export or manufacture in the target country should not change the basic marketing program for the product in a market. Remember that it is essential to differentiate clearly the sourcing plan and the marketing plan so that each is given full attention regardless of the source of product supply for a market. The following examples illustrate the principles of export marketing.

▼ Automobiles: From Export to Local Sourcing

The spectacular penetration of the Canadian auto market by Japanese manufacturers began modestly enough. The basic models designed for the Japanese market were adapted for the low-priced compact and subcompact segments of the Canadian market. Toyota's first auto exports to Canada were so unstylish and underpowered that they were not saleable. However, the Japanese persisted and ultimately succeeded in Canada with a relentlessly customer-oriented approach to export marketing. The Japanese would introduce a product and, if it were not successful, they would find out why, make the necessary changes, and return to the market with what customers wanted.

The initial competitive focus of the Japanese manufacturers was on the compact and subcompact segments. After penetrating these segments, the Japanese companies found themselves with higher wage costs at home and a rising yen in the foreign exchange market. Due to the growing protectionist sentiment in the United States and the existence of the Canada-U.S. Auto Pact, they shifted part of their production to Canada and the United States. Both Honda and Toyota built a plants in Canada and the U.S. They also targeted new segments—first the middle-price and then the upper-price segments of the market. By sourcing in the North American market and moving up-market, the Japanese auto makers achieved greater operating margins, which until recently enabled them to continue to operate profitably in spite of rising wage costs and the appreciating yen at home. Now Honda, Toyota, and other Japanese manufacturers are using their North American manufacturing base as a source for export. In 1991, Honda became the first Japanese auto maker to export American-built cars to Europe; the auto maker was motivated in part by the need to sidestep European import restrictions on cars built in Japan.[5]

▼ Perrier Water: Exported from "The Source"

During the 1980s, the Perrier Group of Canada was able to steadily increase sales volume of Perrier mineral water. By 1994, a market share of 65 percent of the carbonated water segment had been achieved. They simply repositioned their product—which was sourced in France—from an "imported water" to a

---

[5] Doron P. Levin, "Honda Sets U.S. Exports to France," *The New York Times* (September 16, 1991) pp.C1, C4.

"new-age beverage." This required an extensive marketing effort: changes in pricing, in positioning (via advertising and promotion), and in the channels themselves. After the success of the repositioning, in 1985 Perrier proceeded to introduce line extensions in the form of flavored water (Lemon, Lime, and Mint, which account for one-quarter of its sales). All Perrier products are exported from France. Indeed, an important part of the positioning of the product is that the water is imported from "The Source." The lesson from these examples is that marketing can be the driving force behind a very successful export strategy. Over time the export strategy may evolve into a different , more involved strategy, as in the Japanese auto case. Or it may remain tied to a home-country sourcing strategy, as in the Perrier water example.

Most companies conclude that exporting is the best way to market product because of the importance of developing a sound marketing plan and strategy prior to investing in bricks and mortar. A marketing plan cannot be developed in "dry dock." It must be tested and refined under live conditions.

LICENSING

Licensing is an alternative entry and expansion strategy with considerable appeal. A company with technology, know-how, or a strong brand image can use licensing agreements to supplement its bottom-line profitability with no investment and very limited expenses.

Licensing is also driven by the ever increasing pace of technological innovation. For smaller companies, their size can become an obstacle to foreign market development: they simply may not have the resources and staff to develop multiple market simultaneously. Licensing agreements can be a speedy way for the diffusion of technology know-how or a strong brand image through partnership arrangements into foreign markets.

Since most licensing arrangements deal with the transfer of "know-how," however, the stage of "realization" or "development" of such know-how is an important aspect for bringing a product to market and for the royalties the licensor can negotiate. European companies' experience (Table 9–4) shows how royalty rates are influenced by the stage of know-how.

It is also important to realize that such contracts are negotiated and depend on a host of other factors, not least the competition. Of licensing contracts signed by foreign companies in Japan, 48 percent were for royalties between 2 and 8 percent, only 6 percent of contracts stipulated royalties of more than 8 percent, and some 23 percent of the agreements had different compensation arrangements altogether.[6] Indeed, licensing offers an infinite return on investment. The only cost is the cost of signing the agreements and of policing their implementation.

---

[6] Poley, op cit., p.36.

TABLE 9–4 Royalty Rates by Stage of Development of Know-How	
Know-How at the:	
Idea stage	up to 2.5%
Patent applied for	1.0 to 4.0%
Patent obtained	1.5 to 5.0%
Patent and functioning prototype	2.0 to 6.0%
Patent and proven market success	3.0 to 12.0%

Source: Adapted from W.L. Poley, *Know-How Export, Lizenzvergabe, Technologie Transfer* (Koeln: Deutscher Wirtschaftsdienst, 1981) p.35.

Trademarks can be an important part of the creation and protection of opportunities for lucrative licenses.[7] Image-oriented American companies such as Coca-Cola and Disney, for example, are licensing their trademarked names and logos to overseas producers of clothing, toys, and watches. In Asia and the Pacific alone, sales of licensed Disney products doubled between 1988 and 1990 and were expected to double again by 1994.[8]

Of course, anything so easily attained has its disadvantages and risks. The principal disadvantage of licensing is that it can be a very limited form of participation. If licensing concerns technology or know-how, those who "do not know what they do not know" are at risk. Potential returns from marketing and manufacturing may be lost, and the agreement may have a short life if the licensee develops its own know-how and capability to stay abreast of technology in the licensed product area. Even more distressing, licensees have a troublesome way of turning themselves into competitors or industry leaders. This is especially true because licensing enables a company to "borrow"—leverage and exploit—another company's resources. In Japan, for example, Meiji Milk produced and marketed Lady Borden premium ice cream under a licensing agreement with the American company Borden, Inc. Meiji learned important skills in dairy product processing and, as the expiration dates of the licensing contracts drew near, rolled out its own premium ice-cream brands.[9]

Perhaps the most famous licensing fiasco is the story of how, in the mid-1950s, Sony co-founder Masaru Ibuka obtained a licensing agreement for the transistor from AT&T's Bell Laboratories in the U.S. Ibuka dreamed of using transistors to make small, battery-powered radios. Bell engineers informed Ibuka that it was impossible to manufacture transistors that could handle the high frequencies required for a radio; they advised him to try making hearing aids. Undeterred, Ibuka presented the challenge to his Japanese engineers, who spent many months improving high-frequency output. Sony was not the first company

---

[7] Private communication, E. M. Lang, president, REFAC Technology Development Corporation, 122 East 42nd Street, New York, New York.

[8] John Huey, "America's Hottest Export: Pop Culture," *Fortune* (December 31, 1990).

[9] Yumiko Ono, "Borden's Breakup with Meiji Milk Shows How a Japanese Partnership Can Curdle," *The Wall Street Journal* (February 21, 1991) p. B1.

to unveil a transistor radio; an American-built product from Texas Instruments, the Regency, featured transistors and a colorful plastic case. However, it was Sony's high-quality, distinctive approach to styling and marketing savvy that ultimately translated into worldwide success.

As the Borden and transistor stories make clear, companies may find that the up-front easy money obtained from licensing turns out to be a very expensive source of revenue. One way of avoiding the danger of strengthening a competitor through a licensing agreement is to ensure that all licensing agreements provide for a cross-technology exchange between licenser and licensee. On the positive side, it is possible to establish license arrangements that create export market opportunities and open the door to low-risk manufacturing relationships. It can also speed diffusion of new products or technologies. For example, when Apple launched its Newton personal digital assistant in the fall of 1993, the company licensed its software to Sharp, Matsushita, and other companies. Apple executives hoped that second-party vendors would create related products that would drive sales of Newton.

In sum, we can list a number of general factors that can contribute to the success or failure of a licensing arrangement (see Table 9–5).

For companies that do decide to license, agreements should anticipate the possibility of extending market participation and, insofar as is possible, keep options and paths open for expanded market participation. One path is joint venture with the licensee.

TABLE 9–5 Success and Failure in Technology Licensing

Success Factors:

- similar goals and objectives
- mutually profitable for both partners
- continuing technological leadership of licensor
- ongoing cooperation between partners in other business areas, e.g., contract manufacturing, mutual agency arrangement
- experience of licensee with required production technology and process
- experience of licensee in target market

Failure Factors:

- disparate size of partner companies
- difference in decision-making and organizational behaviour
- insufficient articulation or partners' responsibilities and autonomy
- use of licensing contract to help a failing company
- strong desire for independence in one of the partners

Source: based on W.L. Poley, *Know-How Export, Lizenzvergabe, Technologie Transfer* (Koeln: Deutscher Wirtschaftsdienst, 1981) p.31.

JOINT VENTURES

A more extensive form of participation in foreign markets than either exporting or licensing is a joint venture with a local partner. The advantages of this strategy include the sharing of risk and the ability to combine different value chain strengths, for example, international marketing capability and manufacturing. One company might have in-depth knowledge of a local market, an extensive distribution system, or access to low-cost labor or raw materials. Such a company might link up with a foreign partner possessing considerable know-how in the area of technology, manufacturing, and process applications. Companies that lack sufficient capital resources might become partners to jointly finance a project. Indeed, considerable effort is put into partner selection. The selection process and variables that influence the future success of the partnership, such as local identity, low costs, and rapid market entry, are important aspects of choosing the joint venture route of market entry.[10] Finally, a joint venture may be the only way to enter a country or region if government bid-award practices routinely favor local companies, or if laws prohibit foreign control but permit joint venture.

For example, Lenwest is a joint venture between West Germany's Salamander AG, a shoe manufacturer, and the Proletarian Shoe factory in St. Petersburg, Russia. The Russian side brought abundant, low-wage labor and plentiful raw materials to the table; the Germans provide machinery and, equally important, the know-how, management techniques, and quality control that are virtually unknown in the former Soviet republic. The joint venture agreement called for both parties to reinvest all profits from the first three years of operation to double production.[11]

It is possible to use a joint venture as a source of supply for third-country markets. This must be carefully thought out in advance. One of the main reasons for joint-venture "divorce" is disagreement about third-country markets where partners face each other as actual or potential competitors. To avoid this, it is essential to work out a plan for approaching third-country markets as part of the venture agreement.

The disadvantages of joint venturing are not insignificant. Of course, a joint venture requires the sharing of rewards as well as risks. The main disadvantage of this form of global expansion is the very significant costs of control and coordination associated with working with a partner. Also, as noted previously with licensing, a dynamic joint-venture partner can evolve into a stronger competitor. Cross-cultural differences in managerial attitudes and behavior can present formidable challenges as well.

Joint ventures are risk- and reward-sharing and thus are usually a compromise strategy for market entry. Often the regulatory and cultural environment of a foreign market point to a joint venture arrangement. China is a case in point. The People's Republic of China has general economic development objectives of

---

[10] J. Michael Geringer, "Strategic Determinants of Partner Selection Criteria in International Joint Ventures," *Journal of International Business Studies* (1991) 22:1, p.56.

[11] Thomas F. O'Boyle, "Western Ways: How a German Firm Joined With Soviets to Make Good Shoes," *The Wall Street Journal* (February 14, 1989) p.A1.

technology transfer, employment, productivity, control of foreign exchange, and self-sufficiency. Joint ventures more than any other market entry methods contribute substantially to these objectives.[12] Companies, however, pursue their own objectives. Three joint ventures in China underline this point.

A small computer software company anticipated using China as an export base to the U.S. Operating problems changed the company's mind and it decided not to remain there. A pharmaceutical multinational was testing the market with a view towards supplying the local market and found any operating problems manageable. Finally, a European automobile company entered with a $500 million joint venture investment with plans to expand to supply the local market.[13]

Nikkei Aluma Systems is a joint venture of Aluma Systems of Toronto and Nippon Light Metal Co. of Japan that was motivated by the Japanese parent's desire for innovative technology and the Canadian parent's interest in participating in the construction boom in Japan. Since 1988, sales have expanded to 3.5 billion yen in 1993, by more than 600 percent. Aluma Systems has successfully used the joint venture route in Brazil, Russia, Switzerland, and France.[14]

Many joint ventures, however, encounter serious difficulties; according to one study of 170 multinational firms, more than one-third of 1,100 joint ventures involving U.S. companies were unstable, ending in "divorce" or a significant increase in the U.S. firm's power over its partner.[15] Another researcher found that 65 joint ventures with Japanese companies were either liquidated or transferred to the Japanese interest in 1976. This was up from six in 1972, a 600 percent increase. The most fundamental problem was the different benefits that each side expected to receive.[16]

Global marketing experts warn that in an alliance, you have to learn the skills of the partner, rather than just using it as a way to get a product to sell while avoiding a big investment. Yet, compared to North American and European firms, Japanese and Korean firms seem to excel in their ability to leverage new knowledge that comes out of a joint venture. For example, Toyota learned many new things from its partnership with GM about U.S. supply and transportation, and managing American workers that it has subsequently applied at its Camry plant in Kentucky. Similarly, Toyota, Honda, and Mitsubishi have successfully transferred production and work management techniques to their Canadian plants. Still, many companies have achieved great successes pursuing joint ventures. Gillette, for example, has used this strategy to introduce its shaving products in the Middle East and Africa.

---

[12] Farhad Simyar and Kamal Argheyd, "China: Crossroads to Fame or Failure," *Business Quarterly* (November, 1986) p.31–4.

[13] ibid.

[14] "The Challenge of the Japanese Market: Manufacturing Success," Japan External Trade Organization (Tokyo: 1991) pp.20–5.

[15] G. Franko, "Joint Venture Divorce in the Multinational Company," *Columbia Journal of World Business* (May–June 1971), pp.13–22.

[16] W. Wright, "Joint Venture Problems in Japan," *Columbia Journal of World Business* (Spring 1979), pp.25–31. See also W. Wright and C. S. Russell, "Joint Venture in Developing Countries: Reality and Responses," *Columbia Journal of World Business* (Summer 1975), pp.74–80.

OWNERSHIP

The most extensive form of participation in global markets is 100 percent ownership, which may be achieved by start-up or acquisition. Ownership requires the greatest commitment of capital and managerial effort and offers the fullest means of participating in a market. Companies may move from licensing or joint-venture strategies to ownership in order to achieve faster expansion in a market, greater control, or higher profits. In 1991, for example, Ralston Purina ended a 20-year joint venture with a Japanese company to start its own pet-food subsidiary. Monsanto Company and Bayer AG, the German pharmaceutical company, have each also recently disbanded partnerships in favor of wholly-owned subsidiaries in Japan.[17]

Large-scale direct expansion can be expensive and require a major commitment of managerial time and energy. Alternatively, acquisition is an instant but less expensive approach to market entry. While full ownership can yield the additional advantage of avoiding communication and conflict of interest problems that may arise with a joint venture or coproduction partner, acquisitions still present the demanding and challenging task of integrating the acquired company into the worldwide organization and coordinating activities.

Table 9–6 lists additional examples grouped by industry of companies that have pursued global expansion via acquisition.

What is the driving force behind many of these acquisitions? Simply put, it is globalization. As Horst Urban, chairperson of Continental, remarked, "The world is changing and we can't do business the way we used to. We used to be very much a company that didn't look much beyond Germany. But the globalization of the industry has meant that we had to expand into the United States and other parts of the world. There is no choice."[18]

Several of the advantages of joint-venture alliances also apply to ownership, including access to markets and avoidance of tariff or quota barriers. Like joint ventures, ownership also permits important experience transfers and provides access to new manufacturing techniques.

Setting up a foreign subsidiary is driven by the need to overcome market and customer barriers that are more difficult to deal with from afar. Markets can be served better and customer needs are understood and met more effectively from within a market. We can see from companies who set up subsidiaries that problems of meeting customer needs and coping with cultural and business practices in foreign markets were considerably fewer.[19]

For example, Trench Electric developed its long-standing presence in Europe from modest beginnings in the early 1960s into a dominant position in

---

[17] Yumiko Ono, "Borden's Breakup with Meiji Milk Shows How a Japanese Partnership Can Curdle," *The Wall Street Journal* (February 21, 1994) p.B1.

[18] Jonathan P. Hicks, "The Takeover of American Industry," *The New York Times*, May 28, 1989, Sec.3, p.8.

[19] Based on J. Mattson, "Initial penetration of European continental markets by small and medium-sized firms," *Advances in International Marketing,* T.S. Cavusgil, ed. (Greenwich, Conn.: JAI Press, 1986) Vol 1, pp.93–114.

TABLE 9–6   Market Entry and Expansion by Acquisition

Product Category	Acquiring Company
Apparel, personal care, and food products	Sara Lee Corporation has acquired companies with total sales in excess of $1 billion in seven different countries, including Douwe Egberts (coffee and tea), and Dim (hosiery).
Automotive tires	Bridgestone Corporation (Japan) bought Firestone Tire and Rubber Company (1988). Continental AG (West Germany) bought General Tire (1987). Pirelli SpA (Italy) bought Armstrong Tire (1988).
Media and entertainment	Sony bought CBS Records ($2 billion, 1987) and Columbia Pictures ($3.4 billion, 1989). Matsushita (Japan) bought MCA/Universal ($6.59 billion, 1990).
Consumer electronics	Thomson SA (France) acquired GE's consumer electronics business as well as its RCA subsidiary, and Telefunken (West Germany).

the 1990s. Their products, heavy duty transmission equipment for the electrical power industry, were initially represented through an agent. The company learned quickly that it needed more committed attention to the market and opened its own sales office to cover Europe. By 1989, Trench Electric acquired one of the remaining major competitors to achieve a dominant market position.[20]

The four alternatives of exporting, licensing, joint ventures, and ownership are in fact points along a continuum of alternative strategies or tools for global market entry and expansion. There are many possible combinations of these four basic alternatives and hybrid strategies are often used. The overall design of a company's global strategy may call for combinations of exporting, licensing, joint ventures, and ownership among different operating units. Such is the case in Japan for Borden, Inc.; it is ending licensing and joint-venture arrangements for branded food products and setting up its own production, distribution, and marketing capabilities for dairy products. Meanwhile, in nonfood products, Borden has maintained joint-venture relationships with Japanese partners in flexible packaging and foundry materials.[21]

A firm may decide to enter into a joint venture or coproduction agreement for purposes of manufacturing and may either market the products manufactured under this agreement in a wholly-owned marketing subsidiary or sell the products from the coproduction facility to an outside marketing organization. Joint ventures may be 50:50 partnerships or minority or majority partnerships. Majority ownership may range anywhere from 51 percent to 100 percent.

---

[20] QDM Ltd., *Link '92: The Experience of Successful Canadian Companies in Europe*, report prepared for External Affairs and International Trade Canada (Ottawa: November 1991) pp.65–6.
[21] Borden, Inc., *Annual Report* (1990), p.13.

MARKET EXPANSION STRATEGIES[22]

Companies must decide whether to expand by seeking new markets in existing countries or, alternatively, seeking new country markets for already identified and served market segments. These two dimensions in combination produce four strategic options, as shown in Table 9–7. Strategy 1 concentrates on a few segments in a few countries. This is typically a starting point for most companies. It matches company resources and market investment needs. Unless a company is large and resource rich, this strategy may be the only realistic way to begin.

In Strategy 2, country concentration and segment diversification, a company serves many markets in a few countries. This strategy was the design of many European companies that remained in Europe and sought growth by expanding into new markets. It is also the approach of the Canadian companies that decide to diversify in the home market as opposed to going international with existing products.

Strategy 3, country diversification and market segment concentration, is the classic global company strategy that seeks out the world market for a product and serves the world customer. The rationale of this strategy is that by serving the world customer, a company can achieve a greater accumulated volume and lower costs than any competitor and, therefore, have an unassailable competitive advantage. This is the strategy of the well-managed business that serves a distinct need and customer category.

Strategy 4, country and segment diversification, is the corporate strategy of a large multibusiness company such as GE or Matsushita. These companies are multicountry in their scope and because they include many departments, business units, and groups, they are multisegment. The combination of these elements produces corporate Strategy 4. It is important to recognize, however, that at the operating business level, managers should be focused on the needs of the world customer in their particular global market. In Table 9–7, this is Strategy 3, country diversification and market segment concentration.

MARKET POSITION—A STRATEGIC GUIDE

An increasing number of firms all over the world are beginning to see the importance of market share not only in the home or domestic market but also in the world market. Since experience effects are independent of where a product is sold, overseas markets are as important as domestic markets in determining a company's total volume and cost position.

We must also recognize that the size of the domestic market shapes companies' strategies and options. Compared to the U.S., the Canadian domestic market is small. As a result, many Canadian companies must look to foreign markets for expansion and growth. The proximity of the large U.S. market has

---

[22] This section draws on Ayal and J. Zif, "Market Expansion Strategies in Multinational Marketing," *Journal of Marketing*, 43 (Spring 1979), 84–94 and "Competitive Market Choice Strategies in Multinational Marketing," *Columbia Journal of World Business* (Fall 1978) pp.72–81.

TABLE 9–7 Market Expansion Strategies

		Market	
		Concentration	*Diversification*
Country	Concentration	1. Narrow Focus	2. Country Focus
	Diversification	3. Country Diversification	4. Global Conglomerate

historically been of importance to Canadian companies. Indeed, research shows that between 89 and 97 percent of companies in the food, machinery, electrical, and service industries export to the U.S.[23]

The pricing implications of experience theory are profound indeed. Low export prices, which enable companies to penetrate foreign markets, can often only be obtained through the additional sales volume generated by exports since the domestic market is too small. The high-tech industries in small countries such as Canada or Austria depend heavily on exports to sustain their competitiveness.[24]

Survival in the foreign competitive environment requires more than allow product price. Food companies whose products compete on price typically face highly intense competition. On the other hand, high-tech products with superior technology compete on product attributes as well as price. For example, over 80 percent of Canadian high-tech exporters saw price as a threat to their ability to compete abroad.[25]

Companies entering foreign markets often encounter strong domestic competitors who want to preserve their domestic base. Pricing (as we will see in Chapter 13) is a critical element.

If a foreign competitor penetrates a firm's domestic market, the domestic firm should lower its domestic prices. In Canada, this could be a problem for a dominant producer if such a price cut damaged smaller Canadian producers and invited government antitrust action. (Has this ever happened or is it purely hypothetical?) This consideration makes an aggressive export pricing policy an even more desirable strategy for Canadian competitors.

The recommended strategic program for the single-product, single-plant firm is investment in both process and product improvement and the maintenance of world market dominance from the single source by developing and dominating new segments of markets and keeping cost competitive in established ones. Exports are absolutely critical to the single-plant firm's continued

---

[23] Philip J. Rosson and F.H. Rolf Seringhaus, *International Trade Fair Practices of Canadian Companies*, Technical Report (October 6, 1993).

[24] F.H. Rolf Seringhaus, "Comparative Marketing Behaviour of Canadian and Austrian High-Tech Exporters," *Management International Review*, (1993) 33:3, p.255.

[25] ibid., p.257.

competitiveness. Thus, the single-plant firm needs an overseas marketing system and strategy. It must seek to reduce overseas marketing costs through integrated logistical systems, and it must invest in country marketing programs to ensure that it reaches customers with an integrated marketing mix.

ALTERNATIVE STRATEGIES: STAGES OF DEVELOPMENT MODEL

Five stages of evolution of the so-called transnational corporation have been suggested: from domestic to international, multinational, global, and transnational.[26] Although the difference in the stages is quite significant, there is no agreement about the usage of the terms to describe each of the stages. The terminology suggested here conforms to the current usage of terminology by leading scholars but the reader should know that executives who do not read the scholarly literature may use the terms in quite different ways. For example, Percy Barnavik of ABB describes his company as a multidomestic. In the stages model outlined above, ABB would be an emerging stage-five or transnational company.

Figure 9–1 outlines the different orientations of management. As you can see in Table 9–8, orientation does not change as a company moves from domestic to international. The difference between the domestic and the international company is that the international is doing business in many countries. Like the domestic company, it is still ethnocentric and home-country oriented, but it sees extension market opportunities outside the home country and develops programs to do business outside the home country. The first change in orientation occurs as a company moves to a stage-three multinational, when it shifts its orientation from ethnocentric to polycentric. The difference is quite important. The stage-one ethnocentric company seeks to extend its products and practices to foreign countries. It sees similarities outside the home country but is relatively blind to differences. The stage-three multinational is the opposite: It sees the differences and is relatively blind to similarities. The focus of the stage-three multinational is on adapting to what is different in a country.

The stage-four global company is a limited form of the transnational. The orientation in this company is mixed. Management focuses upon global markets or global resources, but not on both. For example, Harley-Davidson is focused on global markets, but not on global resources. The company has no interest in conducting R&D, design, engineering, or manufacturing outside the United States. This was the same stage until recently for BMW and Mercedes who marketed globally, but limited their R&D, engineering, design, and manufacturing activity to Germany.

The further evolution of orientation occurs when a company moves to stage five, transnational. The stage-five company is geocentric or world oriented.

---

[26] Christopher A. Bartlett and Sumantra Ghoshal, *Managing Across Borders* (Boston: Harvard Business School Press, 1991) pp.57–66.

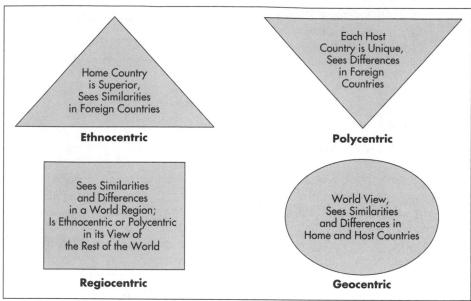

FIGURE 9–1
Orientation of Management and Companies

Management is no longer limited to a focus on similarities or differences but is focused upon similarities and differences. It sees global markets and resources. The stage-five company seeks to serve world markets and to use world resources: human, financial, and material.

Table 9–9 illustrates some other differences in companies at the different stages. The location of key assets shifts from the home country to the world. In the stage-five company, key assets are dispersed, specialized, and interdependent. A transnational automobile company might make engines in one country, transmissions in another, and ship these components to assembly plants located in each of the world regions. Specialized design labs might be located in different countries and work together on the same project. The role of country units changes dramatically as a company moves across the stages of development.

TABLE 9–8	Stages of Development I				
Stage and Company	1 Domestic	2 International	3 Multinational	4 Global	5 Transnational
Strategy	*Domestic*	*International*	*Multidomestic*	*Global*	*Global*
Model	N.A.	Coordinated Federation	Decentralized Federation	Centralized Hub	Integrated Network
View of World	Home Country	Extension Markets	National Markets	Global Markets or Resources	Global Markets and Resources
Orientation	Ethnocentric	Ethnocentric	Polycentric	Mixed	Geocentric

TABLE 9–9   Stages of Development II

	Organization Characteristics				
Stage and Company	*1 Domestic*	*2 International*	*3 Multinational*	*4 Global*	*5 Transnational*
Key Assets	Located in home country	Core centralized, others dispersed	Decentralized and self-sufficient	All in home country except marketing or sourcing	Dispersed, interdependent, and specialized
Role of Country Units	Single country	Adapting and leveraging competencies	Exploiting local opportunities	Marketing or sourcing	Contributions to company worldwide
Knowledge	Home country	Created at center and transferred	Retained within operating units	Marketing or sourcing developed jointly and shared	All functions developed jointly and shared

In the stage-two international company, the role of the country unit is to adapt and leverage the competence of the parent or home-country unit. In the stage-five transnational, the role of each country is to contribute to the company worldwide. For example, in marketing in the international and multinational organization, the responsibility of the marketing organization is to realize the potential of the national market. In the transnational, the responsibility of the marketing unit is to realize the potential of the national market and, if possible, to contribute to the success of marketing efforts worldwide by sharing with the entire organization successful innovations and ideas.

Each of the stages has its strengths. (See Table 9–10.) The international company's strength is its ability to exploit the parent company's knowledge and capabilities outside the home country. The multinational company's strength is its ability to adapt and respond to national differences. The global company leverages its skills and resources by taking advantage of global markets or global resources. The transnational combines the strengths of each of the earlier stages and seeks to serve global markets using global resources and to leverage global learning and experience.

In stage two, the typical product sourcing plan is an export arrangement where, as in stage three, the most frequent or preferred sourcing arrangement is local manufacture. In stage five, product sourcing is based on a sourcing plan that takes into account cost, delivery, and all other factors affecting competitiveness and profitability and produces a sourcing plan that maximizes both competitive effectiveness and profitability. In stage two, the company's key jobs go to home-country nationals in both the subsidiaries and the headquarters. In stage three, key jobs in host countries go to country nationals, whereas headquarters management positions are usually held by some country nationals. In stage five the best person is selected for all management positions regardless of nationality. Research and development in stage two is conducted in the home country and

TABLE 9–10 Stages of Development III

Strengths at Each Level

International
  Ability to exploit the parent company's knowledge and capabilities through worldwide diffusion of products
Multinational
  Flexible ability to respond to national differences
Global
  Global market or supplier reach, which leverages the home-country organization, skills, and resources
Transnational
  Combines the strengths of each of the preceding stages in an integrated network, which leverages worldwide learning and experience

in stage three becomes decentralized and fragmented. In stage five, research is part of an integrated worldwide research and development plan and is typically decentralized, taking advantage of resources as well as responding to local aspirations to produce a worldwide decentralized R&D program.

Control and measurement standards are usually in stage two based on home-country experience, whereas in stage three they become highly decentralized. In stage five, control and measurement standards are both circumstantial and situational and take into account both local conditions and international experience.

▼ SUMMARY

Companies face a wide range of alternative ways of participating in international markets. Those who have had experience in international marketing realize that it is necessary to practice marketing regardless of sourcing arrangements. Companies committed to marketing study the foreign customer and in effect become so knowledgeable about the "foreign" market that it is no longer foreign but rather a market in a geographical location as are all other markets. This is a fundamental application of the marketing concept. If applied, it leads to the formulation of a marketing strategy that integrates product, price, place, and promotion elements in an appropriate way consistent with corporate and product strengths and weaknesses as well as competitive reality.

Companies that have developed an appropriate marketing strategy are then able to reach a decision about the most effective sourcing arrangements. Sourcing plans must take into account organizational resources, strengths and weaknesses, factor costs, transportation costs, conditions of market access and entry, and realistic assessments of political risk and future conditions at entry, as well as security of investments. The choice of an appropriate strategy is complex and always involves an element of risk and uncertainty. In this chapter, we have outlined the major alternative tools and have highlighted factors and conditions that should influence the choice of these tools.

▼ DISCUSSION QUESTIONS

1. What are the alternative tools or strategies for expanding internationally? What are the major advantages and disadvantages of each strategy?

2. The president of XYZ Manufacturing Company of Markham, Ontario comes to you with a license offer from a company in Osaka. In return for sharing the company's patents and know-how, the Japanese company will pay a license fee of 5 percent of the ex-factory price of all products sold based on the Canadian company's license. The president wants your advice. What would you tell the president?

3. What are some of the reasons why technology licensing arrangements might succeed or fail?

4. What are the differences among an international, multinational, and a global company? Can you think of examples of companies that fit the characteristics of each of these types of companies?

5. What is the difference between the strategic options of a small company versus a large company?

▼ BIBLIOGRAPHY

Books

BARTLETT, CHRISTOPHER A. AND SUMANTRA GHOSHAL, *Managing Across Borders*. Boston: Harvard Business School Press, 1991.

CAMPBELL, DENNIS, LOUIS LAFILI, AND MCGEORGE SCHOOL OF LAW, *Distributorship, Agency and Franchising in an International Arena: Europe, the United States, Japan and Latin America*. Boston: Kluwer Law and Taxation Publishers, 1990.

JAMES, HARVEY S., AND MURRAY L. WEIDENBAUM, *When Businesses Cross International Borders: Strategic Alliances and Their Alternatives*. Westport, CT: Praeger, 1993.

LORANGE, PETER, AND JOHAN ROOS, *Strategic Alliances: Formation, Implementation and Evolution*. Cambridge, MA: Blackwell, 1992.

MCCAFFREY, ROGER A., AND THOMAS A. MEYER, *An Executive's Guide to Licensing*. Homewood, IL: Dow Jones-Irwin, 1989.

NADEL, JACK, *Cracking the Global Market: How to Do Business Around the Corner and Around the World*. New York: American Management Association, 1987.

OSTER, SHARON, *Modern Competitive Analysis*. New York: Oxford University Press, 1990.

ROSOW, JEROME M., *The Global Marketplace*. New York: Facts on File, 1988.

SERINGHAUS, F.H. ROLF AND PHILIP J. ROSSON, *Government Export Promotion: A Global Perspective*. London: Routledge Publishers, 1990.

SHERMAN, ANDREW, *Franchising and Licensing: Two Ways to Build Your Business*. New York: American Management Association, 1991.

YIP, GEORGE S., *Total Global Strategy: Managing for Worldwide Competitive Advantage*. Englewood Cliffs, NJ: Prentice Hall, 1992.

Articles

AGARWAL, SANJEEV, AND SRIDHAR N. RAMASWAMI, "Choice of Foreign Market Entry Mode: Impact of Ownership, Location and Internalization Factors," *Journal of International Business Studies*, 23, no. 1 (First Quarter 1992), 1–27.

BERLEW, F. KINGSTON, "The Joint Venture—A Way Into Foreign Markets," *Harvard Business Review* (July/August 1984), 48–54.

CHAN, PENG S., AND ROBERT T. JUSTIS, "Developing a Global Business Strategy Vision for the Next Decade and Beyond," *Journal of Management Development*, 10, no. 2, 38–45.

DAVIDSON, KENNETH, "Strategic Investment Theories," *Journal of Business Studies*, 6, no. 1 (Summer 1985), 1–28.

Doz, Yves L., "Strategic Management in Multinational Companies," *Sloan Management Review* (Winter 1980), 16–27.

———, Christopher A. Bartlett, and C. K. Pralahad, "Global Competitive Pressures and Host Country Demands," *California Management Review* (Spring 1981), 63–73.

———, and C. K. Prahalad, "How MNC's Cope with Host Government Demands," *Harvard Business Review*, 58, no. 2 (March/April 1980), 149–160.

Egelhoff, William G., "Great Strategy or Great Strategy Implementation—Two Ways of Competing in Global Markets," *Sloan Management Review*, 34, no. 2 (Winter 1993), 37–50.

Geringer, J. Michael, "Strategic Determinants of Partner Selection Criteria in International Joint Ventures," *Journal of International Business Studies*, 22, no. 1, 56.

Hamel, Gary, and C. K. Prahalad, "Do You Really Have a Global Strategy?" *Harvard Business Review* (July–August 1985), 139–148.

Harrigan, Kathryn Rudie, "Joint Ventures and Global Strategies," *Columbia Journal of World Business* (Summer 1984), 7–16.

Hill, Charles W. L., Peter Hwang, and W. Chan Kim, "An Eclectic Theory of the Choice of International Entry Mode," *Strategic Management Journal*, 11, no. 2, 117–128.

Hwang, Peter, Willem P. Burgers, and W. Chan Kim, "Global Diversification Strategy and Corporate Profit Performance," *Strategic Management Journal*, 10, no. 1 (January/February 1989), 45–57.

Jatusripitak, Soi'kid, Liam Fahey, and Philip Kotler, "Strategic Global Marketing: Lessons From the Japanese," *Columbia Journal of World Business* (Spring 1985), 47–53.

Kim, W. Chang, Peter Hwang, and Willem P. Burgers, "Multinational's Diversification and the Risk-Return Trade-off," *Strategic Management Journal*, 14, no. 4 (May 1993), 275–286.

Kissin, Warren D., and Julio Herrera, "International Mergers and Acquisitions," *Journal of Business Strategy*, 11, no. 4 (July/August 1990), 51–54.

Koepfler, Edward R., "Strategic Options for Global Market Players," *Journal of Business Strategy*, 10, no. 4, 46–50.

Kogut, Bruce, "Designing Global Strategies: Comparative and Competitive Value-Added Chains," *Sloan Management Review* (Summer 1985), 15–28.

Lee, Chong S., and Yoo S. Yang, "Impact of Export Market Expansion Strategy on Export Performance," *International Marketing Review*, 7, no. 4, 41–51.

McDougall, Patricia, "New Venture Strategies: An Empirical Identification of Eight 'Archetypes' of Competitive Strategies for Entry," *Strategic Management Journal*, 11, no. 6 (October 1990), 447–467.

Miller, Danny, "The Generic Strategy Trap," *Journal of Business Strategy*, 13, no. 1 (January/February 1992), 37–41.

Morrison, Allen J., and Kendall Roth, "A Taxonomy of Business-Level Strategies in Global Industries," *Strategic Management Journal*, 13, no. 6 (September 1992), 399–417.

Negandi, Anant R., and Peter A. Donhowe, "It's Time to Explore New Global Trade Options," *Journal of Business Strategy*, 10, no. 1 (January/February 1991), 27–31.

O'Reilly, Anthony J. F., "Leading a Global Strategic Charge," *Journal of Business Strategy*, 12, no. 4, 10–13.

Perlmutter, Howard V., and David A. Heenan, "How Multinational Should Your Top Managers Be?" *Harvard Business Review* (November/December 1974), 121–132.

Quelch, John A., and James E. Austin, "Should Multinationals Invest in Africa?" *Sloan Management Review*, 34, no. 3 (Spring 1993), 107–119.

Rabstejnek, George, "Let's Go Back to the Basics of Global Strategy," *Journal of Business*

Strategy, 10, no. 5 (September/October 1989), 32–35.

SCHILL, RONALD L., AND DAVID N. MCARTHUR, "Redefining the Strategic Competitive Unit: Towards a New Global Marketing Paradigm?" *International Marketing Review,* 9, no. 3, 5–24.

SCHOEMAKER, PAUL J. H., "How to Link Strategic Vision to Core Capabilities," *Sloan Management Review,* 34, no. 1 (Fall 1992), 67–81.

SEGEV, ELI, "A Systematic Comparative Analysis and Synthesis of Two Business-Level Strategic Typologies," *Strategic Management Journal,* 10, no. 5 (September/October 1989), 487–505.

SERINGHAUS, F.H. ROLF, "Comparative Marketing Behaviour of Canadian and Austrian High-Tech Exporters," *Management International Review,* 33, no. 3, 255.

VAN FLEET, MARK, "Two Sources of Overseas Investment and Export Expertise," *Journal of Business Strategy,* 12, no. 6 (November/December 1991), 62–63.

VAN WOLFEREN, KAREL G., "The Japan Problem," *Foreign Affairs* (Winter 1986), 288–303.

WIND, YORAM, AND SUSAN DOUGLAS, "International Portfolio Analysis and Strategy: The Challenge of the 80's," *Journal of International Business Studies* (Fall 1981), 69–82.

———, SUSAN P. DOUGLAS, AND HOWARD V. PERLMUTTER, "Guidelines for Developing International Marketing Strategies," *Journal of Marketing* (April 1973), 14–23.

———, AND THOMAS S. ROBERTSON, "Marketing Strategy: New Directions for Theory and Research," *Journal of Marketing,* 47, (Spring 1983), 12–25.

YIP, GEORY S., PIERRE M. LOEWE, AND MICHAEL Y. YOSHINO, "How to Take Your Company to the Global Market," *Columbia Journal of World Business,* 23, no. 4 (Winter 1988).

TEN

Competitive
Analysis
and Strategy

Introduction

The essence of marketing strategy is relating an organization to its environment. As the horizons of marketers have expanded from domestic to global markets, so too have the horizons of competitors. The reality in industry after industry today is global competition. This "fact of life" puts an organization under increasing pressure to master techniques for conducting industry analysis, competitor analysis, and developing competitive advantage. These topics are covered in detail in this chapter.

INDUSTRY ANALYSIS: FORCES INFLUENCING COMPETITION

A useful way of gaining insight into competitors is through industry analysis. As a working definition, an industry can be defined as a group of firms that produce products that are close substitutes for each other. In any industry, competition works to drive down the rate of return on invested capital toward the rate that would be earned in the economist's "perfectly competitive" industry. Rates of return that are greater than this so-called competitive rate will stimulate an inflow of capital either from new entrants or from existing competitors making additional investment. Rates of return below this competitive rate will result in withdrawal from the industry and a decline in the levels of activity and competition.

According to Michael E. Porter of Harvard University, a leading theorist of competitive strategy, there are five forces influencing competition in an industry (see Figure 10–1): the threat of new entrants; the threat of substitute products or services; the bargaining power of suppliers; the bargaining power of buyers; and the competitive rivalry between current members of the industry. In industries such as pharmaceuticals, communications, and environmental protection, the favorable nature of the five forces has resulted in attractive returns and prospects for competitors. However, pressure from any of the forces can limit profitability, as evidenced by the current woes of competitors in the personal computer and semiconductor industries. We will discuss each of the five forces in turn.

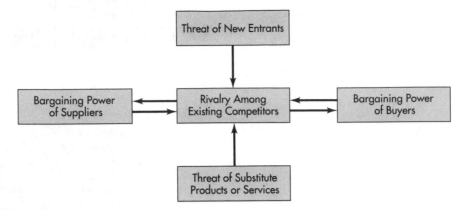

FIGURE 10-1
Forces Influencing Competition in an Industry

Source: Reprinted with the permission of The Free Press, a division of Simon & Schuster, from *Competitive Strategy: Techniques for Analyzing Industries and Competitors,* by Michael E. Porter. Copyright © 1980 by The Free Press.

▼ Threat of New Entrants

New entrants to an industry bring new capacity, a desire to gain market share and position, and very often new approaches to serving customer needs. The decision to become a new entrant in an industry is often accompanied by a major commitment of resources. New players mean that prices will be pushed downward and margins squeezed, resulting in reduced industry profitability. There are eight major sources of barriers to entry, the presence or absence of which determines the extent of the threat of new industry entrants.[1]

The first barrier, **economies of scale,** refers to the decline in product costs per unit as the absolute volume of production increases per period. Although the concept of scale economies is frequently associated with manufacturing, it is also applicable to research and development, general administration, marketing, and other business functions. Honda's efficiency at engine R&D, for example, results from the wide range of products it produces that feature gasoline-powered engines. When existing firms in an industry achieve significant economies of scale, it becomes difficult for potential new entrants to be competitive.

Product differentiation, the second major entry barrier, is the extent of a product's perceived uniqueness, in other words, whether or not it is a commodity. High levels of product differentiation and brand loyalty, whether the result of physical product attributes or effective marketing communication, "raise the bar" for would-be industry entrants. Monsanto Company's Nutrasweet unit, for example, achieved differentiation and erected a barrier in the artificial sweetener industry when it insisted that its logo and brand mark, a red-and-white swirl, appear on diet soft-drink cans.[2]

---

[1] Michael E. Porter, *Competitive Strategy* (New York: The Free Press, 1980), pp. 7–33.
[2] Eben Shapiro, "Nutrasweet's Bitter Fight," *The New York Times,* November 19, 1989.

A third entry barrier relates to capital requirements. Capital is required not only for manufacturing facilities but also for financing R&D, advertising, field sales and service, customer credit, and inventories. The enormous capital requirements in such industries as pharmaceuticals, mainframe computers, chemicals, and mineral extraction present formidable entry barriers.

A fourth barrier to entry is the one-time **switching costs** to the buyer of changing suppliers and products. These might include retraining, ancillary equipment costs, the cost of evaluating a new source, and so on. The perceived cost to customers of switching to a new competitor's product may present an insurmountable obstacle preventing industry newcomers from achieving success.

A fifth barrier to entry is access to **distribution channels.** To the extent that channels are full, or unavailable, the cost of entry is substantially increased because a new entrant must create and establish new channels.

Government policy is frequently a major entry barrier. In some cases, the government will absolutely prohibit competitive entry. This is true in a number of industries that have been designated as "national" industries by their respective governments. For example, utility companies in France are notorious for accepting bids from foreign equipment suppliers but, in the end, favoring national suppliers when awarding contracts. Japan's entire postwar industrialization strategy was based on a policy of reserving and protecting national industries in their development and growth phases. The result was a market that proved difficult for non-Japanese competitors to enter.

Established firms may also enjoy **cost advantages independent of scale** that present barriers to entry. Access to raw materials, favorable locations, and government subsidies are several examples.

Finally, expected **competitor response** can be a major entry barrier. If new entrants expect existing competitors to respond strongly to entry, their expectations about the rewards of entry will certainly be affected. The belief by a potential competitor that entry into an industry or market will be an unpleasant experience may serve as a strong deterrent. Bruce Henderson, former president of the Boston Consulting Group, used the term *brinkmanship* to describe a recommended approach for deterring competitive entry. Brinkmanship occurs when industry leaders convince potential competitors that any market entry effort will be countered with vigorous and unpleasant responses.

Many observers agree that Nutrasweet used brinkmanship to deter competitors from entering the low-calorie artificial sweetener market as Nutrasweet's patents expired. Nutrasweet's tactic of deep price cuts appears to have been motivated by the desire to maintain control over the market and to discourage competitors. In fact, several European producers have already abandoned the business, proof that Nutrasweet's policy of brinkmanship was an effective competitive response to the threat of new entrants.

▼ Threat of Substitute Products

A second force influencing competition in an industry is the threat of substitute products. The availability of substitute products places limits on the prices market leaders can charge in an industry; high prices may induce buyers to switch to the substitute. For example, the pharmaceuticals industry has historically enjoyed high profits in part because of the relative scarcity of substitutes for well-known and effective medications.

Similarly, Monsanto's Nutrasweet unit enjoyed near-monopoly profits on sales of its aspartame sweetener thanks to patent protection and a track record for quality and safety. As patents expired around the world, Nutrasweet has been forced to cut prices to preserve market share. Besides facing a threat from makers of generic aspartame, a new generation of artificial sweeteners is waiting in the wings. One product, Johnson & Johnson's sucralose, offers the benefit of longer shelf life compared to aspartame.[3] For the first time, the threat of substitute products represents a significant negative competitive force for Nutrasweet.

▼ Bargaining Power of Buyers

The ultimate aim of industrial customers is to pay the lowest possible price to obtain the products or services that it uses as inputs. Usually, therefore, the buyers' best interests are served if they can drive down profitability in the supplier industry. To accomplish this the buyers have to gain leverage over firms in the supplier industry. One way they can do this is to purchase in such large quantities that supplier firms depend on the buyers' business for survival. Second, when the supplier's products are viewed as commodities, that is, as standard or undifferentiated, buyers are likely to bargain hard for low prices, since many firms can meet their needs. Buyers will also bargain hard when the supplier industry's products or services represent a significant portion of the buying firms' costs. A fourth source of buyer power is the willingness and ability to achieve backward integration.

Nutrasweet is affected both positively and negatively by several of the factors associated with buyer bargaining power. Soft-drink bottlers such as PepsiCo and Coca-Cola are major buyers of Nutrasweet, which is the most expensive ingredient in diet soft drinks. As Nutrasweet's patents expire, the soft-drink giants' bargaining power will increase as they seek sharply lower prices for this key ingredient. While the soft-drink makers buy in large quantities, Nutrasweet is used in over 5,000 products—a fact that diminishes buyer power by reducing the leverage associated with losing one or a few buyers. Coca-Cola's buyer power is also enhanced because it has developed and patented its own low-calorie sweetener.

▼ Bargaining Power of Suppliers

Supplier power over industry firms is the "flip side of the coin" to buyer power. If suppliers have enough leverage over industry firms, they can raise prices high enough to significantly influence the profitability of their organizational customers. The ability of suppliers to gain leverage over industry firms is determined by several factors. Suppliers will have the advantage if they are large and relatively few in number. Second, when the suppliers' products or services

---

[3] Eben Shapiro, "Nutrasweet's Race With the Calendar," *The New York Times*, April 8, 1992, p. C1.

are important inputs to industry firms, or are differentiated, or carry switching costs, the suppliers will have considerable leverage over buyers. Suppliers will also enjoy bargaining power if their business is not threatened by alternative products. A fourth source of supplier power is the willingness and ability of suppliers to pursue a strategy of forward vertical integration and develop their own products if they are unable to get satisfactory terms with industry buyers.

▼ Rivalry Among Competitors

Rivalry among firms refers to all the actions taken by firms in the industry to improve their positions and gain advantage over each other. Included here are such things as price competition, advertising battles, product positioning, attempts at differentiation, and so on. To the extent that rivalry among firms improves industry profitability and promotes stability within the industry, it is a positive force. To the extent that it drives down prices and, therefore, profitability and creates instability in the industry, it is a negative factor. Several factors can create intense rivalry. Once an industry enters the slow-growth phase, firms focus on market share and how it can be gained at the expense of others. Second, industries characterized by high fixed costs are always under pressure to keep production at full capacity to cover the fixed costs. Once the industry accumulates excess capacity, the drive to fill capacity will push prices—and profitability—down. A third factor affecting rivalry is lack of differentiation or an absence of switching costs, which encourages buyers to treat the products or services as commodities and shop for the best prices. Again, there is downward pressure on prices and profitability. Fourth, firms with high strategic stakes in achieving success in an industry generally are destabilizing because they may be willing to accept unreasonably low profit margins to establish themselves, hold position, or expand.

COMPETITIVE ADVANTAGE

Competitive advantage exists when there is a match between the distinctive competencies of a firm and the factors critical for success within its industry that permits the firm to outperform competitors.[4] There are two basic ways to achieve competitive advantage. First, competitive advantage may be achieved when a firm pursues a strategy of low costs, which enables it to offer products at lower prices than competitors. Competitive advantage may also be gained by a strategy of differentiating products so that customers perceive unique benefits that justify a premium price. Note that both strategies have the same effect: to increase the perceived benefits that accrue to customers.[5]

---

[4] Peter D. Bennett, ed., *Dictionary of Marketing Terms* (Chicago: American Marketing Association, 1988), p. 35.

[5] Michael E. Porter, *Competitive Advantage: Creating and Sustaining Superior Performance* (New York: The Free Press, 1985).

The quality of a firm's strategy is ultimately measured by results—sales, profits, or some other measure. Results, in turn, depend on the level of value created for customers: the greater the perceived consumer value, the better the strategy. A firm may market a better mousetrap, but the ultimate success of the product depends on customers deciding for themselves whether or not to buy it according to the perceived value that it offers them. Value is like beauty—it's in the eye (and the pocketbook) of the beholder. In sum, competitive advantage is achieved by creating more value than the competition, and value is defined by the customer.

Two different models of competitive advantage have received considerable attention. The first offers *generic strategies*, four different routes or paths that organizations choose to offer superior value and achieve competitive advantage. According to the second model, generic strategies alone don't account for the astonishing success of many Japanese companies in recent years. The new model, based on the concept of *strategic intent*, proposes four sources of competitive advantage. Discussion of both models follows.

▼ Generic Strategies for Creating Competitive Advantage

In addition to the five-forces model of industry competition, Michael Porter has developed a framework of generic business strategies based on the two types or sources of competitive advantage mentioned earlier: *low cost* and *differentiation*. Table 10–1 shows that the combination of these two sources with the scope of the target market served (narrow or broad) or product mix width (narrow or wide) yields four **generic strategies:** *cost leadership, differentiation, cost focus,* and *focused differentiation*.

Generic strategies are based on the principle that the achievement of competitive advantage is at the core of a superior marketing strategy. Achieving competitive advantage demands that the firm make choices about the **type** of competitive advantage it seeks to attain (based on cost or differentiation) and the **market scope** or **product mix width** within which competitive advantage will be attained.[6] The nature of the choice between types of advantage and market scope is a gamble, and it is the nature of every gamble that it entails *risk:* By choosing a given generic strategy, a firm always risks making the wrong choice.

Overall Cost Leadership

Cost-leadership advantage is based on a firm's position as the industry's low-cost producer in broadly defined markets or across a wide mix of products. This strategy has become increasingly popular in recent years as a result of the popularization of the experience curve concept. Basically, a firm seeking to base its competitive strategy on overall cost leadership must aggressively pursue a position of cost leadership by constructing the most efficient scale facilities and obtaining the largest share of market so that its cost per unit is the lowest in the

---

[6] Ibid., p. 12.

TABLE 10–1 Generic Competitive Strategies

		Competitive Advantage	
		Lower Cost	*Differentiation*
Competitive Scope	Broad Target	Cost Leadership	Differentiation
	Narrow Target	Cost Focus	Focused Differentiation

Source: Reprinted with the permission of The Free Press, a division of Simon & Schuster, from *The Competitive Advantage of Nations*, by Michael E. Porter. Copyright © 1990 by Michael E. Porter.

industry. These advantages, in turn, give the producer a substantial lead in terms of experience with building the product. Experience then leads to more refinements of the entire process of production, delivery, and service, which leads to further cost reductions.

Whatever its source, cost-leadership advantage can be the basis for offering lower prices (and more value) to customers. Cost leadership has been the cornerstone of other highly successful strategies. In Canada, market pulp, newsprint, and fish processing are examples of international competititve success in natural resource products that have benefited from cost leadership.[7] In Japan, companies and suppliers in the 35mm camera, consumer electronics and entertainment equipment, motorcycle, and automobile industries have achieved leadership on a world basis.

Cost leadership, however, is a sustainable source of competitive advantage only if barriers exist that prevent competitors from achieving the same low costs. In an era of increasing technological improvements in manufacturing, manufacturers constantly leapfrog over one another in pursuit of lower costs. At one time, for example, IBM enjoyed the low-cost advantage in the production of computer printers. Then the Japanese took the same technology, reduced production costs, improved product reliability—and gained the low-cost advantage. IBM fought back by building a highly automated printer plant, where the number of component parts was slashed by more than 50 percent and robots were used to snap many components into place. Despite these successes, IBM ultimately chose to exit the business; the plant was sold.

Differentiation

When a firm's product has an actual or perceived uniqueness in a broad market, it is said to have a **differentiation advantage.** This can be an extremely effective strategy for defending market position and obtaining above-average returns; the uniqueness often allows a company to charge a premium price for its

---

[7] Michael E. Porter, *Canada at the Crossroads—the Reality of a New Competitive Environment* (Ottawa: Business Council on National Issues and Minister of Supply and Services, 1991) p.38.

products. Examples of successful differentiation are Maytag in large home appliances, Canadian Foremost in high-mobility all-terrain vehicles, and almost any successful branded consumer product. IBM traditionally has differentiated itself with a strong sales/service organization and the security of the IBM standard in a world of rapid obsolescence. Among athletic shoe manufacturers, Nike stands out as the technological leader as a result of unique product features found in a wide array of shoes.

The Narrow-Focus Advantage

The preceding discussion of cost leadership and differentiation has considered only the impact on broad markets. By contrast, strategies to achieve a **narrow-focus advantage** target a narrowly defined market/customer. It is an advantage based on an ability to create more customer value for a narrowly targeted segment and results from a better understanding of customer needs and wants. A narrow-focus strategy can be combined with either cost- or differentiation-advantage strategies. In other words, while a *cost focus* means offering a narrow target market low prices, a firm pursuing *focused differentiation* will offer a narrow target market the perception of product uniqueness at a premium price.

Focused Differentiation. Canadian Foremost's exploration and drilling vehicles are an example of focused differentiation. Its international reputation stems from a clear emphasis on world-class production, research, and product design. The company's strategy of product quality over price competition continues despite the mature product life-cycle stage for its vehicles and equipment.[8]

Cost Focus. The final strategy is cost focus, when a firm offers a narrow target market lower prices than the competition based on the firm's lower-cost position. Examples can be found in the world of high-tech electronic products as well as low-tech shipbuilding. Eicon Technology Corporation of Montreal has carved out a global leadership position with such electronics products as the Eicon Card—products through which personal computers can operate as networks. Eicon has differentiated its products on the basis of lower cost and better operating performance against its competitors. The company is focused on customer need and has more than 200 strategic alliances and partnerships to maintain its leadership position.[9] By contrast, the low-tech Chinese shipbuilding industry offers simple, standard vessel types at low prices that reflect low production costs.[10]

The issue of sustainability is central to the strategy concept. As noted earlier, cost leadership is a sustainable source of competitive advantage only if barriers exist that prevent competitors from achieving the same low costs. Sustained differentiation depends on continued perceived value and the absence of imitation by competitors.[11] Several factors determine whether or not focus can be sus-

---

[8] Mary R. Brooks, Donald J. Patton, and Philip J. Rosson, *The Export Edge* (Ottawa: External Affairs and International Trade Canada, October 24, 1990) p.38.

[9] Eicon Technology Corporation, *Annual Report 1994*; "Buyers' Scorecard: Eicon scores highest based on reliability, speed," *Computerworld* (July 4, 1994) and Michael Slater, "Networking Stars," *Report on Business Magazine* (April 1993) p.69.

[10] Michael E. Porter, *The Competitive Advantage of Nations* (New York: The Free Press, 1990) p.39.

[11] Porter, *Competitive Advantage*, p. 158.

tained as a source of competitive advantage. First, focus is sustainable if a firm's competitors are defining their target markets more broadly. A focuser doesn't try to be all things to all people. Competitors may diminish their advantage by trying to satisfy the needs of a broader market segment—a strategy which, by definition, means a blunter focus. Conversely, a firm's focus advantage is only sustainable if competitors cannot define the segment even more narrowly. Second, focus can be sustained if competitors cannot overcome barriers to imitating the focus strategy. Finally, focus can be sustained if consumers in the target segment do not migrate to other segments not served by the focuser.

▼ Competitive Advantage for Global Marketers

An alternative framework for understanding competitive advantage focuses on competitiveness as a function of the pace at which a company implants new advantages deep within its organization. This framework identifies **strategic intent,** growing out of ambition and obsession with winning, as the means for achieving competitive advantage. Writing in the *Harvard Business Review,* C. K. Prahalad and Gary Hamel note that "Few competitive advantages are long lasting. Keeping score of existing advantages is not the same as building new advantages. The essence of strategy lies in creating tomorrow's competitive advantages faster than competitors mimic the ones you possess today. An organization's capacity to improve existing skills and learn new ones is the most defensible competitive advantage of all."[12]

This approach is founded on the principles of W. E. Deming, who insists that a company must commit itself to constant improvement in order to be a winner in a competitive struggle. For years, Deming's message fell on deaf ears in North America, while the Japanese took his view to heart and even named their most prestigious business award after him. Finally, however, North American manufacturers are starting to pay attention.

The significance of Hamel and Prahalad's framework becomes evident when comparing Caterpillar and Komatsu. Caterpillar became the largest manufacturer of earth-moving equipment in the world because it was fanatical about quality and service. Caterpillar is a truly global company, with 35 percent market share worldwide—more than half of which represents sales to developing countries. The differentiation advantage was achieved with product durability, global spare parts service (including guaranteed delivery of spare parts anywhere in the world within 48 hours), and a strong network of loyal dealers.

Unfortunately, Caterpillar has faced a very challenging set of environmental forces during the past decade. Many of Caterpillar's plants were closed by a lengthy strike in the early 1980s; a worldwide recession at the same time caused downturns in the industries that were Caterpillar customers. In addition, the strong dollar gave a cost advantage to foreign rivals.

---

[12] Gary Hamel and C. K. Prahalad, "Strategic Intent," *Harvard Business Review* (May–June 1989), p. 69. See also Gary Hamel and C. K. Prahalad, "The Core Competence of the Corporation," *Harvard Business Review* (May–June 1990), pp. 79–91.

Compounding Caterpillar's problems was a new competitive threat from Japan. Komatsu was the world's number-two construction equipment company and had been competing with Caterpillar in the Japanese market for years. Komatsu's products were generally acknowledged to offer a lower level of quality. The rivalry took on a new dimension after Komatsu adopted the slogan *Maru-c;* that is, "encircle Caterpillar." Emphasizing quality and taking advantage of low labor costs and the strong dollar, Komatsu surpassed Caterpillar as number one in earth-moving equipment in Japan and made serious inroads in North America and other markets. Yet the company continued to develop new sources of competitive advantage even after it achieved world-class quality. New product development cycles were speeded up, manufacturing was rationalized, and so on. Caterpillar struggled to sustain its competitive advantage because many customers found Komatsu's combination of quality, durability, and lower price creates the best overall value. Yet even as recession and a strong yen put new pressure on Komatsu, the company is seeking new opportunities by diversifying into machine tools and robots.[13]

The Komatsu/Caterpillar saga is just one example of how global competitive battles are shaped by more than the pursuit of generic strategies. Many firms have gained competitive advantage by *disadvantaging* rivals through "competitive innovation." Hamel and Prahalad define *competitive innovation* as "the art of containing competitive risks within manageable proportions" and identify four successful approaches utilized by Japanese competitors. These are: *building layers of advantage, searching for loose bricks, changing the rules of engagement,* and *collaborating.*

Layers of Advantage

A company faces less risk in competitive encounters if it has a wide portfolio of advantages. Successful companies steadily build such portfolios by establishing layers of advantage on top of one another. Komatsu is an excellent example of this approach. Another is the television industry in Japan. By 1970, Japan was not only the world's largest producer of black-and-white television sets but was also well on its way to becoming the leader in producing color sets. The main competitive advantage for such companies as Matsushita at that time was low labor costs.

Because they realized that their cost advantage could be temporary, the Japanese also added additional layers of *quality and reliability* advantages by building plants large enough to serve world markets. Much of this output did not carry the manufacturer's brand name. For example, Matsushita Electric sold products to other marketers such as RCA that sold them under their own brand names. Matsushita was pursuing a simple idea: A product sold was a product sold, no matter whose label it carried.[14]

---

[13] Robert L. Rose and Masayoshi Kanabayashi, "Komatsu Throttles Back on Construction Equipment," *The Wall Street Journal,* May 13, 1992, p. B4.

[14] James Lardner, *Fast Forward: Hollywood, The Japanese, and the VCR Wars* (New York: New American Library, 1987) p. 135.

In order to build the next layer of advantage, the Japanese spent the 1970s investing heavily in marketing channels and Japanese brand names to gain recognition. This strategy added yet another layer of competitive advantage: the *global brand franchise*—that is, a global customer base. By the late 1970s, channels and brand awareness were established well enough to support the introduction of new products that could benefit from global marketing, for example, VCRs and photocopy machines. Finally, many companies have invested in *regional manufacturing* so their products can be differentiated and better adapted to customer needs in individual markets.

The process of building layers illustrates how a company can move along the value chain to strengthen competitive advantage. The Japanese began with manufacturing (an upstream value activity) and moved on to marketing (a downstream value activity) and then back upstream to basic research and development. All of these sources of competitive advantage represent mutually desirable layers that are accumulated over time.

Loose Bricks

A second approach takes advantage of the "loose bricks" left in the defensive walls of competitors whose attention is narrowly focused on a market segment or a geographic area. For example, Caterpillar's attention was focused elsewhere when Komatsu made its first entry into the Eastern European market. A similar chain of events occurred in the global motorcycle industry. For many years the American company Harley-Davidson, and the entire British motorcycle industry, focused their efforts on large motorcycles. The market for small engine bikes in North America was neglected by the main domestic producer as well as the main foreign exporters. The Japanese recognized this market niche in North America and began to sell small bikes. At the same time, and not recognized as a potential strategic threat, the Japanese also developed their expertise in large displacement engine design and technology through experimental racing of larger motorcycles on the European circuit.

Honda, along with other Japanese motorcycle manufacturers, expanded North American sales rapidly and began using its core competence in engines to diversify into small automobiles. Its first Honda Civic models were powered by overhead cam motorcycle engines. The market for British motorcycles in North America was decimated by the Japanese. Harley-Davidson, with some help from U.S. protectionist import quotas, was eventually able to reshape itself by dramatically improving product quality and targeting the global market for luxury, super heavyweight motorcycles.

Changing the Rules

A third approach involves changing the so-called rules of engagement and refusing to "play by the rules" set by industry leaders. For example, in the copier market, while IBM and Kodak were imitating the marketing strategies used by Xerox, the American leader, Canon wrote a new rulebook.

While Xerox built a wide range of copiers, Canon built standardized machines and components, reducing manufacturing costs. While Xerox employed a huge direct sales force, Canon chose to distribute through office-product dealers. Canon also designed serviceability, as well as reliability, into its products so that it could rely on dealers for service rather than incurring the expense required to create a national service network. Canon further decided to sell rather than lease its machines, freeing the company from the burden of financing the lease base. In another major departure, Canon targeted its copiers at secretaries and department managers rather than at the heads of corporate duplicating operations.[15]

Smaller companies can sometimes change the rules in a market dominated by large competitors. Nora Beverages Inc. of Mirabel succeeded in capturing 10 percent of the premium spring water market in the United States against such giants as the French Evian brand, which holds a 50 percent market share. It did this by not following industry practice of distributing through grocery brokers and warehouses. By recognizing that distribution is the fundamental basis for success in the beverage industry, Nora opted for direct store distributors who take the product directly to the store, price it, and stock the shelves. This proved a faster, less costly method with a higher level of attention given to the brand.[16]

Collaborating

A final source of competitive advantage is using know-how developed by other companies. Such *collaboration* may take the form of licensing agreements, joint ventures, and partnerships. History has shown that the Japanese have excelled at using the collaborating strategy to achieve industry leadership. As noted in Chapter 9, one of the legendary licensing agreements of modern business history is Sony's licensing of transistor technology from AT&T's Western Electric subsidiary in the 1950s for $25,000. This agreement gave Sony access to the transistor and allowed the company to become a world leader. Beginning with its initial successes in the manufacturing and marketing of portable radios, the Sony name is now synonymous with a wide assortment of high-quality consumer electronics products.

Hamel and Prahalad have continued to refine and develop the concept of strategic intent since it was first introduced in their ground-breaking 1989 article. Recently the authors outlined some broad categories of resource leverage that managers can use to achieve their aspirations: concentrating resources on strategic goals via convergence and focus; accumulating resources more efficiently via extracting and borrowing; complementing one resource with another by blending and balancing; and conserving resources by recycling, co-opting, and shielding.[17]

---

[15] Hamel and Prahalad, "Strategic Intent," p.69.

[16] Michael Slater "Riding the Wave," *Report on Business Magazine* (April 1993) p.67.

[17] Gary Hamel and C. K. Prahalad, "Strategy as Stretch and Leverage," *Harvard Business Review* (March–April 1993), pp.75–84.

GLOBAL COMPETITION
AND NATIONAL COMPETITIVE ADVANTAGE[18]

An inevitable consequence of the expansion of global marketing activity is the growth of competition on a global basis. In industry after industry, global competition is a critical factor affecting success. In some industries, global companies have virtually excluded all other companies from their markets. An example of this phenomenon is the detergent industry where three companies—Colgate, Unilever, and Procter & Gamble—dominate an increasing number of detergent markets. Many companies can make a quality detergent, but the skills required for quality packaging overwhelmed local competition in market after market.[19]

The automobile industry has also become increasingly competitive on a global basis. Part of the reason for the initial success of foreign auto makers in North America was the reluctance of the Big Three to design and make small, inexpensive, high-quality cars. This resistance was based on the economics of car production. The bigger the car, the higher the list price. Under this formula, small cars meant smaller unit profits and domestic manufacturers, therefore, resisted the increasing consumer preference for smaller cars.

Meanwhile, European and Japanese manufacturers' product lines have always included cars smaller than those made in North America because of the different market conditions in Europe: less space, high taxes on engine displacement and on fuel, and a much greater market interest in functional design and engineering innovations. First Volkswagen, then Nissan, Toyota, and other Japanese auto makers discovered that there was a growing demand for their cars in the North American market. Sales of imports, predominantly of small cars, grew rapidly in the late 1950s. The introduction of the American compacts in the early 1960s blunted the import penetration somewhat, but as the size, power, and price of domestic compacts increased each year, import sales continued to expand. While the U.S. began to experience the import surge somewhat earlier than Canada, imported cars now hold about one-third of the share in each market.

The effect of global competition has been highly beneficial to consumers around the world. In the two examples cited of detergents in Central America and automobiles in North America, consumers have benefited. In Central America, detergent prices have fallen as a result of global competition. In Canada and the United States, foreign companies have provided consumers with the automobile products, performance, and price characteristics that they wanted. If the imported cars of the smaller size and lower price had not been available, it is unlikely that the Big Three car makers would have provided a comparable product as quickly. What is true for automobiles here is true for every product class around the world. Global competition expands the range of product and increases the likelihood that consumers will get what they want.

---

[18] This section draws heavily on Michael E. Porter, *The Competitive Advantage of Nations* (New York: The Free Press, 1990) Chapters 3 and 4; and Michael E. Porter, *Canada at the Crossroads* (Ottawa: Business Council on National Issues, and Minister of Supply and Services, October 1991) Part III.

[19] A good illustration of how they have done this is provided by the excellent series of cases on the competition in the detergent industry in the Central American Common Market. Available from Harvard Case Services, Boston, MA, 02163.

The downside of global competition is its impact on the producers of goods and services. Global competition creates value for consumers, but it also destroys jobs. When a company on the other side of the world offers the consumer a better product at a lower price, this company deprives a domestic supplier of a customer. Unless the domestic supplier can create new values and find new customers, the jobs and livelihoods of the domestic supplier's employees are threatened.

A country's trade policy is ultimately a function of its competitive strategy. Owing to Canada's extensive trading relationship with the United States and its unusually high degree of foreign ownership, the shifting character of international competition poses daunting challenges for Canadian companies and public policy-makers. Many companies are in the process of determining how to reconfigure their North American and international activities. NAFTA, the European Union, and trading bloc initiatives in Latin America and South-East Asia all contribute to this process. These decisions do not only concern markets but include deciding on where the "home base" for individual product lines, or indeed for the entire corporate operation, should be, where core research and development should be undertaken and where strategic control should lie.[20]

In order to establish a perspective for this discussion, envision a spectrum measuring degree of "internationalism" in industry or firm activities. At one end is the domestic industry and firm. It has no international operations at all. At the other end are the true global industries and firms. Between the two extremes are various levels of international and multidomestic industries and firms. These firms are characterized by freestanding, or almost freestanding, subsidiaries in several countries. The activities of a unit in any given country are usually independent of activities in units in other countries. The foreign subsidiaries of any particular firm essentially have become "local" firms of the country in which they are operating. There is no integrated global strategy. There are, instead, independent country strategies.

We are not considering such international and multidomestic industries and firms in this section. They gain no advantage or disadvantage from their home nations. Rather, they sink or swim based solely on their abilities to fit into and compete in the local country market.

Global firms, on the other hand, depending on their size, of course, may have integrated global strategies which make the operations of any particular country unit dependent to some degree on the activities of units in other countries.

In this section the following question is addressed: Why is a particular nation a good home base for specific industries? Why, for example, is Canada the home base of leading newsprint, nickel, ice skates, and radiation therapy equipment firms? Why is the United States the home base for the leading competitors in personal computers, software, credit cards, and movies? Why is Germany the home of so many world leaders in printing presses, chemicals, and luxury cars? Why are so many leading pharmaceutical, chocolate/confectionery, and trading companies located in Switzerland? Why are the world leaders in consumer electronics home-based in Japan?

There are four categories of national attributes that contribute to, or detract from, the creation of competitive advantage for the firms of that nation. These attributes form what is known as the national "diamond" (see Figure 10–2).

---

[20] Michael E. Porter, *Canada at the Crossroads* (Ottawa: Business Council on National Issues and Government of Canada, October 1991) p.6.

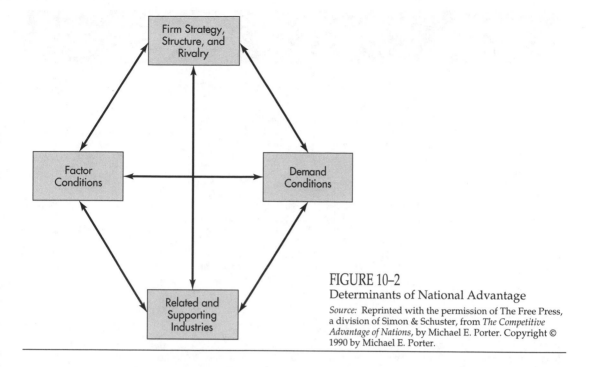

FIGURE 10–2
Determinants of National Advantage

Source: Reprinted with the permission of The Free Press, a division of Simon & Schuster, from *The Competitive Advantage of Nations*, by Michael E. Porter. Copyright © 1990 by Michael E. Porter.

Some 25 industries that figure importantly in Canada's economy and trading relationships are shown in Table 10–2. These industries are singled out because most account for a high share of world exports, several have high investment abroad, and some are of regional significance within Canada.[21] The sources of international competitiveness in these industries are ranked *high, moderate,* or *low* for each of the six components of the complete *diamond,* shown in Figure 10–5.

▼ Factor Conditions

In its simplest form factor conditions refer to a country's land, labor, natural resources, capital, and infrastructure. Of special importance are those factors that are created within a country, as distinguished from those that are inherited. There are five categories of factors: human resources, physical resources, knowledge resources, capital resources, and infrastructure.

Human Resources Factors. The quantity of workers available, the skills possessed by these workers, wage levels, and the overall work ethic of the work force together constitute a nation's human resources factors. Countries with a plentiful supply of low-wage workers have an obvious advantage in the production of low-skill, labor-intensive products. On the other hand, such countries are usually at a *disadvantage* when it comes to the production of sophisticated products requiring highly skilled workers capable of working without extensive supervision.

---

[21] Porter (1991) p.35.

Industry	Factor Conditions	Conditions	Related and Supporting	Strategy, Structure & Rivalry	Role of Government	Role of Chance	% Share of World Export 1989
Resource Based							
Newsprint	(B) High	Low	Low	Low	Low	-	60
Market Pulp	(B) High	Low	Low	Low	Low	-	33
Nickel	(B&A) High	Low	Moderate	Moderate	High	-	60
Aluminum	(B) High	Low	Low	Low	Moderate	High	18
Atlantic Groundfish	(B) High	Low	Moderate	Low	Negative	-	8
Styrene	(B) High	Moderate	Moderate	Low	Low	-	18
Electricity	(B) High	Moderate	High	Moderate	High	-	15
Beef Processing	(B) Moderate	Moderate	Low	Low	Moderate	-	1
Manufactured Housing	(B) High	Moderate	Low	Low	Moderate	-	5
Market-Access Based							
Auto Parts	Low	Low	Low	Low	High	-	10
Auto Assembly	Low	Low	Low	Low	High	-	10
Pulp & Paper Equip.	Low	Low	Moderate	Low	Low	-	11
Innovation-Driven							
Ice Skates	(A) Moderate	High	High	High	Low	-	50
Urban Rail	(A) Moderate	Moderate	Moderate	Low	Moderate	Moderate	7
Flight Simulators	(A) Moderate	Low	Low	Moderate	Low	-	22
Industrial Explosives	(B) Moderate	High	Moderate	Moderate	High	-	n/a
Commuter Aircraft	(A) Moderate	Moderate	Moderate	Low	Moderate	Moderate	10
Central Office Switches	(A) High	High	Moderate	High	Moderate	Moderate	15
Geophysical Contracting	(A) High	Moderate	High	High	High	-	50
Consulting Engineering	(A) Moderate	High	Low	High	High	-	n/a
Whisky	(B&A) Moderate	Low	Low	Moderate	Negative	High	12
Life Insurance	(A) Moderate	Moderate	Low	High	High	-	10
Human Biologicals	(A) Moderate	Low	Low	Low	Moderate	Moderate	n/a
Other							
Waste Management	(A) Moderate	Moderate	Low	Low	Low	Moderate	n/a
Radiation Therapy Equipment	(A) Moderate	Low	High	Low	High	-	30

(B) Advantage stems from basic factor conditions.
(A) Advantage stems from advanced factor conditions.

Source: Michael E. Porter, *Canada at the Crossroads* (Ottawa: Council on National Issues and Industry Canada, Government of Canada, October 1991) p.37, reproduced with the permission of the Council on National Issues and the Minister of Supply and Services Canada, 1994.

Canada has a shortage of such skilled labor in several sectors, but especially in technology-related jobs, such as engineers. We also compare poorly to other industrial nations in the occupational standards for skilled trades.[22]

---

[22] Michael E. Porter, *Canada at the Crossroads* (Ottawa: Council on National Issues, and Government of Canada, October 1991) p.49.

Physical Resources Factors. The availability, quantity, quality, and cost of land, water, minerals, and other natural resources determine a country's physical resources. A country's size and location are also included in this category, since proximity to markets and sources of supply, as well as transportation costs, are strategic considerations. While Canada's physical resources are a significant source of international competitive advantage, proximity to the U.S. market has shaped our economy in a major way.

Knowledge Resources Factors. The availability within a nation of a significant population with scientific, technical, and market-related knowledge means a nation is endowed with knowledge resources. The presence of these factors is usually a function of the number of research facilities and universities, both government and private, operating in the country. These factors are important to success in sophisticated products and services, and to doing business in sophisticated markets. This factor relates directly to Germany's leadership in chemicals; for some 150 years, Germany has been home to top university chemistry programs, advanced scientific journals, and apprenticeship programs.

Capital Resources Factors. Countries vary in the availability, amount, cost, and types of capital available to the country's industries. The nation's savings rate, interest rates, tax laws, and government deficits all affect the availability of these factors. The advantage to industries with low capital cost versus those located in nations with relatively high costs is sometimes decisive. Firms paying high capital costs are frequently unable to stay in a market where the competition comes from a nation with low capital costs. The firms with the low cost of capital can keep their prices low and force the firms paying high costs to either accept low returns on investment or leave the industry. The cost of capital in Canada historically mirrors that in the U.S. and, while the capital market and financial system runs smoothly, smaller companies generally experience more difficulties in obtaining capital to finance growth.[23]

Infrastructure Resources. Infrastructure includes a nation's banking system, health care system, transportation system, communications system, and the availability and cost of using these systems. More sophisticated industries are more dependent on advanced infrastructures for success. Basic physical infrastructure, such as transportation and communications, is well-developed in Canada, although some of the related services (for example, trucking and railways) are burdened by extensive regulation and poor coordination of government policies.[24]

Competitive advantage accrues to a nation's industry if the mix of factors available to the industry is such that it facilitates pursuit of a generic strategy: low-cost production or the production of a highly differentiated product or service. Competitive advantage may also be created by nations that have selective factor *disadvantages.* For example, the absence of sufficient labor may force firms to develop forms of mechanization that give the nation's firms an advantage. High transportation costs may motivate firms to develop new materials that are less expensive to transport.

---

[23] Porter (1991) p.51.
[24] Porter (1991) p.49.

▼ Demand Conditions

The nature of home demand conditions for the firm's or industry's products and services are important because they determine the rate and nature of improvement and innovation by the firms in the nation. These are the factors that either train firms for world-class competition, or which fail to adequately prepare them to compete in the global marketplace. Three characteristics of home demand are particularly important to competitive advantage: the composition of home demand, the size and pattern of growth of home demand, and the means by which a nation's home demand pulls the nation's products and services into foreign markets.

The composition of home demand determines how firms perceive, interpret, and respond to buyer needs. Competitive advantage can be achieved when the home demand gives local firms a better picture of buyer needs, at an earlier time, than is available to foreign rivals. This advantage is enhanced when home buyers pressure the nation's firms to innovate quickly and frequently. The basis for advantage is the fact that when firms are more sensitive to and more responsive to home demand, and when that demand reflects or anticipates world demand, the nation's firms can stay ahead of the market. Canadian consumer-demand conditions have not put strong pressure on companies to innovate, upgrade, or anticipate international needs. Amercian consumers are more demanding of providers of goods and services to enhance their products. Frequently, because of the presence of U.S. consumer goods companies in Canada, advances achieved by American demand conditions spill over into the Canadian market.[25]

The size and pattern of growth of home demand are important only if the composition of the home demand is sophisticated and anticipates foreign demand. Large home markets offer opportunities to achieve economies of scale and learning while dealing with familiar, comfortable markets. For many goods and services the Canadian home market is small. Consequently, companies, especially industrial goods producers, must market their goods abroad. There is less apprehension about investing in large-scale production facilities and expensive R&D programs when the home market is sufficient to absorb the increased capacity. If the home demand accurately reflects or anticipates foreign demand, and if the firms do not become content with serving the home market, the existence of large-scale facilities and programs will be an advantage in global competition.

Rapid home market growth is another incentive to invest in and adopt new technologies faster, and to build large, efficient facilities. For Canada, NAFTA may ultimately have the effect of creating a very large quasi-home market. In Japan, rapid home market growth provided the incentive for Japanese firms to invest heavily in modern automated facilities. *Early home demand,* especially if it anticipates international demand, gives local firms the advantage of getting established in an industry sooner than foreign rivals. Equally important is *early market saturation,* which puts pressure on a company to expand into international markets and innovate. Market saturation is especially important if it coincides with rapid growth in foreign markets.

---

[25] Porter (1991) p.52.

The *means by which a nation's products and services are pulled into foreign countries* is the third aspect of demand conditions. The issue here is whether a nation's people and businesses go abroad and then demand the nation's products and services in those second countries. For example, when the U.S. auto companies set up operations in foreign countries, the auto parts industry followed. The same is true for the Japanese auto industry. Once the auto companies set up operations in the Canada and the U.S., Japanese parts suppliers began to follow suit.

A related issue is whether foreigners come to a nation for training, pleasure, business, or research. After returning home, they are likely to demand the products and services with which they became familiar while abroad. Similar effects can result from professional, scientific, and political relationships between nations. Those involved in the relationships begin to demand the products and services of the recognized leaders.

It is the interplay of demand conditions that produces competitive advantage. Of special importance are those conditions that lead to initial and continuing incentives to invest and innovate, and to continuing competition in increasingly sophisticated markets.

▼ Related and Supporting Industries

The presence in a nation of internationally competitive industries in fields that are related to, or in direct support of, other industries, may give those other industries a competitive advantage. Internationally competitive supplier industries provide inputs to downstream industries that will also be internationally competitive in terms of price and quality. Downstream industries will have easier access to these inputs and the technology that produced them, and to the managerial and organizational structures that have made them competitive. Access is a function of proximity both in terms of physical distance and cultural similarity. It is not the inputs in themselves that give advantage. It is the *contact* and *coordination* with the suppliers—the opportunity to structure the value chain so that linkages with suppliers are optimized.

Similar advantages accrue when there are internationally competitive related industries in a nation. World-class local industries often deliver the most cost-effective or highest-quality inputs. Regional clusters of suppliers and end-users benefit from short lines of communications and an ongoing exchange of ideas and innovations. In Canada, industry clusters have a tendency to source from abroad, which limits the development of world-class related industries. The transportation-equipment industry cluster has created strong, competitive related industries, while the forest products cluster does not. One-half of the latter's equipment is sourced from abroad.[26] Related industries also create "pull-through" opportunities. For example, the development of the Swiss pharmaceuticals industry can be attributed in part to the presence in Switzerland of a large synthetic dye industry; the discovery of the therapeutic effects of dyes in turn led to the development of pharmaceutical companies.

---

[26] Porter (1991) p.54.

▼ Firm Strategy, Structure, and Rivalry

Differences in management styles, organizational skills, and strategic perspectives create advantages and disadvantages for firms competing in different types of industries, as do differences in the intensity of domestic rivalry. In Germany, for example, company structure and management style tend to be hierarchical. Managers tend to come from technical backgrounds and to be most successful when dealing with industries that demand highly disciplined structures, like chemicals, and precision machinery. Italian firms, on the other hand, tend to look like, and be run like, small family businesses that stress customized over standardized products, niche markets, and substantial flexibility in meeting market demands.

Individual and firm goals are shaped by the national environment and, in turn, greatly influence the strategies to be employed. Strategies of many Canadian companies, particularly in manufacturing, favoured a domestic market focus. For example, most Canadian manufacturers do not export. The long-standing tendency by smaller companies to think *domestic* rather than to engage in the more hazardous and time-consuming business of developing foreign markets must give way to a global outlook.[27] Companies have a tendency to offer broad product lines, integrate vertically, and diversify in order to derive growth from the home market. In part, sheltering industries with high tariffs, weak domestic rivalry, high levels of corporate concentration, and interprovincial trade barriers shaped Canadian business strategy.[28]

Perhaps the most powerful influence on competitive advantage comes from domestic rivalry. Domestic rivalry keeps an industry dynamic and creates continual pressure to improve and innovate. Local rivalry forces firms to develop new products, improve existing ones, lower costs and prices, develop new technologies, and improve quality and service. Rivalry with foreign firms lacks this intensity. Domestic rivals have to fight each other not just for market share, but also for employee talent, R&D breakthroughs, and prestige in the home market. Eventually, strong domestic rivalry will push firms to seek international markets to support expansions in scale and R&D investments. The absence of significant domestic rivalry will create complacency in the home firms and eventually cause them to become noncompetitive in the world markets.

It is not the number of domestic rivals that is important; rather, it is the intensity of the competition and the quality of the competitors that make the difference. It is also important that there be a fairly high rate of new business formations to create new competitors and safeguard against the older companies becoming comfortable with their positions and products and services. As noted earlier in the discussion of the forces shaping industry competition, new entrants bring new perspectives and new methods. They frequently define and serve new market segments, which established companies fail to recognize.

Two final elements to consider in the evaluation of national competitive advantage are chance and government.

---

[27] House of Commons, *Canada's Trade Challenge*, Report of the Special Committee on a National Trading Corporation (Ottawa: Minister of Supply and Services, 1981) p.17.
[28] Porter (1991) p.56.

▼ Chance

Chance events play a role in shaping the competitive environment. Chance events are occurrences that are beyond the control of firms, industries, and usually governments. Included in this category are such things as wars and their aftermaths, major technological breakthroughs, sudden dramatic shifts in factor or input cost, like the oil crises, dramatic swings in exchange rates, and so on.

Chance events are important because they create major discontinuities in technologies that allow nations and firms that were not competitive to leapfrog over old competitors and become competitive, even leaders, in the changed industry. For example, the development of microelectronics allowed many firms to overtake American and German firms in industries that had been based on electromechanical technologies traditionally dominated by the Americans and Germans.

From a systemic perspective, the role of chance events lies in the fact that they alter conditions in the "diamond." The nation with the most favorable diamond, however, will be the one most likely to take advantage of these events and convert them into competitive advantage. In the case of insulin, for example, Canada was the first to isolate it, but it could not convert this breakthrough into an internationally competitive product. Foreign firms in the United States and Denmark were able to do that because of their respective national "diamonds."

▼ Government

Although it is often argued that government is a major determinant of national competitive advantage, in fact, government is not a determinant, but rather an important influence on determinants. Government influences demand conditions, both indirectly, through monetary and fiscal policy, and directly, by virtue of its role as a buyer of products and services. It influences resources as a maker of policies on labor, education, capital formation, natural resources, and product standards. It influences competition and the competitive environment by its role as a regulator of commerce, for example, by telling banks and telephone companies what they can and cannot do. By reinforcing determinants in industries where a nation has competitive advantage, government improves the competitive position of the nation's firms. In other words, government can improve or lessen competitive advantage, but it cannot create it.

▼ The System of Determinants

It is important to view the determinants of national competitive advantage as an interactive system where activity in any one of the nodes impacts on all the others and vice versa. This interplay between the determinants is depicted in Figures 10–3 and 10–4. The interaction of all of the forces is presented in Figure 10–5.

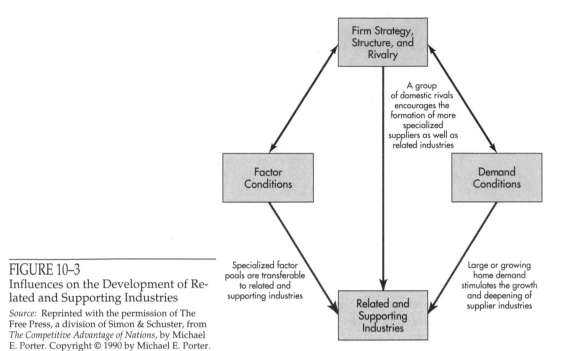

FIGURE 10–3
Influences on the Development of Related and Supporting Industries

Source: Reprinted with the permission of The Free Press, a division of Simon & Schuster, from *The Competitive Advantage of Nations*, by Michael E. Porter. Copyright © 1990 by Michael E. Porter.

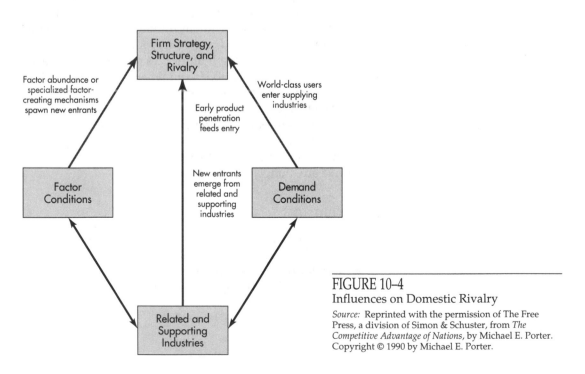

FIGURE 10–4
Influences on Domestic Rivalry

Source: Reprinted with the permission of The Free Press, a division of Simon & Schuster, from *The Competitive Advantage of Nations*, by Michael E. Porter. Copyright © 1990 by Michael E. Porter.

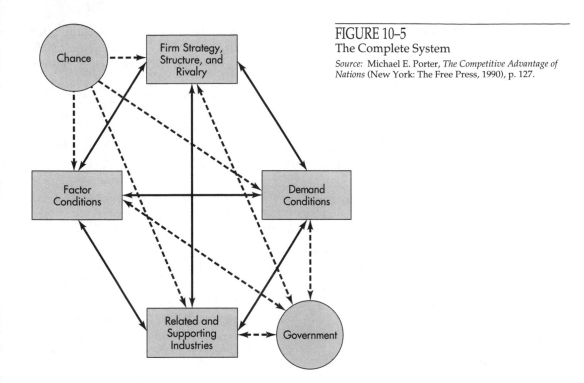

FIGURE 10–5
The Complete System
Source: Michael E. Porter, *The Competitive Advantage of Nations* (New York: The Free Press, 1990), p. 127.

▼ SUMMARY

In this chapter we focused on analyzing industries and the competition from both a national and international perspective and developing strategies for effectively competing in a variety of market and industry situations. The challenges of competing at the early stages of the product life cycle are dramatically different from those at the end of the life cycle. The secret to successful competitive strategy is to recognize the nature of the game and to formulate strategies that are appropriate to the situation. Today, more than ever before, competition is on a global scale. Competitive analysis, in order to be meaningful, must also be carried out on a global scale.

▼ BIBLIOGRAPHY

Books

ABEGGLEN, JAMES C., AND GEORGE STALK, JR., *Kaisha: The Japanese Corporation.* New York: Basic Books, Inc., 1985.

CLIFFORD, DONALD K., JR., AND RICHARD E. CAVANAGH, *The Winning Performance, How America's High-Growth Midsize Companies Succeed.* New York: Bantam Books, 1985.

DAY, GEORGE S., *Market Drive Strategy: Processes for Creating Value.* New York: The Free Press, 1990.

D'CRUZ, JOSEPH R. AND ALAN M. RUGMAN, *New Compacts for Canadian Competitiveness.* Toronto: Kodak Canada Inc., 1992.

DERTOUZOS, MICHAEL L., RICHARD K. LESTER, AND ROBERT M. SOLOW, *Made in America:*

Regaining the Competitive Edge. New York: Harper Collins, 1989.

HALBERSTAM, DAVID, *The Reckoning*. New York: William Morrow and Company, 1986.

OHMAE, KENICHI, *Triad Power*. New York: The Free Press, 1985.

PATTISON, JOSEPH E., *Acquiring the Future: America's Survival and Success in the Global Economy*. Homewood, IL: Dow Jones-Irwin, 1990.

PORTER, MICHAEL E., *Competitive Advantage: Creating and Sustaining Superior Performance*. New York: The Free Press, 1985.

———, *Competition in Global Industries*. Boston: Harvard Business School Press, 1986.

———, *The Competitive Advantage of Nations*. New York: The Free Press, 1990.

———, *Competitive Strategy*. New York: The Free Press, 1980.

WOMACK, JAMES P., DANIEL T. JONES, AND DANIEL ROOS, *The Machine That Changed The World*. New York: Harper Collins, 1990.

Articles

AHARONI, YAIR, "The State-Owned Enterprise as a Competitor in International Markets," *Columbia Journal of World Business* (Spring 1980), 14–22.

BARTMESS, ANDREW, AND KEITH CERNY, "Building Competitive Advantage Through a Global Network of Capabilities," *California Management Review*, 35, no. 2 (Winter 1993), 78–103.

BROUTHERS, LANCER ELIOT, AND STEVE WERNER, "Are the Japanese Good Global Competitors?" *Columbia Journal of World Business*, 25, no. 3 (Fall 1990), 5–11.

CALANTONE, ROGER J., AND C. ANTHONY DI BENEDETTO, "Defensive Marketing in Globally Competitive Industrial Markets," *Columbia Journal of World Business*, 23, no. 3 (Fall 1988), 3–14.

CRAVENS, DAVID W., H. KIRK DOWNEY, AND PAUL LAURITANO, "Global Competition in the Commercial Aircraft Industry: Positioning for Advantage by the Triad Nations," *Columbia Journal of World Business*, 26, no. 4 (Winter 1992), 46–58.

DOUGLAS, SUSAN B., AND C. SAMUEL CRAIG, "Examining Performance of U.S. Multi-nationals in Foreign Markets," *Journal of International Business Studies* (Winter 1983), 51–61.

EGELHOFF, WILLIAM G., "Great Strategy or Great Strategy Implementation—Two Ways of Competing in Global Markets," *Sloan Management Review*, 34, no. 2 (Winter 1993), 37–50.

GARSOMBKE, DIANE J., "International Competitor Analysis," *Planning Review*, 17, no. 3 (May/June 1989), 42–47.

GHOSAL, SUMANTRA, AND D. ELEANOR WESTNEY, "Organizing Competitor Analysis Systems," *Strategic Management Journal*, 12, no. 1 (January 1991), 17–31.

"Global Competition: Confront Your Rivals on Their Home Turf," *Harvard Business Review*, 71, no. 3 (May/June 1993), 10.

HAMEL, GARY, AND C. K. PRAHALAD, "Strategy as Stretch and Leverage," *Harvard Business Review*, 71, no. 2 (March/April 1993), 75–85.

———, "Strategic Intent," *Harvard Business Review* (May/June 1989), 63–76.

———, "The Core Competence of the Corporation," *Harvard Business Review*, 68 (May/June 1990), 79–93.

HENZLER, HERBERT A., "The New Era of Eurocapitalism," *Harvard Business Review*, 70, no. 4 (July/August 1992), 57–68.

HILLIS, W. DANIEL, DANIEL F. BURTON, ROBERT B. COSTELLO, ROBERT M. WHITE, MURRAY WEIDENBAUM, LUKE GEORGHIOU, UMBERTO COLOMBO, LESLIE SCHNEIDER, THOMAS H. LEE, AND JULIE FOX GORTE, "Technology Policy: Is America on the Right Track?" *Harvard Business Review*, 70, no. 3 (May/June 1992), 140–157.

JACQUEMIN, ALEXIS, "The International Dimension of European Competition Policy," *Journal of Common Market Studies*, 31, no. 1 (March 1993), 91–101.

LI, JIATAO, AND STEPHEN GUISINGER, "How Well Do Foreign Firms Compete in the United States?" *Business Horizons*, 34, no. 6 (November/December 1991), 49–53.

LORANGE, PETER, AND JOHAN ROOS, "Why Some Strategic Alliances Succeed and Others Fail," *Journal of Business Strategy*, 12, no. 1 (January/February 1991), 25–30.

MAGRATH, ALLAN J., "Marketing's Agenda for the 1990's," *Journal of Business Strategy*, 13, no. 4 (July/August 1992), 33–37.

MASCARENHAS, BRIANCE, "Order of Entry and Performance in International Markets," *Strategic Management Journal*, 13, no. 7 (October 1992), 499–510.

MORRISON, ALLEN J., AND KENDALL ROTH, "A Taxonomy of Business-Level Strategies in Global Industries," *Strategic Management Journal*, 13, no. 6 (September 1992), 399–417.

NEES, DANIELLE B., "Building and International Practice," *Sloan Management Review* (Winter 1986), 15–26.

PEARSON, ANDRALL E., "Corporate Redemption and the Seven Deadly Sins," *Harvard Business Review*, 70, no. 3 (May/June 1992), 65–75.

PETERS, TOM, "Rethinking Scale," *California Management Review*, 35, no. 1 (Fall 1992), 7–29.

ROBERT, MICHEL M., "Attack Competitors by Changing the Game Rules," *Journal of Business Strategy*, 12, no. 5 (September/October 1991), 53–56.

SCHILL, RONALD L., AND DAVID N. MCARTHUR, "Redefining the Strategic Competitive Unit: Towards a New Global Marketing Paradigm?" *International Marketing Review*, 9, no. 3, 5–24.

SCHOEMAKER, PAUL J. H., "How to Link Strategic Vision to Core Capabilities," *Sloan Management Review*, 34, no. 1 (Fall 1992), 67–81.

SHOSTACK, G. LYNN, "Limitation is the Mother of Innovation," *Journal of Business Strategy*, 9, no. 6 (November/December 1988), 51–52.

WHEELWRIGHT, STEVEN C., "Restoring the Competitive Edge in U.S. Manufacturing," *California Management Review*, 27, no. 3 (Spring 1985), 26–42.

WILLIAMS, JEFFREY R., "How Sustainable Is Your Competitive Advantage?" *California Management Review*, 34, no. 3 (Spring 1992), 29–51.

ELEVEN

Cooperative Strategies and Global Strategic Partnerships

Introduction

In Chapter 9, the discussion focused on the range of strategic options—exporting, licensing, joint ventures, and ownership—traditionally used by companies wishing either to enter global markets for the first time or expand their activities beyond present levels. However, dramatic recent changes in the political, economic, sociocultural, and technological environments of the global firm are all factors that can reduce the effectiveness of those strategies. Trade barriers have fallen, markets have globalized, consumer needs and wants have converged, product life cycles have shortened, and new communications technologies and trends abound. While these developments have created unprecedented opportunities, they also create new challenges for the global marketer.

Increasingly, proactive companies are entering into new types of collaborative arrangements. Once thought of only as joint ventures with the more dominant party reaping most of the benefits (or losses) of the partnership, cross-border alliances are taking on surprising new configurations and even more surprising players. Partnering has become a strategic tool for companies of all sizes across industries. This chapter will focus on global strategic partnerships, *keiretsu*, and various other types of cooperation strategies that are important to the success of the global firm.

REASONS TO COLLABORATE IN GLOBAL STRATEGIC PARTNERSHIPS

Why would an apparently global firm seek to collaborate with another firm, be it local or foreign? Why would a firm dominant in its respective industry or market pursue competitive collaboration with a rival firm? There are two basic reasons. One is to meet the challenge of penetrating and expanding in complex, turbulent, and often unpredictable environments. Collaboration is a way of obtaining the skills, resources, and know-how that can address the complexity of doing business in countries where understanding local culture, law, and practices is essential for business success.

A company faces a fundamental decision: Do we want to expand directly by hiring our own people or do we want to take on partners who will share the effort and bring their expertise and local knowledge and who will, of course, share the reward as well? There is no simple answer to this question although some companies have reduced it to a formula: That is, we always seek a local partner because that is the way we do business. When you ask them why, they reply, "Because this is the only way to succeed." In truth, however, there are many ways to succeed and many ways to fail. Some companies should seek local partners and others should not. There are companies that should seek out partners and alliances in certain countries and not in others. The question of whether or not to collaborate is a fundamental strategic decision and should be carefully thought out.

Another reason for collaboration is the opportunity to leverage capital returns. A firm with limited access to capital will need to find partners in order to expand. This is especially true in diversified companies with businesses at different stages of the life cycle. A company that seeks high targets for growth and return on investment will be unwilling to accept the kind of return that can be earned on manufacturing investments in mature industries. By rationing capital to divisions for manufacturing investment, corporate management forces divisions to develop creative partnerships for manufacturing supply in expansion markets. The net effect of this capital rationing is to increase the return on capital and on equity invested in a mature business. Indeed, by using cooperation strategies a mature business can leverage its capital and know-how to obtain exceptional returns on invested capital.

Partnerships and global strategic alliances open up possibilities for any firm to expand globally. Shortage of capital or lack of expertise is no excuse for sitting back in the home country and hoping that the globalization of the world economy won't endanger your position in the home market. Sitting back and hoping that nothing bad will happen is the beginning of trouble. If you are in a global industry or if your industry is globalizing or if it has the potential for globalizing, you must proactively adopt your own global strategy or you will be overtaken by competition who has beat you to the punch. Eicon Technology Corp., for example, has forged and maintained a global leadership position through continued collaboration and networking with more than 200 alliances and partnerships, including Microsoft and IBM.[1]

If you lack capital or access to capital, or if you know that you will be unable to directly manage research, manufacturing, and marketing operations abroad, you should develop a strategy of cooperation. The trick is to do this without giving up your own competitive advantage. The last thing in the world that you want to do is take on a partner who ends up as a competitor challenging you in the home country and in third-country markets.

---

[1] *Eicon Technology Corporation Corporate Profile* (undated); and *Annual Report 1994*, p.3.

ADVANTAGES OF GOING IT ALONE

There are a number of good reasons to *avoid* cooperation and partnerships. Going it alone has three fundamental advantages: first, there is no issue of control. You own the business and you direct it. There is no conflict concerning short- versus long-term investment horizons, or about third-country markets. You own the business and you decide on these and all issues. Second, there is no danger of transferring technology and know-how to a potential competitor. Today's partner can become tomorrow's competitor. This is especially painful if you helped develop the competitive strength of your new competitor. Finally, when you go it alone there is no issue about sharing the rewards of success. When you go it alone you bear all of the risk and you take all of the gain.

There are two questions that you should ask yourself before taking on a partner.

1. What is the basis for my competitive advantage? What must I do in order to maintain a sustained competitive advantage? Make sure that you do not give up whatever you need to have in order to sustain your competitive advantage. Remember too that if your industry is global or globalizing, your competitive advantage must be global. You must be able to compete with anybody in the world in all markets. If the basis of your advantage is technology, make sure that you continue to develop, control, and own your technology in the partnership. If it is distribution, make sure that you control the distribution channels in the partnership. This might be a 51/49 percent ownership arrangement, for example. Your partner should be in the minority position, and you should be in the controlling position if this is the critical element of a sustained competitive advantage in your business.

2. The second question is: Would I take a partner for the Canadian market? If the answer is no, make a list of the reasons why you would not take a partner. This list of reasons is the cost of partnership: what you are giving up. It is important to make this list because some of the items on the list will be critical to your ability to sustain your competitive advantage. These dimensions of ownership and control can and must be incorporated into your partnership agreement with foreign partners.

THE NATURE OF GLOBAL STRATEGIC PARTNERSHIPS

The terminology used to describe the new forms of cooperation strategies varies widely. The phrases **collaborative agreements, strategic alliances,** and **global strategic partnerships** (GSPs) are frequently used to refer to linkages between companies to jointly pursue a common goal. A broad spectrum of interfirm agreements, including joint ventures, can be covered by this terminology. However, the alliances discussed in this chapter exhibit most or all of the following characteristics. First, they involve contractual, rather than equity, arrangements. Second, ownership is not clear-cut; it is sometimes difficult to identify company "boundaries." Third, they involve forms of technology transfer by other means than the establishment of subsidiaries or via direct investment; thus, successful transfers require new organizational skills. Finally, these collaborative agreements, for the most part, have limited life spans.[2]

Strategic alliances can be classified in different ways. One classification is presented in Table 11–1. According to estimates, the number of strategic alliances has been growing at a rate of 20 to 30 percent since the mid-1980s. The upward trend for GSPs comes in part at the expense of traditional cross-border mergers and acquisitions. According to KPMG Corporate Finance's *Dealwatch*, some 4,106 cross-border mergers and acquisitions took place globally in 1993. This number is 50 percent higher compared with 1990. The most alliance-intensive industries were electrical and electronics, chemical and pharmaceutical, and food, drink, and tobacco, accounting for 25 percent of all deals. Canada accounted for 208, or about five percent, of these outward-bound strategic alliances. Outward-bound here means Canadian companies took the initiative in acquiring or partnering with other companies abroad. Inward-bound strategic alliances, where foreign companies initated linking up with Canadian companies, numbered 178 in 1993.[3]

Roland Smith, chairperson of British Aerospace, offers a straightforward reason why a firm would enter into a GSP: "A partnership is one of the quickest and cheapest ways to develop a global strategy."[4] Former Apple Computer chairperson John Sculley describes the new industrial order as "not necessarily owning layers, but participating in different parts of the value chain."[5] Like traditional joint ventures, GSPs have some disadvantages. Each partner must be willing to sacrifice some control, and there are potential risks associated with strengthening a competitor from another country. Despite these drawbacks, GSPs are attractive for several reasons. First, high product development costs may force a company to seek partners; this was part of the rationale for Boeing's partnership with a Japanese consortium to develop a new jet aircraft, the 777, by the mid-1990s. Second, the technology requirements of many contemporary products mean that an individual company may lack the skills or know-how to go it alone.[6] Third, partnerships may be the best means of securing access to national and regional markets. Fourth, partnerships provide important learning opportunities; in fact, one expert regards GSPs as a "race to learn." Professor Gary Hamel of the London Business School has determined that the partner that proves to be the fastest learner can ultimately dominate the relationship.[7]

---

[2] Riad Ajami and Dara Khambata, "Global Strategic Alliances: The New Transnationals," *Journal of Global Marketing,* 5, 1/2, (1991), 55.

[3] *Dealwatch*, KPMG Corporate Finance, Amsterdam, (1994), No. 2, pp.27–34; (1992) p.33.

[4] Jeremy Main, "Making Global Alliances Work," *Fortune,* December 17, 1990, p. 121.

[5] Stephen Kreider Yoder and G. Pascal Zachary, "Vague New World: Digital Media Business Takes Form as a Battle of Complex Alliances," *The Wall Street Journal,* July 14, 1993, p. A6.

[6] Kenichi Ohmae, "The Global Logic of Strategic Alliances," *Harvard Business Review* (March–April 1989), p. 145.

[7] Main, p. 122.

TABLE 11–1   Types of Strategic Alliances

Type/Focus of Alliance	Description
Technology development	Aimed at reducing costs and hedging the risks associated with technological development. Function by pooling R&D, and/or by technology transfer from "leaders" to "followers."
Operations and logistics	Aimed at improving manufacturing and/or production efficiency through scale and/or learning economies. Function by transferring manufacturing know-how or exploiting country comparative advantage.
Marketing, sales, and service	Cooperation in downstream value chain activities that often must be tailored to individual country conditions.
Single-country and multicountry	Refers to the geographical scope of the alliance.
X and Y	Refer to the value activities undertaken by each partner. In X alliances, value activities are divided (e.g., one partner manufactures, the other markets). Used when partners have different strengths, weaknesses. In Y alliances, the partners work together in the performance of one or more activities to achieve scale economies. Used when partners have similar strengths and weaknesses.

Source: Adapted from Michael E. Porter and Mark B. Fuller, "Coalitions and Global Strategy," in Michael E. Porter, ed., *Competition in Global Industries* (Boston: Harvard Business School Press, 1986), pp. 330–338.

As noted earlier, GSPs and joint ventures differ in significant ways. Traditional joint ventures are basically alliances focusing on a single national market or a specific problem. For example, Lenwest, the joint venture described in Chapter 9 between Germany's Salamander AG and the Proletarian Shoe Factory in St. Petersburg, Russia, fits this description; the basic goal is to make shoes for the Russian market. A true global strategic partnership is different; it is distinguished by the following five attributes:[8]

1. Two or more companies develop a joint long-term strategy aimed at achieving world leadership by pursuing cost leadership, differentiation, or a combination of the two.

2. The relationship is reciprocal. Each partner possesses specific strengths that it shares with the other; learning must take place on both sides.

3. The partners' vision and efforts are truly global, extending beyond home countries and the home regions to the rest of the world.

4. The relationship is organized along horizontal, not vertical, lines. Continual, lateral transfer of resources between partners is required, with technology sharing and resource pooling representing norms.

5. When competing in markets excluded from the partnership, the participants retain their national and ideological identities.

---

[8] Howard Perlmutter and David Heenan, "Cooperate to Compete Globally," *Harvard Business Review* (March–April 1986), p. 137.

One recent and very large multi-national GSP, Motorola's US$3.4 billion Iridium project, is characterized by several of these attributes. When completed, Iridium will consist of a network of 66 powerful low-orbit satellites to allow Motorola to offer global personal communication services that will supplement—and perhaps render obsolete—ground-based cellular telephone service. Motorola is partnering with 12 other participants, each with a specific strength. Lockheed, for example, will build the satellites at a cost of US$13 million each; subcontractors will include Raytheon, Martin Marietta, and Siemens A.G. The participants are from triad countries plus Russia, China, Thailand, and Venezuela.

Iridium embodies several prerequisites that experts believe are the hallmarks of good alliances. First, Motorola is forming an alliance to exploit a core competency, namely, its leadership in wireless communications. Second, the Iridium alliance partners all possess unique strengths of their own. Third, it is unlikely that any of the partners has the ability or the desire to acquire Motorola's core competency. Finally, rather than focusing on a particular market or product, Iridium is an alliance based upon skills, know-how, and technology.[9]

SUCCESS FACTORS

Assuming that a proposed alliance meets the preceding five prerequisites, it is necessary to consider five basic factors that are deemed to have significant impact on the success of GSPs. These are mission, strategy, governance, culture, organization, and management.[10]

1. *Mission.* Successful GSPs create win-win situations, where participants pursue objectives on the basis of mutual need or advantage.
2. *Strategy.* A company may establish separate GSPs with different partners; strategy must be thought out up front to avoid conflicts.
3. *Governance.* Discussion and consensus must be the norms. Partners must be viewed as equals.
4. *Culture.* Personal chemistry is important, as is the successful development of a shared set of values.
5. *Organization.* Innovative structures and designs may be needed to offset the complexity of multicountry management.
6. *Management.* GSPs invariably involve a different type of decision making. They identify potentially divisive issues in advance, and establish clear, unitary lines of authority that will result in commitment by all partners.

Companies forming GSPs must keep these factors in mind. Moreover, successful collaborators will be guided by the following four principles. First, despite the fact that partners are pursuing mutual goals, partners must remember that collaboration is still competition in a different form. Second, harmony is not the

---

[9] Adapted from Michel Robert, *Strategy Pure & Simple: How Winning CEOs Outthink Their Competition* (New York: McGraw-Hill, 1993).

[10] Perlmutter and Heenan, p. 137.

Canadian biotechnology companies export more than 60 percent of their sales and are feeling the competitive pressure from their larger American and European counterparts. Over 1989 to 1993 the industry expanded annually by 24 percent, with exports growing by 19 percent.[11] Of the 310 biotech companies in Canada—worldwide there are between 3,000–4,000 companies— some 88 percent of which have fewer than 135 employees, two-thirds are active in the health-care sector. While these companies are often more innovative and can produce drugs more efficiently than large pharmaceutical companies, they seek synergies through alliances because they lack the capital, the regulatory expertise, and sales and distribution networks.

Two-thirds of these alliances are with foreign partners, mainly in the U.S. and Europe, and to a lesser extent in Japan. Not only did such alliances since 1991 double to eight per firm in 1994, but partnering emphasized three strategic directions: linkages with suppliers for licensing core technology, commercial expertise for marketing and distributors, and access to research and development capabilities.[12]

Quadra Logic Technologies of Vancouver exemplifies the smaller companies with a global perspective. It has developed global strategic partnerships to market its anti-cancer drugs and diagnostic products. By using alliances strategically, Quadra Logic has established distribution networks with partners such as American Cyanamid, Armard-Frappier, Genentech, Guangdong Enterprises of China, and others over several continents.[13]

most important measure of success, some conflict is to be expected. Third, all employees, engineers, and managers must understand where cooperation ends and competitive compromise begins. Finally, as noted earlier, it is critically important to *learn* from partners.[14]

The issue of learning deserves special attention. As one team of researchers notes,

> The challenge is to share enough skills to create advantage vis-à-vis companies outside the alliance while preventing a wholesale transfer of core skills to the partner. This is a very thin line to walk. Companies must carefully select what skills and technologies they pass to their partners. They must develop safeguards against unintended, informal transfers of information. The goal is to limit the transparency of their operations.[15]

---

[11] *Canada's Export Strategy—The International Trade Business Plan 1995/96*, No. 5 Biotechnologies (Ottawa: Minister of Supply and Services, 1995) pp.1–2.

[12] Thierry Roussin, "Biotechnology Alliances Double in Canada," *World Business*, October 1994, pp.8–9.

[13] *How to Form and Manage Successful Strategic Alliances*, A Prospectus Handbook (Ottawa: Industry, Science and Technology Canada, 1990) p.16; and Robert Williamson "Quadra Logic Looks to Japan", *The Globe and Mail*, May 3, 1994, B8.

[14] Gary Hamel, Yves L. Doz, and C. K. Prahalad, "Collaborate with Your Competitors—and Win," *Harvard Business Review* (January–February 1989), p. 134.

[15] Ibid., p. 136.

GSPs abound and the form of such alliances depends on such factors as the competitiveness of the industry and its companies. A wide range of skills and resources can be accessed through a strategic alliance: technology, marketing and contacts, management, sources of financing, distribution networks, and servicing networks. Many partnerships are made between large and small companies. As we saw in Box 11–1 with the example of the Canadian biotechnology industry, typically, small companies possess technological expertise and the ability to keep abreast of fast-changing technology and markets. While the larger partner needs this technology, and may no longer have the flexibility or drive to remain at the cutting edge, it brings other critical resources to the partnership: capital, distribution systems, marketing know-how, and often instant credibility.[16] However, control and coordination of the marketing plan as well as the technology involved can be difficult and some of the key issues are shown in Box 11–2.

▼ Alliances with Competitors

Strategic alliances enable companies to leverage their strengths into larger markets or more diversified market areas. Alliances have been recognized by competitors as a beneficial strategy. While in Canada and the United States competition policy is not receptive to alliances between competitors, in the EU regulatory attitudes have been more flexible, although concentration of market power can reach unacceptable levels.

In a global competitive setting, competitive alliances are quite common, as in the telecommunications industries (Figure 11–1).

Alliances between competitors can take several forms, such as joint ventures in third countries, agreements to market one another's products, technology-sharing arrangements, and combined efforts to build the capabilities of a supplier base. In a recent report, D'Cruz and Rugman suggested that such GSPs between competitors are often forged by so-called flagship companies. A flagship company competes globally and plays a dominant role in exports from an industrial sector. These GSP arrangements are shown in Figure 11–2.

Western companies may find themselves at a disadvantage in GSPs with, for example, an Asian competitor, especially if the latter brings manufacturing skills to the alliance. Unfortunately for western companies, manufacturing excellence represents a multifaceted competence that is not easily transferred. Western managers and engineers must also learn to be more receptive and attentive—they must overcome the "not-invented-here" syndrome and begin to think of themselves as students, not teachers. At the same time, they must learn to be less eager to show off proprietary lab and engineering successes. To limit transparency, some companies involved in GSPs establish a "collaboration section." Much like a corporate communications department, this department is designed to serve as a gatekeeper through which requests for access to people and information must be channeled. Such gatekeeping serves an important control function that guards against unintended transfers.

---

[16] *How to Form and Manage Successful Strategic Alliances*, A Prospectus Handbook (Ottawa: Industry, Science and Technology Canada, 1990) p.19.

Box 11–2
Important Marketing and Technology Issues

Marketing:
- who decides what the product will be?
- who designs the product?
- who chooses the product name?
- how are advertising or marketing campaigns shared?
- who decides on improvements or additions to the product line?
- who is responsible for warranty or service?
- what happens if the product infringes on intellectual property rights?
- what happens to marketing rights if the partnership ends?

Technology:
- who owns the technologies developed by the alliance?
- who has the right to use and market these:
  the technologies to be developed
  the technologies from outside sources
  core technologies?
- how will royalties be divided if a partner markets technology—or products based on technology—developed by the alliance?
- who owns and has rights to use improvements in the technology?
- what is the decision-making process concerning products based on new technology?
- what are the legal rights if another party infringes upon the partnership's technology?

Source: Adapted from *How to Form and Manage Successful Strategic Alliances* (Ottawa: Industry, Science and Technology Canada, and Prospectus Inc., 1991) p.41.

A 1991 report in *The McKinsey Quarterly* sheds additional light on the specific problems of alliances between western and Japanese firms.[17] Often problems between partners had less to do with objective levels of performance than with a feeling of mutual disillusionment and missed opportunity. The study identified four common problem areas in alliances gone wrong. The first problem was that each partner had "different dreams"; the Japanese partner saw itself emerging from the alliance as a leader in its business, or entering new sectors and building a new basis for the future, while the Western partner sought relatively quick and risk-free financial returns. Said one Japanese manager, "Our partners came in looking for a return. They got it. Now they complain that they didn't build a business. But that isn't what they set out to create."

---

[17] Kevin K. Jones and Walter E. Schill, "Allying for Advantage," *The McKinsey Quarterly*, no. 3 (1991), pp. 73–101.

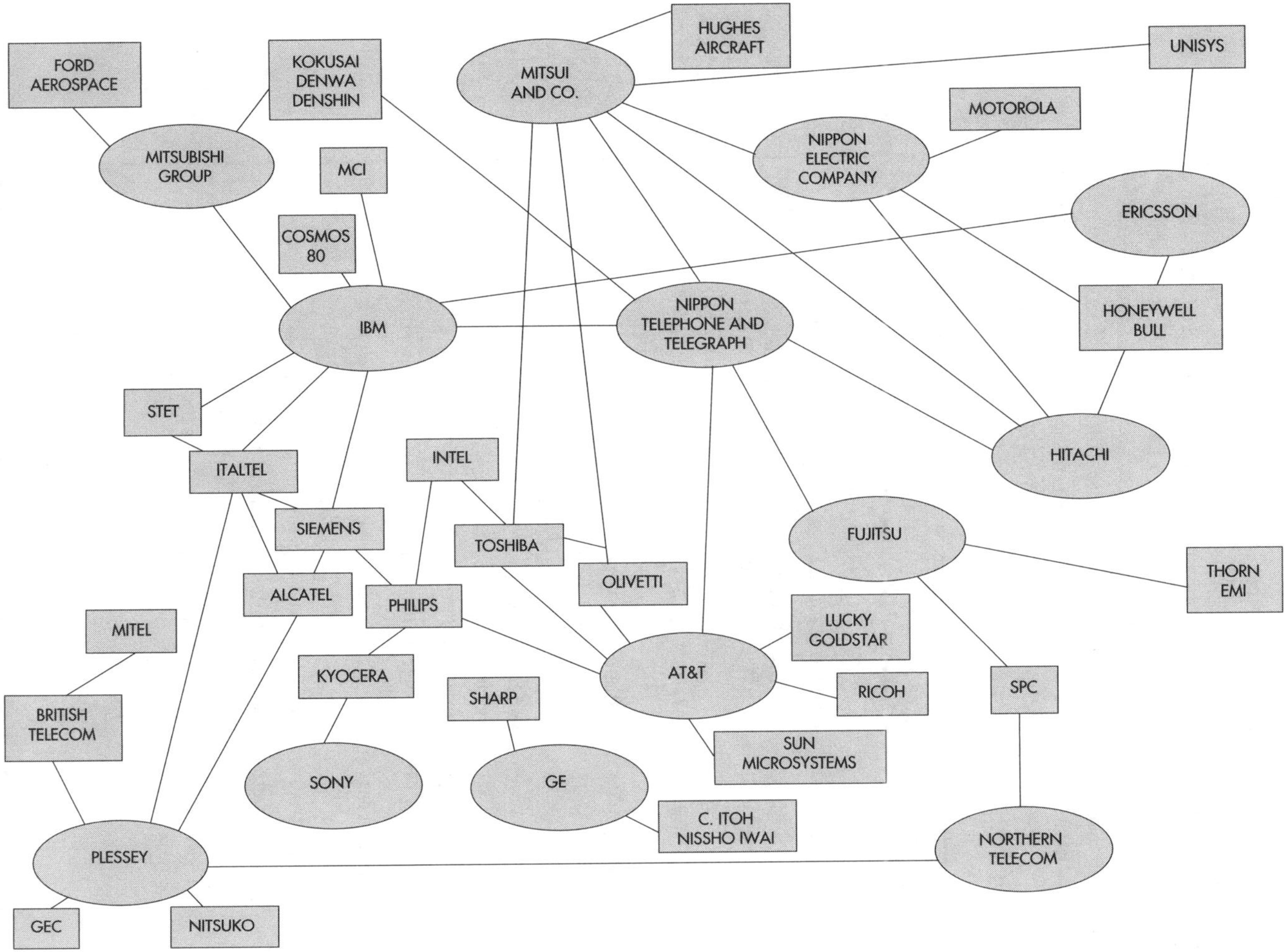

FIGURE 11-1
Competitive Alliances in Telecommunications

Source: Adapted from *How to Form and Manage Successful Strategic Alliances* (Ottawa: Prospectus Inc., 1991), p. 21.

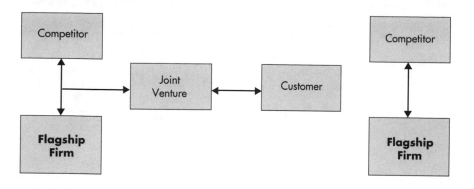

FIGURE 11-2
GSPs: Various Forms of Linkages with Competitors

Source: Joseph R. D'Cruz and Alan M. Rugman, *New Compacts for Canadian Competitiveness* (Toronto: Kodak Canada Inc., 1992) p.33, with permission.

A second area of concern is the balance between partners. Each must contribute to the alliance and each must depend on the other to a degree that justifies participation in the alliance. The most attractive partner in the short run is likely to be a company that is already established and competent in the business with the need to master some new technological skills. The best long-term partner, however, is likely to be a less competent player or even one from outside the industry.[18]

Another common cause of problems is "frictional loss" stemming from differences in management philosophy, expectations, and approaches. All

[18] David Lei and John W. Slocum, Jr., "Global Strategy, Competence-Building and Strategic Alliances," *California Management Review* (Fall 1992), p. 92.

TABLE 11–2 Examples of GSPs

Companies Involved	Purpose of GSP
Hewlett-Packard, Canon Inc.	Leadership in global laser printer market
Daimler-Benz, Mitsubishi	Access to new markets, new products
IBM, Motorola	Develop wireless computer network
IBM, Toshiba Corp., Siemens AG	Develop a new generation of chips for PCs
Apotex Inc., ABI Biotechnology	Synergy to develop, manufacture, and market pharmaceuticals
Komaq Inc., Kobe Steel, Asahi Glass	Access and control over data storage disc materials technology

functions within the alliance may be affected and performance is likely to suffer as a consequence. Speaking of a Japanese counterpart, a Western businessperson said, "Our partner just wanted to go ahead and invest without considering whether there would be a return or not." From the perspective of the Japanese partner, however, "the foreign partner took so long to decide on obvious points that we were always too slow." Such differences often cause much frustration and time-consuming debates which stifle decision making.

Last, the study found that short-term goals can result in the foreign partner limiting the number of people allocated to the joint venture. Those involved in the venture may only perform two- or three-year assignments. The result is "corporate amnesia," that is, little or no corporate memory is built up regarding competing in Japan. The original goals of the venture will be lost as each new group of managers takes their turn. When taken collectively, these four problems will almost always ensure that the Japanese partner will be the only one committed to the alliance for the long haul.

Several recent GSPs are shown in Table 11–2.

▼ Market Access: The Role of Alliances

Alliances to create market access are often motivated by a lack of distribution channels, by a desire for broader control over existing channels, or by a general strategy of market expansion. The following three examples illustrate these points.

Novopharm Ltd., a generic drug producer, recently entered into a distribution partnership with the American Wyeth-Ayerst International Inc. Through this alliance, Novopharm gained access to 7,000 sales people around the globe and anticipates an increase in sales of 5 to 20 percent. Wyeth-Ayerst gains the right to distribute Novopharm's 200 generic drugs outside of North America, making it the leader in the international generic drug field.[19]

Seagram Co. Ltd.'s strategic acquisition of the Colombian distributor Atlas Comercial SA, Bogota, not only provides the company with channel control, but also expands the number of brands it can sell in Colombia, in addition to strengthening its Latin American market presence which includes Brazil, Chile, Costa Rica, Mexico, and Venezuela.[20]

---

[19] "Novopharm signs deal for worldwide distribution," *The Globe and Mail*, December 13, 1994, p.B7.
[20] Ann Gibbon, "Seagram buys Colombian Distributor," *The Globe and Mail*, January 20, 1995, p.B5.

The partnership of CanWest Communications Corp. of Winnipeg with La Red television network of Santiago, the fifth-largest channel in Chile, is key to CanWest's expansion strategy into the Hispanic market of Latin America. Commercial TV is highly profitable in Chile, and CanWest intends to expand La Red to all of the 3.3 million households with TV. Foreign partnerships such as CanWest's, Grupo Televisa SA of Mexico, and Venevision of Venezuela have become a major force in Chile's communications industry.[21]

CFM International/ GE/Snecma: A Success Story

Commercial Fan Moteur (CFM) International, a partnership between GE's jet engine division and Snecma, a government-owned French aerospace company, is a frequently cited example of a successful GSP. GE was motivated in part by the desire to gain access to the European market so it could sell engines to Airbus Industries; also, the development costs, in excess of one billion dollars, were more than GE could risk on its own. While GE focused on system design and high-tech work, the French company handled fans, boosters, and other components. The partnership resulted in the development of a highly successful new engine that, to date, has generated tens of billions of dollars in sales to 125 different customers. The French offered market access and their own ability to advance design and manufacturing technology. GE offered its technology and world leadership position. Each partner brought strength to the alliance.

The alliance got off to a strong start because of the personal chemistry between two top executives, GE's Gerhard Neumann and the late General René Ravaud of Snecma. The partnership thrives despite each side's differing views regarding governance, management, and organization. Brian Rowe, senior vice president of GE's engine group, has noted that the French like to bring in senior executives from outside the industry, while GE prefers to rely on experienced people from within the organization. Also, the French prefer to approach problem solving with copious amounts of data while Americans may take a more intuitive approach.[22] Still, senior executives from both sides involved in the partnership have been delegated substantial responsibility.

▼ Cascade Inc./Groupe Pinault SA: A Learning Experience[23]

In mid-1987, Cascades Inc. of Kinsey Falls, Quebec, now Canada's fifth-largest forestry company,[24] formed a joint venture with Groupe Pinault SA of France for the purpose of acquiring and operating Chapelle Darblay SA, a failing French

---

[21] Harvey Enchin "CanWest buys interest in Chilean network", *The Globe and Mail*, May 31, 1994, p.B1.

[22] Bernard Wysocki, "Global Reach: Cross Border Alliances Become Favorite Way to Crack New Markets," *The Wall Street Journal*, March 26, 1990, p. A12.

[23] This section draws on "Irrevocable Differences," *How to Form Successful Strategic Alliances* (Ottawa: Industry, Science and Technology Canada, and Prospectus Publications) p.33.

[24] "Industry Leaders," *The Financial Post 500* (*The Financial Post Magazine*, 1994) p.114.

newsprint company near Rouen. Each parent controlled 50 percent of the resulting company, La Société Franco-Canadien des Papiers. La Société bought an 85 percent share in Chapelle Darblay, with Credit Lyonnais SA holding the remainder. Cascades was responsible for operating Chapelle Darblay, while Groupe Pinault supplied raw materials.

In 1988 Cascades discovered that it did not actually know its partner as well as it thought it did. The two firms fell out over their different management approaches; unable to resolve their differences, they took their case to a French Commercial Tribunal—with both partners seeking control of the venture. The tribunal found in favor of Groupe Pinault, in part because the French government had given Chapelle Darblay a total of C$300 million, both before and after La Société had acquired it. The tribunal also ruled that Cascades receive C$5.9 million as compensation for its management services. Shortly thereafter Cascades sold its C$2.8 million share in the venture.

North American firms seeking partnerships in Europe need to pay careful attention to differences in corporate culture and philosophy. Cascades discovered that different operating philosophies can create irrevocable problems between partners.

COOPERATIVE STRATEGIES IN JAPAN: *KEIRETSU*

Japan's *keiretsu* represent a special category of cooperative strategy. A *keiretsu* is an interbusiness alliance or enterprise group that, in the words of one observer, "resembles a fighting clan in which business families join together to vie for market share."[25] *Keiretsu* exist in a broad spectrum of markets, including the capital market, primary goods markets, and component parts markets.[26] *Keiretsu* relationships are often cemented by bank ownership of large blocks of stock as well as cross ownership of stock between a company and its buyers and nonfinancial suppliers. Furthermore, *keiretsu* executives can legally sit on each other's boards and share information and coordinate prices in closed-door meetings of "presidents' councils." Thus, *keiretsu* are essentially cartels that have the Japanese government's blessing.

Some observers have disputed charges that *keiretsu* have an impact on market relationships in Japan, claiming instead that the groups primarily serve a social function. Others acknowledge the past significance of preferential trading patterns associated with *keiretsu* but assert that the latter's influence is now weakening. While it is beyond the scope of this chapter to address these issues in detail, there can be no doubt that for companies competing with the Japanese or wishing to enter the Japanese market, a general understanding of *keiretsu* is crucial. Imagine, for example, what it would mean in Canada if an auto maker (e.g.,

---

[25] Robert L. Cutts, "Capitalism in Japan: Cartels and *Keiretsu*," *Harvard Business Review* (July–August 1992) p. 49.

[26] Michael L. Gerlach, "Twilight of the *Kereitsu*? A Critical Assessment," *Journal of Japanese Studies*, 18, no. 1 (Winter 1992), 79.

GM Canada), an electrical products company (Electrohome), a steel maker (Dofasco), and a computer firm (Digital) were interconnected rather than separate firms. Global competition in the era of *keiretsu* means competition exists not only among products, but between different systems of corporate governance and industrial organization.[27]

As the hypothetical example suggests, some of Japan's biggest and best-known companies are at the center of *keiretsu*. For example, Mitsui Group and Mitsubishi Group are organized around big trading companies. These two, together with the Sumitomo, Fuyo, Sanwa, and DKB groups make up the "big six" *keiretsu*. Each group strives for a strong position in each major sector of the Japanese economy. Annual revenues in each group are in the hundreds of billions of dollars.[28] In absolute terms, *keiretsu* constitute less than 0.01 percent of all Japanese companies. However, they account for an astonishing 78 percent of the market valuation of shares on the Tokyo Stock Exchange, a third of Japan's business capital, and approximately one quarter of its sales.[29] These alliances can effectively block foreign suppliers from entering the Japanese market and result in higher prices to Japanese consumers, while at the same time resulting in corporate stability, risk sharing, and long-term employment. The Mitsubishi Group's *keiretsu* structure is shown in detail in Figure 11–3.

In addition to the big six, several other *keiretsu* have formed, bringing new configurations to the basic forms described previously. Vertical supply and distribution *keiretsu* are alliances between manufacturers and retailers. For example, Matsushita controls a chain of 25,000 National stores in Japan through which it sells its Panasonic, Technics, and Quasar brands. About half of Matsushita's domestic sales are generated through the National chain, which generally carries only Matsushita's brands. Japan's other major consumer electronics manufacturers, including Toshiba, Hitachi, and Sony, have similar alliances.

Another type of manufacturing *keiretsu* outside the big six consists of vertical hierarchical alliances between assembly companies and suppliers and component manufacturers. Intergroup operations and systems are closely integrated, with suppliers receiving long-term contracts. Toyota, for example, has a network of about 175 primary and 4,000 secondary suppliers. One supplier is Koito; Toyota owns about one-fifth of Koito's shares and buys about half of its production. The net result of this arrangement is that Toyota produces about 25 percent of the sales value of its cars, compared with 50 percent for General Motors. Manufacturing *keiretsu* show the gains that can result from an optimal balance of supplier and buyer power. Because Toyota buys a given component from several suppliers, discipline is imposed down the network. Also, since Toyota's suppliers do not work exclusively for Toyota, they have an incentive to be flexible and adaptable.[30]

---

[27] Ronald J. Gilson and Mark J. Roe, "Understanding the Japanese *Keiretsu*: Overlaps Between Corporate Governance and Industrial Organization," *The Yale Law Journal*, 102, no. 4 (January 1993), 883.

[28] Clyde V. Prestowitz, Jr., *Trading Places: How We Are Giving Our Future to Japan and How to Reclaim It* (New York: Basic Books, 1989), p. 296.

[29] Carla Rappoport, "Why Japan Keeps on Winning," *Fortune*, July 15, 1991, p. 76. "Why Japan Keeps on Winning," *Fortune*, July 15, 1991, p. 76.

[30] "Japanology, Inc.," *The Economist*, March 6, 1993, Survey 15.

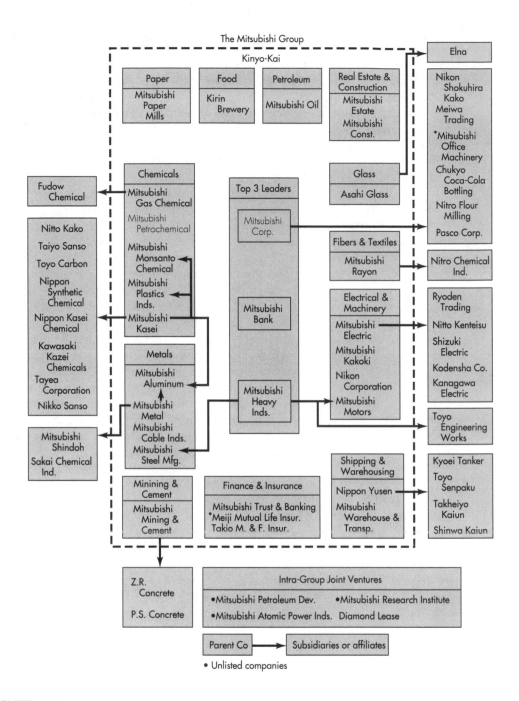

FIGURE 11–3
Mitsubishi Group's *Keiretsu* Structure

Source: Timothy M. Collins and Thomas L. Doorley, *Teaming Up for the 90s* (Homewood, IL: Business One Irwin, 1992), p. 290. Reprinted by permission.

The practices described previously lead to the question of whether or not *keiretsu* violate antitrust laws. As many observers have noted, the interests of the Japanese consumer do not come first in Japan; rather, it is the interests of the producer that come first. In fact, the *keiretsu* were formed in the early 1950s as regroupings of four large conglomerates—*zaibatsu*—that dominated the Japanese economy until 1945. They were dissolved after the occupational forces introduced antitrust as part of the reconstruction. Today, Japan's Fair Trade Commission appears to favor harmony rather than pursuing anticompetitive behavior. As a result, some Japanese companies have been investigated in foreign markets for price fixing, price discrimination, and exclusive supply arrangements.

Keiretsu affect how Japanese companies conduct themselves in foreign markets. For example, Japanese companies preferred to enter the Canadian market in the automotive, electronics, and machinery industries through subsidiaries with majority control.[31] In the Canadian automotive industry, there are some 26 wholly- or majority-owned Japanese manufacturing and marketing companies (not counting the various regional branches many of these companies maintain across Canada), as shown in the Box 11–3. Clearly, there are many more alliances between Canadian and Japanese companies where the latter have a smaller stake.

The impact of Japanese preference for control and maintaining a close relationship with *keiretsu* partners, even when operating in foreign markets, can be challenging for Canadian automotive parts suppliers. In the automotive industry, Canadian suppliers must break through the closely knit tiers of supply arrangements that extend from the first tier—which supplies major parts and subassemblies to the car manufacturer—down three, four, or five levels controlled or linked through ownership or other relationships.[32] The implications are that Canadian companies must recognize and adapt to differing management styles and convince the buying company that purchasing from an outsider (non-*keiretsu*, non-Japanese) does not entail additional risks of quality assurance, reliability, and consistency in products and delivery.

INTERNATIONAL PARTNERSHIPS

Eastern Europe, the former Soviet Union, Asia, India, and Mexico offer exciting opportunities for firms seeking to enter gigantic and largely untapped markets. An obvious tactical alternative for entering these markets is the strategic alliance. Such alliances are used by companies of all sizes. Pop Media Company of Ottawa, a small manufacturer of electronic sign boards, entered the Mexican market initially through a distributor agreement in 1988, then entered a minority partnership with a local publicity firm. Through incremental investment

---

[31] Yiming Tang, "Entry Mode Choice between Wholly-owned Subsidiary and Joint Venture by Japanese Affiliated Manufacturing Firms in Ontario," *Marketing*, Proceedings Administrative Science Association of Canada (1993) 14:3, p.282.

[32] David L. Blenkhorn and Peter M. Banting, "Should North American Parts Suppliers learn Japanese?" *The Journal of Business and Industrial Marketing*, Vol. 7, No. 1, Winter 1992, p. 30

Box 11–3
Japanese-Controlled Companies in the Canadian Automotive Industry 1993–94

Bellemar Parts Industries Canada Inc.	P
Bridgestone/Firestone Canada Inc.	P
Cami Automotive Inc.	P
Canada Suzuki Marketing Service Ltd.	S
Canadian Autoparts Toyota Inc.	P
Canadian Kawasaki Motors Inc.	S
Don Valley North Lexus Toyota Ltd.	S
Fujitsu Ten Canada Inc.	S
General Seating of Canada Ltd.	P
Honda of Canada Manufacturing	P
Mazda Canada Inc.	S
NGK Spark Plugs Canada Ltd.	S
Nichirin Inc.	P
Nippondenso Canada Ltd.	S
Nissan Canada Inc.	S
NSK Bearing Canada Ltd.	S
Ogisaka Canada Inc.	S
SM Cyclo of Canada Ltd.	S
SMC Pneumatics Canada Inc.	P
Subaru Canada Inc.	S
Sumitomo Tire Inc.	S
Suzuki Canada Inc.	S
Toyota Motor Manufacturing Canada Inc.	P
Uni-Ram Corporation	P
Yamaha Motors Canada Ltd.	S
Waterville TG	S

P = production facility, and marketing operations
S = marketing operations, sales and distribution

Source: Adapted from: Ministry of Economic Development and Trade, Edmonton; Ministry of Economic Development, Small Business and Trade, Vancouver; Ministry of Industry, Trade and Technology, Toronto; Centre de Commerce Mondial, Montreal, 1993–1994.

and adaptation to the Mexican market, Pop achieved market dominance and evolved its joint venture into a wholly owned manufacturing and marketing operation.[33] Bombardier Inc. of Boucherville, Canada's largest general manufacturing company, first sold subway cars to Mexico in 1981. Years of relationship-building with buyers and government officials along with the developing

---

[33] "Experience in Mexico: A Small Company—Pop Media Inc.," *Mexico–Canada: Partnering for Success* (Ottawa: Prospectus Publications Limited, 1992) p.68.

market led to the acquisition of Concarril in 1992, through which Bombardier accomplished two goals: a long-term commitment in this market and a base for the development of other Latin American markets.[34]

The addition of Mexico to NAFTA in 1993 has created further interest among Canadian companies in forming alliances to enter this emerging and culturally challenging market.

There is also evidence that joint ventures in Eastern Europe and Russia in particular will evolve at a more accelerated pace. A number of factors make Russia an excellent location for an alliance. There is a well-educated work force; quality is very important to the Russian consumer; and social, political, and economic problems can be turned to success and new growth opportunities. However, there are problems associated with western ventures in Russia: currency convertibility, supply shortages, and a regulatory and a legal environment in a constant state of flux.

Who exactly is in Russia now? For the most part, firms actively participating in joint ventures in Russia are small to midsize companies which can adapt quickly in a still unstable environment. One study noted that of the 6,000 joint ventures registered in Russia since 1987, 20 percent are in operation.[35] Most of the joint-venture relationships studied were initiated by the western partner. The major business activities were evenly divided between services and manufacturing. Some were targeted at westerners visiting or living in Russia, for example, hotel, exhibition, and legal services. Others targeted the domestic market in computer software and systems, telecommunications, music recording, architecture, and medicine. Others focused on both markets: engineering, retail distribution, dentistry, security services, business consulting, banking, construction, and construction equipment leasing. Most of the manufacturing ventures were initially limited to assembly work but have moved on to producing components in Russia. The activities range from computer manufacturing to fish processing. Some of the joint ventures combined manufacturing and services. For example, there is a camera company that both sells and services the equipment it makes and a roofing company that designs, produces, and installs roofing.

In their book on strategic alliances, Collins and Doorley offer a hypothetical scenario illustrating how one western company might seize the opportunity in the former Soviet Union. Chemco (a disguised company name) had long enjoyed high margins and patent protection for its pesticides and herbicides. As its patents expired and sales were lost to producers of generics, however, Chemco found it was harder to replace revenue stream with new products. Chemco needed a world-scale production plant to lower its costs and strong market positions to support volume sales. Collins and Doorley's prescription for a company like Chemco: Enter the market in the CIS to to achieve low-cost production as well as to gain access to a large underserved market and inexpensive raw materials. An alliance partner in the CIS could bring a significant share of the market; much of the plant's output could be sold locally. License fees, royalties, and

---

[34] ibid. p.72.

[35] Paul Lawrence and Charalambos Vlachoutsicos, "Joint Ventures in Russia: Put the Locals in Charge," *Harvard Business Review* (January–February 1993), pp. 44–54.

profits could be paid with hard currency generated from export sales; as its patents neared expiration, Chemco could transfer technology to the CIS. Thus, the CIS partner would gain high-technology products, proprietary production methods, operations experience, and access to export markets.[36]

Other Eastern European markets with huge potential are Poland, the Czech Republic, and Hungary. Hungary already has the most liberal financial and commercial system in Eastern Europe. It has also offered investment incentives to westerners, especially in high-tech industry. Hungary's market of 10.3 million people is quite small; however, its production costs are one-third below western Europe's and its central location makes it attractive. Within a radius of 1,000 kilometres is a population of 240 million. General Woods & Veneers Ltd. of Montreal has set up multiple partnerships with the Hungarian government, a German partner, and another Canadian firm and uses the location to export the majority of its production to western Europe, Asia, South Africa, and the Middle East.

Another Canadian company active in Hungary is ATCO, a Calgary-based manufacturer of construction housing units. This company set up a production facility in 1993 to make construction housing for the Hungarian market as well as for export to the republics of the former Soviet Union.[37] Risk, however, is part of any foreign market activity. Foreign exchange and currency problems are particularly acute in eastern European countries, as is exemplified by the continuing and dramatic loss of value of the Russian ruble since 1990. Like Russia, Hungary also has its share of problems. Take Digital's recent joint-venture agreement with the Hungarian Research Institute for Physics and the state-supervised computer systems design firm, Szamalk. Though the venture was formed so Digital will be able to sell and service its equipment in Hungary, the underlying importance of the venture was to stop eastern bloc firms from cloning Digital's computers.

▼ Asia-Pacific

Global strategic partnerships will undoubtedly become more important in the Asia-Pacific regions. This huge market, with half the world population and one-third of world GNP, includes Japan, Korea, China, Australia, New Zealand, and India. Companies such as Power Corporation, Bombardier, and Babcock and Wilcox have a strategic focus on the region. Babcock recently won a C$1 billion contract for three power plants in Indonesia.[38]

Canadian companies have had partnerships and alliances throughout the region, often as an off-shore production location for exports: Northern Telecom,

---

[36] Timothy M. Collins and Thomas L. Doorley, *Teaming Up for the 90s: A Guide to International Joint Ventures and Strategic Alliances* (Homewood, IL: Business One Irwin, 1991) pp. 327–338.

[37] John Nadler, "Double Agent," *Canadian Business* (January 1995) p.39–40.

[38] "Focus on Indonesia," *Canadexport* (April 1, 1994) 12:6, p.VIII.

for example, has manufacturing joint ventures in Australia, China, Malaysia and Thailand.[39] Dantec Electronics of Waterloo entered into a partnership with Bernas in Malaysia to make process-control systems for rice drying.[40] Although the attraction of the region for infrastructure projects, such as telecommunications, transport, power and energy, is strong, increasingly the several hundred million top income earners present opportunities for companies marketing consumer goods and services.

We pointed out in Chapter 2 that companies need to take a strategic approach to their foreign market activity. The next section emphasises that alliances and partnering can be a win-win approach to foreign markets, provided a number of critical elements are evaluated

STRATEGIC PARTNERSHIP AUDIT: A CHECKLIST

Deciding whether an alliance will satisfy a Canadian company's strategic objectives requires a thorough analysis. The following is a checklist in market analysis, innovation, productivity, financial resources, profitability, and human resources that helps the company to determine its present position in each of its business segments and to pinpoint where and how a partner would contribute.[41]

Market Analysis

► What is your present market position? Consider product life-cycle, market share, marketing strategy, price, quality, market research skills, patents, licenses, agreements.

► What are the current industry trends, how does your company fit in?

► What are your direct and indirect competitors doing with respect to price, quality, originality?

► What are your market opportunities, and what would you like to do?

► How effective are your networks (dealer/distribution and service), and do they need improvement?

► How flexible is your current organizational structure, and what changes could be made in production, personnel, training, equipment?

► What are the current marketing strategies, and how effective have they been?

---

[39] Michael Bociurkiw, "Ontario Firms Team Up To Build Business in Asia," *The Globe and Mail*, May, 30, 1994, p.B5.

[40] *Kitchener-Waterloo Record*, September 13, 1994, p.B8.

[41] Based on *How to Form and Manage Successful Strategic Alliances* (Ottawa: Prospectus Inc.) 1991, pp.49–54.

Innovation

- What is your assessment of your current research and development situation?
- What are your in-house R & D capabilities?
- Any recent successes?
- Were these commercial successes?
- What are your competitors doing in product/process research, and technology imitation?
- Is your staff creative, qualified, reliable, and productive?
- What patents do you have and what do they cover?
- How much do they cost, and how dated is the technology?
- Could you access outside sources of research or technical human resources? Consider suppliers, customers and contractors.
- What is the relationship between your R & D activities and marketing strategy?

Productivity

- Is the company benefiting from economies of scale?
- Are you using appropriate technology?
- Who owns the technology?
- What are the cost advantages?
- How flexible or integrated is your production process?
- At what capacity are you operating, is there room for expansion?
- How effective are your quality control processes?
- Consider issues related to labor force, plant location, transportation costs, and access and cost of raw materials.
- What are your competitors doing?

Financial Resources

- Are your present financial resources sufficient to meet your present objectives in R & D, training, marketing?
- Do you have cash flow problems?
- What is your current equity position?
- What is your borrowing capacity in both the short and the long term?
- How are your finances being managed?
- How important are issues like fluctuating exchange rates, transfer pricing, dividends, the repatriation of funds?
- Are there any changes you want to make to your management and financial accounting systems?

Profitability

- ▶ What is your company's five-year trend in profitability?
- ▶ How does this compare to the industry average and to your competitors?
- ▶ What are the trends in prices and margins for your product?

Human Resources

- ▶ Rate current management on leadership, ability to motivate others, ability to coordinate departments, divisions or functions, and flexibility and adaptability.
- ▶ What are the leadership and motivational qualities of your CEO?
- ▶ Are there managers experienced in managing acquisitions, mergers, joint-ventures, or any form of strategic alliance?
- ▶ Do your managers have international business experience?
- ▶ What kind of attention do you pay to training and development for your staff?
- ▶ What is the level of morale and commitment of the employees to the company? What incentives do they have?
- ▶ How skilled is your work force?
- ▶ What is the age of the work force in relation to that of management?

BEYOND STRATEGIC ALLIANCES

The *relationship enterprise* is said to be the next stage of evolution of the strategic alliance. Consisting of groupings of firms in different industries and countries, reliance enterprises will be held together by common goals which encourage them to act almost as a single firm. Cyrus Freidheim, vice chairperson of the Booz, Allen & Hamilton consulting firm, recently outlined his vision of the relationship enterprise. He suggested that, within the next few decades, Boeing, British Airways, Siemens, TNT (an Australia-based package delivery firm), and Snecma might jointly build several new airports in China. As part of the package, British Airways and TNT would be granted preferential routes and landing slots, the Chinese government would contract to buy all its aircraft from Boeing/Snecma, and Siemans would provide air traffic control systems for all ten airports.[42]

---

[42] "The Global Firm: R.I.P.," *The Economist*, February 6, 1993, p. 69.

More than the simple strategic alliances we know today, relationship enterprises will be superalliances among global giants, with revenues approaching $1 trillion. They would be able to draw on extensive cash resources, circumvent antitrust barriers, and with home bases in all major markets, relationship alliances will enjoy the political advantage of being a "local" firm almost anywhere. This type of alliance is not driven simply by technological change, but by the political necessity of having multiple home bases.

Another perspective on the future of cooperative strategies envisions the emergence of the *virtual corporation*. (The term *virtual* is borrowed from computer science; some computers feature *virtual memory* that allows them to function as though they have more storage capacity than is actually built into their memory chips.) According to a *Business Week* story, the virtual corporation "will seem to be a single entity with vast capabilities but will really be the result of numerous collaborations assembled only when they're needed."[43]

On a global level, the virtual corporation could combine the twin competencies of cost-effectiveness and responsiveness and, therefore, it could easily pursue the "think global, act local" philosophy. This reflects the trend toward *mass customization*. As noted by William Davidow and Michael Malone in their book *The Virtual Corporation*, "The success of a virtual corporation will depend on its ability to gather and integrate a massive flow of information throughout its organizational components and intelligently act upon that information."[44]

Why has the virtual corporation suddenly burst onto the scene? Previously, the technology didn't exist to facilitate this type of data management. Today, distributed databases, networks, and open systems make possible the kinds of data flows required for the virtual corporation. In particular, these data flows permit *supply chain management*. Ford provides an interesting example of how technology is improving information flows among the far-flung operations of a single company. We mentioned earlier how Ford's new "world car"—the Mercury Mystique and Ford Contour in North America, the Mondeo in Europe—was developed using an international communications network linking computer work stations of designers and engineers on three continents.[45]

One of the hallmarks of the virtual corporation will be the production of *virtual products*, a product that practically exists before it is manufactured. As described by Davidow and Malone, the concept, design, and manufacture of virtual products are stored in the minds of cooperating teams, in computers, and in flexible production lines.[46]

---

[43] John Byrne, "The Virtual Corporation," *Business Week,* February 8, 1993, p. 103.

[44] William H. Davidow and Michael S. Malone, *The Virtual Corporation: Structuring and Revitalizing the Corporation for the 21st Century* (New York: Harper Business, 1993) p. 59.

[45] Julie Edelson Halpert, "One Car, Worldwide, With Strings Pulled From Michigan," *The New York Times,* August 29, 1993, Sec. 3, p. 7.

[46] Davidow and Malone, p. 4.

▼ SUMMARY

Changes in the political, economic, sociocultural, and technological environments are leading to new strategies in global competition. Cooperative strategies including global strategic partnerships (GSPs), and the Japanese *keiretsu* have become more important as companies need to share the high cost of product development, pool skills and know-how, gain access to markets, and find new opportunities for organizational learning. GSPs are distinguished by five attributes: They represent long-term strategies for achieving global leadership; they involve reciprocal relationships; the partners' vision is truly global and extends beyond home markets; they involve continual lateral transfer of resources; and the partners retain their identities in markets not included in the partnership. Five factors are critical to the success of a GSP: mission, strategy, governance, culture, organization, and management.

In Japan, a unique cooperative strategy in both manufacturing and distribution, known as *keiretsu,* has had enormous significance for the success of Japanese companies, both in Japan and the rest of the world. In North America, some alliances are resulting in the creation of the virtual corporation, an organization that exists solely in the network of linkages among partners.

▼ DISCUSSION QUESTIONS

1. What are five attributes that distinguish GSPs from traditional joint ventures?

2. What basic factors affect the success of GSPs?

3. What are *keiretsu?*

4. Describe what is meant by a *virtual corporation.*

▼ BIBLIOGRAPHY

Books

BLEEKE, JOEL, AND DAVID ERNST, *Collaborating to Compete.* Somerset, NJ: John Wiley & Sons, 1991.

CARTER, JOHN D., ROBERT FRANK CUSHMAN, AND C. SCOTT HARTZ, *The Handbook of Joint Venturing.* Homewood, IL: Dow Jones-Irwin, 1988.

CONTRACTOR, FAROK, AND PETER LORANGE, *Cooperative Strategies in International Business.* Cambridge, MA: Ballinger, 1987.

CULPAN, REFIK, ed., *Multinational Strategic Alliances.* New York: International Business Press, 1993.

DAVIDOW, WILLIAM H., AND MICHAEL S. MALONE, *The Virtual Corporation.* New York: Harper Business, 1993.

DOORLEY, THOMAS L. III, *Teaming Up for the '90s: A Guide to International Joint Ventures and Strategic Alliances.* New York: Business One Irwin, 1991.

ENEN, JACK, *Venturing Abroad: International Business Expansion Via Joint Ventures.* Blue Ridge Summit, PA: Liberty Hall Press, 1991.

FRUIN, MARK, *The Japanese Enterprise System.* Oxford: Oxford University Press, 1992.

GATES, STEPHEN, *Strategic Alliances: Guidelines for Successful Management.* New York: Conference Board, 1993.

GERINGER, J.M., *Joint Venture Partner Selection: Strategies for Developed Countries.* Westport: Quorum Books, 1988.

GERLACH, MICHAEL L., *Alliance Capitalism: The Social Organization of Japanese Business.* Berkeley: University of California Press, 1992.

GILLESPIE, IAN, *Joint Ventures.* London: Eurostudy, 1990.

LINDSEY, JENNIFER, *Joint Ventures and Corporate Partnerships: A Step-by-Step Guide to Forming Strategic Business Alliances.* Chicago: Probus Publishing Co., 1989.

LYNCH, ROBERT, *The Practical Guide to Joint Ventures and Corporate Alliances: How to Form, How to Organize, How to Operate.* New York: Wiley, 1989.

PRESOTOWITZ, CLYDE V., JR., *Trading Places: How We Are Giving Our Future to Japan and How to Reclaim It.* New York: Basic Books, 1989.

ROBERT, MICHEL, *Strategy Pure and Simple: How Winning CEOs Outthink Their Competition.* New York: McGraw-Hill, 1993.

STARR, MARTIN KENNETH, *Global Corporate Alliances and the Competitive Edge: Strategies and Tactics for Management.* New York: Quorum Books, 1991.

Articles

ADLER, PAUL S., "Time-and-Motion Regained," *Harvard Business Review,* 71, no. 1 (January/February 1993), 97–108.

———, AND ROBERT E. COLE, "Designed for Learning: A Tale of Two Auto Plants," *Sloan Management Review,* 34, no. 3 (Spring 1993), 85–94.

BADARACCO, JOSEPH L., JR., "Alliances Speed Knowledge Transfer," *Planning Review,* 19, no. 2 (March/April 1991), 10–16.

BELL, BRIAN, "Two Separate Teams Should Be Set Up to Facilitate Strategic Alliances," *Journal of Business Strategy,* 11, no. 6 (November/December 1990), 63–64.

BLEEKE, JOEL, AND DAVID ERNST, "The Way to Win in Cross-Border Alliances," *Harvard Business Review,* 69, no. 6 (November/December 1991), 127–135.

BLODGETT, LINDA LONGFELLOW, "Research Notes and Communications Factors in the Instability of International Joint Ventures: An Event Historical Analysis," *Strategic Management Journal,* 13, no. 6 (September 1992), 475–481.

DARNALL, ROBERT J., "Inland Steel's Joint Venture From Competitive Gap to Competitive Advantage," *Planning Review,* 18, no. 5 (September/October 1990), 10–14.

ERDMANN, PETER B., "When Businesses Cross International Borders: Strategic Alliances and Their Alternatives," *Columbia Journal of World Business,* 28, no. 2 (Summer 1993), 107–108.

FERGUSON, CHARLES H., "Computers and the Coming of the U.S. Keiretsu," *Harvard Business Review,* 68, no. 4 (July/August 1990), 55–70.

FLANAGAN, PATRICK, "Strategic Alliances Keep Customers Plugged In," *Management Review,* 82, no. 3 (March 1993), 24–26.

GABOR, ANDREA, "Rochester Focuses: A Community's Core Competence," *Harvard Business Review,* 69, no. 4 (July/August 1991), 116–126.

GOMES-CASSERES, BENJAMIN, "Joint Ventures in the Face of Global Competition," *Sloan Management Review,* 30, no. 3 (Spring 1989), 17–26.

GRANT, ROBERT M., R. KRISHNAN, ABRAHAM B. SHANI, AND RON BAER, "Appropriate Manufacturing Technology: A Strategic Approach," *Sloan Management Review,* 33, no. 1 (Fall 1991), 43–54.

HAIGH, ROBERT W., "Building a Strategic Alliance—The Hermosillo Experience as a Ford-Mazda Proving Ground," *Columbia Journal of World Business,* 27, no. 1 (Spring 1992), 60–74.

HAMEL, GARY, YVES L. DOZ, AND C. K. PRAHALAD, "Collaborate with Your Competitors—and Win," *Harvard Business Review,* 67, no. 1 (January/February 1989), 133–139.

———, AND C. K. PRALAHAD, "Strategic Alliances: Success or Surrender," Mimeo. London Business School.

HERTZFELD, JEFFREY M., "Joint Ventures: Saving the Soviets from Perestroika," *Harvard Business Review*, 69, no. 1 (January/ February 1991), 80–91.

JARILLO, J. CARLOS, AND HOWARD H. STEVENSON, "Co-operative Strategies—The Payoffs and the Pitfalls," *Long Range Planning*, 24, no. 1 (February 1991), 64–70.

JOHNSTON, GERALD A., "The Yin and the Yang: Cooperation and Competition in International Business," *Executive Speeches*, 7, no. 6 (June/July 1993), 15–17.

JORDE, THOMAS M., AND DAVID J. TEECE, "Competition and Cooperation: Striking the Right Balance," *California Management Review*, 31, no. 3 (Spring 1989), 25–37.

KETELHOHN, WERNER, "What Do We Mean by Cooperative Advantage?" *European Management Journal*, 11, no. 1 (March 1993), 30–37.

KODAMA, FUMIO, "Technology Fusion and the New R&D," *Harvard Business Review*, 70, no. 4 (July/August 1992), 70–78.

KRUYTBOSCH, CARLA, "Let's Make a Deal," *International Business*, 6, no. 3 (March 1993), 92–96.

LAWRENCE, PAUL, AND CHARALAMBOS VLACHOUTSICOS, "Joint Ventures in Russia: Put the Locals in Charge," *Harvard Business Review*, 71, no. 1 (January/February 1993), 44–51.

LEI, DAVID, "Offensive and Defensive Uses of Alliances," *Long Range Planning*, 25, no. 6 (December 1992), 10–17.

———, AND JOHN W. SLOCUM JR., "Global Strategy, Competence-Building and Strategic Alliances," *California Management Review*, 35, no. 1 (Fall 1992), 81–97.

LEWIS, JORDAN D., "Competitive Alliances Redefine Companies," *Management Review*, 80, no. 4 (April 1991), 14–18.

———, "The New Power of Strategic Alliances," *Planning Review*, 20, no. 5 (September/October 1992), 45–46.

LODGE, GEORGE, AND RICHARD WALTON, "The American Corporation and Its New Relationships," *California Management Review*, 31, no. 3 (Spring 1989), 9–24.

LORANGE, PETER, AND JOHAN ROOS, "Why Some Strategic Alliances Succeed and Others Fail," *Journal of Business Strategy*, 12, no. 1 (January/February 1991), 25–30.

MCMILLAN, JOHN, "Managing Suppliers: Incentive Systems in Japanese and U.S. Industry," *California Management Review*, 32, no. 4 (Summer 1990), 38–55.

MICHELET, ROBERT, AND ROSEMARY REMACLE, "Forming Successful Strategic Marketing Alliances in Europe," *Journal of European Business*, 4, no. 1 (September/October 1992), 11–15.

MOWERY, DAVID C., AND DAVID J. TEECE, "Japan's Growing Capabilities in Industrial Technology: Implications for U.S. Managers and Policymakers," *California Management Review*, 35, no. 2 (Winter 1993), 9–34.

MURRAY, EDWIN A. JR., AND JOHN F. MAHON, "Strategic Alliances: Gateway to the New Europe?" *Long Range Planning*, 26, no. 4 (August 1993), 102–111.

NILAND, POWELL, "Case Study—U.S.-Japanese Joint Venture: New United Motor Manufacturing, Inc. (NUMMI)," *Planning Review*, 17, no. 1 (January/February 1989), 40–45.

OHMAE, KENICHI, "The Global Logic of Strategic Alliances," *Harvard Business Review*, 67 (March/April 1989), 143–154.

OLSON, PHILIP D., "Choices for Innovation-Minded Corporations," *Journal of Business Strategy*, 11, no. 1 (January/February 1990), 42–46.

PARKHE, ARVIND, "Interfirm Diversity, Organizational Learning and Longevity in Global Strategic Alliances," *Journal of International Business Studies*, 22, no. 4 (Fourth Quarter 1991), 579–601.

PERLMUTTER, H. V., AND D. A. HEENAN, "Cooperate to Compete Globally," *Harvard Business Review* (March/April 1986), 136–152.

ROBERT, MICHEL, "The Do's and Don'ts of Strategic Alliances," *Journal of Business Strategy*, 13, no. 2 (March/April 1992), 50–53.

ROSTEN, KEITH A., "Soviet-U.S. Joint Ventures: Pioneers on a New Frontier," *California Management Review*, 33, no. 2 (Winter 1991), 88–108.

SMART, TIM, PETE ENGARDIO, AND GERI SMITH, "GE's Brave New World," *Business Week*, November 8, 1993, 64–70.

SPENCER, WILLIAM J., AND PETER GRINDLEY, "SEMATECH After Five Years," *California Management Review* (Summer 1993), 9–35.

SPINKS, STEPHEN O., AND ROBERT C. STANLEY, "Joint Ventures Under EC Antitrust and Merger Control Rules: Concentrative or Cooperative?" *Journal of European Business*, 2, no. 4 (March/April 1991), 29–34.

THAKAR, MANAB, AND LUIS MA. R. CALINGO, "Strategic Thinking Is Hip, But Does It Make a Difference?" *Business Horizons*, 35, no. 5 (September/October 1992), 47–54.

VOSS, BRISTOL, "Strategic Federations Frequently Falter in Far East," *Journal of Business Strategy*, 14, no. 4 (July/August 1993), 6.

WEVER, KIRSTEN S., AND CHRISTOPHER S. ALLEN, "Is Germany a Model for Managers?" *Harvard Business Review*, 70, no. 5 (September/October 1992), 36–43.

YABLONSKY, DENNIS, "The US West/Carnegie Group Strategic Alliance," *Planning Review*, 18, no. 5 (September/October 1990), 18–19.

YOSHIDA, KOSAKU, "New Economic Principles in America—Competition and Cooperation: A Comparative Study of the U.S. and Japan," *Columbia Journal of World Business*, 26, no. 4 (Winter 1992), 30–44.

TWELVE

Product Decisions

Introduction

The focus of this chapter is the product, probably the most crucial element of a marketing program. To a very important degree, a company's products define its business. Pricing, communication, and distribution policies must fit the product. A firm's customers and competitors are determined by the products it offers. Its research and development requirements will depend upon the technologies of its products. Indeed, every aspect of the enterprise is heavily influenced by the firm's product offering.

In the past, managers have been prone to committing (often simultaneously) two types of errors regarding product decisions in global marketing. One error has been to fall victim to the "not invented here" (NIH) syndrome, ignoring product decisions made by subsidiary or affiliate managers. Managers who behave in this way are essentially abandoning any effort to influence or control product policy outside the home-country market. The other error has been to impose product decisions policy upon all affiliate companies on the assumption that what is right for customers in the home market must also be right for customers everywhere. This latter error was committed by the German car maker Volkswagen A.G. VW has seen its position in the Canadian and U.S. import market erode from leader to also-ran over the past two decades. While the company once sold more cars in these markets than all other foreign auto makers combined, today VW has less than 2 percent market share. The company's mistake was thinking that what works in Germany should also work in Canada and the U.S. To become better attuned to the tastes of the American car buyer, Volkswagen recently opened a design studio in Los Angeles.[1] Once before, in the 1970s, when the newly set up factory at Westmoreland began to *redesign* the Rabbit model to *American* tastes, the outcome was disastrous. Will history repeat itself?

The challenge facing a company with global horizons is to develop product policies and strategies that are sensitive to market needs, competition, and company resources on a global scale. Product policy must strike a balance between the need for and payoff from adapting products to local market preferences, and the competitive advantages that come from concentrating company resources on a limited number of standardized products.

balance bw standardization and adaptation

---

[1] Steven Greenhouse, "Carl Hahn's East German Homecoming," *The New York Times*, September 23, 1990, Sec. 3, p. 6.

This chapter examines the major dimensions of global product decisions. First, basic product concepts are explored. The diversity of preferences and needs in global markets is then underlined by an examination of product saturation levels. Product design criteria are identified and attitudes toward foreign products are explored. The next section outlines strategic alternatives available to global marketers, and the chapter concludes with an examination of new-product issues in global marketing.

BASIC CONCEPTS

We will begin our introduction to global product decisions by briefly reviewing product concepts. While all basic product concepts are fully applicable to global marketing, several of them apply specifically to global marketing.

▼ Product Definition

What is a product? On the surface, this seems like a simple question. A product is defined by its physical attributes—weight, dimensions, and material. Thus an automobile could be defined as 1200 kilograms of metal, plastic, or fiberglass, measuring about 4.5m long, 1.8m wide, and 1.5m high. This definition could be expanded to include colour, texture, style, shape, and contour. However, marketers know that any description limited to physical attributes is incomplete because it says nothing about the needs a product fills. The automobile, for example, is a product that fulfills many needs. The most obvious is transportation, but marketers cannot ignore the important recreation, status, and power needs and desires satisfied by this product. Indeed, major segments of the automobile market are developed around these consumer desires. As is shown by the renewed success of Harley-Davidson, loyal Harley motorcycle riders get much more than "basic transportation" from their beloved hogs. They get mystique, spirit, and a feeling of freedom.[2] We shall define a product, then, as a collection of physical, service, and symbolic attributes which yields satisfaction, or benefits, to a user or buyer. Product management is concerned with the decisions that affect the customer's perception of the firm's product offering.

As noted in Chapter 1, the shift in emphasis from the actual product to the needs and desires of customers represented an important event in the evolution of marketing thought and the marketing concept. This shift applies equally to consumer and industrial products. Unfortunately, this "new" marketing concept is still lost on many marketers more than 25 years after it was brilliantly expounded by J. B. McKitterick and then expanded upon by Theodore H. Levitt in his classic article "Marketing Myopia."[3]

---

[2] Oliver Bertin, "Harley Finds Success Cultivating Closet Brandos," *The Globe and Mail*, June 6, 1994, p.B8.
[3] See "What Is the Marketing Management Concept?" speech given to the American Marketing Association, Philadelphia, December 27, 1957. Reprinted by Intercollegiate Case Clearinghouse, ICHDCIM et. Also, see Theodore Levitt, "Marketing Myopia," *Harvard Business Review* (July–August 1960).

▼ Product Classifications

Products may be classified according to a variety of criteria. The oldest classification framework is based on users, and distinguishes between consumer and industrial goods. Both types of goods can be further classified on the basis of how they are purchased (convenience, preference, shopping, or specialty goods) and according to their life span (durable, consumable, or disposable). These and other classification frameworks developed for domestic marketing are fully applicable to global marketing.

Local-International-Global Products: A Continuum

It is critically important to evaluate proposed new products in terms of their local-international-global potential. All other things being equal, the product with profitable international-global potential is more attractive than the product whose potential for any reason is basically local. In general, a company should not add a purely local product to its line when an attractive international or global product opportunity is available.

Many international companies find that, as a result of the expansion of existing businesses or acquisition of a new business, they have products for sale in a single national market. General Foods, for example, at one time found itself in the chewing gum business in France, the ice-cream business in Brazil, and the pasta business in Italy. While each of these unrelated businesses in isolation was quite profitable, the scale of each was too small to justify heavy expenditures on R&D, let alone marketing, production, and financial management from international headquarters. *An important question regarding any product is whether it has the potential for expansion into other markets.* The answer to this question will depend upon the company's goals and objectives and upon perceptions of opportunity. There are three product categories in the local-to-global continuum: local products, international products, and global products.

Local Products. A local product is one that, in the context of a particular company, is perceived as having potential only in a single national market. For example, Sony and other Japanese consumer electronics companies produce a variety of products that are not sold outside of Japan. The reason? Japanese consumers have a seemingly insatiable appetite for electronic gadgets, such as video games, pocket translators, and the like.

There are three reasons why the decision to market a local product may represent a substantial opportunity cost to a company even though the product may be quite profitable. First, the existence of a single national business does not provide an opportunity to develop and utilize global leverage from headquarters in marketing, R&D, production, and other functional areas. Second, the local product does not allow for the transfer and application of experience gained in one market to other markets. As noted in Chapter 8, one of the major tools available to the multicountry marketer is comparative analysis. By definition, a single-country marketer cannot use this tool. A third shortcoming of a single-country product is the lack of transferability of managerial expertise acquired in the single-product area. Managers who gain experience with a local product can only utilize their product experience in the single market where the product is sold. Similarly, any manager coming from outside the market area where the single product is sold will not have had any experience in the single-product business. Therefore, while attractive profit opportunities in local products may occasionally present themselves to the global company, a persuasive argument may be made against moving into the single-market area.

International Products. International products are those that are perceived as having potential for extension into a number of national markets. Because industrial products tend to exhibit less environmental sensitivity than consumer products, industrial manufacturers should be especially alert to extension possibilities. For Canadian companies, market niche and focus are critically important when looking at extension to foreign markets. For example, Gennum Corporation, a producer of silicon integrated circuits, derives over 90 percent of its sales from twenty-two countries in seven continents. Gennum's marketing-driven niche strategy has helped it to carve out world market shares of two-thirds in electronics for hearing aids, and one-half in studio video-switching equipment. The twenty-times productivity improvement over 1973 levels have helped keep competitors at bay.[4]

Another example in the fiercely competitive military vehicle market demonstrates the importance of such product/market focus: Western Star Trucks Holdings finds that overseas customers are more interested in having trucks custom designed than North American customers. Such niching is ignored by the major competitors as their focus is on economies of scale, and global cuts in military budgets positions Western Star well to obtain the smaller, customized orders. While its business is well-entrenched in North America, Western Star pursues expansion of its offshore sales from 20 in 1994 to 30 percent of total revenues.[5]

Global Products. Global products are designed to meet the needs of a global market. Although, as noted earlier, Sony markets a number of local products, the company also has a stellar track record with global products. Over fifteen years ago, it introduced the Walkman, making portable, personal music available throughout the world. Sony's latest global product offering is a digital record/playback system called the Minidisc.

When an industry globalizes, companies are under pressure to develop global products. A major driver for the globalization of products is the cost of product R&D. As competition intensifies, companies discover that they can reduce the cost of R&D for a product by developing a global product design. Even products like automobiles, which must meet national safety and pollution standards, are under pressure to become global. With a global product, companies can offer an adaptation of a global design instead of a unique national design in each country.

---

[4] Susan Yellin, "Be all that we can be: Find niche in world winners say," *Hamilton Spectator* May 20, 1993; and "Circuit Stars: A Niche in Noise Enhancers," *Canadian Business* (December 1993) p.34.

[5] Patricia Lush, "Western Star Gears up for the long haul," *The Globe and Mail, Report on Business,* September 20, 1994, pp.B1, B21.

FIVE PRODUCT CHARACTERISTICS

Another way of looking at a product is to consider its characteristics. John Fayerweather suggests five important characteristics that are relevant to global marketing product decisions: primary functional purpose, secondary purpose, durability and quality, method of operation, and maintenance.

Primary function is illustrated by the example of the refrigerator as used in industrialized, high-income countries. The primary function of the refrigerator in these countries is (1) to store frozen foods for a week or more, (2) to preserve perishable food (vegetables, milk, and meat) between car trips to the supermarket, (3) to store products not requiring refrigeration, such as margarine, and (4) to keep bottled drinks cold for short-notice consumption.

In lower-income countries, frozen foods are not widely available. Housewives shop for food on a daily, rather than weekly, basis. Because of lower incomes, people are reluctant to pay for refrigerating items that actually do not require refrigeration to prevent spoilage and cooling beverages. These are luxury uses that require high-income levels to support. The function of the refrigerator in a lower-income country is merely (1) to store small quantities of perishable food for one day and (2) to store leftovers for slightly longer periods. Because the needs fulfilled by the refrigerators are limited in these countries as compared with advanced countries, a much smaller refrigerator is quite adequate.

In some developing countries, refrigerators have an important secondary purpose: They fulfill a need for prestige. In these countries, there is demand for the largest models, which are prominently displayed in the living room rather than hidden in the kitchen.

Durability and quality are important product characteristics that must be appropriate for the proposed market. The durability and quality of home appliances, for example, must be suited to the availability of service within a market. In lower-income markets, appliances are more likely to be repairable—indeed, a repairable appliance is a quality appliance in these markets. Conversely, in advanced countries, where the cost of labor makes it prohibitively expensive to repair appliances costing under $40, appliances are designed without the additional "quality" that would allow a repairperson to take the appliance apart and repair it. Since the availability of small-appliance repair in advanced countries is either nonexistent or prohibitively expensive, to build repairability into appliances would add nothing of value for the consumer. However, an attempt to sell the high-income product in a low-income market may result in failure; it may be perceived as a *lower*-quality product because of its lack of the important benefit of repairability.

The last two product characteristics described by Fayerweather are method of operation and maintenance. For example, the voltage and cycle requirements for an electrical appliance or the driving conditions for an automobile are important method-of-operation considerations in determining product design and characteristics. The same principle is true of maintenance, the availability and cost of which vary in different parts of the world (maintenance costs are discussed later). It is especially important that these factors be taken into account when product characteristics and features are being developed.

GLOBAL BRANDS

A global brand is defined as a brand that is marketed according to the same strategic principles in every part of the world. Specifically, the same positioning and marketing approaches will be used.

▼ Same Positioning

A global brand is positioned the same way in every market. If the brand has a premium price image in the home country, it will carry a similar positioning around the world. For example, Heineken beer is positioned around the world as a premium beverage. By contrast, Corona beer from Mexico and Beck's from Germany are not world brands because in their home countries they are both cheap "working man's" beers. Marlboro is another world brand, positioned around the world as an urban brand. The Marlboro man symbolizes rugged independence, freedom, and space, an image carefully calculated to appeal to the universal human desire for those things. Lack of freedom and physical space are acutely felt by urban dwellers, whose loyalty to Marlboro may be a reflection of their own sense of "macho-ness" or a symbol of freedom and independence. (Not surprisingly, Marlboro is the most popular cigarette brand in the former Soviet Union.) Likewise, if a product is positioned vis-à-vis a particular user—for example, an age segment of the market—the positioning will be the same in every market. Thus, Benetton has positioned its main Benetton line vis-à-vis the youth market of 16- to 24-year-olds around the world.

▼ Same Marketing Approach

A global brand is marketed the same way in every market in the world. However, the marketing mix may be adjusted to meet local consumer and competitive requirements. For example, Coke and Pepsi both increased the sweetness of their beverages in the Middle East where customers prefer a sweeter drink. Only an ideologue would insist that a "global product" cannot be adapted to meet local preferences; certainly no company building a global brand needs to limit itself to absolute product uniformity. The issue is not exact uniformity as much as offering *essentially* the same product. As we will see in the next few chapters, other elements of the marketing mix, such as price, appeal, media, distribution channels, and tactics may also vary.

The essential characteristic of a global brand is not an absolutely uniform marketing mix or execution. A global brand is guided by the same strategic principles; that is, it is positioned the same in every market and follows the same marketing approach in every market with the caveat that the marketing mix may vary.

Coke is an example of a global brand. It is positioned and marketed the same in all countries. Although the product itself may vary to suit local tastes, the price may vary to suit local competitive conditions, and the channels of distribution may differ, the basic, underlying strategic principles that guide the management of the brand are the same worldwide. Coke projects a global image of fun, good times, and enjoyment. A global brand, like a national or regional brand, is a set of consumer beliefs or perceptions about a product. A product is not a brand—it is an objective, physical entity or service. A brand is a perception created in the mind of consumers who ascribe beliefs and values to the product. Thus, it is important to understand that global brands do not exist in nature; rather, marketers must create them.

The possibility of developing a global brand represents an option that should be assessed systematically by global marketers both large and small. Creating a global brand requires a different type of marketing effort than that required to create multiple national brands. In particular, the up-front creative vision necessary to create a great global brand is greater than that required for a national brand. On the other hand, the ongoing effort to *maintain* brand awareness is less for a great world brand than it is for a collection of national brands.

Consider the case of Snickers (United States) and Marathan (United Kingdom). These are just two of the brand names used by Mars for its chocolate-covered caramel bar. In spite of the fact that there were those who argued that consumers in the United Kingdom would associate the name Snickers with knickers, British slang for a woman's undergarment, Mars decided to go ahead with the switch in order to create a global brand out of what had been a global product sold under a variety of national brand names. With a single brand, Mars has the opportunity to leverage all of its communications about this product across national boundaries. In doing this, it must now think globally about the positioning of Snickers, something that it was not obliged to do when it marketed different national brands. Mistakes and successes with the brand are now amplified globally so there is greater positive and negative leverage.

What criteria do marketers use to decide whether or not to establish global brands? One expert has argued that "world branding must, in the final analysis, be an option to be determined by bottom-up consumer driven considerations, not by top-down manufacturer driven business convenience."[6] A major variable in determining success will be whether or not the marketing effort is starting from scratch with a "blank slate," or whether the task is to reposition or rename an existing national brand in an attempt to create a global brand. Starting with a blank slate is vastly easier than repositioning existing brands. Still, many companies have succeeded in transforming national brands into regional or world brands. For example, in the early 1980s Nissan replaced the Datsun name outside Japan. Candymaker Mars Inc. changed the name of its successful European chocolate biscuit from Raider to Twix, the same name used in Canada and the United States. Today there are thousands of global brands, and every day the list grows longer. This includes former national brands. Global marketers should be alert to the advantages accruing to creators of global brands.

---

[6] A. E. Pitcher, "The Role of Branding in International Advertising," *International Journal of Advertising*, no. 4 (1985), 244.

PRODUCT SATURATION LEVELS IN GLOBAL MARKETS

As noted in Chapter 3, many factors determine a product's market potential. Income is clearly a critical factor for many products, but availability, price levels, need, and custom also act as important codetermining influences.

Complementary products—that is, products used in conjunction with other products—can also be an important determinant of demand that will not be revealed by examination of income and general cultural data. Recall from Chapter 3 that differences within Europe in saturation levels for electric vacuum cleaners are due to the type of floor coverings used in the different countries. Virtually all the homes in the Netherlands have rugs on the floor, whereas French and Greek homes tend not to have rugs as floor covering. Thus, in addition to attitudes toward cleanliness, the complementarity factor operates very significantly for electric vacuum cleaners. If the French had more carpets covering their floors, the saturation level for vacuum cleaners would be higher.

The existence of wide disparities in the demand for a product from one market to the next is an indication of the possible potential for that product in the low saturation-level market. For example, a major new-product category in the United States in the early 1980s was mousse, a hair-grooming product for women that is more flexible than stiff, dry hair spray. This product, known as a gel in France, had been available in France and Europe for 25 years prior to its introduction in the United States. The success of the product in Europe was a clear signal of market potential. Indeed, it is more than likely that this opportunity could have been tapped earlier. Every company should have an active global scanning system to identify potential market opportunities based on demand disparities.

PRODUCT DESIGN

Product design is a key factor determining success in global marketing. Should a company adapt product design for various national markets or offer a single design to the global market? In some instances, making a design change may increase sales. However, the benefits of such potential sales increases must be weighed against the cost of changing a product's design and testing it in the market. Global marketers need to consider four factors when making product design decisions: preferences, cost, laws and regulations, and compatibility.

▼ Preferences

There are marked and important differences in preferences around the world for factors such as color and taste. Marketers who ignore preferences do so at their own peril. In the 1960s, for example, Italy's Olivetti Corporation had gained considerable distinction in Europe for its award-winning modern consumer typewriter designs; Olivetti typewriters had been displayed at the Museum of Modern Art in New York City. While critically acclaimed, Olivetti's designs did not enjoy commercial success here. The North American consumer wanted a heavy bulky typewriter that was "ugly" by modern European design standards. Bulk and weight were considered *prima facie* evidence of quality and Olivetti was, therefore, forced to adapt its award-winning design for the Canadian and U.S. markets.

Often, a product design that is successful in Europe meets with success in many other markets around the globe. Kitchen appliances, such as food processors from Germany (Braun) or France (Moulinex), find market acceptance on the basis of their design and performance features. The example of the European designed Ford Mondeo or the Japanese designed Honda Accord emphasizes that product design can indeed create products that have a high degree of cross-national and cross-cultural acceptance.[7] In the fast-paced toy business, Mattel's Barbie doll has become a global toy that has grown to a C$1.4 billion business since its introduction some 35 years ago.[8] Around the globe, a Barbie product is sold every two seconds. Barbie's cultural influence outside of North America is so pervasive that in November 1994, in Italy—where 98 percent of children own a Barbie product—a special exhibit with more than 150 Barbie models and accessory products was featured in the exhibition "Toys of our Time" in Florence.[9]

Management is also aware that product preference is positively influenced by factors such as unique design features, extent of differentiation from existing products, and the degree of improvement a product offers over existing products.[10]

▼ Cost

In approaching the issue of product design, company managers must consider cost factors broadly. Of course, the actual cost of producing the product will create a cost floor. Other design-related costs whether incurred by the manufacturer or the end user must also be considered. Earlier in this chapter we noted that the cost of repair services varies around the world and has an impact on product design. Another example of how labor cost affects product decisions is seen in the contrasting approaches to aircraft design found in the aircraft industry. The British approach, which resulted in the Comet, was to place the engine inside the wing. This produced an aircraft that had lower wind resistance resulting in greater fuel economy, with the disadvantage that the engines were less accessible than externally mounted ones and therefore more time consuming to maintain and repair. The American approach to this question of engine location was to hang the engines from the wings at the expense of efficiency and fuel economy to gain a more accessible engine, thereby reducing the amount of time required for engine maintenance and repair. Both approaches to engine location were rational.

---

[7] "The World Car: Enter the McFord," *The Economist* (July 23, 1994) p.69.

[8] "All dolled up," *The Economist* (February 5, 1994) p.66.

[9] Thomas Martinelli, "La Barbie in mostra a Firenze: Brutta, scema e vincente," *Il Tirreno* (November 24, 1994) p. 10.

[10] Norman W. McGuinness and Blair Little, "The Influence of Product Characteristics on the Export Performance of New Industrial Products," *Journal of Marketing*, 45:2, pp.114–9.

The British approach took into account the relatively lower cost of the labor required for engine repair, and the American approach took into account the relatively high cost of labor for engine repair in the home market.

▼ Laws and Regulations

Compliance with laws and regulations in different countries has a direct impact on product design decisions, frequently leading to product design adaptations that increase costs. This may be seen especially clearly in Europe, where one impetus for the creation of the single market was to dismantle regulatory and legal barriers—particularly in the areas of technical standards and health and safety standards—that prevented pan-European sales of standardized products. In the food industry, for example, there were 200 legal and regulatory barriers to cross-border trade within the EC in ten food categories. Among these were prohibitions or taxes on products with certain ingredients, and different packaging and labeling laws. It is predicted that the removal of such barriers will reduce the need to adapt product designs and will result in the creation of standardized "Euro-products."[11]

The European Commission has created some 230 measures to bring the "single market" to reality. All measures need national legislation to implement them. National governments have been slow with the implementation and the European Commission has limited power to force them. Consequently, Canadian and other non-European companies, while following the measures emanating from the European Commission, still must carefully look at the regulations within each market.[12]

Nontariff Barriers

In Chapter 2 we introduced another important factor for the marketer sourcing across national boundaries, namely, *nontariff barriers* (NTBs) to trade. These barriers are assorted requirements and rulings that may purport to be impartial regulations but in fact serve only to restrict or eliminate foreign competition. Some of these regulations are quite subtle. While the "buy American" policy in the U.S. is an obstacle for Canadian competitors, in the European Union no company can compete for government business without ISO 9000 certification. In addition, tenders must be submitted in the national language, which alone has kept the share of foreign tenders to 5 percent of public service contracts.[13] European businesses recognized the competitive advantage of ISO certification early.[14] In the UK, for example 25,000 businesses are certified, while only 500 Canadian companies had achieved the accreditation by late 1994.[15]

---

[11] John Quelch, Robert Buzzell, and Eric Salama, *The Marketing Challenge of Europe 1992* (Reading, MA: Addison-Wesley, 1991) p. 71.

[12] "Something Dodgy in Europe's Single Market," *The Economist* (May 21, 1994) p.69–70.

[13] "Something Dodgy in Europe's Single Market," *The Economist* (May 21, 1994) p.70.

[14] Charlotte Crystal, "A Weak Commitment to Maintaining Quality," *International Business* (July 1994) p.20.

[15] "Quality Products Mean Business Profits," *Italia Canada: Monthly Report*, 3:1, p.3.

Product standards are often a formidable obstacle to foreign companies. Consider that Germany alone has in excess of 25,000, the United Kingdom 9,000 and Spain 700 product standards.[16]

NTBs are sometimes quite blatant. In France, any company can bid on a contract to supply CAT scanning equipment to hospitals. All hospital purchases must be approved by the Ministry of Health. If the purchase order is for equipment made by a French company, it is immediately approved. If it is for equipment made by a foreign company, it will be delayed in the Ministry of Health for at least a year and a half. NTBs can apply to services as well as products. Britain requires that British firms perform engineering and design work on North Sea oil projects. In Portugal, it is difficult for foreign hotel employees to get work permits. Italy limits seats on domestic flights for international passengers arriving in Italy on foreign carriers.[17]

It is critically important for a company to determine if it is facing a nontariff barrier or if it is indeed facing a legitimate national condition that is nondiscriminatory. The real test here is whether or not there is discrimination, not whether the national conditions are "reasonable." No foreigner has the right to tell a sovereign what is or is not reasonable. However, if it is determined that the government actions are discriminatory, they are then nontariff barriers and the strongest possible action should be taken on the part of any serious competitor.

Other laws, regulations, and practices may be labeled as nontariff barriers when they are, in fact, quite legitimate efforts to promote the public welfare. Automobile safety regulations have, for example, been objected to by some foreign manufacturers as a trade barrier. The intention behind the regulation is important. If a country has a regulation that is designed to reduce or eliminate foreign competition, any effort to comply with it would probably be met with additional legislation or rulings that would keep foreign competitors out of the market. A good test of a country's intention when regulations affect a product is to determine whether a given regulation affects all companies or just foreign companies. If the regulation is universally applicable, this is evidence that it was not motivated by an effort to restrict foreign-based competition. In other words, it is not an NTB.

▼ Compatibility

The last product design issue that must be addressed by company managers is product compatibility with the environment in which it is used. A simple thing like failing to translate the user's manual into various languages can hurt foreign sales of Canadian products. When products are powered by electricity, companies encounter electrical systems from 50 to 230 volts and from 50 to 60 cycles. Product adaptation to the market-specific electrical system is a must to make product and system compatible. Newbridge Networks Corp. has installed its digital communications systems in more than 40 countries and stresses the need

---

[16] Barbara H. Tucker, "Export Tactics Pending Harmonization," *Export Today Magazine* (September 1990).

[17] Leslie Wayne, "Services—the Star of U.S. Trade," *The New York Times,* September 14, 1986, Sec. 3, p. 4.

to adapt to important differences in local standards, whether that is the power supply, appropriate racking or cabinet color, or preparing documentation in the local language.[18]

Another example of the importance of compatibility is provided by the differing technical requirements affecting TV and VCR products. There are three different television broadcast and video systems in the world today: the U.S. NTSC system, the French SECAM system, and the German PAL system. Companies that are targeting global markets design multisystem televisions and VCRs that allow users to simply flip a switch for proper operation with any system. Companies that are not aiming for the global market design products that will only function in one of the systems.

Climate is another environmental characteristic that often demands compatibility. Many products require tropicalization to withstand humidity, whereas other products must withstand extreme cold. Many European automobiles are not suited to the extreme cold winter conditions found in parts of North America. This is particularly true of cars coming from Britain and Italy, two countries that do not have extreme winters.

Measuring systems do not demand compatibility, but the absence of compatibility in measuring systems can create product resistance. The U.S. is the only remaining non-metric country in the world and Canadian companies must calibrate their products in inches and pounds. When companies integrate their worldwide manufacturing and design activity, the metric-English measuring system conflict requires expensive conversion and harmonization efforts.

ATTITUDES TOWARD FOREIGN PRODUCTS

One of the facts of life in global marketing is the existence of stereotyped attitudes toward foreign products. Stereotyped attitudes may either favor or hinder the marketer's efforts. No country has a monopoly on a favorable foreign reputation for its products or a universally inferior reputation. There are marked differences in general in country attitudes toward foreign products. One new enterprise in Brazil, which supplied a sensitive scientific instrument to the oil-drilling industry, discovered the impact of attitudes toward foreign products when it attempted to market its product to an oil-drilling company in Mexico. The company found that its Mexican customers would not accept scientific instruments manufactured in Brazil. To overcome the prejudice in Mexico against instruments from Brazil, the company was forced to export the components for its instruments to Switzerland where they were assembled and the finished product stamped "Made in Switzerland." The company then obtained a very satisfactory level of sales for its product in Mexico.

The manufacturing reputation of a particular country may vary around the world. Nagashima measured business managers' perceptions of products made in the United States, Japan, Germany, France, and England. In a 1977

---

[18] Mary R. Brooks, Donald J. Patton, and Philip J. Rosson, *The Export Edge* (Ottawa, External Affairs and International Trade Canada, October 1990) p.24.

replication of his 1970 study, he reported that the "Made in U.S.A." image has lost ground rather dramatically as compared with the "Made in Japan" image.[19] Japanese consumers, on the other hand, believed that Japanese products are of higher quality.[20] Today, the view of Japanese consumers about quality is shared by the world. This change underlines an important fact: Perceptions of quality lag reality. A recent five-country study by Heslop, Papadopoulos, and Bamossy confirms that consumers' rating of their country's products is affected by the loyalty consumers have for their country. For example, it is interesting that the more positive Canadians' home-country attitudes, the more positively Canadian-made products were perceived.[21] If a country has a reputation for shoddy products or inferior quality, it must resign itself to producing quality products that are perceived as being of lower quality. Over time, as consumers experience higher quality, the perception will change and adjust. Should quality decline, the perception of decline will lag the actual decline. Again, over time, the perception will catch up with the reality.

An experimental study by Curtis C. Reierson tested various communications to determine their impact on attitudes toward foreign products.[22] Reierson found that if prejudice toward foreign products is not too intense, consumer attitudes may be improved by exposure to appropriate communication and promotion messages. However, if there are strong unfavorable attitudes toward a nation's products, such attitudes cannot be changed without substantial efforts. If a marketer is willing to engage in substantial and sustained communications efforts, then even a nation with strong unfavorable attitudes can expect a cumulative effect of communications efforts to change attitudes toward its products.

A very interesting finding of the Reierson study is that association with a prestige retailer is beneficial to the image of a nation's products. Thus, as an alternative to using mass communications to improve product image, global marketers should consider the strategy of obtaining distribution through a prestige retailer. When the budget for a marketing communication effort is limited, the latter strategy may be the only economically feasible method.

In some market segments, foreign products have a substantial advantage over their domestic counterparts simply because they are foreign. In one study, subjects were asked to indicate preference ratings for domestic and foreign beer in a blind test. Subjects indicated a preference for the domestic beers. The same subjects were asked to indicate preference ratings for beers in an open test with labels attached. In this test, the subjects preferred imported beer.[23]

---

[19] Nagashima, "A Comparison of Japanese and U.S. Attitudes Toward Foreign Products," *Journal of Marketing* (January 1970), pp. 68–74. See also Nagashima, "A Comparative 'Made-In' Product Image Survey Among Japanese Businessmen," *Journal of Marketing* (July 1977), pp. 95–100.

[20] Chem L. Narayana, "Aggregate Images of American and Japanese Products: Implications on International Marketing," *Columbia Journal of World Business* (Summer 1981), pp. 31–35.

[21] Louise A. Heslop, Nicolas Papadopoulos, and Gary Bamossy, "Country and Product Perceptions: Measurement Scales and Image Interactions," *Dimensions of International Business*, The International Business Study Group, Carleton University (Spring 1993), 9, p.46.

[22] Curtis C. Reierson, "Attitude Changes Toward Foreign Products," *Journal of Marketing Research* (November 1967).

[23] David T. Meinertz, Michael Nadelberg, William Pelicot, and Michael R. Sullivan, "The 'Imported' Label and Consumer Choice," unpublished Columbia Business School student report, January 8, 1968.

It is a happy situation for the global marketer when foreign origin has a positive influence on perceptions of quality. One way to reinforce foreign preference is by charging a premium price for the foreign product to take advantage of the widespread tendency to associate price and quality.[24] Such a doubly reinforced quality image of foreign origin and high price can put a product in a commanding position in the quality segment of the market. The relative position of imported beer in the Canadian premium-priced beer market is an excellent example of this segmentation strategy.

There are also numerous examples of a *negative* association between perception of quality and foreign origin. The perception varies from product group to product group and from source and market country to source and market country. When a product is found to have a negative quality association because of its foreign source, the global marketer has two alternatives. One is to attempt to hide or disguise the foreign origin of the product. Package and product design can minimize evidence of foreign sourcing. A brand policy of using local names or of using well-known local brand names will contribute to a domestic identity. The other alternative is to continue the foreign identification of the product and attempt to change consumer or customer attitudes toward the product.

Some countries have a very poor image that is not based on product experience. A remarkable example of a change in product image is Japan. In the post–World War II years Japanese products were regarded as being of cheap quality. By the 1970s, constant quality improvement and researching consumers in Western markets had reversed the image of Japanese goods in foreign markets. Their global market success in consumer electronics, automobiles and motorcycles speaks for itself.

Chasin and Jaffe found, in their study of American industrial product buyers, that the images of East European countries were quite poor as compared to the U.S.[25] This means that anyone seeking to market a "Made in East Europe" industrial product has an image problem. Each of the four Ps can be used to attack this problem: Product quality can be offered, price can be lowered, promotion can build an image, and place (distribution) can support the overall image campaign with information and evidence.

More recent studies of the impact of country of origin on product evaluation suggest that country-of-origin effects may be less significant than has generally been believed. There are, however, several important factors that influence the perception of the origin and the attitude towards a product. These include the home country's degree of industrial development, the level of market development, and the consumer's affective feeling towards the home country. A recent eight-country study about the "made in" image of products showed that consumers are aware of weaknesses of domestic producers and hold favorable attitudes towards products from certain foreign origins. This study examined perceived product dimensions (e.g., product integrity, price/value, market presence,

---

[24] The positive correlation between price and perception of quality is well documented in the marketing literature. See, for example, J. Douglas McConnell, "The Price Quality Relationship in an Experimental Setting," *Journal of Marketing Research,* August 1968.

[25] Joseph B. Chasin and Eugene D. Jaffe, "Industrial Buyer Attitudes Toward Goods Made in Eastern Europe," *Columbia Journal of World Business* (Summer 1979) pp.74–81.

and customer response). Respondents in eight countries were asked about a set of thirteen products from Canada, the U.S., Japan, Sweden, and the U.K. One of the findings of the study is that Canadians, Americans, British, French, and Hungarians rated Japanese products highest on product integrity (such as workmanship and quality). Greeks rated U.S. products highest, while Germans rated domestic products and the Dutch rated Swedish products as top. On price-value, consumers rated foreign products better than their own in Canada, the U.S., Great Britain, France, Netherlands, and Hungary. Only in Greece were domestic products perceived as a better price-value.[26]

Global marketers need to understand not only the multiple tangible and intangible attributes that make up a product but also, more importantly, how these attributes are perceived and valued by potential buyers.[27] A costly example of ignoring the customer was Volkswagen's re-design of the interior of its Rabbit model when the Westmoreland factory in the U.S. began producing for the American market. The "North American" looking interior was not what buyers wanted and this error in product management contributed to a drastic drop in demand for the Rabbit. Such effects may occur predominantly in relation to a valuation of specific attributes rather than overall product. Johansson, Douglas, and Nonaka conclude that there is little support for the hypothesis that the country of origin is used as a surrogate variable to evaluate the product when a respondent has limited experience or knowledge about the product.[28] Even if this conclusion is valid, country stereotyping can nevertheless at times present a considerable disadvantage to a competitor in a market. Because of this, global marketers should consider shifting production locations to exploit country-specific advantages. This strategy is more attractive to a competitor who does not have an established brand name. One of the advantages of an established brand name is the ability to avoid the country-of-origin effect.[29]

GEOGRAPHIC EXPANSION— STRATEGIC ALTERNATIVES

Companies can grow in three different ways.[30] The traditional methods of market expansion including the further penetration of existing markets to increase market share and the extension of the product line into new-product market

---

[26] Louise A. Heslop and Nicolas Papadopoulos, "But Who Knows Where or When: Reflections on the Images of Countries and Their Products," *Product-Country Images – Impact and Role in International Marketing* (New York: International Business Press, 1993) pp.61-2.

[27] Nicolas Papadopoulos, Louise Heslop, and Gary Bamossy, "A Comparative Image Analysis of Domestic versus Imported Products," *International Journal of Research in Marketing* (1990) 7:4, p.292.

[28] Johnny K. Johansson, Susan Douglas, and Ikujiro Nonaka, "Assessing the Impact of Country of Origin on Product Evaluations: A New Methodological Prospective," *Journal of Marketing Research*, 12 (November 1985), p. 395.

[29] For further discussion, see Johnny K. Johansson and Hans B. Thorelli, "International Product Positioning," *Journal of International Business Studies* (Fall 1985), pp. 57–76.

[30] This section is adapted from Warren J. Keegan, "Multinational Product Planning: Strategic Alternatives," *Journal of Marketing* (January 1969).

areas in a single national market are available. In addition a company can expand by extending its existing operations into new countries and areas of the world. This method of geographical expansion is one of the major opportunities of international marketing. To pursue geographic expansion effectively, a framework for considering alternatives is required. When a company has a single or multicountry product/market base, it can select from five strategic alternatives to extend this base into other geographic markets.

▼ Strategy 1: Product-Communications Extension (Dual Extension)

Many companies employ product-communications extension as a strategy for pursuing opportunities outside the home market. Under the right conditions, this is the easiest product marketing strategy and, in many instances, the most profitable one as well. American companies pursuing this strategy sell exactly the same product, with the same advertising and promotional appeals used in the United States, in some or all world market countries or segments. Note that this strategy is utilized by companies in stages two, four, and five. The critical difference is one of execution and mindset. In the stage-two company, the dual extension strategy grows out of an ethnocentric orientation; the stage-two company is making the *assumption* that all markets are alike. The company in the fourth or fifth stage does not fall victim to such assumptions; a geocentric orientation allows the company in stage four or five to thoroughly understand its markets and consciously take advantage of similarities in world markets.

Kellogg Co. is using the dual extension strategy in Eastern Europe. The breakfast culture in this region is vastly different from the standard North American cereal breakfast. Kellogg's challenge is to change the ingrained habits of Latvians and Russians through television commercials and in-store "taste testings" with a focus on the fun, nutrition, and variety in breakfast. Due to the relatively high price of the cereal, the initial target was the upper-income consumers.[31]

Capitalizing on such similarities is not the prerogative of large companies such as PepsiCo, whose outstandingly robust performance is a persuasive justification of this practice. Another leading practitioner of this approach, Obus-Forme, a small Canadian designer/manufacturer of back supports, has successfully used the extension approach in a dozen markets and is now the global leader in orthopedic support devices.[32]

Some marketers have learned the hard way that the dual extension approach does not work in every market. When Campbell Soup tried to sell its tomato soup in the United Kingdom, it discovered after substantial losses the English preference for a more bitter taste. Happily, Campbell learned its lesson and subsequently succeeded in Japan by offering seven soup varieties—for example, corn potage—designed specifically for the Japanese markets. Another

---

[31] Joseph B. Treaster, "Kellogg Targets Latvians' Breakfast," *The Globe and Mail*, June 6, 1994, p.B7.
[32] Jared Mitchell, "Show and Sell," *Report on Business*, April 1992, p.47.

multinational food company spent several million dollars in an unsuccessful effort to capture the British cake-mix market. It offered fancy cake mixes with frosting. After the product was launched, the company discovered that the British consume their cake at tea time. The cake they prefer is dry, spongy, and suitable for being picked up with the left hand while the right manages a cup of tea. Closer to home, Canadian Tire entered the U.S. market when it acquired 81 stores from the White Stores Inc. chain in the sunbelt states in 1982. Within four years and after a total cost of C$225 million, Canadian Tire withdrew from the U.S. market. While a myriad of problems, such as poor store locations, poor image with customers, and narrow product lines contributed to the failure, a key issue was a misunderstanding of customers' product preference and buyer behavior. Local customers were used to buying "specials," could not associate White Stores with auto parts and service, and did not respond well to the traditional broad product offering that made Canadian Tire successful in Canada.[33]

Similarly, the 1981 expansion into the U.S. of Mark's Work Wearhouse Ltd., a specialty retailer catering to the "blue collar" worker, had failed by 1987 because the broad product line suitable to the Canadian consumer was inappropriate in the southern U.S.[34]

CPC International hoped to pursue a product extension strategy with Knorr dehydrated soups in the United States. Dehydrated soups dominate the soup market in Europe and CPC managers believed they had an market opportunity in the United States. However, a faulty marketing research design led to erroneous conclusions concerning market potential for this product. CPC's go-ahead decision was based on a strong preference for Knorr found in extensive taste panel comparisons of Knorr dehydrated soups with popular canned soups. Unfortunately, these taste tests did not simulate the actual market environment for soup, which includes not only eating but also preparation. The preparation difference between the 15–20 minute cooking time for dry soup and "heat and serve" benefit of canned soup was a critical factor influencing purchase. In this case, it was only partial extension: Flavors were adapted, but the basic form of the product was extended. The failure was only relative because while the product failed to meet the original expectations, it succeeded in its category (dry soups), but the category market share remains small compared to Europe.

The product-communications extension strategy has an enormous appeal to global companies because of the cost savings that are associated with this approach. The two most obvious sources of savings are manufacturing economies of scale and elimination of duplicate product R&D costs. Less well known but still important are the substantial economies associated with standardization of marketing communications. For a company with worldwide operations, the cost of preparing separate print and television ads for each market is a significant marketing expense. Although these cost savings are important, they should not distract executives from the more important objective of maximum profit performance, which may require the use of an adaptation or invention strategy. As we have seen, in spite of its immediate cost savings, product extension may in fact result in market failure.

---

[33] Mark Baetz, "White Stores Inc.," Wilfrid Laurier University (1986); and Ken Harling, "Canadian Tire: Acquisition of White," mimeo, September 28, 1990.

[34] Henry Lane and Terry Hildebrand, "How to survive in US Retail Markets," *Business Quarterly* (Winter 1990) pp.62–6.

▼ Strategy 2: Product Extension-Communications Adaptation

When a product fills a different need, appeals to a different segment, or serves a different function under use conditions that are the same or similar to those in the domestic market, the only adjustment that may be required is in marketing communications. Bicycles are an example of a product that has been marketed with this approach. Bicycles satisfy recreation needs in Canada but serve as basic transportation in many other countries. Similarly, outboard marine motors are usually sold to a recreation market here, whereas the same motors in many foreign countries are often sold to fishing and transportation fleets. North American lawn and garden power equipment was marketed in less developed countries as agricultural implements because it suited the needs of farmers with small land holdings. Equally important was the lower price: almost a third less than competing equipment especially designed for small-acreage farming, and offered for sale by competing foreign manufacturers.

As these examples show, the product extension-communications adaptation strategy whether by design or by accident results in **product transformation.** The same physical product ends up serving a different function or use than that for which it was originally designed or created. There are many examples of food product transformation. The classic example is Perrier, discussed in earlier chapters; recall that while mineral water has long been advertised and consumed in Europe for its healthful qualities, Perrier became a success in America only after it was marketed as *the* chic beverage to order in restaurants and bars instead of a cocktail. Another product that crossed the Atlantic from Europe with a communication change is dry soup powder, which is sold mainly as soups in Europe and as sauces or cocktail dips in Canada and the United States. On both sides of the ocean, the products are identical; the only change is in marketing communications—specifically, the package labeling. In Europe the label illustrates and describes how to make soup out of the contents; the North American versions illustrate and describe how to make sauce and dip as well as soup.

The appeal of the product extension-communications adaptation strategy is its relatively low cost of implementation. Since the product in this strategy is unchanged, R&D, tooling, manufacturing setup, and inventory costs associated with additions to the product line are avoided. The only costs of this approach are in identifying different product functions and revising marketing communications (including advertising, sales promotion, and point-of-sale material) around the newly identified function.

▼ Strategy 3: Product Adaptation-Communications Extension

A third approach to global product planning is to extend, without change, the basic home-market communications strategy while adapting the product to local use or preference conditions. Note that this strategy (and the one that follows) may be utilized by companies in stages three, four, and five. The critical difference, as noted earlier, is one of execution and mindset. In the stage-three company, the product adaptation strategy grows out of a polycentric orientation; the stage-three company *assumes* that all markets are different. By contrast, the geocentric orientation of managers and executives in a company in stage four or five has sensitized them to actual rather than assumed differences between markets.

Exxon adheres to this third strategy: It adapts its gasoline formulations to meet the weather conditions prevailing in different markets while extending the basic communications appeal ("Put a tiger in your tank") without change. Similarly, Glen Seeds of Blenheim, Ontario, markets different varieties of seed corn that produce optimum yield under different soil and environmental conditions. There are many other examples of products that have been adjusted to perform the same function around the globe under different environmental conditions. Soap and detergent manufacturers have adjusted their product formulations to meet local water and washing equipment conditions with no change in their basic communications approach. Household appliances have been scaled to sizes appropriate to different use environments, and clothing has been adapted to meet fashion criteria. Also, by virtue of their potentially high degree of environmental sensitivity, food products are often adapted. Mueslix, for example, is the name of a mushlike European "health" cereal that is popular in Europe. Kellogg's brought the Mueslix name and product concept to the Canadian market but completely changed the formulation and nature of the product.

▼ Strategy 4: Dual Adaptation

When comparing a new geographic market to the home market, marketers sometimes discover that environmental conditions of use or consumer preferences differ; the same may be true of the function a product serves or consumer receptivity to advertising appeals. In essence, this is a combination of the market conditions of Strategies 2 and 3. In such a situation, a company in stage four or five will utilize the strategy of product and communications adaptation. As was true about Strategy 3, stage-three companies will also use dual adaptation regardless of whether the strategy is warranted by market conditions, preferences, function, or receptivity.

Unilever's experience with fabric softener in Europe exemplifies the classic multinational road to adaptation. For years, the product was sold in ten countries under seven different brand names with different bottles and marketing strategies. Unilever's decentralized structure meant that product and marketing decisions were left to country managers. They chose names that had local-language appeal and selected package designs to fit local tastes. Today, rival Procter & Gamble is introducing competitive products with a pan-European strategy of standardized products with single names, suggesting the European market is more similar than Unilever assumed. In response, Unilever's European brand managers are attempting to move gradually toward standardization.[35]

Greeting card manufacturers, such as Hallmark, have faced genuine market condition and preference differences in Europe, where the function of a

[35] E. S. Browning, "In Pursuit of the Elusive Euroconsumer," *The Wall Street Journal*, April 23, 1992, p. B2.

greeting card is to provide a space for the sender to write an individual message. In contrast, American and Canadian cards contain a prepared message, known in the greeting card industry as "sentiment." The conditions under which greeting cards are purchased in Europe are also different from those here. Thus, manufacturers, like Hallmark, pursuing an adjustment strategy have changed both their product and their marketing communications in response to this set of environmental differences. Cards are handled frequently by customers, a practice that makes it necessary to cellophane wrap greeting cards sold in European markets.

Sometimes, a company will draw upon all four of these strategies simultaneously when marketing a given product in different parts of the world. For example, H. J. Heinz utilizes a mix of strategies in its ketchup marketing. While a dual extension strategy works in England, spicier, hotter formulations are also popular in central Europe and Sweden. Recent ads in France featured a cowboy lassoing a bottle of ketchup and thus reminded consumers of the product's American heritage. Swedish ads conveyed a more cosmopolitan message; by promoting Heinz as "the taste of the big world" and featuring well-known landmarks such as the Eiffel Tower, the ads disguised the product's origins.[36]

▼ Strategy 5: Product Invention

Adaptation and adjustment strategies are effective approaches to international (stage-two) and multinational (stage-three) marketing, but they may not respond to global market opportunities. Nor do they respond to the situation in markets where customers do not have the purchasing power to buy either the existing or adapted product. This latter situation applies to the less developed part of the world, which includes roughly three-quarters of the world's population.

Rather than extend or adapt an existing product, it is often necessary to plan and design for the global market. An example is the rechargeable battery market. As noted earlier, voltage and cycles vary around the world. Anton/Bauer, a small American company, offers a portable power system (batteries and chargers) that will operate anywhere in the world without adjustments by the user. The charger "knows" or reads the type of power that it is plugged into and adjusts accordingly. The product's portability creates added value for customers. The Anton/Bauer approach is to design for the global market: The company manufactures one product instead of many and thereby keeps costs down. This design feature enables Anton/Bauer to manufacture one chassis instead of several, which in turn enables the company to achieve greater economies of scale and greater experience. Scale and experience mean lower costs, and lower costs and higher quality are essential in serving global markets in the 1990s. The winners in global competition are the companies that can develop product designs offering the most benefits, which in turn create the greatest value for buyers. The product invention strategy frequently means higher levels of product performance and lower prices, which translate into greater customer value.

---

[36] Gabriella Stern, "Heinz Aims to Export Taste for Ketchup," *The Wall Street Journal*, November 20, 1992, pp. B1, B9.

In some instances, value is not defined in terms of performance, but rather in terms of customer perception. Customer perception is as important for an expensive perfume or champagne as it is for an inexpensive soft drink. Product quality is essential—indeed, it is frequently a given—but it is also necessary to support the product quality with imaginative, value-creating advertising and marketing communications. This can be done with a global advertising campaign. Most industry experts believe that a global appeal and a global campaign are more effective in creating the perception of value than is a series of separate national campaigns.

When potential customers cannot afford a product, the strategy indicated is invention. In other words, a company may need to develop an entirely new product designed to satisfy the need or want at a price that is within the reach of the potential customer. This is demanding, but if product development costs are not excessive, it is potentially a rewarding product strategy for the mass markets in the less developed countries of the world.

Although there are ample opportunities for the application of the invention strategy in global marketing, it is a strategy that is unfortunately underappreciated and underutilized. For example, an estimated 600 million women in the world still scrub their clothes by hand. These women have been served by soap and detergent companies for decades, yet until recently not one of these companies had attempted to develop an inexpensive manual washing device.

▼ How to Choose a Strategy

Most companies seek a product strategy that optimizes company profits—more precisely, the present value of cash flows—over the long term. Which strategy for global markets best achieves this goal? There is, unfortunately, no general answer to this question. The answer depends upon the specific product-market-company mix.

Recent experience by Canadian companies shows their product/market strategies to be forward and aggressive. Companies are not single-focused when it comes to their strategies; far from it, they employ several approaches simultaneously geared to the opportunities available. Table 12–1 points out that existing foreign markets are pursued for both market penetration and market development by three out of five companies. When it comes to entering new markets, three-fourths of companies do so with already existing products, while one in two perceive the fast pace and competitive pressure of global markets such that they develop new markets with new products.[37]

As we noted in Chapter 2, a product's environmental sensitivity may be assessed in terms of a continuum ranging from low to high. Also recall from Chapter 4 that, in terms of cultural sensitivity, consumer products are more sensitive than industrial products. Another general rule is that food products frequently exhibit the highest degree of cultural sensitivity. What this means to managers is that some products, by their nature, demand significant adaptation. Others require only partial adaptation, and still others are best left unchanged.

---

[37] F.H. Rolf Seringhaus and Philip J. Rosson, *Survey Results of Canadian International Trade Fair Participants in Four Industry Sectors*, Technical Report (October 1994).

TABLE 12-1 Product-Market Strategies of Canadian Companies

Companies Marketing:	
• Existing Products in Existing Markets	64.5%
• New Products in Existing Markets	59.1
• Existing Products in New Markets	73.1
• New Products in New Markets	50.7

Source: Based on data in F.H. Rolf Seringhaus and Philip J. Rosson, *Survey Results of Canadian International Trade Fair Participants in Four Industry Sectors*, Technical Report (October 1994).

Companies differ in both their willingness and capability to identify and produce profitable product adaptations. Unfortunately, there are many stage-one and stage-two companies that are oblivious to the issues presented previously. One new-product expert has described three stages that a company must go through that roughly correspond to the strategies described in this chapter.[38]

1. *Cave dweller.* The primary motivation behind launching new products internationally is to dispose of excess production or increase plant-capacity utilization.

2. *Naive nationalist.* The company recognizes growth opportunities outside the domestic market. It realizes that cultures and markets differ from country to country, and as a result, it sees product adaptation as the only possible alternative.

3. *Globally sensitive.* This company views regions or the entire world as the competitive marketplace. New-product opportunities are evaluated across countries, with some standardization planned as well as some differentiation to accommodate cultural variances. New-product planning processes and control systems are reasonably standardized.

▼ Product-Market Analysis

The first step in formulating global product policy is to identify the product-market relationship of each product in question. Who uses the product, when is it used, for what, and how is it used? Does it require power sources, linkage to other systems, maintenance, preparation, style matching, and so on? Examples of almost mandatory adaptation situations are products designed for 60-cycle power going into 50-cycle markets; products calibrated to a myriad of product standards; products that require maintenance going into markets where maintenance standards and practices differ from those of the original design market; and products that might be used under different conditions than those for which they were originally designed. Renault discovered this last factor too late with the ill-fated Dauphine, which acquired a notorious reputation for breakdown frequency

---

[38] Thomas D. Kuczmarski, *Managing New Products: The Power of Innovation* (Englewood Cliffs, NJ: Prentice Hall, 1992), p. 254.

in Canada and the United States. Renault executives attributed the frequent mechanical failure of the Dauphine to the high-speed highway driving and relatively infrequent maintenance service. The driving and maintenance turned out to be critical differences for a product that was designed for the roads of France and the almost daily maintenance that French people lavish upon their cars.

Even more difficult are the marketing mix adaptations that are not dictated by environmental sensitivity but are of critical importance in determining whether the product will appeal to a narrow market segment rather than a broad mass market. The most frequent offender in this category is price. Too often, companies believe that they have adequately adapted their global product offering when they make mandatory adaptations to the physical features of a product (for example, converting 120 volts to 220 volts) but extend the Canadian price. In foreign markets such as Chile, where average incomes are lower than those in Canada, such a practice may put the product in a different classification and competitive setting. Sometimes the market creates the product's position, as is with the case of blue jeans in Italy. The brand/product image of Levi's is exceptionally strong and has elevated the product to near-cult status, selling it at retail prices of two to three times the North American price. Thus, the product may become a specialty product for the relatively wealthy consumers rather than a convenience good for the mass market. One response to global market price constraints is margin reduction and/or feature elimination. A better response involves "inventing backwards," that is, starting with price and specifications and working backward to a product. Gillette's success in developing countries can be partially attributed to management's decision to make products available in smaller, more affordable packages.

Even if product-market analysis indicates an adaptation requirement, each company must examine its own product-communication development and manufacturing costs. Adaptation costs fall under two broad categories: development and production. Development costs will vary depending on the cost-effectiveness of product-communications development groups within the company. The range in costs from company to company and product to product is great. Frequently the company with international product development facilities has a strategic cost advantage. The vice president of a leading U.S. machinery company has offered an example of this kind of advantage:

> We have a machinery development group both here in the States and also in Europe. I tried to get our U.S. group to develop a machine for making the elliptical cigars that dominate the European market. At first they said "who would want an elliptical cigar machine?" Then they grudgingly admitted that they could produce such a machine for $500,000. I went to our Italian product development group with the same proposal and they developed the machine I wanted for $50,000. The differences were partly relative wage costs but very importantly they were psychological. The Europeans see elliptical cigars every day, and they do not find the elliptical cigar unusual. Our American engineers were negative on elliptical cigars at the outset and I think this affected their overall response.[39]

---

[39] Interview with a vice president of a large U.S. manufacturing company.

Analysis of a company's manufacturing costs is essentially a matter of identifying potential opportunity losses. If a company is reaping economies of scale from large-scale production of a single product, then any shift to variations of the single product will raise manufacturing costs. In general, the more decentralized a company's manufacturing setup, the smaller the manufacturing cost of producing different versions of the basic product. In the company with local manufacturing facilities for each international market, the addition to the marginal manufacturing cost of producing an adapted product for each market is relatively low.

A more fundamental form of company analysis occurs when a firm is considering whether or not to pursue explicitly a strategy of product adaptation. This level of analysis focuses not only on the manufacturing cost structure of the firm but also on the basic capability of the firm to identify product adaptation opportunities and to convert these opportunities into profitable products. The ability to identify preferences will depend to an important degree on the creativity of people in the organization and the effectiveness of information systems in the organization. The existence of salespeople, for example, who are creative in identifying profitable product adaptation opportunities is no assurance that their ideas will be translated into reality by the organization. Information in the form of ideas and perceptions must move through the organization to those who are involved in the product development decision-making process.

To sum up, the choice of product and communications strategy in international marketing is a function of three key factors: (1) the product itself defined in terms of the function or need it serves; (2) the market defined in terms of the conditions under which the product is used, the preferences of potential customers, and the ability to buy the products in question; and (3) the costs of adaptation and manufacture to the company considering these product-communications approaches. Only after analysis of the product-market fit and of company capabilities and costs can executives choose the most profitable international strategy. The alternatives are outlined in Table 12–2.

NEW PRODUCTS IN GLOBAL MARKETING

In today's dynamic, competitive market environment, many companies realize that continuous development and introduction of new products are keys to survival and growth. Which companies excel at these activities? Gary Reiner, a new-product specialist with the Boston Consulting Group, has compiled the following list: Honda, Compaq, Motorola, Canon, Boeing, Merck, Microsoft, Intel, and Toyota. One common characteristic is they are global companies that pursue opportunities in global markets where competition is fierce, thus ensuring that new products will be world class. Other characteristics noted by Reiner are:

1. They focus on one or only a few businesses.
2. Senior management is actively involved in defining and improving the product development process.

TABLE 12–2 Multinational Product-Communications Mix: Strategic Alternatives

Strategy	Product Function or Need Satisfied	Conditions of Product Use	Ability to Buy Product	Recommended Product Strategy	Recommended Communications Strategy	Relative Cost of Adjustments	Product Examples
1	Same	Same	Yes	Extension	Extension	Low	Soft drinks
2	Different	Same	Yes	Extension	Adaptation	Medium	Bicycles
3	Same	Different	Yes	Adaptation	Extension	Low	Gasoline
4	Different	Different	Yes	Adaptation	Adaptation	Medium	Cards
5	Same	—	No	Invention	New communications	High	Hand-powered washing machines

1 = Full extension
2 = Product extension/communications adaptation
3 = Product adaptation/communications extension
4 = Full adaptation
5 = Invention

3. They have the ability to recruit and retain the "best and the brightest" people in their fields.

4. They understand that speed in bringing new products to market reinforces product quality.[40]

What is a new product? Newness can be assessed in the context of the product itself, the organization, and the market. The product may be an entirely new invention or innovation, for example, the VCR or the compact disc. It may be a line extension (a modification of an existing product) such as Diet Coke. Newness may also be organizational, as when a company acquires an already existing product with which it has no previous experience. Finally, an existing product that is not new to a company may be new to a particular market. Theoretically, the combination of three factors (product, company, market) in two levels (new/existing product, new/not new to company, new existing market) results in eight degrees of newness.

Table 12–3 illustrates the degrees of product newness; the shaded columns indicate the degrees of newness relevant to global marketers. Any of the degrees of newness in Table 12–3 may apply to a global new product, but the most characteristic type of newness is category II, an existing product already marketed by a company that is introduced for the first time to a particular national market. For this type of product introduction, the performance of the product in one or more markets is known. A critical task of the product manager is to assess the extent to which the existing record of the product is relevant to the proposed new geographic market. As discussed earlier, the process of investigating this question is called comparative analysis.

Table 12–3 indicates the more difficult product launch situations: Whenever the product is new, new to the company, or introduced to a new international market, there is a greater challenge. It is an open question as to which is the most challenging situation: lack of product experience or lack of market experience.

In column II, a company takes a product already in its product mix and attempts to launch it in new national markets. This was the situation General Mills faced after it decided to enter the cold-cereal market in Europe where it had no previous experience and Kellogg was long entrenched. In order to bring Honey-Nut Cheerios and other brands to Europe, General Mills formed a joint venture with Nestlé. Nestlé's cereal brands were weak, but the company brought distribution clout and market knowledge to the venture.

Column III describes the situation when a company gains a new product (e.g., via acquisition) and introduces it into a market where the company is already operating. This was the situation at CPC International when it attempted to introduce Knorr soups, a European product line. In Canada and the U.S., the marketing plan for Knorr soups was based on the assumption that there would be a substantial increase in the market share of dry soup mixes at the expense of canned soups. Unfortunately, while CPC knew a great deal about the North American market for mayonnaise, peanut butter, and other packaged-food products, inexperience in the dry soup category led managers to underestimate the

---

[40] Gary Reiner, "Lessons from the World's Best Product Developers," *The Wall Street Journal*, April 4, 1990, p. A12.

TABLE 12-3 Degrees of "Newness" and Difficulty of New-Product Launch

	V	IV	III	II	I	
New product						Existing product
New to company						Not new to company
New national market						Existing national markets

Code
Existing Product and Market: unshaded
New Product, New Market: shaded

difficulty of converting canned soup users to the dehydrated soup product. A more difficult situation exists when a company attempts to introduce an existing product that is new to the company and the market.

Column IV describes product launch conditions that present formidable challenges. Here, companies develop new products and introduce them into global national markets or international markets. The products are new, but the markets are known in this case. The best global companies are the ones that rise to these challenges. Innovators such as Sony have enviable track records of developing entirely new products, such as the compact disc and the Walkman, and successfully launching them in the world markets the company serves.

The most difficult situation arises when a company attempts to market an entirely new product in a market where the company has little experience, as shown in column V. This type of product introduction should be avoided.

▼ Identifying New-Product Ideas

The starting point for an effective worldwide new-product program is an information system that seeks new-product ideas from all potentially useful sources and channels these ideas to relevant screening and decision centers within the organization. There are many sources of new-product ideas, including customers, suppliers, competitors, company salespeople, distributors and agents, subsidiary executives, headquarters executives, documentary sources (for example, information service reports and publications), and, finally, actual firsthand observation of the market environment.

For example, the Perrier Group, the French exporter of carbonated mineral water, having identified a distinct flavor preference in the French-Canadian market in Quebec, introduced mint-flavored mineral water.

▼ The International New-Product Department

Davidson and Harrigan found a relationship between organization structure and speed of introduction of new products abroad. In functionally organized firms, 40 percent of the innovations from firms with international divisions went abroad in two years or less as compared with 6 percent of innovations that went abroad in functionally organized firms without international divisions. For firms organized along product lines, the respective figures are 33 percent and 18 percent. For globally integrated organizations, 80 percent of all new products go abroad in two years or less, and *every* innovation in the researchers' sample was introduced abroad in five years or less.[41]

A high volume of information flow is required to scan adequately for new-product opportunities, and considerable effort is subsequently required to screen these opportunities to identify candidates for product development. The best organizational design for addressing these requirements is a new-product department.[42] The function of such a department would be fourfold: (1) to ensure that all relevant information sources are continuously tapped for new-product ideas; (2) to screen these ideas to identify candidates for investigation; (3) to investigate and analyze selected new-product ideas; and (4) to ensure that the organization commits resources to the most likely new-product candidates and is continuously involved in an orderly program of new-product introduction and development on a worldwide basis.

With the enormous number of possible new products, most companies establish screening grids in order to focus on those ideas that are most appropriate for investigation. The following questions are relevant to this task:

1. How big is the market for this product at various prices?
2. What are the likely competitive moves in response to our activity with this product?
3. Can we market the product through our existing structure? If not, what changes will be required and what will the cost be to make these changes?
4. Given estimates of potential demand for this product at specified prices with estimated levels of competition, can we source the product at a cost that will yield an adequate profit?
5. Does this product fit our strategic development plan? (a) Is the product consistent with our overall goals and objectives? (b) Is the product consistent with our available resources? (c) Is the product consistent with our management structure? (d) Does the product have adequate global potential?

▼ Introducing New Products in National Markets

The major lesson of new-product introduction in foreign markets has been that whenever a product interacts with human, mechanical, or chemical elements, there is the potential for a surprising and unexpected incompatibility. Since virtually *every* product matches this description, it is important to test a product under actual market conditions before proceeding with full-scale introduction. A test does not necessarily involve a full-scale test-marketing effort. It may simply involve observing the actual use of the product in the target market.

---

[41] William H. Davidson and Richard Harrigan, "Key Decisions in International Marketing: Introducing New Products Abroad," *Columbia Journal of World Business* (Winter 1977), p. 22.

[42] See, for example, "Introducing a New Product in a Foreign Market," Management Monograph No. 33 (New York: Business International, 1966), p. 7.

Kellogg's introduction of breakfast cereals into Eastern Europe is an example of products that are completely new to the consumer. The general desire for Western products in former Soviet republics and satellite states provides a positive premise for such a product launch.

Failure to assess actual use conditions can lead to big surprises. North American cereals, for example, have not met with great success in Italy because of the absence of a breakfast culture in that country: breakfast is simply not as important as in other European countries. In the case of Singer sewing machines sold in African countries, a slight redesign by the manufacturer in Scotland had a major consequence. The location of a small bolt on the product's base was changed; the change had no effect on product performance but did save a few pennies per unit in manufacturing costs. Unfortunately, when the modified machine reached Africa, it was discovered that this small change was disastrous for product sales. The Scottish engineers had not realized that in Africa, it is customary for women to transport any bundle or load, including sewing machines, on their heads. The relocated bolt was positioned at exactly the place where head met machine for proper balance; since the sewing machines were no longer transportable, demand decreased substantially.

▼ Comparative Analysis

In Chapter 7 one of the most useful techniques in global marketing for aiding the new-product decision was introduced, namely, comparative analysis. Comparative analysis is always possible when an experience record for a product exists in one or more markets at the time of introduction of the product into a new market. The secret to effective comparative analysis is finding market comparability. There are two ways to obtain comparability. One is to find an example of a market that is basically similar in terms of economic and social structural development to that of the target market and to compare the position of the product under study in the two markets. For example, if such comparability exists in Colombia and Mexico, one can take the experience accumulated in Colombia to estimate potential market performance for Mexico.

Another means of achieving comparability is to displace time periods and find points of comparability at different time periods for markets that are not comparable in the same time period. If, for example, one seeks to apply the experience gained with a product in the Canadian market to a marketing problem in Mexico, it is clear that in most cases Canadian experience will not be applicable to current Mexican circumstances. However, it is possible that our domestic experience in some previous period in Canada (for example, say 1954) would be applicable in certain situations to the current marketing situation in Mexico.

If this analogy exists, the time-displacement device can be an effective instrument for obtaining comparability. An interesting example of the time-displacement device is the history of efforts to market Kleenex facial tissues in Germany. The first effort to market this product in Germany centered on a program that promoted Kleenex as a substitute for handkerchiefs. The result of this effort was unsuccessful because Germany had a four-ply heavy paper towel, Tempo, that was stronger than Kleenex and, in the German consumer's judgment, a better substitute for a handkerchief. When this effort failed, Kleenex turned to a second advertising problem, which promoted Kleenex as an all-purpose tissue. Again the effort achieved no success. German consumers were confused by the multiple uses identified in this promotion and concluded that Kleenex had no purposes. A third effort promoted the tissue as a woman's facial tissue. This promotion proved to be very successful. Interestingly, the third approach to marketing the Kleenex tissue was identical to the approach utilized to introduce it to the North Amercian markets in the 1930s.[43]

▼ SUMMARY

The product is the most important element of a marketing program. At any point in time a company is largely defined by the products it offers. Global marketers face the challenge of formulating a coherent global product strategy for their companies. Product strategy requires an evaluation of the basic needs and conditions of use in the company's existing and proposed markets, together with an evaluation and appraisal of the company's basic strengths and weaknesses. Full recognition must be given to the importance of establishing a viable and economic headquarters organization that can develop leverage (that is, the application of useful experience developed in one market to the formulation of a program for another market and the ability to avoid repeating mistakes within the multinational system). To develop leverage, the organization must have at the supranational level an organization that can accumulate and transfer knowledge concerning successful and unsuccessful practices. Another important dimension of the supranational organization's activity is the application of comparative analysis between comparable national markets to further enhance the effectiveness of marketing planning and marketing programs within the global system.

▼ DISCUSSION QUESTIONS

1. What is the difference between a product and a brand?

2. What are the differences among a local, an international, and a global product or brand? Cite examples.

3. What does the trade-cycle model predict will happen to the location of production of a new product? Why does the location of production change at different stages of the product life-cycle?

4. Is the trade-cycle model a valid guide to action today? Why? Why not?

5. What are the conditions and reasons for extending elements of the marketing program internationally?

6. When should a marketing program be adapted to a target market instead of extended from an existing market?

---

[43] This example is taken from Richard Alymer, "Marketing Decisions in the Multinational Firm," unpublished doctoral dissertation, Harvard Business School, 1968.

▼ BIBLIOGRAPHY

Books

KEEGAN, WARREN J., SANDRA MORIARTY, AND TOM DUNCAN, *Marketing*. Englewood Cliffs, NJ: Prentice Hall, Inc., 1992.

KUCZMARSKI, THOMAS D., *Managing New Products; The Power of Innovation*. Englewood Cliffs, NJ: Prentice Hall, Inc., 1992.

MACRAE, CHRIS, *World Class Brand*. Reading, MA: Addison-Wesley, 1991.

PAPADOPOULOS, NICOLAS, AND LOUISE A. HESLOP, *Product-Country Images: Impact and Role in International Marketing*. New York: International Business Press, 1993.

QUELCH, JOHN A., *The Marketing Challenge of Europe 1992*. Reading, MA: Addison-Wesley, 1991.

ROSENTHAL, STEPHEN R., *Effective Product Design and Development: How to Cut Lead Time and Increase Customer Satisfaction*. Homewood, IL: Business One Irwin, 1992.

Articles

AYERS, ROBERT U., AND WILBUR A. STEGER, "Rejuvenating the Life Cycle Concept," *Journal of Business Strategy*, 6, no. 1 (Summer 1985), 6–76.

GRUNE, GEORGE V., "Global Marketing," *Vital Speeches*, 55, no. 19 (July 15, 1989), 580–582.

HANSOTIA, BEHRAN J., AND MUZAFFAR A. SHAIKH, "The Strategic Determinacy Approach to Brand Management," *Business Marketing* (February 1985), 66–82.

HILL, JOHN S., AND WILLIAM L. JAMES, "Product and Promotion Transfers in Consumer Goods Multinationals," *International Marketing Review*, 8, no. 2, 6–17.

JOHANSSON, JOHNNY K., SUSAN P. DOUGLAS, AND IKUIIRO NONAKA, "Assessing the Impact of Country of Origin on Product Evaluations: A New Methodologic Prospective," *Journal of Marketing Research*, 12 (November 1985), 388–396.

JOHANSSON, JOHNNY K., AND HANS B. THORELLI, "International Product Positioning," *Journal of International Business Studies*, 16, no. 3 (Fall 1985), 57–76.

KEEGAN, WARREN J., "Multinational Product Planning: Strategic Alternatives," *Journal of Marketing* (January 1969), 58–62.

KOTABE, MASAAKI, "Corporate Product Policy and Innovative Behavior of European and Japanese Multinational: An Empirical Investigation," *Journal of Marketing*, 54, no. 2 (April 1990), 19–33.

MCGUINESS, NORMAN W., AND BLAIR LITTLE, "The Influence of Product Characteristics on the Export Performance of New Industrial Products," *Journal of Marketing*, Vol. 45, No. 2, 114–9.

NAGASHIMA, "A Comparative 'Made-In' Product Image Survey Among Japanese Businessmen," *Journal of Marketing* (July 1977), 95–100.

———, "A Comparison of Japanese and U.S. Attitudes Towards Foreign Products," *Journal of Marketing* (January 1970), 68–74.

OGBUEHI, ALPHONSO O., AND RALPH A. BELLAS, JR., "Decentralized R&D for Global Product Development: Strategic Implications for the Multinational Corporation," *International Marketing Review*, 9, no. 5, 60–70.

ONKVISIT, SAK, AND JOHN J. SHAW, "An Examination of the International Product Life Cycle and Its Applications Within Marketing," *Columbia Journal of World Business*, 73–79.

PAPADOPOULOS, NICOLAS, LOUISE HESLOP AND GARY BAMOSSY, (1990) "A Comparative Image Analysis of Domestic versus Imported Products," *International Journal of Research in Marketing*, Vol. 7, No. 4, 292.

PITCHER, A. E., "The Role of Branding in International Advertising," *Journal of Advertising*, 4, 241–246.

ROBINSON, WILLIAM T., AND CLAES FORNELL, "Sources of Market Pioneer Advantages in

Consumer Goods Industries," *Journal of Marketing Research* (August 1985).

RONKAINEN, ILKKA A., "Product-Development Processes in the Multinational Firm," *International Marketing Review* (Winter 1983), 57–64.

VENKATESH, ALLADI, AND DAVID WILEMON, "American and European Product Managers: A Comparison," *Columbia Journal of World Business* (Fall 1980), 67–74.

VERNON, RAYMOND, "Gone Are the Cash Cows of Yesteryear," *Harvard Business Review* (November/December 1980).

————, "The Product Life Cycle Hypothesis in a New International Environment," *Oxford Bulletin* (November 1980).

WALTERS, PETER G. P., AND BRIAN TOYNE, "Product Modification and Standardization in International Markets: Strategic Options and Facilitating Policies," *Columbia Journal of World Business*, 24, no. 4 (Winter 1989), 37–44.

THIRTEEN

Pricing Decisions

Introduction

In any country, three basic factors determine the boundaries within which market prices should be set. The first is product cost, which establishes a *price floor*, or minimum price. While it is certainly possible to price a product below the cost boundary, few firms can afford to do this for extended periods of time. Second, competitive prices for comparable products create a *price ceiling*, or upper boundary. International competition almost always puts pressure on the prices of domestic companies. A widespread effect of international trade is to lower prices. Indeed, one of the major arguments favoring international business is the favorable impact of international competition upon national price levels and, in turn, upon a country's rate of inflation. Between the lower and upper boundaries for every product there is an *optimum price*, which is a function of the demand for the product as determined by the willingness and ability of customers to buy.

The interplay of these factors is reflected in the pricing policies adopted by many Canadian companies in the mid-1990s. With inflation in Canada in the low single digits and demand forcing factories to run at or near capacity, companies should be able to raise prices. However, the domestic economic situation is not the only consideration. Worldwide, a combination of idle manufacturing capacity and many jobless workers makes it difficult for Canadian companies to increase prices.

The global manager must develop pricing systems and pricing policies that address these fundamental factors in each of the national markets in which his or her company operates. The following is a list of eight basic pricing considerations for marketing outside the home country.[1]

1. Does the price reflect the product's quality?

2. Is the price competitive?

3. Should the firm pursue market penetration, market skimming, or some other pricing objective?

4. What type of discount (trade, cash, quantity) and allowance (advertising, trade-off) should the firm offer its international customers?

---

[1] Adapted from "Price, Quotations, and Terms," *A Basic Guide to Exporting* (San Rafael: World Trade Press, 1994) p.10–1.

5. Should prices differ with market segment?

6. What pricing options are available if the firm's costs increase or decrease? Is demand in the international market elastic or inelastic?

7. Are the firm's prices likely to be viewed by the host-country government as reasonable or exploitative?

8. Do the foreign country's dumping laws pose a problem?

The task of determining prices in global marketing is complicated by fluctuating exchange rates which may bear only limited relationship to underlying costs. According to the concept of purchasing power parity (PPP) outlined in Chapter 6, changes in exchange rates should be directly linked to changes in domestic prices. Thus, in theory, fluctuating exchange rates should not present serious problems for the global marketer because a rise or decline in the value of the home-country currency should be offset by an opposite rise or decline in domestic price levels. In the real world, however, exchange rates do not move in lock step with inflation. This means that global marketers are faced with difficult decisions about how to deal with windfalls resulting from favorable exchange rates, as well as losses due to unfavorable exchange rates.

A firm's pricing system and policies must also be consistent with other uniquely global constraints. Those responsible for global pricing decisions must take into account international transportation costs, middlemen in elongated international channels of distribution, and the demands of global accounts for equal price treatment regardless of location. In addition to the diversity of national markets in all three basic dimensions of cost, competition, and demand, the international executive is also confronted by conflicting governmental tax policies and claims as well as various types of price controls. These include dumping legislation, resale price maintenance legislation, price ceilings, and general reviews of price levels. For example, Procter & Gamble encountered strict price controls in Venezuela in the late 1980s. Despite increases in the cost of raw materials, P&G was only granted about 50 percent of the price increases it requested; even then, months passed before permission to raise prices was forthcoming. As a result, by 1988 detergent prices in Venezuela were less than what they were in the United States.[2]

While the preceding "textbook" approach is used in part or in whole by most experienced global firms, it must be noted that the inexperienced or part-time exporter does not usually go to all this effort to determine the "best" price for a product in international markets. Such a company will frequently use a much simpler approach to pricing, for example, the cost-plus method explained later in this chapter. As managers gain experience and become more sophisticated in their approach, however, they realize that the factors identified previously should be considered when making pricing decisions.

There is another important internal organizational consideration besides cost. Within the typical corporation there are many interest groups and, fre-

---

[2] Alecia Swasy, "Foreign Formula: Procter & Gamble Fixes Aim on Tough Market: The Latin Americans," *The Wall Street Journal*, June 15, 1990, p. A7.

quently, conflicting price objectives. Divisional vice presidents, regional executives, and country managers are each concerned about profitability at their respective organizational levels. Similarly, the international marketing manager seeks competitive prices in world markets. The controller and financial vice president are concerned about profits. The manufacturing vice president seeks long runs for maximum manufacturing efficiency. In companies with foreign subsidiaries, the tax manager is concerned about compliance with government transfer pricing legislation. And company counsel is concerned about the Competition Act with respect to the implications of international pricing practices.

Taken alone, these divergent and conflicting organizational interests make it difficult to reach consensus on price decisions. Compounding the problem, however, is the rapidly changing global marketplace and the inaccurate and distorted nature of much of the available information regarding demand. It is in the face of all these challenges that the international executive must formulate international pricing strategies and policies that will contribute to company sales and profit objectives worldwide. This can be difficult to accomplish. To manage the pricing function in international marketing effectively, executives and managers must know the factors affecting pricing decisions and have a framework for approaching pricing issues. The purpose of this chapter is to provide the knowledge and the framework required.

GLOBAL PRICING STRATEGIES

An effective pricing strategy for international markets is one in which competition and costs have influenced the pricing decision. Competitive prices can be determined only by examining the price levels of competitive and substitute products in target markets. As we discuss in Chapter 16, an excellent way to get this information is to visit the market personally. Once these price levels have been established, the base price can be determined.

The four steps involved in determining a base price are:

1. Determine the price elasticity of demand. Inflexible demand will allow for a higher price.
2. Estimate fixed and variable manufacturing costs on projected sales volumes. Product adaptation costs must be calculated.
3. Identify all costs associated with the marketing program.
4. Select the price that offers the highest contribution margin.

The final determination of a base price can be made only after the other elements of the marketing mix have been established. These include the distribution strategy and communication strategy. The nature and length of channels utilized in the marketing program will affect margins, as will the cost of advertising and communications. Clearly, the marketing program has a dramatic effect on the final price of the product.

The preceding four steps may sound simple but, in fact, they are not. It is often not possible to obtain the definitive and precise information that would be the basis of an "optimal" price. In many parts of the world, external market information is distorted and inaccurate. The same may be true about internal information. In Russia, for example, market research is a fairly new concept. Historically, detailed market information was not gathered or distributed. Also, managers at newly privatized factories are having difficulty setting prices because cost accounting data relating to manufacturing are frequently unavailable.

There are other problems. When attempting to estimate demand, for example, it is important to consider product appeal relative to competitive products. While it is possible to arrive at such estimates after conducting market research, the effort can be costly and time consuming. The size of many potential export markets is often too small to justify even minimum expenditures on formal market research. As a consequence, as noted earlier, company managers and executives have to rely on intuition and experience. One way of improving the estimates of potential demand is to use analogy. This approach basically means extrapolating potential demand for target markets from actual sales in markets judged to be similar.

▼ Setting Prices: The Japanese Approach

When Sony developed the portable compact disc player in the mid-1980s, the cost per unit at initial sales volumes was estimated to exceed $600. Since this was a "no-go" price in the North American and other target markets, Akio Morita instructed management to price the unit in the $300 range to achieve penetration. Because Sony was a global marketer, the sales volume it expected to achieve in these markets led to scale economies and lower costs.

The Sony example illustrates a fundamental difference in the approach to pricing issues adopted by Japanese companies. As shown in Figure 13–1, the Japanese begin with market research and product characteristics. Up to this point, the process parallels that which is used by most Canadian companies. At the next step, the processes diverge. In Japan, the planned selling price minus the desired profit is calculated, resulting in a target cost figure. It is only at this point that design, engineering, and supplier pricing issues are dealt with; each member of the value chain is forced to meet the target. Once the necessary negotiations and trade-offs have been settled, manufacturing begins, followed by continuous cost reduction. In our process, cost is determined after design, engineering, and supplier considerations have been made; if the cost is too high, the process cycles back to the design stage.[3]

▼ Pricing Objectives

Prices in international markets are not carved in stone; they must be evaluated at regular intervals and adjusted if necessary. Similarly, pricing objectives may

---

[3] Michel Robert, *Strategy Pure and Simple: How Winning CEOs Outthink Their Competition* (New York: McGraw-Hill, 1993), pp. 114–115.

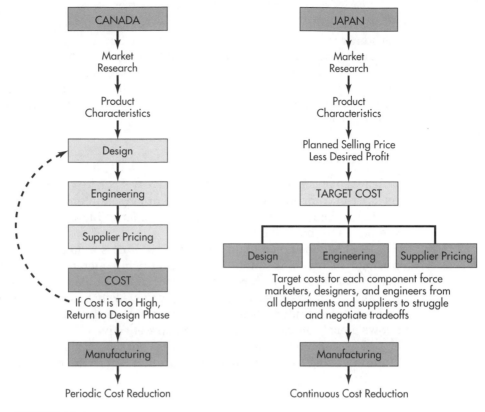

FIGURE 13–1
How the Japanese Keep Costs Low

Source: Adapted from Michel Robert, *Strategy Pure and Simple: How Winning CEOs Outthink Their Competition.* © 1993 McGraw-Hill, Inc. Reproduced with permission of McGraw-Hill, Inc.

vary depending on the stage in the product life-cycle and the country-specific competitive situation. Four of the most frequently encountered approaches are market skimming, market penetration, market holding, and cost-plus pricing.

Market Skimming

The market-skimming pricing strategy is a deliberate attempt to reach a market segment that is willing to pay a premium price for a product. In such instances, the product must create high value for buyers. This pricing strategy is often used in the introductory phase of the product life-cycle when both production capacity and competition are limited. By setting a deliberately high price, demand is limited to early adopters—those who are willing and able to pay the price. One goal of this pricing strategy is to maximize revenue on limited volume and to match demand to available supply. Another goal of market-skimming pricing is to reinforce customers' perceptions of high product value. When this is done, the price is part of the total product positioning strategy.

When Sony first began selling Betamax VCRs in North America in 1976, it used a skimming strategy. The product was clearly targeted at the innovative consumer in the upper income bracket. Those buyers wanted to be the first to have this technologically advanced product at a price of $1300. [4]

The initial success of the Betamax proved that consumers in North America, Japan, and elsewhere were willing to pay a high price for a piece of consumer electronics equipment that would allow them to watch their favorite television shows at any time of the day or night.

Penetration Pricing

Penetration pricing uses price as a competitive weapon to gain market position. The majority of companies using this type of pricing in international marketing are located in the Pacific Rim. Scale-efficient plants and low-cost labor allow these companies to "blitz" the market.

It should be noted that a first-time exporter is unlikely to use penetration pricing. The reason is simple: Penetration pricing often means that the product may be sold at a loss for a certain length of time. Companies that are new to exporting cannot absorb such losses. Nor are they likely to have the marketing system in place (including transportation, distribution, and sales organizations) that allows global companies like Sony to make effective use of a penetration strategy. However, a company whose product is not patentable may wish to use penetration pricing to achieve market saturation before the product is copied by competitors.

Market Holding

The market-holding strategy is frequently adopted by companies that want to maintain their share of the market. In single-country marketing, this strategy often involves reacting to price adjustments by competitors. For example, when one airline announces special bargain fares, most competing carriers must match the offer or risk losing passengers. In global marketing, currency fluctuations often trigger price adjustments. Many Canadian companies used this strategy in the early to mid-1980s when the Canadian dollar appreciated against most currencies other than the U.S. dollar. If Canadian-based companies marketing internationally had maintained their price levels, currency translations tied to the strong dollar would have automatically increased the price of many products. As a result, companies would have priced themselves out of many international markets. To avoid this, companies set prices based not on the Canadian price translated at the current exchange rate but rather on the competitive situation in each market and the ability and willingness of customers to pay. Canadian Foremost markets its high-mobility all-terrain vehicles on its international reputation for world-class quality while some of its competitors have used price discounting to obtain sales.[5]

---

[4] James Lardner, *Fast Forward: Hollywood, The Japanese, and the VCR Wars* (New York: New American Library, 1987), p. 91.

[5] Mary Brooks, Donald Patton, and Philip Rosson, *The Export Edge* (Ottawa: External Affairs and International Trade, 1990) p.36.

Thus, company strategy, product positioning, and market demand influence a company's pricing approaches.

From the mid- to late-1980s, the Canadian dollar was on a rollercoaster ride, initially weakening and then strengthening. When the C$ weakened, companies based in Japan, Germany, France, and elsewhere attempted to hold the line on Canadian prices. Needless to say, adjusting prices to fit the competitive situation may mean lower profit margins.

By early 1993, as the yen approached parity with the U.S. dollar (¥100=US$1), and the Canadian dollar had reached a new six-year low against the U.S. dollar, Nikon, Sharp, and other Japanese companies had abandoned the market-holding strategy and raised prices. A strong home currency may also force a company to consider offshore manufacturing or licensing agreements rather than exporting to maintain market share. Ikea, a Swedish company that sells home furnishings, sourced between 35 and 40 percent of its products in Canada in 1994 to guard against the foreign currency impact on part of its product line.[6] Market holding means that a company must carefully examine all its cost accounting to determine whether or not it can afford to continue marketing in a country.

Cost-Plus/Price Escalation

Companies new to exporting frequently use a strategy known as cost-plus pricing when gaining a toehold in the global marketplace. There are two cost-plus pricing methods: The older is the historical accounting cost method, which defines cost as the sum of all direct and indirect manufacturing and overhead costs. An approach used in recent years is known as the *estimated future cost method*.

Cost-plus pricing requires adding up all the costs required to get the product to where it must go, plus shipping and ancillary charges, and a profit percentage. The obvious advantage of using this method is its low threshold: It is relatively easy to arrive at a quote, assuming that accounting costs are readily available. The disadvantage of using historical accounting costs to arrive at a price is that this approach completely ignores demand and competitive conditions in target markets. Therefore, historical accounting cost-plus prices will frequently be either too high or too low in light of market and competitive conditions. If historical accounting cost-plus prices are right, it is only by chance.

However, novice exporters don't care—they are reactively responding to global market opportunities, not proactively seeking them (for more on the different stages in export marketing, see Chapter 16). Experienced global marketers realize that nothing in the historical accounting cost-plus formula directly addresses the competitive and customer value issues that must be considered in a rational pricing strategy.

---

[6] Paul W. Beamish, *Ikea–Sears* (London: University of Western Ontario, 1988); and communication from Ikea Canada, October 24, 1994.

Item		Price	Percent
Ex-works Calgary		C$30,000	100%
Container freight charges from Calgary to Vancouver	C$1,475.00		
Terminal handling fee	350.00		
Ocean freight for 20-ft container	2,280.00		
Insurance	60.00		
Forwarding fee	150.00		
Total shipping charges		4,315.00	14.4
Total C.I.F. Yokohama value		34,315.00	
V.A.T. (3% of C.I.F. value)		1,029.45	3.4
		35,344.45	
Distributor markup (10%)		3,534.44	11.8
		38,878.89	
Dealer markup (25%)		9,719.72	32.4
Total retail price		$48,598.61	162.0%

* This was loaded at the manufacturer's door, shipped by stack train to Vancouver, and then via ocean freight to Yokohama. Total transit time from factory door to foreign port is about 28 days.

Price escalation is the increase in a product's price as transportation, duty, and distributor margins are added to the factory price. Table 13–1 is a typical example of the kind of price escalation that can occur when a product is destined for international markets. In this example, a manufacturer of agricultural equipment in Calgary is shipping a container load of farm implements to Tokyo, Japan. A shipment of product that costs ex-works C$30,000 in Calgary ends up having a total retail price of almost C$50,000 in Tokyo—a price 162 percent of that ex-works in Calgary.

Let us examine this shipment to see what happened. First, there is the total shipping charge of C$4,315.00, which is 14.4 percent of the ex-works Calgary price. The principal component of this shipping charge is a combination of land and ocean freight.

All import charges are assessed against the landed price of the shipment (C.I.F. value). Note that there is no line item for duty in this example; no duties are charged on agricultural equipment sent to Japan.[7] Duties may be charged in other countries. A nominal distributor markup of 10 percent (C$3,534.44) actually represents 11.8 percent of the C.I.F. Yokohama price because it is a markup not only on the ex-works price but on freight and V.A.T as well. (It is assumed here that the distributor's markup includes the cost of transportation from the port to Tokyo.) Finally, a dealer markup of 25 percent adds up to C$9,719.72— 32.4 percent of the C.I.F. Yokohama price. Like distributor markup, dealer markup is based on the total landed price.

---

[7] Since the Uruguay Round of GATT negotiations, Japan will lower or eliminate duties on 6,000 categories of imports. Japan's average duty rate as of 1994 is 2.5 percent, one of the lowest in the world.

The net effect of this add-on accumulating process is a total retail price in Tokyo of 162 percent of the ex-works Calgary price. This is price escalation. The example provided here is by no means an extreme case. Indeed, as discussed in Chapter 14 , longer distribution channels, or channels that require a higher operating margin typically found in export marketing, can contribute to price escalation. Because of the layered distribution system in Japan, the markups in Tokyo could easily result in a price that is 200 percent of the C.I.F. value.

The preceding example of cost-plus pricing shows an approach that a beginning exporter might use to determine the C.I.F. price. However, experienced global marketers view price as a major strategic variable that can help achieve marketing and business objectives.

▼ Using Sourcing as a Strategic Tool in Pricing Products

The international marketer has several options in addressing the problem of price escalation described in the last section. The choices are dictated in part by product and market competition. Marketers of domestically manufactured finished products may be forced to switch to offshore sourcing of certain components to keep costs and prices competitive. In particular, the Far East and South America are emerging as attractive low-cost sources of production.

Another option is to source 100 percent of a finished product offshore near or in local markets. The manufacturer could enter into one of the arrangements discussed in Chapter 9 such as licensing, joint venture, or a technology transfer agreement. With this option, the manufacturer has a presence in the market it is trying to penetrate; price escalation due to high Canadian manufacturing costs and transportation charges is no longer an issue.

The third option is a thorough audit of the distribution structure in the target markets. In some countries distribution channel intermediaries perform no real function or make no contribution to the total marketing program. Therefore, they unnecessarily drive up the price of the product without adding any value. When this situation exists, a rationalization of the distribution structure can substantially reduce the total markups required to achieve distribution in international markets. Rationalization may include selecting new intermediaries, assigning new responsibilities to old intermediaries, or establishing direct-marketing operations. For example, Toys "R" Us has invaded the Japanese toy market because it bypassed layers of distribution and adopted a warehouse style of selling similar to its approach in the U.S. and Canada. Toys "R" Us has been viewed as a test case of the ability of Western retailers—discounters in particular—to change the rules of distribution.

▼ Dumping

Dumping is the selling of a good in a foreign market for a lower price than in the domestic market or country of origin, or for a lower price than its cost of production.[8] In addition to GATT's 1979 Antidumping Code, which makes dumping illegal, many countries have their own policies and procedures for protecting national companies from dumping.

The Uruguay Round resulted in several changes to the antidumping rules, aiming to make them more transparent. For example, in calculating "fair price" for a given product, any sales of the product at below-cost prices in the exporting country are not included in the calculations; inclusion of such sales would have the effect of exerting downward pressure on the "fair price." Also, governments can no longer penalize price differences between home market and export market of less than 2 percent. Another change relates to the time limit: antidumping actions cannot exceed five years, which, in the Canada/U.S. relationship restricts the ability of the U.S. to maintain countervailing duties against Canadian exports for prolonged periods.[9]

Under NAFTA, any antidumping or countervailing duty determinations and disputes are ultimately reviewed by an independent, binational panel, which is also concerned with the appropriateness of the domestic antidumping laws.[10]

As the nature of these issues and regulations suggests, some countries use dumping legislation as a legitimate device to protect local enterprise from predatory pricing practices by foreign companies. In other nations, they represent protectionism, a device for limiting foreign competition in a market. The rationale for dumping legislation is that dumping is harmful to the orderly development of enterprise within an economy. Few economists would object to long-run or continuous dumping. If this were done, it would be an opportunity for a country to take advantage of a low-cost source of a particular good and to specialize in other areas. However, continuous dumping only rarely occurs; the sale of agricultural products at international prices with farmers receiving subsidized higher prices is an example of continuous dumping. The type of dumping practiced by most companies is sporadic and unpredictable and does not provide a reliable basis for national economic planning. Instead it may injure and hurt domestic enterprise.

The dumping issue has been a part of Canada/U.S. business relations for a long time. Disputes have involved softwood lumber, steel, beer, and hogs and pork, to name a few industries. The softwood lumber issue illustrates the antidumping and countervailing duty action companies may encounter. By the mid-1980s, Canadian lumber had achieved a market share of 30 percent in the U.S. and price-comparisons showed harvested U.S. logs up to 44 percent more expensive than Canadian logs. This was attributed to the greater price-competitiveness (the C$ fell from US$0.85 to US$0.73 between 1980 and 1985), more productive Canadian lumber mills (they were larger and more automated), and higher stumpage fees than those paid in the U.S.[11]

---

[8] Michael Parking and Robin Bade, *Economics: Canada in the Global Environment* (Don Mills, Ontario: Addison-Wesley, 1991) p.987.

[9] *Canada and the Uruguay Round, New Rules and Institutions* (Ottawa, Government of Canada, April 1994) p.10.

[10] *North American Free Trade Agreement: An Overview and Description* (Ottawa: Government of Canada, August 1992) p.9

[11] Charles F. Doran and Timothy J. Naftali, "US-Canadian Softwood Lumber: Trade Dispute Negotiations," Pew Case Studies in International Affairs, Case 141 (Washington: Georgetown University, 1988) pp.2–3.

The U.S. viewed the differential in stumpage fees as subsidies, claimed injury to the U.S. industry and imposed a 15 percent extra duty. Subsequently, Canadian stumpage fees were raised to avoid the duty. A lumber shortage was developing in the U.S. and the building industry opposed the duty because it raised the average house price by US$1,000. Although the appropriate duty had been set at 6.5 percent by 1992, a binational dispute panel took on this issue in 1993 to resolve it.[12]

The last few years have seen a great incidence of antidumping investigation and penalties, imposed primarily in the U.S. but also in the European Union, Canada, and Australia. Companies concerned with running afoul of antidumping legislation have developed a number of approaches to avoid dumping laws. One approach is to differentiate the product sold from that in the home market. An example of this is an auto accessory that one company packaged with a wrench and an instruction book, thereby changing the "accessory" to a "tool." The tariff rate in the export market happened to be lower on tools, and the company also acquired immunity from antidumping laws because the package was not comparable to competing goods in the target market. Another approach is to make nonprice competitive adjustments in arrangements with affiliates and distributors. For example, credit can be extended and essentially have the same effect as a price reduction.

ENVIRONMENTAL INFLUENCES ON PRICING DECISIONS

There are many environmental considerations facing an international marketer. Among these are inflation, devaluation and revaluation, government controls and subsidies, competitive behavior, and market demand. Some of these factors work in conjunction with others; for example, inflation may be accompanied by government controls. A discussion of each consideration follows.

▼ Pricing in an Inflationary Environment

Inflation, or a persistent upward change in price levels, is a worldwide phenomenon. Inflation requires periodic price adjustments. These adjustments are necessitated by rising costs that must be covered by increased selling prices. An essential requirement of pricing in an inflationary environment is the maintenance of operating profit margins. Regardless of cost accounting practices, if a company maintains its margins, it has effectively protected itself from the effects of inflation. To keep up with inflation in Peru, for example, Procter & Gamble has resorted to biweekly increases in detergent prices of 20 percent to 30 percent.[13]

---

[12] Personal communication from Randy Wigle, Wilfrid Laurier University (October 1994).
[13] Swasy, p. 1.

Within the scope of this chapter it is only possible to touch on the many accounting issues and conventions relating to price adjustments in international markets. In particular, it is worth noting that the traditional FIFO (first-in, first-out) costing method is hardly appropriate for an inflationary situation. A more appropriate accounting practice under conditions of rising prices is the LIFO (last-in, first-out) method, which takes the most recent raw material acquisition price and uses it as the basis for costing the product sold. In highly inflationary environments, historical approaches are less appropriate costing methods than replacement cost. The latter amounts to a next-in, first-out approach. Although this method does not conform to Generally Accepted Accounting Principles (GAAP), it is used to estimate future prices that will be paid for raw and component materials. These replacement costs can then be used to set prices. While this approach is useful in managerial decision making, it cannot be used in financial statements. Regardless of the accounting methods used, an essential requirement under inflationary conditions of any costing system is that it maintain gross and operating profit margins. Managerial actions can maintain these margins subject to the following constraints.

▼ Devaluation and Revaluation

Under the floating exchange rate system described in Chapter 6, devaluation and revaluation take place when currency values fluctuate in foreign exchange markets. Devaluation is the reduction in the value of one currency against other currencies; revaluation is an increase.

For example, if the currency of country *A* were devalued relative to country *B*, and if domestic prices in country *A* were unaffected by the devaluation, then the prices of all goods to buyers in country *B* would decline by the amount of the devaluation. However, an importer in country *A* would experience an increase in prices of products imported from country B. Therefore, devaluation actually puts upward pressure on costs and prices in country *A*. This means that part of the price reduction for imports in country *B* resulting from a devaluation is offset by devaluation-induced cost and price increases in country *A*.

In practice, a business executive exporting or sourcing from a country that has devalued its currency must evaluate his or her basic marketing and competitive position. If the competitive position is strong and demand is price inelastic, prices can be maintained in the target market. If this is not the case, it may be necessary to reduce prices in target markets.

Revaluation is an increase in the value of a currency vis-à-vis other currencies. The effect of revaluation on an exporter or a marketer sourcing in a revaluing country is the opposite of devaluation. Assume now that the currency of country *A* is revalued relative to country *B* and that the prices of country *A* export goods are held constant in the home currency. The weaker currency of country *B* does not go as far toward the purchase of imports denominated in the currency of country *A*. The international marketer must decide whether to (1) pass the price increase on to customers in country *B*, (2) absorb the price increase and reduce operating or marketing expenses in an effort to maintain profit levels, or (3) absorb the price increase by reducing prices for the product in country *A*. This is exactly the situation faced by many Japanese companies in the 1990s as the yen hits record highs against the Canadian and U.S. dollar.

In some instances, a slight revaluation has little effect upon export performance. Price increases are passed on to international customers by individual firms with no significant effect upon volume. In more competitive market situations, companies in the revaluing country will often absorb the price increase by maintaining international market prices at prerevaluation levels. In actual practice, a manufacturer and its distributor will work together to maintain market share in international markets. Either party, or both, may choose to take a lower profit percentage. The distributor may also choose to purchase more product to achieve volume discounts; another alternative is to maintain leaner inventories if the manufacturer can provide just-in-time delivery. By using these approaches, it is possible to remain price competitive in markets where revaluation is a price consideration.

▼ Government Controls and Subsidies

If government action limits the freedom of management to adjust prices, the maintenance of margins is definitely compromised. Under certain conditions, government action is a real threat to the profitability of a subsidiary operation. A country that is undergoing severe financial difficulties and is in the midst of a financial crisis (for example, a foreign exchange shortage caused in part by runaway inflation) is under pressure to take some type of action. This has been true in Brazil for many years. In some cases, governments will take expedient steps rather than getting at the underlying causes of inflation and foreign exchange shortages. Such steps might include the wholesale use of price controls or, more likely, selective use of price controls. When selective controls are imposed, foreign companies are more vulnerable to control than local businesses, particularly if the former lack the political influence over government decision making possessed by local managers.

Subsidies have been part of GATT negotiations since the first round in 1947, but it was not until the Uruguay round that specific rules were set up. The widespread use of subsidies in the agricultural sectors in Europe, Canada, and the U.S. affects export prices and the signatories agreed to reduce the expenditures on export subsidies by 36 percent by 1996.[14] This is an important competitive factor in Canada's agri-food sector which exports 22.5 percent of its $60 billion industry.[15] Canadian exporters of processed food, for example, will benefit from this change when competing in European markets.[16]

Government subsidies can also challenge a company to use sourcing strategically in order to be price competitive. A food processor can source its product, say, in France for customers in other European markets and thus benefit from the subsidies, elimination of tariffs and duties by producing within the European Union.

---

[14] GAO Report to Congress, *The General Agreement on Tariffs and Trade*, vol.2 (July 1994) pp.51–67.

[15] Government of Canada, *Canada and the Uruguay Round*, Sectoral Opportunities: Agriculture and Agri-food sectors (April 1994) pp.1–3.

[16] Ibid., p.10.

When subsidies exceed 5 percent of a company's or industry's output, competitors can plead trade distortion, which can lead to the imposition of countervailing duties. The civil aircraft sector, however, is excluded. Here the main competitors are European and American, but Canada also exports three-quarters of its C$5 billion industry.[17] Subsidies up to 1 percent cannot be contested with the positive implication for Canadian exporters that many subsidies will no longer attract U.S. countervail action.[18]

▼ Competitive Pressures

As noted at the beginning of this chapter, all pricing decisions are bounded not only by cost but also by demand and competitive action. Thus, another constraint on management's flexibility to maintain profit margins and profitability is the behavior of the competition. Canadian companies acknowledge that the foreign market environment is more competitive than the domestic one. While this environment includes factors such as competition, technology, or regulation, pricing clearly is an important issue. Four out of five exporters encounter competitive pressures in foreign markets relating to price and profits; on the other hand some 52 percent perceive a competitive advantage in this regard as Table 13–2 shows.[19]

While price is often a dominant concern, Canadian companies see the foreign market environment more broadly. Competitive pressures may result from direct or indirect price competition, non-price competition, or some combination of the two. When Champion Road Machinery competes in a developing country market, it faces price and non-price competition. John Deere roadgraders compete on price, while a combination of cheap and abundant manual labor and lesser equipment provide non-price and "close substitute" competition.

The price sensitivity of a product is an important factor: price sensitivity is low when products compete on unique attributes and the quality of after-sales service and customer care, as with geophysical exploration equipment. Price sensitivity is high in "me-too" products when there are close substitutes, such as in headache remedies, or when technology diffusion occurs rapidly as in the case of computer software.

▼ Market Demand

A final constraint on a manufacturer's ability to adjust prices is the market itself. A company should be alert to the effect of price adjustments upon demand for its products. The objective of a business is not merely to maintain any specific gross or operating margin but to survive and operate as profitably as possible. In some situations, a reduction in margins can lead to more profitable results than the maintenance of margins. Management should be alert to this possibility.

---

[17] Ibid., The Civil Aircraft Sector, p.1.

[18] Ibid., Highlights of the Uruguay Agreement, p.5.

[19] F.H. Rolf Seringhaus, "Export Knowledge and its Role in Strategy and Performance," *The Finnish Journal of Business Economics* (1991) 40:1, p.9.

TABLE 13–2   Competitive Threats and Opportunities in Foreign Markets

Percentage of Companies Perceiving:

Threats:		Opportunities:	
• price/profit pressures	86%	• product line expansion	72%
• large competitors	62	• improved productivity	71
• new technology	43	• export market growth	62
• maturing industry	43	• price/profit advantage	52
• declining markets	25	• expanded/new distribution channels	52

Source: Adapted from F.H. Rolf Seringhaus (1991), "Export Knowledge and its Role in Strategy and Performance," *The Finnish Journal of Business Economics,* Vol. 40, No. 1, p. 9.

TRANSFER PRICING

Transfer pricing is the pricing of goods and services exchanged in intracorporate purchase transactions. As companies expand and create decentralized operations, corporate profit centers have become an increasingly important component in the overall financial picture. A rational system of transfer pricing is required to ensure profitability at each level. Such a system was designed by the OECD in 1979 and is the basis for Canada's rules on international transfer pricing. Domestically, a decentralized profit center is a device for measuring and evaluating performance as well as motivating management of divisions or subsidiaries to achieve corporate goals. When a company extends its operations across national borders, new dimensions and complications are added to the transfer pricing problem.

When global companies determine transfer prices to subsidiaries, they must address a number of issues, including taxes, duties, and tariffs. The legal issues are discussed in Chapter 5. As noted earlier, several additional environmental factors must also be considered: market conditions, ability of potential customers to pay for a company's products, different profit transfer rules, conflicting objectives of joint venture partners, government regulations such as deposit requirements on imports, and so on.

The objective of the transfer pricing rules is to provide a framework to allow companies to report taxable income on the basis of having sold goods and services for a fair price. The complexity arises when one tries to establish the "fair price," when prices charged are either above or below it, and when transactions involve the transfer of technology, rights, patents, various services, and research and development.[20]

---

[20] *International Transfer Pricing and Other International Transactions,* Information Circular 87–2, Revenue Canada.

Recent examples of companies like Coca-Cola, Roche, and Ciba-Geigy, who were assessed for millions of dollars in Japan for using transfer pricing to reduce profits, underline the importance of abiding by transfer pricing rules.[21]

▼ Arm's Length Principle

Underlying the OECD and Canadian transfer pricing rules is the "arm's length principle." This means that a transaction would be seen as reasonable (under the Income Tax Act) when the price reflects fair market value and such a price would have been reached by unrelated parties in a similar transaction. Both OECD and Canadian rules accept that a fair market value price may be difficult to establish. This is the case when products are highly differentiated or unique, innovations may have no substitutes or competitive equals, and semi-finished products or components at various stages of the production process may be transferred. In addition, often combinations of products, components, and services are transferred between company units.

Companies need to clearly define and establish intercompany arrangements. In other words, they need to develop a comprehensive statement on intercompany pricing policy, which, based on a functional analysis of the activities and contributions of each group member, clarifies and quantifies how transfer prices are established. Clearly, factors such as technical assistance or access to technology, reward for economic risk and financing assistance are part of such an analysis.[22]

▼ Transfer Pricing Methods[23]

The Canadian rules specify three main methods of determining transfer prices for goods: comparable, uncontrolled price method; cost-plus method; and resale price method.

The comparable, uncontrolled price method establishes a price in the same market and in circumstances by parties dealing at arm's length. This is the case when a distributor sells identical goods to related and unrelated customers. Because the product, market, credit terms, and reliability of supply may not be identical, a price range would be more realistic than a single price.

The cost-plus method takes the position that costs must be computed with accounting principles and practices generally accepted in Canada. The determination of the transfer price depends on the inclusion of production costs, indirect overheads, and profit.

The resale price method is used when no comparables are available. The home market resale margin and equivalent allowances for marketing expenses (such as advertising) are deducted from the foreign market selling price to determine the transfer price.

---

[21] Samuel Slutsky, "Japan Strikes Back on Transfer Pricing," *The Financial Post*, May, 24, 1994, p. 18.

[22] Ibid, p.2, para 9–11.

[23] This section is based on *International Transfer Pricing and Other International Transactions*, Revenue Canada, Information Circular 87–2, para. 13–22.

The international marketplace, however, does not always fall into such tidy categories and other transfer pricing methods may be needed. Transfer at cost, for example, recognizes that sales by international affiliates contribute to corporate profitability by generating scale economies in domestic manufacturing operations. The expectation is that the affiliate will generate the profit by subsequent resale. The competitive international environment often requires third-country sourcing, particularly when the target market is too small for local manufacturing. Market-based transfer prices may enable a company to develop such a market without local production.

▼ Other Constraints on International Pricing

Company Controls and Information Systems

Transfer pricing to minimize tax liabilities can lead to unexpected and undesired distortions. This was demonstrated when a major American company with a decentralized, profit-centered organization promoted and gave frequent and substantial salary increases to its divisional manager in Switzerland. The reason for the manager's rapid rise was his outstanding profit record. His stellar numbers were picked up by the company's performance appraisal control system, which in turn triggered the salary and promotion actions. The problem in this company was that the financial control system had not been adjusted to recognize that a Swiss "tax haven" profit center had been created. The manager's sky-high "profits" were simply the result of artificially low transfer pricing into the tax haven operations and artificially high transfer pricing out of the Swiss tax haven to operating subsidiaries. It took a team of outside consultants to discover the situation. In this case the company's profit and loss records were a gross distortion of true operating results. The company had to adjust its control system and use different criteria to evaluate managerial performance in tax havens.

Duty and Tariff Constraints

Corporate costs and profits are also affected by the import duty rates. The higher the duty rate, the more desirable a lower transfer price. A country's customs duties and tax rates do not always create the same pressure on transfer prices. For example, a country with a high import duty and a low income tax rate creates pricing pressures that pull in opposite directions. The high duty creates an incentive to reduce transfer prices to minimize the customs duty. The low income tax rate, however, creates a pressure to raise the transfer price to locate income in the low-tax environment. As discussed in Chapter 16, duties in many industry sectors were substantially reduced or eliminated at the Uruguay Round of GATT negotiations.

Notwithstanding the importance of tax and duty considerations, many companies tend to downplay or not address the influence of taxes when developing pricing policies. There are a number of reasons for this. First, some companies consider tax savings to be trivial in comparison with the earnings that can be obtained by concentrating on effective systems of motivation and corporate resource allocation. Second, companies consider any effort at systematic tax minimization to be morally improper. Another argument is that a simple, consistent, and straightforward pricing policy minimizes the tax investigation problems that can develop if sharper pricing policies are pursued. According to this argument, the savings in executive time and the costs of outside counsel offset any additional taxes that might be paid using such an approach. Finally, after analyzing the worldwide trend toward harmonization of tax rates, many CFOs have concluded that any set of policies appropriate to a world characterized by wide differentials in tax rates will soon become obsolete. They have therefore concentrated on developing pricing policies that are appropriate for a world that is very rapidly evolving toward relatively similar tax rates.

Government Controls

As noted in the previous section on environmental influences on pricing, government controls can also affect transfer-pricing decisions. Some government controls directly affect market pricing in a country. The British Monopolies and Mergers Commission, for example, forced the Swiss-based F. Hoffman-La Roche & Company to reduce the price of Librium by 60 percent and Valium by 75 percent and to refund US$27.5 million for overcharging. In a nutshell, the government's case was based on the argument that the company was spending too much on research.

Government control can also take the form of cash deposit requirements imposed on importers. As discussed in Chapter 16, this is a requirement that a company has to tie up funds in the form of a non-interest-bearing deposit for a specified period of time if it wishes to import products. Such requirements clearly create an incentive for a company to minimize the price of the imported product; lower prices mean smaller deposits. Other government requirements that affect the pricing decision are profit-transfer rules that restrict the conditions under which profits can be transferred out of a country. Under such rules the transfer price paid for imported goods by an affiliated company can be interpreted as a device for transferring profits out of a country.

▼ Joint Ventures

Joint ventures present an incentive to set transfer prices at higher levels than would be used in sales to wholly owned affiliates because a company's share of the joint-venture earnings is less than 100 percent. Any profits that occur in the joint venture must be shared. The increasing frequency of tax authority audits is an important reason for working out an agreement that will also be acceptable to the tax authorities. The tax authorities' criterion of arm's-length prices is probably most appropriate for the majority of joint ventures.

To avoid potential conflict, it is important for companies with joint ventures to work out in advance a pricing agreement that is acceptable to both sides. The following are several considerations for joint-venture transfer pricing:[24]

---

[24] Timothy M. Collins and Thomas L. Doorley, *Teaming Up for the 90s: A Guide to International Joint Ventures and Strategic Alliances* (Homewood, IL: Business One Irwin, 1991), pp. 212–213.

1. The way in which transfer prices will be adjusted in response to exchange rate changes.

2. Expected reductions in manufacturing costs arising from learning-curve improvements and the way these will be reflected in transfer prices.

3. Possible increase or reduction of royalty rates as either party to the joint venture improves technology or acquires it from other sources.

4. Shifts in the sourcing of products or components from parents to alternative sources.

5. The effects of competition on volume and overall margins.

GLOBAL PRICING: THREE POLICY ALTERNATIVES

What pricing policy should a global company pursue? Viewed broadly, there are three alternative positions a company can take toward worldwide pricing.

▼ Extension/Ethnocentric

The first can be called an *extension/ethnocentric* pricing policy. This policy requires that the price of an item be the same around the world and that the importer absorb freight and import duties. This approach has the advantage of extreme simplicity because no information on competitive or market conditions is required for implementation. The disadvantage of this approach is directly tied to its simplicity. Extension pricing does not respond to the competitive and market conditions of each national market and, therefore, does not maximize the company's profits in each national market.

▼ Adaptation/Polycentric

The second pricing policy can be termed *adaptation/polycentric*. This policy permits subsidiary or affiliate managers to establish whatever price they feel is most desirable in their circumstances. Under such an approach, there is no control or fixed requirement that prices be coordinated from one country to the next. The only constraint on this approach is in setting transfer prices within the corporate system. Such an approach is sensitive to local conditions, but it does present problems of product arbitrage opportunities in cases where disparities in local market prices exceed the transportation and duty cost separating markets. When such a condition exists, there is an opportunity for the enterprising business manager to take advantage of these price disparities by buying in the lower-price market and selling in the more expensive market. There is also the problem that under such a policy, valuable knowledge and experience within the corporate system concerning effective pricing strategies is not applied to each local pricing problem. The strategies are not applied because the local managers are free to price in the way they feel is most desirable, and they may not be fully informed about company experience when they make their decision.

▼ Invention/Geocentric

The third approach to international pricing can be termed *invention/geocentric.* Using this approach, a company neither fixes a single price worldwide nor remains aloof from subsidiary pricing decisions, but instead strikes an intermediate position. A company pursuing this approach works on the assumption that there are unique local market factors that should be recognized in arriving at a pricing decision. These factors include local costs, income levels, competition, and the local marketing strategy. Local costs plus a return on invested capital and personnel fix the price floor for the long term. However, for the short term, a company might decide to pursue a market penetration objective and price at less than the cost-plus return figure using export sourcing to establish a market. Another short-term objective might be to estimate the size of a market at a price that would be profitable given local sourcing and a certain scale of output. Instead of building facilities, the target market might first be supplied from existing higher-cost external supply sources. If the price and product are accepted by the market, the company can then build a local manufacturing facility to further develop the identified market opportunity in a profitable way. If the market opportunity does not materialize, the company can experiment with the product at other prices because it is not committed by existing local manufacturing facilities to a fixed sales volume.

Selecting a price that recognizes local competition is essential. Many international market efforts have foundered on this point. A major American appliance manufacturer introduced its line of household appliances in West Germany. The exported appliances were priced by simply marking up every item in the product line by 28.5 percent. The result of this pricing method was a line that contained a mixture of underpriced and overpriced products. The overpriced products did not sell because better values were offered by local companies. The underpriced products sold very well, but they would have yielded greater profits at higher prices. What was needed was product line pricing, which took lower than normal margins in some products and higher margins in others to maximize the profitability of the full line.

For consumer products, local income levels are critical in the pricing decision. If the product is normally priced well above full manufacturing costs, the international marketer has the latitude to price below prevailing levels in higher-income markets and, as a result, reduce the gross margin on the product. While no business manager enjoys reducing margins, margins should be regarded as a guide to the ultimate objective, which is profitability. In some markets, income conditions may dictate that the maximum profitability will be obtained by sacrificing "normal" margins. *The important point here is that in global marketing there is no such thing as a "normal" margin.*

The final factor bearing on the price decision is the local marketing strategy and mix. Price must fit the other elements of the marketing program. For example, when it is decided to pursue a "pull" strategy that uses mass-media advertising and intensive distribution, the price selected must be consistent not only with income levels and competition but also with the costs and extensive advertising programs.

In addition to these local factors, the geocentric approach recognizes that headquarters price coordination is necessary in dealing with international accounts and product arbitrage. Finally, the geocentric approach consciously and systematically seeks to ensure that accumulated national pricing experience is leveraged and applied wherever relevant.

Of the three methods, only the geocentric approach lends itself to global competitive strategy. A global competitor will take into account global markets and global competitors in establishing prices. Prices will support global strategy objectives rather than the objective of maximizing performance in a single country.

▼ SUMMARY

Pricing decisions are a critical element of the marketing mix. The general rule of pricing is that over the long run, prices must exceed costs and prices may never exceed those of the competition. There is no absolute maximum price, but for any customer, price must correspond to the customer's perceived value of the product. The aim of most marketing strategies is to set a price that corresponds to the customer's perception of value in the product and at the same time does not leave money on the table, so to speak. In other words, the objective is to charge what a product is worth to the customer and to cover all costs and provide a margin for profit in the process.

International pricing is complicated by the fact that an international business must conform to different rule-making bodies and to different competitive situations in each country. Both the countries and the competition are constraints on pricing decisions. Each company must examine the market, the competition, its own costs and objectives, and local and regional regulations and laws in setting prices that are consistent with the overall marketing strategy.

▼ DISCUSSION QUESTIONS

1. What are the three basic factors affecting price in any market? What considerations enter into the pricing decision?

2. What is *dumping*? Why was dumping such an important issue during the Uruguay Round of GATT negotiations?

3. What is the transfer price? What is the difference, if any, between a transfer price and a "regular" price? What are three methods for determining transfer prices?

4. What are the three alternative approaches to global pricing? Which one would you rec-

ommend to a company that has global market aspirations?

5. If you were responsible for marketing CAT scanners worldwide (average price, C$1.5 million) and the country of manufacture was experiencing a strong and appreciating currency against almost all other currencies, would you adjust your prices to take into account the strong currency situation? Why? Why not?

▼ BIBLIOGRAPHY

Books

ABDALLAH, WAGDY M., *International Transfer Pricing Policies: Decision Making Guidelines For Multinational Companies*. New York: Quorum Books, 1989.

DOORLEY, THOMAS L. III, AND TIMOTHY M. COLLINS, *Teaming Up for the '90s: A Guide to International Joint Ventures and Strategic Alliances*. New York: Business One Irwin, 1991.

NAGLE, THOMAS T., *The Strategy and Tactics of Pricing: A Guide to Profitable Decision Making*. Englewood Cliffs, NJ: Prentice-Hall, 1987.

ROBERT, MICHEL, *Strategy Pure and Simple: How Winning CEOs Outthink Their Competition*. New York: McGraw-Hill, 1993.

SEYMOUR, DANIEL T., *The Pricing Decision*. Chicago: Probus Publishing Co., 1989.

Articles

CANNON, HUGH M., AND FRED W. MORGAN, "A Strategic Pricing Framework," *Journal of Business and Industrial Marketing*, 6, no. 3,4 (Summer/Fall 1991), 59–70.

COHEN, STEPHEN S., AND JOHN ZYSMAN, "Countertrade, Offsets, Barter and Buyouts," *California Management Review*, 28, no. 2, 41–55.

GERSTNER, EITAN, "Do Higher Prices Signal Higher Quality," *Journal of Marketing Research*, 22 (May 1985), 209–215.

GLICKLICH, PETER A., AND SETH B. GOLDSTEIN, "New Transfer Pricing Regulations Adhere More Closely to an Arm's-Length Standard," *Journal of Taxation*, 78, no. 5 (May 1993), 306–314.

KEEGAN, WARREN J., "How Far Is Arm's Length?" *Columbia Journal of World Business* (May/June 1969), 57–66.

LANCIONI, RICHARD, AND JOHN GATTORNA, "Strategic Value Pricing: Its Role In International Business," *International Journal of Physical Distribution and Logistics*, 22, no. 6, 24–27.

MARN, MICHAEL V., AND ROBERT L. ROSIELLO, "Managing Price, Gaining Profit," *Harvard Business Review*, 70, no. 5 (September/October 1992), 84–94.

SCHUSTER, FALKO, "Barter Arrangements with Money: The Modern Form of Compensation Trading," *Columbia Journal of World Business* (Fall 1980), 61–66.

SEIFERT, BRUCE, AND JOHN FORD, "Are Exporting Firms Modifying Their Product, Pricing and Promotion Policies?" *International Marketing Review*, 6, no. 6, 53–68.

SIMON, HERMANN, "Pricing Opportunities—And How to Exploit Them," *Sloan Management Review*, 33, no. 2 (Winter 1992), 55–65.

———, AND MARTIN FASSNACHT, "Price Bundling," Johannes Gutenberg-University, Mainz, Working Papers January 1992.

SINCLAIR, STUART, "A Guide to Global Pricing," *Journal of Business Strategy*, 14, no. 3, 16–19.

WILLIAMS, JEFFREY R., "How Sustainable Is Your Competitive Advantage?" *California Management Review*, 34, no. 3 (Spring 1992), 29–51.

FOURTEEN

Channel
Decisions

Introduction

Channel of distribution is "an organized network of agencies and institutions which, in combination, perform all the activities required to link producers with users to accomplish the marketing task."[1] Distribution is the physical flow of goods through channels; as suggested by the definition, channels are composed of a coordinated group of individuals or firms that perform functions adding utility to a product or service. The major types of channel utility are *place* (the availability of a product or service in a location that is convenient to a potential customer); *time* (the availability of a product or service when desired by a customer); *form* (the product is processed, prepared and ready to use, and in proper condition); and *information* (answers to questions and general communication about useful product features and benefits are available). Since these utilities can be a basic source of competitive advantage and product value, choosing a channel strategy is one of the key policy decisions marketing management must make.

Distribution channels in markets around the world are among the most highly differentiated aspects of national marketing systems. For this reason, channel strategy is one of the most challenging and difficult components of an international marketing program. Smaller companies are often blocked by their inability to establish effective channel arrangements. In larger multinational companies operating via country subsidiaries, channel strategy is the element of the marketing mix that headquarters understands the least. To a large extent, channels are an aspect of the marketing program that is locally led through the discretion of the in-country marketing management group. Nevertheless, it is important for managers responsible for world marketing programs to understand the nature of international distribution channels. Distribution is an integral part of the total marketing program and must be appropriate to the product design, price, and communications aspects of the total marketing program. Another important reason for placing channel decisions on the agenda of international marketing managers is the number and nature of relationships that must be managed. Channel decisions typically involve long-term legal commitments and obligations to other firms and individuals. Such commitments are often extremely expensive to terminate or change. Even in

---

[1] Peter D. Bennett, *Dictionary of Marketing Terms* (Chicago: American Marketing Association, 1988), p. 29.

cases where there is no legal obligation, commitments may be backed by good faith and feelings of obligation, which are equally difficult to manage and painful to adjust.

From the viewpoint of the marketer concerned with a single-country program, international channel arrangements are a valuable source of information and insight into possible new approaches for more effective channel strategies. For example, self-service discount pricing in North America was studied by retailers from Europe and Asia who then introduced the self-service concept in their own countries. Governments and business executives all over the world have examined Japanese trading companies with great interest to learn from their success. This chapter will examine international channel systems by focusing on (1) what the global marketer should know about channels in order to contribute to channel planning and control and (2) what the marketer concerned with a single country should know to exploit channel innovations that have been tried in other countries.

CHANNEL OBJECTIVES AND CONSTRAINTS

The starting point in selecting the most effective channel arrangement is a clear determination of the market target for the company's marketing effort and a determination of the needs and preferences of the target market. Where are the potential customers located? What are their information requirements? What are their preferences for service? How sensitive are they to price? Customer preference must be carefully determined because there is as much danger to the success of a marketing program in creating too much utility as there is in creating too little. Moreover, each market must be analyzed to determine the cost of providing channel services. What is appropriate in one country may not be effective in another.

This has been the experience of Nora Beverages Inc. of Mirabel, Quebec, whose Naya brand of bottled water has been expanding—since the company's founding in 1986—at twice the annual growth rate of 15–20 percent of the North American bottled water market. The company exports sixty percent of its production to the U.S. "Distribution" says George Gaucher, Vice President, Sales and Marketing "is the fundamental basis for success in the beverage industry...if you select the wrong distributor, you risk killing your brand in that market."[2]

Typical distribution channels for branded bottled water are grocery brokers and warehouses, who sell to supermarket chains. Nora Beverages chose to use direct store distributors who take the product directly into the stores, price it and stock the shelves. This assures greater attention to the brand where it counts: on the shelves. Such careful attention to distribution has helped Naya to reach a 10 percent market share in the American imported premium spring water market.[3]

---

[2] Michael Slater, "Riding the Wave," *Report on Business Magazine* (April 1993) p.67.
[3] Ibid., p.67.

Channel strategy in a global marketing program must fit the company's competitive position and overall marketing objectives in each national market. If a company wants to enter a competitive market, it has two basic choices. One option is providing incentives to independent channel agents that will induce them to promote the company's product. Alternatively, the company must establish company-owned or franchised outlets. The process of shaping international channels to fit overall company objectives is constrained by four factors: customers, products, intermediaries, and the environment. Important characteristics of each of these factors will be discussed briefly.

▼ Customer Characteristics

The characteristics of customers are an important influence on channel design. Their number, geographical distribution, income, shopping habits, and reaction to different selling methods all vary from country to country and therefore require different channel approaches. Remember, channels create utility for customers.

In general, regardless of the stage of market development, the need for multiple channel intermediaries increases as the number of customers increases. The converse is also true: The need for channel intermediaries decreases as the number of customers decreases. For example, if there are only ten customers for an industrial product in each national market, these ten customers must be directly contacted by either the manufacturer or an agent. For mass-market products bought by millions of customers, retail distribution outlets or mail-order distribution is required. In a country with a large number of low-volume retailers, it is usually cheaper to reach them via wholesalers. Direct selling that bypasses wholesale intermediaries may be the most cost-effective means of serving large-volume retailers. While these generalizations apply to all countries, regardless of stage of development, individual country customs will vary. For example, Toys "R" Us faced considerable opposition from Japanese toy manufacturers who refused to engage in direct selling after the American company built its first stores in Japan.

▼ Product Characteristics

Certain product attributes such as degree of standardization, perishability, bulk, service requirements, and unit price have an important influence on channel design and strategy. Products with high unit price, for example, are often sold through a direct company sales force because the selling cost of this "expensive" distribution method is a small part of the total sale price. Moreover, the high cost of such products is usually associated with complexity or with product features that must be explained in some detail, and this can be done most effectively by a controlled sales force. For example, computers are expensive, complicated products that require both explanation and applications analysis focused on the customer's needs. A company-trained salesperson or "sales engineer" is well suited for the task of creating information utility for computer buyers.

Computers, photocopiers, and other industrial products may require margins to cover the costs of expensive sales engineering. Other products require margins to provide a large monetary incentive to a direct sales force. In many parts of the world, cosmetics are sold door to door; company representatives call on potential customers. The reps must create in the customer an awareness of the value of cosmetics and evoke a feeling of need for this value that leads to a sale. The sales activity must be paid for. Companies using direct distribution for their products to the end consumer rely upon wide gross selling margins to generate the revenue necessary to compensate salespeople. Two American companies, Amway and Avon, have succeeded in extending their direct-sales systems to overseas markets.

Perishable products impose special form utility demands on channel members. Such products usually need relatively direct channels to ensure satisfactory condition at the time of customer purchase. In less developed countries, producers of vegetables, bread, and other food products typically sell their goods in public marketplaces. In developed countries, perishable food products are distributed by controlled sales forces, and stock is checked by these sales distributor organizations to ensure that it is fresh and ready for purchase.

In 1991, Andersen Consulting assisted the Moscow Bread Company in improving its ability to distribute bread in the Russian capital. For Russians, bread is truly the "staff of life," with consumers queuing up daily to buy fresh loaves at numerous shops and kiosks. Unfortunately, distribution was often hampered by excessive paperwork that resulted in the delivery of stale bread; Andersen found that as much as one-third of the bread produced was wasted. The consulting team arrived at a simple solution: plastic bags to keep the bread fresh. The team found that, although 95 percent of food is packaged in developed countries, the figure was only 2 percent in the former Soviet Union, where open-air markets are the norm. Russian consumers responded favorably to the change; not only did the bags guarantee freshness and extend the shelf life of the bread by 600 percent, the bags themselves created utility. In a country where such extras are virtually unknown, the bags constituted a reusable "gift."[4]

Bulky products usually require channel arrangements that minimize the shipping distances and the number of times products change hands between channel intermediaries before they reach the ultimate customer. Soft drinks and beer are examples of bulky products whose widespread availability is an important aspect of an effective marketing strategy.

▼ Intermediary Characteristics

Channel strategy must recognize the characteristics of existing intermediaries. Intermediaries are in business to maximize their own profit and not that of the manufacturer. They are notorious for "cherry picking," that is, the practice of taking orders from manufacturers whose products and brands are in demand to avoid any real selling effort for a manufacturer's products that may require "push." This is a rational response by the intermediary, but it can present a

---

[4] "Case Study: Moscow Bread Company," Andersen Consulting, 1993.

serious obstacle to the manufacturer attempting to break into a market with a new product. The "cherry picker" is not interested in building a market for a new product. This is a problem for the expanding international company. Frequently, a manufacturer with a new product or a product with a limited market share is forced to set up some arrangement for bypassing the "cherry-picking" segment of the channel. In some cases manufacturers will set up an expensive direct-distribution organization to obtain a share of the market. When they finally obtain a share of the target market, they may abandon the direct-distribution system for a more cost-effective intermediary system. The move does not mean that intermediaries are "better" than direct distribution. It is simply a response by a manufacturer to the newly acquired attractiveness of his or her product to independent distributors.

An alternative method of dealing with the "cherry-picking" problem does not require setting up an expensive direct sales force. Rather, a company may decide to rely on a distributor's own sales force by subsidizing the cost of the sales representatives the distributor has assigned to the company's products. This approach has the advantage of holding down costs by tying missionary and support selling in with the distributor's existing sales-management team and physical distribution system. With this approach it is possible to place managed direct-selling support and distribution support behind a product at the expense of only one salesperson per selling area. The distributor's incentive for cooperating in this kind of arrangement is that he or she obtains a "free" sales representative for a new product with the potential to be a profitable addition to his or her line. This cooperative arrangement is ideally suited to getting a new export-sourced product into distribution in a market.

Selection and Care of
Distributors and Agents

The selection of distributors and agents in a target market is a critically important task. A good commission agent or stocking distributor can make the difference between realizing zero performance and performance that exceeds 200 percent of what is expected. At any point in time, some of any company's agents and distributors will be excellent, others will be satisfactory, and still others will be unsatisfactory and in need of replacement.

To find a good distributor, a firm can begin with a list provided by the foreign country desk of the Department of Foreign Affairs and International Trade or its equivalent in other countries. Bilateral Chambers of Commerce or local chanbers in a country can also provide lists, as can local trade associations. It is a waste of time to try to screen the list by mail. Go to the country and talk to end users of the products you are selling and find out which distributors they prefer and why they prefer them. If the product is a consumer product, go to the retail outlets and find out where consumers are buying products similar to your own and why. Two or three names will keep coming up. Go to these two or three and see which of them would be available to sign. Before signing, make sure there is someone in the organization who will be the key person for your product who will make it a personal objective to achieve success with your product.

This is the critical difference between the successful distributor and the worthless distributor. There must be a personal, individual commitment to the product. The second and related requirement for successful distributors or agents is that they must be successful with the product. Success means that they can sell the product and make money on it. In any case, the product must be designed and priced to be competitive in the target market. The distributor can assist in this process by providing information about customer wants and the competition and by promoting the product he or she represents.

For Canadian companies, the proximity and familiarity of the U.S. market may suggest a simple extension of distribution practices followed at home. As we saw from the example of Nora Beverages Inc., this may be the wrong conclusion. Great care is needed to research and enter into distribution arrangements whether they are overseas or in the U.S. The choice of indirect sales agent—the three main types are agent, distributor, or broker—depends on the company's needs.

For example, an agent or manufacturer's representative can provide market intelligence, may contract with customers and handle payments, or may be used to find and maintain distributors. A distributor, on the other hand, stocks inventory and resells and ᵇutes to customers in his/her region and thereby exercises considerabl℮ ʳr part of the marketing process. A broker pursues individual sᵃˡ ℮ manufacturer and usually represents several suppliers. Tⁱ ·ʸ sensitive to price and conditions that can be offered to · ·

company can expect from any of these three types of in-ᶜ ˢ influenced by the size of margin or commission, the specific maⁱ ᵢbilities agreed to, and the working relationship between the two paᵗ.

The ᵤ ⱼ way to keep a good distributor is to work closely with him or her to ensure that he or she is making money on the product. Any distributor who does not make money on a line will drop it. It is really quite simple. In general, if a distributor is not working out, it is wise to terminate the agreement and find another one. Few companies are large enough to convert a mediocre distributor or agent into an effective business representative. Therefore, the most important clause in the distributor contract is the cancellation clause. Make sure it is written in a way that will make it easy to terminate the agreement. It is not always easy to terminate agreements entered into with channels. This, and the fact that longer term relationships are sought by both partners, are typical reasons why distribution channels are not as pliable and changeable as other components of the global marketing mix. In some countries of Latin America, or the European Union, parting company with a distributor or agent can be difficult and costly because compensation for forgone future profits may have to be paid.[6] The implication is that the manufacturer may have to tolerate poor performance on part of a distributor. However, some successful global marketers have terminated distributors or agents that fail to perform. The key factor is performance: a poorly performing distributor must either shape up or be replaced.

---

[5] *Selecting and Using Manufacturer's Agents in the United States* (Ottawa, Department of External Affairs, undated) p.7.

[6] Phillip J. Rosson, "Success Factors in Manufacturer-Overseas Distributor Relationships in International Marketing," *International Marketing Management*, Erdener Kaynak, Ed. (New York: Praeger Publishers, 1984) pp.91–107.

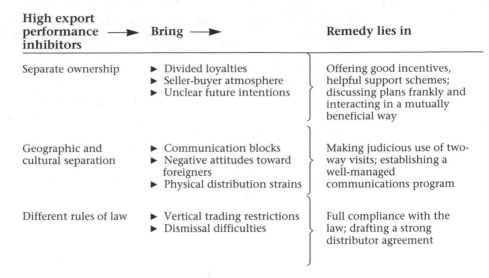

High export performance inhibitors →	Bring →	Remedy lies in
Separate ownership	▶ Divided loyalties ▶ Seller-buyer atmosphere ▶ Unclear future intentions	Offering good incentives, helpful support schemes; discussing plans frankly and interacting in a mutually beneficial way
Geographic and cultural separation	▶ Communication blocks ▶ Negative attitudes toward foreigners ▶ Physical distribution strains	Making judicious use of two-way visits; establishing a well-managed communications program
Different rules of law	▶ Vertical trading restrictions ▶ Dismissal difficulties	Full compliance with the law; drafting a strong distributor agreement

FIGURE 14-1:

Performance Problems and RemediesWhen Using Overseas Distributors

Source: Philip J. Rosson, "Success Factors in Manufacturer-Overseas Distributor Relationships in Third World Markets", *International Marketing Management*, Erdener Kaynak, Ed. (New York: Praeger Publishers, 1984); with permission.

The emphasis is on the relationship between a Canadian company and its foreign distribution channels because it is an important one. Rosson reports on three dimensions of such relationship: commitment, adaptability, and disagreements. Successful manufacturer-distributor relationships were characterized by more intense contact and exchange of resources, more joint decision-making, and consequently fewer disagreements.[7] Because we know that channels of distribution are a social/behavioral system, often the remedies to obtaining high performance are also behavioral.[8] Figure 14-1 shows how management can overcome channel-based inhibitors to high export performance.

▼ Environmental Characteristics

The general characteristics of the total environment are a major consideration in channel design. Because of the enormous variety of economic, social, and political environments internationally, there is a need to delegate a large degree of independence to local operating managements or agents. A comparison of food distribution in countries at different stages of development illustrates how channels reflect and respond to underlying market conditions in a country. In Canada, several factors combine to make the supermarket or the self-service

---

[7] Ibid., p.104.

[8] Louis W. Stern and Jay W.Brown, "Distribution Channels: A Social Systems Approach," *Distribution Channels: Behavioural Dimensions*, Louis W. Stern, Ed. (Boston: Houghton Mifflin Company, 1969) pp.6–19.

one-stop food store the basic food retailing unit. These factors include high incomes, large-capacity refrigerators with large freezer units, automobile ownership, acceptance of frozen and convenience foods, and attitudes toward food preparation. Many shoppers want to purchase a week's worth of groceries in one trip to the store. They have the money, ample storage space in the refrigerator, and the hauling capacity of the car to move this large quantity of food from the store to the home. The supermarket, because it is efficient, can fill the food shoppers' needs at lower prices than are found in butcher shops and other traditional full-service food stores. Additionally, supermarkets can offer more variety and a greater selection of merchandise than can smaller food stores, a fact that appeals to affluent consumers.

The 1970s saw a severe drop in grocery outlet density in nearly all countries. The trend continues even in countries with a low density of stores already. For example, in Canada and the United States, thousands of stores have disappeared in the past several years. Industry observers expect this trend of fewer grocery stores to continue in the future at varying rates in different countries.

CHANNEL STRUCTURE

mail order → time ↑ from consumer persp.

▼ Consumer Products

Figure 14–2 summarizes channel structure alternatives for consumer products. A consumer products manufacturer can sell to customers directly (using a door-to-door sales force), through mail-order selling (using a catalog or other printed materials), or through manufacturer-owned stores. Of the three direct alternatives, the mail-order business is the most widely used. Some observers predict the importance of direct-mail distribution will grow considerably in the next few years because time, one of the most valuable resources, has become increasingly scarce. As consumers trade off the time cost of in-store shopping against the time demands of leisure activity, they are increasingly attracted to the time and place utility created by direct-mail marketing.

Door-to-door selling is a relatively expensive form of distribution that, as noted earlier, requires high gross margins and results in higher prices to the customer. Certain items such as encyclopedias, household brushes, vacuum cleaners, and cosmetics continue to be sold in this manner. Door-to-door selling, however, is growing in popularity in foreign markets. For example, Avon has successfully used this approach in more than 50 countries identified by company executives as having weak retail infrastructures. Also, they recognized that low levels of discretionary income translate into low levels of expenditures on cosmetics and toiletries. Thus, the role of the sales force is to communicate the benefits of cosmetics and build demand. In such countries as China, Hungary, the Czech Republic, and Russia, home direct selling is the perfect channel strategy. In fact, Avon became the first company permitted to sell door to door in China. Since 1990, Avon has operated a joint venture with Guangzhou Cosmetics Factory in the province of Old Canton.

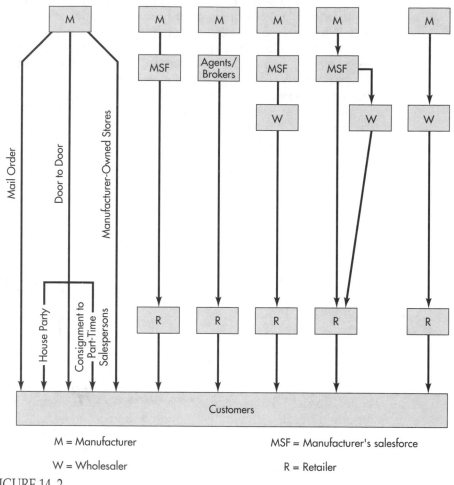

M = Manufacturer MSF = Manufacturer's salesforce

W = Wholesaler R = Retailer

FIGURE 14–2
Marketing Channel Alternatives—Consumer Products

A variation on the door-to-door selling method is the *house-party* selling arrangement where a representative of a manufacturer arranges an informal, semisocial gathering in the home of a cooperating consumer in order to describe and demonstrate the goods he or she is selling. This form of selling has been particularly effective for manufacturers of cosmetics and kitchenware. Although the house-party method originated in the United States, its viability has also been demonstrated in Europe and Asia.

Another variant of the door-to-door selling method, which has achieved some success in Europe, is the consignment sale of merchandise to part-time salespeople who take orders for the company's product from a circle of acquaintances and friends. A French company established a major market position in the liquid household cleaner market in France by using this distribution method.

A third direct-selling alternative is the *manufacturer-owned store*. As noted in Chapter 11, this approach is widely used in Japan in the consumer electronics industry. In other instances, companies choose instead to establish one or two retail outlets for obtaining marketing intelligence rather than as a distribution strategy. In those areas where a manufacturer's product line is sufficient to support a viable retail outlet, the possibilities for this form of distribution are much more attractive. The shoe store, for example, is a viable retail unit, and shoe manufacturers typically have established their own direct outlets as a major element in their distribution strategy, both at home and in important world markets. Singer, one of the first successful international companies, established a worldwide chain of company-owned and operated outlets to sell and service sewing machines.

The other channel structure alternatives for consumer products are various combinations of a manufacturer's sales force and wholesalers calling upon retail outlets, which in turn sell to customers. In a given country at a particular point in time, various product classes will have characteristic distribution patterns associated with them. In Japan, for example, several layers of small wholesalers play an important role in the distribution of food. Attempts to bypass these apparently unnecessary units in the channel have failed because the cost to a manufacturer of providing their service (frequent small deliveries to small grocery outlets) is greater than the margin they require. Channel patterns that appear to be inefficient may reflect rational adjustment to costs and preferences in a market, or they may present an opportunity to the innovative global marketer to obtain competitive advantage by introducing more effective channel arrangements.

▼ Global Retailing

The global retailing environment is highly diversified. For example, in Santiago, Chile, you can buy almost anything from hundreds of uniquely Latin-American street kiosks selling goods inexpensively throughout the city, while at the high fashion Alta Las Condes shopping centre with its *hypermarche* and countless global brand stores, the range and types of goods sold rivals the best European retail environment.

Global retail channels of distribution can be viewed as any retailing activity that spans national boundaries. For centuries venturesome merchants have gone abroad to obtain goods and ideas and to operate retail establishments. The spread of foreign-owned jewelry shops in New York City led *The New Yorker*, in 1929, to speak of "the invasion of Rue de la Paix houses."[9]

The development of trading company operations in Africa and Asia by British, French, Dutch, Belgian, and German retailing organizations progressed extensively during the nineteenth and early twentieth centuries. International trading and retail store operation were two of the economic pillars of the colonial era. The big change taking place in international retailing today involves the gradual dissolution of the colonial retailing structure and, in its place, the creation of global retailing organizations operating in industrialized and developing countries.

---

[9] "On and Off the Avenue," *The New Yorker* (November 23, 1929); quoted in Stanley C. Hollander, "The International Storekeepers," *MSU Business Topics* (Spring 1969).

Examples abound of retailers who have expanded their operations internationally and have become become multinational companies: Bally (footwear), Benetton (leisure clothing), Carrefour (food), Ikea (furniture), Armani (fashion), Laura Ashley (clothing, fabrics), and Toys "R" Us (toys), to name a few.[10]

Hypermarches, discount stores, supermarkets, price club stores, and convenience stores are retailing concepts that can be found in different countries under different names and definitions. *Hypermarches* and superstores, retailing concepts most successful in France where they account for 31 percent of all retail business, contrast sharply with the Italians' preference for small "dedicated" stores, such as a bakery or variety food store. In Italy, less than 2 percent of retail sales is handled by large stores.[11] The development of large superstores is progressing slowly in Italy, on account of worker-protective legislation, and in Japan where small retailers are gradually losing the protection of the "Large Scale Retail Store Law."[12] The structure of the retail industry has undergone great change with large stores gaining dominance. The volume buying power of large retail chains is another factor that has reduced the number of independent retailers in countries like Germany and the U.K.[13]

The diversity of the European retail channels of distribution is evident from Table 14–1. Compared to the Canadian retail store density of 195 people per outlet, the European countries range from a high of 172 in Germany to a low of 42 in Spain. However, the high density of retail outlet in countries like Spain and Italy reflects the many thousands of mobile market stalls, which vendors move throughout a region on a regular pattern of town market days. Similar to the stationary product-diversified kiosks in Santiago, the market stalls offer a large selection of goods.

The economic expansion in Asia has spurred global retailers into the region: Makro, a Dutch superstore is in Malaysia; 7-Eleven in Thailand; Singapore's high class shopping area Orchard Road has Toys "R" Us from the U.S., Galeries Lafayette from France, Marks and Spencer from Britain, and Takashimaya from Japan.[14]

Unsuccessful international retailing ventures, such as Canadian Tire, and Mark's Work Wearhouse in the U.S., and tough competition from local retailers, such as Hong Kong's Giordano, exploiting the market for less expensive casual clothing, suggest that anyone contemplating entry into international retailing should do so with a great deal of caution.[15]

On the other hand, potential advantages do exist. Basically, a retailer has two things to offer consumers. One is the selection of goods at a price, and the second is the overall manner in which the goods are offered in the store setting. This includes such things as the store site, parking facilities, in-store setting, and customer service. Some large American retailers are expanding retailing operations internationally for both reasons. Marketing sophistication, in terms

---

[10] Susan Segal-Horn and Heather Davison, "Global Markets: The Global Consumer and International Retailing," *Journal of Global Marketing* (1992) 5:3, pp.31–62.

[11] European Marketing Data and Statistics 1994, *Euromonitor*, Tables 1203, 1210.

[12] "Japanese Distribution: Too Many Shopkeepers," *The Economist* (January 28, 1989) p.71.

[13] "Retailing in Europe," D.E. Visuals, Sunrise, Fl., p.2.

[14] "Asian Retailing - Teach me Shopping," *The Economist* (December 18, 1993) p.64.

[15] Ibid, p.64.

TABLE 14–1   The West European Retail Market, 1990

	Population (millions)	# Retail Outlets ('000)	# People per Outlet	$ Sales per capita (C$)	# Retail Employees per Outlet
Austria	7.9	39.6	199	4474	6.4
Germany	62.0	359.5	172	6492	7.5
UK	57.2	334.6	171	4690	6.7
Switzerland	6.6	45.0	147	9081	7.6
Iceland	0.3	1.8	141	5016	4.4
Finland	5.0	39.7	126	7054	3.9
Denmark	5.1	42.0	121	5617	4.7
Sweden	8.5	71.9	118	6982	3.5
Luxembourg	0.4	3.3	114	6800	5.0
Ireland	3.5	31.7	110	4396	2.8
France	56.2	518.7	108	6277	2.3
Norway	4.2	38.8	108	5680	3.2
Netherlands	15.2	163.4	93	5332	n.a.
Belgium	10.0	113.0	88	6034	1.5
Portugal	9.8	117.3	83	1760	2.0
Greece	9.9	156.6	63	3315	1.9
Italy	57.7	1052.5	55	7222	n.a.
Spain	38.8	906.8	42	4130	n.a.
Canada	26.2	134.5	195	9920	9.4

Source: Based on data from *World Bank Report 1994; 1991; European Marketing Data and Statistics 1994*, 29th Edition (London: *Euromonitor*, (1994); *International Marketing Data and Statistics 1994*, 18th Edition (London, *Euromonitor.*, 1994).

of displaying products, locating aisles to optimize customer traffic, grouping products, and generally developing an environment that invites the consumer to shop, are all part of successful differentiation in global retailing.[16]

▼ Industrial Products

Figure 14–3 summarizes marketing channel alternatives for the industrial product company. Three basic elements are involved: the manufacturer's sales force, distributors or agents, and wholesalers. A manufacturer can reach customers with its own sales force, or a sales force that calls on wholesalers who sell to customers, or a combination of these two arrangements. A manufacturer can sell directly to wholesalers without using a sales force, and wholesalers in turn can supply customers. Finally, a distributor or agent can call on wholesalers or customers for a manufacturer.

Patterns vary from country to country. Before deciding which pattern to use and which wholesalers and agents to select, managers must study each country individually. In general, the larger the market, the more feasible it is for a manufacturer to use its own sales force. Kyocera Corporation of Kyoto, Japan has

---

[16] Bob Ortega, "Foreign Forays: Penney Pushes Abroad in Unusually Big Way as it Pursues Growth," *The Wall Street Journal*, February 1, 1994, pp.A1, A7.

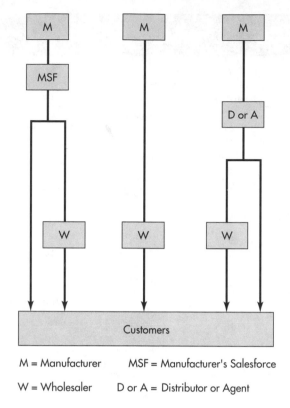

M = Manufacturer   MSF = Manufacturer's Salesforce

W = Wholesaler   D or A = Distributor or Agent

FIGURE 14–3
Marketing Channel Alternatives—Industrial Products

successfully used its own sales force at home and in North America to achieve leadership in the $1.6 billion global market for ceramic microchip covers. This represents a unique strategy in the electronics industry, where reliance on distributors is the norm. However, company founder Kazuo Inamori wants to make sure the spiritual drive of Kyocera's unique corporate culture extends to all parts of the company, including the sales force.

CHANNELS IN LESS DEVELOPED COUNTRIES

Several conspicuous features of channels in less developed countries are the remarkable labor intensity—the large number of people—involved in the selling of very small quantities of merchandise, the large number of intermediaries, and the length of channels.[17] In developing countries, distribution channels are closely linked to economic development and the channel features found in such countries can slow the development process. Figure 14–4 summarizes the channel structure and its consequences for economic development.

---

[17] An excellent discussion of distribution channels in developing countries is found in Erdener Kaynak, *Marketing in the Third World* (New York, Praeger Publishers, 1982).

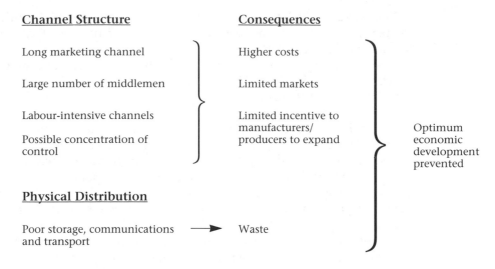

Channel Structure

Long marketing channel

Large number of middlemen

Labour-intensive channels

Possible concentration of control

Physical Distribution

Poor storage, communications and transport ⟶ Waste

Consequences

Higher costs

Limited markets

Limited incentive to manufacturers/producers to expand

Optimum economic development prevented

FIGURE 14–4

Typical Channel Structure in Developing Countries

Source: Joanna Kinsey, *Marketing in Developing Countries* (Houndsmills: Macmillan Education Ltd., 1988) Figure 5–1 with permission of Joanna Kinsey and Macmillan Press Ltd.

The number and variety of channel intermediaries have been criticized by official and unofficial observers. B. P. Bauer comments on these criticisms as follows:

> These criticisms rest on a misunderstanding. The system (in LDCs) is a logical adaptation to certain fundamental factors in the West African economies which will persist for many years to come. So far from being wasteful, it is highly economic in saving and salvaging those resources which are particularly scarce in West Africa (above all, real capital) by using the resources which are largely redundant and for which there is very little demand: and thus it is productive by any rational economic criteria.[18]

Another way of looking at the channel arrangements in less developed countries is to examine the costs of these arrangements to consumers. A study of East Africa revealed that the small *dukas* (small stores typically carrying under 100 items and occupying no more than 5 to 8 square meters of space) indicated that they were operating on average gross margins of approximately 12 percent. This figure seems low when compared with the average gross margin in the typical Canadian supermarket of roughly 22 percent. Clearly, by the measure of markup, the small East African *duka* is a lower-cost form of retail distribution.

Since these *dukas* operate at lower costs, does it mean that they are more efficient than supermarkets? One measure of efficiency is the ratio of productivity or output per worker-hour. In retailing, the measure of productivity is the physical volume or monetary volume of sales per person. By either measure, the East

---

[18] B. P. Bauer, *West African Trade* (Cambridge: Cambridge University Press), p. 22.

African *duka* is a highly inefficient form of distribution compared with a Canadian supermarket. The sales per person in the *duka* are a fraction of sales per person in a Canadian supermarket. *Duka* prices and margins are lower because the total income or salary of the *duka* operator is a fraction of that of even the lowest-level employee of a large North American supermarket. By using overabundant resources that are in surplus (labor), the *duka* employs resources that would otherwise be unemployed.

In the early 1960s the Tanganyika government decided that it would contribute to the general welfare of the nation by opening government-managed supermarkets or food distribution outlets that would compete with the small *duka*. At the time, the government and some of the population mistakenly believed *duka* operators were overcharging the public. The government, after establishing its own food distribution outlets, discovered that it was impossible to compete on price with the *dukas*. It turned out that the operators of the *dukas*, or *dukawallas* as they are known, were earning modest incomes and that, in terms of cost to the consumer, the private retail system of East Africa was a lower-cost arrangement than the government-run stores. The main reason for this was that the *dukawalla* was willing to work from dawn to dusk for the same or less return than the government employee who worked from 9:00 a.m. to 5:00 p.m. with two hours off for lunch.

INTERNATIONAL CHANNEL INNOVATION

As noted at the beginning of this chapter, the nature of channels in markets around the world is highly differentiated. At first glance it appears this differentiation can only be explained in terms of culture and the income level that exists in the market. However, four postulates have been formulated to explain the incidence and rate of innovation in retail channels. These can be used to explain international channel differentiation:

1. Innovation takes place only in the most highly developed systems. In general, channel agents in less developed systems will adapt developments already tried and tested in more highly developed systems.
2. The ability of a system to successfully adapt innovations is directly related to its level of economic development. Certain minimum levels of economic development are necessary to support anything beyond the most simple retailing methods.
3. When the economic environment is favorable to change, the process of adaptation may be either hindered or helped by local demographic/geographic factors, social mores, government action, and competitive pressures.
4. The process of adaptation can be greatly accelerated by the actions of aggressive individual firms.

Self-service—the provision for customers to handle and select merchandise themselves in a store with minimal assistance from sales personnel—is a major twentieth-century channel innovation. It provides an excellent illustration of the postulates just outlined. Self-service was first introduced in the United States. The spread of self-service to other countries supports the hypothesis that the ability of a system to accept innovations is directly related to the level of economic development in the system. Self-service was first introduced internationally into the most highly developed systems. It has spread to the countries at middle and lower stages of development but serves very small segments of the total market in these countries.

If a marketing system has reached a stage of development that will support a channel innovation, it is clear that the action of well-managed firms can contribute considerably to the diffusion of the channel innovation. The rapid growth of Benetton's and McDonald's is a testament to the skill and competence of these firms as well as to the appeal of their product. In some instances, channel innovations are improved, refined, and expanded outside the home country. 7-Eleven stores in Japan, for example, are half the size of Canadian or American stores, carry one third the inventory, yet they ring up twice as much in sales. 7-Eleven Japan boasts a fourth-generation point-of-sale (POS) information system that is more sophisticated than the system used here. Another Japanese 7-Eleven innovation is an in-store catalog, Shop America, that allows Japanese shoppers to order imported luxury products from companies like Tiffany's and Cartier.

Channel innovation is a challenge for global marketers. You can envision the concept of computer-disk-based sales presentations and product demonstrations leading to electronic ordering and contract handling and the impact this will have on global marketing management. Global retailers are also challenged. For example a recent survey shows that two-thirds of German shoppers abhor their weekly grocery shopping and dislike planning such activity. In its concept "Smart Store Europe," Arthur Andersen Consulting suggests ways to overcome weaknesses in the retail system that have led to consumer disenchantment: product assortment and service must have a much stronger focus on customer segments.[19]

CHANNEL STRATEGY FOR NEW MARKET ENTRY

A global company expanding across national boundaries often finds itself in the position of entering a new market. Obtaining distribution can be a major obstacle to establishing a position in a new market. This obstacle is often encountered when a company enters a competitive market where brands and supply relationships are already established. As noted previously, there is little immediate incentive for an independent channel agent to take on a new product when established names are accepted in the market and are satisfying current demands. The global company seeking to enter such a market must either provide

---

[19] "Vom verabscheuten zum erbaulichen Einkaufserlebnis," *Frankfurter Allgemeine Zeitung* (December 15, 1993) p.18.

some incentive to channel agents or establish its own direct-distribution system. Each of these alternatives has its disadvantages. A company may decide to provide special incentives to independent channel agents; however, this approach can be extremely expensive. The company might offer outright payments as either direct cash bonuses or contest awards for sales performance. In competitive markets with sufficiently high prices, incentive could take the form of gross margin guarantees. Both incentive payments and margin guarantees are expensive. The incentive payments are *directly* expensive; the margin guarantees can be *indirectly* expensive because they affect the price to the consumer and the price competitiveness of a manufacturer's product.

The alternative of establishing direct distribution in a new market also has the disadvantage of being expensive. Sales representatives and sales management must be hired and trained. The sales organization will inevitably be a heavy loser in its early stage of operation in a new market because it will not have sufficient volume to cover its overhead costs. Therefore, any company contemplating the establishment of a direct sales force, even one assigned to distributors, should be prepared to underwrite losses for this sales force for a reasonable period of time.

The expense of a direct sales force acts as a deterrent to establishing direct distribution in a new market. Nevertheless, it is often the most effective method. Indeed, in many instances direct distribution is the only feasible way for a new company to establish itself in a market. By using a sales force, the manufacturer can ensure aggressive sales activity and attention to its products. Sufficient resource commitment to sales activity, backed up by appropriate communications programs (including advertising) may in time allow a manufacturer with competitive products and prices to obtain a reasonable share of market. When market-share objectives have been reached, the manufacturer may consider shifting from the direct sales force to reliance on independent intermediaries. This shift becomes a possibility when market share and market recognition make the manufacturer's brand attractive to independent intermediaries.

CASE EXAMPLE: JAPAN

Japan has presented an especially difficult distribution challenge.[20] Distribution in Japan is complex because of a fragmented retail system and the correspondingly high number of intermediaries needed to service these outlets. Perhaps a more apt description of Japanese distribution would be a highly developed system that has evolved to satisfy the needs of the Japanese consumer.

The categories of wholesalers and retailers in Japan are very finely divided. For example, meat stores in Japan do about 80 percent of their business in meat items. Similar specialization exists in other specialty stores as well. This kind of concentration is also true at the wholesale level. This very high degree of specialization in Japan is made possible by the clustering of various types of stores at major street intersections or stops along commuter rail lines.

---

[20] This section is adapted from "Planning for Distribution in Japan," Japan External Trade Organization (JETRO) Marketing Series No. 4, rev. 1978.

Foreigners' distribution headaches in Japan stem, in part, from the longer distribution channels and the proliferation of retailers. Not only does Japan have a much higher density of retail stores (68 people per store compared with Canada's 195) but also many more wholesalers selling to each other: total wholesale turnover is 3.9 times the volume of retail sales. In Canada, the wholesale-to-retail ratio is 1.3.[21] This suggests that Japanese channels of distribution are less efficient than Canadian channels.

There are, of course, many instances in which overseas firms have entered the Japanese market and have been able to overcome difficulties presented by the distribution system. Unfortunately, problems in coping with and adapting to Japanese distribution have also prevented a number of firms from achieving the success they might have had. Historically, foreign marketers in Japan make two basic mistakes. The first is their assumption that distribution problems can be solved the same way they would be in the West, that is, by going as directly as possible to the customer and thus cutting out the intermediary. In Japan, because of the very fragmented nature of retailing, it is simply not cost-effective to go direct.

The second mistake often made is in treating the Japanese market at arm's length by selling to a trading company. The trading company may sell in low volumes to a very limited segment of the market, such as the luxury segment, with the result that there is usually limited interest on the part of the trading company. The experience is likely to be disappointing to all parties involved.

The Japanese system is changing and some of the practices, such as the sole agent arrangement and the system of secret rebates, that tie channels to manufacturers are being challenged.[22]

Successful distribution in Japan (or any other market), however, requires adaptation to the realities of the marketplace. In Japan, this means first and foremost adaptation to the reality of fragmented distribution. Second, it requires research into the market itself including customer needs and competitive products. Then a company must develop an overall marketing strategy that (1) positions the product vis-à-vis market segment identified according to need, price, and other issues; (2) positions the product against competitors; and (3) lays out a marketing plan—including a distribution plan—for achieving volume and share-of-market objectives.

▼ Six Steps to a Japanese Distribution Strategy

Shimaguchi and Rosenberg recommend six steps for mastering a distribution strategy for Japan.[23]

1. Find a Japanese partner. As long as the trade practices and thinking of Japanese business managers remain mysterious, it is wise to find a partner

---

[21] Based on *International Marketing Data and Statistics 1994*, Euromonitor, table 1201; "Market Research Handbook," *Statistics Canada*, Catalog 63-224, table 3.12, 3.51; *Annual Retail Trade 1989*, (1991; 1992) Catalog 63-223, table 1.

[22] "Japanese Distribution—Too Many Shopkeepers," *The Economist* (January 28, 1989) pp.70–1.

[23] Mitsuaki Shimaguchi and Larry R. Rosenberg, "Demystifying Japanese Distribution," *Columbia Journal of World Business* (Spring 1979), pp. 38–41.

who can navigate the strange waters. The most common partners are import agents ranging from small local distributors to the giant *sogo-sosha* (general trading companies).

2. Seek a distinctive market position. The best bet in Japan is better quality or a lower price or a distinctive positioning as a foreign product.

3. Identify available alternative distribution routes. Also consider alternatives to present channels. Philips, for example, has devised a way of marketing its shavers and coffee makers in both large and small outlets. S. C. Johnson Son linked up with the wholesalers who reach 300,000 individually operated retailers with 60 percent of the market and terminated all direct dealings with large retailers. This strategy achieved a very high penetration because the wholesalers sold to the large retailers as well.

4. Focus your distribution resources. The market is too big for a shotgun approach.

5. Prepare for a long-term effort and modest returns. Nothing happens quickly in Japanese distribution. Be patient.

6. Cultivate personal relationships in distribution. Remember, loyalty and trust are important.

▼ SUMMARY

Channel decisions are difficult to manage globally because of the variation in channel structures from country to country. Nevertheless, certain patterns of change associated with market development offer the astute global marketer the opportunity to create channel innovations and gain competitive advantage. The characteristics of customers, products, intermediaries, and environment all impact channel design and strategy.

Consumer channels may be relatively direct, utilizing direct mail or door-to-door selling as well as manufacturer-owned stores. A combination of manufacturer's sales force, agents/brokers, and wholesalers may also be used. Channels for industrial products are less varied, with manufacturer's sales force, wholesalers, and dealers or agents being utilized.

In developed countries, retail channels are characterized by the substitution of capital for labor. This is evident in the self-service store,

which offers a wide range of items at relatively low gross margins. The opposite is true in less developed countries with abundant labor. Such countries disguise their unemployment in "inefficient" retail and wholesale channels suited to the needs of consumers; such channels may have gross margins that are 50 percent lower than those in self-service stores in developed countries. A global marketer must either tailor the marketing program to these different types of channels or introduce a new retail concept that creates value for customers.

Japan exhibits special channel challenges. To establish Japanese distribution, companies are advised to work with a Japanese partner, seek a distinctive market position, seek alternatives to established distribution routes, focus resources, and prepare for long-term efforts by building relationships.

▼ DISCUSSION QUESTIONS

1. In what ways can channel intermediaries create utility for buyers?

2. What factors influence the channel structures and strategies available to global marketers?

3. What is "cherry picking"? What approaches can be used to deal with this problem?

4. Compare and contrast the typical channel structures for consumer products and industrial products.

5. Outline the framework that can be used to explain the incidence and rate of innovation in global retail channels.

6. What special distribution challenges exist in Japan? What is the best way for a non-Japanese company to deal with these challenges?

▼ BIBLIOGRAPHY

Books

BOWERSOX, DONALD J., *Strategic Marketing Channel Management*. New York: McGraw-Hill, 1992.

FIELDS, GEORGE, *From Bonsai to Levi's: An Insider's Surprising Account of How the Japanese Live*. New York: Macmillan, 1983.

HARVEY, MICHAEL G., AND ROBERT F. LUSCH, eds., *Marketing Channels: Domestic and International Perspectives*. Norman, OK: Center for Economic & Management Research, 1982.

STERN, LOUIS W., AND ADEL L. EL-ANSARY, *Marketing Channels*, 3rd ed. Englewood Cliffs, NJ: Prentice-Hall, 1988.

Articles

ALLEN, RANDY L., "The Why and How of Global Retailing," *Business Quarterly*, 57, no. 4 (Summer 1993), 117–122.

BELLO, DANIEL C., DAVID J. URBAN, AND BROHISLAW J. VERHAGE, "Evaluating Export Middlemen in Alternative Channel Structures," *International Marketing Review*, 8, no. 5 (1991), 49–64.

BUCKLEY, PETER J., C. L. PASS, AND KATE PRESCOTT, "Foreign Market Servicing by Multinationals: An Integrated Treatment," *International Marketing Review*, 7, no. 4 (1990), 25–40.

CAVUSGIL, S. TAMER, "The Importance of Distributor Training at Caterpillar," *Industrial Marketing Management*, 19, no. 1 (February 1990), 1–9.

FERNIE, JOHN, "Distribution Strategies for European Retailers," *European Journal of Marketing*, 26, nos. 8, 9 (1992), 35–47.

FRAZIER, GARY L., JAMES D. GILL, AND SUDHIR H. KALE, "Dealer Dependence Levels and Reciprocal Actions in a Channel of Distribution in a Developing Country," *Journal of Marketing*, 53, no. 1 (January 1989), 50–69.

HILL, JOHN S., RICHARD R. STILL, AND UNAL O. BOYA, "Managing the Multinational Sales Force," *International Marketing Review*, 8, no. 1 (1991), 19–31.

KALE, SUDHIR, AND ROGER P. MCINTYRE, "Distribution Channel Relationships in Diverse Cultures," *International Marketing Review*, 8, no. 3 (1991), 31–45.

KLEIN, SAUL, "Selection of International Marketing Channels," *Journal of Global Marketing*, 4, no. 4 (1991), 21–37.

———, AND VICTOR ROTH, "Satisfaction With International Marketing Channels," *Journal of the Academy of Marketing Science*, 21, no. 1 (Winter 1993), 39–44.

NOVICH, NEIL S., "Leading-Edge Distribution

Strategies," *Journal of Business Strategy*, 11, no. 6 (November/December 1990), 48–53.

OLSEN, JANEEN E., AND KENT L. GRANZIN, "Economic Development and Channel Structure: A Multinational Study," *Journal of Macromarketing*, 10, no. 2 (Fall 1990), 61–77.

SAMIEE, SAEED, "Retailing and Channel Considerations in Developing Countries: A Review and Research Propositions," *Journal of Business Research*, 27, no. 2 (June 1993), 103–129.

SHERWOOD, CHARLES, AND ROBERT BRUNS, "Solving International Transportation Problems," *Review of Business*, 14, no. 1 (Summer/Fall 1992), 25–30.

WEIGAND, ROBERT E., "Parallel Import Channels—Options for Preserving Territorial Integrity," *Columbia Journal of World Business*, 26, no. 1 (Spring 1991), 53–60.

FIFTEEN

Global Marketing Communications Decisions: Advertising

Introduction

Marketing communications—the promotion "P" of the marketing mix—refers to all forms of communications that organizations use to establish meaning and influence buying behavior among existing and potential customers. Marketing communications should be designed to tell customers about the benefits and values that a product or service offers. The principal forms of marketing communications, that is, the elements of the promotion mix, are advertising, personal selling, publicity, and sales promotion. All of these elements can be utilized in global marketing; however, the environment in which marketing communications programs are implemented can vary from country to country. In this chapter, we will examine advertising from the perspective of the global marketer.

Advertising may be defined as any sponsored, paid communication placed in a mass-medium vehicle. Advertising plays a more important communication role in the marketing of consumer products than industrial products. Frequently purchased, low-cost products generally require heavy advertising support. Not surprisingly, consumer products companies top the list of big advertising spenders. According to *Advertising Age*, in 1989 Procter & Gamble spent C$3.2 billion worldwide on advertising (nearly C$100 million in Canada). Among non-North American consumer products companies, Unilever spent C$2 billion on global advertising (C$38 million in Canada).[1]

GLOBAL ADVERTISING AND BRANDING

Global advertising is the transfer of advertising appeals, messages, art, copy, photographs, stories, and video and film segments from one country to another. The ability to transfer a successful campaign worldwide is a critical advantage to a global company. Today, regional trading centers such as Europe are experiencing an internationalization of brands as clients align themselves, buy up other companies, and get their pricing policies and production plans organized

---

[1] *A Report of Advertising Revenues in Canada* (Toronto: CARD Media Information Network, September 1993) p.11.

for a united region. From a marketing point of view, there is a great deal of activity going on that will make brands truly pan-European in a very short period of time. This phenomenon is accelerating the growth of global advertising.[2]

Why do many global advertising campaigns fail? It is not always because of the differences in culture or consumer experience among the peoples around the world. Rather, they often fail because the people responsible for executing the global campaigns locally exhibit strong resistance to the global campaign before quality or market effectiveness is even considered. For example, Bruce Steinberg, ad sales director for MTV Europe, reports that he sometimes has to visit as many as 20 marketing directors for the same company to get approval for a pan-European MTV ad.[3]

The potential for effective global advertising is increasing as new concepts such as *product cultures* are emerging. Today, *bounding* is based on global demography—youth culture, for example—rather than ethnic or national culture. Instead of ethnic culture, we can think in terms of product culture. As an example, clothing products can be targeted to males 18 to 25 years old, throughout the world to a worldwide segment. William Roedy, director of MTV Europe, sees clear implications of such product culture for advertising. "Eighteen-year-olds in Paris have more in common with 18-year-olds in New York than with their own parents. They buy the same products, go to the same movies, listen to the same music, sip the same colas. Global advertising merely works on that premise," he says.[4]

MTV is just one of the reasons the people of the world are seeing each other nightly on television and they are making choices from other cultures. Human wants and desires are very similar if presented within recognizable experience situations—people everywhere want value, quality, the latest technology made available and affordable; everyone gets hungry, wants to be loved and respected.[5]

The notion of cultural universals—concepts, ideas, values that are shared across cultures—is relevant here and caution is needed not to extend the assumption of universality too far. For example, religion may have profound influence on the acceptance or rejection of products because they are incompatible with certain teachings. The Hindu religion does not value the notion of convenience.[6] Islam restricts personal adornment and indulgence products, and places a different value on time.[7]

Differences in language, taste, and custom can be insurmountable barriers to the establishment of global food brands. Supermarket shelves around the world abound with thousands of products known only nationally or regionally.[8]

[2] Ann Cooper, "As the World Turns," *Advertising Age*, April 2, 1990, pp. SS16-SS19, SS22-SS23, SS35.

[3] Ken Wells, "Selling to the World: Global Ad Campaigns, After Many Missteps, Finally Pay Dividends," *The Wall Street Journal*, August 27, 1992, p. A1.

[4] Ibid.

[5] Dean M. Peebles, "Executive Insights: Don't Write Off Global Advertising," *International Marketing Review*, 6, no. 1 (1989), 73–78.

[6] Vern Terpstra and Kenneth David, *The Cultural Environment of International Business*, 2nd Ed. (Cincinnati: South-Western Publishing Company) p.90.

[7] Ibid. pp.98–101.

[8] "Marketing Foods Brands—Pass the Marmite", *The Economist* (December 22, 1990) p.96.

On the other hand, the most successful global brands have used advertising to create a culture around the brand: Coca-Cola, Marlboro, Gillette.[9]

The advantages of global branding include economies of scale in advertising as well as improved access to distribution channels. In cases where shelf space is at a premium, as with food products, a company has to convince retailers to carry its products rather than those of competitors. Having a global brand may help persuade them, since from the retailer's standpoint, a global brand is less likely to languish on the shelves. A Landor Associates study showed Coke to have the number-one brand-awareness and esteem position in the United States, number-two position in Japan, and number-six position in Europe. Nestlé's Nescafé is marketed as a global brand even though advertising messages and product formulation vary to suit cultural differences.

In the final analysis, the decision of whether or not to use a global or localized campaign depends on recognition by managers of the trade-offs involved. On the one hand, a global campaign will result in the substantial benefits of cost savings and increased control as well as the potential creative leverage of a global appeal. On the other hand, localized campaigns have the advantages of appeals that zero in on the most important attributes of a product in each culture.

The list of products "going global," once confined to a score of consumer and luxury goods, is growing. Sales of disposable diapers and diamond watches, shampoos, and fine Scotch are growing on the global advertising wave. And some longtime global advertisers are benefiting from fresh campaigns. American Jeans maker Levi Strauss & Co. racked up record sales in Europe in 1991 on the strength of a campaign extended unchanged to Europeans, Latin Americans, and Australians.

As explained in detail later in this chapter, it is important to distinguish between the selling proposition and the creative presentation, between *what* one says, and *how* one says it. For example, the selling proposition for many products is fun or pleasure, and the creative presentation shows people having fun with the product.

According to one recent survey, experienced advertising executives indicated that strong buying propositions can be transferred more than 50 percent of the time. An example of a buying proposal that transfers well is "top quality." The promise of low price or of value for money regularly surmounts national barriers. In the same survey, most executives indicated that they did not believe that creative presentations traveled well. The obstacles are cultural barriers, communications barriers, legislative problems (for example, children cannot be used in France to merchandise products), competitive positions (the advertising strategy for a leading brand or product is normally quite different from that for a minor brand), and execution problems.

These are real barriers, but there are powerful reasons to try to create an effective global campaign. To do so means that the company is forced to discover the global market for its product. The first company to find a global market for any product is always at an advantage over those who discover this later. *The search for a global advertising campaign can be the spearhead of the search for a coherent global strategy.* Such a search should bring together all the people who are involved with the product so they can share information and experience.

---

[9] Marieke De Mooij, *Advertising Worldwide*, 2nd Ed., London, Prentice-Hall, 1994, p.233.

Knowledge of cultural diversity is essential to any global marketer's efforts, especially the symbolism associated with cultural traits. Companies with a local partner or subsidiary have the benefit of sharing important information, such as when to use caution in advertising creativity. Use of colors and man/woman relationships can often be stumbling blocks. For example, white in Asia is associated with death; in Japan intimate scenes between men and women are considered to be in bad taste. Global advertisers need to be careful with social etiquette, as one veteran advertiser explains:

> Transplanted American creative people always want to photograph European men kissing women's hands. But they seldom know that the nose must never touch the hand or that this rite is reserved solely for married women. And how do you know that the woman in the photograph is married? By the ring on her left hand, of course. Well, in Spain, Denmark, Holland, and Germany, Catholic women wear the wedding ring on the right hand.

> When photographing a couple entering a restaurant or theater, you show the woman preceding the man, correct? No. Not in Germany and France. And this would be laughable in Japan. Having someone in a commercial hold up his hand with the back of it to you, the viewer, and the fingers moving toward him should communicate "come here." In Italy it means "good-bye."[10]

The creation of a common database can be the foundation for the development of a truly global campaign, and the global campaign can be the conceptual glue that pulls together a truly global strategy. Of course, this task is an enormous undertaking in markets such as Russia where the mountains of data that marketers take for granted in the West simply do not yet exist. Advertisers that can normally acquire target market statistics such as information on income, age, and geographic distribution suddenly find these tasks difficult, if not impossible.

Global campaigns attest to the conviction on the part of some advertisers that unified themes not only spur short-term sales but also help build long-term product identities and offer significant savings in production costs.[11] Still, not every company is embracing the concept of global advertising. Colgate has departed from a global advertising strategy and is taking a different approach:

> Colgate's advertising and marketing in the 90's will be tailored specifically to local markets and countries; there will be little global advertising. To underscore this point, TV commercials from different countries were shown and no two were alike.

---

[10] John O'Toole, *The Trouble with Advertising* (New York: Chelsea House, 1981), pp. 209–210.

[11] Ken Wells, "Global Ad Campaigns, After Many Missteps, Finally Pay Dividends," *The Wall Street Journal*, August 27, 1992, pp. A1, A8.

Once market penetration and positioning is established in the targeted country, Colgate moves the product into similar markets in other countries. Product introduction has matched this approach with the introduction of Ajax bathroom spray in France. Once a market is established there, plans are made to extend the product to other market areas. Colgate products such as actibrush plaque-fighting mouth rinse, currently in the U.K., France and Brazil, is approved for marketing in Australia and Italy.[12]

Global advertising is aimed at more cultures than the one in which it originated and the main idea is to achieve a universally recognized brand. The challenge, then, is to convey in the advertising theme what the brand means to consumers. The problem of advertising execution can be regarded as one of achieving sufficient context (see chapter 4 for detailed discussion). Companies like Benetton, Coca-Cola, or Mercedes-Benz have accomplished this.

Domzal and Kernan researched the characteristics that make advertisements "globally understood."[13] They suggest that whether an ad travels well or poorly transnationally depends on how six creative dimensions are employed. These dimensions—brand portrayal, target consumer portrayal, the ad's appeal, communication mode, the ad's representations, and the ad's story—combine to render an ad either culture-free or culture-bound. Typically, an ad that fails to "travel well" is too contexted and anchored to a specific culture. Of 321 print ads from seventeen countries, across four product categories, culture-free ads were primarily product-focused, while culture-bound ads emphasized the consumer, mood creation, or testimonials.

The implications for global advertising are straightforward: A global advertising theme must be clear and simple, yet flexible enough that nuances of different cultures can be applied by target consumers without losing the ad's meaning.

ADVERTISING AND STAGES OF ECONOMIC DEVELOPMENT

In some countries, increases in per capita GNP and increases in advertising as a percentage of GNP are directly correlated; that is, the higher the per capita GNP, the higher percentage of GNP accounted for by advertising expenditures. In Spain, for example, economic development has been spurred by a number of factors, including membership in the European Community in 1986 and the Barcelona Olympics in 1992. Spain's economy is growing at nearly 3 percent a

---

[12] Laurie Freeman, "Colgate Axes Global Ads: Thinks Local," *Advertising Age,* November 26, 1990, pp. 1, 59.

[13] This section draws heavily on Teresa J. Domzal and Jerome B. Kernan, "Creative Features of Globally-Understood Advertisements," *Journal of Current Issues and Research in Advertising* (1994) 16:1, pp.29–46.

year and per capita income is C$13,912. Between the mid-1980s and 1990, Spain's per capita advertising expenditures jumped from C$75 to C$306; during the same period, advertising expenditures as percentage of GNP increased from about 1 percent to 2.4 percent (compare this to Canadian advertising expenditures at 1.6 percent of GNP). (See Appendix Tables 15–2 and 15–3.)

As a country's income rises, countervailing forces emerge. On one hand, rising incomes create an even larger potential market for goods and services and thus create a greater incentive to engage in advertising. On the other hand, this increasing level of advertising in response to the growing potential and size of the market results in higher intensity of communications messages, which are directed toward customers and reduce the effectiveness of any particular message.

An intriguing question for global marketers that has not yet been empirically studied is the marginal efficiency of advertising expenditures in countries at different stages of economic development. In a developing country the media environment, that is the types of media available, and the number and frequency of messages to which people are exposed, differs drastically from that of an industrialized country like Canada. Because people in such a developing country are not bombarded daily with thousands of different commercial messages, their receptivity to additional advertising messages is presumably much higher than in Canada. When advertising decisions are made in a multi-market context, we must assess in which market an additional marginal advertising dollar has greater payoff in terms of sales, awareness, or some other company objective. Optimizing global allocation of advertising expenditures is an important question.

Advertising managers at global companies need to determine the optimum total level of worldwide advertising expenditure as well as the optimum allocation of expenditure among countries. Under optimum allocation conditions, the marginal payoff (sales/awareness impact) of country advertising expenditures is equal.

This can be expressed as follows.

Let

A = advertising sales/awareness effect
C = country markets, 1 . . . nth
M = marginal advertising expenditure

At the optimum allocation point,

$$A = M_1 = M_2 = M_3 = M_{n\text{th}}$$

GLOBAL ADVERTISING CONTENT: THE "EXTENSION" VERSUS "ADAPTATION" DEBATE

The overall requirements of effective communication and persuasion are fixed and do not vary from country to country. This is also true of the components of the communication process: The marketer's/sender's message must be encoded, conveyed via the appropriate channel(s), and decoded by the customer/receiver. Communication takes place only when meaning is transferred. The Global Marketing Checklist in this chapter addresses some of the barriers that can prevent communication.

The key question for global marketers is whether the *specific* advertising message and media strategy must be changed from region to region or country to country because of environmental requirements. Proponents of stand- ardization believe that the era of the global village is fast approaching, and that tastes and preferences are converging. According to the standardization argument, since people everywhere want the same products for the same reasons, companies can achieve great economies of scale by unifying advertising around the globe. Advertisers who follow the localized approach do not buy into the "global village" argument; rather, they assert that consumers still differ from country to country and must be reached by advertising tailored to their respective countries. Proponents of localization point out that most blunders occur because advertisers failed to understand and adapt to foreign cultures.

During the 1950s the widespread opinion of advertising professionals was that effective international advertising required delegating the preparation of the campaign to a local agency. In the early 1960s this idea of local delegation was repeatedly challenged. For example, Eric Elinder, head of a Swedish advertising agency, wrote: "Why should three artists in three different countries sit drawing the same electric iron and three copywriters write about what after all is largely the same copy for the same iron?"[14] Elinder argued that consumer differences between countries were diminishing and that he would more effectively serve a client's interest by putting top specialists to work devising a strong international campaign. The campaign would then be presented with insignificant modifications that mainly entailed translating the copy into idiomatic local language.

As the decade of the 1980s began, Pierre Liotard-Vogt, former CEO of Nestlé, expressed similar views in an interview with *Advertising Age.*

> *Advertising Age:* Are food tastes and preferences different in each of the countries in which you do business?
>
> *Liotard-Vogt:* The two countries where we are selling perhaps the most instant coffee are England and Japan. Before the war they didn't drink coffee in those countries, and I heard people say that it wasn't any use to try to sell instant coffee to the English because they drink only tea and still less to the Japanese because they drink green tea and they're not interested in anything else.
>
> When I was very young, I lived in England and at that time, if you spoke to an Englishman about eating spaghetti or pizza or anything like that, he would just look at you and think that the stuff was perhaps food for Italians. Now on the corner of every road in London you find pizzerias and spaghetti houses.
>
> So I do not believe [preconceptions] about "national tastes." They are "habits," and they're not the same. If you bring the public a different food, even if it is unknown initially, when they get used to it, they will enjoy it too.
>
> To a certain extent we know that in the north they like a coffee milder and a bit acidic and less roasted; in the south, they like it very dark. So I can't say that taste differences don't exist. But to believe that those tastes are set and can't be changed is a mistake.[15]

The "'standardized versus localized" debate picked up tremendous momentum after the publication, noted in earlier chapters, of Ted Levitt's 1983 *Harvard Business Review* article titled "The Globalization of Markets." Levitt's thesis in a nutshell: The world is becoming increasingly homogeneous. Global companies, he wrote, should sell standardized products around the world with standardized ad campaigns. That article set the agenda for discussion, debate, and scholarly research for the rest of the decade of the 1980s. In 1988, an article appeared on the front page of *The Wall Street Journal* that was highly critical of Levitt's view; among other things, the article contains a remark by the CEO of a major ad agency that "Theodore Levitt's comment about the world becoming homogenized is bunk."[16]

---

[14] Eric Elinder, "International Advertisers Must Devise Universal Ads, Dump Separate National Ones, Swedish Ad Man Avers," *Advertising Age,* November 27, 1961, p. 91.

[15] "A Conversation with Nestle's Pierre Liotard-Vogt," *Advertising Age,* June 30, 1980, p. 31.

[16] Joanne Lipman, "Ad Fad: Marketers Turn Sour on Global Sales Pitch Harvard Guru Makes," *The Wall Street Journal,* May 12, 1988, p. A1.

Yet less than five years after the appearance of that article, a second article in *The Wall Street Journal* suggested the paper had done an about-face. "Global Ad Campaigns, After Many Missteps, Finally Pay Dividends," the headline declared; ironically, Mr. Levitt was not mentioned by name in the article.

In contrast to the view expounded by Levitt and Liotard-Vogt, some recent scholarly research suggests that the trend is toward the increased use of *localized* international advertising. Kanso (1992) reached that conclusion in a study surveying two different groups of advertising managers—those taking localized approaches to overseas advertising and those taking standardized approaches. Another finding was that culturally oriented managers tended to prefer the localized approach, while nonculturally oriented managers preferred a standardized approach. As Kanso correctly notes, the controversy over advertising approaches will probably continue for years to come. Localized and standardized advertising both have their place and both will continue to be used. Kanso's conclusion is that what is needed for successful international advertising is a global commitment to local vision.[17] The question of *when* to use each approach is discussed in the next section.

ADVERTISING APPEALS
AND PRODUCT CHARACTERISTICS

Advertising must communicate appeals that are relevant and effective in the target market environment. Because products are frequently at different stages in their life cycle in various national markets, and because of the basic cultural, social, and economic differences that exist in markets, the most effective appeal for a product may vary from market to market. Yet, marketers should attempt to identify situations where (1) potential cost reductions exist because of the presence of economies of scale; (2) barriers to standardization such as cultural differences are not significant; and (3) products satisfy similar functional and emotional needs across different cultures.

Green, Cunningham, and Cunningham conducted a cross-cultural study to determine the extent to which consumers of different nationalities use the same criteria to evaluate two common consumer products: soft drinks and toothpaste. Their subjects were college students from the United States, France, India, and Brazil. In relation to France and India, the U.S. sample placed more emphasis on the subjective and less functional product attributes, and the Brazilian sample appeared even more concerned with the subjective attributes than did the U.S. sample. The authors concluded that advertising messages should not use the same appeal for these countries if the advertiser is concerned with communicating the most important attributes of his or her product in each market.[18]

---

[17] Ali Kanso, "International Advertising Strategies: Global Commitment to Local Vision," *Journal of Advertising Research* (January/February 1992), pp. 10–14.

[18] Robert T. Green, William H. Cunningham, and Isabella C. M. Cunningham, "The Effectiveness of Standardized Global Advertising," *Journal of Advertising* (Summer 1975), pp. 25–30.

Effective advertising may also require a difference between a product's basic appeal and the creative execution of the appeal. If the creative execution in one key market is closely tied to a particular cultural attribute, the execution may have to be adapted to other markets. For example, Club Med attempted to use a unified global advertising campaign featuring beautiful photos of vacationers in revealing swimming suits. Many Americans, for whom modesty in public is important, saw the ads as risqué and titillating, with appeal only to "swinging singles." Europeans, who are accustomed to partial nudity on public beaches, did not consider the ads to be improper. Although Club Med retained its basic selling proposition keyed to the theme "The antidote to civilization," the creative execution had to be brought in line with the tastes, perceptions, and experiences of the American market.

As noted in Chapter 9, certain consumer products also lend themselves to advertising extension. If a product appeals to the same need around the world, there is a possibility of extending the appeal to that need. The basic issue is whether or not there is in fact a global market for the product because if the market is global, appeals can be standardized and extended. Coke and Pepsi, Scotch whiskey, expensive Swiss watches, and Italian designer clothing are examples of products whose markets are truly global. For example, Seagrams recently ran a global campaign keyed to the theme line, "There will always be a Chivas Regal." The campaign ran in 34 countries and was translated into 15 languages. In 1991, Seagrams launched a global billboard campaign to enhance the universal appeal for Chivas. The theory: The rich all over will sip the brand, no matter where they made their fortune.

Gillette took a standardized "one product/one brand name/one strategy" global approach when it introduced the Sensor razor beginning in early 1990. The campaign slogan was "Gillette. The best a man can get," an appeal that was expected to cross boundaries with ease. Peter Hoffman, vice president of marketing of the North Atlantic Shaving Group, noted in a press release: "We are blessed with a product category where we're able to market shaving systems across multinational boundaries as if they were one country. Gillette Sensor is the trigger for a total Gillette megabrand strategy which will revolutionize the entire shaving market." Gillette's standardized advertising campaign differs strikingly from that of arch-rival Schick in the Japanese market. Prior to the Sensor launch, Gillette custom-made advertising for the Japanese market; now, except for the fact that the phrase "the best a man can get" is translated into Japanese, the ads shown in Japan are the same as those shown in North America and the rest of the world. Schick, meanwhile, uses Japanese actors in its ads.

As noted in earlier chapters, food is the product category most likely to exhibit cultural sensitivity. Thus, marketers of food and food products must be alert to the need to localize their advertising. A good example of this is the recent effort by H. J. Heinz Co. to develop the overseas market for ketchup. Adapting both the product and advertising to target country tastes is integral to this effort.[19]

---

[19] Gary Levin, "Ads Going Global," *Advertising Age,* July 22, 1991, pp. 4, 42.

In Greece, for example, ads show ketchup being poured on pasta, eggs, and cuts of meat. In Japan, they instruct Japanese homemakers on using ketchup as an ingredient in western-style food such as omelets, sausages, and pasta. Barry Tilley, London-based general manager of Heinz's Western Hemisphere trading division, says Heinz uses focus groups to determine what foreign consumers want in the way of taste and image. Canadians and Americans like a relatively sweet ketchup, but Europeans prefer a spicier, more piquant variety. Significantly, Heinz's foreign marketing efforts are most successful when the company quickly adapts to local cultural preferences and does not dwell on the fact that the company is American-owned. For instance, because of the name, Swedes think the company is German.

In contrast to this, American themes work well in Germany. Kraft and Heinz are trying to outdo each other with ads featuring strong American images. In Heinz's latest television ad, American football players in a restaurant become very angry when the 12 steaks they ordered arrive without ketchup. The ad ends happily, of course, with plenty of Heinz ketchup to go around.[20]

In general, the fewer the number of purchasers of a product, the less important advertising is as an element of the promotion mix. Thus, industrial products, which are infrequently purchased, expensive, and technically complex, can be sold only by a highly trained direct sales force. The more and technically complicated an industrial product is, the truer this statement is. For such products, there is no point in letting national agencies duplicate each other's efforts. Even for the latter type of product, however, advertising has a role in setting the stage for the work of the sales force. A good advertising campaign can make it significantly easier for a salesperson to get in the door and, once in, can make it easier to make the sale.

CREATING ADVERTISING

▼ Art Direction

Art direction is concerned with visual presentation—the "body language" of print and broadcast advertising. Some forms of visual presentation are universally understood. Revlon, for example, has used a French producer to develop television commercials in English and Spanish for use in international markets. These commercials, which are filmed in Parisian settings, communicate the appeals and advantages of Revlon products in international markets. By producing its ads in France, Revlon obtains effective television commercials at a much lower price than it would have to pay for similar-length commercials produced in its various major markets.

PepsiCo has used four basic commercials to communicate its advertising themes. The basic setting of young people having fun at a party or on a beach has

---

[20] Gabriella Stern, "Heinz Aims to Export Taste for Ketchup," *The Wall Street Journal*, November 20, 1992, p. B1.

been adapted to reflect the general physical environment and racial characteristics of North America, South America, Europe, Africa, and Asia. The music in these commercials has also been adapted to these five regions: rock for North America, bossa nova for Latin America, high life for Africa, and so on.

The international advertiser must make sure that advertisements are not inappropriately extended into markets. Benetton, for example, which started its "United Colors of Benetton" campaign in 1985, has been promoting themes of harmony and equality between races in its advertising. These campaigns appear primarily in print and on billboards in more than one hundred countries, although recently Benetton carried out a billboard campaign unique to France.[21] In 1989, the art direction focused on interracial juxtapositions: for example, a white hand and a black hand handcuffed together. Another version of the campaign depicted a black woman breastfeeding a white baby. While they were shown in Canada, the campaign created controversy in the U.S. because the image evoked the history of slavery in the U.S. market. The woman-baby advertisement, which won acclaim in France, Holland, Denmark, Italy, and Austria, was, therefore, not shown in the U.S. market.[22] In 1994, the publicity surrounding two particularly controversial images, a dying AIDS patient and the blood-stained clothes of a Croatian soldier, contributed to a dispute between some German store owners and Benetton and resulted in the closing of one hundred stores.[23] The photographic philosophy and images of Oliviero Toscani, Benetton's photographer, have unquestionably had a global impact on the use of images in advertising.[24]

▼ Copy

Translating copy, or the written text of an advertisement, has been the subject of great debate in advertising circles. Copy should be relatively short and contain no slang or idioms. This is because other languages invariably take more space to convey the same message; thus, the increased use of visual presentations, pictures, and illustrations. More and more European and Japanese advertisements are purely visual, conveying a specific message, and invoking the company name.[25] Certainly, low literacy in many countries seriously impedes communications and calls for greater creativity and use of verbal media.

It is important to recognize the overlap in the use of languages in many areas of the world (e.g., the European Community, Latin America, and the English-language Canada–U.S. market). Capitalizing on this, global advertisers can realize economies of scale in producing advertising copy in the same language and with the same message for these homogenous markets, when product preferences and

---

[21] Presentation by Oliviero Toscani, Universita di Trieste, Trieste, November 28, 1994.

[22] *United Colors of Benetton Advertising—A Brief History* (New York: Benetton Services Corporation, 1994).

[23] "The World This Week," *The Economist* (January 21, 1995) p.7.

[24] Erica Orsini, "A lezione con un genio dell'imagine," *Il Piccolo* (November 29, 1994) p.16.

[25] Vern Terpstra and Ravi Sarathy, *International Marketing* (Orlando, FL: The Dryden Press, 1991), p. 465.

appeals are the same for the targeted buyer group. Advertisers must also recognize that the use of language differs in many subtle as well as obvious ways, as, for example, with German in Germany, Austria, and Switzerland.

Advertising slogans often present the most difficult translation problems and are, hence, most often subject to hilarious errors. Stories are plentiful about such cases as when Kentucky Fried Chicken's "Finger lickin' good" came out in Chinese as "Eat your fingers off;" or how Pepsi's "Come alive" copy line was misunderstood in its Asian version as a call to bring ancestors back from the grave.[26] Before deciding whether to prepare new copy for a foreign market or simply to translate the English copy, an advertiser must consider whether the message as translated can be received and comprehended by the foreign audience to which it is directed. Anyone with a knowledge of foreign languages realizes that it is usually necessary to be able to think in that language in order to communicate accurately. One must understand the connotations of words, phrases, and sentence structures, as well as their translated meaning, in order to be fully aware of whether or not a message will be received and how it will be understood.

We know from the global success of Benetton that one image, one message (in this case generally visual) can indeed be used across cultures. Recent experience by Nike, a sportswear company, demonstrated the challenge of using one message in many languages. Early in 1994, Nike launched an ad in the U.K. featuring a Kenyan runner. In addition to the simple line "just do it," a copy line "in my mind I am Kenyan" was part of the ad. In French, the translation was simple enough, *"Dans ma tête, je suis Kenyan"* ("In my head I am Kenyan"). Translation of the copy into the Latin languages Italian and Spanish would not convey the original meaning and the copy line had to be re-created: In Spanish the copy line became *"Mi fe es la de un keniata"* ("My faith is that of a Kenyan"), and in Italian it became *"Nel mio cuore io mi sento keniano"* ("In my heart I feel Kenyan"). In Nordic languages, however, translation from the original was possible as meaningful equivalent words for *mind* existed.[27]

The same principle applies to advertising—perhaps to an even greater degree. Difficulty of communication in advertising is compounded because it is essentially one-way communication, with no provision for immediate feedback. The most effective appeals, organization of ideas, and the specific language, especially colloquialisms and idioms, are those developed by a copywriter who thinks in the language and understands the consumer to whom the advertisement is directed. Thinking in a foreign language involves thinking in terms of the foreigner's habits, tastes, abilities, and prejudices: One must assimilate not only words but customs and beliefs.[28]

When formulating television and print advertising for use in industrialized countries such as Canada, the U.S. or Japan, the advertiser must recognize major style and content differences. When searching for similarities in cultures and markets, the global advertiser is interested in appeals. A substantial amount of comparative research of advertising styles across countries has been undertaken. For

[26] Richard N. Weitz, "How Do You Say Oops!" *Business Marketing* (October 1990), pp. 52–53.

[27] David Short, "One Message in Many Languages," *The European* (February 25–March 3, 1994) p.21.

[28] Gordon E. Miracle, "Management of International Advertising," Michigan International Business Studies Number 5, University of Michigan, 1966, p. 12.

Canadian companies, comparisons between the U.S. and other countries are the main source of such information. For example, between the U.S. and the European community, print advertisements across countries showed that the differences outnumbered the similarities, suggesting that standardizing advertisements within the European Union is far from simple.[29]

To return to the comparison between the U.S. and Japan, research found that the emphasis on individualism in the West, for example, and on group norms in Asia tend to be reflected in advertising.[30] Other intriguing differences are that American ads make more frequent use of spokespersons and direct product comparisons, and use logical arguments to try to appeal to the reason of audiences. Ads that look irritating to the Japanese viewer may not necessarily be perceived that way by an American, and vice versa. Japanese advertising is more image oriented and appeals to the sentiment of the audience. In Japanese, what is most important frequently is not what is stated explicitly but rather what is implied by the speaker or writer.

Kishii (1988) identified seven characteristics that distinguish Japanese from American creative strategy.

(1) Indirect rather than direct forms of expression are preferred in the messages. This avoidance of directness in expression is pervasive in all types of communication among the Japanese, including their advertising. Many television ads do not mention what is desirable about the brand in use and let the audience judge for themselves.

(2) There is often little relationship between ad content and the advertised product.

(3) Only brief dialogue or narration is used in television commercials, with minimal explanatory content. In the Japanese culture, the more one talks, the less others will perceive him or her trustworthy or self-confident. A 30-second advertisement for young menswear shows five models in varying and seasonal attire, ending with a brief statement from the narrator: "Our life is a fashion show!"

(4) Humor is used to create a bond of mutual feelings. Rather than slapstick, humorous dramatizations involve family members, neighbors, and office colleagues.

(5) Famous celebrities appear as close acquaintances or everyday people.

(6) Priority is placed on company trust rather than product quality. Japanese tend to believe that if the firm is large and has a good image, the quality of its products should also be outstanding.

(7) The product name is impressed on the viewer with short, 15-second commercials.[31]

---

[29] Bob D. Cutler and Rajshekhar G. Javagli, "A Cross-Cultural Analysis of the Visual Components of Print Avertising: The United States and the European Community," *Journal of Advertising Research* (January/February 1992).

[30] Barbara Mueller, "Reflections of Culture: An Analysis of Japanese and American Advertising Appeals," *Journal of Advertising Research* (June/July 1987).

GLOBAL MEDIA DECISIONS

▼ Media Vehicles and Expenditures

In 1990 world advertising expenditures for the 53 countries reported exceeded C$310 billion. Canada, with expenditures of more than C$10 billion, was in seventh place in terms of total advertising expenditures. As might be expected, the largest per capita advertising expenditures occurred for the most part in the more highly developed countries of the world. The lowest per capita expenditures were in the less developed countries.

Per capita advertising expenditures in 1990 averaged C$128 for the 53 countries covered, and a total of 17 countries spent more than C$150 per capita on media advertising. Eleven of these spent over C$300 per capita. Switzerland tops the list with C$715 in per capita advertising expenditures.

Spain and the United States were the only countries that spent more than 2 percent of their gross national product on advertising in 1990; 22 other countries reported percentages in excess of 1 percent.

A key issue in advertising is which of the measured media—print, broadcast, transit, and so on—to utilize. Print advertising (see Appendix Table 15–4) continues to be the number-one advertising vehicle in most countries. In Canada, C$6.5 billion was spent on print media in 1990, the fifth-largest expenditure in the world. Japan, the second-largest print media spender behind the U.S., spent twice as much as Canada. Fourteen other nations, apart from Canada, surpassed the C$1 billion spending mark for print media. Per capita print expenditures (see appendix Table 15–5) were highest in Switzerland, Finland, and Canada.

The use of newspapers worldwide for print advertising is so varied as to almost defy description. In Mexico, an advertiser who can pay for a full-page ad may get the front page, while in India, paper shortages may require booking an ad six months in advance.

In some countries, television and radio stations can broadcast only a restricted number of advertising messages; in Saudi Arabia, there is no commercial television advertising. In such countries the proportion of advertising funds allocated to print is extremely high.

The United States and Japan continued to be the two leaders in television advertising during 1990 accounting for two-thirds of expenditures, with Canada in 10th place. (See Appendix Table 15–7.)

On a per capita basis, advertisers in the United States were the foremost users of television, with per capita expenditures of over C$132. It is interesting to note that in Japan, per capita spending on advertising in 1990 was C$105, while Canada, with C$69, was in eighth place.

---

[31] C. Anthony di Benedetto, Mariko Tamate, and Rajan Chandran, "Developing Creative Advertising Strategy for the Japanese Marketplace," *Journal of Advertising Research* (January/February 1992), pp. 39–48. A number of recent studies have been devoted to comparing ad content in different parts of the world, including Mary C. Gilly, "Sex Roles in Advertising: A Comparison of Television Advertisements in Australia, Mexico, and the United States," *Journal of Marketing* (April 1988), pp. 75–85; Marc G. Weinberger and Harlan E. Spotts, "A Situation View of Information Content in TV Advertising in the U.S. and U.K.," *Journal of Advertising*, 53 (January 1989), 89–94.

Television is also important in the Latin American market (see Appendix Table 15–9). Of the ten countries that allocated more than 50 percent of their measured media expenditures to television, nine were located in Central/South America or the Caribbean. As ownership of television sets increases in other areas of the world such as Southeast Asia, television advertising will become more important as a communication vehicle.

Worldwide, radio continues to be a less important advertising medium than print and television. As a proportion of total measured media advertising expenditures, radio trailed considerably behind print, television, and direct advertising. However, in countries where advertising budgets are limited, radio's enormous reach can provide a cost-effective means of communicating with a large consumer market. Radio accounted for more than 20 percent of the total measured media in only two countries.

As countries add mass-transportation systems and build and improve their highway infrastructures, advertisers are utilizing more indoor and outdoor posters and billboards to reach the buying public. Japan is by far the leader in the use of outdoor and transit advertising, spending more than four times as much as the United States, but more than fifty times as much as Canada (Appendix Table 15–12). Transit advertising was recently introduced in Russia, where drab streetcars and buses have been emblazoned with the bright colors of Western products.

▼ Media Decisions

The availability of television, newspapers, and other forms of electronic and print media varies around the world. Newspaper availability, measured by circulation per 1,000 people, ranges from 9 in Nigeria to 566 in Japan. We observe great variations across regions: In Western Europe, Finland has the highest circulation with 543 and Spain the lowest with 75. In Latin America, Venezuela records a circulation of 186 while Brazil only 48.

While markets are becoming increasingly similar in industrial countries, media situations still vary to a great extent. For example, consider the case of television advertising in Europe: It either does not exist or is very limited in Denmark, Sweden, and Norway. The time allowed for advertising each day varies from 12 minutes in Finland to 80 in Italy, with 12 minutes per hour per channel allowed in France, and 20 in Switzerland, Germany, and Austria. Regulations concerning content of commercials vary, and there are waiting periods of up to two years in several countries before an advertiser can obtain broadcast time.

In Saudi Arabia, where all advertising is subject to censorship, regulations prohibit a long list of subject matter including the following:

▶ Advertisements of horoscope or fortune-telling books, publications, or magazines are prohibited.

▶ Avoid advertisements that frighten or disturb children.

- ▶ Avoid use of preludes to the advertisements, which may appear to be a news item or official statement.
- ▶ Use of comparative advertising claims is prohibited.
- ▶ Noncensored films cannot be advertised.
- ▶ Women may only appear in those commercials that relate to family affairs and their appearances must be in a decent manner that ensures their feminine dignity.
- ▶ Female children under six years of age may appear in commercials provided that their roles are limited to a childhood-like activity.
- ▶ A woman should wear a long suitable dress, which fully covers her body except face and palms. Training suits or similar garments are not allowed.[32]

▼ Selecting Advertising Agencies

Another global advertising issue companies must face is whether to invite advertising agencies to serve product accounts on a multicountry or even global basis. There is a growing tendency for clients to designate global agencies for product accounts in order to support the integration of the marketing and advertising function. Agencies have seen this trend and are themselves engaged in a major program of international acquisition and joint venturing to extend their international reach and their ability to serve clients on a global account basis. While there are several large Canadian advertising agencies, the international agencies, many of whom have subsidiaries in Canada, are available to provide companies with global coverage.[33]

In selecting an international advertising agency, the alternatives are to select a local agency in each national market or an agency with domestic and overseas offices. Selection criteria should be based on the marketing organization and markets covered by the hiring firm. Major areas of consideration include:

Company Organization. Companies that are decentralized may want to leave the choice to the local subsidiary.

National Responsiveness. Is the global agency familiar with local culture and buying habits in a particular country, or should a local selection be made?

Area Coverage. Does the candidate agency cover all relevant markets?

Buyer Perception. What kind of brand awareness does the company want to project? If the product needs a strong local identification, it would be best to select a national agency.

Although the trend seems to be in the direction of international agency selection, companies that are geocentrically organized will adapt to the global

---

[32] National Trade Data Bank: The Export Connection, USDOC, *International Trade Administration, Market Research Reports*, October 2, 1992.

[33] *A Report of Advertising Revenues in Canada* (Toronto: CARD Media Information Network, September 1993).

market requirements and select a combination of both international and national agencies. PepsiCo, for example, largely uses American international agencies, but when it moved into Japan, it chose a Japanese agency because of the complexity of the market.[34]

As political systems shift toward free-market economies, and economic systems bring markets together through alliances such as the European Union and the North American Free Trade Agreement, companies producing internationally marketed products are taking their advertisers abroad. When Coca-Cola crossed the oceans, McCann-Erickson Worldwide followed. When Ford Motor Company entered overseas markets, J. Walter Thompson was close behind. However, markets such as Korea and Japan are still too complex for Western agencies to operate in, and similarly, Japanese and Korean global advertisers find it just as difficult to establish local agency presence in western markets.[35] For example, even very large Japanese agencies—two of them rank among the top ten agencies in the world—have almost no business outside their home market. Unlike Western agencies, they have not followed their multinational clients abroad.[36]

▼ SUMMARY

Marketing communications—the promotion "P" of the marketing mix—include advertising, sales promotion, personal selling, and public relations. Advertising presents opportunities for global extension and requirements for local adaptation. Comparative advertising expenditures can be measured in various ways but some countries are clearly more advertising intensive than others. Canada accounts for some 3 percent and the U.S. for 50 percent of world advertising expenditures. Spain and the U.S. both spend 2.4 percent, and Canada 1.6 percent of GNP on advertising. Switzerland spends the most per capita, C$715, nearly twice as much as Canada. The availability of media varies considerably from country to country. Television is the leading medium in many markets and is unavailable in others.

In spite of the many failures, there are powerful reasons to try to create a global campaign: The exercise of creating a global campaign forces a company to identify a global market for its product, and this is the beginning of the development of a global marketing strategy. In addition, the identification of global appeals and benefits forces a company to probe deeply to identify basic as opposed to superficial needs and buying motives. The success of Coke, Pepsi, Marlboro, and Nestlé is a testament to the payoff of a successful global brand strategy.

[34] Vern Terpstra and Ravi Sarathy, *International Marketing* (Orlando, FL: The Dryden Press, 1991), pp. 456–461.

[35] Julie Skur Hill, "World Brands: Asians See World as Their Oyster," *Advertising Age*, September 11, 1989, pp. 77–87.

[36] "The Enigma of Japanese Advertising," *The Economist* (August 14, 1993) pp.59-60.

▼ DISCUSSION QUESTIONS

1. What is the role of advertising in the promotion mix? What is the role of sales promotion in the marketing mix? How do these roles differ for industrial and consumer products?

2. Does the role of promotion in the marketing mix vary from one country to the next for the same product?

3. What factors should be considered in deciding whether or not to centralize the formulation of advertising strategy or disperse it to company subsidiaries?

4. Why should global advertising messages be concerned with the level of consumer involvement?

5. Are standardized or local advertising campaigns more appropriate for today's global brands? Support your position.

6. Explain the concept of *culture-bound products.*

▼ BIBLIOGRAPHY

Books

HASSAN, SALAH S., AND ROGER D. BLACKWELL, *Global Marketing.* Orlando, FL: The Dryden Press, 1994.

KAYNAK, ERDENER, *The Management of International Advertising: A Handbook and Guide for Professionals.* New York: Quorum Books, 1989.

MOOIJ, MARIEKE K. DE, AND WARREN KEEGAN, *Advertising Worldwide: Concepts, Theories and Practice of International, Multinational, and Global Advertising.* Englewood Cliffs, NJ: Prentice Hall, 1991.

NEELANKAVIL, JAMES P., AND ALBERT B. STRIDSBERG, *Advertising Self-Regulation: A Global Perspective.* New York: Hastings House, 1980.

O'TOOLE, JOHN, *The Trouble with Advertising.* New York: Chelsea House, 1981.

PEEBLES, DEAN M., *Management of International Advertising: A Marketing Approach.* Boston: Allyn and Bacon, 1984.

———, AND JOHN K. RYANS, JR., *Management of International Advertising.* Newton, MA: Allyn and Bacon, Inc., 1984.

STARCH INRA HOOPER INC., AND INTERNATIONAL ADVERTISING ASSOCIATION, *World Advertising Expenditures, 1990 edition.* Mamaroneck, New York, 1992.

TERPSTRA, VERN, AND RAVI SARATHY, *International Marketing.* Orlando, FL: The Dryden Press, 1991.

VARDAR, NUKHET, *Global Advertising: Rhyme or Reason?* London: P. Chapman Publisher, 1992.

Articles

BOURGERY, MARC, AND GEORGE GUIMARAES, "Global Ads: Say It with Pictures," *Journal of European Business,* 4, no. 5 (May/June 1993), 22–26.

CUTLER, BOB D., AND RAJSHEKHAR G. DAVALGI, "A Cross-Cultural Analysis of the Visual Components of Print Advertising: The United States and the European Community," *Journal of Advertising Research,* 32, no. 1 (January/February 1992), 71–80.

DI BENEDETTO, ANTHONY, MARIKO TAMATE, AND RAJAN CHANDRAN, "Developing Creative Advertising Strategy for the Japanese Marketplace," *Journal of Advertising Research* (January/February 1992), 39–48.

FOXMAN, ELLEN R., PATRIYA S. TANSUHAJ, AND JOHN K. WONG, "Evaluating Cross-National Sales Promotion Strategy: An Audit

Approach," *International Marketing Review*, 5, no. 4 (Winter 1988), 7–15.

FREEMAN, LAURIE, "Colgate Axes Global Ads: Thinks Local," *Advertising Age*, 1, 59.

GILLY, MARY C., "Sex Roles in Advertising: A Comparison of Television Advertisements in Australia, Mexico and the United States," *Journal of Marketing* (April 1988), 75–85.

GRAHAM, JOHN L., MICHAEL A. KAMINS, AND DJOKO S. OETOMO, "Content Analysis of German and Japanese Advertising in Print Media from Indonesia, Spain and the United States," *Journal of Advertising*, 22, no. 2 (June 1993), 5–15.

GREEN, ROBERT T., WILLIAM H. CUNNINGHAM, AND ISABELLA C. M. CUNNINGHAM, "The Effectiveness of Standardized Global Advertising," *Journal of Advertising* (Summer 1975), 25–30.

JAMES, WILLIAM L., AND JOHN S. HILL, "International Advertising Messages: To Adapt or Not to Adapt (That Is The Question)," *Journal of Advertising Research*, 31, no. 3 (June/July 1991), 65–71.

JOHNSON, BRADLEY, "Apple Wants a Unified Worldwide Image," *Advertising Age*, 64, no. 15 (April 12, 1993), 2.

KANSO, ALI, "International Advertising Strategies: Global Commitment to Local Vision," *Journal of Advertising Research*, 32, no. 1 (January/February 1992), 10–14.

LEVIN, GARY, "Ads Going Global," *Advertising Age*, 62, no. 30 (July 22, 1991), 4, 42.

LEVITT, THEODORE, "The Globalization of Markets," *Harvard Business Review* (May/June 1983), 92–102.

LIOTARD-VOGT, PIERRE, "Nestlé—At Home and Abroad," *Harvard Business Review* (November/December 1976), 80–88.

MARSTON, MAUREEN R., "Transferring Equity Across Borders," *Journal of Advertising Research*, 32, no. 3 (May/June 1992), RC-3–RC-5.

MUELLER, BARBARA, "Multinational Advertising: Factors Influencing the Standardized vs. Specialized Approach," *International Marketing Review*, 8, no. 1 (1991), 7–18.

NEVETT, TERENCE, "Differences Between American and British Television Advertising: Explanations and Implications," *Journal of Advertising*, 21, no. 4 (December 1992), 61–71.

PEEBLES, DEAN M., "Don't Write Off Global Advertising: A Commentary," *International Marketing Review*, 6, no. 1, 73–78.

ROTH, MARTIN S., "Depth Versus Breadth Strategies for Global Brand Image Management," *Journal of Advertising*, 21, no. 2 (June 1992), 25–36.

SKUR HILL, JULIE, "World Brands: Asians See World as Their Oyster," *Advertising Age*, September 11, 1989, 77–87.

SMITH, PATRICK J., "How to Present Your Firm to the World," *Journal of Business Strategy*, 11, no. 1 (January/February 1990), 32–36.

SYNODINOS, NICOLAOS E., CHARLES F. KEOWN, AND LAURENCE W. JACOBS, "Transnational Advertising Practices: A Survey of Leading Brand Advertisers in Fifteen Countries," *Journal of Advertising Research*, 29, no. 2 (April/May 1989), 43–50.

WEINBERGER, MARC G., AND HARLAN E. SPOTTS, "A Situational View of Information Content in TV Advertising in the U.S. and U.K.," *Journal of Advertising*, 53 (January 1989), 89–94.

▶ APPENDIX A:
World Advertising Expenditures[37]

Table 15–1 shows, by rank, the 30 top spending countries. Advertising expenditures in each of these countries exceeded C$500 million in 1990. Japan held second place with expenditures of C$44.8 billion, well behind the U.S. with C$150.0 billion. Canada was in seventh place with C$10.2 billion.

▼ Per Capita Advertising Expenditures

Details on per capita expenditures for all countries for which this information is available are shown in Table 15–2.

▼ Advertising Expenditures as a Percent GNP

The countries in which the proportion of gross national product allocated to advertising was the lowest were the less developed countries of Africa and Asia, and some of the oil-rich countries of the Middle East. Table 15–3 shows, in rank order, those countries with advertising expenditures exceeding 1 percent of gross national product.

▼ Print Advertising

Print advertising (see Table 15–4) continues to be the number-one advertising vehicle in most countries. In 1990, Canada spent C$6.5 billion on print. In total, some 16 countries spent more than C$1 billion.

Per capita printed expenditures (see Table 15–5) were highest in Switzerland, Finland, Canada, Sweden, and Denmark.

Six countries in Table 15–6 expended over 80 percent, compared with Canada's 64 percent, of their 1990 measured media expenditures in print.

▼ Television Advertising

The United States and Japan continued to be the two leaders in television advertising during 1990. Their combined expenditure was over C$46 billion and accounted for most of the world's expenditures in the medium (see Table 15–7).

---

[37] This section is excerpted from *World Advertising Expenditures*, 1990 edition, sponsored by Starch INRA Hooper Inc., in cooperation with International Advertising Association, Copyright © 1990, by Starch INRA Hooper, used with permission. Total expenditures include all print, television, radio, cinema, outdoor/transit, direct advertising and miscellaneous expenditures reported. Canadian data are based on *A Report of Advertising Revenues in Canada*, September 1993, published by CARD Media Information Network.

TABLE 15–1 Total Advertising Expenditures—Top 30 Countries, 1990

Country	In C$ millions
United States	150,097
Japan	44,844
United Kingdom	18,454
Germany, Federal Republic of	16,270
France	15,042
Spain	12,076
Canada	10,234
Italy	6,662
Netherlands	5,057
Switzerland	4,781
Australia	4,489
Brazil	3,718
Korea, South	3,297
Sweden	3,184
Mexico	2,566
Finland	2,100
Taiwan	1,830
Denmark	1,609
Belgium	1,497
Norway	1,439
Austria	1,180
India	1,045
Hong Kong	1,005
Argentina	968
New Zealand	728
Israel	685
Greece	613
China, People's Republic of	610
Colombia	555
Venezuela	512

TABLE 15–2 Per Capita Advertising Expenditures, 1990

Country	In C$
Switzerland	715
United States	598
Finland	422
Canada	383
Sweden	372
Japan	362
Norway	339
Netherlands	338
United Kingdom	320
Denmark	312
Spain	306
France	266
Australia	263
Germany, Federal. Republic of	262
New Zealand	213
Hong Kong	173
Austria	154
Belgium	149
Israel	148
Singapore	135

TABLE 15–3 Advertising Expenditures as a Percentage of Gross National Product

Country	Percent
Spain	2.4
United States	2.4
Switzerland	1.9
United Kingdom	1.7
Netherlands	1.7
Canada	1.6
New Zealand	1.4
Finland	1.4
Bolivia	1.4
Sweden	1.3
Norway	1.3
Hong Kong	1.3
Costa Rica	1.3
Australia	1.3
Panama	1.2
Korea, South	1.2
Japan	1.2
Israel	1.2
France	1.2
Denmark	1.2
Colombia	1.2
Argentina	1.1
Mexico	1.0
Dominican Republic	1.0

TABLE 15–4 Advertising Expenditures in Print Media

Country	In C$ millions
United States	49,208
Japan	13,967
United Kingdom	10,566
Germany, Federal. Republic of	9,835
Canada	6,536
Spain	4,727
France	4,231
Italy	2,878
Netherlands	2,604
Switzerland	2,211
Australia	2,181
Sweden	1,991
Korea, South	1,518
Finland	1,362
Brazil	1,308
Denmark	1,046

TABLE 15–5 Per Capita Print Media Advertising Expenditures

Country	In C$
Switzerland	330
Finland	273
Canada	244
Sweden	232
Denmark	203
Norway	201
United States	196
United Kingdom	183
Netherlands	174
Germany, Federal Republic of	158
Australia	128
Spain	120

TABLE 15–6 Percent of Measured Media Advertising Expenditures Allocated to Print Media

Country	Percent
Norway	93.0
Sweden	92.9
Denmark	83.0
Zambia	82.5
Netherlands	82.3
Israel	81.1
Canada	64.1

TABLE 15–7 Advertising Expenditures in Television Media

Country	In C$ millions
United States	33,142
Japan	13,026
United Kingdom	4,841
Italy	3,393
France	2,944
Spain	2,793
Brazil	2,130
Germany, Federal Republic of	1,993
Mexico	1,924
Canada	1,858
Australia	1,584

TABLE 15–8 Per Capita Television Media Advertising Expenditures

Country	In C$
United States	132
Japan	105
Australia	93
Hong Kong	85
United Kingdom	84
New Zealand	72
Spain	71
Canada	69
Italy	58
France	52
Finland	49
Singapore	40
Austria	40
Belgium	37

On a per capita basis, advertisers in the United States were the foremost users of television, with per capita expenditures of C$132, nearly double that of Canada. As can be seen in Table 15–8 fourteen other countries spent over C$30 per capita on television advertising.

The importance of television in Latin America is clearly evident in Table 15–9. All of the Latin American countries listed allocated more than 57 percent of their measured media expenditures to television in 1990. By comparison, Canada allocated 18.2 percent to television.

TABLE 15–9 Percent of Measured Media Advertising Expenditures Allocated to Television Media

Country	Percent
Mexico	75.0
Bolivia	72.3
Ecuador	66.2
Venezuela	65.0
Dominican Republic	64.4
Guatemala	64.0
Colombia	59.5
Panama	59.3
Brazil	57.7
Italy	50.9
Canada	18.2

TABLE 15–10 Advertising Expenditures in Radio Media	
Country	In C$ millions
United States	10,181
Japan	1,880
Spain	915
Canada	881
France	723
Germany, Federal Republic of	642
Australia	391
United Kingdom	339
Mexico	275
Brazil	178
Korea, South	157
Austria	139
Italy	106
Colombia	104

▼ Radio Advertising

As shown in Table 15–10, fourteen countries reported radio expenditures of more than C$100 million.

Per capita radio expenditures in 1990 were above C$10 in eleven countries and above C$6 in five others (see Table 15–11).

TABLE 15–11 Per Capita Radio Media Advertising Expenditures	
Country	In C$
United States	40
Canada	33
New Zealand	28
Spain	23
Australia	22
Austria	18
Japan	15
Finland	14
France	12
Ireland	11
Germany, Federal Republic of	10
Hong Kong	7
Israel	7
Switzerland	7
Taiwan	6
United Kingdom	6

TABLE 15–12 Expenditures in Outdoor Advertising Media	
Country	In C$ millions
Japan	5,072
France	1,328
United States	1,264
United Kingdom	587
Korea, South	555
Germany, Federal Republic of	491
Spain	423
Switzerland	348
Italy	283
Australia	257
Belgium	156
India	106
Canada	92

▼ Outdoor and Transportation Advertising

Table 15–12 outlines the top twelve countries spending more than C$100 million for outdoor advertising. Canada ranks just below the C$100 million mark.

▶ APPENDIX B:

International Trade Fairs in Global Marketing Communications

International trade fairs have long been recognized by management as an important part of the marketing mix. The enormous scale of trade-fair activity throughout the world underlines the significance of this form of communication between buyers and sellers: over 2,000 major trade fairs are held worldwide each year. Some 60 percent of these take place in Europe, 10 percent in North America, 20 percent in South-East Asia, and the remaining 10 percent in Latin America, Africa, and Australia.[38]

The major trade fair countries include Germany, Italy, France, and the United Kingdom. For example, in 1993 Germany staged 103 trade fairs with 131,000 exhibitors—44 percent from abroad—attracting more than 9 million visitors, of whom 18 percent were from abroad.[39]

For the global marketer, international trade fairs combine features that cannot be easily duplicated elsewhere:

▶ companies show and demonstrate their products

▶ in a competitive setting

▶ in a favorable atmosphere

---

[38] K. Palka, "Trade Secrets," *Business Traveller, The Globe and Mail*, October 1992, p. 34.

[39] *Calendar of International Trade Fairs and Exhibitions*, 1995 Edition, Deutsche Lufthansa A.-G., Cologne, p.6.

- to the desired target audience
- at a pre-arranged time and place
- through personal contact and interaction of buyers and sellers

The size of the major international trade fairs makes them a potentially crowded and confusing environment. For example, the Hanover trade fair for industrial goods has more than 5,900 exhibitors and half a million visitors. The task of communicating and selling in such an intense and competitive setting is challenging for both buyers and sellers.

Companies must approach the decisions relating to the use of trade fairs as a communications and promotion tool with the same level of commitment and care as other marketing decisions. That is, the role of a trade fair should be consistent with, and thus reflect, the company's marketing strategy and goals. Table 15–A summarizes how marketing goals for a company's target customer segments relate to its communications goals, trade fair goals, and eventually to the style of exhibit used.

A research report on Canadian companies and their use of international trade fairs shows (see Table 15–B) that the majority of trade fairs attended were in the U.S., followed by Germany, France, the United Kingdom, Australia/New Zealand, and China.

The implications of the trade fair attendance and market region profile for global marketers is clear: the U.S. market can often be reached through U.S. trade fairs that are national, while off-shore export markets require the use of the major, largely European, international trade fairs.

International trade fairs are often thought most appropriate for companies seeking to expand their foreign market involvement. In other words, a novice without foreign market experience seeking to assess whether exporting

TABLE 15–A Marketing and Trade Fair Goals

Marketing goal	Target groups	Communications goal	Trade fair goal	Style of exhibit
Gain market share with new products	Old and new customer groups	Emphasize essential uses and features	Introduce and display new product	Product-oriented
Gain market share with old products	New users	New uses and application for old	Reach new customers	Solution-oriented
Protect market share with existing products	Old users	Assurance, appeal to security, needs and relationship	Treat old customers as friends	Contact-oriented
Market development with new product solutions	Potential users	Create awareness of problem/solution	Demonstrate problem/solution	Counsel- and advice-oriented

Source: F.H. Rolf Seringhaus and Philip J. Rosson, "International Trade Fairs and Foreign Market Involvement: Review and Research Directions," *International Business Review* (1994) 3:3, p.317.

TABLE 15–B Location of International Trade Fairs Attended by Canadian Companies and Export Markets

United States	137
Germany	18
France	14
United Kingdom	10
Italy	8
Australia/New Zealand	4
China	3

	International Trade Fairs Attended in:	Market Regions Exported to:
United States	61.2%	92.9%
Western Europe	25.9	61.5
Pacific Rim	7.1	59.5
Latin/Central America	4.5	44.3
Middle East/Africa	1.3	26.7

Source: Based on F.H. Rolf Seringhaus and Philip J. Rosson, unpublished research report, *International Trade Fairs and Canadian Companies*, 1994.

potential exists should visit various markets first, before embarking on the major financial and time commitment required to exhibit at a trade fair.

Interestingly, a recent study shows that nearly half of Canadian exhibitors at international trade fairs had either no or less than one year of experience in the markets reached by the trade fair. One-third of companies had more than three years of experience.[40]

▼ Before Going to the Trade Fair

Companies must make several decisions regarding the use of international trade fairs. On one hand, management needs to clearly set out its objectives—which markets should be reached, should products be sold or agents or distributors sought, or both—and plan, prepare, and manage the exhibition process. On the other hand, the company has to be clear about the target customer segments it plans to reach through the fair, and to understand the expectations of visitors who attend the fair.

▼ During the Trade Fair

The management of the exhibit is a challenge in itself. The exhibit should be well designed, visually attractive, and compatible with company image and products, as well as staffed with knowledgeable and congenial personnel who

---

[40] Philip J. Rosson and F.H. Rolf Seringhaus, "International Trade Fairs: Firms and Government Exhibits," *Export Development and Promotion: The Role of Public Organizations*, F.H. Rolf Seringhaus and Philip J. Rosson, eds. (Boston: Kluwer Academic Publishers, 1991) pp.161–187.

are able to communicate professionally with visitors to the stand. The use of experienced personnel is very important since they should be able to qualify visitors, that is to determine how "serious" they are about purchase, what their role and influence in the buying decision is, and what the time frame and competitive context of their purchase might be. The emphasis here is on communication. Although English is widely spoken, the exhibitor should carefully consider the visitors and customer groups attending the fair, where they come from and which of their characteristics need to be catered to: language, cultural and business practices, and so on.

▼ After the Trade Fair

The investment in time and marketing dollars to exhibit at international trade fairs can be substantial and management must weigh the commitment of resources against the results. While sales are the ultimate objective, they do not follow automatically upon exhibition at a trade fair. A company's follow-up efforts often determine the outcome of what may have been a "successful" exhibit. Tangible results, such as bidding on contracts, frequently require a concerted effort and negotiation after a trade fair. We can regard a trade fair as one component in the global marketing process: it serves to create awareness and interest in a company and its products and in its ability to meet the customers needs. Whether a company can create a desire and preference for its products is very much dependent on its effort after the trade fair.

▼ Profile of Canadian Companies: International Trade Fair Decisions and Performance

The profile is based on a survey of 303 Canadian companies, using international trade fairs, across five industry sectors.

Nearly four out of five companies include international trade fairs as a regular part of their marketing plan. Of the four marketing mix components, product was ranked as the most important, followed by promotion, pricing, and distribution. Within a company's promotional efforts, trade fairs were ranked second-most important, after the sales force. Sales promotion, advertising, and publicity were considered less important.

Companies most often choose trade fairs on the basis of the industry or sector focus (80.1 percent) of the fair. Geographic scope (72.6 percent), visitor profile (53.5 percent), and level of specialization of the fair (38.0 percent) were the next selection criteria. Other factors also matter when selecting a trade fair. For example, four out of five companies mentioned that making contacts with target customers was very important, while three out of five felt this way about the publicity and exposure gained and the effect of the fair on the company's image.

Interestingly, planning for participation in the trade fair was mostly the responsibility of the sales or marketing manager, or the president of the company.

About two-thirds of the trade fairs companies participated in were global: Canadian companies recognize the need to exhibit in the company of global competitors, and to reach visitors from around the world.

The style of a company's exhibit should mirror the exhibitor's knowledge of its target customers. Based on that understanding a particular emphasis would be designed into the exhibit. Some 48.3 percent of exhibits had a clear product focus, 21.6 percent were primarily contact-oriented, 13.2 percent were problem/solution-oriented, and only 9.8 percent set their exhibit up as mainly information-oriented. To achieve the appropriate orientation of the exhibit, most companies designed and built the exhibits themselves. (Few used a professional designer—one in four—or a contractor—one in three.)

The objectives, achievements, and the overall contribution a trade fair makes to a company's global marketing effort are all important when assessing the role of international trade fairs.

There are five most often mentioned objectives for going to an international trade fair: making business contacts, gaining exposure for the company or products, maintaining or establishing a presence in the market, meeting customers, and obtaining market information. A very interesting observation was that sales at the trade fair was one of the least-mentioned objectives. Sales, then, are seen as the outcome of the global marketing process rather than an as immediate result expected from participation in an international trade fair.

Companies see trade fairs as a tool in this process and find their greatest contribution as identifying market opportunities, understanding customer requirements, and improving their knowledge of foreign target markets.

Exporting
and Importing

Introduction

Exporting and importing are two sides of the same coin. Exports supply customers with products manufactured in another country; imports do exactly the same thing. However, there is one important difference between importing and exporting. Importers are buyers/customers, while exporters are sellers/marketers. While the discussion in this chapter focuses on exporting, readers should understand that many of the concepts apply equally to importing if taken from a different perspective.

It is important to distinguish between export *selling* and export *marketing*. As in the product-focused era discussed in Chapter 1, export selling is *not* marketing. Export selling does not involve tailoring the product, the price, or the promotional material to the international market. The only marketing mix element that differs is the place, that is, the country where the product is sold. This selling approach may work for some products or services; for unique products with little or no international competition, such an approach is possible. Similarly, companies new to exporting may initially experience success with selling. Often, the managerial mindset in many companies still favors export selling. But as companies mature in the international marketplace, or as new competitors enter the picture, it becomes necessary to engage in export *marketing*.

Export marketing focuses on the customer in context, the total environment and strategic marketing. The export marketer does not take the domestic product "as is" and simply sell it to international customers. To the export marketer, the product offered in the home market represents a starting point. It is modified as needed to meet the preferences of international target markets. For example, a furniture manufacturer would downsize the physical dimensions of its products in order to export to Japan and other Asian countries. Similarly, the export marketer sets prices to fit the marketing strategy and does not merely extend home-country pricing to the target market. As noted earlier in Chapter 13, there are charges incurred in export preparation, transportation, and financing that must be taken into account in determining prices. Finally, the export marketer also adjusts the communications strategy and plan and the distribution strategy and plan to fit the market. In other words, to communicate product features or uses to buyers in export markets, it may be necessary to create brochures with different copy, photographs, or artwork. It is necessary to approach the international market with *marketing*, as opposed to *sales* literature.

Export marketing is the integrated marketing of goods and services destined for customers in international markets. Export marketing requires

1. An understanding of the target market environment; and
2. The application of all the conceptual and analytical tools of marketing, specifically
   a. The use of marketing research and the identification of market potential;
   b. Product design decisions, pricing decisions, distribution and channel decisions, and advertising and promotion decisions; and
   c. Organization, planning, and control.

We have covered topics 1, 2a, and 2b in preceding chapters. The topics noted in 2c are addressed in Chapter 17. The purpose of this chapter is to provide an overview of the issues and problems facing companies engaged in export marketing.

EXPORT DEPENDENCE: THE CANADIAN EXAMPLE

As we discussed in Chapter 3, Canadian companies have historically exported most of their goods to the U.S. market. This reliance has further increased from 73.3 percent in 1983 to 80.3 percent in 1993. Over the same period Canadian exporters also sold a higher share of manufactured goods: 51.5 percent in 1993 compared with 43.7 percent of all merchandise exports in 1983. We have to consider that of the C$93.2 billion manufactured goods exported in 1993, nearly one half (45.8 percent) were automotive products exported to the U.S. market. The top three exporters are automobile companies: GM Canada, Ford Canada, and Chrysler Canada. Among Canada's top twenty exporters in 1992, five were automotive companies. The largest fifty exporters, shown in Table 16–1, accounted for 44.4 percent of all Canadian merchandise exports.

Out of the total merchandise exports of C$181 billion, some 27.9 percent were manufactured goods sold to other global markets. The implication is clear: while the Canadian economy is highly export-dependent, our exporters rely to a very large extent on a single market, the United States.

ORGANIZATION OF EXPORT ACTIVITIES

The unmistakable fact is that exporting is becoming increasingly important as companies in all parts of the world step up efforts to supply and service markets located outside their national boundaries. Fewer than 1 percent of Canada's 61,000 exporting companies account for 86 percent of its exports, while 99 percent are responsible for the remaining 14 percent. Many small and medium-sized companies are not exporting and have no export objectives or programs for developing international markets. It is clear that, for many of these companies, exporting is a tremendous untapped market opportunity. This is especially so in

TABLE 16–1 The Largest 50 Canadian Exporters, 1992

Exporter	Industry	Export Sales (C$ million)	Exports as % of Total Sales
GM Canada	automaker	13,000	67
Ford Canada	automaker	7,780	64
Chrysler Canada	automaker	7,055	85
IBM Canada	computers	3,907	62
Noranda	resources	3,389	41
Canadian Pacific	diversified	2,418	24
Canadian Wheat Board	grain trading	2,310	66
Honda Canada	automaker	2,000	80
Inco	nickel products	1,354	45
Alcan Aluminum	aluminum	1,300	17
Fletcher Challenge Canada	forest products	1,200	67
Pratt Whitney Canada	aerospace	1,195	85
Amoco Canada	energy	1,180	29
TransCanada Pipelines	energy	1,126	36
Mobil Oil Canada	energy	1,100	63
Falconbridge	mining	1,098	62
Bombardier	diversified	1,084	35
Magna	auto parts	953	40
Shell Canada	energy	913	19
Abitibi-Price	forest products	880	31
Alberta & Southern	energy	820	88
Nova	energy/chemicals	816	27
Cominco	mining	808	61
Xcan Grain	grain trading	664	92
Canfor	forest products	637	77
McDonnell Douglas Canada	aerospace	630	100
Canadian Reynolds	aluminum	569	77
Westinghouse Canada	electrical	542	65
Maple Leaf Foods	food	532	29
Digital Equipment Canada	computers	520	48
Petro Canada	energy	511	11
Repap	forest products	499	47
Du Pont Canada	chemicals	476	36
Dow Chemical Canada	chemicals	458	32
Seaboard Lumber	forest products	451	100
Weldwood	forest products	448	68
Dofasco	steel	434	21
Cargill	grain trading	430	25
Stelco	steel	400	20
Canpotex	potash	363	100
CAE	aero electronics	362	35
Doman	forest products	360	72
Procter & Gamble	consumer goods	356	20
GE Canada	electrical	352	26
Donohue	forest products	349	74
Domtar	forest products	348	11
Hydro-Quebec	energy	304	5
Celanese Canada	chemicals	285	63
Rio Algom	metals	282	27
Xerox Canada	office equipment	230	22

Source: Based on data from *Report on Business Magazine* (April 1993) p. 71.

services, such as knowledge-based exports.[1] For many other companies, exporting also presents an untapped market opportunity, and governments concerned about the trade balance or economic development should focus their attention on educating uninvolved companies about the potential gains from exporting. This is true at the national and at provincial levels of government. We will be looking at the role of government in exporting in the next section.

Bilkey reviewed 43 studies on the export behavior of firms and reached two main conclusions.[2] The first is that exporting is essentially a developmental process. This process can be divided into the following distinct stages:[3]

1. The firm is unwilling to export; it will not even fill an unsolicited export order. This may be due to perceived lack of time ("too busy to fill the order"), or to apathy or ignorance.

2. The firm fills unsolicited export orders but does not pursue unsolicited orders. Such a firm would be an export seller. *Richardson Mfg.*

3. The firm explores the feasibility of exporting. (This stage may bypass Stage 2.)

4. The firm exports to one or more markets on a trial basis.

5. The firm is an experienced exporter to one or more markets.

6. After this success, the firm pursues country- or region-focused marketing based on certain criteria (e.g., all countries where English is spoken; all countries where it is not necessary to transport by water, and so on).

7. The firm evaluates global market potential before screening for the "best" target markets to include in its marketing strategy and plan. *All* markets, both domestic and international, are regarded as equally worthy of consideration.

Bilkey's second conclusion is that the probability of a firm going from one stage to the next depends on different factors. Moving from Stage 2 to Stage 3 depends on management's attitude toward the attractiveness of exporting and its confidence in the firm's ability to compete internationally. However, *commitment* is the most important aspect of a company's international orientation. Before a firm can reach Stage 4, it must receive and respond to unsolicited export orders. The quality and dynamism of management are important factors that can lead to such orders. Success in Stage 4 can lead a firm to stages 5 and 6. Stage 7 is the mature, geocentric company that is relating global resources to global opportunity. To reach this stage requires vision and commitment on the part of management.

Companies with new and innovative products have a better than average chance of succeeding in export markets. However, the most significant factors

---

[1] *Towards A New Cohesive Export Strategy* (Ottawa: Canadian Exporters' Association, January 4, 1994), p.1.

[2] Warren J. Bilkey, "Attempted Integration of the Literature of the Export Behavior of Firms," *Journal of International Business Studies*, 9 (Spring–Summer 1977), 33–46.

[3] The stages are based on Rogers's adoption process. See Everett M. Rodgers, *Diffusion of Innovations* (New York: Free Press, 1962).

affecting export performance are not product characteristics but, rather, firm characteristics. One of those characteristics is the level of knowledge of management. For example, we know from a study of the relationship among knowledge, strategy and performance that the level of knowledge influences the success of Canadian exporters in foreign markets. Increasingly, foreign markets attract competitors from around the globe. Competition is becoming more intense, and the need for management's knowledge of the market environment, competition and buyers, how to make contact with key target market segments, and how to reach markets with messages and products is more critical than ever before.[4] Indeed, Canadian high-tech companies acknowledge that two factors are very important to their export growth: developing their own technology, and export marketing know-how.[5]

Table 16-2 shows how the exporting know-how of Canadian high-tech exporters compares with that of similar Austrian companies.

Canadian companies from this study have an edge when it comes to finding information and knowing what customers want, but are at a disadvantage, compared to Austrian companies, in speaking the language of the customer and in using appropriate promotion methods to communicate with those customers.

TABLE 16–2 Relative Level of Exporting Skills in Canadian and Austrian High-Tech Exporters, 1991 (ranked from highest skill (1) to lowest skill (14) in company)

	CANADA	AUSTRIA
Company has skills in:		
Export procedures	1	2
Developing contacts	2	1
Acquiring market information	3	3
Foreign business practices	4	5
Identifying information sources	5	10
Anticipating customer needs	6	9
Identifying sales opportunities	7	7
Interpreting market information	8	8
Distribution methods/practices	9	11
Promotion methods	10	6
Analysing competitive products	11	13
Understanding regulatory information	12	12
Foreign languages	13	4
Undertaking market research abroad	14	14

Source: Based on data from F.H. Rolf Seringhaus, "A Comparison of Export Marketing Behavior of Canadian and Austrian High-Tech Firms," *Journal of International Marketing,* (1993) 1:4, p.58.

---

[4] F.H. Rolf Seringhaus, "Export Knowledge and its Role in Strategy and Performance," *The Finnish Journal of Business Economics,* (1991) 40:1, pp.3-21.

[5] F.H. Rolf Seringhaus, "Comparative Marketing Behaviour of Canadian and Austrian High-Tech Exporters," *Management International Review,* 33:3, 1993, pp. 247-269.

In a study of the factors influencing exports, McGuinness and Little, using regression analysis, found that two organizational characteristics—"commitment to exporting" and "high technology"—had a powerful positive effect on exports and their influence overwhelmed the influence of product characteristics. The implications of these findings are clear. New product advantages such as relative improvement are definitely a plus in influencing export performance. However, an emphasis on product improvement is not enough. As noted, the single most important factor in determining export success is company attitude and commitment.[6]

(something Richardson Mfg doesn't seem to have)

NATIONAL POLICIES
GOVERNING EXPORTS AND IMPORTS

It is hard to overstate the importance of exporting to economies around the world. In Canada alone, exports expanded by 65 percent over the past decade. A favorable export climate created by national policies often underlies the expansion of export trade. Policies toward exports and imports, however, are far from consistent across countries or within countries, for that matter. For centuries, the nation-states of the world have combined two opposing policy attitudes toward the movement of goods across national boundaries. Nations take steps to encourage exports by outright subsidy and by indirect measures. The latter include tax rebates and extensive government support programs in the area of promotion and producer education. The flow of imported goods is generally restricted by national policy. Measures such as tariffs, import control, and a host of nontariff barriers are designed to limit the inward flow of goods. Thus, the international situation is a combination of measures designed to simultaneously encourage exports and restrict imports.

The fastest growing countries in the world have all relied upon an export strategy encouraged by government. Consider Japan, Singapore, Korea, and the so-called "greater-China" market, which includes Taiwan, Hong Kong, and the People's Republic of China. In the last four decades, Japan totally recovered from the destruction of World War II and became an economic superpower as a direct result of MITI's export lead strategy. The "four tigers," Singapore, Korea, Taiwan, and Hong Kong, built upon the Japanese experience and all have export-based economies. And there soon may be a "fifth tiger": China, or, as it is now called, greater China.

In this section, we will highlight the framework for global trade (for detailed discussion of the GATT and WTO refer to Chapter 5), government support for exporters, and licensing and control of exporting.

▼ Trade Negotiations

Since 1947, the member countries of GATT have completed eight rounds of multilateral trade negotiations. The sixth round, popularly known as the Kennedy

---

[6] Norman W. McGuinness and Blair Little, "The Influence of Product Characteristics on the Export Performance of New Industrial Products," *Journal of Marketing* (Spring 1981), pp. 110–122.

Round, took place from 1963 to 1967. During these negotiations, tariffs on some 60,000 industrial goods were cut by an average of 35 percent, while there were only modest reductions (20 percent) for agricultural products, excluding grains. After the cuts the remaining tariffs averaged about 9 percent on manufactured goods, an all-time low by historical standards.

The seventh round of GATT negotiations was launched in Tokyo and ran from 1973 to 1979. These talks succeeded in cutting duties on industrial products, valued at $150 billion, by another 30 percent so that the remaining tariffs averaged about 6 percent. In terms of agricultural trade, there was a major clash between the U.S. and protectionist EC and Japanese markets. The clash pitted the American farmer, the world's most efficient producer, against the high-cost but politically powerful farmers of Europe and Japan. These deep-rooted differences resulted in little change in the agricultural area during the Tokyo Round. The most notable feature of the Tokyo Round was not the duty cuts, but rather a series of nine new agreements on nontariff trade barriers.

Trade representatives from seventy-eight countries launched the eighth round of negotiations at Punta del Este, Uruguay, in September 1986. These talks were scheduled to be completed by the end of 1990, but they dragged on through 1993 due to the participants' inability to come to agreement on the major issues. The intent was to significantly liberalize world trade, open more markets to the service sector, and revitalize the GATT system of trading rules. Negotiators finally succeeded in reaching agreement by the December 15, 1993 deadline. A stalemate over agricultural subsidies was broken, with France and the EC nations agreeing to reductions. Tariffs on agricultural goods will be reduced by 36 percent between 1995 and 2001. Markets for services will become more open over the next decade allowing for improved market access in financial, professional, telecommunications, computer, transportation, tourism and other services. As well, government procurement will be opened up to international competition.[7]

Many Canadian exporters, will benefit as tariffs are cut or eliminated entirely. The triad nations agreed to end tariffs in pharmaceuticals, construction, agricultural equipment, Scotch whiskey, furniture, paper, steel, and medical equipment. Also, Canadian restrictions on textile and apparel imports from Third World countries will be phased out over a ten-year period.

▼ Government Support for Exports

Exporting has long been of considerable interest and importance to the Canadian government, and tangible assistance to companies interested or involved in foreign markets began in Canada with the establishment of the trade commissioner service over one hundred years ago. Thus, companies' export involvement as a trade or commercial policy issue has been around for some time. Simply stated, export support programs are intended to improve the international competitiveness of companies and thus trade performance (which, in turn, creates jobs). For the most part, government support of export marketing is targeted towards

---

[7] *Canada and the Uruguay Round*, information kit (Ottawa: Government of Canada, April 1994) pp. 2–4.

small and medium-sized companies because they often lack the resources to prepare for and participate in the global competitive environment.

All industrialized countries, and many developing countries, have programs designed to help exporters, although, such support is not always government-based. In some countries, such as Italy, Sweden, the Netherlands, and the U.K., support comes through a cooperative effort of government and the private sector. In other countries, for example in Germany and Austria, export promotion takes place entirely in the private sector.[8]

Indeed, it is of interest to the exporter that such programs are quite similar across countries and typically fall into three broad groups: (1) those aimed at raising awareness, motivating companies, and providing information about foreign markets and opportunities; (2) those assisting with market entry, through market research, visits to markets, going on trade missions and fairs; and (3) those supporting ongoing export operations, such as further market development and expansion through export insurance and financing, and market information.[9]

There are nine categories of export assistance that are acceptable internationally under GATT: market research services, international trade missions, trade fairs and shows, trade promotion offices in foreign countries, government-sponsored research, trade financing and insurance programs (as offered by the Export Development Corporation), rebate of indirect taxes (exporters are exempted from the GST and PST), and free trade zones.[10]

Strictly speaking, such trade stimulation is interventionist and an obstacle to free and economically efficient trade. When any of the gains from trade (in this case exporting) result from governmental support of marketing or production costs, then these costs are not paid by the buyer, but instead are borne by the sources of government revenue in the exporting country.[11]

There are many restrictions through GATT on the type and extent of assistance government can provide to companies. Subsidies, for example, are not permitted.[12] The Uruguay round of GATT, however, agreed that certain subsidies, for example up to 75 percent of basic industrial research costs, or up to 50 percent of pre-competitive development activity, are permissible.[13]

The Canadian federal government, and all provincial governments, provide export support services to varying degrees. Table 16–3 provides a listing of the main trade development programs and services of the federal government.

---

[8] F.H. Rolf Seringhaus, "Export Promotion, the Role and Impact of Government Services," *Irish Marketing Review* (1987) 2, p.110.

[9] Ibid., p. 107.

[10] C.M. Korth, *International Business – Environment and Management*, 2nd ed. (Englewood Cliffs, Prentice-Hall, 1985), p. 94. GATT policies and procedure are continued under the WTO as of January, 1995.

[11] Ibid., pp. 95-7.

[12] For a detailed discussion of the legal barriers to government export support see Chapter 4 in F.H. Rolf Seringhaus and Philip J. Rosson, *Government Export Promotion: A Global Perspective* (London, Routledge, 1990).

[13] "New rules and institutions— Agreement on Subsidies and Countervailing Measures," *Canada and the Uruguay Round*, information kit, (Ottawa: Government of Canada, April 1994) pp.6-7.

TABLE 16-3 Trade Development Programs and Services

- Trade counseling and assistance through International Trade Centers in St.John's, Charlottetown, Halifax, Moncton, Montreal, Toronto, Winnipeg, Saskatoon, Edmonton, Calgary, and Vancouver
- Geographic Trade Divisions in Africa and the Middle East, Asia and Pacific, Europe, Latin America and Caribbean, and the United States
- Trade Commissioner in Canada and abroad (at the Trade Divison offices)
- Access North America Program with focus on Mexico
- Defense Programs, to compete for defense contracts in the U.S.
- Export Orientation/Training, the NEBS program for the U.S., and the NEXOS program for Europe
- Program for Export Market Development (PEMD) for industry- and government-initiated export marketing activities (develop strategy, identify markets, visit markets)
- Renaissance Eastern Europe positions companies for market entry and expansion
- Canadian International Development Agency (CIDA) companies can participate in development assistance projects
- Export Development Corporation (EDC) provides export financing and insurance
- Canadian Commercial Corporation (CCC) assists companies to compete for contracts with foreign governments and institutions
- Trade data and information, such as WIN Exports products and services sourcing, CanadExport trade newsletter, and diverse research reports on foreign markets and trade opportunities

Source: Based on *Trade Development Programs and Services*, Department of Foreign Affairs and International Trade, Ottawa, Government of Canada, 1994.

Exporters, and companies thinking of exporting, are pragmatic about their needs for information and knowledge about foreign markets. While many export support services are available to them, what matters most is what their benefit is to the company.

The services most frequently used by Canadian exporters are the Trade Commissioner Service, and support of participation in foreign trade fairs.[14] In order to understand what benefit exporters see in support programs and services, it helps to take a look at a specific service, such as help with trade fair participation. The exporter's perception, however, is also influenced by the company's export strategy, and newness to exporting.

Table 16–4 shows that new exporters and experienced exporters differ in their views on when the trade fair was of greatest benefit.

---

[14] F.H. Rolf Seringhaus, *Empirical Investigation of Awareness, Use and Impact of Export Marketing Support by Government in Manufacturing Firms*, Working Paper Series No. 104.85, School of Business and Economics, Wilfrid Laurier University, (1985) p.21.

TABLE 16–4 How Exporters View the Benefit of Trade Fair
Percent of companies reporting greatest benefit

	New Exporters	Experienced Exporters
Export Strategy:		
Preparing for Entry	23.6%	13.8%
Entering Export Market	35.7	27.9
Expand/Develop Markets	28.6	41.8
Maintain Export Presence	13.0	18.3

Note: New exporters have been exporting five years or less. Experienced exporters have been exporting for more than five years
Source: Data based on *Participants Survey – Fairs and Missions Evaluation* (Toronto: SPR Associates Incorporated, July 15, 1994) p.5.

Experienced exporters assign greatest benefit to trade fairs for market expansion and development, while new exporters place much greater importance on fairs early in the exporting process, namely during preparation and market entry.

▼ Export Controls and Licenses

The Canadian government controls the exportation of goods to all countries through the Export and Import Permits Act, the Export Control List, and the Area Control List. Export control is exercised primarily over natural resources and military or strategic goods. The Export Control List details specific product categories, such as advanced materials, electronics, or propulsion products, for which export permits are necessary, and/or which have export restrictions. This list is very detailed and exporters must carefully review them for compliance. The Area Control List specifies countries or regions to which all exports require permits. The countries in this list change from time to time depending on political events and developments.[15]

Canada has a bi-lateral agreement with the United States to waive export permits for most goods, although certain goods pertaining to atomic energy or nuclear technology are excluded from this waiver. Export permits are of two types: an Individual Export Permit (IEP) or a General Export Permit (GEP). The IEP is needed to export any goods controlled under the Export Control List or any goods to an Area Control List country. The GEP is a general permit issued to make exporting of "less sensitive goods" easier for companies. In addition, temporary export permits can be obtained when exporters want to take goods abroad for a short period of time, such as for use in trade fair exhibits or shows.

---

[15] Department of Foreign Affairs and International Trade, *A Guide to Canada's Export Controls* (Ottawa: Government of Canada, April, 1994).

In general, article XI of the GATT provides the framework for export/import regulations within which countries set their own regulations. As far as Canada is concerned, the NAFTA specifically emphasizes the applicability of the GATT.[16]

MARKET ACCESS CONSIDERATIONS

The phrase *market access considerations* refers to all conditions that apply to the importation of goods produced outside of the buyer's country. The major categories to be considered are import duties, import restrictions or quotas, foreign exchange regulations, and preference arrangements. Non-tariff and tariff barriers, although briefly covered in Chapter 5, are discussed in this section because, as they impact a company's ability to provide goods and services to customers in foreign markets, they are important considerations for exporters.

▼ Non-Tariff Barriers

A nontariff trade barrier (NTB) is defined by economists as any measure, public or private, that causes internationally traded goods and services to be allocated in such a way as to reduce potential real-world income. Potential real-world income is attainable when resources are allocated in the most economically efficient manner. To the business manager, a nontariff barrier is any measure, other than tariffs, that provides a barrier or obstacle to the sale of products in a foreign market. The five major types of nontariff trade barriers or hidden trade barriers, as they are sometimes called, are discussed next.

Quotas and Trade Control

These are specific limits, restrictions, and controls. The trade distortion caused by a quota is even more severe than a tariff because once the quota has been filled, market price mechanisms are not allowed to operate. The phrase *state trade controls* refers to the practice of monopolizing trade in certain commodities. In the former Soviet Union, all commodities were monopolized; there are also many examples of noncommunist government monopolies. The Swedish government, for example, controls the import of all alcoholic beverages and tobacco products and the French government controls all imports of coal.

For example, there are machine tool agreements with Japan and Taiwan, twenty steel trade agreements, textile quotas for most Southeast Asian and Third World countries, the Semiconductor Agreement between the U.S. and Japan, and Japanese "voluntary" restraints on the export of cars and televisions to the United States. Canada has a "Memorandum of Understanding on Softwood Lumber" with the United States, its largest trading partner. The extent of these and other similar agreements on a worldwide basis has led some critics to argue that trade is "managed" rather than free.

---

[16] *North American Free Trade Agreement* (Ottawa, Government of Canada: 1993), Section C, p. 3-9.

Government and Private Procurement Policies

These are the rules and regulations that discriminate against foreign suppliers and are commonly referred to as "Buy Canadian" or "Buy American" policies. GATT has opened government procurement to international competititon, which, for Canadian exporters, provides significantly greater opportunities to compete.

Restrictive Customs Procedures

For example, under NAFTA, the Harmonized System for the classification of goods, and thus tariffs, helps to simplify the complexities of compliance with, say U.S. customs regulations. Still, the classification of goods used by the U.S. Department of Commerce may differ from that used by the Canadian exporter. While such disagreements are generally resolved between exporters and customs officials, they cause time delays and add additional expense for both exporter and importer.

When goods contain foreign-made components or materials, the Rules of Origin, set up under NAFTA, require an elaborate accounting and apportioning of the various components by the Canadian exporter before the appropriate tariff can be obtained. Exporters can now avail themselves of commercial software programs that seek to make such rules more user-friendly.

Selective Monetary Controls and Discriminatory Exchange Rate Policies

Discriminatory exchange rate policies distort trade in much the same way as selective import duties and export subsidies. Selective monetary policies are definite barriers to trade. For example, many countries from time to time require importers to place on deposit at no interest an amount equal to the value of imported goods. In effect, these regulations raise the price of foreign goods by the cost of money for the term of the required deposit.

Restrictive Administrative and Technical Regulations

These include antidumping regulations, size regulations, and safety and health regulations. Some of these regulations are intended to keep out foreign goods, while others are directed toward legitimate domestic objectives. For example, the safety and pollution regulations being developed in the United States for automobiles and generally used as a standard in Canada, are motivated almost entirely by legitimate concerns about highway safety and pollution. However, an effect of these regulations has been to make it so expensive to comply with the safety requirements that some auto makers have withdrawn certain models from the market.

Despite a GATT agreement concerning technical barriers to trade, sometimes technical standards unrelated to performance are used to bar products from the market.

Another example of a restrictive technical regulation is found in Germany, which requires that imports of feed meal contain only 5 percent fat. An exporter producing a feed meal that contains about 10 percent fat could then not export to

Germany. To change the meal's fat content would involve special machinery which would increase production costs. According to the company it may not be worth it.

As discussed in earlier chapters, there is a growing trend to remove all such restrictive trade barriers on a regional basis. The largest single effort was undertaken by the EC—the alliance is now known as the European Union (EU)—in an effort to create a single market starting January 1, 1993. The intent is to have one standard for all of Europe for such things as automobile safety, drug testing and certification, food and product quality controls as well as the development of a single currency, the ECU, to facilitate trade and commerce. Some observers believe that elimination of these intra-European barriers will result in the creation of a so-called Fortress Europe with new external barriers designed to keep out the foreign (e.g., Japanese) competition. The creation of a single North American market consisting of the United States, Canada, and Mexico is another example. The North American Free Trade Agreement has been in force since January 1, 1994.

TARIFFS AND DUTIES

▼ Tariff Classification

Before World War II specific duties were widely used and the tariffs of many countries, particularly those in Europe and Latin America, were extremely complex. Since the war the trend has been toward the conversion to ad valorem duties. Between 1959 and 1988, tariff administration was simplified by the use of the Brussels nomenclature (BTN). This nomenclature was worked out by an international committee of experts under the sponsorship of the Customs Cooperation Council, which in 1955 produced a convention that took effect in 1959.

The rules of this convention were used by most GATT member countries until the Harmonized Tariff System (HTS) went into effect in January 1989. The importer has to determine the correct import classification number. With the harmonized schedule B, the export classification number for any exported item is now the same as the import classification number. Under the BTN system, these numbers differed. HTS, adopted by over 65 countries, has standardized a common classification system for all products.[17] This makes it easier for buyers and sellers to determine export classifications. Also, exporters are encouraged to include the harmonized tariff schedule B number on their invoices to facilitate customs clearance.

In spite of the progress made in simplifying tariff procedures, the task of administrating a tariff presents an enormous problem. Even a tariff schedule of several thousand items cannot clearly describe every product that enters into international trade. The constant flow of new products and new materials used in manufacturing processes introduces new problems. Often, two or more alternative classifications must be considered in assessing the rate on a particular article depending upon how it is used or its component material.

---

[17] Thomas E. Johnson, *Export/Import Procedure and Documentation* (New York: Amacom, 1991), p. 201.

The classification of a product can make a substantial difference in the duty applied. Under the BTN, it was sometimes possible to seek a more favorable classification to minimize the duty levied in the importing country.

Tariff Systems

Tariff systems provide either a single rate of duty for each item applicable to all countries, or two or more rates, applicable to different countries or groups of countries. Tariffs are usually grouped into two classifications.

Single-Column Tariff

The single-column tariff is the simplest type of tariff and consists of a schedule of duties in which the rate applies to imports from all countries on the same basis.

Two-Column Tariff

Under the two-column tariff, the initial single column of duties is supplemented by a second column of "conventional" duties, which shows reduced rates agreed through tariff negotiations with other countries. The conventional rates, for example, those agreed upon by "convention," are supplied to all countries enjoying MFN (most favored nation) status within the framework of GATT. Under GATT, nations agree to apply their most favorable tariff or lowest tariff rate to all nations who are signatories to GATT, with some substantial exceptions.

Canada maintains MFN status with most countries around the world so the name is really a misnomer. MFN status is sometimes used as a political tool more than an economic one. The U.S., for example, has threatened China with the loss of MFN status because of alleged human rights violations. Loss of MFN status could increase the price of the country's goods, imported by trade partners, significantly.

Preferential Tariff

A preferential tariff is a reduced tariff rate applied to imports from certain countries. GATT prohibits the use of preferential tariffs with three major exceptions. First are historical preference arrangements such as the British Commonwealth preferences and similar arrangements that existed before the GATT convention. Second, preference schemes as part of a formal economic integration treaty, such as free trade areas or common markets, are excluded. Third, the granting of preferential access to industrial country markets to companies based in less developed countries is permitted.

Customs Valuation Code

Canada is a signatory to the GATT Customs Valuation Code. Under the code, the primary basis of customs valuation is known as *transaction value*. As the name implies, transaction value is defined as the actual individual transaction price paid by the buyer to the seller of the goods being valued. In instances where the buyer and seller are related parties (as in the case of most multinational corporate sales), customs authorities have the right to scrutinize the transfer price to make sure it is a fair reflection of market value. If there is no established transaction value for the goods, alternative methods are used to compute the customs value, which sometimes result in increased values and, consequently, increased duties. Exporters should be aware whether or not the country of their trading partner is a signatory to the GATT.

Types of Duties

Customs duties are divided into two categories. They may be calculated either as a percentage of the value of the goods (ad valorem duty), or as a specific amount per unit (specific duty), or as a combination of both of these methods.

Ad Valorem Duties. This duty is expressed as a percentage of the value of goods. The definition of customs value varies from country to country. Therefore, an exporter is well advised to secure information about the valuation practices applied to his or her product in the country of destination. A uniform basis for the valuation of goods for customs purposes was elaborated by the Customs Cooperation Council in Brussels and was adopted in 1953. In countries adhering to HTS conventions on customs valuation, the customs value is landed C.I.F. cost at the port of entry. This cost should reflect the arm's-length price of the goods at the time the duty becomes payable.

Specific Duties. These duties are expressed as a specific amount of currency per unit of weight, volume, length, or number of other units of measurement, for example, "50 cents per pound," "$1.00 per pair," or "25 cents per square meter." Specific duties are usually expressed in the currency of the importing country, but there are exceptions, particularly in countries that have experienced sustained inflation. In the Chilean tariff, rates are given in gold pesos and, therefore, must be multiplied by an established conversion factor to obtain the corresponding amount of the exporter's currency.

Alternative Duties. In this case both ad valorem and specific duties are set out in the custom tariff for a given product. Normally, the applicable rate yields the higher amount of duty, although there are cases where the lower rate is specified.

Compound or Mixed Duties. These duties provide for specific plus ad valorem rates to be levied on the same articles.

Antidumping and Countervailing Duties. Dumping and countervailing duties were discussed in Chapter 13. To offset the impact of dumping and to penalize guilty companies, most countries have introduced legislation providing for the imposition of antidumping duties if injury is caused to domestic producers. Such duties take the form of special additional import charges equal to the dumping margin. Antidumping duties are almost invariably applied to articles that are also produced in the importing country. Countervailing duties seek to target a specific category of goods with a tariff as a measure of retaliation against subsidies.

Other Import Charges

Variable Import Levies. Several countries, including Sweden and some members of the EU, apply a system of variable import levies to certain categories of imported agricultural products. In instances where the prices of imported products would undercut those of domestic products, the effect of these levies would be to raise the price of imported products to the domestic price level.

Temporary Import Surcharges. Temporary surcharges have been introduced from time to time by certain countries, such as the United Kingdom and the United States, to provide additional protection for local industry and, in particular, in response to balance-of-payments deficits.

Compensatory Import Taxes. In theory these taxes correspond to various internal taxes, such as value-added taxes and sales taxes. Such "border tax adjustments" must not, according to GATT, amount to additional protection for domestic producers or to a subsidy for exports.

EXPORT DECISIONS

▼ Investigating Export Markets

A company committed to growth has four basic expansion alternatives. Vertical integration involves moving from a finished product back to basic materials, or vice versa. For a steel manufacturer, this would involve moving forward from the manufacture of steel to the fabrication of metal products. For the metal fabricator, vertical integration would involve moving back to the manufacture of steel. A second expansion alternative is horizontal expansion of the product line. This involves moving to configurations and adaptations in the product that are variations on the company's basic line. For example, a sled manufacturer might introduce a low-priced utility model and a high-priced luxury model, thus expanding the line from one basic, medium-priced sled to three. A third and more venturesome expansion alternative is product diversification. This involves moving into an entirely new product technology area via acquisition. A fourth expansion alternative is geographical diversification, or the extension of existing products to new geographic markets. If the move into foreign markets involves the use of goods manufactured in the home or domestic market, the fourth expansion alternative is export marketing or export selling, depending on the degree of involvement in foreign markets.

When should a company investigate export markets? This question must be answered by comparing the business opportunity in export markets with that in domestic markets. For each market, determine the export opportunity as shown:

M = potential market size in market X_1

C = competitive offering

P_1 = product

P_2 = price (sum of manufacturing cost plus transportation, insurance, taxes, duty, and trade margins)

P_3 = product distribution or availability

P_4 = advertising and promotion

TR = total revenue in market

cost = manufacturing, marketing, tariff, and overhead costs

$$TR = f(M, C, P_1, P_2, P_3, P_4)$$
$$\text{then export opportunity} = TR - \text{cost}$$

Export opportunities should be compared with each other and with domestic opportunities to determine strategy priorities.

▼ Creating a Product-Market Profile

The first step in choosing export markets is to establish the key factors influencing sales and profitability of the product in question. If a company is getting started for the first time in exporting, its product-market profile will have to be based upon its experience in the home market. The basic questions to be answered can be summarized as the nine Ws:

1. Who buys our product?
2. Who does not buy our product?
3. What need or function does our product serve?
4. What problem does our product solve?
5. What are customers currently buying to satisfy the need and/or solve the problem for which our product is targeted?
6. What price are they paying for the products they are currently buying?
7. When is our product purchased?
8. Where is our product purchased?
9. Why is our product purchased?

Any company must answer these critical questions if it is going to be successful in export markets. Each answer provides an input into decisions concerning the four Ps. Remember, the general rule in marketing is that if a company wants to penetrate an existing market, it must offer more value than competitors—better benefits, lower prices, or both. This applies to export marketing as well as marketing in the home country.

▼ Market Selection

Once a company has created a product-market profile, the next step in choosing an export market is to appraise possible markets. Six criteria should be assessed.

Market Potential

What is the basic market potential for the product? To answer this question, the library is a good start. The federal and provincial governments have numerous publications available to help the exporter focus the search for markets. Market profiles are available for many countries. Market data are also available from export census documents compiled by Statistics Canada. Another important source of market data is the Trade Commissioner Service.

A number of electronic communication resources have been developed in recent years, including WIN Exports (World Information Network for Exports), which collects data on Canadian companies and products for export. The International Trade Data Bank with trade statistics from the United Nations covers more than sixty countries. The CanadExport newsletter is a very useful source of up-to-date export opportunities.

Whatever source of information is used, the ultimate goal is to determine the major factors affecting demand for a product. Then, using the tools and techniques described in Chapter 7 and available data, it is possible to arrive at a rough estimate of total potential demand for the product in one or more particular international markets.

As noted in Chapter 3, national income is often a good starting indicator on which to base estimates of demand. Additional statistical measures will considerably sharpen the estimate of total demand. For example, when estimating the demand for automobile tires, data on the total number of cars registered in any country in the world should be easy to obtain. These data, combined with data on gasoline consumption, should permit estimation of the total mileage driven in the target market. When this figure is combined with tire life predictions, demand estimates are easy to calculate.

In some instances, it will be difficult to accurately estimate demand on the basis of published statistics. If specific data are unavailable, the most useful approach to estimating market potential is analogy, as described in Chapter 7. Briefly, if information on consumption or use of the product is available in a single market, and if there is a solid basis for assuming demand conditions for the product are similar in other markets, then analogy can yield a good rough estimate of demand potential.

Market Access Considerations for Importers

This aspect of market selection concerns the entire set of national controls that applies to imported merchandise. It includes such items as import duties, import restrictions or quotas, foreign exchange regulations, and preference arrangements. This topic requires in-depth consideration and is discussed in detail in the next section.

Shipping Cost

As discussed in Chapter 13, export preparation and shipping costs can affect the market potential for your product. If a product similar to yours is already being manufactured in your target market, shipping costs may render your product uncompetitive. Investigate alternative modes of shipping as well as ways to differentiate your product to offset your price disadvantage.

Appraising the Level and Quality of Competition in the Potential Market

Discussions with exporters, bankers, and other industry executives are extremely useful at this stage. Using a country's commercial representatives abroad can also be valuable. When contacting country representatives abroad, it is important to provide as much specific information as possible. If a manufacturer simply says, "I make lawn mowers. Is there a market for them in your territory?" the representative cannot provide much helpful information. If, on the other hand, the manufacturer provides information (1) such as the sizes of lawn mowers manufactured, (2) descriptive brochures indicating features and advantages, and (3) estimated C.I.F. and retail price in the target market, then the commercial representative could provide a very useful report based upon a comparison of the company's product with market needs and offerings.

Product Fit

With information on market potential, cost of access to the market, and local competition, the next step is to decide how well your company's product fits the market in question. In general, a product fits a market if it satisfies the following criteria: (1) the product is likely to appeal to customers in the potential market; (2) the product will not require more adaptation than is economically justifiable by the volume expected in the potential market; (3) import restrictions and/or high tariffs do not exclude or make the product so expensive in the target market as to effectively eliminate demand; (4) shipping costs to the target market are in line with the requirements for competitive price; and (5) the cost of assembling sales literature, catalogs, and technical bulletins is not out of line with the market potential. The last factor is particularly important in selling highly technical products.

Service

If service is required for the product, can it be delivered at a cost that is consistent with the size of the market?

Table 16–5 presents a market selection framework that incorporates the information elements just discussed. Three countries, A, B, and C, are arranged in order of declining size of market. At first glance, market A might appear to hold the greatest potential simply on the basis of size. While it is true that population is a major factor in assessing market potential, there are other important issues to be considered.

First, the competitive advantage of our hypothetical firm is zero in market A, 10 percent in market B, and 20 percent in market C. Multiplying the market size and competitive advantage index yields a market potential of 5 in market B and 4 in C.

The next stage in our analysis requires an assessment of the relevant *market access considerations*. In Table 16–5 all these conditions or terms are reduced to an index number, which is 60 percent for market B and 90 percent for market C. In other words, the market access considerations are more favorable in market C than in B. By multiplying the market's potential and the index of market

TABLE 16–5   Market Selection Framework

Market	Market Size	Competitive Advantage		Market Potential	Terms of Access	Export Potential
A	100	0	=	0	100.00	0
B	50	0.10	=	5	0.60	3.0
C	20	0.20	=	4	0.90	3.6

access considerations, we discover that market C, despite its small size, holds greater potential than A or B. In this example, a company with limited resources would want to begin its export marketing program in market C because this country (all things considered) offers the highest export market potential.

▼ Visiting the Potential Market

After the research effort has zeroed in on potential markets, there is no substitute for a personal visit to size up the market firsthand and begin the development of an actual export marketing program. A market visit should do several things. First, it should confirm (or contradict) assumptions regarding market potential. A second major purpose is to gather additional data necessary to reach the final go/no-go decision regarding an export marketing program. There are certain kinds of information that simply cannot be obtained from secondary sources. For example, an export manager or international marketing manager may have a list of potential distributors provided by the Trade Commissioner Service or the local office of the bilateral Chamber of Commerce. He or she may correspond with distributors on the list and form a tentative idea of whether they meet the company's international criteria. It is difficult, however, to negotiate a suitable arrangement with international distributors without actually meeting face to face to allow each side of the contract to appraise the capabilities and character of the other party. A third reason for a visit to the export market is to develop a marketing plan in cooperation with the local agent or distributor. Agreement should be reached on necessary product modifications, pricing, advertising and promotion expenditures, and a distribution plan. If the plan calls for investment, agreement on the allocation of costs must also be reached.

One way to visit a potential market is through a trade show or a government-sponsored trade mission. Hundreds of trade fairs usually organized around a product, a group of products, or activity are held in major markets. For example, the federal government suports participation in dozens of trade fairs annually in major markets abroad.

By attending trade shows and missions, company representatives can conduct market assessment, develop or expand markets, find distributors or agents, or locate potential end users (i.e., engage in direct selling). Perhaps most important, by attending a trade show it is possible to learn a great deal about competitors' technology, pricing, and the depth of their market penetration. For example, while walking around the exhibit hall, one can gather literature about products that often contains strategically useful technological information. Overall, it is possible to get a good general impression of your competitors in the marketplace while at the same time trying to sell your product.

It is important to remember that trade shows and trade missions differ in the opportunities and potential benefits they provide to participants. Table 16–6 gives a summary of the different roles trade missions and trade fairs play for companies at various stages of export involvement.

▼ Developing an Export Program

After an export market has been selected, the export program must be developed. The best checklist for ensuring a complete program composed of the four Ps: product (P_1), price (P_2), place (P_3), and promotion (P_4). In developing the export program, the issue for each of the four Ps is whether to extend, adapt, or create. For example, can the product be exported as is (extended) or must it be adapted to suit a particular export market?

EXPORT ORGANIZATION: HOME/HOST COUNTRY

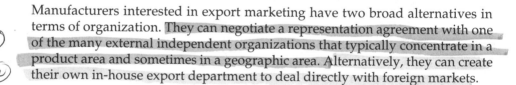

Manufacturers interested in export marketing have two broad alternatives in terms of organization. They can negotiate a representation agreement with one of the many external independent organizations that typically concentrate in a product area and sometimes in a geographic area. Alternatively, they can create their own in-house export department to deal directly with foreign markets.

▼ Home Country

External Independent Export Organizations

If a company chooses not to perform its own marketing and promotion in house, there are numerous export services available, including those provided by export merchants, export brokers, combination export managers, manufacturer's export representatives or commission agents, and export distributors. The definitions in the Appendix are guides to industry usage. Because of the variations in usage of these terms, the reader is warned to check and confirm the services performed by an independent export organization.

There are several hundred independent trading houses in Canada whose services offer an alternative for companies who do not wish direct involvement in the exporting process.

TABLE 16–6 International Trade Missions and Trade Fairs and Their Different Roles for Exporters

Export Involvement	Key questions to ask	Key decisions to make	Role for trade mission	Role for trade fair
Non-Exporter	Should we consider consider exporting as a vehicle for growth?	• Notional interest in exporting • Exportability of product or service • Resources that could be available for exporting	• Trade mission not appropriate for these companies	• Trade fair not appropriate for these companies
First-Time Exporter	Should we initiate exporting?	• Growth potential from exports vs. domestic market • Problems to be overcome to tap export potential • Likely cost/benefit of export invovement	• Potential to investigate market, buyers, competitors, distrbutors at first-hand; opportunity to discuss exporting with other, more experienced mission particpants; make initial contacts • Chance to better define what is involved in exporting – resources, commitments	• Trade fair not generally appropriate for these companies, unless market research, potential and segmentation support exhibiting
Expanding Exporter	Which market(s) should we enter next? What market entry method is best?	• Determine market potential and barriers to entry • Choose between between feasible market entry alternatives • Select foreign market partner (where applicable)	• Opportunity to meet buyers, members of trade, and government officials; do market size-up; check on competiton • Advice from mission participants experienced in market and/or own government officials covering market • Chance to meet prospective agents/ distributors and/or trading partners	• Chance to present product/service to the market and test response prior to entry decision • Since key competitors are likely to be ex-hibiting, able to check out rivals in an efficient manner • Opportunity to make useful future contacts with buyers and prospective trading partners
Continuing Exporters	How can we maintain/improve our performance?	• Need to adjust/ change existing operations for the market in question • Decide what new initiatives look best	• Trade mission normally not appropriate for these companies	• Provides an opportunity to renew contacts with buy ers, trading partners and to solidify company position in market.

TABLE 16–6 *Continued*

- Presents chance to test out new ideas for product features, price, promotion, etc., prior to making final decisions
- Opportunity to scout out new trading partners if changes viewed as necessary

Source: Adapted from F.H. Rolf Seringhaus , *The Changing Role of Trade Fairs and Missions*, discussion paper prepared for External Affairs and International Trade Canada (1994).

In-House Export Organization

Most companies handle export operations within their own organization. Depending on the company's size, responsibilities may be incorporated into an employee's domestic job description. Alternatively, these responsibilities may be handled as part of a separate division or organizational structure.

The possible arrangements for handling exports include the following:

1. As a part-time activity performed by domestic employees.
2. Through an export partner affiliated with the domestic marketing structure that takes possession of the goods before they leave the country.
3. Through an export department that is independent of the domestic marketing structure.
4. Through an export department within an international division.
5. For multidivisional companies, each of the foregoing possibilities exists within each division.

A company that assigns a sufficiently high priority to its export business will establish an in-house organization. It then faces the question of how to organize effectively. This depends on two things: the company's appraisal of the opportunities in export marketing and its strategy for allocating resources to markets on a global basis. It may be possible for a company to make export responsibility part of a domestic employee's job description. The advantage of this arrangement is obvious: It is a low-cost arrangement requiring no additional personnel. However, this approach can only work under two conditions. First, the domestic employee assigned to the task must be thoroughly competent in terms of product/customer knowledge. Second, that competence must be applicable to the target international market(s). The key issue underlying the second condition is the extent to which the target export market is different from the domestic market. If customer circumstances and characteristics are similar, the requirements for specialized regional knowledge are reduced.

▼ Host County

The export organization must make arrangements to distribute the product in the market country. This is true regardless of whether it is located within the manufacturing company or in an external independent export organization. The basic decision that every exporting organization faces is: To what extent do we rely upon direct market representation as opposed to representation by independent intermediaries?

Direct Market Representation

There are two major advantages to direct representation in a market. The first is control; the second is communications. Control is an important feature of direct representation. When a marketer wishes to develop a particular program, commit resources to some activity such as advertising, or change price, direct representation allows such decisions to be implemented unilaterally. When a product is not yet established in a market, special efforts are necessary to achieve sales. The advantage of direct representation is that these special efforts are ensured by the marketer's investment. With indirect or independent representation, such efforts and investment are often not forthcoming; in many cases, there is simply not enough incentive for independents to invest significant time and money in representing a product.

The other great advantage to direct representation is that the possibilities for feedback and information from the market are much greater. This information can vastly improve export marketing decisions concerning product, price, communications, and distribution.

Direct representation does not mean that the exporter is selling directly to the consumer or customer. In most cases, direct representation involves selling to wholesalers or retailers.

Independent Representation

For smaller markets, some companies are using the electronic media in innovative ways. Product details and sales presentations are placed on personal computer disks, which are sent to distributors or prospective customers. The programmed electronic presentation might even have an interactive part, thus allowing customers to view, for example, product performance, while considering their particular requirements. Customers can then place orders with independent agents. Yet another form of representation emerging as a result of communications technology is telemarketing through "call centers." These call centers, staffed by multilingual well-trained personnel, straddle the concept of direct telemarketing and independent representation and offer exporters a fast entry into market regions. Ireland, Scotland and the Netherlands are some of the key locations for call centers that offer cost-effective export marketing in Europe.[18]

---

[18] Tony Glover, "Call of the Wilds," *Eurobusiness* (November 1994) pp. 43–46.

Piggyback Marketing

Piggyback marketing or the use of a *mother hen* sales force is an innovation in international distribution that has received much attention in recent years. This is an arrangement whereby one manufacturer obtains distribution of products through another's distribution channels. The motivation for this arrangement exists on both sides of the contract. The active distribution partner obtains a fuller use of its distribution system and thereby increases the revenues generated by the system. The manufacturer using the piggy-back arrangement does so at a cost that is much lower than that required for any direct arrangement. Successful piggyback marketing requires that the combined product lines be complementary. They must appeal to the same customer, and they must not be competitive with each other. If these requirements are met, the piggyback arrangement can be a very effective way of fully utilizing an international channel system to the advantage of both parties.

EXPORT FINANCING/METHODS OF PAYMENT[19]

The decision as to the appropriate method of payment for a given international sale is a basic credit decision. A number of factors must be considered, including currency availability in the buyer's country, creditworthiness of the buyer, and the seller's relationship to the buyer. Finance managers at companies that have never exported often express concern regarding payment. Many CFOs with international experience know that a comparison of international receivables with domestic receivables often demonstrates that there is less of a problem collecting on international sales than on domestic sales, provided the proper financial instruments are used. The reason is simple: As explained later, using a letter of credit in export sales guarantees payment for a product. Domestic sales, on the other hand, are usually conducted on an open-account basis; collecting thus hinges on the creditworthiness of the buyer. After an exporter and importer have established a good working relationship, and the finance managers' level of confidence increases, it may be possible to move to a documentary collection or open-account method of payment. The different methods for arranging payment for export merchandise sales to buyers abroad are explained next.

▼ Letters of Credit

Letters of credit are the payment method most often used in international trade. Excluding advance payment terms, a letter of credit offers the exporter the best assurance of being paid for products sold internationally. That assurance arises from the fact that the payment obligation under a letter of credit lies with the buyer's bank and not the buyer.

A letter of credit (L/C) is essentially a "letter" by which a bank substitutes its creditworthiness for that of the buyer. A letter of credit can be considered a

---

[19] Thanks to Patricia F. Rourke of Bankers Trust in Des Moines, Iowa, for supplying several of the definitions in this section.

conditional guarantee issued by the bank on behalf of the buyer to a seller assuring payment if the seller complies with the terms set forth in the L/C. For importers, however, the letter is more expensive since funds might have to be deposited in their bank to secure the credit line. If a letter of credit is the method of financing, the exporter ordinarily receives payment at the time shipping documents are presented to the bank negotiating the L/C in the seller's country.

▼ Documentary Collections (Drafts)

A documentary collection is a method of payment using a bill of exchange, also known as a draft. A bill of exchange is a negotiable instrument which is easily transferable from one party to another. In its simplest form, it is a written order by one party directing a second party to pay to the order of a third party.

A documentary draft is an important instrument in an export transaction. With a documentary draft, the documents which are required to clear the goods through customs and convey title plus other important shipping documents are sent to a bank in the importer's country. The draft is presented to the importer along with these documents, which are delivered against the importer's honoring of the draft.

▼ Cash in Advance

There are a number of conditions which may prompt the exporter to request cash payment in whole or in part in advance of shipment. Examples include times when credit risks abroad are high, when exchange restrictions within the country of destination may delay return of funds for an unreasonable period, or when, for any other reason, the exporter may be unwilling to sell on credit terms. Because of competition and restrictions against cash payment in many countries, the volume of business handled on a cash-in-advance basis is small.

▼ Sales on Open Account

Open-account terms generally prevail in areas where exchange controls are minimal and exporters have had long-standing relations with good buyers in nearby or long-established markets. Open-account terms also prevail when sales are made to branches or subsidiaries of the exporter. The main objection to open-account sales is the absence of a tangible obligation. Normally, if a time draft is drawn and is dishonored after acceptance, it can be used as a basis of legal action, whereas in the case of a dishonored open-account transaction, the legal procedure may be more complicated.

▼ Sales on a Consignment Basis

As in the case of sales on open account, no tangible obligation is created by consignment sales. In countries with free ports or free trade zones, it can be arranged to have consigned merchandise placed under bonded warehouse control in the name of a foreign bank. Sales can then be arranged by the selling agent and arrangements made to release partial lots out of the consigned stock against regular payment terms. The merchandise is not cleared through customs until after the sale has been completed.

BARTER AND COUNTERTRADE[20]

In recent years, barter and countertrade have become increasingly important means of exchange in international trade. These methods of completing international transactions are an alternative to trade based only on the exchange of money for goods or services. In some instances, exchange controls prevent companies from expatriating earnings; in such instances, companies may be forced to spend money in the country for products that are then exported and sold in third-country markets. Unconfirmed estimates of the barter and countertrade share of world trade volume put it as high as 25 to 30 percent. For East-West trade, the share is estimated to be even higher.

Huszagh and Barksdale developed a typology of barter and countertrade to clarify the differences among the various approaches to what is potentially a very confusing mixture of trade and financing. Their work is summarized in Table 16–7 and in the discussion that follows.

▼ Barter

Simple Barter

Also termed *straight*, *classical*, or *pure barter*, this term describes the least complex and oldest form of bilateral, nonmonetized trade. Simple barter is a direct exchange of goods or services between two parties. Although no money is in-

---

TABLE 16–7   Types of International Transactions*

Conventional	Barter	Countertrade
Exporting	Simple	Counterpurchase
Importing	Closed-end barter	Offset
Licensing	Clearing account barter	Compensation trading
Management contract	Indirect barter	Cooperation agreements
Overseas sales office or marketing subsidiary†	Switch trading	Switch trading
Overseas production† Assembly operations Complete manufacturing operations		

* It is possible that any of the forms given can be combined, for example, licensing with a cooperation agreement joined to classical barter.
† Ownership and control may be shared in a joint venture or be wholly owned by the investing firm.
Source: Adapted from Sandra M. Huszagh and Hiram C. Barksdale, "Barter and Countertrade; A 'New' Approach to International Marketing," College of Business Administration, University of Georgia (Athens), no date.

---

[20] This section is adapted from the paper "Barter and Countertrade: A 'New' Approach to International Marketing," by Sandra Huszagh and Hiram C. Barksdale, College of Business Administration, University of Georgia (Athens), no date.

volved, both partners construct an approximate shadow price for products flowing in each direction. One contract formalizes simple barter transactions, which are generally less than one year to avoid problems in price fluctuations. However, for some transactions, the exchange may span months or years, with contract provisions allowing adjustments in the exchange ratio to handle fluctuations in world prices. Generally, distribution is direct between trading partners with no intermediaries included. Sometimes companies seek the help of barter specialists.

The most high-profile company involved in barter deals is PepsiCo Inc., which has done business in the Soviet market for over twenty years. Russia and other CIS countries "pay" Pepsi for soft-drink syrup concentrate with Stolichnaya vodka that is in turn exported to the United States by Pepsi's PepsiCo Wines & Spirits subsidiary and marketed.

Closed-End Barter

This type of transaction modifies simple barter in that a buyer is found for goods taken in barter before the contract is signed by the two trading parties. Obviously, risk related to product quality is significantly reduced in closed-end barter arrangements. Again, no money is involved in the exchange.

Clearing Account Barter

Also termed *clearing agreements, clearing arrangements, bilateral clearing accounts,* or simply *bilateral clearing,* this approach is based on the principle that exchanges balance without either party having to acquire hard currency. In this form of barter, each party agrees in a single contract to purchase a specified and usually equal value of goods and services. The duration of these transactions is commonly one year, although occasionally they may extend over a longer time period. The contract's value is expressed in nonconvertible, clearing account units (also termed *clearing dollars*) that effectively represent a line of credit in the central bank of that country with no money involved. Clearing account units are universally accepted for the accounting of trade between countries and parties whose commercial relationships are based on bilateral agreements.

The contract sets forth the goods to be exchanged, the ratio of exchange, and the length of time for completing the transaction. Limited export or import surpluses may be accumulated by either party for short periods. Generally, after one year's time, imbalances are settled by one of the following approaches: credit against the following year, acceptance of unwanted goods, payment of a previously specified penalty, or payment of the difference in hard currency. Trading specialists also have initiated the practice of buying clearing dollars at a discount for the purpose of using them to purchase salable products. In turn, the trader may forfeit a portion of the discount to sell these products for hard currency on the international market. Compared with simple barter, clearing accounts offer greater flexibilities in length of time for drawdown on the lines of credit and the types of products exchanged.

▼ Countertrade

Countertrade incorporates a real distinction from barter, since money or credit is involved in the transaction. *Countertrade* is a generic term that broadly defines an arrangement in which firms both sell to and buy from their customers' customers. Countertrade generally involves a seller from the West and a buyer in a developing country; the countries in the former Soviet bloc have historically relied heavily on countertrade. Countertrade generally means that Western products or technology are paid for in full or in part with products produced in the importing countries.

This approach, which reached a peak in popularity in the mid-1980s, is now used in some one hundred countries. Perhaps the single most important driving force behind the proliferation of countertrade has been the decreasing ability of developing countries to finance imports through bank loans. This trend has resulted in debt-ridden governments pushing for self-financed deals.[21] Two conditions determine the probability that importing nations will demand countertrade: (1) the priority attached to the western import, and (2) the value of the transaction. Overall, the advantages to nonmarket and developing economies are access to Western marketing expertise and technology in the short term, and creation of hard-currency export markets in the long term.

Counterpurchase

This form of countertrade, also termed *parallel trading* or *parallel barter*, is distinguished from other forms in that each delivery is paid for in cash. Generally, products offered by the foreign principal are not related to the Western firm's exports and thus cannot be used directly by the firm. In most counterpurchase transactions, two separate contracts are signed. In one the supplier agrees to sell products for a cash settlement (the original sales contract); in the other the supplier agrees to purchase and market unrelated products from the buyer (a separate, parallel contract). The dollar value of the goods the supplier agrees to market generally represents a set percentage—and sometimes the full value—of the products sold to the foreign principal. When the Western supplier sells these goods, the trading cycle is complete.

Offset

Offset is used to recover hard-currency drains resulting from purchases of expensive items. Often occurring at the government level, offset may be distinguished from counterpurchase because the latter is characterized by smaller deals over shorter periods of time.[22] On occasion, offset may involve cooperation in manufacturing. For example, a foreign principal may include requirements to

---

[21] Pompiliu Verzariu, "Trends and Developments in International Countertrade," *Business America*, November 2, 1992, p. 2.

[22] Patricia Daily and S. M. Ghazanfar, "Countertrade: Help or Hindrance to Less-Developed Countries?" *The Journal of Social, Political, and Economic Studies*, 18, no. 1 (Spring 1993), 65.

place subcontracts locally and/or to arrange local assembly or manufacturing equal to a certain percentage of the contract value.[23]

This type of countertrade has emerged from foreign purchases of machinery and equipment for large-scale industrial projects, commercial and military aircraft, and defense-related products and services. Other countries practicing offset include some highly developed nations such as Switzerland, and Australia. The major distinction between offset and other forms of countertrade is that the agreement is not contractual but reflects a memorandum of understanding that sets out the dollar value of products to be offset and the time period for completing the transaction. In addition, there is no penalty on the supplier for nonperformance. Typically, requests range from 20 to 50 percent of the value of the supplier's product, with highly competitive sales requiring over 100 percent.

Compensation Trading

This form of countertrade is also called buyback, and involves two separate parallel contracts. In one contract, the supplier agrees to build a plant or provide plant equipment; patents or licenses; or technical, managerial, or distribution expertise for a hard-currency down payment at the time of delivery. In the other contract, the supplier company agrees to take payment in the form of the plant's output equal to its investment (minus interest) for a period of as many as 20 years. Essentially, the transaction rests on the willingness of each firm to be both a buyer and a seller. Compensation differs from counterpurchase in that the technology or capital supplied is related to the output produced.[24] In counterpurchase, the goods taken by the supplier typically cannot be used directly in its business activities.

In general, the terms are set so the value of goods taken back and the costs of the Western firm's offering are balanced over the life of the agreement. Financing may include Western banks as well as lending institutions in the host country. The cash-to-goods ratio in East-West compensation contracts generally averages 20 percent cash to 80 percent goods, which is the inverse of the situation in the mid-1970s.

Cooperation Agreements

Cooperation agreements meet the needs of Western firms doing business with nonmarket economies, which are reluctant to link selling and buying. What distinguishes these arrangements from other types of countertrade is the specialization of each Western firm for either buying or selling, but not both. Each of the three forms of cooperation agreements represents an increasingly complex accommodation to the needs of trading partners. They include cooperation and

---

[23] The commitment to local assembly or manufacturing under the supplier's specifications is commonly termed a *coproduction agreement,* which is tied to the offset but does not in itself represent a type of countertrade.

[24] Daily and Ghazanfar, p. 66.

simple barter (triangular deals); cooperation and counterpurchase; and cooperation, counterpurchase, and credit by a bank. As an example of cooperation and simple barter, the parties to the transaction might be two unrelated Western firms with a Canadian company specialized as a seller, a Western European firm as a buyer, and an Eastern European Foreign Trade Organization (FTO). The Canadian firm may perform the selling function by delivering goods to the FTO. In payment for the goods, the FTO might deliver raw materials to the Western European firm, which carries out the buying function. The Western European firm then pays the Canadian firm for the raw materials an amount equivalent to the value of goods originally sent to the Eastern European FTO. The advantage to the Canadian firm offering goods is in removing the obligation to buy and, for the Western European firm receiving raw materials, a considerable reduction in transport costs. Problems associated with these arrangements include finding two Western firms with the appropriate supply-demand fit and the flexibilities to handle time delays in receipt of payment or in delivery of goods.

Hybrid Countertrade Arrangements

Hybrid forms of countertrade are becoming more prevalent in trading arrangements. For example, the investment performance contract in Third World markets is an additional condition of offset arrangements. Canada and other countries such as Brazil and Mexico now condition official approval of investment proposals to commitments by the investors to export. As a second example, *project accompaniment* typifies an arrangement in which a Western supplier is encouraged to buy a greater volume and/or wider range of products, compared with the countertrade commitment. Project accompaniment has surfaced as a condition to the exchange of industrial goods by the West for oil from Middle Eastern producers.

Switch Trading

Also called triangular trade and swap, switch trading is a mechanism that can be applied to barter or countertrade. In this arrangement, a professional switch trader, switch trading house, or bank steps into a simple barter arrangement, clearing agreement, or a countertrade arrangement when one of the parties is not willing to accept all the goods or the clearing credits received in a transaction. The switching mechanism provides a secondary market for countertraded or bartered goods and credits and reduces the inflexibilities inherent in barter and countertrade. Fees charged by switch traders range from 5 percent of market value for commodities to 30 percent for high-technology items. Switch traders develop their own networks of firms and personal contacts and are generally headquartered in Vienna, Amsterdam, Hamburg, and London. If a party anticipates that the products he or she receives will be sold eventually at discount by a switch trade, the common practice is to price products higher or build in special charges for port storage or consulting, or require shipment by the national carrier.

The advantages of switching are that (1) its multilateral character offers a greater decree of economic efficiency in pricing and in increasing trade, and (2) discounted prices can open new markets more rapidly, and Western firms can shed the responsibilities of marketing goods received in countertrade. Disadvantages include (1) disruptions of producers' established markets, when switch dealers offer their products at discount to such markets; (2) products that may be in oversupply or difficult to sell on the world market; (3) the foreign principal assessing the Western firm as uncommitted to a long-term trade relationship, particularly if the foreigner's established markets are threatened by discounted products; and (4) the complex and cumbersome nature of switching transactions. Switch trading's complexity is rooted in the mechanics of the transaction; typically, the switch trader sells a commodity for "soft" (i.e., nonconvertible) currency, uses the soft currency to purchase another commodity, and repeats the process until he or she can purchase a commodity that can be sold for hard currency.

▼ SUMMARY

This chapter provides an overview of export marketing and the decisions company personnel have to make to become successful exporters. Governments exert a strong influence on exports, through support programs, regulations, nontariff barriers, and tariff classifications.

In choosing export markets, companies must assess market potential, market access, shipping costs, competition, product fit, and service requirements. It is definitely a good idea to visit a potential market before developing an export program. Market access considerations are particularly important for the exporter and the importer. The exporter must understand that tariffs and duties affect the prices that must be paid by the importer. Successful exporting entails organizational decisions (e.g., regarding internal or external expertise) in both the manufacturer's country and the market country.

Exporters and importers must also have a thorough understanding of international financial instruments, especially letters of credit. Exporters and importers must also be familiar with the various forms of barter and countertrade that represent nonmonetary methods of conducting trade with cash-poor countries new to market-driven economies.

▼ DISCUSSION QUESTIONS

1. Why is exporting from Canada dominated by large companies? What, if anything, could be done to increase exports from smaller companies?

2. What six criteria should be assessed when evaluating potential export markets?

3. How do trade missions and trade fairs help exporters with their global marketing efforts?

4. What are the various types of duties that export marketers should be aware of?

5. What is the difference between barter and countertrade? Why do companies barter?

6. What does it take to be a successful exporter?

7. Overall, what effect has the Uruguay Round of GATT negotiations had on the ability of Canadian companies to export?

▼ BIBLIOGRAPHY

Books

BRANCH, ALAN E., *Elements of Export Marketing Management*. London: Chapman and Hall, 1990.

GORDON, JOHN S., *Profitable Exporting: A Complete Guide to Marketing Your Products Abroad*. New York: Wiley, 1993.

JOHNSON, THOMAS E., *Export/Import Procedure and Documentation*. New York: Anacom, 1991.

MAGGIORI, HERMAN J., *How to Make the World Your Market: The International Sales and Marketing Handbook*. Los Angeles: Burning Gate Press, 1992.

PATTISON, JOSEPH E., *Acquiring the Future: America's Survival and Success in the Global Economy*. Homewood, IL: Dow Jones-Irwin, 1990.

RAYNAULD, ANDRE, *Financing Exports to Developing Countries*. Paris, France: Development Centre of the Organisation for Economic Cooperation and Development, 1992.

RODGERS, EVERETT M., *Diffusion of Innovations*. New York: Free Press, 1962.

SCHAFFER, MATT, *Winning the Countertrade War: New Export Strategies for America*. New York: John Wiley & Sons, 1989.

SERINGHAUS, F.H. ROLF AND PHILIP J. ROSSON, *Government Export Promotion: A Global Perspective*. London: Routledge Publishers, 1990.

SERINGHAUS, F.H. ROLF AND PHILIP J. ROSSON, Eds., *Export Development and Promotion: The Role of Public Organizations*. Boston: Kluwer Academic Publishers, 1991.

TULLER, LAWRENCE W., *The McGraw-Hill Handbook of Global Trade and Investment Financing*. New York: McGraw-Hill, 1992.

U.S. COMMISSION ON INTERNATIONAL TRADE, *Assessment of the Effects of Barter and Countertrade Transactions on U.S. Industries: Report on Investigation N. 332-185 Under Section 332 of the Tariff Act of 1930*. Washington, DC: U.S. International Trade Commission, 1985.

U.S. DEPARTMENT OF COMMERCE, *A Basic Guide to Exporting*. Washington, DC: U.S. Department of Commerce, 1992.

U.S. TRADE PROMOTION COORDINATING COMMITTEE, *Toward A National Export Strategy: U.S. Exports = U.S. Jobs: Report to the United States Congress*. Washington, DC: Trade Promotion Coordinating Committee, 1993.

VENEDIKIAN, HARRY M., *Export-Import Financing*. New York: Wiley, 1992.

VERZARIU, POMPILIU, *Countertrade, Barter, and Offsets: New Strategies for Profit in International Trade*. New York: McGraw-Hill, 1985.

ZURAWICKI, LEON, *Global Countertrade: An Annotated Bibliography*. New York: Garland Publishers, 1991.

Articles

AKE, JEFFREY J., "Easier Done Than Said," *Inc.*, 15, no. 2 (February 1993), 96–99.

BILKEY, WARREN J., "An Attempted Integration of the Literature on the Export Behavior of Firms," *Journal of International Business Studies*, 9, no. 1 (1978), 33–46.

CAVUSGIL, S. TAMER, AND V. H. KIRPALANI, "Introducing Products into Export Markets: Success Factors," *Journal of Business Research*, 27, no. 1 (May 1993), 1–15.

CHAN, T. S., "Emerging Trends in Export Channel Strategy: An Investigation of Hong Kong and Singaporean Firms," *European Journal of Marketing*, 26, no. 3, 18–26.

DAILY, PATRICIA, AND S. M. GHAZANFAR, "Countertrade: Help or Hindrance to Less-Developed Countries," *Journal of Social, Political and Economic Studies*, 18, no. 1 (Spring 1993), 65.

DOMINGUEZ, LUIS V., AND CARLOS G. SEQUEIRA, "Strategic Options for LDC Exports to Developed Countries," *International Marketing Review*, 8, no. 5 (1991), 27–43.

"Economics Focus: From Sublime to the Subsidy," *Economist*, 314, no. 7643 (February 24, 1990), 71.

"Export Promotion: Pushing It Together," *Economist*, 320, no. 7725 (September 21, 1991), 70.

FOUST, DEAN, AND MARIA MALLORY, "The Boom Belt," *Business Week*, September 27, 1993, 98–104.

FRIEDMANN, ROBERT, "International Marketing Synergy," *International Marketing Review*, 7, no. 3 (1990), 6–17.

HENNART, JEAN-FRANÇOIS, AND ERIN ANDERSON, "Countertrade and the Minimization of Transaction Costs: An Empirical Examination," University of Illinois at Urbana-Champaign, Working Paper, May 1993.

HOLSTEIN, BILL, "An Export Service of Great Import," *Business Week*, September 28, 1992, 138.

HOWARD, DONALD G., AND JAMES M. MASKULKA, "Will American Export Trading Companies Replace Traditional Export Management Companies?" *International Marketing Review*, 5, no. 4 (Winter 1988), 41–50.

KORTH, CHRISTOPHER M., "Managerial Barriers to US Exports," *Business Horizons*, 34, no. 2 (March/April 1991), 18–26.

KOSTECKI, MICHEL M., "Marketing Strategies Between Dumping and Anti-Dumping Action," *European Journal of Marketing*, 25, no. 12 (1991), 7–19.

KUTTNER, ROBERT, "How 'National Security' Hurts National Competitiveness," *Harvard Business Review*, 69, no. 1 (January/February 1991), 140–149.

LOUTER, PIETER J., COK OUWERKERK, AND BEN A. BAKKER, "An Inquiry into Successful Exporting," *European Journal of Marketing*, 25, no. 6 (1991), 7–23.

MAGEE, JOHN F., "1992: Moves Americans Must Make," *Harvard Business Review*, 67, no. 3 (May–June 1989), 78–84.

McGUINNESS, NORMAN W., AND BLAIR LITTLE, "The Influence of Product Characteristics on the Export Performance of New Industrial Products," *Journal of Marketing* (Spring 1981), 110–122.

PARKHE, DAVID, "US National Security Export Controls: Implications for Global Competitiveness of US High-Tech Firms," *Strategic Management Journal*, 13, no. 1 (January 1992), 47–66.

RAJAN, MAHESH N., AND JOHN L. GRAHAM, "Nobody's Grandfather Was a Merchant: Understanding the Soviet Commercial Negotiation Process and Style," *California Management Review*, 33, no. 3 (Spring 1991), 40–57.

RAO, C. P., M. KRISHNA ERRAMILLI, AND GOPALA K. GANESH, "Impact of Domestic Recession on Export Marketing Behavior," *International Marketing Review*, 7, no. 2 (1990), 54–65.

REICH, MICHAEL R., "Why the Japanese Don't Export More Pharmaceuticals: Health Policy as Industrial Policy," *California Management Review*, 32, no. 2 (Winter 1990), 124–150.

ROBOCK, STEFAN H., "The Export Myopia of US Multinationals: An Overlooked Opportunity for Creating US Manufacturing Jobs," *Columbia Journal of World Business*, 28, no. 2 (Summer 1993), 24–32.

SCHAFFER, MATT, "Countertrade as an Export Strategy," *Journal of Business Strategy*, 11, no. 3 (May/June 1990), 33–38.

SERINGHAUS, F.H. ROLF, "Comparative Marketing Behaviour of Canadian and Austrian High-Tech Exporters," *Management International Review*, 33 (1993) no.3, 247–269.

SERINGHAUS, F.H. ROLF AND PHILIP J. ROSSON, "International Trade Fairs and Foreign Market Involvement: Review and Research Directions," *International Business Review*, 3 (1994), no.3, 311–329.

SPIERS, JOSEPH, "A Coming Surge in Capital Spending," *Fortune*, April 22, 1991, 113–119.

TUNCALP, SECIL, "Strategy Planning in Export Marketing: The Case of Saudi Arabia," *Columbia Journal of World Business*, 23, no. 3 (Fall 1988), 69–76.

WOOLLEY, SUZANNE, "Shaping Up By Shipping Out," *Business Week*, no. 3315 (April 19, 1993), 119.

▶ APPENDIX

Export Agents and Organizations—Glossary of Terms

A. NO ASSIGNMENT OF RESPONSIBILITY FROM CLIENT

▼ Purchasing Agent

Foreign purchasing agents are variously referred to as *buyer for export, export commission house,* or *export confirming house.* They operate on behalf of, and are remunerated by, an overseas customer. They generally seek out the United States manufacturer whose price and quality match the demands of their overseas principals.

Foreign purchasing agents often represent large users of materials abroad, governments, utilities, and railroads, for example. They do not offer the Canadian manufacturer stable volume except when long-term supply contracts are agreed upon. Purchases may be completed as domestic transactions with the purchasing agent handling all export packing and shipping details, or the agent may rely on the manufacturer to handle the shipping arrangements.

Export Broker

The export broker receives a fee for bringing together the Canadian seller and the overseas buyer. The fee is usually paid by the seller, but sometimes the buyer pays it. The broker takes no title to the goods and assumes no financial responsibility. A broker usually specializes in a specific commodity, such as grain or cotton, and is less frequently involved in the export of manufactured goods.

Export Merchant

Export merchants are sometimes referred to as *jobbers.* They seek out needs in foreign markets and make purchases in Canada to fill these needs. Conversely, they often complement this activity by importing to fill needs in the United States. Export merchants often handle staple, openly traded products, for which brand names or manufacturers' identifications are not important.

B. ASSIGNMENT OF RESPONSIBILITY FROM CLIENT

▼ Export Management Companies

Export management company (EMC) is the term used to designate an independent export firm that acts as the export department for more than one manufacturer. The EMC usually operates in the name of a manufacturer-client for export markets but it may operate in its own name. It may act as an independent distributor, purchasing and reselling goods at an established price or profit margin, or as a commission representative taking no title and bearing no financial risks in the sale.

▼ Manufacturer's Export Representative

Combination export management firms often refer to themselves as manufacturer's export representatives whether they act as export distributors or export commission representatives.

▼ Export Distributor

The export distributor assumes financial risk. The firm usually has exclusive right to sell a manufacturer's products in all or some markets outside Canada. The distributor pays for goods in Canada in a domestic transaction and handles all financial risks in the foreign sale. The firm ordinarily sells at manufacturer's list price abroad, receiving an agreed percentage of list price as remuneration. The distributor may operate in its own name or in the manufacturer's name. It handles all shipping details. The export distributor usually represents several manufacturers and hence is a combination export manager.

▼ Export Commission Representative

The export commission representative assumes no financial risk and is sometimes termed an *agent*, although this term is generally avoided because of the legal connotations of the term. The commission representative is assigned all or some foreign markets by the manufacturer. The manufacturer carries all accounts, although the representative often provides credit checks and arranges financing. The representative may operate in its own name or in the manufacturer's name. Generally, export commission representatives handle several accounts and hence are combination export managers.

▼ Cooperative Exporter

The cooperative exporter, sometimes called a *mother hen, piggyback exporter,* or *export vendor,* is an export organization of a manufacturing company retained by other independent manufacturers to sell their products in some or all foreign markets. Cooperative exporters usually operate as export distributors for other manufacturers, but in special cases they operate as commission representatives. They are regarded as a form of export management company.

▼ Freight Forwarder

Freight forwarders are specialists in traffic operations, customs clearance, and shipping tariffs and schedules. While exporters can choose to make their own shipping arrangements, freight forwarders belong to, and abide by the standards and procedures of, the Canadian International Freight Forwarders Association, and thus offer expertise and cost effectiveness.

They assist exporters in determining and paying freight, fees, and insurance charges. Forwarders may also do export packing when necessary. They usually handle freight from port of export to overseas port of import. They may also move inland freight from factory to port of export and, through affiliates abroad, handle freight from port of import to customer. Freight forwarders also perform consolidation services for air and ocean freight. They contract for blocks of space on a ship or airplane and resell that space to various shippers at a rate lower than generally available to individual shippers.

SEVENTEEN

Leading, Organizing, and Controlling the Global Marketing Effort

Introduction

This chapter focuses on the integration of each element of the marketing mix into a total plan that responds to expected opportunities and threats in the global marketing environment. In the global firm, leadership is a critical need. Without leadership, no firm can resolve the complex mix of effort and response that integrates the need for local responsiveness, global efficiency and leverage, and a coherent global vision and strategy. The challenge is to integrate the efforts and creativity of everyone in the company into a global effort that best utilizes organizational resources to exploit global opportunities.

CHAPTER OUTLINE

LEADERSHIP

Global marketing demands exceptional leadership. The truly global company is capable of formulating and implementing global strategies that leverage worldwide learning, respond fully to local needs and wants, and draw on all of the talent and energy of every member of the organization. This is a heroic task requiring global vision and a sensitivity to local needs. It must inspire members of each operating unit to address their immediate responsibilities and at the same time cooperate with functional, product, and country experts in different locations.

▼ Core Competence

In the 1980s, top executives were assessed on their ability to reorganize their corporations; in the 1990s top executives are "judged on their ability to identify, cultivate, and exploit core competencies that make growth possible."[1]

Core competence is defined by the following three criteria:

1. It provides potential access to a wide variety of markets.
2. It makes a significant contribution to the perceived customer benefits of the end product.
3. It is difficult for competitors to imitate.

---

[1] C. K. Prahalad and Gary Hamel, "The Core Competence of the Corporation," *Harvard Business Review* (May/June 1990), p. 79.

Few companies are likely to build world leadership in more than five or six fundamental competencies. In the long run, if the organization is to be competitive in the global marketplace, it will derive its competitiveness from its ability to bring high-quality, low-cost products to market faster than its competitors. In order to do this, an organization will need to consist of "a portfolio of competencies rather than a portfolio of businesses."[2]

Many companies have the technical resources to build competencies but key executives lack the vision to do so. The concept challenges executives to rethink the concept of the corporation itself. If you accept the notion of a company as a set of core competencies, the task of management "is to build competencies and the administrative means for assembling resources spread across multiple businesses."[3]

▼ Teams

The use of self-directed work teams as a way of responding to competitive challenges is gaining in popularity. There is a tendency in larger companies to involve more employees in teams.[4] Indeed, work teams are seen by some companies as the link to goal achievement and superior performance.[5] The implementation of self-directed work teams is another example of the pressures organizations are facing to remain competitive. This is precisely why Ford Motor Co. is restructuring its North American and European operations as well as its automotive components group into a single operating unit.[6] Ford's product development, for example, has been organized into five teams, called vehicle platform centers: four in the U.S. at Dearborn, and one in Europe, split between Germany and the U.K. Not only does this approach eliminate duplication but video conferencing and linked computer networks make it unnecessary to bring together members of each team at a single site.[7]

The make-up of such teams and their task seem critically important to their effectiveness. It has been found that teams consisting of a "single culture" are generally of average effectiveness, while "cross-cultural teams" are either much less effective or highly effective. The key to team performance appears to be the way in which such cultural diversity is managed.[8]

Thus, teams represent another corporate response to the need to flatten the organization, to reduce costs and overheads, and to be more responsive. As Tom Peters put it, "You can't survive, let alone thrive, in a time-competitive

---

[2] Ibid., p. 81.

[3] Ibid., pp. 81, 86.

[4] Susan G. Cohen, *Designing Effective Self-Managing Work Teams*, CEO Publication G93-9, University of Southern California, July 1993, p.3.

[5] Nancy K. Austin, "Workers Unite," *Incentive* (February 1993), p.15; and Jon R. Katzenbach and Douglas K. Smith, "The Discipline of Teams," *Harvard Business Review* (March–April 1993) p.119.

[6] Kevin Done, "Tomorrow the World," *Financial Times*, April 22, 1994, pp.15–16.

[7] "Ford's New Product Teams Span Globe," *The Globe and Mail*, January 10, 1995, p.B9.

[8] Nancy J. Adler, *International Dimensions of Organizational Behavior*, 2nd Ed. (Belmont: Wadsworth Publishing Company, 1991) p.134; and "The Melting Pot Bubbles Less," *The Economist* (August 7, 1993) p.63.

world with a six-to-eight-layer organization structure. The time-obsessed organization is flat—no barriers among functions, no borders with the outside."[9]

ORGANIZATION

Organization is a subject of major importance to any company that has decided to market globally. Enormous amounts of energy are expended on organization because organizational structure is the mechanism through which critical issues get resolved.[10] When a domestic company decides to expand internationally, the issue of how to organize arises immediately. Who should be responsible for this expansion? Should product divisions operate directly or should an international division be established? Should individual country subsidiaries report directly to the company president or should a special corporate officer be appointed to take full-time responsibility for international activities? Once the first decision of how to organize initial international operations has been reached, a growing company is faced with a number of reappraisal points during the development of its international business activities. Should a company abandon its international division and, if so, what alternative structure should be adopted? Should an area or regional headquarters be formed? What should be the relationship of staff executives at corporate, regional, and subsidiary offices? Specifically, how should the marketing function be organized? To what extent should regional and corporate marketing executives become involved in subsidiary marketing management?

The goal in organizing for international marketing is to find a structure that enables the company to respond to relevant differences in international market environments and at the same time enables the company to extend valuable corporate knowledge, experience, and know-how from national markets to the entire corporate system. It is this pull between the value of centralized knowledge and coordination and the need for individualized response to the local situation that creates a constant tension in the international marketing organization. A key issue in global organization is how to achieve balance between autonomy and integration. Subsidiaries need autonomy in order to adapt to their local environment. But the business as a whole needs integration to implement global strategy.[11]

At the outset it is important to recognize that there is no single correct organizational structure for international marketing. Even within an industry, worldwide companies have developed very different strategic and organizational responses to changes in their environment.[12] Geographical diversity is a consequence of a strategy of international expansion. The effect of operations

---

[9] Tom Peters,"Time Obsessed Competition," *Management Review* (September 1990), p.18.

[10] Michael Hammer and James Champy, *Reengineering the Corporation* (New York: Harper Business, 1993), p. 78.

[11] George S. Yip, *Total Global Strategy* (Englewood Cliffs, NJ: Prentice Hall, 1992), p.179.

[12] Christopher A. Bartlett and Sumantra Ghoshal, *Managing Across Borders: The Transnational Solution* (Boston, MA: Harvard Business School Press, 1989), p. 3.

in different countries and areas is to present a major new dimension of required response to the organization. A geographically dispersed company in addition to its knowledge of product, function, and the home territory must acquire knowledge of the complex set of social, political, economic, and institutional arrangements that exist within each international market. Most companies, after initial *ad hoc* arrangements (all foreign subsidiaries reporting to a designated vice president or to the president, for example) establish an international division to manage their geographically dispersed new business. It is clear, however, that the international division in the multiproduct company is an unstable organizational arrangement and that as a company grows, this initial organizational structure gives way to various alternative structures.[13]

In today's fast-changing competitive global environment, corporations are having to find new and more creative ways to organize in order to meet the challenges of the decade. New forms of flexibility, efficiency, and responsiveness are required to meet the market demands. Being customer-driven, delivering the best quality, and delivering that quality quickly are only being compounded by the need to be cost-effective.

The most recent report of the Club of Rome notes that current dramatic changes represent the first global revolution because the entire world is experiencing these events together at the same time.[14] Leading-edge global competitors share one key organizational design characteristic. Their corporate structure is simple and flat, rather than tall and complex. The message is clear: The world is complicated enough, no need to add to the confusion with a complex internal structuring. Simple structures increase the speed and clarity of communication and allow the concentration of organizational energy and valuable resources on learning, rather than on controlling, monitoring, and reporting.[15] According to David Whitwam, CEO of Whirlpool, "You must create an organization whose people are adept at exchanging ideas, processes, and systems across borders, people who are absolutely free of the 'not-invented-here' syndrome, people who are constantly working together to identify the best global opportunities and the biggest global problems facing the organization."[16]

Recently there have been several authors who have described new organization designs that are appearing in response to the necessity of being market-driven in order to be competitive. They all build on the realities of needing to find more responsive and flexible structures, of needing to flatten the organization and to employ teams. There is also the recognition of the need to develop networks, to develop stronger relationships among participants, and to exploit technology.

They also reflect an evolution in the thinking of what makes an organization effective. At the turn of the century, Fredrick Taylor claimed that all managers had

---

[13] John M. Stopford and Louis T. Wells, *Managing the Multinational Enterprise* (New York: Basic Books, 1972).

[14] Willian E. Halal, "Global Strategic Management in a New World Order," *Business Horizons* (November-December 1993), pp. 7–8.

[15] Valdimir Pucik, "Globalization and Human Resource Management," reprinted from V. Pucik, N. Tichy, and C. Barnett, *Globalizing Management: Creating and Leading the Competitive Organization* (New York: J. Wiley & Sons; 1992), p. 70.

[16] Regina Fazio Maruca, "The Right Way to Go Global: An Interview with Whirlpool CEO David Whitwam," *Harvard Business Review* (March-April 1994), pp. 136–137.

to see the world the same way. Then came the contingency theorists who said that effective organizations design themselves to match their conditions. These two basic theories are reflected in today's popular management writings. "To Michael Porter, effectiveness resides in strategy, while to Tom Peters it is the operations that count—executing any strategy with excellence."[17]

▼ Patterns of International Organizational Development

The conflicting pressures of the need for (1) product and technical knowledge, (2) functional expertise in marketing, finance, planning, and so on, and (3) area and country knowledge make it difficult to achieve performance and balance in organizations that typically have country operations that range over a long spectrum of size, potential, and local management competence. Because the matrices of pressures that shape organizations are never exactly the same, no two organizations pass through organizational stages in exactly the same way, nor do they arrive at precisely the same organizational pattern. Nevertheless, some general patterns have developed.

Most companies undertake initial foreign expansion with an organization similar to that in Figures 17–1 and 17–2. When a company is organized on this basis, foreign subsidiaries report directly to the company president or other designated company officer, who carries out his or her responsibilities without assistance from a headquarters staff group. This is a typical initial arrangement for companies getting started in international marketing operations.

▼ International Division Structure

As a company's international business grows, the complexity of coordinating and directing this activity extends beyond the scope of a single person. Pressure is created to assemble a staff group that will take responsibility for coordination and direction of the growing international activities of the organization. Eventually, this pressure leads to the creation of the international division, as illustrated in Figures 17–3 and 17–4.

Four factors contribute to the establishment of an international division. First, the international commitment of the firm has reached an absolute size and a relative importance within the enterprise to justify an organizational unit headed by a senior manager. Second, the complexity of international operations requires a single organization unit that can resolve within it such conflicts as the best means for entering new markets outside the home country based on a broad view of the firm's global opportunities. Third, the firm has recognized the need for internal specialists to deal with the special features of international

---

[17] Henry Mintzberg, "The Effective Organization: Forces and Forms," *Sloan Management Review* (Winter 1991), pp. 54–55.

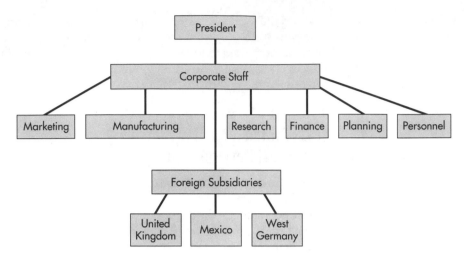

FIGURE 17-1
Functional Corporate Structure, Domestic Corporate Staff Orientation, Preinternational Division

FIGURE 17-2
Divisional Corporate Structure, Domestically Oriented Product Division Staff, Preinternational Division

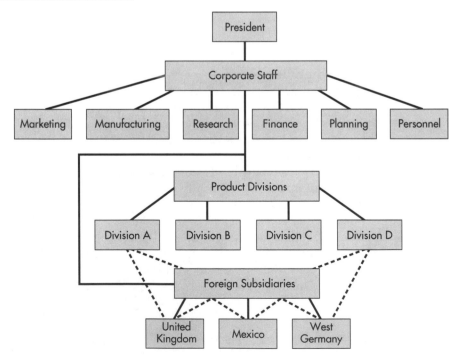

operations. And finally, the enterprise wants to develop an affirmative capability for scanning the global horizon for opportunities or competitive threats rather than simply responding to situations that are presented to the company.

The corporate staff may or may not be involved in the management of international marketing activities at this point. If the international division is fully developed in terms of staff appointments, there is a tendency for it to operate autonomously and independently of corporate staff. On the other hand, if the international division staff is small and limited, there is a tendency for a service such as marketing research to be supplied by the corporate staff organization.

The international division structure occurs in both the functional and the divisional organization. It allows an organization to concentrate in one headquarters location all its expertise in dealing with foreign markets. In companies that have the bulk of their sales in a domestic market, this arrangement assures that an organizational location in the corporation gives its full attention to international markets. But many American companies are disbanding international divisions and assigning world responsibility to product and functional executives. This move eliminates a split in the organization between executives responsible for the home country and those responsible for the rest of the world.

FIGURE 17–3
Functional Corporate Structure, Domestic Corporate Staff Orientation, International Division

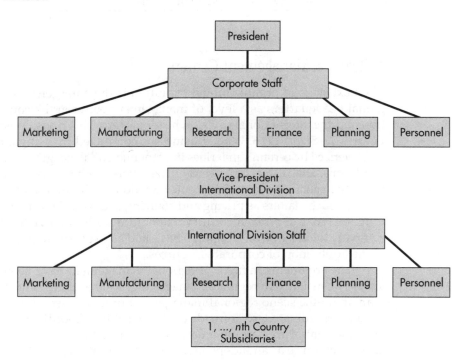

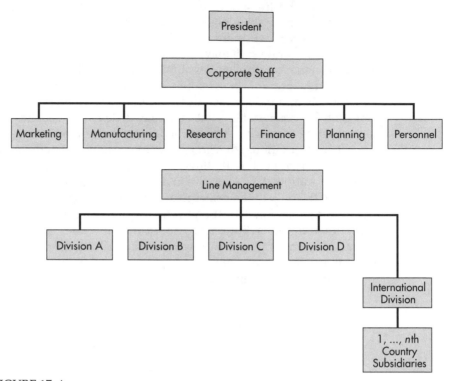

FIGURE 17-4
Divisional Corporate Structure, Domestically Oriented Corporate Staff, Domestically Oriented Product Divisions, International Division

▼ Regional Management Centers

The next stage of organizational evolution is the emergence of an area or regional headquarters as a level of management between the country organization and the international division headquarters. This division is illustrated in Figures 17–5 and 17–6. When business is conducted in a single region that is characterized by certain similarities in economic, social, geographical, and political conditions, after it reaches a certain size, there are both justification and need for a management center. The center would coordinate interdependent decisions on such matters as pricing and sourcing and would participate in the planning and control of each country's operations with an eye toward applying company knowledge on a regional basis and also toward regional optimization of the application of corporate resources.

The arguments in favor of regional management have been stated as follows: The majority of regional managers agrees that there is no better solution than an on-the-scene regional management unit, at least where there is a real need for coordinated, regionwide decision making. Coordinated regional planning and control are becoming necessary as the national subsidiary continues to lose its relevance as an independent operating unit. Regional management can

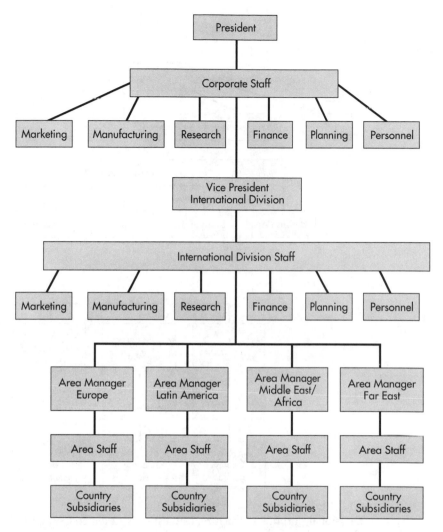

FIGURE 17–5

Functional Corporate Structure, Domestic Corporate Staff Orientation, International Division, Area Divisions

probably achieve the best balance of geographical, product, and functional considerations required to implement corporate objectives effectively. By shifting operations and decision making to the region, the company is better able to maintain an insider advantage.[18]

The pressure for the creation of a regional headquarters comes from two sources. One is the scale and complexity of a company's operation within a re-

---

[18] See, for example, Allen J. Morrison, David A. Ricks, and Kendall Roth, "Globalization versus Regionalization: Which Way for the Multinational?" *Organizational Dynamics* (Winter 1991), p. 25.

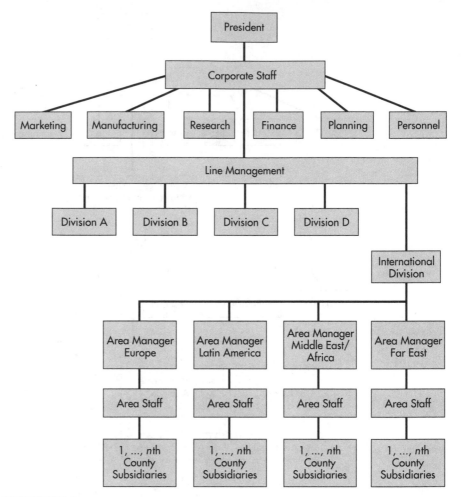

FIGURE 17–6

Divisional Corporate Structure, Domestically Oriented Corporate Staff, International Division, Area Subdivisions

gion. Size generates revenues that can cover the cost of a regional headquarters, and complexity creates a pressure to respond at the regional level. A second important source of pressure is the nature of regions. A geographical region is by definition a group of countries related to each other by geographic proximity. When a region is additionally unified by tariff reduction applying within the regional boundaries, by interregional communication media, by the development of interregional transportation systems, by various regional moves toward economic, social, and political cooperation, and by basic economic and cultural similarities, then the development of the region itself generates a pressure for the creation of a regional headquarters that will guide corporate activities in a way that will take advantage of the economic, social, and political integration that exists within the region. But the creation of a regional headquarters is not easy for the parent.

The rise of regional trading blocks has led many companies to reassess the anticipated rise of globalization. Increasingly, regionalization is being viewed by managers as a stepping stone to more effective global competition. One of the best examples of the combination of economic, social, and political integration with geographic proximity and relatively large-scale operations has occurred in the European Union. In the EU, the progress toward economic, social, and political integration during the past two decades has created preconditions for the integration of business activities in EU countries. However, these pressures in themselves are not sufficient to make it desirable for every company to create a regional headquarters. The company situation itself must be considered. Companies in a region can be placed in four categories:

1. Initial operations, small annual sales in a handful of countries
2. Regional operations dominated by one or two sizable national subsidiaries, each of which has its own substantial management staff
3. Regional operations composed of several large, strong, historically independent national operating subsidiaries
4. Regional operations of companies of national subsidiaries that have been closely integrated according to a worldwide plan

Categories 1 and 2 are the type of operations that have little need for a regional headquarters. The principal subsidiaries are so large that they can effectively function as operating units and in many cases are multicountry companies in their own right. In any event, there is really little coordination between companies of vastly different size to be pursued.

Whenever a company's operations become sizable and are scattered over a number of subsidiaries, the pressure for regional integration grows. This pressure is perhaps the greatest in the Category-3 situation, where large unintegrated subsidiary companies are operating relatively autonomously and have therefore avoided the cost savings and rationalization moves that an overall direction would provide. Most companies today feel that the Category-4 situation merits a regional headquarters in an area such as Europe where the opportunities for rationalization and areawide coordination are significant.

A major disadvantage of a regional center is its cost. Whenever operations are under profit pressure, these costs become quite apparent and have in many companies been responsible for the abandonment of a regional headquarters. Extra compensation for living abroad and the cost of replacing incompetent employees can run up an enormous bill simply for transportation. Overhead cost for office space is expensive. Aside from the desirability or necessity to set up a local office or subsidiary, the costs of maintaining such a location must be part of the decision on regional management centers. Rental costs vary a great deal across and within countries, as we see from Table 17–1, and this fact may influence the location choice. Thus, creating an organizational unit adds personnel, transportation, and communication costs that must be justified by the unit's contribution to organizational effectiveness. Even a two-person office could cost in excess of C$600,000 per year. The scale of regional management must be in line with the scale of operations in a region. A regional headquarters is premature

City	Country	Annual Office Rent[1] Downtown	Annual Warehouse Rent[2]	Annual Retail Rent[1]
Atlanta	U.S.	272.00	46.92	557.60
Berlin	Germany	590.92	91.52	553.92
Budapest	Hungary	515.16	92.07	1317.16
Hong Kong	H.K.	1109.76	214.20	9805.60
Jakarta	Indonesia	267.24	62.83	720.80
London	U.K.	505.64	106.21	5258.71
Mexico City	Mexico	795.60	91.12	61.20
Milan	Italy	546.17	70.72	549.84
Seoul	Korea	321.64	180.06	4311.20
Shenzen-Guangdong	China	657.28	66.91	4277.20
Singapore	Singapore	485.52	221.81	307.90
Sydney	Australia	570.92	110.56	2559.11
Tokyo	Japan	1649.13	165.92	1931.20
Toronto	**Canada**	338.64	35.90	820.08

[1] includes all operating expenses and taxes
[2] excludes all operating expenses, insurance, taxes

Source: Adapted from "International Business Real Estate Mart," *International Business* (March, September, October, November 1994).

whenever the size of the operations it manages is inadequate to cover the costs of the additional layer of management. Thus, the basic issue with regard to the regional headquarters is: Does it contribute enough to organizational effectiveness to justify its cost?

▼ Beyond the International Division

As companies develop their capability to operate globally with an international division, they usually find that the growing size and complexity of their international operation demands organizational modifications that fully apply organizational capabilities to market opportunities. In the functional single-product company, or product group, one modification involves the creation of geographical structure. In the multidivisional company, this involves the creation of the worldwide product division.

▼ Geographical Structure

The geographical structure involves the assignment of operational responsibility for geographic areas of the world to line managers. The corporate headquarters retains responsibility for worldwide planning and control, and each

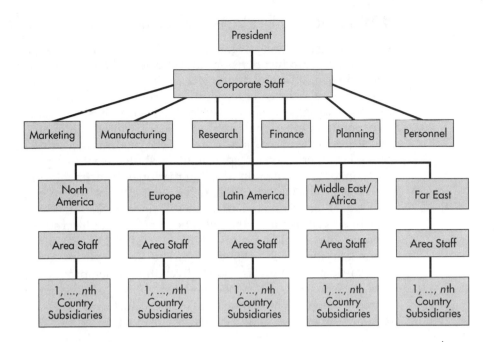

FIGURE 17–7
Geographic Corporate Structure, World Corporate Staff Orientation, Area Divisions Worldwide

area of the world including the "home" or base market is organizationally equal. While for a company with Canadian origins Canada is simply another geographic market under this organizational arrangement, the U.S. market, because of its size, often warrants a separate division or even subsidiary office. The most common appearance of this structure is in companies with closely related product lines that are sold in similar end-use markets around the world. For example, the major international oil companies utilize the geographical structure, which is illustrated in Figure 17–7.

A strong country manager has great power over all of the businesses in his or her country. This power structure was more popular in the early days of multinational expansion when communications and travel were far more difficult than today. The strong country manager was particularly in favor with European companies because of their colonial administration heritage. With the improvement of communications technology, companies have been able to extend the "normal" command structure and process to any location on the globe. It doesn't matter where you are today: You can be reached by fax, telephone, travel, and the internet. Without doubt, the expansion of communications technology has diminished the power of the country manager.

▼ Worldwide Product Division Structure

When an organization assigns worldwide product responsibility to its product divisions, the product divisions must decide whether to rely upon an international division, thereby dividing their world into domestic and foreign, or to rely upon an area structure with each region of the world organizationally treated on an equal basis. In most cases when a divisional company shifts from a corporate international division to worldwide product divisions, there are two stages in the internationalization of the product divisions. The first stage occurs when international responsibility is shifted from a corporate international division to the product division international departments. The second occurs when the product divisions themselves shift international responsibility from international departments within the divisions to the total divisional organization. In effect, this shift is the utilization of a geographical structure within each product division. The worldwide product division with an international department is illustrated in Figure 17–8. The product structure works best when a company's product line is widely diversified, when products go into a variety of end-use markets, and when a relatively high technological capability is required. Foreign-owned companies with product mandates—whether global or regional—operate as a mix of area and product structure.

▼ Strategic Business Units

One of the important organizational expressions of the growing importance of strategy is the strategic business unit (SBU). This term, first used at General Electric, refers to the organizational unit that is responsible for preparing the business plan. The SBU may or may not correspond to the divisions, groups, or other organizational units in the company. The criterion for the definition of an SBU is that it be a group of products and technologies that serves an identified market and competes with identified competitors—in other words, a business.

In some companies, SBUs are not part of the formal structure of the company but, rather, represent a process or system overlay for the purpose of developing a business strategy. The implementation of the strategy may be carried out by divisions or groups that are organized along more functional lines.

One of the problems with the SBU structure is that it does not, in itself, encourage cooperation between SBUs in addressing customers and countries. AT&T is an example of a company that felt the need to reorganize around SBUs in order to push P&L responsibility further down in the organization.

▼ The Matrix Structure

The most sophisticated organizational arrangement brings to bear four basic competencies on a worldwide basis. These competencies are as follows:

1. Geographic knowledge. An understanding of the basic economic, social, cultural, political, and governmental market and competitive dimensions of a country is essential. The country subsidiary is the major structural device employed today to enable the corporation to acquire geographic knowledge.

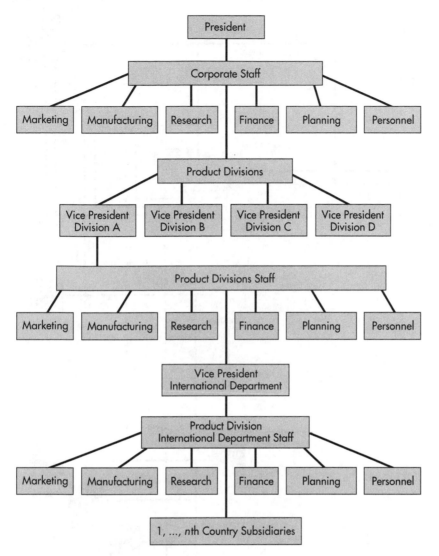

FIGURE 17-8
Divisional Corporate Structure, International Product Division with an International Department in the International Product Division

2. Product knowledge and know-how. Product managers with a worldwide responsibility can achieve this level of competence on a global basis. Another way of achieving global product competence is simply to duplicate product management organizations in domestic and international divisions, achieving high competence in both organizational units.

3. Functional competence in such fields as finance, production, and especially marketing. Corporate functional staff with worldwide responsibility contributes

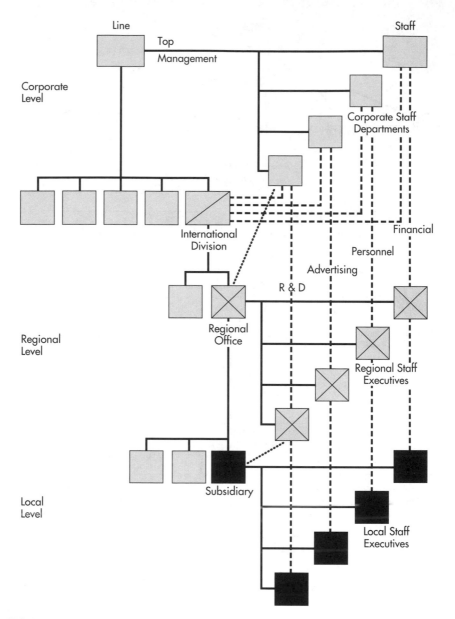

FIGURE 17–9
Organization Chart Showing Relationships Between Staff Executives in Corporate
Departments, Regional Office, and Subsidiary

toward the development of functional competence on a global basis. In a handful of companies, the appointment of country subsidiary functional managers is
reviewed by the corporate functional manager who is responsible for the development of his or her functional activity in the organization on a global basis.

What has emerged in a growing number of companies is a dotted-line relationship among corporate, regional, and country staff. These relationships are illustrated in Figure 17–9. The dotted-line relationship ranges from nothing more than advice offered by corporate or regional staff to regional country staff to a much "heavier" line relationship where staff activities of a lower organizational level are directed and approved by higher-level staff. The relationship of staff organizations can become a source of tension and conflict in an organization if top management does not create a climate that encourages organizational integration. Headquarters staff wants to extend its control or influence over the activities of lower-level staff.

For example, in marketing research, unless there is coordination of research design and activity, the international headquarters is unable to compare one market with another. If line management instead of recognizing the potential contribution of an integrated worldwide staff wishes to operate as autonomously as possible, the influence of corporate staff is perceived as undesirable. In such a situation the "stronger" party wins. This can be avoided if the level of management to which both line and staff report creates a climate and structure that expects and requires the cooperation of line and staff, and recognizes that each has responsibility for important aspects of the management of international markets.

4. A knowledge of the customer or industry and its needs. In certain large and very sophisticated international companies, staff with a responsibility for serving industries on a global basis exists to assist the line managers in the country organizations in their efforts to penetrate specific customer markets.

In the fully developed large-scale international company, product, function, area, and customer know-how are simultaneously focused on the organization's worldwide marketing objectives. This type of total competence is a matrix organization. In the matrix organization the task of management is to achieve an organizational balance that brings together different perspectives and skills to accomplish the organization's objectives. Under this arrangement, instead of designating national organizations or product divisions as profit centers, both are responsible for profitability: the national organization for country profits, and the product divisions for national and worldwide product profitability. Figure 17–10 illustrates the matrix organization. This organization chart starts with a bottom section that represents a single-country responsibility level, moves to representing the area or international level, and finally moves to representing global responsibility from the product divisions to the corporate staff, to the chief executive at the top of the structure.

The key to successful matrix management is the extent to which managers in the organization are able to resolve conflicts and achieve integration of organization programs and plans. Thus, the mere adoption of a matrix design or structure does not create a matrix organization. The matrix organization requires a fundamental change in management behavior, organizational culture, and technical systems. In a matrix, influence is based on technical competence and interpersonal sensitivity, not on formal authority. In a matrix culture, managers recognize the absolute need to resolve issues and choices at the lowest possible level and do not rely upon higher authority.

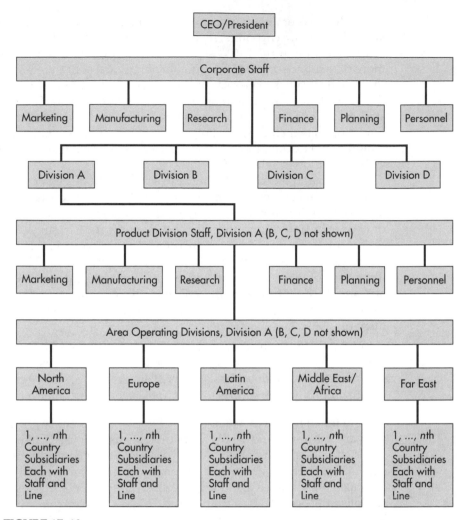

FIGURE 17–10
Divisional Corporate Structure, Globally Oriented Corporate Staff, Global Product Division (globally oriented product division staff with area subdivisions)

A sure sign that managers do not understand matrix organizations is when issues and problems are regularly pushed to the chief executive officer for resolution. Matrix organizations develop because companies refuse to accept the trade-offs of alternative traditional structures. For example, in traditional hierarchical structures, there is a choice between country or national organization and worldwide product divisions as the profit center or accountability location for strategic business management. Which is more important—in-depth knowledge of language, customs, laws, and customers, or in-depth knowledge of technology, products, and markets? In the traditional design, organizations must choose. In the matrix, both the product and country organizations are responsible for profits. Traditional structures minimize conflict, whereas matrix structures are acknowledged generators of conflict. The potential conflict in a matrix is accepted as inherent in the structure rather than as the consequence of poor management. Finally, a matrix requires a substantial investment in control systems—dual accounting, transfer pricing, corporate budgets, and so on.

Matrix Variations

The divisional company that assigns direct responsibility for global operations to its product divisions is seeking an organizational structure that is capable of directing the organization's full product-market competence toward opportunities in global markets. Unfortunately, a company utilizing this structural arrangement will have multiple division organizational units operating simultaneously and independently in many countries where the market may not be large enough to fully employ the resources committed.

A matrix solution to this problem might involve the creation of so-called *umbrella companies* in each country that are responsible for specified pooled activities such as administering reporting requirements to national authorities and coordinating corporate image-building activities, cash management, and pooled services such as office management and transportation. Product divisions would have responsibility for country strategies and programs and would directly employ their own staff. They would have profit and loss accountability, and the umbrella organization would be a cost center whose costs would be allocated to each of the product divisions on the basis of a formula. This would be a matrix with heavy emphasis on product division responsibility and is illustrated in Figure 17–11. Another matrix could shift major emphasis for profit and loss to the country or national organization. Still another matrix variation would be the attempt to divide responsibility equally between product and national organization.

▼ Relationship Among Structure, Foreign Product Diversification, and Size

John Stopford and Louis Wells, Jr. have hypothesized the relationship among structure, foreign product diversification (defined as sales of a firm outside its major product line expressed as a percentage of the total sales), and size. This formulation posits that when size abroad grows, the emergence of an area division develops so that whenever size abroad is 50 percent of total size or more, several area divisions will probably be adopted. On the other hand, as foreign product diversification increases, the likelihood that product divisions will operate on a worldwide basis increases. In a company where there is both worldwide product diversity and large-scale business abroad as a percentage of total business, foreign operation will tend to move toward the matrix structure. Companies with limited foreign product diversification (under 10 percent) and limited size as a percentage of total size will utilize the international structure. This formulation is summarized schematically in Figure 17–12.

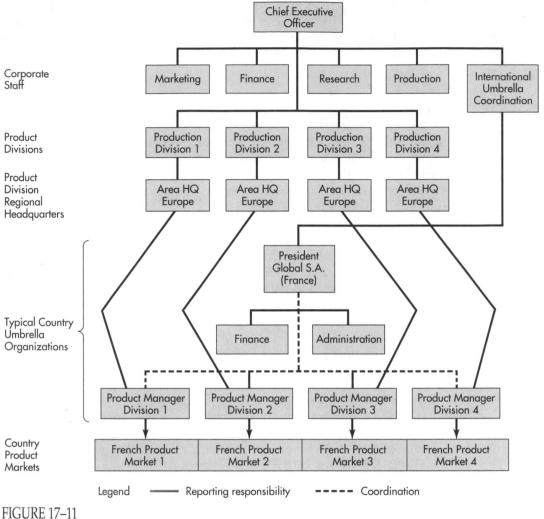

FIGURE 17–11
Umbrella Reporting Relationships and Structure

▼ Organization Structure and National Origin

The multidivisional structure was introduced in the United States as early as 1921 by Alfred P. Sloan at General Motors. This structure had three distinctive characteristics. First, profit responsibility for operating decisions was assigned to general managers of self-contained business units. Second, there was a corporate headquarters that was concerned with strategic planning, appraisal, and the allocation of resources among the business divisions. Third, executives at the corporate headquarters were separated from operations and were psychologically committed to the whole organization rather than the individual businesses.[19] During the 1960s European enterprises underwent a period of unprecedented reorganization. Essentially they adopted the American divisional-structure model. Today at the overall level there is little difference between large European and North American organizations.

Japanese and other Asian company organizations, however, are quite different. Japanese organizations, for example, rely upon generalists as opposed to functional specialists and make greater use of project teams to design and manufacture products. They also form much closer relationships with suppliers than do Canadian or American companies, and are in a different relationship to sources of capital and have a fundamentally different governance structure. The success of Japanese companies has recommended their organizational structure and design for careful evaluation, and many non-Japanese companies have successfully adopted Japanese organizational design features.

Bartlett's study of U.S. multinational companies found three stages of development.[20] First, companies recognized the diversity of the world and made the transition from ethnocentric and polycentric orientations to a geocentric orientation. Second, companies built channels of communications between managers and various parts of the organization. An example of this would be a first-time meeting of management at a conference center. There, executives from the company's businesses from around the globe would get a chance to meet each other and to learn about the business strategies of their counterparts in other countries.

Third, the company develops norms and values within the organization to support shared decisions and corporate—as opposed to country or product—perspectives. The highest value is placed on corporate goals and a cooperative ef-

---

FIGURE 17–12

The Relationship Among Structure, Foreign Product Diversification, and Size Abroad (as a % of total size)

Source: John M. Stopford and Louis T. Wells, Jr., *Managing the Multinational Enterprise* (New York: Basic Books, 1972); adapted by author.

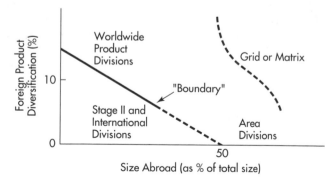

Size Abroad (as % of total size)

---

[19] Lawrence G. Franko, "The Move Toward a Multidivisional Structure in European Organizations," *Administrative Science Quarterly,* 19, no. 4 (December 1974), 493–506.

[20] Christopher A. Bartlett, "MNC's: Get Off the Reorganization Merry-Go-Round," *Harvard Business Review* (March–April 1983), pp.138–146.

fort. Japanese companies fit this description perfectly, which is a major reason why they have been so successful.

The important task of top management is to eliminate a one-dimensional approach to decisions and encourage the development of multiple management perspectives and an organization that will sense and respond to a complex and fast-changing world. By thinking in terms of changing behavior rather than changing structural design, companies can free themselves from the static nature and limitations of the structural diagram and instead can focus on achieving the best possible results with available resources.

D'Cruz and Rugman have analyzed the competitiveness of Canadian business and suggest that organizations need to move away from the traditional command and control structure toward "market focus," that is, staff and workers become the front line in serving customer needs.[21] Indeed, organizational structure will need to recognize increasingly the importance of networking with suppliers, customers, channels of distribution and competitors, along the lines of the network linkages shown in Chapter 10.[22]

GLOBAL MARKETING MANAGEMENT CONTROL

Global marketing presents formidable problems to managers responsible for marketing control. Each national market is different from every other market. Distance and differences in language, custom, and practices create communications problems. In larger companies, the size of operations and number of country subsidiaries often result in the creation of an intermediate headquarters, which adds an organizational level to the control system. This chapter reviews global marketing control practices, compares these practices with domestic marketing control, and identifies the major factors that influence the design of a global control system.

Every plan is conceived in the midst of uncertain internal and external forces that influence marketing success. Market growth, customer response to a new product, competitive moves, government regulations, and costs are just a few of the uncertain factors about which assumptions must be made to formulate a plan. Therefore, when a company plans, it must also make provisions to monitor the results of plan implementation programs and make adjustments to plans where necessary. Planning necessitates control.

In the managerial literature, control is defined as the process by which managers assure that resources are used effectively and efficiently in the accomplishment of the organization's objectives. Control activities are directed toward programs initiated by the planning process. In the ongoing enterprise, however, the data measures and evaluations generated by the control process are

---

[21] Joseph R. D'Cruz and Alan M. Rugman, *New Compacts for Canadian Competitiveness* (Toronto: Kodak Canada Inc., March 1992) p.40.

[22] Ibid., p.33.

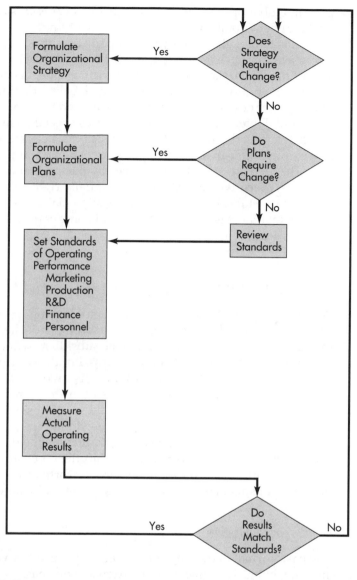

FIGURE 17–13
Relationship of Strategic Control and Planning

also a major input to the planning process. Thus, planning and control are intertwined and interdependent. The planning process can be divided into two related phases: (1) strategic planning is the selection of opportunities defined in terms of products and markets, and the commitment of resources, both human and financial, to achieve these objectives; and (2) operational planning is the process in which strategic product-market objectives and resource commitments to these objectives are translated into specific projects and programs. The relationship among strategic planning, operational planning, and control is illustrated in Figure 17–13.

In global operations, marketing control presents additional challenges. The rate of environmental change in a global company is a dimension of each of the national markets in which the company operates, and the multiplicity of environments, each changing at a different rate and each exhibiting unique characteristics, adds to the complexity of this dimension. In addition, the multiplicity of national environments challenges the global marketing control system with much greater environmental heterogeneity and therefore greater complexity in its control. Finally, global marketing causes special communications problems associated with the great distance between markets and headquarters and differences among managers in languages, customs, and practices.

The need for control is underlined by the fact that when making marketing decisions, executives are right or substantially right considerably less than 100 percent of the time. Indeed, if an organization makes no mistakes, it is a good indication that there is an excessive level of conservatism in decision making. So, mistakes are given.

▼ Formal Control Methods

When a company decides that it wants to develop a global strategy, it is essential that control of the subsidiary operations of the company shifts from the subsidiary to the headquarters. The subsidiary will continue to make vital inputs into the strategic planning process, but the control of the strategy must shift from subsidiary to headquarters. This involves a shift in the balance of power in the organization and may result in strong resistance to change.

In many companies there is a tradition of subsidiary autonomy and self-sufficiency that limits the influence of headquarters. To acquire control, there are three types of mechanisms: (1) data management mechanisms, (2) managers' management mechanisms that shift the perception of self-interest from subsidiary autonomy to global business performance, and (3) conflict resolution mechanisms that resolve conflicts triggered by necessary trade-offs.

Planning and Budgeting

The basic formal marketing control technique used by companies is planning and budgeting. This practice is an extension of a basic technique used by companies in domestic marketing to global marketing. It involves expressing planned sales and profit objectives and expenditures on marketing programs in unit and money terms in a budget. The budget spells out the objectives and necessary expenditures to achieve these objectives. Control consists of measuring actual sales and expenditures. If there is no variance or favorable variance between actual and budget, no action is usually taken. If variance is unfavorable, this is a red flag that attracts the attention of line and staff executives at regional and international headquarters, and they will investigate and attempt to determine the cause of the unfavorable variance and what might be done to improve performance.

▼ Evaluating Performance

In evaluating performance, actual performance is compared with budgeted performance as described in the previous section. Thus, the key question is: How is the budget established? Most companies in both domestic and global operations place heavy reliance upon two standards—last year's actual performance and some kind of industry average or historical norm. A more normative approach is to develop at headquarters an estimate concerning the kind of growth that would be desirable and attainable in each national market. This estimate can be based upon exhaustive studies of national and industry growth patterns.

In larger companies there is enough business volume in a number of products to justify staff product specialists at corporate headquarters who follow the performance of products worldwide. They have staff responsibility for their product from its introduction to its withdrawal from the company's product line. Normally, a new product is first introduced in the largest and most sophisticated markets. It is subsequently introduced in smaller and less developed markets. As a result, the company's products are typically at different stages of the product life cycle in different markets. A major responsibility of staff specialists is to ensure that lessons learned in more advanced markets are applied to the management of their products in smaller, less developed markets. Wherever possible, they try to avoid making the same mistake twice, and they try to capitalize on what they have learned and apply it elsewhere. They also ensure that useful ideas from markets at similar stages of development are fully applied. Smaller companies focus on key products in key markets. Key products are those that are important to the company's sales, profit objectives, and competitive position. They are frequently new products that require close attention in their introductory stage in a market. If any budget variances develop with a key product, headquarters intervenes directly to learn about the nature of the problem and to assist local management in dealing with the problem.

In theory, if conditions in the subsidiary's business environment change during a planning period, the budget would be changed to reflect changes in underlying assumptions. In practice, budgets of the companies studied are not changed during an operating period. Companies recognize that refusing to change a budget can result in unfavorable variances that are not controllable by the subsidiary management, but the view of most companies is that it is better to allow these unfavorable variances to occur than it is to allow budget revision during an implementation period. When a company does not permit budget revision, it is emphasizing the importance of careful planning and of achieving plan objectives. If uncontrollable and unforeseeable changes do occur, these can be noted as mitigating reasons or even as a full explanation for failure to achieve budget.

▼ Influences on Marketing Budgets

In preparing a budget or plan, the following factors are important:

Market Potential

How large is the potential market for the product being planned? In every domestic market, management must address this question in formulating a product plan. An international company that introduces a product in more than one national market must answer this question for each market. In most cases new products are introduced on a serial rather than simultaneous basis and can be defined as new international products as opposed to new products per se. A new international product is analogous to a product that has been introduced in a test market. The major opportunity of a test market is the chance to project the experience in the test market to a national market, whereas its major pitfall is that the characteristics of the test market will be unlike those of the national market, thus invalidating the projections made. The same opportunities and pitfalls apply in an amplified way to new international products.

Competition

A marketing plan or budget must be prepared in light of the competitive level in the market. The more entrenched the competition, the more difficult it is to achieve market share and the more likely a competitive reaction will occur to any move that promises significant success in the target market. Competitive moves are particularly important as a variable in international market planning. Often, companies move from strong competitive positions in their base markets to foreign markets where they have a minor position and must compete against both entrenched companies and other foreign competitors. Domestic market standards and expectations of marketing performance are based on experience in markets where the company has a major position. These standards and expectations frequently are different in a market where the company is in a minor position trying to break into the market.

Impact of Substitute Products

One of the sources of competition for a product in a market is the frequent existence of substitute products. As a product is moved into markets at different stages of development, improbable substitute products often emerge. For example, in Colombia a major source of competition for manufactured boxes and other packaging products is woven bags and wood boxes made in the handicraft sector of the economy. Marketing officials of multinational companies in the packaging industry report that the garage operator producing a handmade product is very difficult competition because of costs of materials and labor in Colombia.

Process

The manner in which targets are communicated to subsidiary management is as important as the way in which they are derived. One of the most sophisticated methods used today is the so-called *indicative planning method*. Headquarters estimates of regional potential are disaggregated and communicated to subsidiary management as *guidance*. The subsidiaries are in no way bound by guidance. They are expected to produce their own plan, taking into account the headquarters guidance that is based on global data and their own data from the market, including a detailed review of customers, competitors, and other relevant market developments. This method produces excellent results because it combines a global perspective and estimate with specific country marketing plans that are developed from the objective to the program by the country management teams themselves.

Headquarters, in providing guidance, does not need to understand a market in depth. For example, it is not necessary that the headquarters of a manufacturer of electrical products know how to sell electric motors to a French consumer. What headquarters can do is gather data on the expected expansion in generating capacity in France and use experience tables drawn from world studies that indicate what each megawatt of additional generating capacity will mean in terms of the growth in demand in France for electrical motors. The estimate of total market potential together with information on the competitiveness of the French subsidiary can be the basis for a guidance in terms of expected sales and earnings in France. The guidance may not be accepted by the French subsidiary. If the indicative planning method is used properly, the subsidiary educates the headquarters if its guidance is unrealistic. If headquarters does a good job, it will select an attainable but ambitious target. If the subsidiary does not see how it can achieve the headquarters goal, discussion and headquarters involvement in the planning process will either lead to a plan that will achieve the guidance objective or it will result in a revision of the guidance by headquarters.

▼ Share of Market

Another principal measure of marketing performance is share of market. This is a valuable measure because it provides a comparison of company performance with that of other competitors in the market. Companies that do not obtain this measure, even if it is an estimate, are flying blind. In larger markets data are reported for subsidiaries and, where significant sales are involved, on a product-by-product basis. Share-of-market data in larger markets are often obtained from independent market audit groups. In smaller markets share-of-market data are often not available because the market is not large enough to justify the development of an independent commercial marketing audit service. In smaller markets, it is possible for a country manager or agent to hide a deteriorating market position or share of market behind absolute gains in sales and earnings.

▼ Informal Control Methods

In addition to budgeting, informal control methods play an important role, particularly in multinational companies. The main informal control method is the transfer of people from one market to another. When people are transferred, they take with them their experience in previous markets, which will normally include some standards for marketing performance. When investigating a new market that has lower standards than a previous market, the investigation will lead to revised standards or to discovery of why there is a difference. Another valuable informal control device is face-to-face contact between subsidiary staff and headquarters staff as well as contact among subsidiary staff. These contacts provide an opportunity for an exchange of information and judgments that can be a valuable input to the planning and control process. Annual meetings that bring together staff from a region of the world often result in informal inputs to the process of setting standards.

▼ Variables Influencing Control

Domestic Practices and the Value of Standardization

One of the major assets of any organization is its operational and successful managerial practices. If a company has successfully developed and used a control system in its home or domestic operation, then this system is clearly a candidate for export because (1) it works, (2) there are people who understand it, and (3) these people can in most instances be persuaded to transfer their know-how to a foreign subsidiary. Today companies are using a standard reporting format for both domestic and foreign operations. The amount of detail and frequency of reports should be a function of the size of the foreign subsidiary and the nature of the markets: so, reporting frequency will be greatest for key markets.

The advantage of a standard system (adapted for market size differences) is that it allows comparisons to be made on a global basis, and it facilitates the easy transfer of people and ideas because all managers in the organization are working with the same system.

Communications System

A major development affecting control in international marketing operations is the communications infrastructure. A century ago international marketers had at their disposal various means of surface travel—horse, carriage, and train—as well as various means of water travel, such as sailboats and steamships. Electronic communications were limited to the telegraph. The businessperson who wanted to control international operations had two choices: traveling by land, sea, or a combination of both or transmitting written messages either by post or by telegraph. Given the speed, cost, and comfort of the communications methods available a century ago, it is understandable that businesses operated on a highly decentralized basis. Operating policies consisted of sending out hand-picked people with instructions as to their general areas of operations. These individuals were versed in the ways of the company, and therefore it was assumed that company policies and procedures would be implemented by them. They had total responsibility for carrying out the company's operations in their area. At the end of the designated operating period, which was typically a year, the results of operations would be reported. In those days, subsidiaries were controlled according to Saint Augustine's rule for Christian conduct: "Love God and do what you like!" The implication of this is that if you love God, then you will only ever want to do things that are acceptable to him. Men who were sent out to manage company affairs were expected to approach things in the approved manner.

Today the communications infrastructure is vastly enlarged. In addition to surface and sea travel, the airplane is now the major form of long-distance travel in the world. Face-to-face and written communications possibilities are vastly extended by high-speed jet aircraft. They allow managers to maintain regular direct contact with operating units all over the world. Given the importance of face-to-face communications in the information acquisition process, it seems reasonable to conclude that the jet aircraft has been a major tool in making it possible to manage a global enterprise. The very limited success of small businesses in international operations can be attributed to the reluctance or inability of the small business owner to invest money and time to travel to achieve instant familiarity with customers, agents, and distributors in foreign markets. The larger enterprise spends enormous sums to maintain contact with managers in foreign markets who are in direct contact with employees, customers, agents, and distributors in their markets.

In addition to the face-to-face communications possibilities, electronic communication is also vastly expanded. The fax machine and telephone enable rapid, direct, high-speed voice and data communication to take place on a global basis. Increasingly, the communications systems of both large and small corporations are being developed so that communication of voice and data will be available on a worldwide basis. Technological advances by telecom companies will make global "internal" company communications possible.

Distance

All other things being equal, the greater the distance between headquarters and an operating unit, the more autonomous the operating unit will be from headquarters. This relationship is due to physical and psychological differences. The physical distance imposes a time and cost barrier on communications because to travel to a distant point takes more time and therefore is more costly. To communicate by telephone, fax, or other telecommunications methods is also more costly and time consuming as distances increase. Thus, with less communication, particularly face-to-face communication, there is a greater delegation of responsibility as distances increase in international operations. Nevertheless, one of the major changes in the environment of international business is the development of communications technology, which has reduced the time and cost barriers of distance by increasing the speed, raising the quality, and covering the cost of voice, data, facsimile, telex, television, and air travel methods of communications.

The Product

A major factor affecting the type of marketing control system developed for international operations is the product being controlled. A product that is technically sophisticated can be more extensively controlled because the product use is highly similar around the world. This similarity creates opportunities to apply standards of measurement and evaluation on an international basis. Computers, for example, are products that are applied today in the same manner in technologies wherever they are located in the world. The process control computer for the petrochemical industry is the same type of application in Rotterdam as it is in Calgary, Alberta. The technology for the application of microcircuitry is a universal technology that is applied in the same way in Japan as it is in Canada.

Environmental sensitivity is the relevant product dimension influencing the extent to which international control can be exercised. If a product is similar or identical in the way it is applied and used around the world, that is, if it is culturally insensitive, then international standards and measures of performance can be developed. Computers and many industrial products fit this category. If a product is sensitive to environmental differences, then it is more difficult to apply international standards. Drugs and packaged food are two examples of environmentally sensitive products that normally require adaptation to meet the preferences of different cultures and systems of medical practice.

Environmental Differences

The greater the environmental difference, the greater the delegation of responsibility and the more limited the control of the operating unit. For example, U.S.-owned subsidiaries in Canada are extensively controlled by their American parent companies. Although some of the Canadian operations have considerable autonomy, others function as if Canada and the U.S. were the same market. Similarly, U.S. subsidiaries of Canadian companies are also closely controlled from Canada. A major reason for this situation is that both Canadian and American business perceive each others' market as very similar. As we saw earlier with the example of Canadian Tire in the United States, the assumption of market similarity may be unwarranted and thus lead to failure. When Wal-Mart entered Canada in 1994, its use of English-language promotional material in Québec caused an uproar in the French-speaking community of the province. In this case also, the assumption of market similarity was applied too broadly. In general, the standards of measurement and evaluation applicable in Canada are also seen as applicable and relevant to U.S. operations.

The development that has most accelerated the extension of control of international operations in regions that are highly different from the home-country area is the regional headquarters. Regional headquarters copes with environmental differences by focusing on a group of countries that is formed to maximize within-group similarities and between-group differences.

Environmental Stability

The greater the degree of instability in a country, the less the relevance of external or planned standards and measures of performance. When a country moves into a period of sweeping political change, it is often impossible to predict environmental conditions. One company decided that whenever a subsidiary country went into a period of revolutionary change or turmoil it would scrap all plans and adopt a policy of simply delegating total on-the-spot discretion to local management to do whatever the managers thought best. Its experience had been that local management usually achieved much more than headquarters expected.

Subsidiary Performance

A major variable influencing the kind of control exercised over international operations is the performance of subsidiary units. A subsidiary that is achieving budget is normally left alone. When a subsidiary fails to achieve budget, the variance between budgeted and actual performance is a sign that triggers intervention by headquarters. In addition, managers of successful profit centers have more leverage in holding off headquarters involvement in their operations. Subsidiaries reporting unfavorable variances find that headquarters is anxious to determine the cause of the problem, to correct the problem, and to maintain closer surveillance of operations to ensure that further difficulties do not emerge and develop undetected. Therefore a well-managed, successful subsidiary operation will be more loosely controlled than will an operation in difficulty. At the same time, the sophisticated multinational company headquarters wants to know how everybody, including successful units, is doing. It needs data on performance to help establish standards and comparisons to use in evaluating the performance of subsidiaries.

▼ Communications Guidelines

Effective communications requires both cooperation and adaptability on the part of home office and subsidiary management. Each manager walks a thin line between chaos and rigidity. Systems are absolutely necessary to provide the possibility of integration and comparison across the international network. On the other hand, a rigid adherence to standardized systems results in useless reports that provide the appearance of standardized and comparable information but actually are nothing of the sort.

All data reported by subsidiaries should meet the following test: Is this information necessary to help manage the subsidiary or the broader worldwide operation? Is the information worth the cost of collection? What is the cost of collection? These are routine questions in a well-managed market research operation, particularly when the information is being purchased in an outside buy. Inevitably there is a tendency within a company to assume that management time is a free good. This, of course, is not true.

▼ The Global Marketing Audit

A global marketing audit can be defined as a comprehensive, systematic, and periodic examination of a company's or business unit's marketing environment, objectives, strategies, programs, policies, and activities, which is conducted with the objective of identifying existing and potential problems and opportunities and recommending a plan of action to improve a company's marketing performance.

The global marketing audit is a tool for evaluating and improving a company's global marketing operations. The audit is an effort to assess effectiveness and efficiency of marketing strategies, practices, policies, and procedures vis-à-vis the firm's opportunities, objectives, and resources.

A full marketing audit has two basic characteristics. The first is that it is formal and systematic. Asking questions at random as they occur to the questioner may come up with useful insights, but this is not a marketing audit. The effectiveness of an audit normally increases to the extent that it involves a sequence of orderly diagnostic steps as is the case in the conduct of a public accounting audit.

The second characteristic of a marketing audit is that it is conducted periodically. Most companies in trouble are well on their way to disaster before the trouble is fully apparent. It is therefore important that the audit be conducted periodically and that this should include even periods when there are no apparent problems or difficulties inherent in the company's operations.

The audit may be broad or it may be a narrowly focused assessment. A full marketing audit is comprehensive. It reviews the company's marketing environment, competition, objectives, strategies, organization, systems, procedures, and practices in every area of the marketing mix including product, pricing, distribution, communications, customer service, and research strategy and policy.

There are two types of audit: independent and internal. An independent marketing audit is conducted by someone who is free from influence of the organization being audited. The independent audit may or may not be objective: It is quite possible to influence a consultant or professional firm that you are paying. The company that wants a truly independent audit should discuss with the independent auditor the importance of objectivity. A potential limitation of an independent marketing audit is the lack of understanding of the industry by the auditor. In many industries, there is no substitute for experience because if you don't have it, you are simply not going to see the subtle clues that any pro would easily recognize. On the other hand, the independent auditor may see obvious indications that the experienced pro may be unable to see.

An internal or self-audit may be quite valuable because it is conducted by marketers who understand the industry. However, it may lack the objectivity of an independent audit. Because of the strengths and limitations of the two types of audit, we recommend that both be conducted periodically for the same scope and time period, and that the results be compared. The comparison may lead to insights on how to strengthen the performance of the marketing team.

Setting Objectives and Scope of the Audit

The first step of an audit is a meeting between company executives and the auditor to agree on objectives, coverage, depth, data sources, report format, and time period for the audit.

Gathering Data. One of the major tasks in conducting an audit is data collection. A detailed plan of interviews, secondary research, review of internal documents, and so forth is required. This effort usually involves an auditing team.

A basic rule in data collection is not to rely solely on the opinion of people being audited for data. In auditing a sales organization, it is absolutely essential to talk to field sales personnel as well as sales management, and of course, no audit is complete without direct contact with customers and suppliers.

Creative auditing techniques should be encouraged and explored by the auditing team. For example, if you are auditing an organization and you want to determine whether or not the chief executive or operating officer of the organization unit is really in touch with the organization and all of its activities, send an auditor into the mail room. Find out if the chief executive has ever visited the mail room. If he or she has never been there, it tells you volumes about the management style and the degree of hands-on management in the organization. If an organization has developed an elaborate marketing incentive program, which is purported to generate results with customers, an audit should involve customer contact to find out if indeed the program is actually having any impact. For example, you can be certain that 99 percent of the material that is associated with frequent flier plans is never read or noted by fliers who have got better things to do with their time than read complicated rules and announcements.

Preparing and Presenting the Report. After data collection and analysis, the next step is the preparation and presentation of the audit report. This presentation should restate the objectives and scope of the audit, present the main findings, and present major recommendations and conclusions as well as major headings for further study and investigation.

Components of the Marketing Audit. There are six major components of a full global marketing audit. They are:

Marketing environment audit

Marketing strategy audit

Marketing organization audit

Marketing systems audit

Marketing productivity audit

Marketing function audit

Problems, Pitfalls, and Potential of the Global Marketing Audit

The marketing audit presents a number of problems and pitfalls. Setting objectives can be a pitfall, if indeed the objectives are blind to a major problem. It is important for the auditor to be open to expand or shift objectives and priorities while in the conduct of the audit itself.

Similarly, new data sources may appear during the course of an audit and the auditor should be open to such sources. The approach of the auditor should simultaneously be systematic, following a predetermined outline, and perceptive and open to new directions and sources that appear in the course of the audit investigation.

Report Presentation. One of the biggest problems in marketing auditing is that the executive who commissions the audit may have higher expectations about what the audit will do for the company than the actual results seem to offer. An audit is valuable even if it does not offer major new directions or panaceas. It is important for all concerned to recognize that improvements at the margin are what truly make a difference between success and mediocrity. In major league baseball, the difference between a batter with a .350 batting average (3.5 hits out of 10 times at bat) and a .250 (2.5 hits out of 10 times at bat) is the difference between a major-league hitter and someone who is not even good enough for the minor leagues. Major-league marketers understand this fact and recognize it in the audit. Don't look for dramatic revolutionary findings or panaceas. Accept and recognize that improvement at the margin is the winner's game in global marketing.

Global marketers, even more than their domestic counterparts, need marketing audits to assess far-flung efforts in highly diverse environments. The global marketing audit should be at the top of the list of programs for strategic excellence and implementation excellence for the winning global company.

▼ SUMMARY

To respond to the opportunities and threats in the global marketing environment a firm must have a global vision and strategy. By providing leadership, organizing a global effort, and establishing control procedures, a firm can exploit global opportunities. Leaders must have the vision in addition to the technical resources to build global competencies. In organizing the global marketing effort, a structure that enables the company to respond to relevant differences in international market environments and enables the company to extend valuable corporate knowledge is the goal. A balance between autonomy and integration must be established. Within this organization firms must establish core competencies to be competitive. For global marketing control practices to be effective, differences from purely domestic control must be recognized and implemented in planning and control practices.

▼ DISCUSSION QUESTIONS

1. What are the major variables influencing control in a global company?

2. What is the major complaint of managers in subsidiary companies about the control practices of headquarters?

3. What is a global marketing audit?

4. What kind of planning problems develop in the headquarters of a global company?

5. What are the problems in planning at the country or subsidiary level in a global company?

6. How would you advise a company manufacturing a line of construction equipment to group its market for planning purposes?

▼ BIBLIOGRAPHY

Books

ADLER, NANCY J., *International Dimensions of Organizational Behavior*, 2nd edition, Belmont: Wadsworth Publishing Company, 1991.

BARTLETT, CHRISTOPHER A., AND SUMANTRA GHOSHAL, *Managing Across Borders: The Transnational Solution*. Boston, MA: Harvard Business School Press, 1989.

DAVIDOW, WILLIAM H., AND MICHAEL S. MALONE, *The Virtual Corporation*. New York: Harper Business, 1993.

GERLACH, MICHAEL L., *Alliance Capitalism: The Social Organization of Japanese Business*. Berkeley: University of California Press, 1992.

HAMMER, MICHAEL, AND JAMES CHAMPY, *Reengineering the Corporation*. New York: Harper Collins Publishers, Inc., 1993.

KATZENBACH, JON R., AND DOUGLAS K. SMITH, *The Wisdom of Teams: Creating the High Performance Organization*. Boston, MA: Harvard Business School Press, 1993.

NAKATANI, IWAO, *The Japanese Firm in Transition*. Tokyo, Japan: Asian Productivity Organization, 1988.

ROBOCK, STEFAN H., AND KENNETH SIMMONDS, *International Business and Multinational Enterprises*. Homewood, IL: Irwin, 1989.

———, *Going Global: Succeeding in World Markets*. Boston: Harvard Business School Press, 1991.

STOPFORD, JOHN M., AND LOUIS T. WELLS, *Managing the Multinational Enterprise*. New York: Basic Books, 1972.

TULLER, LAWRENCE W., *Going Global: New Opportunities for Growing Companies to Compete in World Markets*. Homewood, IL: Business One Irwin, 1991.

YIP, GEORGE S., *Total Global Strategy*. Englewood Cliffs, NJ: Prentice Hall, 1992.

Articles

AUSTIN, NANCY K., "Workers United," *Incentive* (February 1993).

BYRNE, JOHN, "The Horizontal Corporation," *Business Week*, December 20, 1993.

———, "The Virtual Corporation," *Business Week*, February 8, 1993.

COHEN, SUSAN G., "Designing Effective Self-Managing Work Teams," *CEO Publication—University of Southern California*, G93–9.

FLORIDA, RICHARD, "The New Industrial Revolution," *Futures* (July/August 1991).

HALAL, WILLIAM E., "Global Strategic Management in a New World Order," *Business Horizons* (November/December 1993).

HAX, ARNOLDO C., "Building the Firm of the Future," *Sloan Management Review*, 30, no. 3 (Spring 1989), 75–82.

KASHANI, KAMRAN, "Beware the Pitfalls of Global Marketing," *Harvard Business Review*, 67, no. 5 (September/October 1989), 91–98.

KATZENBACH, JON R., AND DOUGLAS K. SMITH, "The Discipline of Teams," *Harvard Business Review* (March/April 1993).

KRUGMAN, PAUL, "Competitiveness: A Dangerous Obsession," *Foreign Affairs*, 73, no. 2 (March/April 1994), 28–44.

KUNIYASU, SAKAI, "The Feudal World of Japanese Manufacturing," *Harvard Business Review* (November/December 1990), 38–49.

MARUCA, REGINA FAZIO, "The Right Way to Go Global: An Interview with Whirlpool CEO David Whitwam," *Harvard Business Review*, 72, no. 2 (March–April 1994), 134–145.

MINTZBERG, HENRY, "The Effective Organization: Forces and Forms," *Sloan Management Review* (Winter 1991).

MORRISON, ALLEN J., DAVID A. RICKS, AND KENDALL ROTH, "Globalization Versus Regionalization: Which Way for the Multinational?" *Organizational Dynamics* (Winter 1991).

O'REILLY, ANTHONY J. F., "Leading a Global Strategic Charge," *Journal of Business Strategy*, 12, no. 4 (July/August 1991), 10–13.

PETERS, TOM, "Time Obsessed Competition," *Management Review* (September 1990).

PRAHALAD, C. K., AND GARY HAMEL, "The Core Competence of the Corporation," *Harvard Business Review*, 68 (May–June 1990), 79–93.

QUIGLEY, PHILIP J., "The Coming of the Rabbiphant Toward Decentralized Corporations," *Vital Speeches*, June 15, 1990.

SCHILL, RONALD L., AND DAVID N. MCARTHUR, "Redefining the Strategic Competitive Unit: Towards a New Global Marketing Paradigm?" *International Marketing Review*, 9, no. 3, 5–24.

THUROW, LESTER, "Who Owns the Twenty-First Century?" *Sloan Management Review*, 33, no. 3 (Spring 1992), 5–17.

WEBSTER, FREDERICK E., JR., "The Changing Role of Marketing in the Corporation," *Journal of Marketing*, 56, no. 4, 1–17.

▶ APPENDIX
Asea Brown Boveri (ABB): Leadership in Action

Percy Barnevik, president and CEO of Asea Brown Boveri (ABB), has moved aggressively to build an organization that combines global scale and world-class technology with deep roots in local markets.[1] He is dedicated to giving substance to the endlessly invoked corporate mantra, "Think global, act local."[2] The company was formed in 1987 when Asea, a flagship of Swedish industry, was combined with Brown Boveri, an industrial giant of Switzerland. Barnevik had to rationalize and consolidate the operations of these two giant organizations, which resulted in layoffs, plant closings, and product exchanges between the two. The creation of this new organization was the first step in a trans-Atlantic journey of acquisition, restructuring, and growth.[3]

ABB earned a profit of $505 million in 1992 on sales of almost $30 billion. The company employs more than 200,000.[4] In expanding through acquisitions, the company now employs 29,000 in North America, nearly 20,000 in Asia Pacific, and 20,000 in Eastern and Central Europe.[5] ABB has over 1,300 companies and operates in 65 business areas in 140 countries. ABB is a world leader in the generation, transmission, and distribution of electricity, in industrial process automation, in systems and products for environmental control, and in rail transport systems.[6]

ABB is a merger between Swedish and Swiss companies, but is it a Swedish or a Swiss company? Barnevik was born and educated in Sweden but headquarters are not in Sweden. Headquarters are in Switzerland, but only 100 professionals work at the Zurich headquarters. ABB reports its financial results in U.S. dollars, English is ABB's official language, and ABB acquired Combustion Engineering, an American firm. Maybe ABB is an American company.[7]

Actually, ABB is a company with no geographical center, no national "ax to grind." But according to Barnevik, ABB is not homeless. ABB is a company with homes.[8] ABB strives to be a local company everywhere and as a result has many "home countries."[9] ABB is a multidomestic corporation made up of strong national companies that have local manufacturing and engineering facilities along with local and individual market characteristics.[10] And multidomestic is

---

[1] William Taylor, "The Logic of Global Business: An Interview with ABB's Percy Barnevik," *Harvard Business Review* (March–April 1991), p. 91.

[2] Ibid.

[3] Ibid.

[4] "Reorganizing for Europe: ABB's New Regional Approach," *Business Europe,* October 4–10, 1993, p. 6.

[5] Ibid., p. 6.

[6] Romy Joyce, "Global Hero," *International Management* (September 1992), p. 82.

[7] Stephen D. Harlan, "Becoming a Global Thinker," *Vital Speeches,* January 15, 1992, p. 205.

[8] William Taylor, "The Logic of Global Business: An Interview with ABB's Percy Barnevik," p. 92.

[9] Ted Agres, "Asea Brown Boveri—A Model for Global Management," *R&D Magazine* (December 1991), p. 30.

[10] Klaus E. Agthe, "Managing the Mixed Marriage," *Business Horizons* (January–February 1990), p. 37.

ABB's favored designation rather than multinational because multidomestic more aptly defines its highly decentralized national operations.[11] One of ABB's secrets is its seemingly paradoxical management approach: global yet local, and radically decentralized with centralized reporting and control.[12]

ABB boasts a unique matrix system that has each local company president reporting to not one but two bosses, each with a different perspective.[13] According to Barnevik, there is no magic or originality in the matrix structure of ABB. If you have global product lines and you operate in many countries, "you have a matrix whether you like it or not . . . you have two rules, a global one and a national one, not fighting but complementing each other. One is set in a global framework and the other is managing a day-to-day business."[14]

An executive committee is made up of Barnevik and key executives with responsibilities for the eight business segments, regional or functional responsibilities, and in some cases responsibilities for both.[15] This committee meets every three to four weeks in a variety of locations and is responsible for ABB's global strategy and performance.[16] The executives are Swedes, Swiss, Germans, and Americans and not all are based in Zurich.

Worldwide business activities are grouped into eight business segments that oversee 50 or so business areas. Each business segment is responsible for global strategies, business plans, allocation of manufacturing responsibilities, and product development.[17] Each of the business areas has a leader who is responsible for optimizing the business on a global basis. These leaders are also responsible for sharing expertise by rotating people across borders, creating mixed-nationality teams to solve problems, and building a culture of trust and communication.[18]

For management purposes, ABB is also organized into geographical markets. There is a separate ABB company in each Western industrialized country.[19] These country member companies each has its own president and board of directors. The companies have their own ledgers and are responsible for profits and losses.[20] And these companies are established to be multidomestic, meaning that English managers in England, Thais in Thailand, and Swedes in Sweden run their individual companies with the cultural and market knowledge that will help them be perceived for what they are—local manufacturers, not foreign importers. The use of English as the company's official language is the only element of homogeneity.[21] Where appropriate, country companies are grouped into regions, or in the case of smaller countries, a regional company manages the operations.

---

[11] Carol Kennedy, "ABB: Model Merger for the New Europe," *Long Range Planning,* 25, no. 5 (1992), 13.

[12] Ted Agres, "Asea Brown Boveri—A Model for Global Management," p. 30.

[13] Ibid.

[14] Carol Kennedy, "ABB: Model Merger for the New Europe," p. 13.

[15] Ibid.

[16] William Taylor, "The Logic of Global Business: An Interview with ABB's Percy Barnevik."

[17] Klaus E. Agthe, "Managing the Mixed Marriage," p. 37.

[18] William Taylor, "The Logic of Global Business: An Interview with ABB's Percy Barnevik," p. 93.

[19] Klaus E. Agthe, "Managing the Mixed Marriage," p. 37.

[20] Ted Agres, "Asea Brown Boveri—A Model for Global Management," p. 32.

[21] Romy Joyce, "Global Hero," p. 85.

The business area structure meets the national structure at the level of ABB's member companies. Wherever possible the operations are decentralized and the separate companies do the work of the business areas in the different countries.[22] The two parts of the matrix intersect at the level of the group's 1,300 companies, whose heads report both to their national company president and their business area leader, wherever he or she may be based.[23]

ABB has over 5,000 profit centers with an average of 50 employees and over 1,300 companies with an average of 200 employees.[24] By being so decentralized, the small units have real profit and loss responsibility and meaningful autonomy. It also helps that the corporate headquarters is only around 100 people. Barnevik is convinced that in order to be responsive, you have to have a flat organization with profit centers measured on business results.

In October 1993, ABB reorganized in order to further cut costs and to exploit emerging pan-European sales and contract opportunities.[25] The existing matrix organization was retained, but ABB strengthened its cross-border management of Europe by creating a new post of executive vice president for Europe. The membership of the executive committee was reduced from twelve to eight. Individual committee members now have responsibility for either countries or products.[26] There are now three regional executive vice presidents with sales responsibilities in Europe, Americas, and Asia Pacific. There are four product segment executive vice presidents each responsible for individual business segments. All have responsibility for business performance. Functional heads such as finance and R&D now report directly to Barnevik and are not members of the committee. Barnevik has created a new discussion group of 70 top managers, a top-management council, who will meet three or four times a year to review operations and talk strategy.[27]

Mr. Barnevik says that the slimmed-down executive committee clarifies responsibility and optimizes transnational decision making. He believes that the new organization will strengthen the operating advantages of ABB's matrix and enable ABB to react even faster to market developments.[28]

As admired as ABB's management is, and as successful as its organization structure has been, it is not without its problems. Decentralization in a multidomestic environment poses a problem according to Gasser, who before the merger was head of BBC Brown Boveri. The ambiguity of evolving in a multicultural environment with multiple management structure is a further problem, raising the possibility of conflict or confusion. And then there is the question of the capabilities and skills of Barnevik. Could his successor ever hope to be able to lead such a complex organization?

---

[22] William Taylor, "The Logic of Global Business: An Interview with ABB's Percy Barnevik," p. 93.

[23] Carol Kennedy, "ABB: Model Merger for the New Europe," p. 14.

[24] William Taylor, "The Logic of Global Business: An Interview with ABB's Percy Barnevik," p. 99.

[25] "Reorganizing for Europe: ABB's New Regional Approach," p. 6.

[26] Ibid.

[27] Ibid., p. 7.

[28] Ibid.

EIGHTEEN

The Future of Global Marketing

Introduction

Anyone who maintains that he or she can predict the future is either a charlatan or a fool. Nevertheless, one of the more fascinating and valuable enterprises in human endeavor is the effort to forecast future developments on the basis of patterns, trends, and underlying factors that can be observed in the present situation. These forecasts are vitally important as an input to the strategic planning process for both domestic and international enterprises.

THE CHANGING WORLD ECONOMY

The world economy, however, has never been in better shape. It has undergone revolutionary changes during the past 50 years. Perhaps the greatest and most profound change is the emergence of global markets and global competitors who have steadily displaced local competitors. Even as recently as 25 years ago, the world was far less integrated than it is today. Goods were generally produced for the home market buyer and the many companies and products resulted in great differentiation. To be sure, trade has always been important to many nations. But such trade was often in natural resources or in products, produced for the domestic market, for which a need or want was also discovered in foreign markets. Often, cultural affinity of markets, such as between Canada and the United States, or between Germany, Austria, and Switzerland, was an important stimulus to trade. The pace of change and interdependence of nations and markets has been steadily increasing. In addition, the past decade witnessed four major changes:

- ▶ The poor countries of the world, which have always been poor, are getting rich.
- ▶ Capital movements rather than trade have become the driving force of the world economy.
- ▶ The old trade-cycle model, which said that as a product matures, the location of production must shift to low-wage countries, has been repealed.
- ▶ The world economy is in control. The macroeconomics of the nation-state no longer control economic outcomes in countries, and even the large superpower countries like the United States can no longer dictate to poorer countries how they should behave.

▶ The 75-year "contest" between capitalism and socialism is over. The clear success of the capitalist system over the communist centrally controlled model has led to the collapse of communism as a model for the organization of economic activity and as an ideology.

These remarkable changes are contrary to much of the received doctrine of economic theory, and they are of great significance and importance to government and business practitioners. Practitioners cannot wait until there is a new theory—the likelihood of success is much greater when actions are based on the new reality of the changed world economy.

The first change is that poor countries are getting rich! The emergence of the newly rich countries from among the ranks of the former less developed (LDC) group breaks the long monopoly of Western Europe, the United States and Canada, and Japan on the rich-nation status. These countries are proving that you don't have to be Western European or Japanese to be rich. Countries like Singapore and Hong Kong are already high-income countries (i.e., countries with an income of C$14,500 per capita or higher in 1994) and especially in East Asia there are many countries that are growing at annual rates of 5 percent per annum or higher. A 5 percent real growth rate will double real income in 14 years. The emerging rich countries include smaller countries like Korea as well as the largest countries in the world, China and India. For the first time in the history of the world, there is a prospect for *global* prosperity.

The second change is that capital movements rather than trade have become the driving force of the world economy. World trade is greater than ever before. Trade in goods and so called *invisibles* (services) is running at more than C$3 trillion per year. We also know that capital movements have become more influential than trade flows. Foreign exchange transactions of C$270 trillion per year are some 38 times the volume of global trade in goods and services. Some 60 percent of all foreign exchange reserves in the world are held in U.S. dollars. Thus, capital and trade both influence the value of currencies.

The third change is that the old trade-cycle model, which said that as a product matures, the location of production must shift to low-wage countries, has been repealed. The trade-cycle model was the discovery of Professor Ray Vernon of the Harvard Business School based upon his study of U.S. trade data from the 1950s, 1960s and 1970s. The shift of the location of production of a mature product from high-wage to low-wage countries affected a wide range of industries, from textiles to television sets.

The economic rationality of this approach had particularly profound implications for the U.S. in terms of replacing high-paying jobs with lower-paying, lower-skill jobs in services. Canada was affected differently in that free trade with the United States altered and reduced the importance of Canadian production locations. Subsidiaries became distribution locations or were upgraded with global product mandates. Japan, on the other hand, responded to the challenge of competition from lower-wage countries by increasing the efficiency and productivity of their work force.

As a business strategy, there was a fatal flaw with the U.S.'s approach to management: It offered a one-time advantage, but what do you do when wages start to go up in the country to which you have moved? What do you do when your competitor increases quality via new production methods and design processes? In other words, chasing cheap labor is really an exit strategy when your competitors are innovating and constantly improving quality and reducing costs in place. Today, even if your company is located in a high-wage country, there is no reason to shift the location of manufacturing simply because wages are high if you innovate and drive down labor as a percentage of total costs.

A good example of an executive who knows this is Nicolas Hayek, the CEO of the Swiss watch company SMH. He recently observed that he doesn't care if the workers for his competitors get paid nothing. His company will still win in competition because even though wages in Switzerland are the highest in the world, labor costs for SMH are low because of their creative design and manufacturing methods.

The fourth major change is the emergence of the world economy as the dominant economic unit. Companies and countries that recognize this fact have the greatest chance of success. An important aspect of this is the power of regional economic blocs, such as the European Union, NAFTA, or the emerging Latin American Mercosur. Companies and countries that recognize this fact have the greatest chance of success. The economic power of individual countries is shifting and with it their ability to influence other nations' internal affairs. For example, the United States, still a very large economic power, has diminished in global influence; Japan has emerged as the economic powerhouse in Asia; and Germany fills this role in Europe. As poor countries grow richer, they perceive their own values as the main reason for their success.

Changes in global competition are bringing countries into more direct confrontation with their main economic rivals than was the case in the past. Yesterday's global forces were founded on exports of products and services not available to competing nations. It used to be that countries relied on exports of products that others did not produce (whether this was natural resources or high-tech products). Today, countries in the same industries in different countries and regions compete ferociously with each other in manufactured goods, agricultural products, natural resources, and services.

These are the new economic realities. The rich are getting richer, and the poor are getting richer, and the world is becoming more and more integrated. This means new opportunities and new challenges for companies and countries.

GLOBAL CORPORATIONS IN THE EVOLVING INTERNATIONAL ECONOMIC ORDER

Four major trends will undoubtedly affect the role and future of global corporations in the evolving international economic order. The first is the trend toward symmetry in the relative importance of global corporations based in different parts of the world. A country's power and influence, relative to the world economy, is not constant, as the current economic importance of Japan shows. What is clear is that no country or region has a monopoly on drive, creativity, and energy for commercial effort. Today, there are major new global companies emerging in the lower,

lower middle, and upper middle income countries, and for the first time, countries at these stages of development appear to have excellent prospects as major developing markets.

A second trend that is clearly observable is the emergence of an increasingly large number of world-scale industries. Today we are witnessing a shakeout of firms in industries ranging from electronics to automobiles. As the scope of competition broadens into world markets and many world-scale industries emerge, increasingly the benchmark for survival and success will be competitive competence, the ability to understand the diversity of market needs, and to meet these with world standard quality and value. Experience shows that company size is not necessarily a critical factor, as many highly successful small and medium-size companies demonstrate.

The implications of this trend are of enormous significance from both a private and a public policy perspective. From the point of view of the corporation, it is necessary to identify and recognize the world-scale trend if it applies to the company's industry. Zenith and RCA, for example, made the mistake of assuming that they were leaders in the color television industry because of their leading position in the North American market in the 1960s and 1970s. This proved to be a disastrous illusion, as both companies found it increasingly difficult to compete with Japanese companies that were operating not only in the North American market but throughout the world.

Companies that find themselves in world-scale industries must choose between going for positions as high-volume, low-cost producers for the volume markets of the world or carefully positioning themselves in niche markets where the value they create is based as much on knowing their customer as it is on being a low-cost producer. Each of these positions is a winning strategy. The losing strategy, which has been demonstrated by the now defunct British motorcycle industry, is to be a high-cost producer trying to compete in the volume market against a low-cost producer.

A third trend is the steady shift toward a geocentric or world corporate orientation as opposed to an ethnocentric or home-country orientation or, alternatively, a polycentric or host-country orientation. A geocentric company is one that consciously recognizes that it is operating in the international economic order and that its stakeholders are customers, employees, and shareholders in every area of operation. In addition, a geocentric company is one that recognizes the possibility of creating a global strategic plan for each of its businesses in order to allocate and apply resources most effectively.

A fourth trend relates to the role of cooperation, among countries and companies. Clearly, the European Union and NAFTA are the most significant examples of efforts toward cooperation and economic integration. Companies within those spheres of increasing economic and trade interdependence find rapid expansion of potential and opportunities. At the company level, alliances and partnerships, to complement one another's strengths for the purpose of competitive advantage, are fast becoming a critical strategic global marketing option in today's dynamic and fast-paced business environment. Such cooperative and partnering efforts are a direct result of the shift in management orientation toward the geocentric point of view.

The new openness of economies has major implications for Canadian companies competing locally or globally. Companies must increasingly monitor developments taking place at home and in other parts of the world to stay abreast of the most advanced practices and the most important new-product development and introduction activities. In the past, if one was informed about what was going on in one's home or key markets, one was informed about the frontiers of marketing practice. Today this is no longer the case. Marketing professionals who are committed to keeping up with the latest developments in the field must scan the world. In effect, there is no longer a separation between domestic and international marketing: They have become a part of a unified field.

▼ SUMMARY

The opportunities in global marketing have never been greater than they are today. The companies that seize these opportunities will offer the best combination of product, price, promotion, place, and service: in short, greater value. In addition, over the long term, successful companies will also be sensitive to the aspirations and needs not only of the individual customers in each national market but also the collective aspirations of countries.

▼ DISCUSSION QUESTIONS

1. What are the implications of the four major global changes for a global marketing manager?

2. Discuss how the four main trends are likely to impact the global marketing strategy of small- and medium-sized companies?

▼ BIBLIOGRAPHY

Books

DRUCKER, PETER F., *The New Realities*. New York: Harper & Row, 1989.

FALLOWS, JAMES, *Looking at the Sun*. New York: Pantheon Books, 1994.

HIGASHI, CHIKARA, AND G. PETER LAUTER, *The Internationalization of the Japanese Economy*. Morwell, MA: Kluwer Academic Publishers, 1990.

OHMAE, KENICHI, *The Borderless World: Power and Strategy in the Interlinked Economy*. New York: Harper Business, 1990.

———, *Triad Power*. New York: The Free Press, 1985.

PORTER, MICHAEL E., *Competition in Global Industries*. Boston: Harvard Business School Press, 1986.

THUROW, LESTER, *Head to Head: The Coming Economic Battle Among Japan, Europe, and America*. New York: William Morrow and Company, Inc., 1992.

TICHY, NOEL M., AND STRATFORD SHERMAN, *Control Your Destiny or Someone Else Will: How Jack Welch Is Making General Electric the World's Most Competitive Corporation*. New York: Currency, Published by Doubleday, a Division of Bantam Doubleday, Dell Publishing Group, Inc., 1993.

TOFFLER, ALVIN, *The Third Wave*. New York: Bantam Books, 1981.

Articles

BARNEVIK, PERCY (interviewed by William Taylor), "The Logic of Global Business: An Interview with ABB's Percy Barnevik," *Harvard Business Review*, 69, no. 2 (March–April 1991), 90–105.

DAS, GURCHARAN, "Local Memoirs of a Global Manager," *Harvard Business Review*, 71 (March–April 1993), 38–47.

FARLEY, LAURENCE J., "Going Global: Choices and Challenges," *Journal of Consumer Marketing*, 3, no. 1 (Winter 1986), 68.

MORRIS, CHARLES R., AND CHARLES H. FERGUSON, "How Architecture Wins Technology Wars," *Harvard Business Review*, 71 (March–April 1993), 86–96.

TAYLOR, WILLIAM, "Message and Muscle: An Interview with Swatch Titan Nicolas Hayek," *Harvard Business Review*, 71 (March–April 1993), 99–110.

► APPENDIX

Establishing a Presence Around the Globe[1]

by Ron K. Glover

I want to talk about establishing a global presence. Now that task is, in part, about establishing an image or a brand that represents your company to external audiences around the world. And, in part, it is about establishing and changing the internal substance and practices of your company.

But above all, I think the challenge of establishing a global identity is about the relationship between the external and the internal. That crucial relationship, I believe, must be governed by three principles. They are:

Principle number one: Over time, an external image must reflect internal practices. Less formally, I call this the "reversible raincoat" principle.

Principle number two: All significant corporate change proceeds from a profound effort by leaders to change perceptions, patterns, and practices—in short, from an irresistible plea to change paradigms. Less formally, I call this principle "Brother, can you paradigm?"

Principle number three: In the new, more unified global marketplace, persistent differences in language, culture and perception make it a delicate balancing act to establish a unified global presence which also reflects local nuance. Less formally stated, this principle says that, even in the global village, the biggest building is still the Tower of Babel.

Before we look more closely at each of these principles, let's look briefly at what establishing a global presence looks like to a company like Dun & Bradstreet. Dun & Bradstreet has a wide variety of products and services. Those separate products are not generally identified in the public mind by their separate names. In that sense, our products are not like, say, Procter & Gamble's product, Ivory Soap, or Pampers Diapers. In the case of these P&G products, many—probably most—customers have an opinion about them without connecting them to the parent company.

The Dun & Bradstreet Corporation is the world's largest marketer of information and related services, with operations in more than 60 countries. The company's divisions include Dun & Bradstreet Information Services, A. C. Nielsen, IMS International, D&B Software, Reuben H. Donnelley and Moody's Investors Service.

[1] Ron K. Glover, President, North America, Dun & Bradstreet Information Services, Remarks to The Conference Board, January 26, 1993, The Waldorf-Astoria, New York City. *D&B Executive Forum* is a continuing series that presents white papers, articles and speeches of interest to the international business community.

But in our case, what customers think about each of our products is entirely bound up with what they think about Dun & Bradstreet. So, when we talk about D&B's presence around the world, we are talking about the Dun & Bradstreet name. In that sense, we are a brand just like Coca-Cola soft drinks or Jaguar sports cars or Ninja Turtles.

But what does that mean? What is a brand? Consider a simple can of soup. A can of soup has a wide variety of characteristics—taste, smell, color, texture, price, weight, etc. Those characteristics are found in the product itself, and when the product is transported across borders by trucks or boats or trains or airplanes, all those characteristics go with it.

But however closely you examine that can of soup, no matter how powerful your microscope, you'll never find the brand. Of course, you'll find the brand *name* and the brand *logo* printed on the side. But the brand identity itself—what the marketers call the brand equity—is different, because the brand identity or the brand equity is outside of the product. The brand identity is a combination of the set of expectations, the positive or negative past experiences, and the positive or negative emotional feelings that are associated with that brand in the public mind.

In other words, the product's brand, unlike its other characteristics, is found not in the product or its package, but in the minds of consumers and prospects.

Consider the implications: That means the brand is not transported across borders by trucks or planes, but by various forms of communication. Word of mouth. Advertising. Unpaid media. And as we will see later, in a global marketplace the same message can be perceived very differently in different contexts, while the color remains the same from Lisbon to London to Los Angeles.

So there are important distinctions between the concrete product and the brand identity. But while the brand can be conceptually distinguished from the product, the two must be in sync. Essentially, the brand holds out to customers a "promise of quality"—and there are many examples of products which fail precisely because they don't live up to their promise. When that happens the brand name plummets and the sales of products dry up.

And that's a good introduction to the first principle—what I call informally the "reversible raincoat" principle. This principle simply asserts that external images must, in the end, reflect the internal practices and substance of the company. Over time, the inside becomes outside, as with a reversible raincoat. Brands are promissory notes, and if the product doesn't deliver on that promise, both the brand and the product are doomed.

Certainly you can choose a high-sounding name for your product. You can get that name copyrighted and you can protect it with the force of law. But if your new name doesn't reflect substantial internal change, you haven't helped yourself.

Here's a story that makes that point. Perhaps you've heard about the man who insisted on calling a certain countess a pig. So the countess hauled this fellow into court. Sure enough, the judge ordered the man to stop. The man asked the judge, "You mean, Your Honor, that I can't call the countess a pig?" "That's right," the judge replied, "never again call her a pig."

"Well, Your Honor," the man said, "Suppose I see a pig—can I call the pig a countess?" The judge thought for a minute and said, "Yes, I suppose if you see a pig you can call it 'countess.' " Whereupon the man turned directly to the countess and said, "Hi, Countess!"

The point is that you can protect your name with the force of law, but if the name or the brand or the image is not in sync with reality, you won't fool anybody for long. The inside becomes outside. That's the reversible raincoat principle. And, of course, it has a corollary—that the outside can become the inside.

Here's what I mean. When a company sets out to construct an identity, an image, or a brand name, it usually does so because it's new to a market . . . or because it's expanding or deepening its traditional array of products and services . . . or because it is trying to overcome some negative publicity. The internal practices must live up to the external image. But a wise business leader will also leverage the external image—that is, the advertising and communication efforts intended for outside audiences—to help change the internal culture.

At Dun & Bradstreet Information Services (DBIS), we've undertaken a significant culture change over the past few years. That change was motivated by a number of different factors: we have increased almost exponentially the range of products and services we provide; we have expanded into new geographical areas; we've revolutionized our commitment to quality; and we have worked to overcome some negative publicity of a few years ago.

As part of our efforts to expand, enhance and more firmly position ourselves for external audiences in light of those internal changes, we've considered new avenues of advertising, including television advertisements. And I never pass up an opportunity to show to internal audiences the ads, the commercials and the other elements of our new communications plan, even when we haven't finally approved them.

And to tell the truth, the more these efforts differ from our traditional style, the more they suit my purpose. Because, frankly, part of my motivation is sheer shock therapy—to communicate as clearly as I possibly can that we are undertaking thoroughgoing change at DBIS. We're serious about it. It's irreversible. It opens up new possibilities that have been hidden from us before.

That brings me to my second principle. Formally stated, this is the principle that cultural change for companies only occurs when the company leaders seek to transform the corporate paradigm. I use the term "paradigm" in the sense that Thomas Kuhn did in his ground-breaking book, *The Structure of Scientific Revolutions*. That is, a paradigm is the entire set of semi-conscious ways of perceiving, judging, practicing and speaking that underlie and shape the daily pattern of business as usual. Paradigms define—and they limit—the range of possibilities for any institution. Changing a company in significant ways is a matter of breaking through those old paradigms in order to free up new energies and open up new possibilities. It's hard to do. It requires leadership by example as well as by communication. It requires leaders to constantly invite and request change: "Brother, can you paradigm?"

It's hard to do because the old paradigms have such a strong and hidden hold on all of us. Here's an example of what I mean. A few years ago the Queen of England was taken to a demonstration of the British army's cannons. The particular cannon being demonstrated that day was served by a crew of five soldiers. When the order to fire was given, four of the five men immediately went to work at their assigned tasks on the cannon—loading, priming, aiming and so on. But the fifth man simply executed a left-face. The Queen asked why. The general who was accompanying her answered that the fifth man executed a left face because it was the job of the number five man to execute a left face. Always had been.

The Queen wasn't satisfied, so the general promised to investigate. He found out that the practice dated back to the days when the cannon were dragged to the battlefield by horses. Back then, when the order to fire was given, the fifth man turned left to grab the horses' reins in case they got spooked by the loud noise. Of course, by the time of the Queen's visit, it had been several decades since horses were used to transport cannon. Nevertheless, the cannon was still served by a five man crew, and the fifth man still executed a left face when the order to fire was given.

It was Mark Twain who once said that the past isn't dead—in fact, it isn't even past. As in the example of that cannon, the past persists in the present through the habits and practices which are never questioned, and whose original purpose may have been obsolete for decades if not centuries.

Here's an example from my own company. More than a century ago, Robert Dun concluded that the economies of scale of his time meant that it was not economically feasible to sell credit reports in units of less than 100. Now, in the century since Dun made that decision, technological innovations have exploded, the cost structure of the business revolutionized. But Dun's decision was never revisited until a couple of years ago, when I looked at the question again. I found that we could make money selling in units of less than 100. And so, I changed that policy.

So we start by forming our habits, and we end with our habits forming us . . . almost unconsciously. Why does the number five man make a left-face? Well, because that's what the number five man has always done!

The first task of change is to make conscious all those habits that might have outlived their usefulness. But as you undertake that change, you have to convince the institutional culture that the change you propose is consistent with its identity and self-image—that is not something alien and threatening.

In an earlier job, I had the task of rapidly expanding the Japanese division of an American company. At first I met a lot of resistance. This resistance was expressed in the endless repetition of the phrase that the action plan I sought was, "Not the Japanese way!" I heard that phrase over and over, "Not the Japanese way! Not the Japanese way!"

I was stymied at first. But then I pointed to the example of Sony, and to the examples of Honda and other Japanese companies that have rapidly expanded. Finally I said, "Perhaps this has not been the Japanese way of the future." I was trying to give them a way to buy into this process of change without feeling like they had to sacrifice their identity. And, fortunately, it seemed to work.

But the force of accumulated habit is only one of the institutional barriers to meaningful change. Change is also likely to be resisted by those who fear that it will diminish their power. For that reason, when we undertook a major change in the direction of quality improvement at DBIS, I first brought in all of my direct reports and asked each associate to pick their best person to serve on the steering committee. The first question they all asked was whether they should pick someone from finance, or marketing, or production, or whatever.

But I told them I just wanted the best person, without any further specifications. Because I wanted it to be clear that our quality effort was not a matter of concern only to one department or to one area of specialization or expertise. Quality efforts have to be across-the-board, multidisciplinary, thoroughgoing. In short, they have to be everybody's business.

The people who report directly to the senior executive of a company have a high level of motivation to change. And it's a motivation that is constantly reinforced through their interactions with the senior executive. The people who are in the entry-level positions are also receptive to change because they haven't been acculturated in the old habits for decades. But the people in between those two levels—the middle managers—are often the most resistant to change. They might feel stuck in their mid-level positions, and conclude that if they just hunker down and dig in their heels, they can thwart the attempts at change.

So, in our quality efforts, we started with middle managers. We focused our efforts on those middle managers for a full year before we brought in more senior executives. We took the middle managers through a period of training at the beginning of the process because we knew it was essential to give them a sense of ownership.

Through a long process that built slowly over the past couple of years, we expanded that initial effort into all parts of the corporation. Following the first group of middle managers to go through the process, a second group, comprised of the first group's direct reports, underwent quality training. That process was replicated throughout the ranks of middle management. Soon the quality initiative spread throughout the company.

In short, we're in the process of changing the paradigm for doing business at DBIS. And that's the second governing principle in trying to establish a new global presence.

Part of the new story we wanted to tell was a story of improved quality and customer sensitivity. But there were other parts of our image we also wanted to change in order to bring it further in line with our evolving reality, especially our movement into markets where we did not have an historical identity.

That brings up the third principle: It requires a very subtle balancing act to establish a unified image that also reflects different cultures. Less formally stated, even in the global village, the biggest building is still the Tower of Babel.

In the U.S., D&B has always been seen as an authoritative voice. For example, in Ernest Hemingway's famous novel *The Sun Also Rises*, the hero, Jake Barnes, says about another character that he "believed everything he read, as if it had come from Robert Dun himself."

That enviable reputation attached to Dun & Bradstreet's long history and success in providing basically one product—the credit report—was an identity that was acquired primarily in the United States. But a few years ago, we realized that the information in our huge proprietary databases could be used for a large variety of other business purposes. Thus, we began to expand our product line, our customer base and our geographical areas. At the same time, we worked to hold onto the solid base of positive perceptions. It was a classic case of extending the brand.

And so we faced the task of confronting all marketers who want to position or reposition their corporate identities or images in the world marketplace. Can communications establish and support a truly global brand?

What, exactly, is a global brand, anyway? In the strictest possible definition, a global brand would be a product that is identical in every way in every corner of the world: identical in the content of the product, identical in name and in logo, identical in price structure, identical in packaging, advertising and promotion and identical in the mind set of customers everywhere.

The problem with defining global brands in this strict sense is that I don't think there are any: Coca-Cola changes the content and the taste of its product slightly by changing the sweetener in its diet versions in different parts of the world. Spirit alcohol, while tasting the same in Trieste, Tampa, Toulouse, Taiwan or Timbuktu, takes on a different character in different countries. In Japan, for example—unlike in the U.S.—I. W. Harper is viewed as a premium whiskey, and is priced accordingly.

Nevertheless, a number of companies have successfully established names with coherent identities and images around the world. So, how is it done? The first step, I believe, is to recognize that whether you like it or not, whether you try to manage it or not, you already have an image out there in the marketplace. And you have to start by finding out exactly what that image is.

By the way, don't ask the question if you don't want to know the answer. You probably will not like the results of your research, but knowing how you are currently perceived is a crucial part of getting where you want to be.

Changing your image is not simply a matter of erasing the old image and writing up what you want. To be credible, the new identity you seek to establish must have some connection with the image that people already have. The trick is to put the current perception into a positive light, rather than simply to try to erase it off the blackboard.

D&B celebrated its 150th Anniversary recently. Our long history and dominant market position have helped to feed the view, in some quarters, that we are remote, detached, perhaps even a bit arrogant.

It would have been a meaningless exercise for us to try to say, "Look, forget about our size and market position: we're really a small, struggling company."

Instead, our strategy has been to capitalize on our existing image, to tell the marketplace that our size, history, and marketplace position are all unique strengths that benefit our customers. To that, we added the message that if in the past we had seemed remote and unconcerned, we have moved aggressively to be more fully focused on our customers. And, to repeat the first principle, you've got to be telling the truth when you make a claim like that.

Now, the ultimate judges of the success of your identity program are your customers out there in your marketplace. Customers can't create your corporate identity—you can't invite a couple dozen of them in to create an ad campaign for you. But once you have come up with the ideas for an identity campaign, you've got to take it to the marketplace and test, test and test again.

If you're taking your campaign around the world, you have to test in each market to find out its nuances and subtle differences. That's especially true when you are trying to formulate what I call a "descriptor" for your identity. I don't mean a slogan or an advertising tag line, I mean the two or three words or the phrase that defines your activity. Your logo and name are, in a sense, a picture of your company: the descriptor says what the picture is about. A descriptor is like the headline on a news photograph. An inappropriate descriptor, like a misleading headline, can lead to trouble.

Here's an illustration. Several years ago a small newspaper in the Midwest was all set to run a front-page story, complete with photograph, about the re-opening of a power plant that had been shut down for years. Right before deadline a bigger story broke: the area's aging congressman had just married a 19-year-old student. So the newspaper ran a photograph of this 65-year-old congressman with his 19-year-old bride in place of the photograph of the power plant. But they forgot to change the headline. It still read, "Old power house gets new spark of life."

The moral of the story is that you've got to take great care with the descriptors because they give meaning and context to your name and logo.

Moreover, translating your descriptor into other languages almost always raises very subtle but significant challenges. Often, a translation can be technically correct but nevertheless misleading. Here are some examples:

► A dry cleaners in Bangkok has a sign that says, "Drop your trousers here for best results."

► A cleaning shop in Rome says, "Ladies, leave your clothes here and spend the afternoon having a good time."

► And a sign at the desk in a Paris hotel says, "Leave your values here before going upstairs."

Small wonder then, that when it comes to translating your message into other languages, you've got to do a lot more than just refer to a foreign language dictionary. Right now, for example, we at Dun & Bradstreet Information Services are researching ways to translate a possible descriptor, "Decision information." It's a complicated process.

We've found, for example, that in some languages the juxtaposition of the literal translation of those two terms seems awkward and artificial. So we are looking for descriptors in the local languages that suggest the same understanding of what we are about as the phrase "decision information" suggests in English.

Sending messages across borders can sometimes cause translation problems even when there are no language differences. For example, a few years ago the British division of McDonald's was damaged by a persistent rumor that the company supported the Irish Republican Army. They spent a lot of time and money tracing that rumor to its source. They found that the rumor began when a CNN program seen in England reported that McDonalds' senior management encourages its employees to invest in IRAs. Of course, IRA in the U.S. means "Individual Retirement Accounts," while in Britain it means "Irish Republican Army."

That incident is a handy reminder of George Bernard Shaw's observation that "England and America are two countries divided by a common language."

Now, let's quickly review the three basic principles that govern successful efforts to establish a global presence:

First, the "reversible raincoat" principle—internal practices must live up to the external images.

Second, the "Brother, can you paradigm?" principle—that internal change is a laborious process of breaking through encrusted perceptions, patterns and practices in order to redefine markets and seize new possibilities.

Third, the principle that even in the global village the most prominent feature is the Tower of Babel. It requires extremely delicate and creative work to carry around the globe a single, coherent message that can fit into the fabric of each separate culture. And it requires hard work.

But from my long experience in operating in the global marketplace, it's extremely exhilarating and rewarding work to accomplish. Dun & Bradstreet is the world's leading provider of business information. Recent events—from the fall of the Berlin Wall to the finishing touches on the North American Free Trade Agreement—show that the demand for the fruits of unconstrained enterprise has changed our world. And that demand has been awakened and strengthened by the flow of information. It has brought down barriers and opened up the globe to new possibilities.

And all those changes give testimony to the power of the central theme of my remarks, the central term in the title of this conference, and the centerpiece of your careers—the power of images, ideas and communication.

For a long time it was fashionable to denigrate images as pale reflections of reality, to discount ideas as powerless to affect events, and to dismiss communication as mere talk. We came to view relations among nations and across cultures not as a great debate but as a game of grab. What mattered was not the force of international communication, but the calculus of national force—not the potency of principles, but the perception of power.

But the world reaffirms the power of communication, including the communication of advertising image and messages from which people in regressive and stagnant command economies receive information about living standards in free economies. And when they find out about such living standards, they want them for themselves.

For centuries, people gave evidence that they were citizens of the world by declaring "Nothing human is foreign to me." Today, people are saying, "Nothing foreign is forbidden to me—if it is a product I like!" Increasingly, global maps are viewed as international shopping catalogues: India is where madras cloth comes from; Germany is a great source of beer and cars; Thailand has wonderful wall hangings; France is the best source for perfume and women's couture.

In this world market, the task is to make your product brand identified as the best product in its category from New Delhi to New York. That's an enormous task. It increases exponentially the challenge for all of us who are responsible for establishing a global presence by communicating messages and images across borders. We face a world marketplace that is hedged with dangers of misunderstanding and fraught with cultural and linguistic ambiguity . . . but which also churns with new possibilities.

And for that reason, I'm sure that, like me, you wouldn't trade places with anybody!

CASES

CASE	MAIN CHAPTER	OTHER RELEVANT CHAPTERS	GEOGRAPHIC FOCUS
1. Which Company Is Transnational?	1	10, 17	Global
2. Euro Disney in Trouble	2	3, 4	Europe
3. Club Med Inc.: The Special Challenge of Growth	4	7, 10, 12	Global, North America
4. Revenue Canada: The Special Import Measures Act	5	16	North America
5. Swatch Watch U.S.A.: Creative Marketing Strategy	7, 8	10	North America
6. Choufont-Salva, Inc.	7, 8	2, 4, 12, 14, 15	Asia/Pacific
7. Curtis Automotive Hoist	9	12, 16	Europe
8. Neilson International in Mexico (A,B)	10	9, 12, 16	Latin America
9. Metro Corporation: Technology Licensing Negotiation	9, 11	4, 6, 9	Latin America
10. Odysseus, Inc.	9, 11	13	Europe
11. I.M.P. Group Limited	10, 11	4, 5	Latin America
12. Logitech	12	7, 8	Europe
13. Fortron International Inc.	14	8, 9	Europe
14. A.S. Norlight	14	12	Europe
15. Wuhan Art and Advertising Co.	15	4, 8	Asia/Pacific
16. Grasse Fragrances S.A.	15	4, 17	Global
17. Richardson Manufacturing	(16)	2, 6, 9, 12, 13, 15	Asia/Pacific
18. Parker Pen (A, B, C)	17, 18	2, 12, 15	Global

Which Company Is Transnational?

Four senior executives of companies operating in many countries speak:

COMPANY A

We are a transnational company. We sell our products in over 80 countries, and we manufacture in 14 countries. Our overseas subsidiaries manage our business in their respective countries. They have complete responsibility for their country operations including strategy formulation. Most of the key executives in our subsidiaries are host-country nationals, although we still rely on home-country persons for the CEO and often the CFO slots. Recently we have divided the world into geographic regions and North America (the U.S and Canada). Each of the world regions reports to our world trade organization, which is responsible for all of our business outside North America.

The overseas companies are responsible for adapting to the unique market preferences that exist in their country or region and are quite autonomous. We are proud of our international reach: We manufacture not only in Canada and the United States but also in Europe and the United Kingdom, Latin America, and Australia.

We have done very well in overseas markets, especially in the high-income countries with the exception of Japan. We would like to enter the Japanese market, but let's face it, Japan is a protected country. There is no level playing field, and as you no doubt know, the Japanese have taken advantage of the protection they enjoy in their home country to launch an export drive that has been a curse for us and the industry. Our industry has been a principal target of the Japanese, who have taken a real bite out of our market share here in North America. We are currently lobbying for more protection from Japanese competition.

COMPANY B

We are a unique transnational media company. We do not dominate any particular area, but we have an important presence on three continents in magazines, newspapers, and television. We have a global strategy. We are a global communications and entertainment company. We're in the business of informing people around the world on the widest possible basis. We know how to serve the needs of our customers who are readers, viewers, and advertisers. We transfer people and money across national boundaries, and we know how to acquire and integrate properties as well as how to start up a new business. We started out as Australian, and then the weight of our effort shifted to the United Kingdom and today our main effort is in the United States. We go where the opportunity is because we are market driven.

Sure, there are lots of Australians in the top management of this company, but we started in Australia, and those Aussies know our business and the company from the ground up. Look around and you'll see more and more Americans and Brits taking the top jobs. We stick to English because I don't believe that we could really succeed in foreign print or broadcast. We know English, and so far the English-speaking world is big enough for us. The world is shrinking faster than we all realize, and to be in communications is to be at the center of all change. That's the excitement of what we're doing—and also the importance.

COMPANY C

We're a transnational company. We are committed to being the number-one company in our industry worldwide. We do all of our manufacturing in our home country because we have been able to achieve the lowest cost and the highest quality in the world by keeping all engineering and manufacturing in one location. The constantly rising value of our home currency is forcing us to invest in overseas manufacturing in order to maintain our cost advantage. We are doing this reluctantly but we believe that the essence of being global is dominating markets and we plan to do whatever we must do in order to maintain our position of leadership.

It is true that all of our senior managers at home and in most of our foreign markets are home-country nationals. We feel more comfortable with our own nationals in key jobs because they speak our language and they understand the history and the culture of our company and our country. It would be difficult for an outsider to have this knowledge, which is so important to smooth-working relationships.

COMPANY D

We are a transnational company. We have 24 nationalities represented on our headquarters staff, we manufacture in 28 countries, we market in 92 countries, and we are committed to leadership in our industry. It is true that we are backing off on our commitment to develop business in the Third World. We have found it extremely difficult to increase sales and earnings in the Third World, and we have been criticized for our aggressive marketing in these countries. It is also true that only home-country nationals may own voting shares in our company. So, even though we are global, we do have a home and a history and we respect the traditions and sensibilities of our home country.

We want to maintain our number-one position in Europe, and over time achieve the same position of leadership in our target markets in North America and Japan. We are also keeping a close eye on the developing countries of the world, and whenever we see a country making the move from low income to lower middle, or from lower middle to upper middle, or from upper middle to high income we commit our best effort to expand our positions, or, if we don't have a position, to establish a position. Since our objective is to achieve an undisputed leadership position in our industry, we simply cannot afford not to be in every growing market in the world.

We have always had a European CEO, and this will probably not change. The executives in this company from Europe tend to serve all over the world, whereas the executives from the United States and Japan serve only in their home countries. They are very able and valuable executives, but they lack the necessary perspective of the world required for the top jobs here at headquarters.

▼ DISCUSSION QUESTIONS

1. Which company is transnational?

2. What are the attributes of a transnational company?

3. What is the difference between a domestic, international, multinational, global, and transnational company?

4. What stage of development is your company and your LOB at today? Where should you be?

Euro Disney in Trouble[1]

INTRODUCTION

Michael Eisner, chairperson of Walt Disney Company, was sitting in his Los Angeles office. It was New Year's Eve 1993, and Eisner had one meeting left before he could go home to celebrate a quiet holiday. The meeting was with yet another group of high-powered consultants from one of the world's most prestigious general management and strategy consulting companies. The consultants had assembled a multi-disciplinary team including financial, marketing, and strategic planning experts from the New York and Paris offices. The meeting couldn't wait until after the holidays—the topic, what to do about Euro Disney, was that critical. The consultants were asked by the consortium of bank lenders to provide an additional perspective on the problems of Euro Disney and to make recommendations to Eisner and Disney management on what should be done.

In the ten years since Eisner and his senior management team had arrived, they had turned Disney into a company with annual revenues of $8.5 billion, compared with $1 billion in 1984. For Eisner, his track record was impeccable. "From the time they came in, they had never made a single misstep, never a mistake, never a failure," according to a former Disney executive. "There was a tendency to believe that everything they touched would be perfect." Eisner was particularly proud of

the success of the immensely profitable Tokyo Disneyland, which had more visitors in 1993 than even the two parks in California and Florida. Based on the company's success in the United States and Japan, Eisner had vowed to make Euro Disney, located outside of Paris, the most lavish project that Disney had ever built. Eisner was obsessed with maintaining Disney's reputation for quality and he listened carefully to the designers who convinced them that Euro Disney would have to brim with detail to compete with the great monuments and cathedrals of Europe. Eisner believed that Europeans, unlike the Japanese, wouldn't accept carbon copies. Construction of the park alone (excluding the hotels) was approaching $2.8 billion. In developing Euro Disney, Eisner had learned from some of the mistakes made on other projects. For example, in Southern California, Disney let other companies build the hotels to house visitors and in Japan, Disney merely collected royalties from the park rather than having an equity ownership stake.

In preparing for the meeting with the consultants, Eisner was shuffling through some of the papers on his desk. An article in that week's French news magazine Le Point quoted Eisner as saying that Euro Disney might be shut down if Disney failed to reach an agreement with its creditor banks on a financial rescue plan by March 31. The company's annual report for 1993 said that Euro Disney was the company's ". . . first real financial disappointment" since Eisner had taken over in 1984. Eisner's defense had been to publicly blame the performance on external factors including the severe European recession, high interest rates, and the strong French franc. Eisner picked up the financials from the comparable periods from the initial two years' operations of Euro Disney (Table 1)

---

[1] This case was prepared by James L. Bauer, Vice President, Consumer Market Management at Chemical Bank and doctoral candidate, Pace University Lubin School of Business under the direction of Dr. Warren J. Keegan, Professor of International Business and Marketing and Director of the Institute for Global Business Strategy as a basis for class discussion rather than to illustrate either effective or ineffective business leadership and management. © 1994 by Dr. Warren J. Keegan.

TABLE 1 Euro Disney P&L		
Six Months Ending Sept 30		
	1993	**1992**
Revenues (French francs)	1.8 billion	3.1 billion
Profit/(Loss)	(1.1 billion)	0.7 billion

TABLE 2 Annual Attendance Figures		
Year Ending April **(Initial Opening in April 1991)**		
	1993	**1992**
Attendance	9.5 million	10.5 million

TABLE 3 European Population Proximity to Euro Disney	
Population	**Time to Euro Disney**
17 million	2-hour drive
41 million	4-hour drive
109 million	6-hour drive
310	2-hour flight

and then quickly, after reviewing the numbers, put them down. The situation was deteriorating quickly, he thought.

Eisner then turned to the attendance figures, which were also trending downward (Table 2).

REVIEW OF PROJECTIONS/ THE INITIAL PLAN

Eisner walked to his bookshelf from which he took down a bound copy of the initial 30-year business plan for Euro Disney. The plan was done in the typical detailed and methodical Disney fashion. The table of contents was exhaustive, appearing to cover virtually every detail. Over 200 locations in Europe were examined before selecting the site just outside Paris, with Paris being Europe's biggest magnet for tourism. A huge potential population could get to Euro Disney quickly (see Table 3).

European vacation habits were also studied. While Americans average two to three weeks' vacation, French and Germans typically have five weeks' vacation. Longer vacations should translate into being able to spend more time at Euro Disney.

The French government was spending hundreds of millions of dollars to provide rail access and other infrastructure improvements. Within 35 minutes, potential visitors could get to the park from downtown Paris. The opening of the Channel Tunnel in 1993 would make the trip from London 3 hours and 10 minutes.

While the weather in France was not as warm as that in California or Florida, waiting areas and moving sidewalks would be covered to protect visitors from wind, rain, and cold. Tokyo Disney had been built in a climate similar to Euro Disney and the company had learned a lot about how to build and run a park in a climate that was colder and wetter than those of Florida and California.

The attractions themselves would be similar to those found in the American parks, with some modifications to increase their appeal to Europeans. Discoveryland, for example, would have attractions based on Frenchman Jules Verne's science fiction; a theater with a 360-degree screen would feature a movie on European history. The park would have two official languages, English and French, a multilingual staff would be on hand to assist Dutch, German, Italian, and Spanish visitors. Basically, however, Euro Disney's strategy was to transplant the American park. Robert Fitzpatrick, a U.S. citizen with extensive ties to France and the chairperson of Euro Disney, felt "it would have been silly to take Mickey Mouse and try to do surgery to create a transmogrified hybrid, half French and half American."

Other aspects of the American parks would also be transferred to France. These include Main Street U.S.A., Frontierland as well as Michael Jackson's Captain EO 3-D movie. Like the American parks, wine and other alcoholic beverages would not be served.

Fitzpatrick's greatest fear was ". . . that we will be too successful" and that too many people would come at peak times, forcing the park to shut its gates.

Eisner turned to the financing plan, which had been prepared by CFO Gary Wilson, a man known as a tough negotiator with a knack for creating complex, highly leveraged financing packages that placed the risk for many projects outside of Disney while keeping much of the upside potential for the company. Wilson had subsequently left Disney to become CEO of the parent company of Northwest Airlines.

The plan had set up a finance company to own the park and lease it back to an operating company. Under the plan, Disney held a 17 percent stake in the company, which was to provide tax losses and borrow capital at relatively low rates. Disney was to manage the resort for large fees and royalties, while owning 49 percent of the equity in the operating company, Euro Disney SCA. The remaining shares were sold to the public, largely to small individual European investors. A total of $3.5 billion in construction loans was raised from dozens of banks eager to finance the project.

Euro Disney was just the cornerstone of a huge real estate development planned by Disney in the area. Initially, the area was to have 5,200 hotel rooms, more than are available in the entire city of Cannes. The number of rooms was expected to triple after a second theme park opened in the area. Subsequent phases of the plan also included office space that would rival the size of France's largest office complex, La Defense, in Paris. Other plans showed shopping malls, golf courses, apartments, and vacation homes. Key to the plan's financial success was that Euro Disney would tightly control the design and build almost everything itself and then sell off the completed properties at a large profit.

THE JAPANESE EXPERIENCE

Eisner put the book down and picked up another file that contained an assessment of the incredible success of Tokyo Disneyland. Seeking to determine if there were any parallels between the Japanese and European experiences, he had commissioned a study of why the Japanese venture was doing so well.

Tokyo Disneyland had been open about 11 years and had been drawing larger crowds than the U.S. parks. Located less than ten miles from Tokyo, the park drew over 16 million visitors from throughout Asia in 1993. Tokyo Disneyland is a near replica of the American original. Most of the signs are in English with only occasional Japanese; the Japanese flag is never seen but variations on the Stars and Stripes appear throughout the park. In the file, Eisner found a study written by Masako Notoji, a Tokyo University professor, who studied the hold that Tokyo Disneyland has over Japanese people. Notoji wrote that the "Japanese who visit Tokyo Disneyland are enjoying their own Japanese dream, not the American dream. In part, this is because the park is so sanitized and precise in how it depicts an unthreatening, fantasy America that it has become totally Japanese, just the way that Japanese want it to be." It has been compared to the Japanese garden, which is a controlled and confined version of nature that becomes more satisfying and perfect than nature itself. The Japanese Disneyland, some say, outdoes the American parks because it is probably cleaner due to the Japanese obsession with cleanliness.

Notoji's report also noted that Tokyo Disneyland opened in 1983, a period in which the Japanese economy was especially strong. During that time period, the United States was perceived as a model of an affluent society. At the same time, as a result of its growing affluence, Japan was starting to feel part of world culture. Tokyo Disneyland became a symbol for many people of Japan's entry into world culture.

In commenting on the differences between Tokyo and France, Notoji's research hypothesized that ". . . the fakeness of (Tokyo) Disneyland is not evident because (the Japanese) only had fantasy images of these things before" while "Europeans see the fakeness because they have their own real castles and many of the Disney characters come from European folk tales."

Eisner's secretary announced that the consulting team had arrived and that the meeting would be held in his conference room. The meeting started with Eisner explaining the assignment and the short time frames in which solutions had to be developed.

EURO DISNEY PROBLEMS

In early February, a team of consultants returned to Eisner's office with the first phase of their study completed. Given the size and complexity of the problems that they expected to find, the study had been divided into three phases. The first phase was a top-level assessment of the problems that they had uncovered in the initial month of the study, without any recommendations as to what should be done. The second phase was to identify the most critical problems that needed to be addressed immediately and to develop action plans. The third phase was to identify the remaining, less critical problems, and develop recommended plans of action.

The consultants' report identified six critical major problem areas that they felt had contributed to the problems. The team felt that, even though not all of the problems could be rectified, it was critical that Disney management understand the fundamental problems so that they could fix the problems at Euro Disney and not repeat the same mistakes again should they expand to other countries. The six critical problem areas were:

1. Management hubris
2. Cultural differences
3. Environmental and location factors
4. French labor issues
5. Financing and the initial business plan
6. Competition from U.S. Disney parks

Management Hubris

The first issue addressing the way in which Disney management had approached the development of the project and tactical errors made by members of the management team was the most sensitive. Because of the sensitivity of this subject, the consulting firm had brought in the head of their European practice, based in Paris, to analyze the problem and make the presentation. Extensive interviews had been conducted with members of the Disney management teams, both in the United States and in France; academicians who have studied French and American culture; and executives of the European banks that had made many of the construction loans as well as workers at the park.

"The initial premise of Euro Disney in the mid-1980s was that there was no limit to the European public's appetite for American imports given the success of Big Mac's, Coke and Hollywood movies," the presentation started off. That initial assumption totally failed to take into consideration the fact that "the French flatter themselves that they are more resistant to American cultural imperialism." The "hermetically sealed world of the theme park did not give the French an ability to put their own mark on the park. Disney was exporting the American management system, experience and values with a management style that was brash, frequently insensitive and often overbearing." The Americans were overly ambitious and always sure that it would work because they were Disney, and it had always worked in the past. By starting off on this premise, Euro Disney quickly became known as a "cultural Chernobyl" and it created hostility from the French people. The initial arrogance of American management further demoralized the work force, creating a spiraling effect that cut down on the number of French visitors.

Much of this arrogance, the report continued, created tension and hostility among the management team. The first general manager, Robert Fitzpatrick, an American, spoke French and was married to a French woman; however, he was distrusted by some American as well as French executives. Management, unfamiliar with the French construction industry, had made a number of critical mistakes including selecting the wrong local contractors, some of whom went bankrupt. Fortunately, Fitzpatrick had already been replaced with a French native.

Cultural Differences/Marketing Issues

The firm's senior marketing strategist presented the second part of the report, which focused on cultural and marketing differences between the U.S. and European markets.

The first phase of the analysis had uncovered a number of obvious problems, some of which had already been rectified. The purpose in identifying these problems, the consultants said, was to be able to be sensitive and to identify other possibly more subtle cultural and marketing problems.

While attendance was initially strong at the park, the length of the average stay was considerably different than at the U.S. parks. Europeans stayed in Euro Disney an average of two days and one night, arriving early in the morning of the first day and checking out early the next day. By comparison, the average length of the visit in the United States was four days. In large part, this was because the American parks in Florida and California had multiple parks in the immediate areas, while there was only one park at Euro Disney.

Attendance at the park was also highly seasonal with peaks during the summer months when European children had school vacations and troughs during nonvacation periods. Unlike American parents who would take their children out of school for vacations, European parents were reluctant to do this. Europeans were also accustomed to taking one or more longer vacations, while Americans favored short, mini-vacations.

Revenues from food were also significantly lower at Euro Disney compared with the other parks, the report found. Three of the reasons that had been identified just after the park had opened were related to misunderstandings about European lifestyles. The initial thinking was that Europeans did not generally eat a big breakfast and, as a result, restaurants were planned to seat only a small number of breakfast guests. This proved incorrect, with large numbers of people showing up for fairly substantial breakfasts. This problem was corrected by changing the menus as well as providing expanded seating for breakfast through the expansion of cafeteria facilities. While the park offered fast-food meals, they were priced too high, restraining the demand. This problem, too, had been taken care of by reducing the prices at the fast-food restaurants. At the U.S. parks, alcohol was not served, in keeping with the family-oriented values. The decision not to serve alcohol at Euro Disney failed to account for the fact that alcohol is viewed as a normal part of daily life and a regular beverage with meals. This error, too, was rectified after it was discovered.

Revenues from souvenir shop sales were also considerably below those in the other parks, particularly Tokyo Disneyland. In Japan, great value was placed on purchasing a souvenir from the park and giving the souvenir as a gift to friends and family upon one's return home. Europeans were far less interested in purchasing souvenirs.

In the initial design of the project, it was assumed that Europeans would be like Americans in terms of transportation around the park and from the hotels to the park attractions. In the United States, a variety of trains, boats, and tramways carried visitors from the hotels to the park. While it was possible to walk, most Americans chose to ride. Europeans, on the other hand, chose to walk rather than ride, leaving the vehicles significantly underutilized. While not directly affecting revenue, the capital as well as ongoing costs for this transportation were considerable.

It was also assumed, given the automobile ownership statistics in Europe, that the majority of visitors would drive their own cars to Euro Disney and that a relatively small number of tourists would arrive by bus. Parking facilities were built accordingly, as were facilities for bus drivers who would transport passengers to the park. Once again, the initial planning vastly underestimated the proportion of visitors who would arrive by bus as part of school, community, or other groups. Facilities for bus drivers to park their buses and rest were also inadequate. This, too, was a problem that was initially solved.

The consultant concluded this portion of the presentation by saying that these were just a few examples of problems that resulted from a misunderstanding of the differences between the U.S. and

Japanese parks that had already been identified. Most likely, he said, there were a number of other similar problems that needed to be identified and fixed.

Environmental and Location Factors

Next to speak was a team that included experts from an environmental planning firm. This presentation would be brief, since the problems that they identified were virtually impossible to correct at this stage in the project.

They initially noted that given the location in middle to northern Europe and the fact that there were only about six months of temperate weather when it was truly pleasant to be outside, the park was clearly sited in a location that did not encourage visitors on a year-round basis. While accommodations were made (including the covered sidewalks), the fact that off-season visits had to be heavily discounted and promoted to groups to get even reasonable attendance, this still represented a major problem that needed to be corrected. Whether through pricing changes, the development of other attractions or other marketing and promotional vehicles, attendance in the off-peak months had to be increased.

The second problem that they identified, the location east of Paris rather than to the west, was also something that could not be rectified. It was reported that this was again related to overconfidence on the part of the initial planning team, which thought that even though most Parisians who would visit the park currently live west of the city, the longer-term population growth would be in the east. Consequently, it was felt that the park should be built in the east. Again, they noted, Disney executives disregarded the initial advice of the French.

French Labor Issues

Next to speak was a European labor economist. This problem, which stemmed from differences in the United States and Europe, could potentially be solved. Disney did not understand the differences in U.S. versus European labor laws, he said. In the United States, given the cyclicality and seasonality of the attendance at the parks, U.S. workers were scheduled based on the day of the week and time of year. This provided U.S. management with a high degree of flexibility and economy in staffing the park to meet peak visitor demand. French labor laws, however, did not provide this kind of flexibility and, as a result, management could not operate Euro Disney as efficiently and labor costs were significantly higher than the U.S. parks.

Financing and the Initial Business Plan

The consulting team had hired a major global investment banking concern to review the plan, identify the problems, and develop a restructuring plan.

The firm's senior managing director spoke: "Financing and the assumptions of the initial business plan is the area that has created the greatest problems for the park; its restructuring is most critical to the ability of the venture to continue operating and become profitable and, as a result, is the most important problem that needed to be addressed short term."

His presentation identified the following problem areas.

1. The initial plan was highly optimistic and extraordinarily complex. There was little room for error in this plan, which was based on overleveraged financial scenarios that depended on the office parks and hotels surrounding the park to pay off, rather than the park itself.

In addition to the plan being highly leveraged, significant cost overruns in the construction of the park further increased the start-up costs, making the achievement of the promised returns even more unlikely.

Disney itself had imposed an arbitrary deadline of March 31 to develop a refinancing package with the creditor banks, further putting pressure on developing a credible and viable restructuring plan. A separate team was already at work to develop such a restructuring plan.

2. The initial plan was presented as financially low risk; shares were largely sold to individual investors with little tolerance for risk.

The plan was constructed in the mid-1980s, a period of high-flying free-market financing in the United States. European investors did not understand these kinds of deals and propositions.

3. A severe European recession, a drop in the French real estate market, and revaluation of European currencies against the French franc severely undercut all of the assumptions on which the plan was depending in order to succeed.

4. Euro Disney management, faced with the problem of trying to achieve an unrealistic plan, had made serious errors in pricing.

Among the mistakes were charging $42.25/day for admission to the park compared with a $30 daily fee for the U.S. and Tokyo parks. Hotel prices were set similarly, with a room costing $340, equivalent to a top hotel room in Paris. Inside the park, food prices were also priced too high.

Competition from U.S. Disney Parks

Finally, given the strengthening of the European currencies against the French franc and U.S. dollar, it was often less expensive for Europeans to travel to the United States, especially Florida. Not only did their currencies buy more, but there were other attractions surrounding Orlando and the weather was warm and sunny year around. In addition, the U.S. park provided the real experience compared with the European simulation.

WHAT TO DO?

The consultants' phase-one report was concluded. As these problems were identified, teams had already been formed to develop potential solutions to the problems that could be solved. The investment bankers were already examining restructuring options. While critical to enable the park to remain open beyond the March 31 deadline, the long-term issues appeared to be in the area of marketing.

In particular, park attendance and revenues per visitor needed to be increased while providing value and meeting Europeans' expectations about the Euro Disney experience.

The meeting adjourned after the group had agreed that phase two of the consultants' report, identifying action plans for the most critical issues, would be presented on March 15.

▼ DISCUSSION QUESTIONS

1. What did Disney do wrong in its planning for Euro Disney?

2. What recommendations would you make to Disney to deal with the problems of Euro Disney?

3. What lessons can we learn from Disney's problems with Euro Disney?

Club Med, Inc.: The Special Challenge of Growth[1]

INTRODUCTION

Gerald Martin, assistant vice president/marketing, and Jean Prevert, vice president/marketing,[2] had what each called a good working relationship as well as an understanding of each other's point of view. Martin, a native of New York City with extensive experience in the American leisure and lodging industry, had been lured to Club Med, Inc.[3] by Prevert, a Parisian whose 20 year affiliation with Club Med had been mostly spent with the parent firm, Club Mediterranee, S.A.

The two men had been wrestling with the issue of how to broaden Club Med's appeal to capture a bigger piece of the American market. Prevert, who had seen Club Med successfully market a basically

standardized product offering on a global scale, felt that success depended on edu-

[1] This case was prepared by Charles Anderer, case writer and research associate, under the supervision of Warren J. Keegan, Professor of International Business and Marketing, as part of the Leading Edge Case Study Project, the Center for International Business Studies, Pace University. This project was funded in part by a grant from the United States Department of Education.
[2] These characters, as well as their discussions, are fictitious. Their purpose is to highlight some of the issues facing the company described herein.
[3] Club Med, Inc. is a Grand Cayman Island company, traded on the New York Stock Exchange; 73 percent of its shares outstanding are owned by its French parent, Club Mediterranee S.A. It has exclusive rights to the sale of Club Med packages and the operation of Club Med resorts in North and Central America and the Caribbean, the Pacific Basin, Oceania, Asia and the Indian Ocean (see Table 1).

cating American consumers rather than tailoring the product to them. Once Americans understood what made Club Med a different and rewarding experience, he reasoned, they would naturally choose to spend their hard-earned vacation time in one of his company's lovely villages. Martin saw things a little differently. While he agreed that educating the American consumer was important, he felt that certain concessions had to be made to American tastes as well. He believed that the Club Med product concept had global appeal, but he was more inclined to make adjustments to local market conditions than Prevert. Whatever their disagreements on methods, both agreed that the key to long-term success of Club Med, Inc. would lie in its ability to succeed in America.

THE STRATEGIC PROBLEM

After three decades of nearly unqualified success, Club Mediterranec, S.A. was at a crossroads. Both outside and internal research reports confirmed that its subsidiary, Club Med, Inc., had enormous and untapped growth potential. Part of Club Med, Inc.'s territory included North America, and a considerable effort was being made to expand its share of potential customers. The fundamental issue facing Gerald Martin and Jean Prevert was how to win the maximum share of the American market while at the same time retaining the identity and the formula that had always served Club Med so well.

THE CLUB MED CONCEPT

That Club Med would distinguish itself as a unique company should have been apparent from the start. How many successful companies, after all, are run by former journalists whose political inclinations are decidedly to the left, and the far left at that? Club Med's chairman, Gilbert Trigano, was a member of the French Resistance and, subsequently, a reporter for the Communist paper L'Humanite. Trigano joined Club Med as managing director in 1954 and founded the company's first "village" in Greece the following year. Under his leadership, Club Med became a veritable tourism empire composed of 104 villages (and three "auxiliary" ones), located in France and some 30 foreign countries or French overseas territories.

Central to Club Med's success is its concept of what vacationers need in order to truly feel removed from the everyday pressures they seek to escape. Villages are typically located in beautiful, warm-weather areas (see Table 2). Within each village, Club Med creates an environment that stresses the similarities between people. Its villages are closed societies where beads are used instead of money (everything is prepaid except for side trips and drinks, so the need for money is hardly acute), where there are no locks on doors, where the rooms are identical, where dining is done together at round tables and where the style of dress, excepting the company's ski villages, is minimalist (some might call it skimpy). Simply put, the spirit of competition in the outside world is replaced by a spirit of cooperation that evokes a simpler, less complicated way of life.

Nowhere is the spirit of cooperation more apparent than in the relationship between Club Med guests, who are called GMs (gentils membres—congenial members) and Club Med staff, who are known as GOs (gentils organisateurs—congenial organizers). The GOs are the constant companions of the GMs. They eat with the guests, their rooms are similar as is their style of dress. Each village has around 100 GOs. They work 14-hour days and serve as the guests' teachers, entertainers and friends.

TABLE 1 Club Med, Inc.

Income Data (Million $)

Year Ended Oct. 31	Revs.	Oper. Inc.	% Oper. Inc. of Revs.	Net Bef. Taxes	Net Inc.	% Net Inc. of Revs.
1985	280	23.8	8.5%	16.8	14.2	5.1%
1984	235	21.2	9.0	13.4	12.0	5.1
1983	211	16.6	7.8	10.9	9.7	4.6
1982	207	13.3	6.4	9.0	7.1	3.5

Balance Sheet Data (Million $)

Oct. 31	Cash	Current Assets	Current Liab.	Ratio	Total Assets	Ret. on Assets	Ret. on Equity
1985	47.5	78.4	46.5	1.7	269	5.9%	10.5%
1984	38.7	75.5	40.9	1.8	212	5.6	11.7
1983	27.3	47.1	40.9	1.2	158	7.1	19.8
1982	20.6	38.3	38.7	1.0	115	NA	NA

Revenues (Million $)

Quarter	1985–6	1984–5	1983–4	1982–3
Jan.	85.4	71.9	62.1	—
Apr.	107.9	87.3	76.0	123.8*
Jul.		62.3	47.6	—
Oct.		58.2	49.6	87.7*

* Six months

Source: Standard NYSE Stock Reports.

The prepaid package that Club Med offers includes accommodations, all meals, sports and leisure activities, as well as air transportation, and land transfers (see Table 3). Unlike any number of "package deals" that are available to consumers, Club Med's offerings are decidedly upscale. The company only builds villages in exclusive coastal or mountainside locations. The villages themselves are normally equipped with everything from tennis courts to discotheques and the food is reputed to be excellent.

1985 – A WARNING AGAINST COMPLACENCY

Club Mediterranee, S.A. received a warning of sorts when its financial results for the year ended October 31, 1985 were reported. In a marked contrast to previous years, the company experienced a modest rise in net profit of 8.3 percent to FFr 266.6 million ($28.5 million) on revenues that increased by 17.3 percent to FFr 6 billion. This represented an increase in earnings per share of only 0.8 percent in a year when consumer prices in France rose by 5 percent. This per share decline in real terms was all the more surprising in that the Paris stock market experienced a boom year in 1985. As a result of its lackluster performance, Club Med fell from its position of the 16th largest firm on the Paris exchange in terms of stock market capitalization to the 28th largest.

The parent company bounced back in the first six months of 1986 and realized a 22 percent increase in net profits. In fact, this figure would have been even greater had the

TABLE 2 Club Med Inc.—Operations

Geographic Region	Villages	Number of Beds
North America/Caribbean	Eleuthera-Bahamas	600
	Paradise Island-Bahamas	750
	Punta Cana-Dominican Republic	600
	Caravelle-Guadeloupe	600
	Fort Royal-Guadeloupe	304
	Magic Isle-Haiti	700
	Buccaneer's Creek-Martinique	750
	Cancun-Mexico	750
	Ixtapa-Mexico	750
	Playa Blanca-Mexico	580
	Sonora Bay-Mexico	750
	Copper Mountain-Colorado, USA	470
	Turkoise-Turks and Caicos	490
	St. George's Cove-Bermuda	680
	Five Archeological Inns-Mexico	400
Pacific Basin	Chateau Royal-New Caledonia	550
	Bora Bora-Tahiti	102
	Moorea-Tahiti	700
Indian Ocean	Pointe aux Canonniers-Mauritius	374
	Le Lagon-Reunion	120
Asia	Cherating-Malaysia	600
	Thulagiri-Maldives	60
	Farukolhufushi-Maldives	250
	Phuket-Thailand	600
	Bali-Indonesia	700

Source: Drexel Burnham Lambert.

dollar not weakened. This impressive first-half reinforced Club Med's overall image as a highly profitable, well-run company. Those who run the company had been at it for over three decades and had developed some fool-proof ways to generate revenues and cut costs.

Firstly, since all of its vacations are paid anywhere from three to eight weeks in advance, Club Med makes upwards of $3 million a year in annual interest income from this source alone. Furthermore, since it transports most of its guests in groups, Club Med can strike a hard bargain with airlines for bulk rates. The company makes a substantial amount of money (17½ percent of gross operating profits in 1983) buying air transport at wholesale prices and selling it to its vacationers at the going retail rate. While this policy often resulted in taxing the patience of its clientele (flights were often with "second-tier" airlines at odd hours of the day and rarely non-stop), the profits realized were too good to pass up. As for its villages, Club Med often builds at the request of host country governments in remote areas that would not otherwise be developed. The company can afford to do this because the success of its concept does not hinge on a specific locale or destination. By bringing business to distant areas, Club Med often gets the host country to put up much of the necessary capital (more than one-third of its $240 million North American/Asian expansion plan was being financed this way), while it takes a less than 10 percent ownership position in order to minimize tax liabilities (*The Economist,* 7/12/86.)

In spite of its strong financial condition, however, Club Med was not about to be lulled into a false sense of security. The company's product was at different levels

TABLE 3 The Price of a Club Med Vacation: The Caribbean Example		
One Week Stays (Not Including Airfare)		
Villages	_Lowest Price (Early Nov.)_	_Highest Price (Early March)_
Caribbean		
Buccaneer's Creek	$470	$980
Caravelle	600	980
Magic Isle	525	600
Punta Cana	450	660
St. Lucia	—	700
Turkoise	735	1,070
One Week Rates with Air & Transfers		
Villages	_Lowest Price (Early Nov.)_	_Highest Price (Early March)_
Caribbean		
Buccaneer's Creek	$879	$1,470
Caravelle	999	1,470
Magic Isle	824	925
Punta Cana	799	1,080
St. Lucia	—	1,090
Turkoise	1,049	1,425

Note: Rates are for the winter/spring 1986–87 season. All rates are per person, double occupancy, and subject to Club Med's terms and conditions.

Source: Company brochure.

of life cycle in each of its major markets. In France, for example, the product was fast reaching saturation. The United States and West Germany were still in the growth stage, and the product was still in the introductory phase in markets such as Japan and Brazil. Of all these markets, none carried the importance that the American market held. It was becoming more and more obvious that, in order for Club Med to realize its true growth potential, its American customer base had to be expanded.

SELLING CLUB MED TO AMERICA

Gerald Martin just knew he had the answers. When Jean Prevert asked him what he thought Club Med, Inc. needed to do in order to expand in America, he submitted the following:

1. The villages had to be internationalized. That is, English-speaking villages where the number of French GMs was necessarily limited needed to be created. Even more importantly, the number of American GO's needed to be substantially increased.

2. The popular perception of Club Med as a haven for young and virile singles had to be altered somewhat. The demographics of the travel industry and Club Med's clientele had changed. More mature customers, many of whom were married and had children, needed to feel that a Club Med village was an appropriate place for them to spend a vacation. American consumers, in short, needed to be better informed on the advantages that Club Med offered them.

3. Americans took less vacation time than almost any other country in the developed world. They were far more likely to take a long weekend than a week or two in the sunshine. It was therefore a considerable challenge for Club Med to persuade them that it was beneficial for them to spend an important portion of the time they had away from their jobs in one of its villages.

4. Americans are very attached to convenience. While Club Med finds it lucrative to place many of its customers on flights that are marked by poor service and erratic scheduling, Martin felt that Club Med's long-term interests would be better served by a more flexible approach to air travel. Martin also pushed for added amenities in the villages, such as telephones in the rooms.

THE NEED FOR MORE AMERICAN GOs

Martin considered GOs to be the key to the success of any American expansion. He felt that the same personnel policies used with French GOs could not work with American GOs because their expectations are different. French GOs had a significantly lower turnover rate than American GOs and it appeared that the major problem was money. Martin felt that it would be beneficial to the company to reward those American GOs who show promise or who are already good at what they do with good salaries. American GOs needed to feel that they were not making an unnecessary financial sacrifice by staying with Club Med (See Appendix). Presently, they had that feeling (they are paid $100 per week including room and board) and it showed in their turnover rate.

Prevert thought it would be destabilizing to pay American GOs more than the French GOs who worked alongside them. Of course, they could raise everybody's salary, but that would be too costly. Prevert also thought Martin was overestimating the importance of American GOs to begin with. Club Med, Inc.'s French GOs were required to speak fluent English, so what was the big deal?

American GOs were important, Martin thought, because American GMs feel so much more comfortable around them than is the case with French GOs. Martin knew that the French GOs, whether deservedly or not, sometimes had a reputation among American GMs as being arrogant toward them. This could simply be a result of the misunderstanding that takes place between members of different cultures or the result of a popularly held perception amongst Americans who travel that the French are simply an arrogant group of people. Martin believed that many French were guilty until proven innocent when it came to the question of arrogance. However unfair this might be, it remained absolutely necessary, in Martin's view, that Club Med cultivate a solid group of American GOs.

THE FRENCH ACCENT: ASSET OR LIABILITY?

Even though the Club Med concept stresses the similarities between people, the village themselves inevitably have a strong French feeling to them. The dominant language in the large majority of Club Med's enclosed villages is, quite naturally, French. While the French accent does lure Americans to underdeveloped countries that they would be otherwise hesitant to visit, it can be intimidating to non-French speakers. Many Americans have no doubt either heard the usual horror stories from friends about those legendary, ill-mannered Parisians or have themselves had humbling experiences during the course of their visit(s) to France. Some industry observers surmise that the company's strong French accent serves as a barrier to growth. For example, France's sometimes playfully antagonistic neighbor from across the Channel, the United Kingdom, accounted for only 10,800 GMs in 1985 (a 48 percent increase from the previous year) compared to the French total of 365,200. The British, it might be added, can also vacation at the villages of Club Mark Warner, an anglicized version of the Club Med concept.

Being French, Prevert was naturally sensitive about the charge of arrogance. Although he thought Americans such as Martin exaggerated the problem, he favored the development of "international villages." At these villages, English is the dominant language spoken and the proportion of French GMs is limited to 25 percent. In

Europe, 18 such villages were established in 1986 whereas another 14 were planned for the rest of the world. It remained to be seen, according to Martin, if "internationalizing" a mere one-third of its villages would be enough to enable Club Med to substantially increase the American GMs.

JUGGLING THE IMAGE TO SATISFY THE MARKET

For years, the mere mention of the name "Club Med" evoked an alluring imagery of hedonism that only single people could enjoy in good conscience. In fairness to the company, Club Med had only passively cultivated this sort of image. Of course, the gates to its villages were not graced with signs reading "For Singles Only." On the other hand, once inside a Club Med village, one was far more likely to encounter single people than married couples. An example of how firmly entrenched this image was (and still is) in the minds of some was provided by members of Bermuda's political opposition in March of 1986 who called Club Med and its villages in the harbors of Castle and St. George immoral.

By 1984, Club Med would state in its annual report that significant changes in the makeup of its guest population had taken place. Nowhere was this change more apparent than among the American GMs. About half of them were married, the median age was said to be 37 years old, and more than half of them reported an annual income of at least $50,000. Club Med has catered to this demanding group of affluent baby boomers by offering more luxury, more options, special clubs for parents with children and a wider range of villages within reasonable travel time from the northeastern United States. American GMs are therefore steered to the village that best fits their personal tastes.

Even though Club Med's unstated goal was to portray itself as a provider of vacations for a maturing group of people, it initially found it difficult to resist the lure of selling the simple concept of sun and fun with beautiful people. A 1986 advertising campaign which revolved around the theme, "The perfect climate for body and soul," illustrates this point. Although the ads promoted such ideas as self-discovery, friendship, and improved communications between married couples, these messages were clearly marked by visuals of young, beautiful people flaunting toned-up physiques.

AMERICANS: ANYTHING BUT VACATION

As of 1986, in spite of some undeniable gains Club Med, Inc. still saw itself as underperforming with respect to the number of American guests it attracted per year. This view was no doubt reinforced by a 1985 study done by the investment bank Drexel Burnham Lambert (see Tables 4–7). Drexel calculated that the French were over nine times more likely to be a Club Med GM than Americans. If the concept could only become half as popular in the United States as it is in France (meaning an increase in GM's per 1,000 people from 0.7 to 3.0), then North America alone could support 90 villages or six times the number of villages it had in 1985.

Drexel's optimistic numbers notwithstanding, Martin still saw a large problem. The group that was to fuel Club Med's ambitious growth plans, the Americans, took less vacation time than the French, the British or the Germans (see Table 8). Europeans, who were responsible for Club Med's initial success, enjoy a decidedly more relaxed lifestyle than Americans. Vacations in Europe are traditionally taken in four to six week blocks in July or August.

Why is there such a big difference in vacation time between America and other developed countries? The reasons are mainly cultural in nature. American society is outwardly more competitive than those in Western Europe. The difference might be summed up by a commonly held notion among Europeans who have either worked in America or for American companies in Europe: Americans live to work and Europeans work to live. In any event, a typical American manager would be downright afraid to take that much time off in one stretch and most wouldn't even begin to contemplate the notion. In order to ease the guilt, Martin was able to convince Prevert, after some arm-twisting, to equip 7 villages with computer workshops.

TOYING WITH THE CONCEPT

Martin's controversial approach to the Club Med concept was largely based on his interpretation of Club Med's initial success with the French. At the heart of this success, he believed, was Club Med's ability to give people a home away from home. Martin believed very little in the notion of global Club Med villages where the peoples of the world comfortably coexist. He saw room for a little international flair, but he felt that Americans, in particular, did not want to spend their vacations in an environment basically alien to them and surrounded by GOs who do not speak their language.

On the other hand, Martin saw the Club Med concept as a natural for Americans because of their basic social in-

TABLE 4 Club Mediterannee, SA and Club Med, Inc. Membership by Nationality (Percent of Total)

	1981	1982	1983	1984	1985E	1986E
Europe and Africa						
France	49.0	46.6	44.6	43.4	42.0	40.0
Italy	5.9	5.6	5.3	5.1	4.8	4.6
Belgium	5.2	5.1	4.8	4.7	4.5	4.4
W. Germany	4.5	4.4	3.8	4.5	4.4	4.4
Switzerland	2.9	2.7	2.6	2.5	2.3	2.2
Other	7.1	47.6	8.1	7.2	6.5	6.4
	74.6	72.0	69.2	67.4	64.5	62.0
North and Central America						
U.S./Canada	16.2	17.5	19.5	21.9	24.0	26.0
Other	1.5	2.1	2.3	1.7	2.0	2.0
	17.7	19.6	21.8	23.6	26.0	28.0
Asia, Indian Ocean and South Pacific						
Australia	2.7	2.6	2.2	1.7	1.8	2.0
Japan	0.9	1.2	1.5	1.5	1.5	1.7
Other	2.1	2.4	2.8	2.7	2.7	2.8
	5.7	6.2	6.5	5.9	6.0	6.5
South America	2.0	2.2	2.5	3.1	3.5	3.5
TOTAL	100.0	100.0	100.0	100.0	100.0	100.0

Source: Drexel Burnham Lambert.

TABLE 5   Selected Propensities to Visit Club Med

Country	Approx. No. of Native G.M.'s Per Year	% of Total G.M.'s	Pop. (1980)	G.M.'s Per Thousand Inhabit.
Europe				
France	356,000	39.6%	53,580,000	6.6
Italy	106,000	11.8	57,080,000	1.9
Belgium	38,800	4.3	9,890,000	3.9
W. Germany	35,000	3.9	61,480,000	0.6
Switzerland	20,800	2.3	6,250,000	3.3
North America				
USA/Canada	179,800	20.0%	258,302,604	0.7
Asia, Indian Ocean and South Pacific				
Japan	12,000	1.3%	119,680,000	0.1
Australia	18,000	2.0	15,535,000	1.2

Source: Drexel Burnham Lambert.

stincts. There was no reason why the concept could not be successful here. The main problem, as Martin saw it, was management's ability to properly implement its growth strategy. One area where Martin was successful was in air travel. As stated above, the company buys air travel wholesale and sells it retail. Martin fought hard to ensure that the company would not risk losing customers for the sake of avoiding a decrease in interest income from the sale of airfare. As a result of his efforts, air travel for the American market was upgraded.

Martin was still worried by Prevert's reluctance to change the company's winning ways. An example was the horror with which Prevert greeted Martin's proposal to put telephones in guests' rooms.

TABLE 6   Estimated Potential Club Med Market

	Current Propensity to Visit Club Med (G.M.'s Per 1,000 Pop.)	Estimated Potential Propensity (G.M.'s Per 1,000 Pop.)	Extrapolated Potential Number of G.M.'s
Europe			
France	6.6	6.6	356,000
Italy	1.9	2.0	114,200
Belgium	3.9	4.0	39,600
W. Germany	0.6	3.5	215,250
Switzerland	3.3	4.0	25,200
North America			
Canada	0.7	2.5	62,750
U.S.A.	0.7	3.0	717,300
Asia, Indian Ocean and South Pacific			
Japan	0.1	2.5	299,250
Australia	1.2	2.5	38,750

Source: Drexel Burnham Lambert.

TABLE 7 Current vs. Estimated Potential

	Approx. Current No. of GM's	Estimated Potential	Estimated % Growth Potential	Approx. Growth Potential as a % of Total Growth Potential
Europe				
France	356,000	356,000	0%	0.0%
Italy	106,000	114,000	8	0.6
Belgium	38,000	39,600	2	0.1
W. Germany	35,000	215,250	515	12.6
Switzerland	20,800	25,200	21	0.3
North America				
USA/Canada	179,800	780,050	334%	42.1%
Asia, Indian Ocean and South Pacific				
Japan	12,000	299,250	2,934%	20.1%
Australia	18,000	38,750	115	1.5

Source: Drexel Burnham Lambert.

"A telephone is a direct link with the outside world and all of its miseries," sniffed Prevert, fully aware of the fact that his company had somehow managed to survive before Gerald Martin was hired. "Cut off the outside world, and you cut off the very anxieties that the guests are trying to escape. Computer workshops and better travel arrangements, yes. Telephones in the rooms, never."

TABLE 8 Holidays With Pay (annual averages)

	Statutory	Collective Agreements and Practice	Paid Public Holidays
Belgium	4 weeks	4 weeks	10 days
Canada	2 weeks	3 weeks	6–9 days
France	5 weeks	5 weeks	*
W. Germany	3 weeks	5–6 weeks	11–13 days
Italy	10 days	4 weeks	10 days
Japan	6 days	—	12 days
The Netherlands	3 weeks	4–4.5 weeks	8 days
Sweden	5 weeks	5 weeks	11 days
Switzerland	2–3 weeks	3–4 weeks	4–5 days
England	*	4 weeks	8 days
USA	*	1–2 weeks	*

* No generally applicable statutory provisions.
Source: International Labor Office.

A Day in the Life of a Club Med GO[1]

What are the difficulties that Club Med faces in cultivating a solid group of American GOs? One problem is that, by American standards, the GOs actually are underpaid for the amount of work they do. One former American GO who lasted six months as a dance instructor at the Punta Cana resort in the Dominican Republic said that a major factor in her decision to leave was the rigorous schedule that she faced every day of the week:

7:30–10 a.m.	Breakfast duty. Greet and seat guests.
11–12	Teach dance class in the theater.
12–1:30 p.m.	Host luncheon buffet or perform mime skit with the animateur (club jester) in the dining room as guests eat lunch.
1:30–3 p.m.	Rehearsals in the theater.
3–6 p.m.	FREE! If I didn't have Arrivals and Departures, a GO meeting or a team meeting, or have to help prepare the set or costumes for the evening performance.
6–7 p.m.	Teach another dance class in the theater.
7–8 p.m.	Cocktail hour. Model a dress from the boutique and flirt with guests at the bar.
8–9:30 p.m	SMILE! Host dinner or perform a mime skit.
9:30–10 p.m.	Change out of boutique dress or mime costume and gulp down dinner.
10–11 p.m.	Change into another costume and perform in show.
11–12 p.m.	Clean up backstage and mingle with guests at the bar.
12–1 a.m.	Midnight rehearsal if scheduled.
1–?	Disco. Lure shy guests onto the dance floor.

Revenue Canada—The Special Import Measures Act

Shahin Gupta had just received a complaint filed, in August, 1991, by Canada's only manufacturer of flat, wooden toothpicks under the Special Import Measures Act. As Senior Import Trade Administrator with the Department of National Revenue (Revenue Canada), it was her job to review the activities of the Canadian importer and the American producer of toothpicks to make a preliminary determination of dumping. If she determined that dumping occurred and that it had or was likely to cause material injury to the production, in Canada, of similar goods, she would recommend to the Deputy Minister that a special import duty be assessed on imports from the American company.

---

[1] *The Hartford Courant*, February 16, 1986.

THE SPECIAL IMPORT MEASURES ACT

Enacted in 1984, the purpose of the Special Import Measures Act (SIMA) was to protect Canadian producers from two important forms of unfair competition from foreign countries:

(1) exporting goods to Canada at lower prices than they were sold in their home market. This was dumping. Dumping also occurred when goods were sold for export over an extended period of time at prices below full cost; or

(2) exporting goods to Canada which were produced with the benefit of foreign government subsidies. This was subsidizing.

SIMA provided protection to Canadian producers if it was established that dumped or subsidized imports had caused material injury or threatened to cause future injury to the Canadian production of like goods. The injury test was required because non-injurious dumping or subsidizing usually benefitted the consumer through lower prices and such practices were not, therefore, discouraged. If material injury (past, present or future) was established, however, protective anti-dumping or countervailing duties were levied on these imports to offset the price advantage caused by the dumping or subsidizing.

In considering evidence of dumping, it was not adequate to demonstrate that the price of imports was lower than

This case was prepared by Marvin Ryder using both public and private sources. Some key personalities have been disguised. This case is intended as a basis for class discussion rather than to indicate effective or ineffective handling of managerial situation. Copyright 1993 by Marvin Ryder, Michael G. DeGroote School of Business, McMaster University.

Canadian manufacturers' prices. It was generally necessary to provide evidence that the imported goods were being sold to the Canadian importer at less than the price at which they were sold in the exporter's home market in the ordinary course of trade or at less than their full cost. When the exporter and the importer were related, evidence that the importer was selling the goods in Canada at a price which did not cover the full cost plus a profit was required. Some examples of evidence of dumping included:

(1) invoices or price lists showing that the goods were sold to importers in Canada at less than the market price in the country of export, plus delivery costs and duty and tax, if applicable; and

(2) a comparison of the complainant's manufacturing cost with an estimate of the exporter's manufacturing cost, suggesting that the sales to importers in Canada were below full costs.

Canada's international obligations under the General Agreement on Tariffs and Trade (GATT) required that there be evidence that dumped imports were causing or threatening injury before an anti-dumping investigation could be initiated. The question of whether there was or was likely to be injury to domestic production was therefore an important aspect of any anti-dumping proceeding. The following was a list of factors which indicated that material injury had occurred to Canadian producers:

1. loss or orders, market share, profits, or declining sales;
2. reduction in employment;
3. reduction in capacity utilization;
4. price erosion or degradation;
5. failure to achieve projected realistic goals for increased profits, production, or sales;

6. inability to raise capital for investment;

7. negative effects on cash flow, inventories and wages;

8. slowing of anticipated market growth; and

9. delay or cessation of planned plan expansion or purchase of additional machinery by Canadian producers.

COMPLAINT PROCEDURES UNDER SIMA

Once a formal written complaint was received, the Department of National Revenue had 21 days to examine the documents and ask for any additional information. Once the documentation was completed, the Deputy Minister of the Department of National Revenue had 30 days to decide whether to initiate an investigation. Within 90 days of the opening of an investigation, the Deputy Minister was usually in a position:

1) to issue a preliminary determination as to whether dumping or subsidizing had occurred on a scale sufficient to cause injury to Canadian producers; and

2) to estimate the margin of dumping or the amount of subsidizing.

If no dumping or subsidizing was uncovered, the investigation was terminated. Otherwise, a preliminary determination resulted in provisional duty being levied on dumped or subsidized imports, to protect Canadian producers. Within 90 days of issuing a preliminary determination, if the Deputy Minister was satisfied that the evidence of dumping or subsidizing was conclusive, a final determination was issued. This more accurately specified the margin of dumping or amount of the subsidy.

The Canadian International Trade Tribunal (CITT) was a court of record, one of whose functions was to investigate the effect of dumped or subsidized goods on Canadian producers. The Tribunal issued a finding within 120 days of receiving notice of the preliminary determination by the Deputy Minister. If the Tribunal found that injury had occurred to domestic producers, protective anti-dumping or countervailing duties were levied on all goods imported from the date of the preliminary determination.

When the Tribunal found that imports of dumped or subsidized goods had not caused injury in the past, but that they threatened to cause injury in the future, duties were levied only on those goods imported after the date of the Tribunal's decision. Any provisional duties paid on goods prior to that date were refunded. When the Tribunal found no injury, all provisional duties were refunded and all proceedings in the case stopped.

THE COMPLAINANT

Jackson Industries Ltd. of Coquitlam, British Columbia, could trace its roots to an 1896 lumber wholesaler. In later years, it became a sawmill operation making wooden refrigerating iceboxes, screen doors and snow fencing. In 1975, Tony Mazzetti acquired the company which had, by then, focussed production on wooden toothpicks, wire frames, floral wreaths and floral posts. Because the products experienced seasonal sales demand, employment varied from a low of 35 to a high of 55. In 1979, he moved the operation from the city's bay shore to the new industrial park. In July, 1985, the only other manufacturer of toothpicks in Canada closed its doors after 50 years in operation. It was also Canada's only importer of wooden clothespins. Seizing the opportunity, Jackson added the importation of clothespins and coffee stir sticks from Brazil to its product mix.

Flat, wooden toothpicks were made from white birch trees because their wood was hard, white, straight-grained, tasteless and odourless. Birch bolts were trucked to the 1,575 square metre plant from various parts of Northern British Columbia. Bolts were short logs, between two and three feet in length. One birch tree yielded an average of five bolts. When they reached the plant, the bark was removed. They were placed in veneer lathes, which peeled off the wood in a continuous strip. The width of these strips was about the same as the length of a finished toothpick—2.2 inches.

The strips were put through machines which had very sharp knives. At the rate of 10,000 per minute, the knives chopped the strips of wood into toothpicks with a width of 0.10 inches at one end and a width of 0.05 inches at the tapered end. An average birch tree produced nearly 400,000 toothpicks. The toothpicks were then dried, polished and screened to remove all dust and chips.

The clean toothpicks went to packaging machines to be boxed 650 at a time. Filled packages were placed in cases by workers and the cases piled onto wooden platforms called pallets to be taken by truck to a storage warehouse. Jackson produced approximately 4.5 billion toothpicks per year with a retail value of $5 million. With the retail Canadian market estimated to be $2.5 million annually, Jackson was an exporter of toothpicks to Puerto Rico, the Dominican Republic, Denmark, Norway, England, Jamaica, New Zealand and Australia, though, to date, little was exported to the United States. For the past five years, demand had remained constant in Canada with most toothpicks being purchased by restaurants and hobbyists. In the latter case, consumers purchased toothpicks and "stir sticks" to build things. In international markets, Jackson faced competition from far eastern countries, some

with much lower production costs, like China and Korea.

In April, 1990, Gaulin-Manon Inc. of Trois Rivieres, Quebec acquired Jackson Industries from Tony Mazzetti to establish a full service toothpick supply company. Gaulin-Manon had operated in Trois Rivières from 30 years and had been purchased two and a half years earlier by Jacques Blais, a former insurance executive. Gaulin-Manon imported round wooden toothpicks from Japan and flavoured them in its Quebec plant with cinnamon, lemon and mint. The flavoured toothpicks were then individually wrapped for the restaurant trade. They were also popular in the United States. In its complaint, Jackson Industries made it clear that the markets for the two types of toothpicks were different. No complaint was being lodged about the importation of round toothpicks.

THE DEFENDANTS

In 1962, Scherff and Niles Co. Ltd. of Windsor, Ontario was established as an importer and broker of many food and food-related products including tuna, mushrooms, olive oil, plastic garbage bags, household cleaners and disposable picnic/party ware (i.e., plastic and styrofoam cups, plastic and paper plates, napkins, drinking straws, etc.). While many products came from Canada and the United States, it also imported from Italy, China, Thailand and Malaysia. The company was well respected in Ontario for its sales agency skills.

In 1970, Scherff and Niles became the Ontario sales agent for Jackson Industries and its line of "Jaylee" toothpicks. While most food brokers received a 5% commission on wholesale sales, Scherff and Niles received a 15% commission because it additionally offered warehousing, distribution and invoicing services. Out of a wholesale price of thirty cents for a box of

650 toothpicks, Scherff and Niles received five cents as commission. The variable cost of goods sold for Jackson was thirteen cents. The remainder, twelve cents, went to Jackson for overhead and profits. For nearly twenty years, both parties enjoyed an amicable business arrangement.

In the fall of 1990, Jacques Blais, the new owner of Jackson, visited the Scherff and Niles offices. He felt the broker was not being aggressive enough with retailers in Ontario even though Scherff and Niles had arranged contracts with all major Ontario retailers and Jaylee enjoyed a 100% market share in Ontario. Twice that fall, Jackson announced wholesale price increases culminating in a forty-five cent per box price. Scherff and Niles' commission had increased to seven cents but the remainder of the increase flowed to Jackson's bottom line. Price increases were not stimulated because of changes in the cost of goods sold. Hoping to generate more profits and to find a more aggressive broker, Scherff and Niles was dropped as Ontario sales agent at the end of 1990.

Stung by the loss of the product line, Scherff and Niles began the hunt for another toothpick producer. It discovered that Jackson had a toothpick monopoly in Canada so it turned to the United States where three producers were available. With a good deal in hand, it started to import flat, wooden toothpicks from Swindler Mfg. Co. of Pierre, Vermont and began selling them under its disposable picnic/party ware brand name—"Happy Days."

Knowing the reaction from retailers to the recent Jackson price increases, Scherff and Niles knew that a lower price could convince retailers to switch suppliers. In the United States, Swindler was a full service producer and distributor of toothpicks. Working hard to promote its own brand name, it developed co-operative advertising, point-of-purchase displays and floor racks. Given the range of services provided, it sold its product to retailers for fifty-five cents (Cdn.) per box of 750 toothpicks. Scherff and Niles did not want any of the services provided by Swindler nor did it require use of its brand name. It only wanted the base product. Thus Swindler was able to sell to Scherff and Niles for twenty-five cents (Cdn.) per box. Allowing for a commission to Scherff and Niles, Happy Days toothpicks had a wholesale price of thirty cents (Cdn.) per box.

In the first four months of 1991, Scherff and Niles signed contracts with a number of small, independent, Ontario retailers and one major retailing chain. In Ontario, Scherff and Niles captured 20% of the market from Jackson. In May and June, Jackson responded by lowering its wholesale price to thirty-five cents per box which stopped any further switching of retail accounts to Scherff and Niles.

THE CHARGE

According to Jacques Blais, "it doesn't bother me if (Scherff and Niles) import at the same price that the toothpicks sell in the United States. But they're selling at 40 or 50 percent less than they sell in the U.S. market. To keep my big clients, I'm selling at 20 percent less than last year." In essence, Blais argued that the thirty cent per box price by Scherff and Niles was predatory and represented a margin of dumping of 45% (calculated as 1–30/55). Correcting for package sizes (650 Jaylee vs. 750 Happy Days) meant that consumers were also getting 15% more product at the "dumping" price. Looking strictly at the price from Swindler, Jackson charged that the actual margin of dumping was 55% (Calculated as 1–25/55).

Jackson noted that it had been forced to reduce price, that it had lost market share and that inventories of unsold product had grown by 16 percent. If these trends continued, Jackson was considering a lay-off of production staff from the 45 workers it currently employed. "We should fight all the time if we think there is dumping," said Blais.

Joan Farrugia, President of Scherff and Niles commented, "surely to God, a single Canadian manufacturer can stand the scrutiny of one competitor. If the toothpick monopoly is allowed to continue, it will ultimately be the consumer who is going to suffer." She insisted that Swindler never sold the base product to Scherff and Niles at a price that was better than that offered domestic American customers. In the late fall of 1990, retail prices for Jaylee had climbed to ninety-nine cents per box. In July 1991, a box of 750 "Happy Days" toothpicks sold at retail for seventy-nine cents. Wholesale price cuts by Jackson had seen Jaylee's price fall at retail by fifteen cents per box.

"To find dumping, Jackson would have to attach no value to the marketing programs undertaken by Swindler in the United States," said Farrugia. "I can't believe in that concept." Jackson wanted financial compensation for injuries due to past dumping in 1991 and countervailing duties imposed on Swindler toothpicks to protect against future injury.

THE DECISION

If the case moved forward, it was estimated that both sides would need to hire legal counsel which could cost between $15,000 and $20,000. As well, Revenue Canada would need to incur staff time including a visit by two officials to Vermont to verify Swindler's records. Such trips could take three to five days.

Shahin would need to determine: 1) if dumping of American toothpicks had occurred; 2) if that dumping was, is or would be injurious to Jackson; and 3) the level of countervailing duty that would be required to stop the injury to Jackson. Ms. Farrugia's words echoed in her mind, "on it's own merits, this case is ludicrous. This industry is so small, any action taken by the government would be sheer stupidity." Shahin wondered if every company was entitled to the same protection from the government, no matter how big or how small.

Swatch Watch U.S.A.: Creative Marketing Strategy[1]

"Vision is the art of seeing things invisible."

JONATHAN SWIFT

INTRODUCTION

As speaker after speaker paid tribute to the extraordinary skills that had earned him the award of "Marketing Executive of the Year," Max Imgruth, President of Swatch Watch U.S.A. grew more and more uneasy. Fully confident that the product that changed the watch industry forever, the Swatch watch, would enjoy continued success, Imgruth nonetheless felt the need to change gears. The competition, which was at first slow to react, had begun to implement strategies that stood to erode Swatch's position. Gazing from his privileged place on the dais, Imgruth saw an

[1] This case was prepared by Charles Anderer, case writer and research associate, under the supervision of Warren J. Keegan, Professor of International Business and Marketing, as part of the Leading Edge Case Study Project, Center for International Business Studies, Pace University. This project was funded in part from a grant from the United States Department of Education. Copyright © 1986, Pace University.

audience that was content to rehash past successes for a night, which was nice, but not at all his style.

Imgruth had recently guided his company through a fast paced and, some would say, controversial diversification program. Having already achieved spectacular success with the Swatch watch, Imgruth spearheaded a plan to establish Swatch as a total fashion enterprise. This move was accompanied by a good deal of skepticism from colleague and competitor alike. His next objective was to make sure that this year's #1 marketing executive did not become one of the decade's more memorable disappointments.[2]

BACKGROUND— THE SWISS WATCH INDUSTRY

1985 was a good year for the Swiss watch industry. The number of finished watches shipped abroad rose 41% to 25.1 million and the value of watch exports increased by 12.2%. Luxury watches still comprised the backbone of the Swiss watch trade, accounting for only 2.1% of total shipments but 41.8% of total earnings. In 1985, the Swiss raised their share of the world market to 10% by volume (number of units sold) and 45% by value (Figures 1–3). For the first time in 15 years, an increase in employment was registered as 1,000 new jobs were created. The industry's good performance in 1985, combined with a strong year in 1984, gave every indication that the Swiss watch industry was back on its feet after struggling for much of the previous decade.

The comeback had been led by the success of Swatch (a blend of Swiss and watch). Over 10 million of its brightly colored, plastic wristwatches were sold worldwide in 1984–85. Success had been most notable in the United States, where Swatch's latest move was the launching of a diversification program aimed at making the company a total fashion enterprise.

Whether or not this expansion of the Swatch product line proved successful remained to be seen. What was certain, on the other hand, is that the Swatch watch had given new life (and increased market share) to an industry that was recently engaged in a very difficult struggle with Asian competitors. What was also clear is that Swatch's willingness to break with convention, especially in the area of marketing strategy, gave it a head start in what had become a vast new market—the low-priced watch as a fashion accessory.

Some might say that the Swatch watch was just another in a long line of Swiss successes. In the 1950s, few other industries enjoyed the domination known by the Swiss watch industry. In that decade, the Swiss possessed an estimated 80% share of the (non-Communist) world watch market. Production was centered in the Jura region where snowed-in farming families, doubling as skilled watchmakers, supplemented their incomes by assembling mechanical watch parts during the winter months. At the industry's peak in 1956, there were 2,332 such maisons. Two large watchmaking groups, Allgemeine Schweitzer Uhren AG (Asuag) and Societe Suisse pour l'Industrie Horlogere (SSIH), controlled most of the Swiss brands at this time.

The Swiss remained industry leaders until the mid-1970s when the mass production of electronic watches changed the watch industry forever. The most important difference between an electronic watch and a mechanical watch is that the former is much easier to manufacture. A mechanical watch is an intricate piece of machinery whose assembly necessitates a highly skilled work force. The electronic watch is typically composed of microchips and printed units and lends itself well to mass production and automated processes.

---

[2] This situation is fictional. Its purpose is to highlight the issues faced by the company described herein.

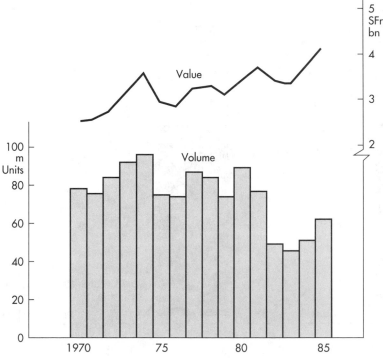

FIGURE 1

It's All in the Price Swiss Watch Production*

*Including unassembled movements

Source: Federation of the Swiss Watch Industry.

After having ruled supreme over the watch industry for decades, the Swiss suddenly found themselves faced with strong competition from Japan and such low wage producers as Hong Kong, Singapore, Taiwan and Korea. These newcomers produced inexpensive watches with digital faces that were more accurate than mechanical watches.

Even though it was the Swiss who introduced the first electronic quartz watch in 1968, they were slow to accept the importance of the new technology. Hindsight suggests that small and fragmented producers had a vested interest in keeping things as they were—the new technology was still unproven in the marketplace and the Swiss proposition was secure. In any event, the Swiss were late and reluctant

entrants into a new market whose rules were different. In the 1970s, for example, watches were introduced to mass outlets such as department stores and supermarkets. This was nothing short of blasphemous to the proud Swiss who required their watches to be sold in approved watch and jewelry stores. The Swiss continued to produce watches whose styles were no longer in touch with consumer demands, and they displayed a noticeable lack of marketing creativity. In reality, the Swiss had ceased to be leaders in the watch industry. The Swiss luxury watch market was still healthy, but they had lost a huge amount of market share at the lower end of the market. In 1974 Swiss watch exports still accounted for 60% of the world's total. By 1979, the Swiss represented about a

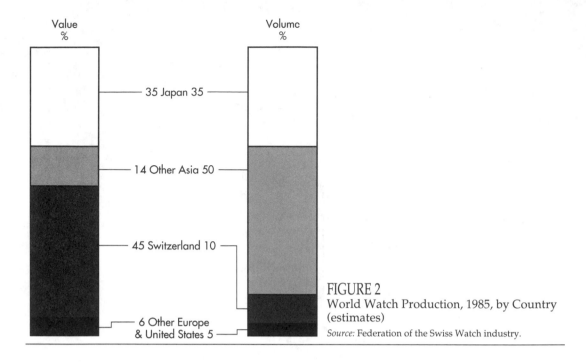

FIGURE 2
World Watch Production, 1985, by Country (estimates)
Source: Federation of the Swiss Watch industry.

FIGURE 3
Swiss Watch Exports,* 1985, by Destination
Source: Federation of the Swiss Watch Industry.
*Including unassembled movements

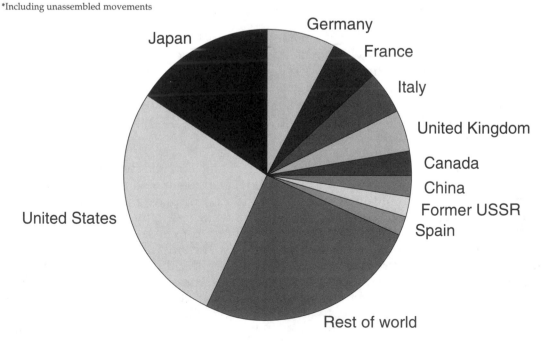

third of the world's watch exports. Economic recession and a sharp rise in the value of the Swiss franc played a part in the industry's problems. Most observers, however, now attribute the decline of the Swiss watch industry to too many years of unqualified success that gave it an aura of invincibility. As one watch executive put it:

> Just imagine the situation in the early post-war years when the Swiss were the only people making and selling watches; the industry had a waiting list of months; and selling prices were set to enable even inefficient firms to survive. The more efficient ones were making enormous profits. Why would any manager in his senses want to change things? (*Management Today,* 12/80)

As Switzerland entered the 1980s, the structure of its watchmaking industry, which had more or less retained its form since the late eighteenth century, finally began to adapt to the electronic age. This meant rationalization of production, automation, concentration and the corollary of fewer jobs. Between 1980 and 1983, production of watches dropped by 50%. By 1983, only 686 maisons remained and overall employment stood at about 40,000 jobs, down from 90,000 in the early 1970s.

THE MERGER OF ASUAG-SSIH

The merger of Asuag, whose flagship brand is Longines, and SSIH, whose best known brand is now Swatch but also boasts Omega and Tissot, was Switzerland's first response to the Asian challenge. The new group was granted a financial package worth $310 million, representing the largest rescue scheme in the history of Swiss banking. Heavy reorganization took place in both groups, especially SSIH which had lost $77 million in the year ending March 31, 1981. Most of SSIH's management was sacked and control of the watch division was transferred to Ernst Thomke, a rank outsider to the industry, who possessed both a medical doctor's degree and an advanced degree in chemistry.

The merger, as it turns out, was a sensible move because Asuag was far better technologically equipped to face the 1980s than SSIH, having already made a substantial commitment to the research and development of electronic watches. SSIH, for its part, possessed the better known brand names. (In the summer of 1985, Asuag-SSIH was renamed the Swiss Corporation for Microelectronics and Watchmaking Industries, SMH in short.)

Dr. Thomke made two important, tradition-breaking decisions in his first year. The first was to sell Swiss watch movements all over the world instead of restricting such sales to Switzerland, a move that allowed Asuag-SSIH to improve its technological base through increased production. The second was to recapture the lower end of the watch market by developing a product that was inexpensive to manufacture, low-priced, durable, technically advanced and stylish. The result was the Swatch watch, which was especially successful in the United States, with total retail sales increasing from $3 million in 1983 to $150 million in 1985.

PRODUCT DESCRIPTION

The Swatch is a lightweight (¾ ounce), shock proof, water resistant (up to 100 feet), electronic watch with a plastic band that uses a quartz analog (with dial and hands) movement. It is manufactured by robots and sealed by lasers in a state of the art factory in Switzerland. The watch is comprised of only 51 components (the average is 91), which lends itself well to the thin look that is currently in vogue, and is manufactured off a single assembly line (the Japanese use three). What most distinguishes the product is its design and its departure from convention. A wide variety of faces have been used and even glow in the dark and scented bands (banana, raspberry and mint) have been tried. Battery life is estimated to be three years, and the watch retails from $30 to $35, which represents a substantial markup on cost.

THE SWATCH MARKETING STRATEGY

Central to the marketing strategy of the Swatch watch is the notion of the watch as a fashion accessory. This is a novel approach in that it is typically used as a selling point for gold and diamond-studded watches at the higher end of the market. Watches in the $30–$35 range normally compete on the basis of price, performance or, in the case of digitals in the late 1970s and early 1980s, on accessory features such as a stopwatch and/or calculator. Swatch, on the other hand, describes its target market as "fashion-oriented 12-to-24 year olds."

One trend that worked in Swatch's favor from the start is that, during the period 1976–1986, more and more people bought watches. No longer was the watch primarily a gift item and no longer was it only the rich who owned more than one. In 1976, 240 watches per 1,000 inhabitants were sold in America. Ten years later the figure was 425 watches per 1,000 inhabitants. About 90% of sales were composed of inexpensive electronic watches of various styles and brands. (*The Economist*, 5/17/86)

Of course, Swatch never would have been able to take advantage of this trend without a sound marketing strategy. According to Imgruth, his company's strategy is divided into three elements: design, distribution and production.

1. *Design.* An essential feature of the fashion oriented approach is a constant variety of product lines whose designs suit seasonal fashions. According to Imgruth, the company has "a clear product concept based on four directions: young and trendy; active and sporty; cool and clean high style; and classic. These four lines are available at all times. There are 12 small-faced models, and 12 larger ones. Every face is only out a restricted amount of time, sometimes only three months, sometimes 12 months, depending on the design concept of the watch." Each line is given a distinct theme such as the "Cosmic Western" group which was described as a combination of Buck Rodgers and the Wild, Wild West. New models are introduced four times a year, the seasons being spring/summer/fall/ holiday (see Figure 4). In addition, special versions of the Swatch Watch such as the $100 diamond-studded Limelight and limited edition art watches are added periodically. Generally speaking, the trendier the design, the shorter it will remain available; the more classic the design, the longer it will remain on the market. Says Imgruth: "This is done on purpose, to create collecting and spur multiple ownership." (*Marketing and Media Decisions*, Spring/1985) Advertising media are chosen based on the product concept. There are four campaigns running simultaneously, each geared to a specific element of the four-tiered product mix.

2. *Distribution.* Distribution was originally limited to fashion outlets and now includes upscale department stores such as Bloomingdale's, Saks Fifth Avenue, Macy's, etc. Such stores never used to handle Swiss watches and still only account for 10% of all watches sold. Imgruth scrupulously avoids distributing through drugstores and mass merchandisers such as Sears and J.C. Penney, even though these are the usual paths for watches priced under $100. Distribution is limited to 5,000 locations in

the United States, although Imgruth claims that 5,000 more would love to sell his products. As one Swatch executive puts it: "You have to control dstribution and not flood the market, or people lose their hunger for the product." (Sales and Marketing Management, 3/11/85)

3. *Production.* The production process described above makes the design strategy possible. The flexibility that Swatch enjoys is unknown elsewhere in the industry. Design changes for other watchmakers typically require a substantial capital investment whereas Swatch can make changes without adding cost. Such flexibility is absolutely essential because of Swatch's product strategy. Without it, design runs of three months would be out of the question.

SWATCH MARKETING STRATEGY IN ACTION

In view of the fact that Swatch's strategy is unorthodox, it is not at all surprising that its marketing executives would look out of place in most corporate boardrooms. All advertising, marketing and promotion activities are handled by 27-year-old Steve Rechtschaffner, vp/marketing, and Nancy Kadner, director of advertising, 31. Rechtschaffner, a former member of the U.S. Ski Team and self-described workaholic who recently overcame a bout with thyroid cancer, has no formal business education. He began his career by forming his own sports promotion business. As for Kadner, prior to her work at Swatch she spent over 4 years in the marketing department at MTV.

Rechtschaffner and Kadner are the creative forces behind Swatch's novel marketing strategy. Before Swatch entered the market, watches priced under $50 competed on the basis of price or performance. To gain an appreciation of just how dif-

ferent the Swatch strategy is, a glance at a typical advertisement for a low-priced watch would suffice. Normally, the watch is placed against a background in the hope that the right message is communicated. Timex developed one of the more creative performance-oriented campaigns in the early 1980s when it strapped a watch to an auto tire and proclaimed that the product "Takes a lickin' and keeps on tickin'." Others have not been so imaginative. For example, it is not uncommon to see digital watch advertisements where product features are simply listed next to a black and white photograph of the watch.

Swatch, for its part, has taken roads previously untraveled by watch producers. It employs the use of colorful (and often humorous) print ads, multi-page advertising inserts in magazines such as Vogue and Rolling Stone, concert and event sponsorship, and the use of music videos and MTV.

A good example of the Swatch strategy in action is its use of a rap music group and a graffiti artist to promote and develop its products. In September, 1984, Swatch sponsored the World Breakdancing Championships. One of the participating rap music groups, the Fat Boys, was hired to do a commercial on MTV on which its lead singer, the Human Beat Box, incessantly chants "BrrrSWATCHUM ha ha ha SWATCHUM." In addition, Swatch wanted an artist to help promote the breakdancing championships so it hired Keith Haring, New York's best known graffiti artist. The result was a four-watch-series called the Keith Haring Swatch.

The Haring watches were promoted under the banner of "Great Modern Art That Tells Time." Swatch produced 9,999 of each edition. Each watch is numbered and, in Imgruth's words, is "a collectible piece of art, a distinctive fashion accessory, and a sturdy timepiece." The watches were introduced in separate months, the

FIGURE 4

Source: Company records.

first being released in December, followed by new editions in April, May and June.

THE COMPETITION

The under $50 watch segment is the most competive in the watch industry in terms of the number of companies involved. Based on 1984 watch sales, this segment of the watch market also was responsible for the large majority of all U.S. watch sales:

1984 Watch Sales By Price	
Under $10	29%
$10–50	52
Over $50	19
Source: Timex.	

Because the Swatch watch was such a novelty at its introduction, the company had free reign over the plastic fashion watch market (some have called it "cheap chic") for well over a year. The picture has now changed considerably as strong competitors in the under $50 segment such as Casio, Timex, Lorus, Armitron and Parker Watch have entered the fray. In addition to imitating some of the very styling and advertising techniques that Swatch employs (Figure 5), the new competition has targeted drug stores and mass retail outlets, the very areas Swatch has shied away from, as their primary points of distribution.

While it remained to be seen if the new entries could match Swatch's creativity and design flexibility (one Swatch insider said that technology-conscious Casio's bid to enter the fashion watch market was "like John Deere getting into sportscars"), the new array of low-cost watches was certain to exert downward pressure on retail prices. Lorus' initial line of plastic watches sold for $19.95 at full mark-up, Timex's Fun Timers sold for $17.95 and Casio's ColorBurst line started at $19.95. Most drug retailers feel prices will eventually fall to the $12–$14 range. (*Drug Store News,* 5/27/85)

Swatch has also had to concern itself with the sale of phony Swatch watches and unlicensed sales. In October, 1985, 5,000 fakes were uncovered by U.S. Customs and Asuag-SSIH quickly sued three Swiss imitators. There is also a thriving "gray market" in which unlicensed traders exploit price differences between the United States and Europe (the watch sells at a lower price in Europe). Swatch elected to buy up all such watches in 1985, spending an estimated $500,000 in order to maximize control over the sale of its products.

THE NEXT STEP: SWATCH AS A TOTAL FASHION ENTERPRISE

It was perhaps with an eye to an increasingly competitive environment that Swatch embarked on a fast-paced diversification program in late 1985. The company created over 470 "Swatch Shops" within major department stores nationwide selling, in addition to watches, a new ready-to-wear line called "Funwear" and an accessories line called "Fungear" (see Figure 6).

Swatch will continue to employ the same strategies that it uses to sell its watches. The new product groups are aimed at the same fashion-oriented 12-to-24 year olds who are the target market for Swatch. Funwear is described as "a bright and whimsical line of unisex casual wear including shorts, T-shirts, tank tops, slip-on-pants, big shirts, and beachwear." Each collection has a theme that ties in with a Swatch watch theme. Swatch's own marketing and design people will introduce new collections every eight weeks, and prices range between $10 and $50. Fungear

FIGURE 5

is a collection of leather and rubber knapsacks, belts, bags, and the jacketpack, which is a backpack containing a windbreaker and a hood. Prices range from $10 to $65.

Swatch offers more than just the above two product lines. There are Swatch Shields, which are described as high-fashion sunglasses; Swatch Guards, small, colorful devices that cover watch faces; Swatch Chums, which are eyeglass holders, and umbrellas and sweats that feature current watch designs. Swatch also imports and markets pens, notebooks, address books, key rings and safety razors.

The Swatch drive to open shops within major department stores is based on management's conviction that products should be sold in a total Swatch environment—an environment that has the Swatch "personality." The company president, Max Imgruth, has predicted that ready-to-wear and accessories will represent from 30% to 40% of total 1986 sales. In the long term, he expects the new product lines to account for the majority of Swatch sales.

OTHER EXAMPLES OF BRAND TRANSFER

There are several examples of companies that have attempted, for better or worse, to build on the success of its first product by using its brand name on other, not necessarily related products. One of the more infamous examples is that of Bill Blass, who put his name on chocolates only to see the idea fail miserably. Another example of failure is that of Nike, which unsuccessfully expanded its collection of footwear to runningwear and leisurewear. A Nike spokesman looking back at that experience notes: "When you're tremendously successful in one area, there's a tendency to develop an arrogance about your

ability to transfer the value of a brand name." (*Forbes*, 1/27/86)

On the other side of the coin, there was the example of Conran's, which successfully expanded from a producer of home furnishings to a retailer of everything from towels to desk lamps. Like Swatch, Conran's started out catering to the needs of young people and, when expansion took place, stayed with the same target market. Another point in Swatch's favor was its Swatch Shops, which spared the company from having its new product lines being placed on shelves next to competitors who had the advantage of an established image as quality producers of ready-to-wear. In order to keep its shops and continue to avoid head to head competition with more established companies, Swatch had to remain a trend setting, creative company. In this way they could avoid the fate of Bill Blass chocolates, which were sometimes found placed next to boxes of Godiva chocolates, leaving the consumer with what might be a choice easily made.

▼ DISCUSSION QUESTIONS

1. Swatch is a unique success story. Why has the company been so successful? Was it important that the Swiss watch industry recapture the lower end of the market? Why? Why not?

2. Do you see any parallels between the decline of the Swiss watch industry and other Western industries?

3. Evaluate the cultural dimension of the Swatch story, taking into account such practices as the willingness to bring in people from other industries, to delegate authority to younger executives, and to employ new media such as rock concerts and music videos.

4. Swatch created a new market—can they continue to expand that market? What must they do to defend their position in

SWATCH FUNWEAR & FUNGEAR
The NEFERTITI COLLECTION is out there. In Watches, Shirts, Shorts, Sweaters and Sweats.
In Swim Suits, Sarongs and Beach Towels. It's all over the map. In Leather Knapsacks. Even
Sun Shields. See how it fits. See how it feels. It's all SWATCH and IT'S REALLY OUT THERE!
swatch
Design © 1986 SWATCH WATCH U.S.A., Inc.
bloomingdale's

FIGURE 6

this market?

5. What do you think of Swatch's chances for success as a total fashion enterprise? Do you agree with management's extension of the Swatch brand name to other products? Why? Why not?

6. Swatch is a classic example of marketing success through creativity. What lessons can be learned from their experience?

Choufont-Salva, Inc.[1]

On January 10, 1991, the marketing committee[2] of Choufont-Salva, Inc., the Philippine subsidiary of A. L. Choufont et Fils, S.A., decided to add to the company's product line an oral contraceptive developed by the laboratories of the parent company. Choufont-Salva's marketing division (see Figure 1) now was faced with the task of designing a marketing plan that would effectively sell this product.

THE COMPANY

Choufont-Salva, Inc., was founded in 1973 by Mr. Lorenzo J. Salva. The company was known as the L. J. Salva Drug Company until 1984, when the company became a subsidiary of A. L. Choufont et Fils, S.A., of

Belgium, the second largest drug company in Europe and a company with operations in 39 countries, including the Philippines. Many of the subsidiaries of A. L. Choufont et Fils, S.A., marketed both ethical[3] and proprietary[4] drugs. Choufont-Salva, however, had followed the policy established by Mr. Salva when he founded the company of dealing only in ethical drugs.

In 1990 Choufont-Salva marketed 67 different drug products and had sales of approximately P184,963,000.[5] Penicillin accounted for 47 percent of the sales and streptomycin, 16 percent. Thirteen other products were responsible for an additional 21 percent of the company's income.

For all products, Choufont-Salva had three prices: the retail price,[6] the semi-wholesale price, which was 5 percent less

---

[1] This case was prepared by Dr. Ralph Z. Sorenson, Dean, College of Business Administration, University of Colorado at Boulder. Used by permission.

[2] The marketing committee was composed of the general manager, the marketing manager, the sales manager, and the manager of marketing services.

[3] Ethical drugs were promoted directly to the medical profession, whose members in turn recommended or prescribed drugs to the ultimate consumers. Ethical drugs could be divided into two groups: (1) prescription pharmaceuticals, which were ethical products that legally were available only by prescription, and (2) over-the-counter drugs, which were ethical products that could be purchased legally without prescription,

although physicians frequently did write prescriptions for these drugs. Over-the-counter products typically were manufactured by firms that specialized in prescription pharmaceuticals.

[4] Proprietary drugs were promoted directly to the consumers; the manufacturers of proprietary products usually engaged in heavy consumer advertising and promotions, including extensive in-store display advertising.

[5] One peso = .0382 U.S.

[6] Retail price, as used by Choufont-Salva and other drug companies, referred to the price charged to retail drug outlets and similar purchasers, not to the price paid by the ultimate consumers. The price paid by the ultimate consumers generally was about 10 percent higher than this retail price.

than the retail price, and the wholesale price, which was 10 percent less than the retail price. Because of the difficulty in determining whether a purchaser was functioning primarily as a wholesaler or a retailer, Choufont-Salva used the volume of business done annually with the company as the basis for determining which of the price lists was applicable to the customer. Approximately 30 percent of the company's sales were retail; 10 percent, semiwholesale; and 60 percent, wholesale.

In 1990 Choufont-Salva realized an average gross profit of 59 centavos on every peso of sales. Five centavos of this gross profit was paid out in commissions,[7] 9.5 centavos was spent on advertising and promotions, and 21.5 centavos was expended on other marketing and administrative expenses. However, the gross profit that the company received on sales of a particular product and the expenditures made in promoting the sale of a product frequently varied greatly from this average.

SALES ACTIVITIES

Choufont-Salva had divided the Philippines into 26 sales territories. In each territory, there were between 150 and 300 doctors in private practice on whom the sales representative assigned to the territory called once per month.

Since Choufont-Salva dealt only in ethical drugs, management believed that the doctor was the most important person to reach in the company's marketing activities. Sales representatives in the provinces spent approximately 70 percent of their time calling on physicians. Sales representatives in Manila and other large cities devoted an estimated 80 percent of their time to this activity.

Because of the busy schedules of the doctors, most visits with physicians did not last longer than 15 minutes. During this time a sales representative normally made two product presentations. During each presentation, the sales representative described how the drug being discussed had been developed, noted the benefits of the product, pointed out how this drug differed from comparable products on the market, and presented clinical evidence attesting to the effectiveness of the drug. At the close of the visit, the sales representative left samples of the two products he had discussed and also of two or three other drugs that the company marketed.

Approximately 40 percent of the doctors on whom Choufont-Salva salespersons called dispensed their own drugs. During visits to these doctors, the salesperson also took orders and made collections for previous purchases.[8] Approximately 10 percent of Choufont-Salva's sales in 1990 were made to this group of doctors, most of whom were located in the provinces.

A sales representative who had a territory in Manila or another large city and devoted his day exclusively to calling on doctors could make 15 to 18 calls if the doctors had their offices at a hospital, and 12 to 15 calls if the doctors had private offices away from a hospital. A provincial sales rep calling only on doctors could average 10 to 12 calls per day.

Choufont-Salva sales reps called on an estimated 25 percent of the doctors in the Philippines. Management believed, however, that these doctors were the ones with the highest professional standing and with the largest and most important practices.

In addition to the doctors, Choufont-Salva salespersons called monthly on 1,500 of the estimated 5,000 drugstores in the

---

[7] Sales representatives received commissions of 4.5 percent, and district sales managers received commissions of .5 percent on all sales made in their respective territories.

[8] Commissions on a sale were not paid until the company had received payment.

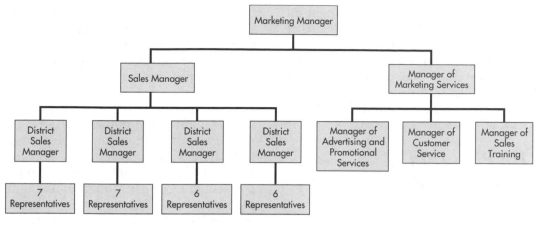

FIGURE 1
Organizational Chart of the Marketing Division

Philippines. Approximately 85 percent of the company's sales were made to these pharmaceutical outlets. When calling on drugstores, the sales reps answered any questions that the personnel had about different products, discussed with the employees new or improved products that the company was introducing, took back old stocks of drugs, accepted orders, and made collections.

Drugstores in the Philippines were free to dispense pharmaceutical products without prescriptions. According to one expert in the field, the Philippines probably had the least restrictive drug laws of any major country in the world. It was not uncommon for antibiotics and similar drugs to be promoted directly to the consumer through media advertising, posters, and point-of-purchase displays.

The sales reps also called each month on approximately 50 clinics. Sales to these clinics, which were either government health centers or industrial clinics attached to large manufacturing facilities, were responsible for 5 percent of Choufont-Salva's sales. During the visits to the clinics, the sales representatives promoted Choufont-Salva products, left samples, took orders, and received payments for previous orders.

Choufont-Salva supported the activities of its sales representatives with advertising and promotional efforts. The company spent P214,450 on advertising in 1990. Since Choufont-Salva dealt only in ethical drugs, the entire advertising expenditure was for ads placed in the three leading professional medical journals— *The PMA[9] Journal, Family Physician,* and *The Philippine Journal of Surgeons.* (See Table 1.)

In 1990 Choufont-Salva also spent P17,424,000 on promotional activities. Of this amount 14,743,500 was invested in samples given to physicians. This reflected management's belief that samples were the most effective way of promoting the company's drugs. When samples of drugs were left with doctors it reminded them of the products and encouraged them to prescribe them to their patients. Also, the company believed that doctors like samples because samples enabled them occasionally to give away medicine free to patients, thus generating goodwill among the recipients.

---

[9] Philippine Medical Association.

The remaining P2,680,600 spent on promotions in 1990 was used to print cards, folders, and booklets about various drugs sold by Choufont-Salva. These printed materials were used by the sales representatives in discussing the products with the doctors and were left with the doctor at the close of the call.

THE PHILIPPINE MARKET FOR CONTRACEPTIVES

When Choufont-Salva decided to enter the contraceptive market in 1991, the population of the Philippines was approximately 63,600,000. The country had an estimated 11,200,000 households, 85 percent of which were located in rural areas. According to government statistics, the population was increasing at the rate of 2.4 percent per year, one of the highest population growth rates in the world. If this rate of population growth continued, the country would have 106,000,000 inhabitants by 2005.[10] (See Tables 2 through 5.)

In early 1990 the Family Planning Association of the Philippines, Inc. (FPAP), was organized by a group of Catholic laypersons. Although three small Protestant family planning groups already were in existence, the FPAP was the first nationwide family planning movement in the Philippines, a country in which 84 percent of the population was Catholic.[11]

By the time that Choufont-Salva decided to enter the market in 1991, the management of the company estimated that there were approximately 100 government or private clinics from which persons could receive information on family planning and, if they desired, birth control products. The majority of these centers were affiliated with either the FPAP or the Planned Parenthood Movement of the Philippines. Birth control products were also available at most drug outlets.

The management of Choufont-Salva estimated that in 1990 Filipinos spent P134,031,000 on contraceptive products. Approximately 70 percent of these products were dispensed through drugstores, 25 percent through clinics, and 5 percent directly by doctors. Management predicted that in 1991 the market for contraceptives would be P201,647,000 and that the market would continue to grow at least 50 percent per year for the next three years.

---

[10] See Tables 2, 3, and 4 for selected demographic data based on the 1980 Census and Table 5 for a summary of the results of a Family Limitation Survey taken by the Bureau of the Census and Statistics in 1990.

[11] See Appendix I for a statement of the position of the Roman Catholic Church concerning family planning and Appendix II for additional information on the FPAP.

TABLE 1	Journals in Which Choufont-Salva Advertised		
Journal	**Frequency of Publication**	**Circulation**	**Cost Per Page***
Family Physician	Quarterly	3,000	6,030
The Philippine Journal of Surgeons	Quarterly	3,000	6,030
The PMA Journal	Monthly	7,000	18,095

*The journals accepted only full-page advertisements.

TABLE 2   Population by Marital Status, 1960* (10 years and over)

Individuals 10 Years Old and Over	Total Philippines		Greater Manila Only	
	Pop	Percent	Pop	Percent
Single	16,646,314	45.9%	904,080	54.6%
Married	17,837,478	49.2	678,122	41.0
Widowed	1,644,824	4.5	66,064	4.0
Divorced or separated	162,350	.4	6,044	.4
Total	36,290,966	100.0%	1,654,310	100.0%

* Rate of marriages per 1,000 persons: 13.56.

Source: Based on data from the Bureau of Census and Statistics.

In 1990 an estimated P107,225,000 was spent on oral contraceptives in the Philippines. The popularity of this method of birth control was attributed to the fact that oral contraceptives were virtually 100 percent effective and extremely easy to use. Although there were 15 brands of oral contraceptives on the Philippine market, 5 brands controlled 75 percent of the market. (See Table 6.)

The second most popular contraceptive product in the Philippines was the intrauterine contraceptive device (I.U.D.). Filipinos in 1990 spent an estimated P20,104,700 on I.U.D.s, including fees paid to doctors for inserting the devices. The charges made by private doctors for this service ranged from a low of P134 to a high of P2,680 per patient. Planned parenthood clinics, on the other hand, had a policy of inserting I.U.D.s completely free or at a charge of P134 or less.

I.U.D.s were in strong favor with governmental and private agencies in the Philippines who promoted planned parenthood to low-income groups. This method of birth control was inexpensive and did not require instructions that women had to remember. Yet, I.U.D.s had a major drawback. Approximately 20 percent of all women were unable to retain I.U.D.s. This method of birth control, however, was 98 percent effective in preventing pregnancy among the other 80 percent of the women.

Condoms, diaphragms, and spermicidal jellies and creams were not widely used in the Philippines. In 1990 these products together accounted for only an estimated P6,701,600 of the total contraceptive market.

CHOUFONT-SALVA'S ORAL CONTRACEPTIVE

Choufont-Salva's oral contraceptive was developed in the A. L. Choufont laboratories in Belgium. In early 1990 the product was first introduced on the market in Canada. By 1991 it was being marketed in 14 countries. the parent company had not yet published for its subsidiaries any detailed information on the market performance of the contraceptive. The bits of data that had been received from the company's Brussels headquarters indicated that the acceptance of the new contraceptive by the market had ranged from fair in Brazil to excellent in Mexico and Denmark.

TABLE 3 Female Population in the Philippines, 10 Years and Over, 1990 (in thousands)

| | Last Census (1960) | | Current |
| | | No. of Ever | Estimated |
Age (years)	Total No. of Women	Married Women*	No. of Women
10–14	3410	4	4292
15–19	2802	348	3604
20–24	2316	1378	2944
25–29	1918	1584	2416
30–34	592	1382	1992
35–39	1350	1328	1644
40–44	1160	994	1378
45–49	978	928	1170
50–54	768	624	986
55–59	576	436	778
60–64	428	360	568
65 +	818	668	924
Total	18,116	10,034	22,696

* Women who currently were married or had been married at one time. Choufont-Salva executives believed that common law marriages were included in these data.

Source: Bureau of Census and Statistics.

Oral contraceptives were manufactured in the form of tablets that were taken by women for 20 to 22 days during each menstrual cycle. Most oral contraceptive tablets were a combination of a progestin and an estrogen, and tablets containing these two hormonal products were virtually 100 percent effective as contraceptives.

Oral contraceptives, however, produced in one out of every five women undesirable side effects, such as weight gain, nausea, and headaches. In general the incidence of these side effects was related to the dose of the progestin in the oral contraceptive. As a result, pharmaceutical companies had been trying to develop new progestational agents that could be given in dosages of 1 milligram or less but still be effective in controlling fertility.

A. L. Choufont et Fils, S.A., was the first to achieve this breakthrough in steroid research. The company in its laboratories developed a new, totally synthesized and

TABLE 4 Distribution of Households by Income, 1985

| | Percent of Families | | |
| | | Other Metropolitan | |
Annual Income	Greater Manila	Areas	Rural Areas
Under P500	.9%	11.3%	21.2%
P500 to P999	4.6	20.0	36.0
P1,000 to P1,499	13.2	16.8	18.0
P1,500 to P1,999	12.2	15.7	10.5
P2,000 to P2,499	10.8	8.8	5.4
P2,500 to P2,999	8.1	6.2	2.8
P3,000 to P3,999	13.3	7.8	2.8
P4,000 to P4,999	7.8	4.4	.9
P5,000 to P5,999	6.8	2.9	.7
P6,000 to P7,999	9.4	2.9	.6
P8,000 to P9,999	4.0	1.0	.1
P10,000 +	8.7	2.3	.2
Number of families	722,000	2,888,000	5,842,000
Total number of families:	9,452,000		

Source: Based on data from the Bureau of Census and Statistics.

TABLE 5   Summary of Family Limitation Survey

A total of 3496 women representing approximately 59 percent of the 8414 ever-married women* in the Philippines covered in the inquiry indicated not wanting more children than what they had in 1990. A significant 39 percent of the total knew how to go about limiting the number of children. In fact, 31 percent of such women had already done something† about the matter. The survey further indicated that of women aged below 45 years and who did not know anything about children limitation, 24 percent welcomed the idea of learning possible means of limiting their number of offspring. These indications were revealed by the sample survey conducted in May 1990, covering 14,296 ever-married women from 18,292 sample households throughout the country.

In terms of the level of education attained by the ever-married women included in the inquiry, 32.0 percent belonged to the primary level; 29.5 percent, intermediate; 13.6 percent, high school; 7.0 percent, college; and no grade completed, 16.7 percent. Those whose level of education was not stated represented only 1.2 percent.

According to religious affiliation, on the other hand, 86.5 percent comprised Roman Catholics; 2.4 percent, Aglipayans; 1.2 percent, Iglesia ni Kristo; 2.5 percent, Protestants; and "Others" representing Moslems, Buddhists as well as those not reporting any religion at all, 6.4 percent.‡

Among the questions asked of the women were: "If all of your children are living, do you think you would like to have more?" "Do you know or have you heard of certain ways by which the number of children in the family may be limited?" "Have you and your husband done anything to limit the number of your children?" And for women aged below 45 years only, the question, "Are you willing to learn any means to limit the number of your children?" was asked. Less than .5 percent did not give answers to any of the four questions.

Answers to the inquiries showed that in all the sectors of the ever-married women there was widespread refusal to have a bigger size of family and that a sizable portion was practicing means of limiting their number of children.

To the first question, an appreciable 60 percent of the women in the urban areas did not want more children than what they had at the time of the survey; meanwhile, 57.4 percent of the rural ever-married women included in the inquiry were of the same opinion. The desire to have more children was concentrated among women of ages below 30 years—a common finding to both the urban and rural sectors. It seems that the desire for more children among these young ever-married women is geared toward acquiring a family—to them, the number of children is rather uncertain.

By religious affiliation, 66.7 and 62.9 percent of the Aglipayan respondents in the urban and rural communities, respectively, did not want to have more children. This indication was followed by the Roman Catholic group with 61.0 and 59.3 percent and the Iglesia ni Kristo group with 56.9 and 50.0 percent for the urban and rural sectors, in that order.

It is interesting to note that the desire not to have more children than what they actually have is inversely related to the level of education and this holds true to both the urban and rural ever-married women.

In the urban sector, 72.4 percent, 64.1 percent, 60.1 percent, 55.8 percent, and 43.5 percent of the ever-married women with corresponding level of education of no grade completed, primary, intermediate, high school, and college, respectively, expressed not wanting more children as compared with the rural ever-married women with 65.0 percent, 61.1 percent, 49.6 percent, 46.9 percent, and 33.8 percent, in the same order of level of education.

The survey further revealed that 45.1 and 31.6 percent of the urban and rural ever-married women, respectively, knew or have heard ways of family limitation. Some 45.4 percent of the Roman Catholic group, 45.6 percent of Aglipayan, 44.8 percent of Iglesia ni Kristo, and 45.3 percent of Protestant ever-married women in the urban areas knew ways of limiting family sizes as compared with the women in the same order of religion in the rural areas with only 32.4 percent, 32.6 percent, 20.8 percent, and 25.3 percent, respectively. It was noted that the Aglipayan women in both urban and rural areas alike proved to be most apprised regarding ways of family limitation than women belonging to the other religious affiliations. This observation was followed by the Roman Catholic, Protestant, and Iglesia ni Kristo groups.

The survey also showed that the higher the level of education, the greater is the number of women knowing about family limitation. And this pattern is common in both urban and rural areas. However, in the urban areas, women with high school educations exercised the least family limitation practice, while in the rural areas it was found that the women with no grade completed manifested the same attitude.

It was observed from the answers to the inquiries that a sizable portion among those who knew means of limiting their number of children were actually practicing or doing something to limit their family size. Some 32.5 percent§ in the urban areas were practicing family limitation compared to 27.1 percent represented by the rural sector. From among the four major religious groups, 38.5 percent for both Aglipayan and Iglesia ni Kristo groups in the urban centers were noted doing something about family limitation. In the rural areas, however, 38.1 percent of the Protestant women practiced family limitation fol-

TABLE 5 (Cont.)

lowed by the Roman Catholic with 27.9 percent, Iglesia ni Kristo with 20.0 percent, and Aglipayan with 18.6 percent.

Finally, among those women aged below 45 years who did not know ways of family limitation, many signified intentions of learning about it. This number represented 24.3 percent among the urban women and 23.2 percent from the rural group.

Special Note to Readers from the Bureau: Readers should bear in mind that these data were gathered from a sample survey conducted simultaneously last year with the annual labor force survey made by the Bureau of Census and Statistics. This being a sample survey, it should, therefore, be treated with certain limitations in mind.

---

* Includes common law marriages.
† Includes both artificial and natural methods of birth control.
‡ The Aglipayan and Iglesia ni Kristo religions were both relatively minor religious sects indigenous to the Philippines. Neither sect objected to artificial means of birth control on theological grounds.
§ That is, 32.5 percent of those women who knew about family limitation.

Source: This summary was prepared by the Bureau of Census and Statistics and is based on a survey conducted by the Bureau in May 1990.

---

extremely potent progestational hormone. By using this new progestational agent, Choufont et Fils was able to produce a new oral contraceptive that combined in each daily dose only 1 milligram of progestin with one-tenth of a milligram of an estrogenic agent.

There was only one oral contraceptive compound available in the Philippines that contained as little as 1.5 milligrams of progestin per daily dose. This was a new contraceptive that had been on the market for less than three months. The strength of the progestin in the other compounds on the market varied from 2 to 10 milligrams per tablet.

The low dosage of progestin in the Choufont-Salva contraceptive lessened the chance that a patient would experience undesirable side effects from taking the medication. Clinical data compiled by A. L. Choufont et Fils, S.A., indicated that in only 4 percent of the patients taking the oral contraceptive developed by the company did the patient experience nausea, headaches, or similar unpleasantness. No other oral contraceptive had such a low incidence of side effects.

The Choufont-Salva oral contraceptive consisted of 21 tablets per course of medication. The woman was to take the first tablet on the fifth day of her menstrual cycle and take one tablet daily for 21 days. She was then to stop taking the tablets for 7 days. On the eighth day she was to start the next 21-day series of tablets. This meant that each new course of medication started on exactly the same day of the week as the initial course. Always starting the medication on the same day of the week lessened the chance of a woman forgetting to begin the cycle anew. Choufont-Salva felt that this attribute would give the product a slight competitive advantage over most of the other oral contraceptives on the market. Only two other contraceptives on the market had dosages of 21 tablets per 28-day period.

Because of the heavy financial investment in equipment required for producing oral contraceptives, Choufont-Salva had signed a contract with Companie Nationale de Pharmacie, S.A., the French subsidiary of A. L. Choufont et Fils, S.A. According to the contract, the French company would supply Choufont-Salva with the contraceptive tablets at a cost equivalent to P19.03 per course of medication. This price included shipping to Manila but did not include packaging.

TABLE 6 Five Leading Brands of Oral Contraceptives

Brand	Usual Progestin Strengths (mg)	Est. Market Share	Retail Price*,† (Pesos)	Comments
Brand A	2.5 or 5.0	35%	87.12	Company concentrated on drug outlets for promotion and distribution.
Brand B	4.0	17	80.42	Company concentrated on family planning centers for distribution.
Brand C	2.0 or 10.0	10	120.63	
Brand D	3.0	8	147.43	An improved version of Brand B; made by same company.
Brand E	10.0	5	214.45	

* Price per course of medication.
† Retail price refers to the price charged by the drug firms to retail drug outlets and similar purchasers. The prices to the

DEVELOPING A MARKETING PLAN

In 1990, 63 percent of Choufont-Salva's revenue came from the sales of penicillin and streptomycin. Management wanted to lessen the company's dependence on these two products and felt that its new oral contraceptive had the potential of developing into a major drug in the company's product line. The marketing manager said that to help achieve this goal, the sales representatives would devote at least 15 percent of their time to promoting the contraceptive during the first 18 months that it was on the market.

The task of developing a marketing plan that would effectively promote Choufont-Salva's oral contraceptive was the responsibility of the company's marketing committee. Deciding on a name for the tablets, selecting the packaging that would be used, determining the price that would be charged, and deciding on what advertising and promotional activities to employ were among the decisions facing the committee.

Name

The oral contraceptive developed by A. L. Choufont et Fils, S.A., was marketed by the company's Canadian subsidiary under the brand name Controva. This name was formed by combining the prefix contra, which makes up the first half of the word contraceptive and means against, with ova, the plural of ovum, which means egg. Since entering the market in Canada, the product had been introduced in three other English-speaking countries—Great Britain, the United States, and Australia. In all three countries the product was also being sold under the name Controva.

Because contraceptive and ovum were not words commonly used by Filipinos, some in the marketing organization at Choufont-Salva felt that the company should select another brand name for the product. These persons felt that the name should be easy to remember, be suggestive of a characteristic of the product, and sound western. Two names had been suggested: Combitabs, which was formed from the words combination and tablets and suggested that the tablets were a combination of progestin and estrogen, and Periodez, which suggested that the tablets were taken during a definite period in the menstrual cycle.

Packaging

Management was considering four packaging possibilities for the oral contraceptive: a glass bottle, a simple aluminum strip, a comb case, and a compact case. (See Table 7.) The company was also faced with the question of what color combinations to use on the packaging. Three combinations had been suggested: black and white, gold and white, and light pink and pale green. An advocate of the pastel colors claimed that they were "feminine and inviting to the woman."

Price

Primarily because of its lower progestin content, the progestin-estrogen compound developed by Choufont et Fils cost less to manufacture than did other oral contraceptives. Since the tablets were costing Choufont-Salva only P19.03 plus packaging for each dosage of 21 tablets, management was considering making the company's retail price for the medication P67.02 or P73.72 per bottle or package. This would give the company a competitive advantage in price since the retail price[12] of other oral contraceptives on the market ranged from P80.42 to P268.06 per course of medication.

Advertising and Promotional Activities

Choufont-Salva did not engage in consumer advertising. The company had the policy of advertising in medical journals because the management wanted Choufont-Salva to have the image of being a responsible pharmaceutical organization that worked closely with and through the medical profession. Some members of management, however, felt that the company should advertise its oral contraceptive directly to the general public. The decision made regarding this matter would influence the theme of the advertising campaign as well as the size of the advertising budget for the product.

Management also was undecided about how to promote Choufont-Salva's oral contraceptive. (A memo from the company's advertising and promotional staff containing suggestions regarding promotional activities is reproduced in Table 8; representative consumer-oriented media costs are shown in Table 9.)

NEW COMPETITION

A week after Choufont-Salva decided to enter the oral contraceptive market, the company learned that within a year a competing Philippine drug company probably would be marketing an oral contraceptive containing only .5 milligram of progestin. North American Drugs, Inc., the American parent company of the Philippine company, had just developed the new oral contraceptive in its laboratories. The American company planned to test market the product in the United States. If the test marketing was successful, North American Drugs would then release the product to its subsidiaries. Because of the test marketing, Choufont-Salva's management felt that it would be at least 9 months and probably 12 months before North American Drug's oral contraceptive would appear on the Philippine market.

---

[12] Price charged to retail drug outlets and similar purchasers.

TABLE 7 Kinds of Packaging Being Considered

Description of the Package*	Estimated Cost†	Major Advantages	Major Disadvantages
Glass bottle with label on the outside.	P3.48	Very low cost Adequate protection to the tablets	Not attractive Little room on label for product description or instructions on usage Impossible to mark the package; the woman cannot easily ascertain the number of pills she has taken
Aluminum strip 5" long and 1¾" wide to which the tablets would be affixed by being encased in thin plastic. Strip would be packaged in aluminum foil.	P5.90	Relatively low cost Permits instructions on a separate sheet to be enclosed with the strip Strip can be marked with the days of the week so the woman can easily ascertain the number of pills she has taken	Inadequate protection to the tablets—would have some breakage
Comb case in which tablets would be affixed (by being encased in plastic) to an aluminum strip 5" long and 1¾" wide; the strip would be placed in a comb carrying case 5½" long and 2¼" wide. The aluminum strip and carrying case would be packaged in a cardboard container 6" × 2¾" × ½".	P7.77	Excellent protection to the tablets Relatively attractive carrying case Permits ample room for instructions to be enclosed separately and/or printed on the package Aluminum strip can be marked so woman can easily ascertain the number of pills she has taken	Relatively high cost
Compact case in which tablets would be affixed (by being encased in plastic) to an aluminum disc 2¾" in diameter; disc would be placed in a compact 3¼" in diameter; perforated holes in the bottom of the compact would permit the woman to push the label through the bottom of the compact, separating the tablet from the aluminum disc; compact would be packaged in a cardboard container 3¾" × 3¾" × ¾".	P20.37	Very attractive carrying case Excellent protection to the tablets Permits ample room for instructions to be enclosed separately and/or printed on the package Aluminum disc can be marked so woman can easily ascertain how many pills she has taken	Very high cost

* Each package would contain 21 tablets.
† This estimated cost includes the price of the container and the cost of labor and other expenses involved in packaging the tablets.

TABLE 8   Memo on Possible Promotional Activities

DATE: FEBRUARY 16, 1991

TO: Mr. Jose J. Lim, Manager of Marketing Services
FROM: Mr. Manuel D. Pineda, Manager of Advertising and Promotional Activities
RE: Possible Promotional Activities for the Oral Contraceptive Product

The sales promotional staff submits the following sales promotional ideas for consideration in the formulation of the marketing plan for the new oral contraceptive product.

I. Sampling. The sales promotion staff suggests that the following sampling activities be considered:
   A. Comprehensive sampling of all the doctors upon whom Choufont-Salva salesmen call. Almost every doctor in the Philippines has patients who are potential customers for our oral contraceptive. Extensive sampling will give broad coverage to our product.

   To get the desired penetration and to develop brand loyalty among doctors, it might be desirable for the company to engage in heavy sampling for at least six months. This could be accomplished:
      1. By giving to gynecologists, obstetricians, and general practitioners with clientele likely to use contraceptives from one to four dozen sample packets per month, depending upon the doctor's location and practice. (We estimate that this group of doctors constitutes no more than one-fourth of the doctors on whom our salesmen call.)
      2. By giving to all other doctors upon whom our salesmen call four sample packets of our oral contraceptive during the product's introductory month and two packets per month for the next five months.
   B. That the approximately one hundred government and private clinics disseminating birth control information and products be heavily sampled. Most of these clinics recommend—and often insert either free or for a very nominal charge—I.U.D.s. For example, at one Manila family planning clinic last year, only 2 percent of the couples that came to the clinic decided to take oral contraceptives. The others are using I.U.D.s. To help alter this situation, the company might give one to four dozen samples monthly to each of the clinics, the number of samples depending upon the size of the clinic.

II. The printing of both brochures and posters that will be used by the salesmen in describing to physicians our oral contraceptives and will be left with the physicians at the end of the visit. A five-color, eight-page brochure measuring 8″ × 11″ will cost approximately P15,815.70 per 1,000 with a minimum order of 5,000 required. A five color 12″ × 15″ poster will cost approximately P13,403.14 per 1,000 with a minimum order of 5,000 required.

III. Mailing to all physicians on whom our salesmen do not call the eight-page brochure mentioned above. The cost of printing a cover letter and mailing the brochure would be approximately P5.36 per physician not counting the cost of the brochure.

IV. Engaging in outlet promotions. Because of the nature of the product and the large number of potential consumers, the company might consider altering its policy against outlet promotions and engage in the following subtle promotional activities:
   A. Encourage the salesclerks in drugstores to recommend our oral contraceptive to contraceptive customers. This could be accomplished (1) by the sales representatives discussing with the clerks both the characteristics of the product and its advantages over similar products on the market and (2) by giving the clerks a sample packet of our contraceptive.
   B. Print small booklets on family planning and have them displayed on the sales counter in an attractive heavy cardboard rack. The booklet would define family planning, discuss the various methods of birth control, give the answers to the questions people most frequently ask about family planning, and contain semihumorous illustrations. Printing a three-color, thirty-page booklet that would be 5″ × 3½″ in size would cost approximately P6701.57 per 1,000 with a minimum order of 5,000 required. Each display rack would cost approximately P134.03. Consideration might also be given to placing these racks in the offices of doctors. Both the booklets and the display racks would carry the name and trademark of Choufont-Salva.

TABLE 9 Consumer-Oriented Media Costs

Print

Publication	Circulation	Percent of Copies to Households Earning P15,000 and Above	Rates per Column Inch
Newspapers			
Evening News	58,000	N.A.	214.45
Manila *Chronicle*	144,000	22%	294.87
Manila *Daily Bulletin*	118,000	71	254.66
Manila *Times*	240,000	31	509.32
Mirror	48,000	N.A.	160.84
Philippine Herald	94,000	18	227.85
The Sunday Times	310,000	48	562.93
Weekly magazines			
Free Press	172,000	42	402.09
Graphic	176,000	55	321.66
Weekly Women's Magazine	186,000	65	375.29
Woman & the Home	162,000	22	348.48

N.A. = Not available.

Radio
Class Time: 6:00 A.M.—9:00 A.M.

Units	60 Seconds (per spot)	30 Seconds (per spot)	5–10 Seconds (per spot)
1–12	335.09	251.17	83.64
13–25	318.46	238.84	79.61
26–38	301.57	226.25	75.33
39–51	284.95	213.65	71.30
52–103	268.06	227.08	67.02
104–259	249.30	188.45	62.73
260+	234.55	175.85	58.71

Class B Time: 5:00 A.M.—6:00 A.M. 9:00 A.M.—2:00 P.M., and 5:00 P.M.—6:00 P.M.

Units	60 Seconds (per spot)	30 Seconds (per spot)	5–10 Seconds (per spot)
1–12	227.08	150.65	61.12
13–25	191.13	143.41	50.13
26–38	180.94	135.64	45.30
39–51	171.02	128.13	42.62
52–103	160.84	120.63	40.21
104–259	150.91	113.39	37.80
260+	140.73	104.28	35.12

Class C Time: 2:00 P.M.—5:00 P.M. 6:00 P.M.—12:00 Midnight, and 4:00 A.M.—5:00 A.M.

Units	60 Seconds (per spot)	30 Seconds (per spot)	5–10 Seconds (per spot)
1–12	120.62	90.34	30.02
13–25	114.73	86.05	28.68
26–38	108.57	80.49	27.07
39–51	102.67	76.93	25.73
52–103	96.50	72.38	24.73
104–259	22.65	67.82	22.79
260+	84.44	63.26	21.18

TABLE 9 (Cont.)

Class D Time: 12:00 Midnight—5:00 A.M.

Units	60 Seconds (per spot)	30 Seconds (per spot)	5–10 Seconds (per spot)
1–12	80.42	60.31	20.14
13–25	76.40	57.36	19.03
26–38	72.38	54.42	17.96
39–51	68.36	51.20	17.16
52–103	64.34	48.25	16.08
104–259	60.31	45.30	15.01
260+	56.29	42.09	13.94

Production Costs*

Length	Estimated Costs
60 seconds	13,403
30 seconds	13,403
10 seconds	10,723
5 seconds	10,723

Television
1. Rates

Midprogram breaks	Prime Time 6:30 P.M.—10:00 P.M. (per spot)	Class B Time (all other hours) (per spot)
60 seconds	13,403	6,702
30 seconds	6,702	3,351
10 seconds	3,351	1,742
5 seconds	1,742	938
Station breaks (between programs)		
60 seconds	10,723	5,361
30 seconds	5,361	2,681
10 seconds	2,681	1,340
5 seconds	1,340	670

2. Production Costs

a. A 30-second film commercial would cost approximately P5,000 to produce.
b. The estimated costs of producing a T.V. slide commercial are as follows:

Length	Estimated Costs
60 seconds	9,382
30 seconds	8,712
10 seconds	8,310
5 seconds	8,176

* In estimating costs, it was assumed that (1) two announcers would be used in producing a 30- or 60-second ad and that only one announcer would be used in producing a 5- or 10-second ad and (2) a combo would furnish simple background music for the ads. The estimated costs also include the studio fees, the costs of tapes, and similar expenses.

▶ APPENDIX I

Position of the Roman Catholic Church Concerning Contraception

At the present time (1991), the Church holds the position stated by Pope Pius XI in *Casti Connubii,* an encyclical issued in 1930. This excerpt is a summary of it:

> Any use whatsoever of matrimony exercised in such a way that the act is deliberately frustrated in its natural power to generate life is an offense against the law of God and nature, and those who indulge in such are branded with the guilt of a great sin. (para. 56)

> The only methods of family limitation which meet with the approval of the Church are continence and periodic continence, or the rhythm method. The Catholic Church does, however, permit the use of artificial contraception for medical (as distinct from birth control) reasons.

▶ APPENDIX II

Excerpts from "The Family Planning Association of the Philippines—Its Performance and Program of Activities"[1]

The present status of the family planning movement in the Philippines has been very favorable and progressing in spite of its predominantly Catholic population, about 84 percent of the total population. Because of this strong religious affiliation, before the year 1990 although there were about three Protestant family planning groups already existing, the mere mention of birth control was strongly tabooed and no public forum on the subject was allowed even by a private organization. Any press publication on family planning and birth control materials was censured and not permitted to enter the country and be transmitted through mails (old custom and postal laws).

In the early part of 1990, the Family Planning Association of the Philippines, Inc. (FPAP), organized by progressive Catholic leaders, launched a nationwide family planning movement which was never done before. Since this concept was very new to the general public, the FPAP's intensified and relentless efforts have been concentrated on dissemination of informative knowledge of family planning methods and motivation programs to change the attitude and behavior of the people through continuing series of lectures and speaking tours in public meetings and forums all over the country, and through extensive use of mass media communications, such as endless publication of articles and news in newspapers, magazines, medical journals, nationwide distribution of pamphlets, handouts, brochures, and lately the use of TV and radio. Note that the first article in the Graphic-Kislap magazine was censured, but the favorable public opin-

---

[1] Published by the FPAP, May 1992.

ion changed the attitude of authorities which later just ignored the old law, and which was recently repealed "by implication" by the Republic Act No. 4729 of June, 1991.

Training seminars to create man-power are being conducted locally for physicians, nurses, and health educators. Family planning leaders and workers, including those of other allied organizations (PPMP, RPA, PFPA, Manila Health Dept., Municipal Health Officers) were sent through the FPAP under IPPF and other foreign grants to attend training seminars, international conferences, university studies, and observation tours of family planning programs in other countries. To date, the FPAP has 162 assisted clinics and 3 fully supported and maintained clinics in different areas of the country. Including the Manila Health Department, PPMP, RPA, and the Pathfinder Fund to which the FPAP is closely associated, there are now about 300 family planning clinics all over the country. The strongly conservative Catholic sector is starting to establish rhythm clinics, and there are strong indications that other institutions, especially the educational, may follow soon.

The present population of the Philippines is about 63 million, with an annual rate of growth of 3.2 percent, the highest in Asia. The annual birth rate is 45 to 46 per thousand and the annual death rate is 12 to 14 per thousand. The average family size is 6.7. The land area is 115,700 sq. miles. The population density is 560 persons per sq. mile which is already five times the world average. The city of Manila has 160,000 persons per sq. mile. The country cannot feed its population adequately; therefore, it is over-populated. Food supply and increasing unemployment are two very serious major problems. The annual net income per capita is only P10,454, or about $400. Two-thirds of the population are in poverty and medically indigent, and depend very much on government agencies which, at this time, cannot give family planning services and in participation of private medical sectors, without the participation of government health agencies, it would be far from its goal—the promotion of the well-being of the Filipino family and helping in the socioeconomic development of this country.

There is at present increasing awareness and demand from government health officers and agencies relative to the knowledge and methods of family planning. Cognizant of this, the Family Planning Association of the Philippines, Inc. is also exerting its efforts to offer its help to introduce a family planning program in the Maternal and Child Health agencies of the government.

▼ DISCUSSION QUESTIONS

1. Formulate a marketing strategy for Choufont-Salva. Identify your objectives, target markets, product, price, promotion, and distribution policies and your research plan.

2. Would you respond to the North American Drug announcement? How and why, or why not?

Curtis Automotive Hoist

In September 1990, Mark Curtis, president of Curtis Automotive Hoist (CAH), had just finished reading a feasibility report on entering the European market in 1991. CAH manufactured surface automotive hoists, a product used by garages, service stations, and other repair shops to lift cars for servicing (Exhibit 1). The report, prepared by CAH's marketing manager, Pierre Gagnon, outlined the opportunities in the European Economic Community and the entry options available.

Mr. Curtis was not sure if CAH was ready for this move. While the company had been successful in expanding sales into the United States market, Mr. Curtis wondered if this success could be repeated in Europe. He thought, with more effort, that sales could be increased in the United States. On the other hand, there were some positive aspects to the European idea. He began reviewing the information in preparation for the meeting the following day with Mr. Gagnon.

CURTIS AUTOMOTIVE HOIST

Mr. Curtis, a design engineer, had worked for eight years for the Canadian subsidiary of a U.S. automotive hoist manufacturer. During those years, he had spent considerable time designing an above-ground (or surface) automotive hoist. Although Mr. Curtis was very enthusiastic about the unique aspects of the hoist, including a scissor lift and wheel alignment pads, se-nior management expressed no interest in the idea. In 1980, Mr. Curtis left the company to start his own business with the express purpose of designing and manufacturing the hoist. He left with the good wishes of his previous employer who had no objections to his plans to start a new business.

Over the next three years, Mr. Curtis obtained financing from a venture capital firm, opened a plant in Lachine, Quebec, and began manufacturing and marketing the hoist, called the Curtis Lift (Exhibit 1).

From the beginning, Mr. Curtis had taken considerable pride in the development and marketing of the Curtis Lift. The original design included a scissor lift and a safety locking mechanism that allowed the hoist to be raised to any level and locked in place. As well, the scissor lift offered easy access for the mechanic to work on the raised vehicle. Because the hoist was fully hydraulic and had no chains or pulleys, it required little maintenance. Another key feature was the alignment turn plates that were an integral part of the lift. The turn plates meant that mechanics could accurately and easily perform wheel alignment jobs. Because it was a surface lift, it could be installed in a garage in less than a day.

Mr. Curtis continually made improvements to the product, including adding more safety features. In fact, the Curtis Lift was considered a leader in automotive lift safety. Safety was an important factor in the automotive hoist market. Although hoists seldom malfunctioned, when they did, it often resulted in a serious accident.

This case was prepared by Professor Gordon H. McDougall. This case is intended as a basis for class discussion rather than to indicate effective or ineffective handling of a managerial situation. Copyright 1988, by Gordon H. McDougall, School of Business and Economics, Wilfrid Laurier University.

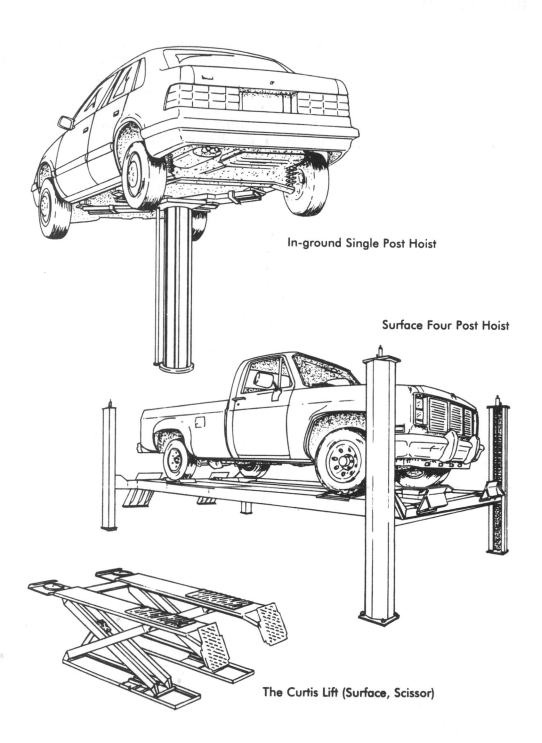

In-ground Single Post Hoist

Surface Four Post Hoist

The Curtis Lift (Surface, Scissor)

	1989	1988	1987
Sales	$9,708,000	$7,454,000	$6,218,000
Cost of sales	6,990,000	5,541,000	4,540,000
Contribution	2,718,000	1,913,000	1,678,000
Marketing expenses*	530,000	510,000	507,000
Administrative expenses	840,000	820,000	810,000
Earnings before tax	1,348,000	583,000	361,000
Units sold	1,054	847	723

Source: Company records

*Marketing expenses in 1989 included advertising ($70,000), four salespeople ($240,000), marketing manager and three sales support staff ($220,000).

The Curtis Lift developed a reputation in the industry as the "Cadillac" of hoists; the unit was judged by many as superior to competitive offerings because of its design, the quality of the workmanship, the safety features, the ease of installation, and the five-year warranty. Mr. Curtis held four patents on the Curtis Lift including the lifting mechanism on the scissor design and a safety locking mechanism. A number of versions of the product were designed that made the Curtis Lift suitable (depending on the model) for a variety of tasks, including rustproofing, muffler repairs, and general mechanical repairs. $7600 ca.

In 1981, CAH sold 23 hoists and had sales of $172,500. During the early years, the majority of sales were to independent service stations and garages specializing in wheel alignment in the Quebec and Ontario market. Most of the units were sold by Mr. Gagnon, who was hired in 1982 to handle the marketing side of the operation. In 1984, Mr. Gagnon began using distributors to sell the hoist to a wider geographic market in Canada. In 1986, he signed an agreement with a large automotive wholesaler to represent CAH in the U.S. market. By 1989, the company sold 1,054 hoists and had sales of $9,708,000 (Exhibit 2). In 1989, about 60% of sales were to the United States with the remaining 40% to the Canadian market.

INDUSTRY

Approximately 49,000 hoists were sold each year in North America. Typically hoists were purchased by an automotive outlet that serviced or repaired cars including new car dealers, used car dealers, specialty shops (for example, muffler shops, transmission, wheel alignment), chains (for example, Firestone, Goodyear, Canadian Tire), and independent garages. It was estimated that new car dealers purchased 30% of all units sold in a given year. In general, the specialty shops focused on one type of repair, such as mufflers or rustproofing, while "non-specialty" outlets handled a variety of repairs. While there was some crossover, in general, CAH competed in the specialty shop segment and, in particular, those shops that dealt with wheel alignment. This included chains such as Firestone and Canadian Tire as well as new car dealers (for example, Ford) who devote a certain percentage of their lifts to the wheel alignment business and independent garages who specialized in wheel alignment.

The purpose of a hoist was to lift an automobile into a position where a mechanic or service person could easily work on the car. Because different repairs required different positions, a wide variety of hoists had be developed to meet specific needs. For example, a muffler repair shop required a hoist that allowed the mechanic to gain easy access to the underside of the car. Similarly, a wheel alignment job required a hoist that offered a level platform where the wheels could be adjusted as well as providing easy access for the mechanic. Mr. Gagnon estimated that 85% of CAH's sales were to the wheel alignment market to service centres such as Firestone, Goodyear, and Canadian Tire and to independent garages that specialized in wheel alignment. About 15% of sales were made to customers who used the hoist for general mechanical repairs.

Firms purchasing hoists were part of an industry called the automobile aftermarket. This industry was involved in supplying parts and service for new and used cars and was worth over $54 billion at retail in 1989, while servicing the approximately 11 million cars on the road in Canada. The industry was large and diverse; there were over 4,000 new car dealers in Canada, over 400 Canadian Tire stores, over 100 stores in each of the Firestone and Goodyear chains, and over 200 stores in the Rust Check chain.

The purchase of an automotive hoist was often an important decision for the service station owner or dealer. Because the price of hoists ranged from $3,000 to $15,000, it was a capital expense for most businesses.

For the owner/operator of a new service centre or car dealership the decision involved determining what type of hoist was required, then what brand would best suit the company. Most new service centres or car dealerships had multiple bays for servicing cars. In these cases, the decision would involve what types of hoists were required (for example, in-ground,

surface). Often more than one type of hoist was purchased, depending on the service centre/dealership needs.

Experienced garage owners seeking a replacement hoist (the typical hoist had a useful life of 10 to 13 years) would usually determine what products were available and then make a decision. If the garage owners were also mechanics, they would probably be aware of two or three types of hoists but would not be very knowledgeable about the brands or products currently available. Garage owners or dealers who were not mechanics probably knew very little about hoists. The owners of car or service dealerships often bought the product that was recommended and/or approved by the parent company.

COMPETITION

Sixteen companies competed in the automotive lift market in North America: four Canadian and twelve United States firms. Hoists were subject to import duties. Duties on hoists entering the U.S. market from Canada were 2.4% of the selling price; from the U.S. entering Canada the import duty was 7.9%. With the advent of the Free Trade Agreement in 1989, the duties between the two countries would be phased out over a ten-year period. For Mr. Curtis, the import duties had never played a part in any decisions: the fluctuating exchange rates between the two countries had a far greater impact on selling prices.

A wide variety of hoists were manufactured in the industry. The two basic types of hoists were in-ground and surface. As the names imply, in-ground hoists required that a pit be dug "in-ground" where the piston that raised the hoist was installed. In-ground hoists were either single post or multiple post, were permanent, and obviously could not be moved. In-ground lifts constituted approximately

21% of total lift sales in 1989 (Exhibit 3). Surface lifts were installed on a flat surface, usually concrete. Surface lifts came in two basic types, post lift hoists and scissor hoists. Surface lifts, compared to in-ground lifts, were easier to install and could be moved, if necessary. Surface lifts constituted 79% of total lift sales in 1989. Within each type of hoist (for example, post lift surface hoists), there were numerous variations in terms of size, shape and lifting capacity.

The industry was dominated by two large U.S. firms, AHV Lifts and Berne Manufacturing, who together held approximately 60% of the market. AHV Lifts, the largest firm with approximately 40% of the market and annual sales of about $60 million, offered a complete line of hoists (that is, in-ground and surface) but focused primarily on the in-ground market and the two post surface market. AHV Lifts was the only company that had its own direct sales force; all other companies used (1) only wholesalers or (2) a combination of wholesalers and company sales force. AHV Lifts offered standard hoists with few extra features and competed primarily on price. Berne Manufacturing, with a market share of approximately 20%, also competed in the in-ground and two post surface markets. It used a combination of wholesalers and company salespeople and, like AHV Lifts, competed primarily on price.

Most of the remaining firms in the industry were companies that operated in a regional market (for example, California or British Columbia) and/or offered a limited product line (for example, four post surface hoist).

Curtis had two competitors that manufactured scissor lifts. AHV Lift marketed a scissor hoist that had a different lifting mechanism and did not include the safety locking features of the Curtis Lift. On average, the AHV scissor lift sold for about 20% less than the Curtis Lift. The second competitor, Mete Lift, was a small regional company with sales in California and Oregon. It had a design that was very similar to the Curtis Lift but lacked some of its safety features. The Mete Lift, regarded as a well-manufactured product, sold for about 5% less than the Curtis Lift.

MARKETING STRATEGY

As of early 1990, CAH had developed a reputation for a quality product backed

---

EXHIBIT 3 North American Automotive Lift Unit Sales, By Type (1987 to 1989)

	1987	1988	1989
In-ground			
Single post	5885	5772	5518
Multiple post	4,812	6,625	5,075
Surface			
Two post	27,019	28,757	28,923
Four post	3,862	3,162	3,745
Scissor	2,170	2,258	2,316
Other	4,486	3,613	3,695
Total	48,234	50,187	49,272

Source: Company records

by good service in the hoist lift market, primarily in the wheel alignment segment.

The distribution system employed by CAH reflected the need to engage in extensive personal selling. Three types of distributors were used: a company sales force, Canadian distributors, and a U.S. automotive wholesaler. The company sales force consisted of four salespeople and Mr. Gagnon. Their main task was to service large "direct" accounts. The initial step was to get the Curtis Lift approved by large chains and manufacturers and then, having received the approval, to sell to individual dealers or operators. For example, if General Motors approved the hoist, then CAH could sell it to individual General Motors dealers. CAH sold directly to the individual dealers of a number of large accounts including General Motors, Ford, Chrysler, Petro-Canada, Firestone, and Goodyear. CAH had been successful in obtaining manufacturer approval from the big three automobile manufacturers in both Canada and the United States. As well, CAH had also received approval from service companies such as Canadian Tire and Goodyear. To date, CAH had not been rejected by any major account but, in some cases, the approval process had taken over four years.

In total, the company sales force generated about 25% of the unit sales each year. Sales to the large "direct" accounts in the United States went through CAH's U.S. wholesaler.

The Canadian distributors sold, installed, and serviced units across Canada. These distributors handled the Curtis Lift and carried a line of noncompetitive automotive equipment products (for example, engine diagnostic equipment, wheel balancing equipment) and noncompetitive lifts. These distributors focused on the smaller chains and the independent service stations and garages.

The U.S. wholesaler sold a complete product line to service stations as well as manufacturing some equipment. The Curtis Lift was one of five different types of lifts that the wholesaler sold. Although the wholesaler provided CAH with extensive distribution in the United States, the Curtis Lift was a minor product within the wholesaler's total line. While Mr. Gagnon did not have any actual figures, he thought that the Curtis Lift probably accounted for less than 20% of the total lift sales of the U.S. wholesaler.

Both Mr. Curtis and Mr. Gagnon felt that the U.S. market had unrealized potential. With a population of 248 million people and over 140 million registered vehicles, the U.S. market was over ten times the size of the Canadian market (population of 26 million, approximately 11 million vehicles). Mr. Gagnon noted that the six New England states (population over 13 million), the three largest mid-Atlantic states (population over 38 million), and the three largest mid-eastern states (population over 32 million) were all within a day's drive of the factory in Lachine. Mr. Curtis and Mr. Gagnon had considered setting up a sales office in New York to service these states, but they were concerned that the U.S. wholesaler would not be willing to relinquish any of its territory. They had also considered working more closely with the wholesaler to encourage it to "push" the Curtis Lift. It appeared that the wholesaler's major objective was to sell a hoist, not necessarily the Curtis Lift.

CAH distributed a catalogue type package with products, uses, prices, and other required information for both distributors and users. In addition, CAH advertised in trade publications (for example, *Service Station & Garage Management*), and Mr. Gagnon travelled to trade shows in Canada and U.S. to promote the Curtis Lift.

In 1989, Curtis Lifts sold for an average retail price of $10,990 and CAH received, on average $9,210 for each unit sold. This average reflected the mix of sales through the three distribution channels:

(1) direct (where CAH received 100% of the selling price), (2) Canadian distributors (where CAH received 79% of the selling price), and (3) the U.S. wholesaler (where CAH received 78% of the selling price).

Both Mr. Curtis and Mr. Gagnon felt that the company's success to date was based on a strategy of offering a superior product that was primarily targeted to the needs of specific customers. The strategy stressed continual product improvements, quality workmanship, and service. Personal selling was a key aspect of the strategy; salespeople could show customers the benefits of the Curtis Lift over competing products.

THE EUROPEAN MARKET

Against this background, Mr. Curtis had been thinking of ways to continue the rapid growth of the company. One possibility that kept coming up was the promise and potential of the European market. The fact that Europe would become a single market in 1992 suggested that it was an opportunity that should at least be explored. With this in mind, Mr. Curtis asked Mr. Gagnon to prepare a report on the possibility of CAH entering the European market. The highlights of Mr. Gagnon's report follow.

HISTORY OF THE EUROPEAN COMMUNITY

The European Community (EC) stemmed from the 1953 "Treaty of Rome" in which five countries decided it would be in their best interest to form an internal market. These countries were France, Spain, Italy, West Germany, and Luxembourg. By 1990, the EC consisted of 12 countries (the additional seven were Belgium, Denmark,

Greece, Ireland, and the Netherlands, Portugal, and the United Kingdom) with a population of 325 million people.[1] In 1992, virtually all barriers (physical, technical, and fiscal) in the EC were scheduled to be removed for companies located within the EC. This would allow the free movement of goods, persons, services, and capital.

In the last five years many North American and Japanese firms had established themselves in the EC. The reasoning for this was twofold. First, these companies regarded the community as an opportunity to increase global market share and profits. The market was attractive because of its sheer size and lack of internal barriers. Second, in 1992, companies that were established within the community were subject to protection from external competition via EC protectionism tariffs, local contender, and reciprocity requirements. EC protectionism tariffs were only temporary, and would be removed at a later date. It would be possible for companies to export to or establish in the community after 1992, but there was some risk attached.

MARKET POTENTIAL

The key indicator of the potential market for the Curtis Lift hoist was the number of passenger cars and commercial vehicles in use in a particular country. Four countries in Europe had more than 20 million vehicles in use, with West Germany having the largest domestic fleet of 30 million vehicles followed in order by France, Italy, and the United Kingdom (Exhibit 4). The number of vehicles was an important indicator because the more vehicles

---

[1] As of September 1990, West Germany and East Germany were in the process of unification. East Germany had a population of approximately 17 million people.

in use meant a greater number of service and repair facilities that needed vehicle hoists and potentially the Curtis Lift.

An indicator of the future vehicle repair and service market was the number of new vehicle registrations. The registration of new vehicles was important as this maintained the number of vehicles in use by replacing cars that had been retired. Again, West Germany had the most new cars registered in 1988 and was followed in order by France, the United Kingdom, and Italy.

Based primarily on the fact that a large domestic market was important for initial growth, the selection of a European country should be limited to the "Big Four" industrialized nations: West Germany, France, the United Kingdom, or Italy. In an international survey companies from North America and Europe ranked European countries on a scale of 1 to 100 on market potential and investment site potential.

The results showed that West Germany was favoured for both market potential and investment site opportunities while France, the United Kingdom, and Spain placed second, third, and fourth respectively. Italy did not place in the top four in either market or investment site potential. However, Italy had a large number of vehicles in use, had the second

largest population in Europe, and was an acknowledged leader in car technology and production.

Little information was available on the competition within Europe. There was, as yet, no dominant manufacturer as was the case in North America. At this time, there was one firm in Germany that manufactured a scissor-type lift. The firm sold most of its units within the German market. The only other available information was that 22 firms in Italy manufactured vehicle lifts.

INVESTMENT OPTIONS

Mr. Gagnon felt that CAH had three options for expansion into the European market: licensing, joint venture, or direct investment. The licensing option was a real possibility as a French firm had expressed an interest in manufacturing the Curtis Lift.

In June 1990, Mr. Gagnon had attended a trade show in Detroit to promote the Curtis Lift. At the show, he met Phillipe Beaupre, the marketing manager for Bar Maisse, a French manufacturer of wheel alignment equipment. The firm, located in Chelles, France, sold a range of wheel alignment equipment throughout Europe. The best-selling product was an electronic modular aligner that enabled a

EXHIBIT 4 Number of Vehicles (1988) and Population (1989)

| Country | Vehicles in Use(000s) | | New Vehicle Registrations (000s) | Population (000s) |
	Passenger	Commercial		
West Germany	28,304	1,814	2,960	60,900
France	29,970	4,223	2,635	56,000
Italy	22,500	1,897	2,308	57,400
United Kingdom	20,605	2,915	2,531	57,500
Spain	9,750	1,750	1,172	39,400

mechanic to utilize a sophisticated computer system to align the wheels of a car. Mr. Beaupre was seeking a North American distributor for the modular aligner and other products manufactured by Bar Maisse.

At the show, Mr. Gagnon and Mr. Beaupre had a casual conversation in which each explained what their respective companies manufactured, they exchanged company brochures and business cards, and both went on to other exhibits. The next day, Mr. Beaupre sought out Mr. Gagnon and asked if he might be interested in having Bar Maisse manufacture and market the Curtis Lift in Europe. Mr. Beaupre felt the lift would complement Bar Maisse's product line and the licensing would be of mutual benefit to both parties. They agreed to pursue the idea. Upon his return to Lachine, Mr. Gagnon told Mr. Curtis about these discussions, and they agreed to explore the possibility.

Mr. Gagnon called a number of colleagues in the industry and asked them what they knew about Bar Maisse. About half had not heard of the company, but those who had, commented favourably on the quality of its products. One colleague, with European experience, knew the company well and said that Bar Maisse's management had integrity and would make a good partner. In July, Mr. Gagnon sent a letter to Mr. Beaupre stating that CAH was interested in further discussions and enclosed various company brochures including price lists and technical information on the Curtis Lift. In late August, Mr. Beaupre responded stating that Bar Maisse would like to enter a three-year licensing agreement with CAH to manufacture the Curtis Lift in Europe. In exchange for the manufacturing rights, Bar Maisse was prepared to pay a royalty of 5% of gross sales. Mr. Gagnon had not yet responded to this proposal.

A second possibility was a joint venture. Mr. Gagnon had wondered if it might not be better for CAH to offer a counter proposal to Bar Maisse for a joint venture. He had not worked out any details, but Mr. Gagnon felt that CAH would learn more about the European market and probably make more money if they were an active partner in Europe. Mr. Gagnon's idea was a 50-50 proposal where the two parties shared the investment and the profits. He envisaged a situation where Bar Maisse would manufacture the Curtis Lift in their plant with technical assistance from CAH. Mr. Gagnon also thought that CAH could get involved in the marketing of the lift through the Bar Maisse distribution system. Further, he thought that the Curtis Lift, with proper marketing, could gain a reasonable share of the European market. If that happened Mr. Gagnon felt that CAH was likely to make greater returns with a joint venture.

The third option was direct investment where CAH would establish a manufacturing facility and set up a management group to market the lift. Mr. Gagnon had contacted a business acquaintance who had recently been involved in manufacturing fabricated steel sheds in Germany. On the basis of discussions with his acquaintance, Mr. Gagnon estimated the costs involved in setting up a plant in Europe at: (1) $250,000 for capital equipment (welding machines, cranes, other equipment), (2) $200,000 in incremental costs to set the plant up, and (3) carrying cost to cover $1,000,000 in inventory and accounts receivable. While the actual costs of renting a building for the factory would depend on the site location, he estimated that annual building rent including heat, light, and insurance would be about $80,000. Mr. Gagnon recognized these estimates were guidelines but he felt that the estimates were probably within 20% of actual costs.

THE DECISION

As Mr. Curtis considered the contents of the report, a number of thoughts crossed his mind. He began making notes concerning the European possibility and the future of the company.

- ► If CAH decided to enter Europe, Mr. Gagnon would be the obvious choice to head up the "direct investment" option or the "joint venture" option.

  Mr. Curtis felt that Mr. Gagnon had been instrumental in the success of the company to date.

- ► While CAH had the financial resources to go ahead with the direct investment option, the joint venture would spread the risk (and the returns) over the two companies.

- ► CAH had built its reputation on designing and manufacturing a quality product. Regardless of the option chosen, Mr. Curtis wanted the firm's reputation to be maintained.

- ► Either the licensing agreement or the joint venture appeared to build on the two companies' strengths; Bar Maisse had knowledge of the market and CAH had the product. What troubled Mr. Curtis was whether this apparent synergy would work or would Bar Maisse seek to control the operation.

- ► It was difficult to estimate sales under any of the options. With the first two (licensing and joint venture), it would depend on the effort and expertise of Bar Maisse; with the third option, it would depend on Mr. Gagnon.

- ► CAH's sales in the U.S. market could be increased if the U.S. wholesaler would "push" the Curtis Lift. Alternatively, the establishment of a sales office in New York to cover the eastern states could also increase sales.

As Mr. Curtis reflected on the situation he knew he should probably get additional information—but it wasn't obvious exactly what information would help him make a "yes" or "no" decision. He knew one thing for sure—he was going to keep his company on a "fast growth" track—and at tomorrow's meeting he and Mr. Gagnon would decide how to do it.

Neilson International in Mexico (A)

In January, 1993, Howard Bateman, Vice President of International Operations for Neilson International, a division of William Neilson Limited, was assessing a recent proposal from Sabritas, a division of Pepsico Foods in Mexico, to launch Neilson's brands in the Mexican market. Neilson, a leading producer of high quality confectionery products, had grown to achieve a leadership position in the Canadian market and was currently producing Canada's top selling chocolate bar, "Crispy Crunch". In the world chocolate bar market, however, Neilson was dwarfed

This case was prepared by Gayle Duncan and Shari Ann Wortel under the supervision of Professors P.W. Beamish and C.B. Johnston of the Western Business School. Copyright 1995, The University of Western Ontario. This material is not covered under authorization from CanCopy or any reproduction rights organization. Any form of reproduction, storage or transmittal of this material is prohibited without written permission from Western Business School, The University of Western Ontario, London, Canada N6A 3K7. Reprinted with permission, Western Business School.

by major players such as M&M/Mars, Hershey/Lowney and Nestlé/Rowntree. Recognizing their position as a smaller player with fewer resources, in a stagnant domestic market, Neilson in 1990 formed its International Division to develop competitive strategies for their exporting efforts.

Recent attempts to expand into several foreign markets, including the United States, had taught them some valuable lessons. Although it was now evident that they had world class products to offer to global markets, their competitive performance was being constrained by limited resources. Pepsico's joint branding proposal would allow greater market penetration than Neilson could afford. But, at what cost?

Given the decision to pursue international opportunities more aggressively, Bateman's biggest challenge was to determine the distributor relationships Neilson should pursue in order to become a global competitor. *(Biggest problem)*

THE CHOCOLATE CONFECTIONERY INDUSTRY[1]

The "confectionery" industry consisted of the "sugar" segment, including all types of sugar confectionery, chewing gum, and the "chocolate" segment which included chocolates and other cocoa based products. Most large chocolate operations were dedicated to two major products; boxed chocolates and bar chocolates which represented nearly 50% of the confectionery industry by volume.

Competition from imports was significant with the majority of products coming from the United States (39%). European countries such as Switzerland, Germany, the United Kingdom and Belgium were also major sources of confectionery, especially for premium products such as boxed chocolates. (See Exhibit 1 for a profile of chocolate exporting countries). In order to maintain production volumes and to relieve the burden of fixed costs on operations, Canadian manufactures used excess capacity to produce goods for exporting. Although nearly all of these products were traditionally exported to the United States, in early nineties, the world market had become increasingly more attractive.

Films in the confectionery industry competed on the basis of brand name products, product quality and cost of production. Although Canadian producers had the advantage of being able to purchase sugar at the usually lower world price, savings were offset by the higher prices for dairy ingredients used in products manufactured for domestic consumption. Other commodity ingredients, often experiencing widely fluctuating prices, caused significant variations in manufacturing costs. Producers were reluctant to raise their prices due to the highly elastic demand for chocolate. Consequently, they sometimes reformatted or reformulated their products through size or ingredient changes to sustain margins. Three major product types were manufactured for domestic and export sales:

Blocks These products are molded blocks of chocolate that are sold by weight and manufactured in a variety of flavours, with or without additional ingredients such as fruit or nuts. Block chocolate was sold primarily in grocery outlets or directly to confectionery manufacturers. (Examples: baking chocolate, Hershey's Chocolate Bar, Suchard's Toblerone).

Boxed These products included a variety
Choco- of bite-sized sweets and were gen-
lates erally regarded as "gift" or "occa-

---

[1] Some information in this section was derived from: James C. Ellert, J. Peter Killing and Dana G. Hyde, "Nestlé-Rowntree (A)", in *Business Policy, A Canadian Casebook*, Joseph N. Fry et al. (eds.), Prentice Hall Canada Inc., 1992, pp. 655-667.

sion" purchases. Sales in grocery outlets tended to be more seasonal than for other chocolate products, with 80% sold at Christmas and Easter. Sales in other outlets remained steady year round. (Examples: Cadbury's Milk Tray, Rowntree's Black Magic and After Eights).

Count- These were chocolate covered prod-
lines ucts sold by count rather than by weight, and were generally referred to by consumers and "chocolate bars". The products varied widely in size, shape, weight and composition, and had a wider distribution than the other two product types. Most countlines were sold through non-grocery outlets such as convenience and drug stores. (Examples: Neilson's Crispy Crunch, Nestlé-Rowntree's Coffee Crisp, M&M Mars' Snickers, and Hershey/Lowney's Oh Henry!)

Sweet chocolate was the basic semi-finished product used in the manufacture of block, countline, and boxed chocolate products. Average costs of sweet chocolate for a representative portfolio of all three product types could be broken down as follows:

Raw Material	35%
Packaging	10
Production	20
Distribution	5
Marketing/Sales	20
Trading profit	10
Total	100%
(of manufacturer's selling price)	

For countline products, raw material costs were proportionately lower because a smaller amount of cocoa was used.

In value terms, more chocolate was consumed than any other manufactured food product in the world. In the late eighties, the world's eight major markets (representing over 60% of the total world chocolate market) consumed nearly three million tonnes with a retail value close to $20 billion. During the 1980's countline was the fastest growing segment with close to 50% of the world chocolate market by volume and an average annual rate of growth of 7%. An increasing trend towards indulgence in snack and "comfort" foods strongly suggested that future growth would remain strong.

COMPETITIVE ENVIRONMENT

In 1993, chocolate producers in the world included: M&M/Mars, Hershey Foods, Cadbury-Schweppes, Jacob Suchard, Nestlé-Rowntree, United Biscuits, Ferrero, Nabisco and George Weston Ltd. (Neilson). Chocolate represented varying proportions of these manufacturers' total sales.

For the most part, it was difficult to sustain competitive advantages in manufacturing or product features due to a lack of proprietary technology. There was also limited potential for new product development since the basic ingredients in countline product manufacturing could only be blended in a limited variety of combinations. This forced an emphasis on competition through distribution and advertising.

Product promotion played a critical role in establishing brand name recognition. Demand was typified by high-impulse and discretionary purchasing behaviour. Since consumers, generally, had a selection of at least three or four favourite brands from which to choose, the biggest challenge facing producers was to create the brand awareness necessary to break into these menus. In recognition of the wide selection of competing brands and the broad range of snack food substitutes available, expenditures for media and trade promotions were considerable. For example, Canadian chocolate bar makers spent more than $30 million for advertising in Canada, in 1992, mostly on television. This was often a barrier to entry for smaller producers.

MAJOR COMPETITORS

M&M/Mars

As the world leader in chocolate confectionery M&M/Mars dominated the countline sector, particularly in North America and Europe, and such famous global brands as Snickers, M&Ms and Milky Way. However, in Canada, in 1992, M&M/Mars held fourth place with an 18.7% market share of single bars. (Exhibits 2 and 3 compare Canadian market positions for major competitors).

M&M/Mars' strategy was produce high quality products which were simple to manufacture and which allowed for high volume, and automated production processes. They supported their products with heavy advertising and aggressive sales, focusing marketing efforts on strengthening their global brands.

Hershey/Lowney

Hershey's strength in North America was in the block chocolate category in which it held the leading market position. Hershey also supplied export markets in Asia, Australia, Sweden, and Mexico from their chocolate production facilities in Pennsylvania. In Canada, in 1992, Hershey held third place in the countline segment with a 21.6% share of the market.

Hershey's strategy was to reduce exposure to volatile cocoa prices by diversifying within the confectionery and snack businesses. By 1987, only 45% of Hershey's sales came from products with 70% or more chocolate content. This was down from 80% in 1963.

Cadbury Schweppes

Cadbury was a major world name in chocolate, with a portfolio of brands such as Dairy Milk, Creme Eggs and Crunchie. Although its main business was in the United Kingdom, it was also a strong competitor in major markets such as Australia and South Africa.

Cadbury Schweppes diversified its product line and expanded into new geographic markets throughout the 1980s. In 1987, Cadbury International sold the Canadian distribution rights for their chocolate products to William Neilson Ltd. Only in Canada were the Cadbury incorporated into the Neilson confectionery division under the name Neilson/Cadbury. In 1988, Cadbury sold its U.S. operations to Hershey.

Nestlé-Rowntree

In 1991, chocolate and confectionery comprised 16% of Nestlé's SFr 50.5 billion revenue, up sharply from only 8% in 1987. (In January 1993, 1SFr = $0.88 CAD = .69 U.S.) This was largely a result of their move into the countline sector through the acquisition in 1988 of Rowntree PLC, a leading British manufacturer with strong global brands such as Kit Kat, After Eights and Smarties. In 1990, they also added Baby Ruth and Butterfinger to their portfolio, both "Top 20" brands in the U.S. Considering these recent heavy investments to acquire global brands and expertise, it was clear that Nestlé-Rowntree intended to remain a significant player in growing global markets.

NEILSON

Company History

William Neilson Ltd. was founded in 1893, when the Neilson family began selling milk and home made ice cream to the Toronto market. By 1905 they had erected a house and factory at 277 Gladstone Ave., from which they shipped ice cream as far west as Winnipeg and as far east as Quebec City. Chocolate bar production was initiated to offset the decreased demand for ice cream during the colder winter months and as a way of retaining the skilled labour pool. By 1914, the company was producing one million pounds of ice cream and 500,000 pounds of chocolate per year.

William Neilson died in 1915, and the business was handed down to his son Morden, who had been involved since its inception. Between 1924 and 1934, the "Jersey milk", "Crispy Crunch" and "Malted Milk" bars were introduced. Upon the death of Morden Neilson in 1947, the company was sold to George Weston Foods for $4.5 million.

By 1974, "Crispy Crunch" was the number one selling bar in Canada. In 1977, "Mr. Big" was introduced and became the number one teen bar by 1986. By 1991, the Neilson dairy operations had been moved to a separate location and the ice cream division had been sold to Ault Foods. The Gladstone location continued to be used to manufacture Neilson chocolate and confectionery.

Bateman explained that Neilson's efforts under the direction of the new president, Arthur Soler, had become more competitive in the domestic market over the past three years, through improved customer service and retail merchandising. Significant improvements had already been made in Administration and Operations. All of these initiatives had assisted in reversing decades of consumer share erosion. As a result, Neilson was now in a position to defend its share of the domestic market and to develop and international business that would enhance shareholder value. (Exhibit 4 outlines the Canadian chocolate confectionery market.)

Neilson's Exporting Efforts

Initial export efforts prior to 1990 were contracted to a local export broker—Grenadier International. The original company objective was to determine "what could be done in foreign markets" using only working capital resources and avoiding capital investments in equipment or new markets.

Through careful selection of markets on the basis of distributor interest, Grenadier's export manager, Scott Begg, had begun the slow process of introducing Neilson brands into the Far East. The results were impressive. Orders were secured for containers of "Mr. Big" and "Crispy Crunch" countlines from local distributors in Korea, Taiwan, and Japan. "Canadian Classics" boxed chocolates were developed for the vast Japanese gift ("Omiyagi") market. Total 1993 sales to these markets were projected to be $1.6 million.

For each of these markets, Neilson retained the responsibility for packaging design and product formulation. While distributors offered suggestions as to how products could be improved to suit local tastes, they were not formally obliged to do so. To secure distribution in Taiwan, Neilson had agreed to launch the "Mr. Big" bar under the distributor's private brand name "Bang Bang" which was expected to generate a favourable impression with consumers. Although sales were strong, Bateman realized that since consumer loyalty was linked to brand names, the brand equity being generated for "Bang Bang" ultimately, would belong to the distributor. This put the distributor in a powerful position from which they were able to place significant downward pressure on operating margins.

Market Evaluation Study

In response to these successful early exporting efforts Bateman began exploring the possible launch of Neilson brands into the United States (discussed later). With limited working capital and numerous export opportunities, it became obvious to the International Division that some kind of formal strategy was required to evaluate and to compare these new markets.

Accordingly, a set of weighted criteria was developed during the summer of 1992 to evaluate countries that were being considered by the International Division. (See Exhibit 5 for a profile of the world's major chocolate importers). The study was intended to provide a standard means of evaluating potential markets. Resources could then be allocated among those markets that promised long term incremental growth and those which were strictly opportunistic. While the revenues from opportunistic markets would contribute to the fixed costs of domestic production, the long term efforts could be pursued for more strategic reasons. By the end of the summer, the study had been applied to thirteen international markets, including the United States. (See Exhibit 6 for a summary of this study).

Meanwhile, Grenadier had added Hong Kong/China, Singapore and New Zealand to Neilson's portfolio of export markets, and Bateman had contracted a second local broker, CANCON Corp. Ltd, to initiate sales to the Middle East. By the end of 1992, the International Division comprised 9 people who had achieved penetration of 11 countries for export sales (See Exhibit 7 for a description of these markets).

THE U.S. EXPERIENCE

In 1991, the American chocolate confectionery market was worth U.S.$5.1 billion wholesale. Neilson had wanted to sneak into this vast market with the intention of quietly selling off excess capacity. However, as Bateman explained, the quiet U.S. launch became a Canadian celebration:

Next thing we knew, there were brands in the streets, Neilson t-shirts and baseball caps, and newspaper articles and T.V. specials describing our big U.S. launch!

The publicity greatly increased the pressure to succeed. After careful consideration, Pro Set, a collectible trading card manufacturer and marketer, was selected as a distributor. This relationship developed into a joint venture by which the Neilson Import Division was later appointed distributor of the Pro Set cards in Canada. With an internal sales management team, full distribution and invoicing infrastructures and a 45-broker national sales network, Pro Set seemed ideally suited to diversify into confectionery products.

Unfortunately, Pro Set quickly proved to be an inadequate partner in this venture. Although they had access to the right outlets, the confectionery selling task differed significantly form card sales. Confectionery items demand more sensitive product handling and a greater amount of sales effort by the Pro Set representatives who were used to carrying a self-promoting line.

To compound these difficulties, Pro Set sales plummeted as the trading-card market became over-saturated. Trapped by intense cashflow problems and increasing fixed costs, Pro Set filed for Chapter 11 bankruptcy, leaving Neilson with huge inventory losses and a customer base that associated them with their defunct distributor. Although it was tempting to attribute the U.S. failure to inappropriate partner selection, the U.S. had also ranked poorly relative to other markets in the criteria study that had just been completed that summer. In addition to their distribution problems, Neilson was at a serious disadvantage due to intense competition from the major industry players in the form of advertising expenditures, trade promotions and brand proliferation. Faced with duties and a higher cost of production, Neilson was unable to maintain price competitiveness.

The International Division was now faced with the task of internalizing distribution in the U.S., including sales management, broker contact, warehousing, shipping and collections. Neilson managed to reestablish a limited presence in the American market using several local brokers to target profitable niches. For example, they placed strong emphasis on vending-machine sales to increase product trial with minimal advertising. Since consumer purchasing patterns demanded product variety in vending-machines, Neilson's presence in this segment was not considered threatening by major competitors.

In the autumn of 1992, as the International Division made the changes necessary to salvage past efforts in the U.S., several options for entering the Mexican confectionery market were also being considered.

MEXICO

Neilson made the decision to enter the Mexican market late in 1992, prompted by its parent company's, Weston Foods Ltd., own investigations into possible market opportunities which would emerge as a result of the North American Free Trade Agreement (NAFTA). Mexico was an attractive market which scored very highly in the market evaluation study. Due to their favourable demographics (50% of the population was within the target age group), Mexico offered huge potential for countline sales. The rapid adoption of American tastes resulted in an increasing demand for U.S. snack foods. With only a limited number of competitors, the untapped demand afforded a window of opportunity for smaller players to enter the market.

Working through the Ontario Ministry of Agriculture and Food (OMAF), Neilson found two potential independent distributors:

Grupo Corvi a Mexican food manufacturer, operated seven plants and had an extensive sales force reaching local wholesalers. They also had access to a convoluted infrastructure which indirectly supplied and estimated 100,000 street vendor stands or kiosks (known as "tiendas" representing nearly 70% of the Mexican confectionery market. (This informal segment was usually overlooked by market research services and competitors alike.) Grupo Corvi currently had no American or European style countline products.

Grupo Hajj a Mexican distributor with some experience in confectionery, offered access to only a small number of retail stores. This limited network made Grupo Hajj relatively unattractive when compared to other distributors. Like Grupo Corvi, this local firm dealt exclusively in Mexican pesos, historically, a volatile currency. (In January 1993, 1 peso = $0.41 CAD.)

While considering these distributors, Neilson was approached by Sabritas, the snack food division of Pepsico Foods in Mexico, who felt that there was a strategic fit between their organizations. Although Sabritas had no previous experience handling chocolate confectionery, they had for six years been seeking a product line to round out their portfolio. They were currently each week supplying Frito-Lay type snacks directly to 450,000 retail stores and tiendas (The trade referred to such extensive customer networks as "numeric distribution"). After listening to the initial proposal, Neilson agreed to give Sabritas three months to conduct research into the Mexican market.

Although the research revealed strong market potential for the Neilson products, Bateman felt that pricing at 2

Handwritten at top: Don't go by company — just prod name.

pesos (at parity with other American style brands) would not provide any competitive advantage. Sabritas agreed that a one peso product, downsized to 40 grams (from a U.S.-Canadian standard of 43 to 65 grams), would provide an attractive strategy to offer "imported chocolate at Mexican prices".

Proposing a deal significantly different from the relationships offered by the two Mexican distributors, Sabritas intended to market the "Mr. Big", "Crispy Crunch" and "Malted Milk" bars as the first brands in the "Milch" product line. "Milch" was a fictitious word in Spanish, created and owned by Sabritas, and thought to denote goodness and health due to its similarity to the work "milk". Sabritas would offer Neilson 50% ownership of the Milch name, in exchange for 50% of Neilson's brand names, both of which would appear on each bar. As part of the joint branding agreement, Sabritas would assume all responsibility for advertising, promotion, distribution and merchandising. The joint ownership of the brand names would provide Sabritas with brand equity in exchange for building brand awareness through heavy investments in marketing. By delegating responsibility for all marketing efforts to Sabritas, Neilson would be able to compete on a scale not affordable by Canadian standards.

Under the proposal, all "Milch" chocolate bars would be produced in Canada by Neilson. Neilson would be the exclusive supplier. Ownership of the bars would pass to Sabritas once the finished goods have been shipped. Sabritas in turn would be responsible for all sales to final consumers. Sabritas would be the exclusive distributor. Consumer prices could not be changed without the mutal agreement of Neilson and Sabritas.

ISSUES

Bateman reflected upon the decision he now faced for the Mexican market. The speed with which Sabritas could help them gain market penetration, their competitive advertising budget, and their "store door access" to nearly a half million retailers were attractive advantages offered by this joint venture proposal. But what were the implications of omitting the Neilson name from their popular chocolate bars? Would they be exposed to problems like those encountered in Taiwan with the "Bang Bang" launch, especially considering the strength and size of Pepsico Foods?

The alternative was to keep the Neilson name and to launch their brands independently, using one of the national distributors. Unfortunately, limited resources meant that Neilson would develop its presence much more slowly. With countline demand in Mexico growing at 30% per year, could they afford to delay? Scott Begg had indicated that early entry was critical in burgeoning markets, since establishing market presence and gaining share were less difficult when undertaken before the major players had dominated the market and "defined the rules of play."

Bateman also questioned their traditional means of evaluating potential markets. Were the criteria considered in the market evaluation study really the key success factors, or were the competitive advantages offered through ventures with distributors more important? If partnerships were necessary, should Neilson continue to rely on independent, national distributors who were interested in adding Neilson brands to their portfolio, or should they pursue strategic partnerships similar to the Sabritas opportunity instead? No matter which distributor was chosen, product quality and handling were of paramount importance. Every chocolate bar reaching consumers, especially first time buyers, must be of the same freshness and quality as those distributed to Canadian consumers. How could this type of control best be achieved?

Handwritten: Freshness — Very important

EXHIBIT 1 World Chocolate Exports (Value as % of Total)–1990

	1987	1988	1989	1990
Africa	x1.5	x1.0	x1.1	x0.7
Americas	8.1	9.1	9.2	x9.1
LAIC[1]	2.1	1.9	1.4	x1.4
CACM[2]	0.1	x0.1	x0.1	x0.1
Asia	2.5	3.2	3.4	2.9
Middle East	x0.5	x0.5	x0.7	x0.4
Europe	86.4	85.0	84.2	85.4
EEC (12)[3]	73.3	71.8	71.3	73.5
EFTA[4]	12.5	12.7	12.1	11.5
Oceania	x1.5	1.8	x2.1	x1.8

Figures demoted with an "x" are provisional or estimated.
Adapted from: The United Nations' "International Trade Statistics yearbook", Vol. 11, 1990

[1]LAIC = Latin American Industrialists Association.
[2]CACM = Central American Common Market.
[3]EEC (12) = The twelve nations of the European Economic Community.
[4]EFTA = European Free Trade Association.

EXHIBIT 2 Single Bars Canadian Market Share: 1991–1992

Manufacturer	1992	1991
Neilson	28.1%	29.4%
Nestlé/Rowntree	26.9%	26.2%
Hershey/Lowney	21.6%	21.9%
M&M/Mars	18.7%	19.0%
Others	4.7%	3.5%

Source: Neilson News–Issue #1, 1993

EXHIBIT 3 Top Single Bars in Canada: 1991–1992

Top Single Bars	Manufacturer	1992	1991
Crispy Crunch	Neilson	1	1
Coffee Crisp	Nestlé/Rowntree	2	3
Kit Kat	Nestlé/Rowntree	3	2
Mars Bar	M&M/Mars	4	4
Caramilk	Cadbury Schweppes	5	6
Oh Henry!	Hershey/Lowney	6	5
Smarties	Nestlé/Rowntree	7	7
Peanut Butter Cups	Hershey/Lowney	8	8
Mr. Big	Neilson	9	11
Aero	Hershey/Lowney	10	10
Snickers	M&M/Mars	11	9
Crunchie	Cadbury Schweppes	12	12

Source: Neilson News–Issue #1, 1993

EXHIBIT 4 Canadian Confectionery Market–1993

	Dollars (millions)	%
Total Confectionery Category	$1,301.4	100.0
Gum	296.5	22.8
Boxed Chocolates	159.7	12.3
Cough Drops	77.0	5.9
Rolled Candy	61.3	4.7
Bagged Chocolates	30.3	2.3
Easter Eggs	22.0	1.7
Valentines	9.4	0.7
Lunch Pack	3.6	0.3
Countline Chocolate Bars	641.6	49.3
Total Chocolate Bar Market Growth	+8%	

Source: Neilson Marketing Department Estimates

EXHIBIT 5 World Chocolate Imports (Value as % of Total)–1990

	1987	1988	1989	1990
Africa	x0.7	x0.7	x0.7	x0.7
Americas	x15.6	x15.0	x13.9	x13.2
LAIC[1]	0.2	0.4	1.1	x1.3
CACM[2]	x0.1	x0.1	x0.1	x0.1
Asia	11.7	x13.9	15.6	12.9
Middle East	x3.5	x3.3	x3.9	x2.8
Europe	70.8	68.9	67.7	71.4
EEC (12)[3]	61.1	59.5	57.7	59.3
EFTA[4]	9.3	9.0	8.9	8.4
Oceania	x1.3	1.7	x2.1	x1.8

Figures demoted with an "x" are provisional or estimated.
Adapted from: The United Nations' "International Trade Statistics Yearbook", Vol. 11, 1990

[1]LAIC = Latin American Industrialists Association.
[2]CACM = Central American Common Market.
[3]EEC (12) = The twelve nations of the European Economic Community.
[4]EFTA = European Free Trade Association.

EXHIBIT 6   Summary of Criteria for Market Study (1992)

Criteria	Weight	Aust ralia	China	Hong Kong	Indo nesia	Japan	Korea	Malaysia	New Zealand	Sing- apore	Taiwan	Mexico	EEC	USA
U.S. Countline	-	4	4	4	4	4	4	4	4	4	4	4	4	4
1 Candybar Economics	30	20	20	30	20	20	28	20	15	25	15	20	10	10
2 Target Market	22	12.5	14	13	15.5	19	15	10	7	9.5	12.5	21	22	22
3 Competitor Dynamics	20	12	15	8	7.5	11	13.5	10	12	14.5	12	11	20	6.5
4 Distribution Access	10	9	4	4	3.5	5	6	6.5	9	3.5	7.5	9.5	9	9
5 Industry Economics	9	2.5	3.5	6	5.5	2	5	2.5	7	4.5	3	3.5	3.5	4.5
6 Product Fit	8	7	6	6	6	3	7.5	7.5	7.5	8	4	8	5	8
7 Payback	5	4	4	1	2.5	4	5	2.5	4	2	2	5	2	1
8 Country Dynamics	5	5	1	4	3	5	3.5	4.5	4.5	5	4	3	2	4
Total	109	72	67.5	72	63.5	69	83.5	63.5	66	72	60	81	73.5	65

Due to Neilson/Cadbury's limited resources, it was not feasible to launch the first western-style brands into new markets. The basic minimum criterion for a given market, therefore, was the presence of major western industry players (i.e., Mars or Hershey). Countries were then measured on the basis of 8 criteria which were weighted by the International Group according to their perceived importance as determinants of a successful market entry. (See above table). Each criterion was then subdivided into several elements as defined by the International Group, which allocated the total weighted score accordingly. (See table, right).

This illustration depicts a single criterion, subdivided and scored for Mexico.

Source: Company Records

Competitor Dynamics	Score	Mexico
Financial Success of Other Exporters	0-8	5
Nature (Passivity) of Competition	0-6	2.5
Brand Image (vs Price) Positioning	0-6	3.5
Score/20	20	11

EXHIBIT 7   Neilson Export Markets–1993

Agent (Commission)	Country	Brands
Grenadier International	Taiwan	Bang Bang
	Japan	Canadian Classics, Mr. Big, Crispy Crunch
	Korea	Mr. Big, Crispy Crunch
	Hong Kong/China	Mr. Big, Crispy Crunch, Canadian Classics
	Singapore	Mr. Big, Crispy Crunch
Cancon Corp. Ltd.	Saudi Arabia	Mr. Big, Crispy Crunch, Malted Milk
	Bahrain	Mr. Big, Crispy Crunch, Malted Milk
	U.A.E	Mr. Big, Crispy Crunch, Malted Milk
	Kuwait	Mr. Big, Crispy Crunch, Malted Milk
Neilson International	Mexico	Mr. Big, Crispy Crunch, Malted Milk
	U.S.A	Mr. Big, Crispy Crunch, Malted Milk

Source: Company Records

Metro Corporation: Technology Licensing Negotiation

Details of negotiations between Metro Corporation and Impecina Construcciones S.A. of Peru, for the licensing of Petroleum Tank Technology follow.

THE LICENSOR FIRM

Metro Corporation is a diversified steel rolling, fabricating, and construction company based in the Midwest and considers itself to be in a mature industry. Innovations are few and far between. With transport and tariff barriers, and the support given by many governments to their own companies, exporting as a means of doing foreign business is rather limited. Similarly, given the large investment, modest return, and political sensitivity of the industry, direct foreign investment is all but a closed option. In a global strategic sense then, Metro Corporation has far more frequently focused on licensing as a market entry method, with technologies confined to (1) processes and engineering peripheral to the basic steel-making process, for example, mining methods, coke oven door designs, galvanizing, and so on, and (2) applications of steel in construction and other industries, for example, petroleum tank design, welding methods, thermoadhesion, and so on.

All Metro's licensing is handled by its international division, International Construction and Engineering (ICE), which is beginning to develop a reputation in Western Europe and South America as a good source for specialized construction technology.

THE PROPOSED LICENSEE

Impecina, a private firm, is the largest construction company in Peru and operates throughout Latin America. Impecina has a broad range of interests including residential and commercial buildings, hydraulic works, transportation, and maritime works. Employing several thousand personnel, engineers and technicians, its sales had doubled in the last five years. It was still primarily a Peruvian business with most turnover in Peru, but was in the process of expanding into Colombia, the North African Mediterranean countries, and Argentina, Brazil, and Venezuela. Impecina has advanced computer capacity with a large IBM and other computers at their branches. In oil-storage tanks, Impecina experience was limited to the smaller fixed-cone roof designs under 150-feet diameter.

THE TECHNOLOGY

National Tank Inc., a fabrication division of Metro, had developed a computerized design procedure for floating-roof oil-storage tanks, which minimized the use of steel within American Petroleum Institute or any other oil industry standards. Particularly for the larger tanks, for instance, 150-feet diameter and above, this would confer upon the bidding contractor a significant cost advantage. National Tank had spent one labor-year at a direct cost of $225,000 to write the computer program alone. Patents were involved in an incidental manner, only for the seals on the floating roof. Metro had not bothered to file for this patent except in the United States.

THE MARKET

Peru's indigenous oil output is very low, but it imports and refines annually 50 million tons mostly for domestic demand. Following the escalation of oil prices and tightening of supplies in 1973, the Peruvian government determinedly set about to formulate a program to augment Peru's oil-storage capacity. Impecina's representatives at a preliminary meeting with ICE in U.S. headquarters said their government planned $200 million expenditures on oil-storage facilities over the next three years (mostly in large-sized tanks). Of this, Impecina's "ambition" was to capture a one-third market share. That this appeared to be a credible target was illustrated by their existing 30 percent share of the fixed-cone type under 150-feet diameter. Additionally, they estimated private-sector construction value over the next three years to total $40 million.

Approximately half of a storage system's construction cost goes for the tank alone, the remainder being excavation, foundation, piping, instrumentation, and other ancillary equipment, all of which Impecina's engineers were very familiar with.

Neighboring Colombia was building a 12 million ton refinery, but the tank installation plans of other South American nations were not known, according to the Impecina representative.

Each of Impecina's competitors in Peru for this business were affiliated with a prominent company: Umbertomas with Jefferson Inc. in the United States, Zapa with Philadelphia Iron & Steel, Cosmas with Peoria-Duluth Construction Inc., and so on. Thus, association with Metro would help Impecina in bidding.

THE FIRST MEETING

National Tank had in the past year bid jointly with Impecina on a project in southern Peru. Though that bid was unsuccessful, Impecina had learned about Metro's computerized design capabilities and initiated a formal first round of negotiations, which were to lead to a licensing agreement. The meeting took place in the United States. Two Impecina executives of subdirector rank were accompanied by an American consultant. Metro was represented by the vice president of ICE, the ICE attorney, and an executive from National Tank.

Minutes of this meeting show it was exploratory. Both genuine and rhetorical questions were asked. Important information and perceptions were exchanged and the groundwork laid for concluding negotiations. Following is a bare summary of important issues from the somewhat circular discussion:

1. *Licensee Market Coverage:* Impecina tried to represent itself as essentially a Peruvian firm. It reviewed its government expenditure plans and its hoped-for market share. Yet through the meeting, there kept cropping up the issue of the license also covering Libya, Algeria, Morocco, Colombia, Argentina, Brazil, and Venezuela.

2. *Exclusivity:* For Peru, Metro negotiators had no difficulty conceding exclusivity. They mentioned that granting exclusivity to a licensee for any territory was agreeable in principle, provided a minimum performance guarantee was given. At this, the question was deferred for future discussion. At one point a Metro executive remarked, "We could give Impecina a nonexclusive—and say, for example, we wouldn't give another (licensee) a license for one year (in those nations)," proposing the idea of a trial period for Impecina to generate business in a territory.

3. *Agreement Life:* Impecina very quickly agreed to a ten-year term, payment in U.S. dollars, and other minor issues.

4. *Trade Name:* The Impecina negotiators placed great emphasis on their ability to use

Metro's name in bidding, explaining how their competition in Peru had technical collaboration with three U.S. companies (as noted previously). "Did that mean Metro's National Tank Division could compete with Impecina in Peru?" they were asked rhetorically. (Actually both sides seem to have tacitly agreed that it was not possible for Metro to do business directly in Peru.)

5. *Licensee Market Size:* Attention turned to the dollar value of the future large (floating-roof) tank market in Peru. Impecina threw out an estimate of $200 million government expenditures and $40 million private-sector spending, over the coming three years, of which they targeted a one-third share. Later, a lower market-size estimate of $150 million (government and private) with a share of $50 million received by Impecina over three years was arrived at (memories are not clear on how the estimates were revised). "Will Impecina guarantee us they will obtain one-third of the market?" brought the response "That's an optimistic figure that we hope we can realize." Impecina offered as evidence their existing one-third share of the "fixed roof under 150 feet" market, an impressive achievement.

6. *Product Mix Covered by License:* It became clear that Impecina wanted floating-roof technology for all sizes, and fixed roof over 100-feet diameter. They suggested the agreement cover tanks over 100 feet in size. Impecina was asked if it would pay on all tanks (of any size) to simplify royalty calculation and monitoring. After considerable discussion, Metro seems to have acceded to Impecina's proposal (to cover both types, only over 100 feet) based on consensus over three points.

a. The competition probably does not pay (its licensors) on small tanks and, therefore, Impecina would be at a disadvantage if it had to pay on small tanks also.

b. The market in floating-roof tanks was usually over 100 feet.

c. Impecina claimed that customers normally dictate the dimensions of the tanks, so Impecina cannot vary them in order to avoid paying a royalty to Metro.

7. *Compensation Formula:* Metro proposed an initial lump-sum payment (in two installments, one when the agreement is signed, the second on delivery of the computer program and designs), plus engineers and executives for bid assistance on a per diem rate, plus a royalty on successful bids based on the barrel capacity installed by Impecina. Impecina's American consultant countered with the idea of royalties on a sliding scale, lower with larger-capacity tanks, indicating talk about "1 million barrel capacity tanks." The (rhetorical?) question about Peru's oil capacity seems to have brought the discussion down to earth and veered it off on a tangent, while both sides mentally regrouped.

On returning to this topic, Impecina executives ventured that as a rule of thumb their profit markup on a turn-key job was 6 percent. (However, on excluding the more price-sensitive portions such as excavation, piping, and ancillary equipment, which typically constitute half the value, Impecina conceded that on the tank alone they might mark up as much as 12 percent, although they kept insisting 5 to 6 percent was enough.)

Impecina executives later offered only royalties (preferably sliding) and per diem fees for bid assistance from Metro executives and engineers.

Metro countered by pointing out that per diem fees of $225 plus travel costs amounted at best to recovering costs, not profit.

The compensation design question was left at this stage, deferred for later negotiation, the broad outlines having been laid. Metro's starting formal offer, which would mention specific numbers, was to be telexed to Lima in a week.

8. *The Royalty Basis:* Metro entertained the idea that Impecina engineers were very

familiar with excavation, piping, wiring, and other ancillary equipment. Metro was transferring technology for the tank alone, which typically comprised half of overall installed value.

9. *Government Intervention:* Toward the end of the discussions, Impecina brought up the question of the Peruvian government having to approve of the agreement. This led to their retreat from the idea of a ten-year term agreed to earlier, and Impecina then mentioned five years. No agreement was reached. (Incidentally, Peru had in the last two years passed legislation indicating a "guideline" of five years for foreign licenses.)

INTERNAL DISCUSSION IN METRO LEADING TO THE FORMAL OFFER

The advantages derived by the licensee would be acquisition of floating-roof technology, time and money saved in attempting to generate the computerized design procedure in house, somewhat of a cost and efficiency advantage in bidding on larger tanks, and finally the use of Metro's name.

It was estimated that National Tank had spent $225,000 (one labor-year = two executives for six months, plus other costs) in developing the computer program. Additionally, it may cost $40,000 (three-quarters of a labor-year) to convert the program into Spanish, the metric system, and adapt it to the material availability and labor cost factors peculiar to Peru. Simultaneously, there would be semiformal instruction of Impecina engineers in the use of the program, petroleum industry codes, and Metro fabrication methods. All this had to be done before the licensee would be ready for a single bid.

It was visualized that Metro would then assist Impecina for two labor-weeks for each bid preparation, and four labor-weeks on successful receipt of a contract award. Additionally, if Metro's specialized construction equipment were used, three labor-months of on-site training would be needed.

As the licensee's personnel moved along their learning curve, assistance of the type just described would diminish until it was no longer needed after a few successful bids.

Additional considerations that went into a determination of the initial offer:

1. Metro obligations (and sunk costs) in development and conversion were fairly determinate, whereas their obligations to assist Impecina in bidding depended on the technical sophistication and absorbtive capacity of the licensee's engineers, their success rate in bidding, and so on.

2. If Impecina's market estimates were used, over the next three yers, they would generate large tank orders worth $50 million, on which they would make a profit of $3 million (at 6 percent on $50 million or 12 percent on half the amount).

3. The market beyond three years was an unknown.

4. Exclusive rights might be given to Impecina in Peru and Colombia, with perhaps ICE reserving the right of conversion to nonexclusive if minimum market share was not captured.

5. While Impecina's multinational expansion plans were unknown, their business in the other nations was too small to justify granting them exclusivity. They may be satisfied with a vague promise of future consideration as an exclusive licensee in those territories.

6. Metro would try to meet an agreement term of ten years. It was felt that Impecina computer and engineering capability was strong enough so they would not need Metro assistance after a few bids.

Surprisingly, the discussions reveal no explicit consideration given to the idea that Impecina may emerge some day as a multinational competitor.

In view of the uncertainty about how successful the licensee would actually be in securing orders, the uncertainty surrounding the Peruvian government's attitude, a safe strategy seemed to be to try and get as large a front-end fee as possible. Almost arbitrarily, a figure of $400,000 was thrown up. (This was roughly 150 percent of the development costs plus the initial costs of transferring the technology to the licensee.) There would be sufficient margin for negotiations and to cover uncertainties. In order that the licensee's competitiveness not be diminished by the large lump-sum fee, a formula as described later may be devised whereby the first five years' royalties could be reduced.

THE FORMAL OFFER

The formal offer communicated in a telex a week later called for the following payment terms:

- ▶ $400,000 lump-sum fee payable in two installments.

- ▶ A 2 percent royalty on any tanks constructed of a size over 100-feet diameter, with up to one half of royalties owed in each of the first five years reduced by an amount up to $40,000 each year, without carryovers from year to year. The royalty percentage would apply to the total contract value less excavation, foundation, dikes, piping, instrumentation, and pumps.

- ▶ Agreement life of ten years.

- ▶ Metro to provide services to Impecina described earlier in consideration of the lump-sum and royalty fees.

- ▶ For additional services, as described earlier, Metro would provide on request personnel paid up to $225 per day, plus travel and living costs while away from their place of business. The per diem rates would be subject to escalation based on a representative cost index. There would be a ceiling placed on the number of labor-days Impecina could request in any year.

- ▶ All payments to be made in U.S. dollars, net, after all local withholding, and other taxes.

- ▶ Impecina would receive exclusive rights for Peru and Colombia only, and nonexclusive rights for Morocco, Libya, Algeria, Argentina, Venezuela, and Brazil. These could be converted to an exclusive basis on demonstration of sufficient business in the future. For Peru and Colombia, Metro reserves the right to treat the agreement as nonexclusive if Impecina fails to get at least 30 percent of installed capacity of a type covered by the agreement.

- ▶ Impecina would have the right to sublicense only to any of its controlled subsidiaries.

- ▶ Impecina would supply free of charge to ICE all improvements made by it on the technology during the term of the agreement.

- ▶ Impecina would be entitled to advertise its association with Metro in assigned territories on prior approval of ICE as to wording, form, and content.

THE FINAL AGREEMENT

ICE executives report that the Peruvians "did not bat an eyelid" at their demands, and that an agreement was soon reached in a matter of weeks. The only significant change was Metro agreeing to take a lump sum of $300,000 (still a large margin over costs). In return, the provision for reducing one half of the royalties up to $40,000 per year was *dropped*. The final agreement called for a straight 2 percent royalty payment (on tank value alone, as before). Other changes were minor: Impecina to continue to receive benefit of further R&D; ICE to provide at cost a construction engineer if specialized welding equipment was used; the per diem fee fixed at $200 per day (indexed by an average hourly wage escalation factor used by the U.S. Department of Labor); and the $300,000 lump-sum fee to be paid in installments over the first year.

In other respects such as territory, royalty rate, exclusivity, travel allowances, and so on, the agreement conformed with Metro's initial offer.

AN UPSET

The Peruvian government disallowed a ten-year agreement life. By then, both parties had gone too far to want to reopen the entire negotiations and Metro appears to have resigned itself to an agreement life of five years, with a further extension of another five years subject to mutual consent. Given Impecina's in-house engineering and computer capability, extension of the agreement life was a very open question.

▼ DISCUSSION QUESTIONS

Analyze the negotiations from each party's perspective:

1. List what each party is offering and what it hopes to receive.

2. Identify the elements in each list that are "musts" and those where flexibility may be shown, and state why.

3. Describe negotiating tactics or ploys each party used or could have used.

4. Compute net cash flows for each party under several scenarios. For example:

   a. Licensee fails to get a single order.

   b. Licensee gets one-third market share in Peru for three years, no orders thereafter, and no orders in any other nation.

   c. Licensee gets one-third share in Peru for ten years and half again as much in business in other nations, and so forth.

5. Compute the share of net present value of profits that each of the two parties will capture under various market scenarios.

6. What do you think of the rule of thumb, encountered in licensing literature, that licensors should settle for roughly one quarter to one half of the licensee's incremental profit?

7. a. Are sunk costs relevant here?

   b. What, if any, are the opportunity costs?

   c. In computing the licensor's cash flows, remember that in addition to the direct costs of implementing an agreement, there are sometimes substantial indirect costs. What are they? How would you apply the licensor's development costs to this exercise?

8. Why did the licensee accept the offer (with small changes) without "batting an eyelid"? (Hint: Calculate break-even sales for both parties.)

9. Should the licensor have threatened to pull out when the government limited the agreement life to five years? (Hint: Recalculate question 5 under a five-year limit.)

10. Do you think the licensee knew this all along?

11. Discuss the role of government intervention in licensing negotiations in general.

Odysseus, Inc. (The Decision to Go "International")

She faced him waiting. And Odysseus came, debating inwardly what he should do; embrace this beauty's knees in supplication or stand apart and use honeyed speech, inquire the way to town and beg some clothing? In his swift reckoning, he thought it best to trust in words to please her—and keep away; he might anger the girl, touching her knees.

HOMER, *THE ODYSSEY*, BOOK SIX, *"THE PRINCESS AT THE RIVER," ROBERT FITZGERALD TRANS.*

In early 1991, Mr. Donald R. Odysseus, president of the Odysseus Manufacturing Company of Kansas City, Kansas, was actively considering the possibilities of major expansion of the firm's currently limited international activities and the form and scale such expansion might take.

Odysseus was founded in 1926 by Edward Odysseus as a small machine shop. By 1991, the head office and production facilities of the company were located in a 500,000-square-foot modern factory on a 30-acre site near the original location. Odysseus products were sold throughout the United States and Canada. In 1990, net sales were over $83,800,000 while after-tax profits were about $4,835,000. In early 1990, Odysseus employed just over 1,000 people, and its stock was held by 1,000 shareholders. (The company's 1990 income statement and balance sheet are given in Tables 1 and 2.)

Odysseus produced a line of coupling and clutches including flange, compression, gear type, flex pin, and flexible disc couplings, and overrunning and multiple disc clutches. In all, the company manufactured about 600 different sizes and types of its eight standard items. The company's single most important product was the Odysseus Flexible Coupling, which its research department had developed in 1985 and which, produced in about 70 different sizes and combinations, now accounted for one-third of Odysseus's sales. Odysseus held patents throughout the world on its flexible coupling as well as several other devices. By 1991, Odysseus had carved itself a secure niche in the clutch and couplings market, despite the competition in this market of larger firms with widely diversified product lines.

Odysseus was not dependent on any single customer or industry. Sales were made through distributors to original equipment manufacturers for use in small motor drives for a wide range of products including machine tools, test gear, conveyors, farm implements, mining equipment, hoisting equipment, cranes, shovels, and so on. No more than 10 percent of its output went to any single industry; its largest single customer took less than 4 percent of production. Speaking generally, Odysseus couplings and clutches were used more by small- and medium-sized producers of general-purpose equipment than by large manufacturers of highly automated machines. Odysseus's sales manager believed that demand for the company's couplings and clutches would benefit from continuation of a long-term trend toward increased installation of labor-saving equipment in medium enterprises. This trend and the breadth of its market had provided some protection against cyclical fluctuations in business activities. During the period 1977 to 1990, sales had increased from $32 million to over $84 million; the largest annual decline during the period had been 8 percent, while in the most recent recession year sales had actually increased by 5 percent.

TABLE 1 Consolidated Income Statement, Year Ending December 31, 1990 (in thousands of dollars)

Income		
Net sales	$84,700	
Royalties, interest, and other income	174	
	$84,874	$84,874
Costs and expenses		
Cost of goods sold	$54,019	
Depreciation	1,773	
Selling, administrative, and general expense	18,845	
Interest on long-term debt	219	
	$74,856	$74,856
Income before income taxes		10,018
Federal taxes on income (estimated)		5,157
Net income		$4,861

TABLE 2 Balance Sheet, December 31, 1990 (in thousands of dollars)

Assets		
Cash	5,667	
Marketable securities	3,688	
Accounts receivable	6,399	
Inventories	25,578	
Total current assets	41,332	41,332
Investments and other assets		1,351
Property, plant, and equipment (net)		23,177
Total assets		65,860
Liabilities		
Accounts payable	2,015	
Dividends payable	745	
Accruals	3,394	
Federal income tax liability (estimated)	3,752	
Installment on long-term debt	277	
Total current liabilities	10,183	10,183
Long term debt (20-year 67/8% notes, final maturity 1987)		5,051
Preferred stock		6,370
Common stock and retained earnings		44,256
Total liabilities		65,860

The company's commercial objective was to operate as a specialist in a product field in which its patents and distinctive skills would give it a strong competitive position. In the past, the company had experimented with various products outside its coupling and clutch line; it had tried to make components for egg-candling machinery, among other things. The investment in these products was initially considered a means of more efficiently utilizing the company's forging and machining capacity, but the firm had not been particularly successful. The Odysseus management had come to the conclusion that it should concentrate its efforts on its line of couplings and clutches; and in 1991, Mr. Odysseus stated the company's corporate objectives explicitly as being a coupling and clutch manufacturer. New investments were made to develop better products within this field, and to open new markets for Odysseus products.

Odysseus's production and assembly facilities were located in its modern factory near Kansas City, Kansas. The site offered ample room for expansion and was well located for both rail and highway transportation. The company maintained warehousing facilities in Boston, Jersey City, Atlanta, Columbus, Ohio, and Oakland, California. The scale economies stemming from concentrating production in one factory can be seen from the following examples. One of the company's largest selling items, product K-2A (a flexible coupling component) produced in lots of 750, cost $5.19 each; in lots of 1,200, $4.22 each. The incremental 450 units produced after the initial 750, therefore, cost only $2.60 each. Put differently, on this particular product, a 50 percent cost saving could be realized on the marginal production from the 750-unit level to the 1,200-unit level. Although specific cost savings from higher volume varied among its products a fundamental characteristic of Odysseus's cost structure was that marginal cost typically was significantly less than average cost and that important economies of scale could be obtained by achieving larger lot sizes and longer production runs.

Odysseus's cost structure was, of course, dictated by its manufacturing process. In the first of three major steps in the manufacture of couplings or clutches, steel bars or tubing were cut and forged. Apart from the unit cost reductions stemming from more complete utilization of the existing forging facilities, economies of scale in this department were limited. Second, the forged steel pieces were machined to close tolerances in the machine shop. Here costs varied significantly with lot sizes. For most products, the choice among two or three alternative methods of production depended on the lot size. If a large lot size were indicated, special-purpose automatic machines with large setup costs and lower variable unit costs were used. Smaller lot sizes were produced on general-purpose turret and engine lathes where setup time was less but unit costs were higher.

Typically, production of smaller lot sizes was more labor intensive than the larger runs. For example, one operator running three automatic machines could perform all the boring and cutting operations on 300 2½-inch coupling flange units in an hour. The same out-put on general-purpose lathes and boring machines would require about six person-hours. To set up the automatic machines required a day and a half, however, while the lathes could be set up in about two hours. Furthermore, the burden charge on the automatics was considerably higher. On the other hand, the cost of the third step, assembly, did not vary under different lot sizes. (Table 3 presents a breakdown of the costs of some representative components.)

Mr. Odysseus regarded Odysseus's U.S. and Canadian market position as a strong one. The patented Odysseus Flexible Coupling possessed unique characteristics that no other coupling device duplicated, and many other Odysseus products served special functions not performed by competitive devices. Of course, other coupling and clutch systems competed with Odysseus, but no single company could be said to compete directly by introducing an identical product line. Mr. Odysseus estimated that Odysseus accounted for roughly 10 percent of total sales of its products in the American market and that was ample room for Odysseus to expand its sales in this domestic market as the total market grew and through an increase in its share of industry sales. Odysseus products were sold by distributors who generally, but not always, carried the entire line of Odysseus couplings and clutches. These distributor organizations were complemented by a 45-person Odysseus sales force.

TABLE 3 Typical Variation of Production Costs with Lot Sizes Product N-15Cl

Operation	Lots of 150	Lots of 400
I. Foundry	$51.67	$51.67
II. Machine Shop		
1. Boring	55.67	32.69
2. Turning	14.17	11.43
3. Facing	19.79	16.25
4. Drilling	32.23	26.30
5. Turning	18.95	15.41
6. Facing	19.95	14.76
7. Finishing	18.76	18.76
8. Finishing	17.95	18.24
III. Assembly	7.96	7.96
	257.10	$213.49

Product L-36G:
  Lots of 3: $108.6 each
  Lots of 4: $90.6 each

In 1990, export sales were $1,353,862, on which the company made a $161,174 operating profit. Although export sales had never been actively solicited, a small but steady stream of orders for export trickled into the Kansas City sales office. These orders were always filled expeditiously, but the active exploitation of export markets was considered too difficult in view of the barriers of language, custom, and currency. Furthermore, although he recognized that foreign wages were increasing more rapidly than those in the United States, Mr. Odysseus had always believed that Odysseus could not compete in export markets because its costs in Kansas City were too high. Also, tariffs imposed on Odysseus products by foreign governments were typically 10 percent ad valorem or higher.

Odysseus sold all products on flat price basis (F.O.B. warehouse) to all customers. In competing with other suppliers of similar products, Odysseus stressed delivery time, quality, service, and merchandising, but not price.

In its management's view, improvements in its products or in delivery or service promised more than temporary competitive advantage. Price-cutting moves, in contrast, would likely be matched by competitors the same day. No added sales would be gained, and total revenues would be cut. The company's export pricing policy was identical to its domestic policy. This meant that the foreign importer paid the U.S. F.O.B. price plus freight and import duties.

Along with filling orders, Odysseus's activities outside the United States and Canada consisted of a licensing agreement with an English coupling manufacturer. In 1985, on a vacation trip in England, where Odysseus's vice president in charge of engineering had spent his youth, he met the chairperson of Siren Ltd. of Manchester. Siren, a manufacturer of related equipment with sales of $14.6 million in 1984, was anxious to diversify by adding other power transmission products. Consequently, Siren became interested in several Odysseus patents, particularly those on the Odysseus Flexible Coupling. In late 1985, Odysseus granted the English concern an exclusive 15-year license to manufacture and sell all present and future Odysseus products in the United Kingdom. The licensing arrangement specifically defined the United Kingdom to include England, Scotland, Wales, and Northern Ireland. Siren was granted also a nonexclusive license to sell products produced from Odysseus patents in all other countries except the United States, Canada, Mexico, and France. The terms of the license agreement stipulated a 1.5 percent royalty on the ex-factory sales price of all products in which devices manufactured from Odysseus patents were incorporated. The 1990 royalty income from Siren amounted to $128,939 and was expected to rise to $161,174 in 1991.

Mr. Odysseus had noted Siren's success with considerable interest. The royalty payments were a welcome addition to Odysseus income, especially since they had not necessitated any additional investment. Mr. Odysseus felt that the licensee was receiving very generous profits from this deal, as Siren had almost tripled its sales (which by 1990 were equivalent to $35.5 million) during its five-year association with Odysseus and its equity had appreciated many times the total royalties of about $483,522 that Odysseus had received.

During the five years Odysseus and Siren had worked together, however, the English firm had made it understood that in general it considered its territory to be the Eastern Hemisphere, while Odysseus's was in the Western Hemisphere. Siren was especially interested in the German market for couplings and clutches and was a licensee of a German brake shoe manufacturer.

In addition, Odysseus had a licensing agreement on the same terms (1.5 percent royalty) with Scylla, S.A. Scylla was a medium-sized French manufacturer of clutches and complementary lines located near Paris. The company was financially sound and well headed by a young and aggressive management team. Scylla had been granted an exclusive license in France and a nonexclusive license in Belgium to sell products incorporating Odysseus-patented devices. Odysseus had entered the agreement during 1989 for an initial period of ten years. Royalty income in 1990, the first full year of operation in France, had totaled roughly $32,200. Odysseus expected a doubling of this figure in 1991.

In February 1991, M. Scylla, the president of the French firm, had proposed to Mr. Odysseus a closer association of their two companies. M. Scylla was anxious to expand his operations and needed capital to do this. He, therefore, proposed that Odysseus form a joint venture with Scylla. According to the terms of the proposal, Odysseus would bring $645,000 into the joint venture, paid in cash, while Scylla would provide a 40,000-square-foot plant, equipment, a national distribution system, and managerial personnel. Scylla S.A. would cease to exist as a corporate entity; its expanded organization and plant would become Scylla Odysseus, S.A. (SOSA). The original owners of Scylla, S.A. (the Scylla family) would own 60 percent of SOSA, and their return would be in the form of dividends plus salaries of members of the Scylla family employed by SOSA. Odysseus would own 40 percent of SOSA and, for tax reasons, would receive fees and royalties rather than dividends totaling 5 percent of the ex-factory price of all products incorporating Odysseus patents.

Mr. Odysseus thought that he should give this proposal serious attention. The French market for couplings looked very attractive. Moreover, the geographical lo-cation of SOSA within the European Community would make it possible to supply the even larger German market from the SOSA plant near Paris. M. Scylla had indicated that he considered Germany a primary target for future expansion.

So far, Odysseus had not actively pursued business leads in Germany in spite of several inquiries about licensing from German companies. Odysseus even had the possibility of acquiring an existing German manufacturer of couplings, Charybdis Metallfabrik GmbH (CMF) of Kassel. Mr. Odysseus had learned that CMF's aging owner-managers were anxious to sell their equity interest in the company but would stay on in managerial capacity. Odysseus's British licensee, Siren, had made it clear, however, that although it had no sizable business in Germany, it considered this market to be in Siren's sales territory and a move into Germany by Odysseus without Siren an "unfriendly act." In the light of Odysseus's growing royalty income from Siren, Mr. Odysseus did not want to antagonize the British licensee.

Mr. Odysseus had no ready means of precisely quantifying the market potential for clutches and couplings in Germany and in France. He knew, however, that the total market for Odysseus's "type L" couplings in the United States was $72.5 million in 1990, or 14 percent of the U.S. market. Odysseus assumed that the coupling market in France was correlated with sales of durable equipment in France, which were 12 percent of the U.S. total. The French type-L coupling market, therefore, would be $8.7 million a year, of which SOSA should expect to capture 14 percent, or $1,218,000. Similarly in Germany, durable equipment sales were 20 percent of those in the United States. The type-L coupling market could, therefore, be expected to be about $14.5 million, of which a company using Odysseus patents and know-how should obtain between 10 percent and 15 percent. Sales of comparable lines by both Scylla, S.A. and CMF appeared to justify these estimates; Scylla had sold $870,000 of a device closely comparable to the type-L coupling, or 10 percent of the assumed French market, and CMF had sold $1,160,000 of virtually the same device, or 8 percent of the assumed German market.

In 1991, the European market with its accelerating pace of industrial development and mechanization appeared to offer great opportunities for Odysseus. Mr. Odysseus, therefore, was most anxious to capitalize on these opportunities, presumably by manufacturing in Europe in cooperation with a European firm. He saw three reasons why Odysseus should expand its foreign operations.

First, the corporate objectives of focusing on a single line of products sold in as large a market as possible—the policy of area instead of products diversification—dictated expansion into markets outside the United States and Canada. The nature of the demand for Odysseus's products appeared to limit near-term sales potential in less developed areas but especially in Europe. Odysseus couplings and clutches appeared to find ready acceptance. Proof of this seemed to be contained in Siren's success in the United Kingdom.

Second, an important improvement on the Odysseus multiple disc clutch had been the result of European research. Mr. Odysseus felt that by becoming an active participant in the European market, the company could obtain valuable recent innovations that would be important to its competitive position in the United States. There was considerable activity in the clutch and coupling field in Europe, and Mr. Odysseus wanted to be in touch with the latest developments in the industry.

Third, Mr. Odysseus was seriously worried about the trend of costs in his Kansas City plant. He had heard that a French firm was planning to invest in a manufacturing plant in Mexico where wages were 16 percent of those in the United States. How could Odysseus compete against this kind of cost advantage? Ultimately, Odysseus might have to follow the lead of U.S. watch and bicycle firms and perform much of its manufacturing abroad and import parts, or even finished products, into the United States. At the present time, Mr. Odysseus felt that there was some reluctance on the part of American manufacturers to buy foreign couplings and clutches, and foreign competition was virtually nil in this market in 1991. But Mr. Odysseus was worried about the future and wanted to preserve Odysseus's competitive position by assuring a foreign source of supply. Also, the company would be in a better position to withstand exorbitant demands from the local labor union if it possessed alternative manufacturing facilities.

Before definitely deciding whether Odysseus should become more deeply involved in foreign operations, Mr. Odysseus wanted to review the ways this might be done. First, Odysseus could establish foreign markets by expanding export sales. Mr. Odysseus believed, however, that Odysseus's costs might be too high for it to compete successfully on this basis. Second, the company could enter into additional licensing agreements. This it had done with Siren in England and Scylla in France, but there was a definite ceiling on the possible profit potential from exclusive use of this method. Third, the company could enter joint ventures with a firm already established in foreign markets. Presumably, Odysseus would supply capital and know-how and the foreign firms would supply personnel (both local managerial skill and a labor force), market outlets, and familiarity with the local business climate. This approach appeared particularly promising to Mr. Odysseus. Finally, the company could establish wholly-owned foreign subsidiaries. Mr. Odysseus saw formidable barriers to such action, since Odysseus lacked managerial skill in foreign operations. They were unfamiliar with foreign markets and business practices. They did not have executives to spare from the Kansas City operations who might learn the intricacies of foreign business, and the development of wholly-owned operations from scratch would require significant investment of time and money.

As he reflected on these issues, he looked at a set of tables on global trade, productivity, output, and wages (Appendices I to III) and decided to attempt to comprehend what, if any, significance the data in these tables had for Odysseus. Mr. Odysseus recognized that certain deep-seated ideas of his tended to make him predisposed toward active development of overseas business. These included a view that his business should not shrink from difficult tasks—organizations, he believed, couldn't stand still—the choice was one of moving forward or falling backward. He considered "taking the plunge" into less familiar areas and learning from the experience was generally preferable to long-extended and expensive inquiry before taking action. Nonetheless, he wanted to be sure that the most basic issues related to expansion overseas by Odysseus were thought through before firm decisions were made.

▼ DISCUSSION QUESTIONS

1. Should Odysseus expand international business operations?

2. Rightly or wrongly, Odysseus management has decided in the affirmative. What form should these operations take? What *scope* will be required for Odysseus's international activities to achieve success? Possible forms, which in turn may be combined, include (a) exporting, (b) licensing, (c) joint ventures, and (d) wholly-owned subsidiaries, either by starting them from scratch or by acquiring one or more existing companies. This decision should take into account Odysseus's capabilities (as determined, for example, by its products, its capital and labor strength, and its marketing and research needs) as well as the industry's competitive requirements and foreign conditions, such as trade and business barriers, the number and sizes of countries to be covered, and political and business risk.

3. Evalute the arrangement with Siren, particularly the following questions:

   a. What assumptions were in Mr. Odysseus's mind when he concluded the licensing arrangement with Siren?

   b. Do you consider it a success?

   c. How does the timing of this arrangement fit into Odysseus's overall business strategy?

4. Evaluate the Scylla, S.A. proposal and the Charybdis possibility.

5. Recommend a global strategic plan to Mr. Odysseus.

Global Trade and Investment

Exports and Imports of the World to and from the Areas Listed (in Millions of U.S. Dollars)

	Exports (F.O.B.)			Imports (C.I.F.)		
	1988	*1989*	*1990*	*1988*	*1989*	*1990*
Areas						
IFS World Total (US$ Bi)	2,699.3	2,913.8	3,325.0	2,774.8	3,009.4	3,455.0
DOTS World Total	2,693.4	2,912.8	3,339.6	2,773.8	3,002.2	3,450.6
Ind. Countries (US$ Bi)	1,958	2,118	2,449	2,016.1	2,160.9	2,500.1
Developing Countries	689,839	744,726	835,509	746,592	832,674	935,954
Africa	64,507	65,103	73,846	66,131	74,466	86,196
Asia	342,136	381,836	433,172	362,822	403,131	456,448
Europe*	80,139	83,095	95,105	84,684	85,714	86,086
Middle East	99,008	100,572	105,801	103,082	124,568	150,387
Western Hemisphere†	104,048	114,120	127,585	129,874	144,794	156,837
USSR and selected other countries n.i.e.††	81,676	86,095	73,905	78,319	78,997	68,476
Memorandum Items						
EEC (US$ Bi)	1,043	1,125	1,357	1,058	1,122	1,359
Triad** (US$ Bi)	1,740	1,881	2,182	1,780	1,909	2,208
Oil Exporting Countries	96,543	98,488	108,864	132,497	160,121	195,419
Nonoil Developing Countries	593,296	646,238	726,646	614,095	672,553	740,535
Annual Percent Change						
World	14.4	8.1	14.7	14.6	8.2	14.9
Industrial Countries	13.2	8.2	15.7	14.9	7.2	15.7
Developing Countries	18.1	8.0	12.2	14.1	11.5	12.4
Africa	12.1	0.9	13.4	5.9	12.6	15.8
Asia	29.0	11.6	13.4	22.5	11.1	13.2
Europe	5.7	3.7	14.5	11.4	1.2	0.4
Middle East	7.4	1.6	5.2	−3.1	20.8	20.7
Western Hemisphere	11.4	9.7	11.8	15.1	11.5	8.3
USSR and selected other countries n.i.e.	14.8	5.4	−14.1	8.5	0.9	−13.2

† Latin America, Greenland, Netherland Antilles, and other not spec.
DOTS = Direction of Trade Statistics.
IFS = International Financial Statistics.
* Defined as: Albania, Bulgaria, Cuba, East Germany, the Mongolian Republic, North Korea, Czechoslovakia, and the USSR, which are not included in the world trade table published in the IFS.
†† In the absence of a more suitable term that would conveniently cover the countries included in the third category (Europe), they are referred as USSR and selected other countries n.i.e.

▶ APPENDIX II

Global Productivity, Investment, and Output

Gross Output Per Worker, 1986 – 1990 (as a Percentage of World Total)

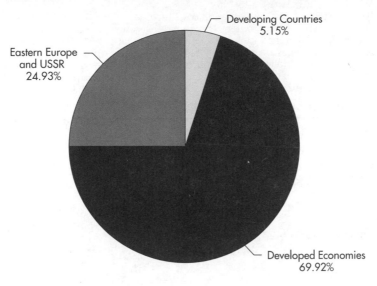

Source: Prepared by author.

Productivity and Investment in the World Economy, 1971–1990 (Thousands of 1980 Dollars)

	1971–75	1976–80	1981–85	1986–90
Gross Product per Worker				
Developed market economies	20.2	22.2	23.0	25.8
Eastern Europe and USSR	6.0	7.3	8.2	9.2
Developing Countries of which:	1.5	1.7	1.8	1.9
Africa	1.8	2.0	1.8	1.8
Asia, exluding West Asia	0.6	0.8	0.9	1.2
Latin America, and Caribbean	5.4	6.0	5.9	5.8
World	5.5	6.0	6.2	6.6
Investment per Worker				
Developed market economies	5.1	5.2	5.1	6.2
Eastern Europe and USSR	1.9	2.3	2.3	2.4
Developing Countries of which:	0.3	0.4	0.5	0.5
Africa	0.4	0.5	0.4	0.3
Asia, exluding West Asia	0.2	0.2	0.3	0.4
Latin America, and Caribbean	1.2	1.5	1.1	0.9
World	1.4	1.5	1.5	1.6

Source: World Economic Survey 1992; United Nations.

Hourly Compensation Costs—Industrial Structure

Hourly Compensation Costs—Industrial Structure

Indexes of Hourly Compensation Costs for Production Workers in Manufacturing
Selected Countries: 1975 to 1989
[United States=100. Compensation costs include pay for time worked, other direct pay,
employer expenditures for legally required insurance programs, and contractual and private benefits plan, and for some countries, other labor taxes. Data adjusted for exchange
rates. Area averages are trade-weighted to account for difference in countries' relative importance to U.S. trade in manufactured goods. The trade weights used are the sum of U.S.
imports of manufactured products for consumption (customs value) and U.S. domestic
exports of manufactured products (x.a.s. value) in 1986; see source for detail.]

Area or Country	1975	1980	1985	1987	1988	1989
The United States	100	100	100	100	100	100
Total (1)	62	70	54	75	82	82
OECD (2)	75	83	85	91	99	97
Europe (3)	82	103	63	101	105	100
Asian newly ind. economies (4)	6	12	13	16	19	23
Canada	91	85	83	89	98	103
Brazil	14	14	9	10	11	12
Mexico (5)	31	30	16	12	14	16
Australia	67	66	63	70	81	85
Hong Kong (6)	12	15	13	16	17	19
Israel	35	39	31	47	55	54
Japan	48	57	50	81	92	88
South Korea	6	10	10	13	16	25
New Zealand	50	54	34	51	59	55
Singapore	13	15	19	17	19	22
Sri Lanka	4	2	2	2	NA	NA
China: Taiwan	6	10	12	17	20	25
Austria (6)	68	87	56	98	101	95
Belgium	101	133	69	112	112	106
Denmark	99	111	63	109	115	106
Finland (7)	72	84	62	100	113	116
France	71	91	58	93	94	89
Germany (8)	100	125	74	126	131	123
Greece	27	38	26	34	36	38
Ireland	47	60	45	60	70	66
Italy	73	81	56	91	93	92
Luxembourg	100	122	59	97	100	NA
Netherlands	103	123	69	116	117	109
Norway	107	119	82	129	136	131
Portugal	25	21	12	19	19	19
Spain	41	61	37	59	64	64
Sweden	113	127	75	113	121	122
Switzerland	96	113	75	127	130	117
United Kingdom	52	76	49	67	76	73

N.A. Not Available.
(1) The 27 foreign economies for which 1989 data are available.
(2) Canada, Australia, Japan, New Zealand and the 16 European countries for which 1989 data are available.
(3) The 16 European countries for which 1989 data are available.
(4) Hong Kong, Singapore, South Korea and China: Taiwan.
(5) Average of selected manufacturing industries.
(6) Excludes workers in establishments considered handicraft manufacturers (including all printing and publishing and miscellaneous manufacturing in Austria.)
(7) Includes workers in mining and electrical power plants.
(8) Data refer to September.

Source: Bureau of Labor Statistics, Report 787, August 1990. Extracted from *Statistical Abstract of the United States 1991*, p. 851.

I.M.P. Group Limited

It is January 1989 and the I.M.P. team is just arriving in Rio de Janeiro, Brazil for what is expected to be the final meeting with the Brazilian military concerning I.M.P.'s proposal to re-engine the military's Tracker aircraft. The only other contender for the contract is Grumman Aerospace of Bethpage, New York.

About the Company

I.M.P. Group Limited (I.M.P.) is a diversified, Halifax-based company, employing nearly 1500 people in 13 divisions. It is one of Canada's largest non-civilian aircraft engineering, repair and overhaul firms and handles major military aircraft contracts for the Department of National Defence. Although I.M.P.'s operations are predominately in the high technology aerospace industry, a substantial portion stems from the company's original specialty—marine service contracts. In addition to many of the aircraft operated by the Department of Defence, I.M.P. provides structural and systems engineering support to Canada's new C.P. 140 *Aurora* long range patrol aircraft.

Ken Rowe, I.M.P.'s CEO, president, and majority owner, founded the company in 1967 when he and several partners bought two struggling foundries which they redirected into the marine equipment industry. Later, Rowe bought out his partners. In the early 1970s I.M.P. diversified into the aerospace industry when Rowe

This case was prepared by Professor Mary R. Brooks, with the assistance of Mary Ann Hultoy and Kim Stephenson, Dalhousie University MBA students, as a basis for classroom discussion rather than to illustrate effective or ineffective handling of a managerial situation. The financial assistance of the Secretary of State, Canadian Studies Program, in developing the case is gratefully acknowledged. Copyright 1990, by Mary R. Brooks, Dalhousie University.

bought the equipment and hired the employees of Fairey Aviation, a struggling aircraft repair and overhaul company in nearby Dartmouth, Nova Scotia.

In 1989, the *Financial Post* ranked the I.M.P. Group Limited as the 400th largest company in Canada on the basis of its sales, estimated at $180 million. In aircraft engineering, only deHavilland and Canadair were larger.

I.M.P. Group Limited is organized into the following divisions: Aerospace Division, General Aviation Services, Marine Supplies, Foundry Castings, Steel Fabrication, Tool and Machining, Plastics Manufacturing, Hotel and Catering, Properties and Investments, and Research and Development. Headquarters staff is lean, with 9 managers and 59 support staff providing common services, such as accounting and payroll, to all operating divisions.

Within the Aerospace Division, two units will provide the services required for this contract: the Aircraft Repair and Overhaul unit and the Aerospace Engineering Services unit. The former, according to company brochures conducts "a full range of equipment modifications, repair and overhaul programs" on military and commercial aircraft. The Aerospace Engineering Services unit offers integrated services for aerospace units including the systems installation design engineering and analysis necessary for the contract as well as the systems ground and flight testing.

About the Tracker

The Tracker was the carrier-borne aircraft standard for the U.S. Navy's post-War anti-submarine warfare program; its maiden flight was in July 1953. The Canadian Navy followed suit and acquired Grumman-designed deHavilland-built CS2F-1 and CS2F-2 Trackers, stationing four of the five squadrons at CFB Shearwater in Nova Scotia and operating them from HMCS *Bonaventure*. The aircraft used Pratt & Whitney of Canada (Wright R-1820-82) engines and incorporated Grumman manufacturing expertise.

As the Defence priorities of the Canadian government shifted in the early 1970s, so did the role for the Tracker. By 1980, demand required that the Tracker add search and rescue, vessel traffic management and other coastal duties to its role of fisheries surveillance. The role changes were accompanied by base location changes from CFB Shearwater to CFB Summerside on Prince Edward Island and CFB Comox in British Columbia.

Although the aircraft proved to be an extremely flexible workhorse, its engines continue to provide new challenges to its operations. Fuel availability, cold weather reliability and maintenance problems plague the Tracker. One solution investigated by the Canadian Department of National Defence is to replace the Tracker fleet with a modern alternative; both deHavilland and Canadair can offer acceptable designs based on the Dash 8M and the Challenger CL-601 respectively. Another option, re-engining, can extend the life of the existing Tracker fleet, as the airframe has a life expectancy of 40 years. As new military aircraft cost more than many governments are willing to pay, refurbishing existing planes is favoured by many countries as a cost effective alternative.

The Re-Engining Technology

In addition to replacing an aging aircraft component, re-engining also allows the re-specification of aviation fuel. The original Tracker piston engines require 100/130 Avgas fuel which provides less power, but more importantly, is scarce and therefore more expensive. Secondly, parts are hard to find making the engines difficult to maintain. In addition, the engines

have a short overhaul cycle, costing more than $200,000 an engine every 600 hours; the Pratt & Whitney turbine engine costs only $500,000 new and only needs to be overhauled every 3000 hours of flying time. There are clear economies favouring conversion to turbine (turboprop) engines.

The re-engining of an aircraft is not a simple process whereby one engine is replaced with another. The conversion of an aircraft is considered by those associated with this technology to be a more difficult technical process than designing a new aircraft. Due to changes in the load distribution as well as differing engine and aerodynamic responses, the aircraft must also undergo major structural alterations. The addition of mass ballast is needed to re-balance the aircraft and maximize its aerodynamic performance. Poor attention to detail may result in reduced airworthiness or cause the aircraft to be completely unsafe.

Development of a prototype, using the buyer's aircraft, is the industry norm to prove the technology works. If, for some reason, the prototype does not meet the conditions of sale outlined in the sale contract, the buyer is refunded 100 percent. The seller, because of his inventory in the aircraft, will usually buy the aircraft back and then resell it to recover his investment, advertising its real capability.

Once an aircraft has been re-engined, ground testing, flight testing, component qualification testing and engineering data documentation are required to obtain certification. Certification approval is granted by the country of operation; in this case, the CTA, Certificao Technologico Aeronautica in Brazil will certify the modification. I.M.P. has agreed to meet U.S. Federal Aviation Administration (FAA) requirements (as the standard of performance for the contract) and the prototype must be certifiable on delivery for the contract to be fulfilled. On acceptance of the prototype by CTA, 11 more Trackers will be re-engined at the fixed contract price.

644   Cases

The Tracker is designed as a carrier-based aircraft and, as no carrier-based aircraft has been re-engined to date, the engineering data produced in the course of fulfilling the contract is an important element in the certification process, and therefore the landing engineering data rights is a possible area for technology transfer.

The Brazilian Opportunity

The Brazilians wish to modernize a dozen of their Tracker aircraft and have narrowed the contenders for the contract to two companies—I.M.P. Group Limited and the U.S.-based Grumman Aerospace, the original designer and manufacturer of the aircraft. Initially, two other companies were competing for the Brazilian deal: Marsh Aviation of Arizona, who had already flown a proof-of-concept aircraft equipped with a Garrett engine, and Trecor, who are working on a prototype design under contract to Grumman. Both these companies dropped out, leaving only I.M.P. and Grumman in the running.

Grumman has had a long relationship with the Brazilian military but the engine they are proposing to use is more expensive than the Pratt & Whitney engine being proposed by I.M.P. On the other hand, Grumman has manufactured and sold carrier-borne aircraft for over 50 years, and its reputation has been enhanced by the film *Top Gun*.

Various I.M.P. personnel made a total of 5 visits to Brazil between receipt of the Request For Proposals (RFP) in the spring of 1988 and December, 2 of these visits were on technical elements alone. The

contract's initial deadline was April 30, but by December details were still being discussed and the Brazilian Air Force had not reached a decision. Grumman, throughout this period, has cut their price three times while I.M.P. has stuck to their initial bid. The Grumman price remains high.

December 22nd I.M.P. received from their agents in Brazil a translation of the final contract the Brazilians are prepared to sign. The contract calls for work to begin on contract signature and to end 10 months 1 week later. The structure of the contract is illustrated in Exhibit 1.

The I.M.P. team is now preparing for what they expect to be the final meeting on this contract. Success will mean the contract is theirs; failure will give the deal to Grumman.

EXHIBIT 1 The Structure of the Contract

Main Body:

The contract terms and conditions, which include the relevant portions of the RFP as issued, and the I.M.P. proposal in its entirety.

Annexes:

A. A technical annex for the re-engining and deliverables;
B. Schedules of work;
C. Additional work required;
D. Details of after-sales service; and
E. Certification standards for the project.

THE AEROSPACE INDUSTRY*

The Global Environment

The aerospace industry is a technology-intensive one requiring a great deal of capital investment in high-tech machinery, skilled labour and R & D, thus creating enormous barriers to entry. In spite of this, competition among producers is fierce. Recently the competition has intensified because of government budget cutbacks and the deregulation occurring in the global aviation industry.[1]

Traditionally the Americans enjoyed the dominant position, but in recent years the industry has experienced a boom of new producers in other developed countries. Even though there are no precise statistics available, based on 1984 data analysts estimate that the Americans service 70 percent of the market.[2] Slowly more and more non-American companies have penetrated the diverse sub-sectors, starting in those with the least formidable barriers to entry. Today the American industry shares the civil aircraft sub-sector with Airbus, a European firm. The Americans are reacting to this competition by forming a variety of consortia.[3]

To remain competitive in the industry, firms rely heavily on R&D, further increasing their capital commitment. Because the recovery of an investment may take many years, companies have developed a number of strategies to reduce the risk involved in the development of projects.[4]

One manoeuvre is horizontal diversification. Recently, aerospace producers have invested in other industries, while industries such as transport, MIS, and telecommunications have begun to invest in the aerospace industry.[5]

Another form of risk-sharing involves delegating to the smaller, specialized subcontractors a part of the investment in new project development. Only firms which are financially sound can participate, thus creating a need for more and more investment capital. This is further encouraged as assemblers rationalize their operations and choose fewer component manufacturers.[6]

Such trends create opportunities for the Canadians. Canadian aerospace manufacturers possess specialized capabilities. The Canadian industry does not manufacture or overhaul the full range of aircraft and engines, or the multiple of different components which make up the end product. Instead, particular products and processes are concentrated on, and such a niche strategy combines the Canadians' expertise with sound economic potential.

The environment in which the aerospace industry operates is marked by changes in domestic and foreign government policies on market access, technology transfer, defence, and investment. Also product liability has become a major threat for aircraft manufacturers; the number of lawsuits in which manufacturers are being blamed for crashes because of negligent aircraft design is increasing.[7]

Growth in both the European and Asian civilian aerospace markets appears to be promising. Established aircraft carriers in both regions are being challenged by newcomers who are acquiring large fleets.

---

*This industry note essentially summarizes two main profiles done of the aerospace industry: Lambert, Daniel, *Analyse de l'industrie aeronautique canadienne et quebecoise: perspective de development* (CETAI: Montreal, Mai 1989), p. 3 and *Industry Profile: Aerospace,* Industry, Science and Technology Canada: Ontario, 1988, p. 1. It was prepared by Kim Stephenson under the direction of Mary R. Brooks for use with the case I.M.P. Group Limited.

[1] Lambert, Daniel, *Analyse de l'industrie aeronautique canadienne et quebecoise: perspective de development* (CETAI: Montreal, Mai 1989), p. 3.
[2] *Ibid.,* p. 3.
[3] *Ibid.,* p. 4.
[4] *Ibid.,* p. 5.
[5] *Ibid.,* p. 5.
[6] *Ibid.,* p. 5.
[7] Barnard, Thomas, "Courts and Crashes," *Canadian Aviation,* July 1985, p. 34.

In addition, European restrictions on the age of aircraft and on noise levels are becoming more stringent, creating a need for new aircraft and components. The demand will be further enhanced by 1992 when the industry will experience deregulation. It is estimated that these factors, coupled with a healthy European economy, will double passenger air travel in Europe in the next 15 years.[8]

The Canadian Industry

The Canadian aerospace industry is the fifth largest in the western world, after the United States, Great Britain, France, and West Germany. It is one of Canada's most dynamic industries, employing more than 60,000 people in 1988.[9] Total sales in the industry are essentially divided between Ontario and Quebec, which have 51.8 percent and 40.5 percent of sales respectively. Nova Scotia has a small 1 percent while Western Canada is responsible for 6.7 percent.[10] Larger firms are predominately foreign-owned, accounting for about 70 percent of sales.[11] A greater percentage of Ontario firms are American subsidiaries than those in Quebec.

Approximately 20 percent of Canadian R&D funds goes specifically to this industry.[12] In 1986, sales were $4.7 billion; 28 percent of these ($1.36 billion) were domestic sales. Exports of aircraft components topped $3.4 billion, with approximately 70 percent of this to the U.S.[13]

The largest domestic customer is the Canadian government; in 1986, the Department of National Defence purchased $866 million of goods and services.

Canadian government procurement equals nearly 20 percent of total industry sales and 70 percent of domestic sales. The industry's other markets include general aviation aircraft manufacturers, regional airlines, business aircraft users, and major defense and commercial aerospace contractors.[14]

Based on relative size, market autonomy, capabilities and products, Canadian aerospace firms can be divided into three tiers.[15]

1. *The Largest Firms*—Their strength lies in their abilities to design, develop, manufacture, market, and repair complete aircraft, engines, and systems. They account for approximately 45 percent of industry sales. Pratt & Whitney Canada Inc., Canadair Inc., The deHavilland Aircraft Company Canada Limited an Bell Helicopter constitute this group.

2. *Medium Sized Firms*—These firms generally supply other prime aerospace manufacturers (predominately foreign) with specially made components. As well, these firms specialize in the repair and overhaul of aircraft, engines, and components. There are approximately 40 companies in this tier who enjoy 45 percent of industry sales. Major firms include McDonnell Douglas Canada Ltd., Menasco Aerospace Ltd., Garrett Canada, Fleet Aerospace Corp., and Spar Aerospace Limited.

3. *Small Businesses*—The remaining 10 percent of sales is accounted for by approximately 140 firms. These small businesses are special process and precision machining shops which predominately handle short-term orders from large companies, aerospace parts distributors, and foundries.

[8] Mongelluzzo, Bill, "Aerospace firms bullish on future in Europe, Asia," *Journal of Commerce*, May 9, 1989, p. 5B.
[9] Lambert, Daniel, *Op. Cit.*, p. 3.
[10] *Ibid.*
[11] *Ibid.*, p. 12.
[12] *Ibid.*, p.16.
[13] *Industry Profile: Aerospace*, Industry, Science and Technology Canada: Ontario, 1988, p. 1.

[14] *Ibid.*, p. 1.
[15] *Ibid.*, p. 1,2.

As Canada's largest aerospace defence contractor, I.M.P. Group is considered to be a second tier company.

The Canadian industry's capabilities in product development have gained it respect in world markets. Independent product development by firms, government supported R&D, technology transfer, and innovative engineers and managers have been critical to industry competitiveness. This has been furthered by Canadian firms' ability to adapt to rapidly changing manufacturing technologies, allowing improved manufacturing competitiveness. Particularly strong are the second- and third-tier firms. Many are at the leading edge in technology and in manufacturing. Technical performance, coupled with efficient quality and cost structures, make these firms competitive internationally. Canadians have also earned a reputation for commitment to after-sales support.

Because many of Canada's first- and second-tier firms are predominately foreign-owned, the ability to develop uniquely Canadian design capabilities is limited. On the other hand, such foreign involvement has provided easier access to state-of-the art technology, management skills, and foreign markets, thus benefiting the industry on the whole.[16]

As mentioned, R&D is the essential factor in this competitive industry. The Canadian industry invests much less than the U.S., France, or the U.K. However, it must be noted that these countries have large defence needs backing much of the industry's R&D, while Canadian firms' expenditures are driven by the demand of international markets.[17]

Therefore, the world demand for defence products is an important driving force in the aerospace industry. Yet many markets are difficult for Canadians to access because countries with well-developed aerospace industries tend to turn to domestic suppliers. Since 1959, the U.S. military markets have been open to Canadian companies by the Defence Production Sharing Arrangement (DPSA).

As with many other Canadian industries, exports are crucial to the aerospace industry. Seventy percent of exports go to the U.S., but exports to Asian countries are increasing. The industry's global dependence is also illustrated by the number of imported components used in products (26.8–27.9 percent); these components are mostly U.S.-made. This dependence is inevitable given the large foreign ownership levels in the Canadian industry and the global nature of the industry.[18]

Tariff barriers have little impact on this industry. The GATT agreement on Trade in Civil Aircraft has eliminated tariffs. Many reciprocal defence production agreements, such as DPSA, encourage trade. It is the non-tariff barriers in foreign markets which limit Canadian aerospace export opportunities. Government procurement and national preferences for indigenous products make market penetration difficult for Canadian firms competing directly with domestic firms.

[16] *Ibid.*, p. 3.
[17] *Ibid.*, p. 3.
[18] Lambert, *Op. Cit.*, p. 10.

Logitech

[handwritten: problem: "slow to react. · how to maintain"]

Early in the spring of 1990, Pierluigi Zappacosta, CEO of Logitech, reflected on the changing market conditions in North America and Europe and wondered what would be required to maintain and expand Logitech's position in the computer peripherals marketplace. Logitech had become one of three companies that dominated the global market for pointing devices for computers. While Logitech had captured a large unit share of the OEM (Original Equipment Manufacturer) mouse market, Microsoft was the clear leader in terms of industry standards and dollar share of the retail market, and KYE (Genius), having a strong retail presence in Europe, was poised to complete aggressively in North America.

Zappacosta recognized that Logitech had been slow to react to changes in market conditions, such as the 1987 introduction of Microsoft's "white mouse", a shapely design that had developed considerable consumer appeal. This, combined with eroding margins on the OEM mouse business, had left Zappacosta wondering whether Logitech could maintain a leadership position in the pointing device market. Logitech had been successful in developing leadership positions in other niches, such as scanners, and other opportunities existed. Committed to their mission of "connecting the computer to the world" by giving it "senses", Zappacosta wondered what direction(s) the company should take and what the priorities should be.

[handwritten: How they got their start]

This case was prepared by Brock Smith under the supervision of Professor Adrian B. Ryans of the Western Business School. Copyright 1992, The University of Western Ontario. This material is not covered under authorization from CanCopy or any reproduction rights organization. Any form of reproduction, storage or transmittal of this material is prohibited without written permission from Western Business School, the University of Western Ontario, London, Canada N6A 3K7. Reprinted with permission, Western Business School.

COMPANY BACKGROUND

[handwritten: pos. focussed too much on product. customer]

Logitech SA was founded in October 1981 by Mr. Zappacosta and Daniel Borel in Switzerland after Bobst Graphics, the company with which the two had been developing a European word-processing/DTP package, was sold and the new owners did not want to continue the project. Zappacosta had met Borel at Stanford University while they were completing their MS (Computer Science) degrees. After an initial attempt to bring US technology to Europe with their own software company, Borel, and then Zappacosta, had joined Bobst to gain industry contacts. They had then formed their own software company with Bobst as the major client. Giacomo Marini, a software manager at Olivetti and a friend of Zappacosta's from the time when they had both worked in Pisa, Italy, joined in founding Logitech together with a group of young engineers.

Two contacts set the stage for the initial growth and development of the organization. First, they won a $1 million contract with Ricoh to develop hardware and software for use with Ricoh printers and scanners. Shortly thereafter, Logitech won a contract with Swiss Timing to develop hardware and software for use at the Olympic Games. Wanted to be close to Ricoh and developments in Silicon Valley Zappacosta, and later Borel, and then Marini, moved to Palo Alto, California and created Logitech Inc. In March 1982, Logitech Inc. learned of a Swiss watch company, Depraz, that had developed a mouse. Recognizing the advantages of the mouse relative to other pointing devices such as cursor keys, light pens, and touch screens, Logitech secured the rights to market the Depraz mouse in the U.S. and packaged it with software for the operation of text and graphics programs.

A major turning point in the strategic direction of the organization came after Logitech secured a contract with Hewlett-Packard to supply 25,000 mice under an OEM contract. It quickly became evident that Hewlett-Packard's price and quality requirements could not be met by Logitech's initial strategy of contracting out manufacturing to Depraz. Adhering to a philosophy of having direct control of the critical elements of the business, Logitech bought the rights to manufacture and market a mouse designed by CC Corp. With help from Hewlett-Packard, Logitech redesigned the mouse for mass production and set up a manufacturing operation in Redwood City, California in 1984. Production was moved to Fremont, California in 1987 to a facility across the street from Logitech's U.S. headquarters.

Control over manufacturing and a commitment to quality led to rapid growth in the OEM mouse market with contracts from Apollo, Olivetti, AT&T, and other key computer manufacturers. However, Apple and IBM were wary of Logitech's manufacturing expertise and continued to buy most of their mice from Alps, a Japanese company operating in California, which had purchased Apple's keyboard and mouse facility and was the exclusive supplier to microsoft.

In 1986 two events took place that would help solidify Logitech's future in the mouse market. First, due to slow growth in OEM sales, Logitech entered the retail market with the Series 7 mouse, a product that had been successful in the OEM market. Then, to win a piece of the Apple business and to satisfy the demands of OEM customers for Logitech to lower the cost of mice, Logitech set up a manufacturing base in Hsinchu, Taiwan, with an initial production capacity of 1 million mice per year, but potentially expandable to ten times that volume. In retrospect, Zappacosta thought they had been a bit lucky. For a $300,000 investment, they had secured a high volume, state-of-the-art, manufacturing plant in Taiwan's "Silicon Valley" just before Taiwan became a leader in manufacturing technology and a hot-bed of design creativity, and just as the mouse industry took off under the combined forces of Apple's Macintosh, desktop publishing, Microsoft's Windows, and other applications using graphical user interfaces.

In 1988, anticipating a unified Europe in 1992, and wanting to be close to Apple and potential customers such as IBM and Compaq in Europe, Logitech opened another manufacturing facility in Cork, Ireland, which had a capacity, similar to that of the Fremont plant, of about 1,.5 million mice per year. At the same time, they broadened their product line with the introduction of a hand-held scanner, a product that shared some technological features with the mouse, that capitalized on Logitech's experience in software development, and that could be marketed through established retail channels.

By the end of 1989, Logitech had reached sales of over $100 million, employed about 1000 people, had manufacturing facilities on three continents, and had sales offices in England, Germany, Italy, France, Japan, Sweden, Switzerland, the United States, and Taiwan.

CULTURE

The culture at Logitech reflected the global nature and operations of the organization. Because employees had varied life and educational experiences from around the globe, they were appreciative and accepting of differences in backgrounds, perspectives, and styles. As Fabio Righi, Vice President Sales and Marketing, put it: "our greatest strength as well as our biggest challenge is that Logitech is an international company. It is difficult to be international and local at the same time. Local flavour affects/impacts everything."

Deeply rooted in the Logitech culture was a strong product/technical orientation. Employees gained considerable job satisfaction from being on the leading edge and working on bold, exciting projects. Fabio Righi, for example, talked of the elusive "atomic mouse" like a Grail that helps define the common purpose of the employees. As senior executives admitted, employees tended to be quite internally focused and did not make a great effort to have their beliefs validated before launching a new product into the marketplace. As Ron McClure, Vice President Strategic Marketing, put it: "We are the most critical users of our products. Customer need recognition is limited by their understanding of technology—they don't know what is possible!"

Related to this technical orientation was a strong design and production orientation. According to Chip Smith, Production Manager in Fremont, "Everything revolves around production. The floor, receiving and shipping, traffic, and order processing are key processes by which we satisfy consumers." Therefore, manufacturing was seen as a key marketing success factor.

There was also a strong spiritual component to the culture at Logitech. This was supported in part by the personal philosophies of the founders, but also by the shared vision that employees had for shaping the future. For example, aesthetics were a high priority, not only in the products, but also in the workplace itself. One might infer that if there was a Logitech company handbook, it would probably be *Zen and the Art of Motorcycle Maintenance*.

Working relationships at Logitech tended to be very informal, flexible, open, and close. Employees were genuinely excited to be on the leading edge and found their jobs and the "family" atmosphere fun. This "family" atmosphere was reinforced by Logitech's policy of hiring talented young professionals from around the world and relocating them to enrich their own and others' perspectives. Dislocated from their own families and culture, employees often relied on each other for social, emotional, and cultural support.

Consistent with the informal, close working relationships, there were few formal procedures and structures within Logitech. Executive decisions were generally made by consensus after seeking employee input. Worldwide interaction of management and staff was maintained on a daily basis by an electronic mail system.

BUSINESS STRATEGY

Pierluigi Zappacosta explained the long-term Logitech vision by saying: "Only if the computer becomes a little more human will it become an effective tool for the mind. And evolution of our own brain through computers is our long-term vision. Our more immediate mission is to connect the computer with the world by giving it "senses", humanize the interface to the computer, and help people turn data into meaningful information,. Our goals are to maintain/attain the number one position in whatever markets we play in by redefining and continually changing the products and markets we compete in. We want to have a Logitech product on every computer desk."

To achieve their mission and objectives, Logitech's business strategy was to recognize major trends and technologies early, move fast in bringing quality products to market (forming alliances if necessary), develop in-house expertise for product extensions, become effective and efficient manufacturers, have the best sales force and channels to sell the products, and keep ahead of the competition by an accelerated pace of innovation.

TABLE 1 Estimated Manufacturing Costs and Selling Prices

Mouse	Estimated Manufacturing Cost (Jan 1990)	Estimated Average Selling Price to Channel
Logitech S9	$25.00	$60.00
Microsoft Mouse	27.00	75.00
Pilot Mouse	17.40	33.00
Dexxa	16.30	19.50
Logitech OEM	15.20	22.00
Taiwanese OEM	13.10	16.50
Ergonomic (corded)	19.60	Not on the market
Ergonomic (cordless)	64.30	Not on the market

Source: Company records

Logitech competed aggressively in both the OEM and retail sides of the personal computer accessory business. On the OEM side of the business, they competed using innovation and skill in manufacturing and design that allowed them to bring new technology to market at very competitive prices (see estimated manufacturing costs in Table 1). Toward this end, Logitech had achieved an experience curve in mouse manufacturing of about 70%. On the retail side of the business, Logitech focused on image management. They wanted to be perceived in the marketplace as innovators that develop neat products that were fun to use and were easy to sell. *Too prod'n oriented*

About 60% of Logitech's unit sales were in the OEM segment but more than 60% of their revenue came form the retail segment. In both the OEM and retail markets, Logitech's financial success (see Exhibit 1) had been, and would continue to be, tied to the development and growth of the PC marketplace and recognition of the need to "humanize" the computer.

PRODUCT DEVELOPMENT

don't concentrate on customer needs

Product development at Logitech involved finding or developing technologies that require Logitech's skills in design, mass manufacturing, and distribution to bring them to market. Logitech had three basic development strategies: start from scratch, evolve current in-house technology, or buy required technology at an advanced development stage from others. Starting from scratch added about a year to the product development process since employees had to learn about a technology, decide what to develop, and test product concepts. Building on current expertise to extend or develop new generations of products was the most common approach taken. If required technology was not available internally, then Logitech would buy it, make minor adjustments to bring it to market, then develop internally the skills required for product evolution.

Decisions on product development were usually based on consensus among senior managers and tended to be emotional an based on "gut feel" rather than extensive analysis and research. Some of the decision criteria that were considered, however, included licensing or development costs, manufacturing cost, margins, a six-month payback, whether it was going to be fun to work on, and whether the product could gain a 40% share of its market. Focus groups were sometimes used late in the process to validate the "gut feelings". However, Pierluigi Zappacosta recognized

EXHIBIT 1 Selected Financial Data

Logitech International SA, Applies
(In Swiss Francs)

Full Year Ending	3/31/87	3/31/88	3/31/89	Projected 3/31/90
Consolidated Revenue	33,543,351	62,806,740	124,110,684	180,000,000
Net Income after tax	1,459,888	7,032,066	11,206,922	14,000,000
% of Revenues	4.35%	11.20%	9.03%	7.78%
Cash Flow	2,136,959	9,413,623	14,290,273	17,500,000
% of Revenues	6.37%	14.99%	11.51%	9.72%
Earnings per Bearer Share	-	54	76	96
Dividend per Bearer Share	-	-	12	16
Engineering, Research & Development Expenses	2,579,023	4,663,430	8,396,799	13,700,000
% of Revenues	7.69%	7.43%	6.77%	7.61%
Number of personnel	240	442	731	1,000

	3/31/87	3/31/88	3/31/89	3/31/90
Current Assets	12,117,422	27,026,936	75,526,814	108,000,000
Property, Plant & Equipment Gross	6,212,338	8,843,297	22,421,727	30,600,000
less Accumulated Depreciation	(1,412,316)	(2,139,330)	(5,222,681)	(8,500,000)
Property, Plant & Equipment Net	4,800,022	6,703,967	17,199,046	22,100,000
Other Non-Current Assets	328,775	2,273,945	1,184,542	3,900,000
Goodwill	0	14,214,241	13,093,605	11,200,,000
Total Assets	17,246,219	50,219,089	107,004,007	145,200,000
Current Liabilities	8,945,618	18,701,970	36,775,490	37,200,000
Long-Term Debt & Deferred Taxes	3,858,044	5,517,119	10,541,326	43,500,000
Stockholders' Equity	4,442,557	26,000,000	59,687,191	69,500,000
Total Liabilities & Stockholders' Equity	17,246,219	50,219,089	107,004,007	145,200,000

	1988	1989
Net Sales	62,806,740	124,110,684
Cost of Goods Sold	30,921,004	71,493,833
Gross Profit	31,885,736	52,616,851
Operating Expenses		
Marketing, Sales and Support	10,070,523	21,081,432
General and Administration	5,553,719	10,276,622
Research, Development and Engineering	4,663,430	8,396,799
	20,287,672	39,754,853
Income from Operations	11,598,064	12,861,998
Other Expenses, Net	191,569	59,656
Income Before Income Taxes	11,406,495	12,802,342
Provision for Taxes on Income	4,374,429	1,595,420
Net Income	7,032,066	11,206,922

that more effort was needed to get qualitative feedback at earlier stages of the product development cycle.

At any given time there were 20-39 official projects in various stages of development, as well as others that were "unofficial". The major projects were managed by multifunctional new product teams. Currently, there was no central authority on any particular project, but Zappacosta recognized the need to have someone who knew how the whole picture was coming together. Logitech was spending over 7% of sales on R&D and money could be found for important projects. Zappacosta thought the biggest problem that Logitech faced in new product development was not getting caught up in "the fun of it."

PERSONAL COMPUTER INDUSTRY

After five years of rapid growth, the PC industry was in turmoil in early 1990. The initial standards established by IBM and Apple had given way to a confusing array of technologies, including IBM's Micro-Channel, EISA (the Micro-Channel alternative offered by Compaq and six other major vendors), RISC (various versions of reduced instruction set computing used primarily by engineering/scientific workstations running under Unix operating system), and Apple's Macintosh. Confusing matters ever more were competing operating systems such as DOS, OS/2, and Unix and competing graphical user interfaces such as Microsoft's Window (version 2), IBM's Presentation Manager, the Open System Foundation's "X", AT&T's Unix System 5, and Next's "NextStep." All of these competing operating system and user interfaces, however, used mice or another pointing device to control the operating environment. While it was expected that graphical user interfaces would be adopted on most, if not all, systems, the rate of adoption would depend heavily on the success of Microsoft's newly announced Windows 3.0 for DOS and IBM's OS/2.

The industry itself exhibited characteristics of the maturity phase of the product life cycle. Competition was intense and a shake-out of the market was underway, which affected even some relatively large companies. Consumers were becoming more sophisticated and knowledgeable and did not require the same level of support and sales assistance that they had a few years earlier. Consequently, manufacturers were beginning to make inroads through alternative channels such as mail order, price clubs, and superstores, while traditional full-service retailers such as ComputerLand and Business Land were refocusing their efforts on organizations using outbound direct sales forces. Personal computers themselves were quickly becoming commodity items as limited product differentiation, short technology life-cycles, and steep experience curves combined to put substantial downward pressure on prices. With the early mystique of computers wearing off, users, and in particular corporations, were beginning to question and evaluate the impact of computer technology on employee productivity, health, and other aspects of organizational life. Stress injuries, for example, were gaining prominence and were being linked to workplace computer operation. One of these was carpal tunnel syndrome, which involved painful damage to the nerve that runs through the arm as a result of repetitive strain from the use of typewriters, computers, and other arm- or hand-operated equipment. Carpal tunnel syndrome had received considerable media attention (see example in Exhibit 2) and a recent ordinance in California required corporations to take measures to reduce this type of workplace injury. Other concerns were also being raised about cathode ray tubes in terms of

"Repetitive Strain Repetitive Pain: Carpal Tunnel Becomes Major Workplace Hazard" Himanee Gupta, The Seattle Times, Vol. 112, Iss: 223, September 18, 1989, Section F, Page 1.

... Throughout the country and in Puget Sound, companies are realizing the painful, often crippling condition [carpal tunnel syndrome] has grown into a major workplace hazard. No one's sure just when and how had it will hit, but any worker who types at computers, works with electronic scanners or regularly performs other repetitive tasks on automated equipment is at risk.

Carpal tunnel syndrome, one of several ailments known as repetitive strain injuries, occurs when constant bending of the hands, wrists and arms inflames tendons that squeeze the main nerve that runs through the arm... The problems start with swelling, tingling and discomfort, and can wind up causing numbness, severe pain and paralysis. Treatment often means slow, painful therapy or surgery followed by therapy. And in terms of treatment, therapy and disability claims, the cost for employers can be enormous...

In 1988, the state Department of Labor and Industries paid $6.5 million for 1,910 workers' compensation claims filed for carpal tunnel syndrome. That compares with 1,228 claims in 1986 and 123 in 1979.

"Pressing for New Ways to Type", Ronald Roel, Newsday, Vol. 50 #50, October 22, 1989, Section 1, Page 71.

... Hodges is one of a handful of iconoclasts promoting radical alternatives today's conventional keyboard designs. Their devices, which so far have been roundly rejected by the big U.S. keyboard makers, range from variations on Hodges' split keyboard to keys that are moved much like a computer mouse. Like Hodges, most keyboard inventors say their passion for change has been spurred, in part, by an interest in reducing hand and wrist injuries, known as repetitive strain injuries, or RSI, experienced by thousands of computer users each year. Some medical experts believe that conventional flat keyboard design may contribute to RSI...

IBM and other major manufacturers say they have no plans to radically change the keyboards used by 25 million office workers. If big changes are made within the next decade, it will probably be to eliminate the keyboard altogether, substituting them with other inputting devices that convert handwriting or human speech directly to computer print, says Maryann Karinch, a spokeswoman for the Computer and Business Manufacturers' Association, a Washington D.C. based trade group.

EXHIBIT 2
Carpal Tunnel Syndrome

---

possible harmful emissions from computer screens and in terms of eye strain. Thus, while unit growth in the PC industry was expected to be in the 10-15% range, profits were eroding and consumers were becoming more critical and discerning.

THE MOUSE MARKETPLACE

In the computer sense, "mice" were handheld mobile devices that used a combination of hardware and software to translate physical movement into digital signals that controlled cursor movement on a computer screen and executed commands. Named for their basic shape, mice (and trackballs) were more precise and flexible than other pointing devices such as light pens, touch screens, and cursor keys and were generally more intuitive an easier to use. While the first mice developed in the 1960s were mechanical in design and were used predominantly by engineers, mice were now mostly opto-mechanical in technology and were used by a wide variety of users, including children, for a variety of applications ranging from drawing to interacting with most business software.

Market Development

In December 1985, Logitech entered the retail mouse market, first in North America and then in Europe with the Logitech mouse, a retail version of their successful Series 7 OEM mouse. Adopting a penetration strategy for the more knowledgeable and price-sensitive North American market, Logitech priced the Logitech mouse at $99 U.S., about half the suggested price of both the Microsoft mouse and the mouse offered by Mouse Systems Corporation (the first into the U.S. market). Targeting the computer "techies", Logitech initially sold the Logitech mouse directly to consumers by soliciting phone and mail orders in trade publications. Initial success generated sufficient market pull to enable Logitech to establish a dealer network and increase the price of their *used to pull* mouse by 10-20%. In the less sophisticated European market, Logitech followed Microsoft's lead and used a skimming price strategy, charging about 30% more than it did in the U.S. Instead of using mail-order for distribution, Logitech developed relationships with a strong dealer network in Europe, who were able to support higher prices and margins by meeting the full-service needs of customers with high quality and prestige image products. In 1987, Microsoft launched its new ergonomic "white mouse", for $200 in the U.S., but $350 in Europe. Logitech was slow to react and did not bring out their Microsoft-compatible Series 9 mouse until 1988. This new mouse was priced about 20% below Microsoft in North America and Europe. At this time, Logitech also introduced a "low-end" mouse under the Dexxa brand name to compete against the more than 20 Taiwanese manufacturers, who were pricing their mice in the $20-$35 range. These Taiwanese manufacturers had captured about 40% unit market share, compared to 30% unit shares of both Logitech and Microsoft in the U.S. and Europe.

Supporting their R&D efforts from their high margins in Europe, both Logitech and Microsoft were slow to react to changes in the increasingly sophisticated and price-conscious European mar-

ket. KYE (Genius), the largest of the Taiwanese manufacturers, had introduced a high quality mouse at $50 in mid-1988 and had captured a major share of the European market. In response, Microsoft and Logitech lowered their prices to $200 and $180, respectively, and Logitech began developing a new mouse at a price of $50-$60. This new "Pilot Mouse" was introduced in Europe at the end of 1989. Microsoft had unbundled their "paint" software from their mouse in the U.S., and had lowered the price to within 20% of Logitech's. KYE (Genius) had just bought Mouse Systems Corporation and were poised to bring their "Genius" product into the U.S. under the Mouse Systems brand name, which had a strong user recognition despite its decreasing market share.

The positioning of the major mouse vendors in Europe and North America in early 1990 is shown in Exhibit 3. Worldwide dollar market shares were approximately 40-45% for Microsoft, 30% for Logitech, and 20% for KYE/mouse Systems. Demand for mice was expected to grow about 50% in 1990 and only slightly less in the foreseeable future due to trends towards graphical user interfaces. Sales of portables and laptops were expected to grow 22% in 1990 to 1.2 million units (14% of the PC market) and were expected to account for almost half of PC sales within a few years. Manufacturers of these computers would have to offer a built-in pointing device. Mice or trackballs seemed to be the logical choice for these pointing devices, but other technologies involving track pens and pen-based computing would likely play an increased role. Moreover, there would be increasing retail demand for replacement products and upgrades. Industry observers expected KYE/Mouse Systems to experience unit sales growth of 60% in 1990. Microsoft was expected to experience 50% growth and Logitech was expected to experience slightly

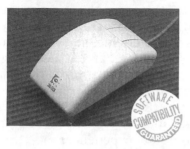

EXHIBIT 3
Illustrative Product Literature

lower growth. Logitech's retail sales were expected to remain at 40% of total unit sales in 1990. Previous years' unit sales are presented in Table 2.

Buyer Behavior

The mouse marketplace could be segmented into home/personal users, home/business users, corporate and educational users. Home/personal buyers, who accounted for about 48% of Logitech retail sales, were thought to be more price-sensitive than other segments and were less concerned about compatibility with software that they did not yet own. These consumers tended to buy from discount houses or no frills dealers and would chose among the alternative mice available at the most convenient location. Home/business buyers, representing about 26% of Logitech's retail sales, were thought to be value-and brand-conscious, but less concerned about compatibility than corporate users. These consumers were thought to be influenced by articles in *PC World*, *Byte* and other trade magazines, and to a lesser extent, advertisements in those magazines. Word-of-mouth and sales representative recommendations were thought to have the most influence of all. Finally, corporate buyers, representing 25% of Logitech's retail sales but 50% of Microsoft's, were thought to be more concerned with the brand name of a mouse and its likely compatibility with future hardware and software products. If use of the mouse was "mission critical" in the sense of being tied to productivity or used extensively, corporate buyers tended to play it safe and bought Microsoft.

While the profile of the Logitech mouse buyer was not completely understood, Logitech did keep track of who their retail customers were. Some 82% were desktop users and 48% of buyers were also the users. For 60%, the Logitech mouse was the second mouse they had purchased and 27% bought the mouse "bundled" with a paint program. Some 50% purchased the product at a retail store, 26% at a super-store, and 13% through mail order. Forty percent made the brand decision at the store. In terms of demographics, 80% were male, 55% were aged 30-45, and over 60% had 5 or more years of computer experience.

Competition

On the retail end of the business, the major competitors were Microsoft, Logitech, and KYE/Mouse Systems. Microsoft was positioned as the compatibility leader for both hardware and software and marketed its product to the premium, brand-conscious segment. It used its software reputation to help sell mice, and often bundled its mouse with Microsoft programs that required one. The second major competitor, Mouse Systems, was a bit of an enigma. It traditionally competed aggressively on price and promotions, but had limited resources and

Calendar Year	Logitech	Microsoft	Mouse Systems	Other	Total Retail	Percentages of Total Market
1988	577	803	630	361	2371	35
1989	883	1321	554	400	3158	40

TABLE 2 Estimated World Retail Sales (in thousands of units)

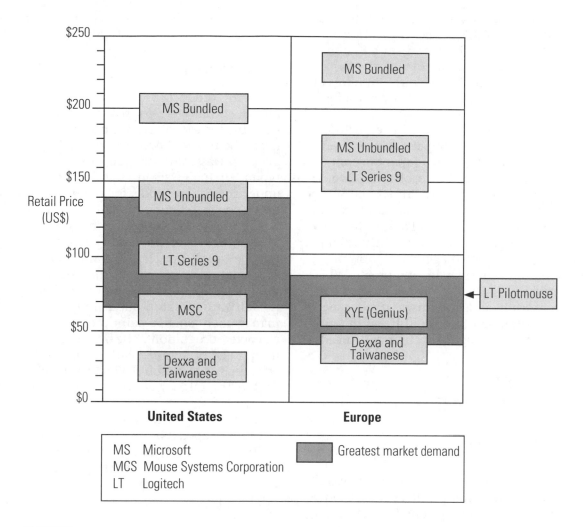

EXHIBIT 4
Positioning of Products in the Retail Market in January 1990

product quality was not believed to be as high as Logitech's or Microsoft's. However, with KYE's purchase of Mouse Systems, KYE was now claiming to be the largest mouse producer in the world (in terms of units) and was expected to become a force in North America.

On the OEM end of the business, Logitech's main competitors were: Alps and Mitsumi, (the two Japanese companies that supplied Microsoft), KYE/Mouse Systems, Z-nix, Truedox, Primax and Silitec (Taiwanese manufacturers). Primax and Silitec were suppliers to Packard Bell, the fourth largest PC vendor. All these competitors competed aggressively on price, resulting in low margins and profits. While Logitech felt it had a superior product both technically and in terms of quality, new users often could not tell the difference and most products met their basic needs.

LOGITECH'S POSITIONING AND MARKETING STRATEGY

Logitech's overall mouse strategy was to compress technology life cycles and give consumers more options for increasing productivity. They competed by developing innovative designs and technologies, producing high quality products, and pricing the products to deliver good customer value. They aggressively managed their costs and tried to maintain strong relationships with their distributors. Traditionally, their products had been positioned to attract the serious and technically oriented user, but were now also attracting creative and aesthetically oriented users looking for fun, form, and function. This overall strategy had led to an increase in unit sales of over 74% in 1989, but because the average selling price had decreased 22%, revenues increased at only about half the rate of unit sales.

Product Strategy

Logitech's product strategy was to develop products that were consistent with, but not obvious extensions of, current offerings. The image they were attempting to develop was that Logitech offered neat products which were fun to use. Marketed under the theme "tools for the imagination", Logitech's current retail product offering included: the Logitech (Series 9) Mouse, the Pilot (Series 15) Mouse (in Europe only), the Dexxa brand mouse, Trackman (a trackball pointing device), ScanMan (a hand-held scanner); and utility software (desktop publishing, a DOS management shell, a paint program, and character recognition). The mice were sold unbundled or bundled with popular software such as Microsoft's Windows (Exhibit 4). On the OEM side, they offered the Series 9 Mouse (a 3-button Microsoft-compatible mouse), the Series 14 Mouse (a uniquely shaped 2-button, Microsoft-compatible mouse that was expected to be very popular), and the new Series 15 mouse.

Pricing Strategy

Logitech's pricing strategy was to support a street price $10-20 below Microsoft by differential channel pricing. This involved starting with a target street price and working back to the manufacturer's selling price using the margins expected by different channels. This was particularly tricky since different channels had very different expectations. Electronic superstores and price clubs worked with 8-25 percent margins, while traditional dealers and department stores worked with 30-40 percent margins and stores would carry the Logitech product, only if they could get their margin. Pricing was further complicated by grey marketing and cross-channel ownership. The former would arise if differential pricing in different countries created opportunities for the product to be bought by distributors in one market to be sold at a profit in another. The latter arose if a holding company owned more than one type of Logitech distributor and was able to supply a superstore, for example, with a product bought for a full-service dealer. Estimated average wholesale prices for Logitech's and Microsoft's mice products are presented in Table 1.

Distribution and Sales Strategy

Logitech used a mix of direct sales, telemarketing, and distributors to achieve their objective of intensive distribution. Six OEM sales reps backed by 11 support staff managed ongoing relationships with key customers. On the retail side, Logitech had four retail channel groups: major retail and corporate accounts, education/government, international corporate accounts, and other retail chains or independents. While traditionally, Logitech's sales force had focused on developing channel relationships, management had increasing concerns about the lack of inroads made into corporate markets. Where Microsoft marketed directly to corporations, Logitech had tried to reach the corporations through dealers.

Logitech's distribution goals were to be everywhere they could be, to have as many stock-keeping units (skus) as possible in each store to maximize their shelf space, and to maintain strong distributor relationships. This required utilizing a mix of wholesaling intermediaries and retailers ranging from small independent computer stores to major international chains. Logitech believed they had successfully covered 98% of the market with their distribution strategy and led the industry with 50% coverage in the rapidly growing channel of consumer electronic super-

stores. However, they actively sought alternative channels of distribution, such as mail-order and telemarketing, as the industry matured and evolved towards commodity products. *good.*

Communication Strategy

Logitech's communication strategy had traditionally been a no-nonsense cognitive feature-function-benefit approach design to present solutions to customer needs. Wanting to develop an upscale image and develop greater affective appeal, Logitech created a new avant-grade visual identity and logo in January 1989. Although Logitech wanted to create an image of being a market leader in design and quality, and to communicate core product benefits of fun, creative freedom, and solution uniqueness, change was not achieved overnight. By the spring of 1990, some Logitech executives were concerned that they had not yet achieved a consistent feeling with their communication strategy. They had used a wide variety of communication media to spread their messages, but relied heavily on print advertising in trade magazines as well as point of purchase materials and packaging. Logitech also paid particular attention to co-operative advertising and special channel programs to motivate and support distributors.

THE SITUATION IN EARLY 1990

While Pierluigi Zappacosta was happy with the performance of Logitech, he was concerned with Logitech's ability to maintain margins in the mouse marketplace and wondered how he could maintain the current rate of growth and profitability into the 1990s. The Series 9 mouse had been a success, but it had been a quick response to Microsoft's sleek redesign and was not perceived internally as leading edge. As most mice now provided the same level of productivity, Zappacosta felt that a move towards ergonomic differentiation might be appropriate. Shortly after the launch of the Series 9 mouse, Logitech had begun developing two versions of a new ergonomic mouse based on the technology of the Series 9. One of these was designed specifically for right-handed users and the other for left-handed users. These new designs were shaped to fit the curve of the hand at rest and would help reduce repetitive stress problems, such as carpel tunnel syndrome. Prototypes of the ergonomic mouse had been completed (Exhibit 5) and had been received well in focus groups. In a second mouse development, Logitech engineers had developed a radio "cordless" mouse that could be used to control a computer without the impediment of a cord and without the line-of-sight requirement of an infrared mouse. This technology could be packaged in the Series 9 mouse shape or the new ergonomic mouse shape at a price about $100 higher than a corded mouse. Finally, Logitech had developed technology for a 3-dimensional mouse that showed promise for high-end CAD/CAM and design applications.

Zappacosta had to decide whether to launch one, two or all of these new products, and if so, how. The cordless mouse and the 3-D mouse were "neat" from a technological perspective and had generated some excitement among the engineers. The ergonomic mouse was not particularly exciting from a technological perspective, but it might help differentiate the Logitech product in the marketplace. In addition, it might provide a "foot in the door" for attracting corporate business. However, from a strategic perspective, not everyone was comfortable with the right- and left-handed approach. Ron McClure, Vice President Strategic Marketing, had expressed concerns about the potential reception for the product among corporate customers and resellers. Corporate buyers would probably not know whether the user would be left-handed or right-handed and many mice would be shared by multiple users. It was not clear, for example, how a purchaser for a school lab would decide how many right-handed versions and how many left-handed versions to buy. Corporate users also might not have much input into the purchase decision to specify brand preference. The "safe" corporate strategy would be to buy a generic "one size fits all" mouse. Ron had a similar concern about OEM customers. An OEM usually bundled the Logitech mouse with the OEM's software or hardware and would probably not want to package left-handed and right-handed versions. Resistance to the new ergonomic mouse was also based on three other factors. Distributor representatives said it could be a sku nightmare for resellers if they had to carry left- and right-handed, corded and cordless mice as well as the current bus, serial port, mouseport, serial and mouseport, IBM and Apple versions, bundled or unbundled. Many employees were concerned that it would be the first Logitech product launched that was not based purely on a technological innovation/advantage. Finally, for many of the reasons outline above, Logitech SA did not think they would want to launch the product in Europe.

While Logitech had been built on mouse technology, there were other directions that seemed to have great long-term potential. Scanner technology was similar to mouse technology and Logitech's hand-held Scanman had been a great success in terms of market share, margins and product image. Driven by increased demand for desktop publishing and multi-media solutions, the scanner market was expected to grow 25-30% per year and opportunities existed to produce better grey-scale or even color scanners. Another opportunity related to scanners

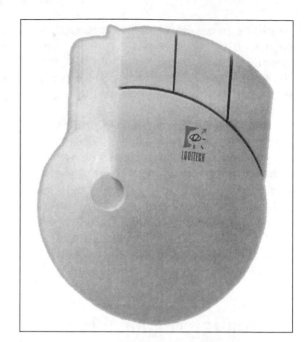

Cordless Radio Mouse

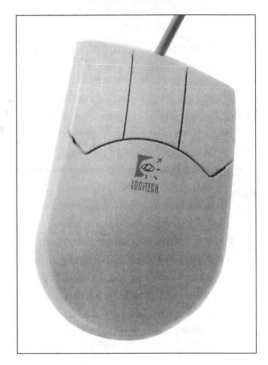

Ergonomic Mouse

EXHIBIT 5
Mouse Prototypes

would be to develop a digital camera that captured black and white images and downloaded them to a computer. Finally, the interactive gloves developed for computer games might be improved upon to use with computers.

There were lots of neat products to develop but Zappacosta knew he needed to act strategically. Personally, he was a strong champion of the new ergonomic mouse, but he recognized that it might be risky. The product was ready to launch and he could not put off the decision much longer. He wondered, if they did launch, how it should be done. Would this be an addition to the line or a re-placement? How could Europe be convinced to carry the product? Should the cordless mouse be launched as part of the new ergonomic product line, or separately, or not at all? How should the products be priced? How would Microsoft react? Would pursuit of other opportunities be a better use of resources? Zappacosta thought the best place to start looking for answers and directions was in their mission statement and long-term vision. He wondered whether "humanizing the computer" by giving senses to the computer adequately reflected their current and potential operation.

Fortron International Inc.

When entering foreign markets, Fortron International Inc., a Hamilton, Ontario based producer of sport whistles, had planned to use renewable sales agency agreements granting exclusive distribution rights to a country-specific distributor. The first such agreement with Allzweck-Sportartikel, a German wholesale catalogue store specializing in soccer equipment, was set to expire in October, 1991. Steve Foxcroft, General Manager of Fortron International Inc., felt the German market could be better exploited and was looking for alternative arrangements.

PRODUCT HISTORY

A conventional whistle produced its shrill "trill" through the movement of a small

This case was prepared by Marvin Ryder as a basis for classroom discussion rather than to illustrate effective or ineffective handling of a managerial situation. Copyright 1992, by Marvin Ryder, Michael G. DeGroote School of Business, McMaster University.

pea (a cork or plastic ball) in its interior. The pea alternately covered and uncovered a hole through which air was released producing a rapid cycle of sound and silence. Unfortunately, the pea would often stick especially if overblown or if water and debris got into the interior.

Ron Foxcroft and Joe Forte, professional basketball referees, perceived a need for a better, more dependable whistle. Along with dependability, they felt a new whistle had to have a louder, more penetrating sound, and an ability to be heard over the noise of a crowd. In short, a whistle that would not fail to perform under any conditions.

With the aid of an industrial designer, three and a half years of extensive development and testing, and $150,000 in start-up capital, the Fox 40 whistle was introduced in 1987 as the only whistle without a pea. It had three air chambers that, when blown, created three different frequencies. As the frequencies were out of phase, they were alternately reinforced and cancelled resulting in a louder, piercing, intense vibrato. The Fox 40 whistle worked in all weather conditions and, also, floated on water. Patent protection for twenty years, from those firms that would try to copy technology, was sought and received worldwide.

The whistle was introduced at the Pan American Games in Indianapolis, Indiana. By 1991, the Fox 40 whistle was used in seven Olympic sports, the National Football League (NFL), the Canadian Football League (CFL), the World Basketball League (WBL), National Collegiate Athletic Association (NCAA) Basketball, and the National Basketball Association (NBA). Since its introduction, many police departments and safety-oriented organizations adopted the whistle for standard use. The U.S. Cavalry and the Royal Life Saving Society endorsed the Fox 40 as their whistle of choice.

Originally designed for a professional referee, the Fox 40 whistle was available in three models. The "Classic" was sold in eight colours (red, orange, yellow, green, blue, pink, black and white), as was the "Mini-Fox." A referee model came in black and had a convenient finger grip.

COMPANY HISTORY

Fortron International Inc. was created in 1987 by Foxcroft and Forte to market the Fox 40 Whistle. It was a lean organization with a staff of three executives, including Foxcroft's son, Steve, as General Manager, who shared responsibility for marketing and financial decisions, and one secretarial assistant. For a dollar each, a nearby company, Promold Plastics, manufactured the whistle using injection moulding equipment and state of the art ultrasonic welding. In 1991, two million Fox 40 whistles would be sold worldwide and sales were expected to double in 1992. Revenue in 1991 exceeded $5 million and profits crossed the $300,000 threshold.

Fortron International's first overseas sales agent was Allzweck-Sportartikel in Trechtingshausen, West Germany. Exclusive distribution rights for West Germany were granted in a three year license agreement signed on October 8, 1988. Under the agreement, Fortron sold the whistles for $3.45 to Allzweck. Though Allzweck was free to negotiate discounts for volume purchases or promotional purposes, the suggested retail selling price was $5.95.

Allzweck was a wholesale catalogue store specializing in soccer equipment. It distributed 5,000 catalogues annually within Germany and had four sales representatives. In addition, it operated a small booth at the most important sporting goods trade show (ISPO) held annually in Munich. Allzweck's sales of Fox 40 whistles are presented in Table 1. All of these sales were from West Germany and most were from an area of thirty

TABLE 1	Sales of Fox 40 Whistles By Allzweck-Sportartikel

Year	Number of Whistles Sold
1989	9,340
1990	19,610
1991	29,850

kilometers around Frankfurt including Trechtingshausen.

[handwritten: no competitors in Germany]

There were no whistle manufacturers located in Germany.

COMPETITION

Conventional "pea" whistles retailed for half the price of the Fox 40. A number of small manufacturers were located in southeast Asia. These whistles were perceived to be a low quality, low price choice and were not used in sporting events. Instead, they were used recreationally and were common as children's gifts.

[handwritten: major competitor] The major sporting whistle was made by ACME Whistles of Birmingham, England. This company had manufactured whistles for more than a century and held the original patents for the British bobby's whistle (registered in 1884) and the original pea whistle (1985). The sales director did not feel that the Fox 40 posed any threat to its major sports whistle—the ACME Thunderer. "If you wish to imply that the Fox 40 is about to sweep ACME into liquidation, I think that's not the case." Nonetheless, it was rumoured that ACME was attempting to develop its own line of pea-less whistles.

A UNIFIED GERMANY

The breaching of the Berlin Wall in November 1989, was the beginning of German reunification. On October 3, 1990, 45 years after being separated, West Germany, the Federal Republic of Germany (FRG), and East Germany, the German Democratic Republic (GDR), were reunited under the former's name. The new FRG covered 356,945 square kilometers and supported a population of 79 million. Of that, *[handwritten: FRG]* 18 million lived in the former GDR.

While more than three-quarters of Germans favoured reunification, 1991 was a difficult year of adjustment. Forty percent of West Germans believed their financial health had worsened through higher taxes, increased interest rates, inflation and higher apartment rents. The unemployment rate rose to 11.3% due to closures of inefficient East German plants.

The currency used was the Deutschmark (DM). In reunification, the former Mark der Deutschen Demokratischen

TABLE 2 Sports Participation in East Germany During 1988

Sport	Number Participating	Individuals in Training
Football (soccer)	575,667	39,207
General sports	513,453	35,265
Gymnastics	408,476	26,542
Track and Field	180,605	15,583
Handball	152,975	13,225
Volleyball	134,924	12,454
Table Tennis	126,376	12,084
Swimming	83,509	6,911
Total	3,792,892	263,512

* Most recent statistic available.

TABLE 3 Sports Participation in West Germany During 1989

Sport	Number of Males	Number of Females
Football (soccer)	4,320,440	484,144
Gymnastics	1,226,507	2,669,562
Tennis	1,217,265	879,301
Hunting/Shooting	1,060,089	263,758
Table Tennis	534,391	179,876
Handball	515,514	257,824
Track and Field	452,437	364,950
Swimming	286,413	273,658
Volleyball	196,449	185,358
Judo	173,239	66,198
Total	11,604,189	6,817,754

*Most recent statistics available.

Republik (DDK-Mark) of East Germany was revalued to equal the DM. For exchange purposes, one DM was worth approximately $1.33 Canadian. In 1990, prior to unification, the GNP of West Germany increased by 4.5% to $1.6 trillion DM. The GNP for a unified Germany was expected to grow by 3.1% in 1991 and 1.6% in 1992. This was the second highest growth rate of the seven largest industrial nations. Inflation in West Germany was 2.7% in 1990. For a unified Germany, inflation was expected to be 3.5% in 1991 and 3.8% in 1992. These rates were among the lowest of the seven largest industrial nations. Under unification, the trade surplus was expected to decline. West Germany had a trade surplus of US$71.9 billion in 1990. A unified Germany would have trade surpluses of US$15 billion in 1991 and US$20 billion in 1992.

In 1991, over DM90 billion (US$50 billion) had been allocated for improving social security, roads, schools and hospitals and merging military forces in the former East Germany. This amount was more than 3% of the new Germany's GNP. Another DM90 billion would be spent over the next decade to move the federal government from Bonn to Berlin. Other spending in-

cluded DM115 billion between 1991 and 1994 for the Germany Unity Fund, DM21 billion in 1991 for privatising East German state firms and payments to the Soviet Union for the withdrawal and resettlement by 1994 of Soviet forces from East Germany costing DM50 billion.

The process of unification also involved sport and sports organizations. The old East German state bodies and associations, from the National Olympic committee (NOK) to the German Gymnastics and Sport Association (DTSB) were dissolved and incorporated into the corresponding West German structure (German Sports League). Many of the special sport schools for children and adolescents of East Germany were closed in favour of a decentralized sports movement. All sports budgets were dramatically cut and hundreds of full-time coaches and trainers were dismissed.

In 1988*, 21% of the East German population participated in sports. Of this number, only seven percent were in training for national and international competition (see Table 2). In 1989*, 30% of the West German population participated in sports. Interestingly, nearly twice as many males participated than did females and

*Most recent statistics available.

Potential market size (handwritten annotation)

TABLE 4   Participation in Sports By Age In West Germany During 1989

Age Group	Number of Males	Number of Females
Under 15	2,009,208	1,567,630
15 to 19	1,094,193	687,183
20 to 23	811,568	465,439
24 and Over	7,689,220	4,097,502
Total	11,604,189	6,817,754

* Most recent statistic available.

18 421 943. participate in sports. (handwritten annotation)

the largest group of participants was 24 years and older (see Tables 3 and 4).

Other German Markets

In addition to the sports market, Foxcroft wondered about the safety, fashion and education markets. Two blasts of a whistle were recognized internationally as an emergency signal. Since the Fox 40 whistle got louder as an individual blew harder and since it operated under any weather conditions, it was an ideal whistle in an emergency. With reunification in Germany came increased racist attacks on the poor and on new immigrants. Community groups were being formed to protect citizens and make neighbourhoods safer. Using a whistle as a signalling device would not require translation to be understood.

In the past decade, high fashion became prevalent in sportswear. The Fox 40 whistle had the potential of becoming a very fashionable, safety-oriented, accessory item. While limiting the extent to which it could spread in the sportswear industry, safety was particularly important in hunting, fishing, hiking, camping, skiing, cycling and boating. Interestingly, the more expensive the apparel for a sport, the easier it could be to sell a whistle. After spending two thousand DM on ski clothing and equipment, the price of a Fox 40 whistle would be almost unnoticeable.

In 1991, there were 4.5 million students enrolled in German schools and an additional 2.6 million enrolled in polytechnic schools. A safety education program coordinated through teachers and the schools could increase awareness of the Fox 40 whistle and lead to sales.

The German Consumer

In the "Guide for Canadian Exporters—The European Community" it was recommended that punctuality, politeness and a degree of formality were part of the keys to success in dealing with German consumers. Also, one needed to have a thorough knowledge of delivery periods, shipping costs, service requirements and performance characteristics. As holidays were very important to German workers, sales visits in July or August were avoided. A list of references was also useful.

By far the best sales vehicle for the German market was the appropriate trade fair. Germany had more world-class specialized industrial trade fairs than any other country. Because of this, many companies from beyond the German market attended, which extended marketing opportunities.

INTERNATIONAL OPTIONS

Generally, there were six levels of involvement in international marketing. Casual

(handwritten annotation: OPP #1)

exporting was the most passive and involved exporting only occasionally when surplus or obsolete inventory was available. This choice often led to losses and a fear of export markets.

Once a firm was making a continuous effort to sell its merchandise abroad, it moved to the level of active exporting. This was usually accomplished through sales agency agreements. A distributor in a foreign country was granted either exclusive or non-exclusive rights to sell a product in a geographic region. The manufacturing company only gained access to a market but no information about the business environment in that country. In return, the sales agency used its knowledge of distribution channels, consumer behaviour and local promotion to earn a healthy margin on each item sold. Foxcroft had such an agreement with Allzweck-Sportartikel. The spectrum of potential sales agents ranged from importers and wholesalers to department stores, mail order houses and buying co-operatives.

Licensing involved a formal agreement with a foreign company to produce Canadian merchandise. Like before, a company gained access to a market but no information about the business environment. The licensee was typically not responsible for sales of the product and so, often, a sales agency agreement was also required before a product could be distributed. Rather than make money through product production, the Canadian licensor would earn royalties either from a lump sum payment or on a per unit basis. Licensing was favoured for either elementary technology or products with short life cycles. The potential was considerable for licenses to copy new or advanced technology or use the technology after the end of an agreement. Historically about 50% of all licensing agreements managed to satisfy both parties.

At a higher level, a Canadian company could maintain a separate sales/marketing operation in a foreign country. The product could be made at home or through foreign contract manufacturers but the Canadian company would control foreign sales either through its own sales force or through supervising a group of local sales agents. This path was often used when a company wanted to gather information about a country before it considered launching its own production facility. It was an especially attractive learning experience if the company could protect its technology with patents and thus have time to grow slowly.

Of course, the ultimate level of involvement occurred with a company both marketing and producing its product in a foreign country. A new plant could be built or an existing plant could be acquired. For Foxcroft, a foreign plant would cost $1 million and would require management time to establish and operate.

Another option at this level, however, would be a joint venture with a foreign firm. While this path offered the advantage of cutting in half the $1 million investment and reducing the commitment of managerial resources, there were some disadvantages. One was the sharing of profits. A second was the lack of control over the strategic and operational decisions which affected the joint venture. Perhaps the biggest drawback was the lack of a potential joint venture partner. One could, no doubt, be found but how long would the process take?

The European Community

If Fortron established a stronger presence in Germany, it could become a base for expanded operations in the European Community. The European Economic Community (EEC) came into being in Rome in 1957. A treaty was signed by Belgium, France, West Germany, Luxembourg, Italy and the Netherlands. In 1973, the EEC became a group of nine as

Denmark, Ireland and the United Kingdom joined. It reached twelve member status when Greece joined in 1981 and Spain and Portugal joined in 1986. It was then that the name was shortened to European Community (EC) to reflect new integration goals of the group rather than the original economic ones. In 1990, the EC decided that a reunified Germany would retain EC membership. The EC represented one of the largest potential consumer markets with its population of 340 million. *→ big potential market*

The EC was striving to: 1) end intra-country customs checks; 2) create uniformity and mutual recognition of technical standards, university diplomas and apprenticeship courses; 3) create a common market in goods and services including a single broadcasting area; and 4) create an equal excise and national value added tax system. As of January, 1989, the standard value added tax rate in Germany was 14%. Value added taxes paid on a good in one EC country could be reclaimed if it entered another EC country.

Since forming, the positive consequences of the EC included the overall improvement of economic conditions in member countries and easier and less costly access to member markets. Patents registered in one member-country would automatically be registered and recognized in all EC countries. For Canadian firms, the EC posed some risks including: 1) intensified competition in EC markets as European firms became more efficient and the interest of non-European firms in the EC increased; 2) more competition in North American markets and non-EC markets as

should go in quickly
intensified comp – as other firms go into us.

the EC became more unified; and 3) another major bloc in the globalized world economy.

A major concern was the EC 1992 agreement. It would eliminate all barriers between member-countries so that people, capital and goods could move freely. The agreement also raised fears, outside the EC, that as internal barriers were lowered, external barriers would be raised, sometimes on very short notice. "Fortress Europe" was the worst possible outcome if a wave of protectionism swept the EC. It would see trade between EC countries stimulated at the expense of trade with non-EC member countries.

THE DECISION

As Steve Foxcroft reviewed the information, he needed to make several preliminary decisions. Should Fortron be selling whistles in the German Market? If so, what level of international marketing involvement was appropriate? Did existing management and financial resources preclude some forms of involvement? Not renewing the Allzweck license agreement would mean dissatisfaction with the number of whistles being sold. Could Fortron do better if it took control of all sales activities? Could a production centre, or other arrangement, be justified on the basis of entering the EC?

Clearly any preliminary decision made would need follow-up research and information before being implemented. Still he could not afford to have his limited managerial staff pursuing a number of non-viable options.

don't have enough staff to get involved

A.S. Norlight[1]

In the middle of March 1992, Mrs. Anne Solbakken (CEO, and a major shareholder of Norlight—a privately owned corporation) had problems hiding her temper when she confronted her marketing manager, Mr. Ole Olsen. "This is a real mess!" she said, referring to a letter received that same morning from the company's Italian agent, Mr. Antonio di Napoli. Mr. di Napoli had in fact informed A.S. Norlight that he terminated the contract they had signed less than a year ago, and that he demanded Lira 500 million in indemnities.

And this was not all. Their representative in Newcastle, GB-Light, had insisted on further changes of the present products in order to satisfy the requirements of the British market. According to Mr. Tore Bu, Norlight's financial officer, and Mr. Knut Johansen, the company's technical manager, the costs of complying with GB-Light's request would lead to a price increase that would virtually eliminate Norlight in the British market.

Fortunately Norlight had a very good position in the home market, with about 30% market share and annual sales approaching NOK 60 million. This should enable them to sustain the costs incurred during the introduction period in new markets. In Norway, they were well entrenched in the market, had excellent relations to the distribution channels, and were technologically well ahead of their competitors. Return on sales had been close to 5% during each of the last four years, and annual net profit after taxes had been above NOK 1 million during the same period.

Their main competitor in the domestic market—it had actually developed into quite a rivalry—was A.S. Lite-Tech, also a Norwegian company, but companies from Germany and Sweden also held considerable market shares. However, it was quite typical for this industry worldwide that the domestic companies held an edge. The major reasons for this were the local design and technical standards, the great number of contractors and the peculiarities of the channels of distribution in each market.

Norlight's export ventures had come about in response to The Single Market Act, and expected increased competition from foreign competitors. After some discussion with representatives of The Norwegian Export Council, and having done some basic research on the marketing opportunities, it was decided to approach the following EC countries: Great Britain, Denmark, Italy, France, and Germany. The markets of Great Britain and Italy were considered to be the most promising, and Mr. Olsen was assigned the task of looking into the opportunities. A primary concern was to find the best possible candidates to work with—either an agent or a distributor.

After some investigation—partly through small advertisements in trade magazines, partly with the assistance of the local representatives of the Export Council—they ended up with a long list of candidates in each country, most of which seemed quite serious and capable. It was the most diverse types of companies, ranging from one-man operations to large, established import firms.

Mrs. Solbakken expressed some doubts as to what kind of company they ideally should tie up with. A large and well introduced import company with an established network of wholesalers and customers would perhaps be best suited, but such a

---

[1] This case was written by Carl Arthur Solberg and Hermann Kopp at the Norwegian Management Institute. Although the background of the story is real, facts and names have been changed to disguise the company.

company might be too big for Norlight. Norlight would only be a small and insignificant supplier to such a company. On the other hand, a "one-man operation" would be advantageous if that person would give all his attention to the Norlight products. After endless discussions, Mrs. Solbakken favored trying both alternatives.

THE BRITISH MARKET

In the UK Norlight negotiated with a company well introduced in this type of business, GB-Light Ltd. in Newcastle-upon-Tyne. This company had been importing electrical fixtures and equipment ever since the early sixties, and had developed a large network of retailers mostly in the North East region of England. The company was chosen primarily because Mr. Jones, their managing director, immediately established a pleasant working relationship both with Mrs. Solbakken and Mr. Olsen, and because the company had excellent financial results and a very solid reputation. Yearly sales were about UK£ 14 million and the sales staff numbered 18–20 people.

The contract negotiations were a new and unexpected experience for both Mrs. Solbakken and Mr. Olsen. In the introductory phases they had met with Mr. Jones alone. He gave a refreshing impression of a professional manager, quite unlike the stereotyped picture of a British manager. When they later met in Newcastle to discuss the final details of the agency agreement, Mr. Jones was joined by three other men: Mr. P. Holloway, Mr. Jones' partner in GB-Light, Mr. A. G. Ressing, the sales manager, and Sir John Lawson, the company lawyer. The four were all equipped with a ten-page standard contract which they would like to use as a starting point for the discussions. Sir John politely presented the details of the contract to the two representatives of Norlight.

Mrs. Solbakken was quite astounded.

This was very different from the relaxed meetings they had previously had with Mr. Jones. During these meetings they had discussed things like commission and sales volume, and had reached a general agreement on these issues. The Norlight representatives believed the contract negotiations would be a mere formalization of this discussion. Instead they were met with a long range of new demands. Accordingly, Norlight was now expected to:

▶ Develop an English version of their product catalogue, manuals and service instructions.

▶ Transfer for one week in Newcastle a product engineer in order to train the sales and service people involved in the project.

▶ Send GB-Light within three weeks a complete set of demos at no cost.

▶ Stock sufficient spare parts and the most popular models in a warehouse in Newcastle.

▶ Guarantee maximum delivery to be no more than one month.

▶ Authorize GB-Light to grant price discounts, accept returns and extend credit beyond four months when necessary.

▶ Contribute at least UK£ 20,000 to the introductory advertising campaign, and pay 25 percent of any future advertising campaigns.

Mrs. Solbakken did not find any clause in the suggested contract that really committed GB-Light in any significant way, and she and Mr. Olsen had a hard time introducing such terms as:

▶ Minimum sales the first year UK£ 200,000 to be increased to UK£ 400,000 in the third year.

▶ A guarantee that GB-Light would not extend credit or pursue sales to customers who had exhibited a notoriously bad credit record.

▶ Changes in prices and terms of payment should be submitted to Norlight for approval.

In order to accept such "concessions," the GB-Light negotiators demanded a new clause entitling their company to a compensation of UK£ 20,000 if any of Norlight's commitments were breached. This was a bitter pill to swallow, but was accepted because Mrs. Solbakken and Mr. Olsen felt confident that Norlight could comply, and because the British representatives seemed quite stubborn on this if they were to accept Norlight's requirements.

Back in Norway, the Norlight organization immediately began their preparations to fulfill their commitments. The brochures and manuals were translated, and the company's development manager was sent to Newcastle to train GB-Light's sales and service people. Arrangements were also made to rent storage space and the demo models were shipped. Finally UK£ 20,000 were transferred to GB-Light's account in Barclay's Bank. A rough calculation indicated that by now NOK 500,000 had been spent on the introduction.

Mr. Bu, the financial officer, persuaded the local bank to extend the company's line of credit, and submitted a request for support from the Export Council. The council was generally prepared to cover part of the costs for translation, initial training and advertising expenses.

THE ITALIAN MARKET

The Italian experience was quite different. Mr. Olsen received a telephone call from Mr. Antonio di Napoli. He was at the Oslo airport, had just landed, and was just starting a two-week holiday with his family. He referred to the ads about representation, and was prepared to stop by Norlight anytime during his visit to discuss the prospects of working together.

Mr. di Napoli arrived at Norlight's headquarters the next morning. He was a charming and knowledgeable man who could refer to a long list of references in Italy. He was an experienced salesman and had worked in the electro fixtures industry for several decades. He knew the dealers better than his own cousins. After a visit to the factory, he expressed great interest in being Norlight's agent in Italy. At the end of a couple of hours of discussion, they agreed in principle on the main points of a representation agreement. The contract would be signed before Mr. di Napoli returned to Italy, about two weeks later. This would give Norlight's management a chance to check some of his references.

All references recommended Mr. di Napoli, and they also double checked with the Milan office of the Norwegian Export Council. Mrs. Solbakken and Mr. Olsen were confident that they had found the right man for the job, but Mr. Bu was somewhat reserved. "We haven't even considered the names on the list of candidates we already have," he said. He was overruled by the two others, who were very impressed with Mr. di Napoli, not least his mastery of English which they considered unusual in Italy.

A contract was signed, and the major terms were:

▶ Mr. di Napoli would get exclusive rights for all of Norlight's products in Italy.

▶ He was committed to sell for at least Lira 200 million in the first full year of operations, increasing to Lira 500 million the following year and reaching Lira 1 billion in the fourth year.

▶ His commission would be 10 percent on total sales.

▶ The two parties would seek to develop a good spirit of cooperation.

No mention was made of advertising expenditures. In fact, Mr. di Napoli did not place any importance on advertising. "What matters," he said, "is a good network of personal contacts. Then the rest comes by itself!" Mr. di Napoli even agreed to return to Norway soon in order to get required technical training, and he was prepared to cover the travel costs himself.

BUSINESS AS USUAL?

After half a year of operations, the status of Norlight's export efforts could be summed up as follows:

In the UK trial orders started to come in already two weeks after the first "introductory months" (when all the preparatory work was done). GB-Light had in fact presented the products at a local trade fair near Newcastle, and received some noticeable interest from one dealer. However, Mr. Jones reported that in order to push the sales, they had to grant substantial discounts, between 12 and 15 percent. Mr. Olsen was not in doubt: "We have to go along with these requirements, otherwise we will not get our products out to the dealers, and then nobody will use them." This made sense, but the other officers of the company were reluctant, and Mr. Bu exclaimed: "Who do they think they are? We've already put more than half a million kroners in this venture and now they are asking for discounts!" However, they agreed to allow GB-Light to grant 5–7 percent discount to select customers.

The reaction from Mr. Jones was one of qualified acceptance. After some weeks he returned with a request for "minor product alterations," as he put it. "Our dealers find it difficult to achieve preference for your products as they now stand and at the price you quote . . . etc. . . . etc." He finally suggested some changes in the design of the products.

Mr. Johansen was furious. "We have had endless discussion with our British representative on just about every tiny issue of our products, and of our marketing program, but so far they haven't achieved a single major sale. In Italy we don't meet any such objections. Both prices and products are being accepted as they are, and Antonio has been successful with about 20 dealers. I think we should look for a new distributor in the UK. I'm fed up with all their 'minor product alterations.' It only adds to our production costs!"

In Italy, things developed nicely. There was an endless stream of orders, initial trial orders, that later reached considerable numbers. In fact, next year's sales target had already been exceeded. Norlight was very happy and executed the orders as they came in. "We certainly have found the right representative in Italy," Mrs. Solbakken said one morning.

However, next week, Mr. Bu entered her office and presented last quarter's figures. It turned out that only 10 percent of all the invoices that were due from the Italian customers had been paid. "I don't like this," he grunted, "I wonder what kind of customers our friend Antonio is selling to?" "I can't understand this," Mr. Olsen said, "last week Antonio reassured me that our customer base was very solid, and based on his references, I find it hard to doubt what he's saying." "That's fine, Ole," the financial officer countered, "but I think that when twelve out of fourteen invoices have not been paid in time—and we've granted liberal credit terms—then it's time to review our credit policies towards our Italian customers!"

Mr. Olsen conceded that something should be done and agreed to write a letter to Mr. di Napoli airing Norlight's concerns. The situation did not improve when they two days later received a message from Banco di Milano that Stella Lucia, their biggest account so far in Italy, had filed for bankruptcy. An inquiry to the Export Council revealed that several of Mr. di Napoli's customers did not exhibit the world's best track record concerning timely payments. In his report the trade officer in Milan added that this is not unusual in Italy,

---

A/S Norlight

Ytterfjord
Norway

Tel (476)330780
Fax (476)330770

Mr. Antonio di Napoli
Villa di Lucia
Genova
Italy

March 2, 1992

Dear Antonio,

We have just received the news of Stella Lucia's bankruptcy, and would like to ask you to do anything in your power to minimize our loss. We have also experienced that some of your other customers are not paying our invoices on time, and this is clearly not acceptable.

So far we have liberally paid your commission and intend to do so in the future, but we are forced to suggest some new routines:

1. All new customers should pay by Letter of Credit, and established customers who do not meet their obligations in time should be required to do the same. This, naturally, is until we get to know them better.

2. We will not transfer any commission on sales before payment has been received from the customer.

I trust you understand this and look forward to hearing from you in the near future.

Sincerely,

Ole Olsen
Sales Manager

and that Norlight would have to be patient if they wanted to retrieve their accounts receivable. Mr. Olsen, nevertheless, tried to be very polite when writing his letter (Exhibit 1).

The response, however, was not very pleasant (Exhibit 2).

Mrs. Solbakken immediately called a management meeting.

"Gentlemen," she said, "we have tried for one year to enter two export markets. The results so far are not satisfactory. We are, of course, newcomers, but what we are experiencing now exceeds any expectation of bad luck. The efforts that we have put into these two markets cannot be quantified, but we spent at least NOK 700,000 in the UK, and our customers in Italy owe us

---

EXHIBIT 2

Antonio di Napoli

Genoa
Italy

Tel. (371)6590034
Telex 78560 agent i

Genova, March 12, 1992

Norlight A/S
POB 13
Ytterfjord
Norway

Att. Ole Olsen

Re terms of payment

I have received your letter of March 2, 1992, and can inform you that I do not see how I can work under the conditions stated in your letter. I thought that I had to do with professional business people, but your suggestions on commission payments and L/C suggest to me that we will have problems in getting along in the future.

I will therefore by April 1, 1992, end our relationship, and will demand that you pay a fee of Lira 500 million in indemnities.

Sincerely yours,

Antonio di Napoli

---

more than Lira 150 million, plus of course Antonio's demand for indemnity. And if this was not enough, I'm sorry to tell you that our business in Norway has suffered. We have not paid enough attention to our domestic business and our market share and profits have been eroding. I think time has come to reassess our strategy. This should be done before we discuss how to proceed with Antonio and GB-Light. I look forward to your comments!"

The Wuhan Art and Advertising Company

INTRODUCTION

Early in November 1987 Mr. Gui Niansheng (Manager), Mr. Song Zhiwei (Deputy Manager), Mr. Peng Shaowen (Head, Advertising Division), and Mr. Li Dali (Head, Planning and Development Section) of the Wuhan Art and Advertising Company met to discuss a new assignment given to their company by the Wuhan Oil Chemical Company, manufacturer of a number of detergent products.

The Wuhan Art and Advertising Company (WAAC) was located in Wuhan, a large industrial city situated on the Yangtze river in the central Chinese province of Hubei, about 750 kilometres to the west of the coastal city of Shanghai (Exhibit 1). Wuhan actually consists of three cities—each with its own distinctive history and personality. Hankou and Hanyang lie on the north bank of the Yangtze. Wuchang (the largest of the three cities) lies on the south bank. Hanyang and Wuchang are linked by the Wuhan Yangtze River Bridge. This bridge was com-

pleted with Russian assistance in 1957, prior to the break with the Soviet Union. It is the second largest bridge over the Yangtze River, and the only railway and highway bridge between Chongqing (Chungking) in the west and Nanjing (Nanking), near Shanghai, in the east. Hanyang and Hankou, in turn, are linked by a bridge over the smaller Han river, which flows into the Yangtze at Wuhan.

Wuhan is a major Chinese centre of iron and steel production and, with metropolitan area population of six million inhabitants, is the fifth largest city in China after Shanghai, Beijing (Peking), Tianjin (Tientsin) and Guangzhou (Canton). It is also a major educational centre, with more than sixty universities and colleges of higher learning. Huazhong University of Science and Technology in Wuchang ranks among China's "top eight" universities.

ADVERTISING IN CHINA

1. Media

China has an abundance of advertising media. In 1989 there were more than 1,300 newspapers and 3,000 periodicals which accepted advertising, 167 radio stations and 65 million television sets. At peak times more than 250 million people watch television—the highest audience for a television program in the world, exceeding even the US Superbowl telecast's audience.

This case was prepared by Professor John R.G. Jenkins with the assistance of Wang Xin, research assistant, with the support of a Laurier Institute case writing grant. This case is intended as a basis for class discussion rather than to indicate effective or ineffective handling of an administrative situation. Copyright 1990 by Laurier Institute, Wilfrid Laurier University and John R.G. Jenkins, Graduate School of International Management, Monterey Institute of International Studies.

EXHIBIT 1

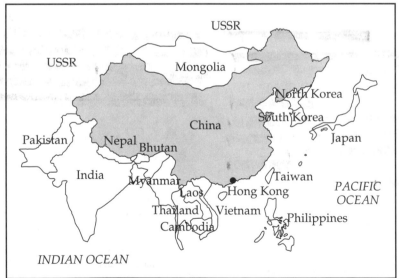

Boundary representations not necessarily authoritative.

2. Historical Development

Advertising has existed both in China and elsewhere for thousands of years. For example, in China during the period of the Shang Dynasty (3,000 years ago), banners were flown to advertise wine shops.

While commercial advertising was banned in China during the Cultural Revolution (which lasted approximately from 1966 to 1976), it has made rapid strides since then. Domestic advertising expenditure increased by more than 50% every year between 1979 and 1989. Advertising aimed at export markets also increased each year.

With the development of a planned consumer-oriented economy and the emergence of competition, it became clear to Chinese government planners that advertising had a major role to play in providing both purchasers of consumer goods and customers for industrial goods with information which would assist them in making the right choice. It was increasingly recognized that advertising in China had to be both honest and informative.

3. Advertising Agencies

In 1989 China could report the existence of 680 *major* advertising agencies (often referred to in China as "advertising companies"). In total, there were approximately 10,000 advertising agencies employing 117,000 people. Some of these operated on a national scale, while others operated on a regional or local basis. Some concentrated purely on domestic advertising, while others already had considerable experience of international business.

A number of Chinese advertising agencies had been established for more than 20 years (for example the Shanghai Advertising Corporation). In Beijing the two major advertising corporations were the Beijing Advertising Corporation and the China International Advertising Corporation.

Chinese advertising corporations played a vital role in assisting their clients with media selection. For instance, in the case of radio, there were not only (as indicated earlier) 167 stations to choose from but, in turn, a number of these radio stations broadcast different programs—aimed at specific segments—on different frequencies.

4. Market Research

While market research was still in its infancy in China in 1989, advertising companies could at least provide the necessary information to develop random samples of certain categories of consumers. This was because advertising agencies had access to comprehensive government family registration data, with up-to-date information on all urban residents including data relating to age, sex, marital status, occupation, and salary level.

Furthermore, door-to-door surveys were particularly productive in a culture where face-to-face exchanges are a common feature of daily life.

HISTORY OF THE WUHAN ART & ADVERTISING COMPANY

The Wuhan Art and Advertising Company is located in the Hankou sector of Wuhan. It was originally established in 1956 by the Government of China on the premises of an earlier advertising firm which had operated prior to the establishment of the People's Republic of China. From its inception it was involved both in the development of advertising materials and in the production of traditional Chinese art for export.

In 1967, soon after the beginning of the Cultural Revolution, the advertising activities of the company were halted and many of the latter's employees were transferred to the company's art production facility, which continued to produce Chinese art works. Mr. Gui (WAAC's manager) was transferred to the art production facility from another government organization in 1972. From 1979, when the company was re-established following the end of the Cultural Revolution, WAAC grew significantly in size and importance until 1989, at which time it had become one of the eight largest advertising companies in China. It was an active member of the China National United Advertising Corporation, an association of 61 advertising companies located across China.

WAAC had produced advertising campaigns, both in Wuhan and the surrounding Hubei Province, for a number of leading consumer branded products produced in various regions of China. These included "Paris" perfume (marketed by an agency based in the northern city of Tianjin). "South China" sewing machines (manufactured in Guangzhou), "Honey" Beer (brewed in Wuhan) and many others. WAAC also specialized in package design work for a number of clients in Wuhan and Hubei province together with a number of nearby provinces including Hunan and Sichuan.

ORGANIZATION

concentrated only on the SC·

By 1988, the Wuhan Art & Advertising Company had a total of approximately 300 employees. As it grew, the company made a determined effort to attract able, intelligent and well-educated young people. Mr. Li Dali[1] (Head of Planning and Development, and a graduate in Economic Management from Zhongnan Finance &

---

[1] As some readers of this case will be aware, it is customary for the Chinese to list an individual family name (surname) first. Li Dali would be referred to in English as "Mr. Dali Li", or "Mr. Li" for short.

Economics University in Wuchang) joined the company in 1983. However, because the advertising business in China was not known to offer such well-paid jobs as did certain other industries (for example, Chinese joint ventures with foreign firms), it was not an easy task to attract capable new employees. An organizational chart of the company is provided in Exhibit 2. Each division will be discussed in turn.

1. The Chinese Art Division

This division of the company was not involved in advertising activities. Rather, it specialized in the production of traditional Chinese art, specifically water-colour paintings on silk fabric. These traditional paintings were particularly popular with customers in western countries. The paintings were exported to dealers located in Hong Kong and overseas, especially Canada, the United States, Japan, Singapore and Australia. The Chinese Art Division employed 140 people. It once accounted for 40 percent of the company's total revenue and profits, but its shares of these had gradually decreased in recent years. It was expected that this division and the rest of the Wuhan Art & Advertising Company would become separate entities in the near future.

2. The Advertising Division

This division, which employed 35 employees and was headed by Mr. Peng Shaowen, was divided into three sections, as follows:

a. *The Customer Service Section*

The Customer Service Section, employing 17 persons and headed by Mr. Wang Huan, maintained liaison with past and present clients, thus corresponding to the Account Management divisions (consisting of account supervisors, account executives, etc.) of North American, Japanese and Western European advertising agencies. This

EXHIBIT 2
Organization Chart of the Wuhan Art & Advertising Company (WAAC)

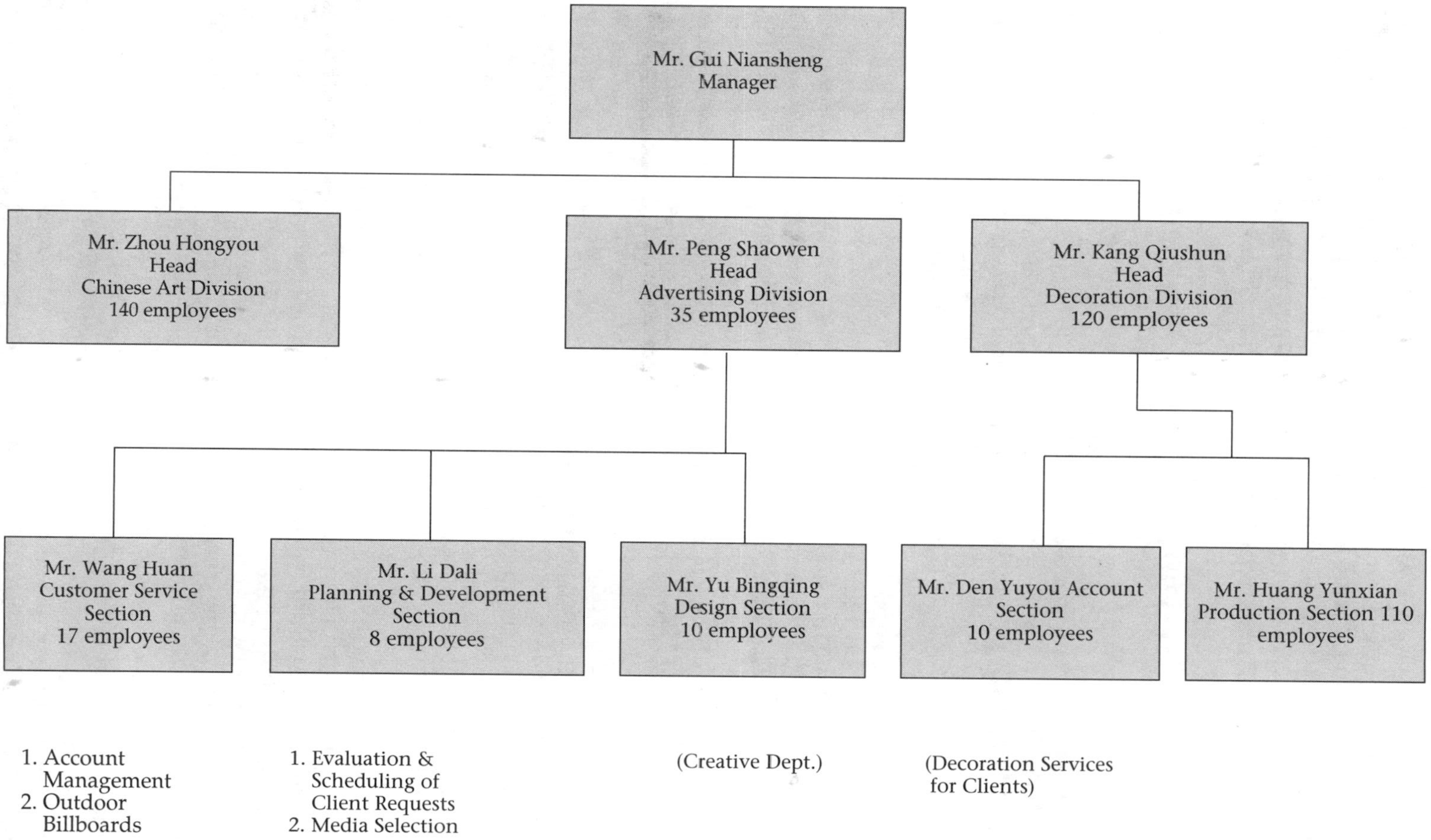

Mr. Gui Niansheng
Manager

Mr. Zhou Hongyou
Head
Chinese Art Division
140 employees

Mr. Peng Shaowen
Head
Advertising Division
35 employees

Mr. Kang Qiushun
Head
Decoration Division
120 employees

Mr. Wang Huan
Customer Service
Section
17 employees

Mr. Li Dali
Planning & Development
Section
8 employees

Mr. Yu Bingqing
Design Section
10 employees

Mr. Den Yuyou Account
Section
10 employees

Mr. Huang Yunxian
Production Section 110
employees

1. Account
   Management
2. Outdoor
   Billboards

1. Evaluation &
   Scheduling of
   Client Requests
2. Media Selection

(Creative Dept.)

(Decoration Services
for Clients)

section was also responsible for all outdoor billboard advertising.

b. *The Planning and Development Section*

The company's Planning and Development Section, headed by Mr. Li Dali, consisted of eight employees. Its function was to evaluate client requests, and decide how they would be executed. This section also reached decisions regarding the precise media vehicles and media schedules to be recommended to clients for their campaigns. In terms of its specific media functions, the Planning and Development Section thus corresponded, in part, with the media departments of advertising agencies in North America, Japan, and Western Europe.

c. *The Design Section*

The Design Section, headed by Mr. Yu Bingqing, employed ten people. These were artists and copywriters who specialized in layouts of the advertisements conceived by the Planning & Development Section in response to client requests. The Design Section thus corresponded to the creative departments of Western and Japanese advertising agencies.

3. The Decoration Division

This division, headed by Mr. Kang Qiushun, employed 120 employees and was divided into two sections. It was equal status to the Chinese Art Division and the Advertising Division.

a. *The Account Section*

This section, employing 10 persons and headed by Mr. Den Yuyou, accepted orders from its own clients who merely required specific indoor and outdoor services to be performed, such as the repainting of billboards. The Account Section also accepted orders from WAAC's own Advertising Division, which would sometimes choose WAAC's Decoration Division to produce a spe-

cific advertisement. The Account Section was also responsible for organizing and planning special decoration assignments, and made all decisions required.

b. *The Production Section*

The Production Section, headed by Mr. Huang Yunxian, employed 110 people. Most of them were carpenters and painters. The job of the Production Section was primarily to provide ad layouts and finished illustrations to implement creative strategies and executions *previously decided* upon by the Account Section, or to have a specific decoration job done. Sometimes, however, the section illustrated concepts which had been developed by the Wuhan Art & Advertising Company's own Advertising Division, and at the latter division's request.

RELATIONSHIPS BETWEEN DIVISIONS

Each of the three divisions of the company constituted a profit centre. The company naturally encouraged collaboration between its divisions and sections if all other things were equal. However, each division also had the right, if it saw fit, to choose another division or independent company to have a particular job done. The Advertising Division, in particular, sometimes gave a production order to an outside company after considering all of its options.

THE COMPANY'S CLIENTS

The Wuhan Art & Advertising Company used the term "clients" to mean those organizations with whom it had enjoyed long-established relationships, and who advertised in a number of different mass media (radio, TV, newspapers, etc.).

The company's clients were mainly located in the Wuhan area, but represented a variety of industries. For example (and in addition to the clients mentioned earlier), in the electric appliance industry the company handled advertising for "Lotus" washing machines (manufactured by the Wuhan Washing Machine Company), "Hongshanhua" electric fans (the Wuhan Electric Fan Company) and "Yangtze" cassette recorders (the Wuhan Radio Company).

In the chemical industry, WAAC advertised the "Flower" line of soap and detergent products (the Wuhan Oil Chemical Company) and the "Sanxi" line of industrial chemicals (the Wuhan Sanxi Industrial Group Co.). In the food industry, in addition to the previously-mentioned "Honey" beer (the Wuhan Beer Company), WAAC was also responsible for advertising the "Yangtze" line of food products (the Changjiang Food Company*).

In the office equipment industry, WAAC advertised "Youyi" ("Friendship") duplicating machines (manufactured by the Wuhan Duplicating Machine Company). In the textile industry, WAAC advertised "Bingchuan" ("Glacier") feather-lined clothes (the Wuhan Feather Clothes Factory) and "Jinlu" ("Golden Deer") sportswear (the Wuhan Knitting Mill).

In addition to its clients who were manufacturers of consumer and industrial goods and services, WAAC also had a number of service industry clients, including a number of hotels and restaurants in Wuhan and other towns and cities in Hubei province.

While a number of the agency's clients (such as the producers of "Paris" perfume and the manufacturers of 'South China' sewing machines) were located in other parts of China, WAAC primarily handled the advertising needs of clients in Wuhan and the surrounding cities of Hubei Province, the neighbouring provinces of Hunan and Sichuan, and certain coastal provinces to the east. Other advertising agencies usually handled the advertising needs of large "national" consumer companies in other regions of China.

SYSTEM OF PAYMENT

Traditionally, WAAC charged a fee for an advertising campaign which featured billboards only. For example, one advertising campaign consisted to ten painted billboards located at various points within the Wuhan metropolitan area. The fee for this particular advertising campaign, as for other billboard campaigns, was based on the amount of work requested from the agency. In this respect, WAAC's fee billing procedure was typical of that of most Chinese advertising agencies. However, when *other* media were used the advertising agency was compensated on a commission basis. This was also the case with other Chinese agencies.

THE CHINESE MARKET FOR CONSUMER GOODS

Because China was a developing country in 1989, the North American concept "The Consumer is King" meant little. Many consumer goods were still in short supply and organizations dedicated to the protection of the rights of Chinese consumers were only just beginning to appear on the scene in the late 1980s.

Many Chinese manufacturers of established consumer goods and services were not market-oriented in the North American sense, reasoning that if their product was a good one, it didn't need to be advertised.

---

* Changjiang is the Chinese name for the Yangtze River.

THE DEVELOPMENT OF ADVERTISING CAMPAIGNS

If a new or existing client company of the Wuhan Art and Advertising Company simply requested, for example, the painting of a single billboard for one of its products, or the production of one hundred 12" x 22" wall posters to be displayed around Wuhan, or 200 wall calendars to be distributed to various organizations, the agency acceded promptly to this request. No major demand was thus made on the time of the advertising company's executives.

However, where an existing or new client was considering a more substantive advertising campaign, the Wuhan Art and Advertising Company involved a significant number of its executives in planning activities. The procedure followed in such cases is indicated in Exhibit 3.

Firstly, the client request was communicated to that member of the Customer Service Section who was assigned to that client. This individual, in turn, contacted Mr. Li Dali, head of the Planning and Development Section. The client liaison man (the "account executive" in North American terms) then met with Mr. Li and one or more of his colleagues to agree on the target market, to establish special objectives, and to decide advertising strategy and tactics. The Planning and Development Section would subsequently select the media to be used.

The next division of the agency to be involved was the Design Section, since it was responsible for the creation of the actual advertising layouts. At this point the Planning & Development Section of the Advertising Division (which, as we have earlier noted, was responsible for the scheduling of all work within the agency) would develop a schedule for the work which would result. Finally, the Production Section would be asked to produce the final art-

work required, such as the assigning of painters to produce billboards to the agreed upon design.

If a major advertising campaign was prepared, a Review Committee, chaired by Mr. Li, would examine it closely and make revisions, if necessary, before presenting it to the client.

Advertising Media

Table 1 summarizes the main advertising media available to advertisers within China. The predominant media recommended by WAAC were billboards, posters, calendars, and magazines. A client, however, would usually go directly to the local television or radio station, or to the local newspaper, if he decided he wished to use any of the later media. He would also call upon a representative of these media for advice with respect to the design and content of such advertisements.

Table 2 provides cost data with respect to certain advertising media available to advertisers in the Wuhan area.

Sources of Media Information

Information regarding the circulations and audiences of Chinese advertising media was still somewhat limited in 1989, due to the relative youth of the advertising industry in China. This meant that decisions on the most appropriate media to use for a given client's campaign often had to be made, in part, on the basis of previous experience with various media and on intelligent judgement.

NEW BUSINESS

New business activity was primarily handled by WAAC's manager, Mr. Gui Niansheng. However, Mr. Gui would be accompanied by other key WAAC executives when a prospective client wished to discuss more specific advertising ideas.

EXHIBIT 3
Wuhan Art & Advertising Company: Procedure Followed in the Development of an Advertising Campaign

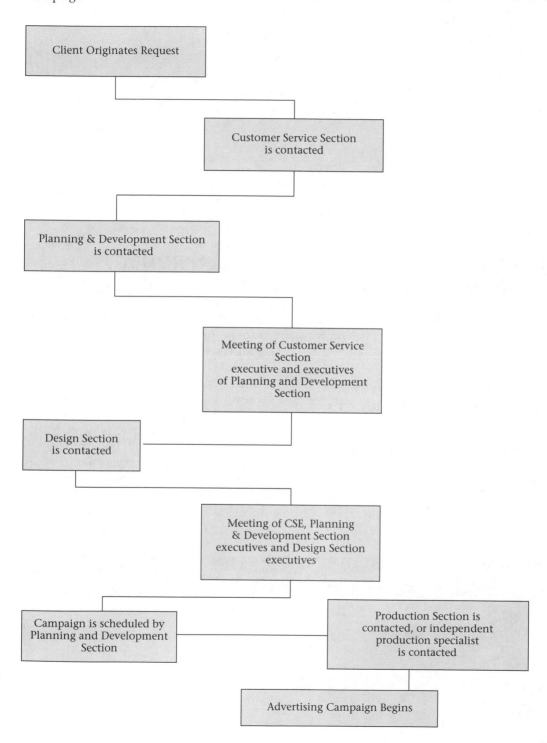

Client Originates Request

Customer Service Section is contacted

Planning & Development Section is contacted

Meeting of Customer Service Section executive and executives of Planning and Development Section

Design Section is contacted

Meeting of CSE, Planning & Development Section executives and Design Section executives

Campaign is scheduled by Planning and Development Section

Production Section is contacted, or independent production specialist is contacted

Advertising Campaign Begins

TABLE 1 Advertising Media Available to Advertisers in China

A.	*Outdoor* Billboards Colored Lanterns Neon Lights Sculptures Banners	D.	*Point of Purchase* Posters Models Coloured Banners Cards
B.	*'Electronic'* Radio TV Theatre	E.	*Novelty Items* Various
C.	*Print* Newspapers Magazines Playbills Product Booklets Calendars		

THE WUHAN OIL CHEMICAL COMPANY

In October 1987 the Wuhan Oil Chemical Company (WOCC) contacted Mr. Gui to inform him that they planned to launch a new consumer detergent in the Wuhan area. Wuhan Oil Chemical Company was founded in the 1900s and was located in Hanyang, Wuhan. Since 1949, it had become a state-owned company.

Direct by Mr. Yang Decong, the company had a total of approximately 1230 employees. Over one hundred of these were engineers. In 1986, WOCC's net sales reached ¥41,734,000. Its net profit after taxes was ¥3,500,000.

WOCC'S PRODUCT LINE

WOCC produced a number of consumer products, primarily in the soap and detergent categories, along with some other industrial chemical products. It marketed six brands of detergent products: "Flower", "Golden Monkey", "Wuhan", "White Goose", "Qintai" (a place in Hanyang in which musical instruments were traditionally played), and "Dragon horse". Although WOCC had spent ¥480,000 on advertising and sales promotion in 1988, WOCC's six brands were advertised as a group. Consumers, consequently, appeared to be confused with respect to the

TABLE 2 Some Selected Media Costs in Wuhan Area

Television	Commercial	Time Cost
Wuhan TV	30 sec.	¥500
Hubei TV	30 sec.	¥600
Jianghan TV	30 sec.	¥600
Newspapers	*Space Unit*	*Unit Cost*
Yangtze Daily	10 x 35 cm	¥3,750
Hubei Daily	10 x 35 cm	¥4,200

Note: The Renminbi yun (¥) was worth approximately 0.30¢ Canadian (0.25¢ U.S.) during the latter part of 1989.

TABLE 3 Wuhan Oil Chemical Company Flower Product Line

Description	Unit	Wholesale Price (¥)	Selling Price @/pack
1. 500g x 20 "Flower" super-concentrated, foamless detergent	Tonne	3,290.80	1.87
2. 500g x 20 "Flower" concentrated, fragrance detergent	"	3,771.90	2.15
3. 100g x 10 "Flower" concentrated, fragrance detergent	"	5,570.20	6.35
4. 450g x 24 "Flower" high-efficiency, bleaching detergent	"	3,372.30	1.73
5. 450g x 24 "Flower" coloury detergent	"	3,879.10	1.99
6. 450g x 24 "Flower" multi-function detergent	"	4,093.50	2.10
7. 450g x 24 "Flower" cleaner	"	2,865.00	1.47
8. 500g x 30 "Flower" liquid detergent	"	4,180.00	2.38
9. 400g x 30 "Flower" liquid detergent	"	5,600.00	2.55
10. 100g x 30 "Flower" liquid detergent	"	4,540.00	2.59
11. 330g x 50 "Flower" foam bath	"	10,151.51	3.89
12. 250g x 50 "Flower" Wool and Silk cleaner	"	5,360.00	1.53
13. 500g x 30 "Flower" Wool and Silk cleaner	"	4,700.00	2.68
14. 400g x 30 "Flower" disinfectant liquid detergent	"	4,452.00	2.03
15. 500g x 30 "Flower" disinfectant liquid detergent	"	4,440.00	2.53
16. 500g x 30 "Flower" toilet cleanser	"	4,620.00	2.63
17. 250g x 50 "Flower" toilet cleanser	"	5,280.00	1.51
18. 250g x 50 "Flower" shampoo	"	9,520.00	2.81
19. 500g x 30 "Flower" shampoo	"	9,510.00	5.62
20. 500g x 30 "Flower" conditioner	"	8,103.00	4.78
21. 300g x 30 "Flower" conditioner	"	8,099.92	7.98
22. 250g x 50 "Flower" conditioner	"	8,320.00	9.81
23. 450g x 24 "White Goose" fragrance detergent	"	2,956.00	1.62
24. 450g x 24 "Golden Monkey" fragrance detergent	"	3,274.00	1.68
25. 1000g x 10 "Dragon Horse" detergent (for export only)	"	3,230.00	3.68

characteristics and benefits of each individual brand, resulting in half of WOCC's production volume remaining unsold and stored in warehouses.

Table 3 includes a complete list of items in the "Flower" product group. Three other WOCC detergent products are also listed. Table 4 is a partial list of some industrial products produced by the company.

THE DETERGENT MARKET IN CHINA

1. The National Market

Since 1980, when semi-automatic washing machines became popular in China, consumer demand for detergents had increased rapidly. During the 1980–85 period

TABLE 4 Some Industrial Products Produced by The Wuhan Oil Chemical Company

	Price (¥)
1. Castor oil in bulk	4,800.00/Tonne
2. Barrelled roll oil	8,500.00/Tonne
3. Bulk DP (bottle-washing) detergent	4,200.00/Tonne
4. Bulk (eiderdown-cleaning) detergent	5,500.00/Tonne

the detergent market grew steadily, and local producers usually dominated local markets. But since 1985 the situation had changed. A Shashi (Hubei Province based competitor (the Shashi Oil Chemical Company, or SOCC) was the first to break the pattern with a new and effective detergent produced called "Power 28" which invaded the Wuhan market and then expanded nationally. Competition in the detergent market subsequently became intense.

Nevertheless, overall consumer demand for detergent continued to increase and detergent production was expanded accordingly. More than 1.3 million tonnes of detergent were produced nationally in 1988. The Wuhan Oil Chemical Company accounted for 2.3 percent of total national production.

2. The Wuhan Market

It was estimated that there were over 1.1 million households in the Wuhan metropolitan area in 1989. Total detergent demand in the Wuhan market was estimated to be 17,800 tonnes. In Wuhan WOCC faced the competitors shown in Table 5.

A recent study indicated that White Cat, Jiamei, Power 28 and WOCC's own "Flower" brand each had Wuhan market shares of over 10 percent. WOCC's Wuhan share of market (achieved by all *six* of WOCC's detergent brands) was only 27 percent. It seemed that WOCC's brands couldn't perform as well as might have been expected in their home market, partly because of the poor product quality of several brands and partly because of poor packaging. WOCC executives also suspected that the company's past advertising campaigns had been ineffective, since only 40 percent of the adult population of the Wuhan area was even *aware* of the existence of WOCC's detergent brands.

MARKETING OBJECTIVES

Carefully examining the situation, WOCC executives first decided to combine the company's six detergent brands into one brand and concentrate marketing efforts on the latter. It would be based on a new detergent formula of high quality that would be launched to combat competitive brands and increase the company's market share. It would be made available to consumers at an attractive price.

There were two ways of selecting the company's brand name. Firstly, a new name could be selected. Alternatively, a brand name could be selected by WOCC from among one of its existing brand names. After careful consideration, one of the latter ("Flower") was selected for the following reasons:

1. The new Flower" formula had been designated as a high-quality product by the National Ministry of Light Industry.
2. "Flower" ranked first in sales among WOCC's six branded detergents.
3. The "Flower" brand name was likely to be more easily recognized by old customers.

After a thorough review and study of the 1987 market situation, it was agreed that the following marketing objectives should be set for "Flower" detergent from March of 1988 to March of 1989:

1. Increase WOCC's market share in the Wuhan area from 27 percent to 40 percent.
2. Increase sales volume by 50 percent within the rest of Hubei Province.
3. Expand sales in other provinces by 35 percent.
4. Increase total annual sales volume from 14,444 to 40,000 tonnes.

TABLE 5

Competitor	City	Head Office Province	Leading Brand(s)
WOCC faced the following competitors in Wuhan:			
SOCC	Shashi	Hubei	Power 28
SOCC	Shanghai	—	White Cat Wuzhou
BOCC	Beijing	—	Golden Fish Temple of Heaven
XOCC	Xuzhou	Jiangsu	Seagull
TOCC	Tianjin	—	Jiamei
NOCC	Nanjing	Jiangsu	Jiajia

While the WOCC executives stated that their company would undertake strong selling efforts to ensure that the new soap would be stocked in all Wuhan-area stores, it was clear that they were looking to their advertising agency for assistance both in persuading retailers to stock the product and in persuading consumers to buy it. Above all, they expected the agency to develop, for them, an exciting and colorful advertising campaign.

BUDGET CONSTRAINTS

After a study of all relevant costs, it was decided that the advertising budget would be ¥550,000, based on the target volume of 40,000 tonnes.

MARKETING STRATEGY AND TACTICS

In order to achieve "Flower's" marketing objectives, it was decided by WOCC that marketing efforts should be focused on the household consumer market, i.e., a "pull" strategy should be adopted.

Specifically, efforts should be directed at that consumer group which appeared to be most responsive to marketing efforts designed to persuade it to buy detergents. This group was composed of married men aged 25 to 45 and married women aged 30 to 50.

Market research information indicated that 86 percent of detergent buyers were in the 25-45 age groups. Over 60 percent of purchasers were married men, since men in the China of the late 1980s played a more active role as household buyers than women. In addition, 60 percent of the purchasers were frequent buyers.

SUBSEQUENT DEVELOPMENTS

WOCC selected WAAC as its exclusive advertising agency to handle its advertising for "Flower" detergent, and asked it to develop an advertising campaign for 1989. As indicated at the beginning of the case, Mr. Gui and his colleagues at WAAC met early in November for a preliminary discussion of the market situation and to prepare for a series of meetings with WOCC executives.

ADVERTISING OBJECTIVES

WOCC and WAAC executives recognized that based on the "Hierarchy of Effects" or "Market Continuum" theories of consumer/customer behaviour[2], in which

---

[2] See, for example, Robert J. Lavidge and Gary A. Steiner, "A Model for Predictive Measurement of Advertising Effectiveness," *Journal of Marketing*, October 1961, p. 61 and John R.G. Jenkins, *Marketing and Customer Behavior*, Pergamon Press, 1974, p. 17.

consumers/ customers for a product are perceived to move along a series of stages—from unawareness of the product's very existence to purchase-evaluation and repurchase—it was essential to increase the brand's awareness level as a prerequisite to increasing brand preference.

ADVERTISING STRATEGY AND TACTICS (EXECUTION)

Following discussions between WOCC and WAAC executives at a series of work sessions in November and December 1987, it was decided that "Flower's" advertising campaign should consist of two stages:

1. The brand name and package should be emphasized in order to increase brand awareness among households aged 24–45. The advertising agency strongly recommended the use of TV commercials for this purpose.

   TV to attract awareness

2. Potential users of "Flower" detergent would need to be moved along the various stages of the Market Continuum following the initial Awareness stage (i.e. Comprehension, Conviction, Preference, Intent-to-Buy, Purchase-Evaluation and Repurchase) through the use of other media in addition to TV.

   Other media to encourage them to repurchase

   Subsequently a line of WOCC products would be introduced bearing the "Flower" brand name. "Flower" itself would be marketed internationally.

MEDIA

In order to re-introduce "Flower" detergent to its present consumers and to potential new consumers as rapidly as possible, WAAC recommended the use of various media, as follows:

1. Outdoor Advertising

▶ *Billboards*

   Billboards should be used mainly in the cities of Wuhan and Shashi, as well as in the big cities of South China. The billboard size would be just over $80m^2$.

▶ *Neon Signs*

   Neon signs would be constructed in the downtown district of Wuhan.

2. Television

▶ A TV commercial would be produced to emphasize "Flower's" package and brand name, and broadcast on Central TV Hubei TV and Wuhan TV for a period of 2–3 months.

▶ A TV series commercial would subsequently be produced to focus on a line of products bearing the "Flower" brand name.

3. Radio

"Flower" should be advertised on Radio Hubei and Radio Wuhan for 1 year.

4. POP Advertising

▶ Posters should be displayed in and around retail stores throughout the Wuhan area.

▶ Lighted models of "Flower" packages would be placed in stores where detergents were sold.

▶ Calendar cards would be printed and presented to shoppers.

5. Public Relations

A "Flower" theme song would be created. This was subsequently done, and the words were as follows:

> "Flower, Flower. Both you and I love her.
> Flower, Flower. I love Flower."

Each of the WAAC recommendations was accepted by WOCC's executives and the "Flower" advertising campaign commenced in March 1988.

THE ADVERTISING BUDGET

Flower's 1989 advertising budget was broken down as indicated in Table 6.

THE FUTURE

While both the WOCC executives and Mr. Gui and his colleagues at WAAC were pleased with the results of their collaboration, and believed that they had produced an effective 1989 "Flower" advertising campaign, they knew that they could not afford to be complacent about the future.

Not only was the Chinese consumer becoming more sophisticated and demanding in terms of consumer goods, but competition—not only from the Shashi firm but from detergent producers elsewhere in China—seemed likely to intensify. WOCC therefore faced the challenge of making continual product improvements, introducing appropriate product line extensions, and launching completely new products to meet newly developing consumer needs.

WAAC, as the Wuhan Oil Chemical Company's sole advertising agency, faced an annual challenge of producing and placing high-calibre advertising to achieve its client's marketing objectives.

In May 1989, WOCC executives informed Mr. Gui and his colleagues at the Wuhan Art & Advertising Company that they wished to meet with them in August to begin planning sessions for "Flower's" 1990 advertising campaign.

TABLE 6

1. *Outdoor Advertising*
   a. *Billboards*
      ▶ *Hankou, Wuhan (size: 100m^2)*
        March 1988 March 1989
        Cost: ¥18/m2 month x 100 x 12
          = ¥21,600

      ▶ *Guanzhou, Guangdong (size: 80m^2)*

   b. *Neon Signs*
      ▶ *Hankou, Wuhan (size: 90m^2)*
        Cost: ¥45/m^2 month x 9 x 12 = ¥48, 600

2. *Television*
   a. *Central TV*
      ▶ 10 times/ month (April-October 1988)
        Cost: ¥120,000

   b. *Beijing TV (Local affiliate of National Network)*
      ▶ Number of times: 30
        Cost: ¥8,000

   d. *TV Commercial Production*
        Cost: ¥50,000

3. *Radio*
   a. *Radio Hubei & Radio Wuhan*
        Cost: ¥16,200

4. *Point of Purchase Items*
   a. *Posters (in and around stores)*
      ▶ Number: 10,000
        Cost: ¥8,000

   b. *Lighted Models*
      ▶ Number: 60
        Size 60 x 100 cm
        Cost: ¥30,000

5. *Newspaper*
        Cost: ¥70,000

6. *Sports and Entertainment Advertising*
        Cost: ¥50,000

7. *Other Media*
        Cost: ¥20,000

   Total Budget

   ▶ *Shashi, Hubei (size: 40 m^2)*
     March 1988–March 1989
     Cost: ¥7,200

   c. *Hubei TV*
      ▶ Number of times: 120
        Cost: ¥40,000

   e. *Wuhan TV*
      ▶ Number of times: 60
        Cost: ¥12,000

   c. *Calendar Cards*
      ▶ Number: 100,000
        Cost: ¥14,000

   ¥540,000

Grasse Fragrances SA[1]

Grasse Fragrances, headquartered in Lyon, France, was the world's fourth largest producer of fragrances. Established in 1885, the company had grown from a small family-owned business, selling fragrances to local perfume manufacturers, to a multinational enterprise with subsidiaries and agents in over 100 countries.

For marketing director Jean-Pierre Volet, the last few years had been devoted to building a strong headquarters marketing organization. In February 1989, however, he was returning to France after an extensive tour of Grasse sales offices and factories, and a number of visits with key customers. As the Air France flight touched down in Lyon Airport, Jean-Pierre Volet was feeling very concerned about what he had learned on the trip. "Our sales force," he thought, "operates much as it did several years ago. If we're going to compete successfully in this new environment, we have to completely rethink our sales-force management practices."

THE FLAVOR AND FRAGRANCE INDUSTRY

Worldwide sales of essential oils, aroma chemicals, and fragrance and flavor compounds were estimated to be around $5.5 billion in 1988.

Five major firms accounted for approximately 50 percent of the industry's sales. The largest, International Flavors & Fragrances Inc. of New York, had 1988 sales of $839.5 million (up 76 percent from

1984), of which fragrances accounted for 62 percent. The company had plants in 21 countries, and non-U.S. operations represented 70 percent of sales and 78 percent of operating profit.

Quest International, a wholly-owned subsidiary of Unilever, was next in size with sales estimated at $700 million, closely followed by the Givaudan Group, a wholly-owned subsidiary of Hoffman-LaRoche with sales of $536 million, and Grasse Fragrances with sales of $480 million. Firmenich, a closely held Swiss family firm, did not disclose results but 1987 sales were estimated at $300 million.

Grasse produced only fragrances. Most major firms in the industry, however, produced both fragrances and flavors (i.e., flavor extracts and compounds mainly used in foods, beverages, and pharmaceutical products). Generally, the products were similar. The major difference was that the flavorist had to match his or her creations with their natural counterparts, such as fruits, meats, or spices, as closely as possible. On the other hand, the perfumer had the flexibility to use his or her imagination to create new fragrances. Perfumery was closely associated with fashion, encompassed a wide variety of choice, and products had to be dermatologically safe. Development of flavors was more limited, and products were required to meet strict toxicological criteria because the products were ingested.

MARKETS FOR FRAGRANCES

While the use of perfumes is as old as history, it was not until the nineteenth century, when major advances were made in organic chemistry, that the fragrance industry emerged as it is known today.

[1] This case was written by Professor Michael Hayes as a basis for class discussion rather than to illustrate either effective or ineffective handling of an administrative situation. All names, including the company name, have been disguised. Copyright © 1989 by IMEDE, Lausanne, Switzerland. Not to be used or reproduced without permission.

Focusing first on perfumes, use of fragrances expanded into other applications. In recent years manufacturers of soap, detergents, and other household products have significantly increased their purchases of fragrances and have represented the largest single consumption category. Depending on the application, the chemical complexity of a particular fragrance, and the quantity produced, prices could range from less than FF40 per kilogram to over FF4,000.[2]

Despite its apparent maturity, the world market for fragrances was estimated to have grown at an average of 5 to 6 percent during the early 1980s, and some estimates indicated that sales growth could increase even further during the last half of the decade. New applications supported these estimates. Microwave foods, for instance, needed additional flavorings to replicate familiar tastes that would take time to develop in a conventional oven. In laundry detergents, a significant fragrance market, the popularity of liquids provided a new stimulus to fragrance sales, as liquid detergents needed more fragrance than powders to achieve the desired aroma. Similarly, laundry detergents designed to remove odors as well as dirt also stimulated sales, as they used more fragrance by volume.

THE NEW BUYING BEHAVIOR

Over time, buying behavior for fragrances as well as markets had changed signficantly. Responsibility for the selection and purchase of fragrances became complex, particularly in large firms. R&D groups were expected to ensure the compatibility of the fragrance with the product under consideration. Marketing groups were responsible for choosing a fragrance that gave the product a competitive edge in the marketplace, and

purchasing groups had to obtain competitive prices and provide timely deliveries.

Use of briefs (the industry term for a fragrance specification and request for quotation) became common. Typically, a brief would identify the general characteristics of the fragrance, the required cost parameters as well as an extensive description of the company's product and its intended strategy in the marketplace. Occasionally, a fragrance producer would be sole sourced, generally for proprietary reasons. Usually, however, the customer would ask for at least two quotations, so competitive quotes were the norm.

GRASSE FRAGRANCES SA

Background

The company was founded in 1885 by Louis Piccard, a chemist who had studied at the University of Lyon. He believed that progress in the field of organic chemistry could be used to develop a new industry—creating perfumes, as opposed to relying on nature. Using a small factory on the Saigne River near Grasse, the company soon became a successful supplier of fragrances to the leading perfume houses of Paris. Despite the interruptions of World Wars I and II, the company followed an early policy of international growth and diversification. Production and sales units were first established in Lyon, Paris, and Rome. In the 1920s, company headquarters were moved to Lyon. At that time, the company entered the American market, first establishing a sales office and then a small manufacturing facility. Acquisitions were made in England, and subsequently the company established subsidiaries in Switzerland, Brazil, Argentina, and Spain.

Faced with increased competition and large capital requirements for R&D, plant expansion, and new-product

---

[2] $1.00 = approximately FF6.00 in 1988.

launches, the Piccard family decided to become a public company in 1968. Jacques Piccard, oldest son of the founder, was elected president and the family remained active in the management of the company. Assisted by the infusion of capital, Grasse was able to further expand its business activities in Europe, the United States, Latin America, and the Far East.

In 1988 total sales were $450 million, up 60 percent from 1984; 40 percent of sales came from Europe, 30 percent from North America, 10 percent from Latin America, 5 percent from Africa/Middle East, and 15 percent from Asia/Pacific. In recent years the company's position had strengthened somewhat in North America.

By the end of 1988, the company had sales organizations or agents in 100 countries, laboratories in 18 countries, compounding facilities in 14 countries, chemical production centers in three countries, and research centers in three countries. Employment was 2,500, of whom 1,250 were employed outside France.

Products

In 1988, the company's main product lines were in two categories:

▶ Perfumery products used for perfumes, eau de cologne, eau de toilette, hair lotion, cosmetics, soaps, detergents, and other household and industrial products.

▶ Synthetics for perfume compounds, cosmetic specialties, sunscreening agents, and preservatives for various industrial applications.

According to Jacques Piccard: "From the production side, flavors and fragrances are similar, although the creative and marketing approaches are quite different. So far we have elected to specialize in just fragrances, but I think it's just a matter of time before we decide to get into flavors."

Following industry practice, Grasse divided its fragrances into four categories:

▶ Fine fragrances
▶ Toiletries and cosmetics
▶ Soaps and detergents
▶ Household and industrial products

MARKETING AT GRASSE

In 1980, Jean-Pierre Volet was appointed marketing director, after a successful stint as country manager for the Benelux countries. At the time, the headquarters marketing organization was relatively small. Its primary role was to make sure the sales force had information on the company's products, send out samples of new perfumes that were developed in the labs, usually with little customer input, and handle special price or delivery requests. As Volet recalled:

In the 1940s, 1950s and 1960s, most of our business was in fine fragrances, toiletries and cosmetics. Our customers tended to be small and focused on local markets. Our fragrance salesman would carry a suitcase of 5 gram samples, call on the customer, get an idea of what kind of fragrance the customer wanted and either leave a few samples for evaluation or actually write an order on the spot. It was a very personal kind of business. Buying decisions tended to be based on subjective impressions and the nature of the customer's relation with the salesman. Our headquarters marketing organization was designed to support that kind of selling and buying. Today, however, we deal with large multinational companies who are standardizing their products across countries, and even regions, and who are using very sophisticated marketing techniques to guide their use of fragrances. Detergents and other household products represent an increasing share of the market. When I came to headquarters, one of my important priorities was to structure a marketing organization which reflected this new environment.

In addition to the normal administrative activities such as field sales support, pricing, and budgeting, Volet had built a fragrance creation group and a product management group. More recently, he had established an international account management group.

The fragrance creation group served as a bridge between the basic lab work and customer requirements. It also ran the company's fragrance training center, used to train both its own sales force and customer personnel in the application of fragrances. The product management group was organized in the four product categories. Product managers were expected to be knowledgeable about everything that was going on in their product category worldwide and to use their specialized knowledge to support field sales efforts as well as guide the creative people. It was Volet's plan that international account managers would coordinate sales efforts.

Field sales in France reported to Piccard through Raoul Salmon, who was also responsible for the activities of the company's agents, used in countries where it did not have subsidiaries or branches. In recent years, use of agents had declined, and the company expected the decline to continue.

Outside France, field sales were the responsibility of Grasse country managers. In smaller countries, country managers handled only sales, thus operating essentially as field sales managers. In other countries, where the company had manufacturing or other nonselling operations, the norm was to have a field sales manager reporting to the country manager. Although individual sales representatives reported to the field sales managers, it was understood that there was a dotted-line relationship from the sales representatives to the ICCs and the product managers.

The company relied extensively on its field sales force for promotional efforts, customer relations, and order-getting activities. There were, however, two very different kinds of selling situations. As Salmon described them:

> There are still many customers, generally small-scale, who buy in the traditional way where the process is fairly simple. One salesperson is responsible for calling on all buying influencers in the customer's organization. Decisions tend to be based on subjective factors, and the sales representative's personal relations with the customer are critically important.

> The other situation, which is growing, involves large and increasingly international customers. Not only do we see that people in R&D and marketing as well as in purchasing can influence the purchase decision, but these influencers may also be located in a number of different countries.

In either case, once the decision had been made to purchase a Grasse fragrance, the firm could generally count on repeat business, as long as the customer's product was successful in the marketplace.

On occasion, however, purchase decisions were revised, particularly if Grasse raised prices or if the customer's product came under strong competitive price pressure, thus requiring that a less expensive fragrance be considered.

The Quotation Procedure

For small orders, the quotation procedure was relatively simple. Popular fragrances had established prices in every country, and the sales force was expected to sell at these prices.[3] In some instances, price concessions were made, but they required management approval and were discouraged.

For large orders, it was the norm to develop a new fragrance. Increasingly, customers would provide Grasse with extensive information on their intended product and its marketing strategy, including the country or countries where the product would be sold. To make sure the fragrance fit the customer's intended marketing and product strategy, Grasse was expected to do market research in a designated pilot country on several fragrances, sometimes combined with samples of the customer's product. According to Volet:

> Once we have found or developed what we think is the best fragrance, we submit our quotation. Then the customer will do his own market research, testing his product with our fragrance and with those of our competitors. Depending on the outcome of the market research, we may get the order at a price premium. Alternatively, we may lose it, even if we are the low bidder. If, on the other hand, the results of the market research indicate that no fragrance supplier has an edge then price, personal relationships or other factors will influence the award.

Because of the extensive requirements for development and testing, headquarters in Grasse was always involved in putting a quotation together, and close coordination was vital between headquarters and the branch or subsidiary. When buying influencers were located in more than one country, additional coordination of the sales effort was required to ensure that information obtained from the customer was shared and also to have a coherent account strategy.

Coordination of pricing was also growing in importance. Many large customers manufactured their products in more than one country and looked for a "world" price rather than a country price. In these situations, country organizations were expected to take a corporate view of profits, sometimes at the expense of their own profit statements. The lead country (i.e., the country in which the purchasing decision would be made) had final responsibility for establishing the price. Increasingly, however, this price had to be approved in Lyon.

Submitting quotations in this environment was both complex and expensive. According to Volet:

> Receiving a brief from a customer starts a complex process. We immediately alert all our salespeople who call on various purchasing influencers. Even though the brief contains lots of information on what the customer wants, we expect our salespeople to provide us with some additional information.

> The next step is for our creative people to develop one or more fragrances which we believe will meet the customer's requirements. They are aided in this effort by our product managers who know what is going on with their products worldwide. If additional informa-

---

[3] Subject to approval by marketing headquarters, each Grasse producing unit established a transfer price for products sold outside the country. Country prices were established, taking into account the country profit objectives and the local market conditions. Transfer prices were usually established for a year. Adjusting transfer prices for fluctuations in exchange rates was a matter of ongoing concern.

tion is needed from the customer, our international account people will contact the appropriate sales-people.

After creating what we think is the right product or products, we may conduct our own market research in a country designated by the customer. This is usually done under the direction of our product manager, working closely with our market research people. Throughout this process, our sales force is expected to stay in close touch with the customer to give us any changes in his thinking or any competitive feedback. Based on the results of this effort, we then submit our proposal, which gives the customer the price, samples, and as much product information as possible.

With some customers, there is little further sales effort after they receive our quotation, and the buying decision is made "behind closed doors." In other instances, we may be asked to explain the results of our research or to discuss possible modifications in our product and, sometimes, in our price. Frequently we find that the customer is more concerned with our price policy (i.e., how firm the price is and for how long) than with the price quoted at the time of the brief.

When you make this kind of effort, you obviously hate to lose the order. On the other hand, even if we lose, the investment made in development work and market research is likely to pay off in winning another brief, either with the original customer or with another customer.

International Accounts

In 1988 about 50 percent of the firm's business came from some 40 international accounts. Looking to the future, it was expected that the number of international accounts would grow, and some estimated that by 1994 as much as 80 percent of the firm's business would come from international accounts.

As of 1988, 18 to 20 international accounts were targeted for coordination by International Client Coordinators (ICCs) in Lyon. The principal responsibility of each ICC was to really know assigned customers on a worldwide basis and put that knowledge to use in coordinating work on a brief. The rest were followed in Lyon, but coordination was a subsidiary responsibility. In either case, it was the view at headquarters that coordination was critical. As Volet described it:

> We rely extensively on account teams. European teams may meet as often as once a quarter. Worldwide teams are more likely to meet annually. For designated accounts, the ICC takes the lead role in organizing the meeting and, generally, coordinating sales efforts. For others, the Parent Account Executive (the sales representative in the country selling the customer component with the greatest buying influence) plays the lead role. In these situations, we hold the Parent Account Executive responsible for all the ICCs daily coordinating work with the customer. We also expect him to be proactive and already working on the next brief long before we get a formal request.

> Here in Lyon, we prepare extensive worldwide "bibles" on international accounts which are made available to all members of the

team. We also prepare quarterly project reports for team members. Our next step will be to computerize as much of this as possible.

Sales Management Practices

In 1988, sales-force management practices were not standardized. Selection, compensation, training, organization, and so on were the responsibility of subsidiary management. Even so, a number of practices were similar.

Sales representatives tended to be compensated by a salary and bonus scheme. A typical minimum bonus was 1.5 month's salary, but could range up to 2.5 month's salary for excellent performance. The exact amount of the bonus was discretionary with sales management and could reward a number of factors.

Sales budgets were established from estimates made by sales representatives for direct orders (i.e., orders that would be placed by their assigned accounts). These estimates were developed from expectations of sales volume for fragrances currently being used by customers, in which case historical sales were the major basis for the estimate, and from estimates of sales of new fragrances. While historical sales of currently used fragrances were useful in predicting future sales, variations could occur. Sales activity of the customer's product was not totally predictable. In some instances, customers reopened a brief to competition, particularly where the customer was experiencing competitive cost pressures.

Predicting sales of new fragrances was even more difficult. Customers' plans were uncertain, and the nature of the buying process made it difficult to predict the odds of success on any given transaction. Grasse Fragrances, nevertheless, relied heavily on these estimates. The sum of the estimates was expected to add up to the company budget for the coming year. When this was not the case, sales managers were expected to review their estimates and increase them appropriately.

The company had recently introduced companywide its own version of management by objectives. Each sales representative was expected to develop a personal set of objectives for negotiation with his or her sales manager. Formal account planning, however, had not been established, although some subsidiaries were starting the practice.

Sales training had two components. Product knowledge tended to be the responsibility of headquarters, relying heavily on the fragrance training center. Selling skills, however, were principally the responsibility of the subsidiary companies.

Selection practices were the most variable. Some subsidiaries believed that company and product knowledge were key to selling success and so tended to look inside the company for individuals who had the requisite company and product knowledge and who expressed an interest in sales work. Others believed that demonstrated selling skills were key and so looked outside the company for individuals with good selling track records, preferably in related industries.

SALES MANAGEMENT ISSUES

A number of sales management practices were of concern, both in headquarters and in the subsidiaries.

Influence Selling

Ensuring appropriate effort on all buying influencers was a major concern. According to Salmon:

> Our sales representatives understand the importance of influence selling, but we have no formal way of recognizing their efforts. A num-

ber of our large accounts, for instance, have their marketing groups located in Paris, and they have lots of influence on the buying decision. If we win the brief, however, purchasing is likely to take place in Germany or Spain or Holland, and my sales representative will not get any sales credit.

In a similar vein, Juan Rodriguez, sales manager for a group of countries in Latin America, commented:

We have a large account that does lots of manufacturing and purchasing in Latin America but does its R&D work in the US. The customer's people in Latin America tell us that without strong support from R&D in the US, it is very difficult for them to buy our fragrances. The sales representative in New York is certainly aware of this, but his boss is measured on profit, which can only come from direct sales in the US, so he's not enthusiastic about his sales representative spending a lot of time on influence business.

In certain instances, the nature of the buying process resulted in windfalls for some sales representatives. Commenting on this aspect, Salmon observed:

It can work the other way as well. Our Spanish subsidiary recently received an order for 40 tons of a fragrance, but the customer's decision to buy was totally influenced by sales representatives in Germany and Lyon. Needless to say, our Spanish subsidiary was delighted, but the people in Germany and Lyon were concerned as to how their efforts would be recognized and rewarded.

While there was general recognition that influence selling was vital, it was not clear how it could be adequately measured and rewarded. As Salmon pointed out:

In some instances (e.g., the order in Spain) we're pretty sure about the amount of influence exerted by those calling on marketing and R&D. In other instances, it is not at all clear. We have some situations where the sales representative honestly believes that his calls on, say R&D are important but, in fact, they are not. At least not in our opinion. If we come up with the wrong scheme to measure influence, we could end up with a lot of wasted time and effort.

Incentive Compensation

Compensation practices were a matter of some concern. The salary component was established at a level designed to be competitive with similar sales jobs in each country. Annual raises had become the norm, with amounts based on performance, longevity, and changes in responsibility. The bonus component was determined by the immediate manager, but there was concern that bonuses had become automatic. Still further, some held the view that the difference between 1.5 and 2.5 times the monthly salary was not very motivating, even if bonus awards were more performance driven.

Whether merited or not, sales representatives expected some level of bonus, and there was concern that any change could cause morale problems. At the same time, there was growing recognition of the increasing importance of team selling.

Overall responsibility for compensation practices was assigned to Claude Larreché, director of human resources. According to Larreché:

Some of our sales managers are interested in significantly increasing the incentive component of salesforce compensation. It has been my view, however, that large incentive payments to the sales force could cause problems in other parts of our organization. Plus, there seems to be considerable variation in country practice with regard to incentive compensation. In the US, for instance, compensation schemes which combine a fixed or salary component and an incentive component, usually determined by sales relative to a quota, are common. To a lesser degree, we see some of this in Europe, and somewhat more in the south, but I'm not sure that we want to do something just because a lot of other companies are doing it.

We're also thinking about some kind of team incentive or bonus. But this raises questions about who should be considered part of the team and how a team bonus should be allocated. Should the team be just the sales representatives, or should we include the ICCs? And what about the customer service people without whom we wouldn't have a base of good performance to build on?

Allocation is even more complicated. We're talking about teams comprised of people all around the world. I think it is only natural that the local manager will think his sales representative made the biggest contribution, which could result in long arguments. One possibility would be for the team itself to allocate a bonus pool, but I'm not sure how comfortable managers would be with such an approach.

Small Accounts

Despite the sales growth expected from international accounts, sales to smaller national accounts were expected to remain a significant part of the firm's revenues and, generally, had very attractive margins. According to one country sales manager:

> With the emphasis on international accounts, I'm concerned about how we handle our smaller single-country accounts. Many of them still buy the way they did 10 and 20 years ago, although today we can select from over 30,000 fragrances. Our international accounts will probably generate 80% of our business in the years to come, but the 20% we get from our smaller accounts is important and produces excellent profits for the company. But I'm not sure that the kind of selling skills we need to handle international accounts are appropriate for the smaller accounts. Personal and long-term relationships are tremendously important to these accounts.

Language

In the early 1980s, it had become apparent to Grasse management that French would not serve as the firm's common language. In most of its subsidiary countries, English was either the country language or the most likely second language. With considerable reluctance on the part of some French managers, it was decided that English would become the firm's official language. Personnel in the United States and England, few of whom spoke a second language, welcomed the change. There were, however, a number of problems. As the Italian sales manager said:

We understand the need for a common language when we bring in sales representatives from all over Europe or the world. And we understand that English is the "most common" language in the countries where we do business. All of my people understand that they will have to speak English in international account sales meetings. What they don't like, however, is that the Brits and Americans tend to assume that they are smarter than the rest of us, simply because we can't express ourselves as fluently in English as they can. It's totally different when my people talk to someone from Latin America or some other country, where English is their second language, too.

A related problem is the attitude that people from one country have toward those of another. This goes beyond language. Frequently, our people from Northern Europe or North America will stereotype those of us from Southern Europe or Latin America as disorganized or not businesslike. My people, on the other hand, see the northerners as inflexible and unimaginative. To some extent, these views diminish after we get to know each other as individuals, but it takes time and there is always some underlying tension.

Language also influenced decisions on rotation of personnel. It was Volet's view that there should be movement between countries of sales managers and marketing personnel. Still further, he felt that sales representatives who aspired to promotion should also be willing to consider transfers to another country or to headquarters in Lyon. As he pointed out, however:

Customer personnel in most of our international accounts speak English. Hence, there is a temptation to feel that English language competency is the only requirement when considering reassignment of sales personnel. In fact, if we were to transfer a sales representative who spoke only English to Germany, for instance, he would be received politely the first time, but from then on it would be difficult for him to get an appointment with the customer. It has been our experience that our customers want to do business in their own language, even if they speak English fluently.

An exception might be an international account whose parent is British and which transfers a lot of British personnel to another country. Even here, however, there will be lots of people in the organization for whom English is not a native tongue.

Therefore, we require that our salespeople speak the language of the country and are comfortable with the country culture. Local people meet this requirement. The real issue is getting all, or most, of our people to be comfortable in more than one language and culture.

Sales Training

One of the most perplexing issues was what, if any, changes to make with regard to sales training. At headquarters there was considerable sentiment for standardization. As Volet put it:

I really don't see much difference in selling from one country to another. Of course, personal relations may be more important in, say, Latin America or the Middle East than in Germany, but I think that as much as 80–85% of the selling job can be harmonized. In addition, it's my view that our international accounts expect us to have a standardized sales approach. Sales training, therefore, should be something we can do centrally in Lyon.

This view was supported by those in human resources. According to Claude Larreché, director of human resources:

We no longer see ourselves as a collection of individual companies that remit profits to Lyon and engage in occasional technology transfer. Our view of the future is that we are a global company that must live in a world of global customers and markets. I think this means we must have a Grasse Fragrance culture that transcends national boundaries, including a common sales approach; i.e., this is the way Grasse approaches customers, regardless of where they are located. A key element in establishing such a culture is sales training here in Lyon.

Others disagreed with this point of view, however. Perhaps the most vociferous was the U.S. sales manager:

I understand what Jean-Pierre and Claude are saying, and I support the notion of a common company culture. The fact is, however, that selling is different in the United States than in other parts of the world. Not long ago we transferred a promising sales representative from Sweden to our office in Chicago. His sales approach, which was right for Sweden, was very relaxed, and he had to make some major adjustments to fit the more formal and fast-paced approach in Chicago. I don't see how a sales training program in Lyon can be of much help. Plus, the cost of sending people to Lyon comes out of my budget, and this would really hit my country manager's profits.

In fact, I think we ought to have more flexibility with regard to all our sales management practices.

As Jean-Pierre Volet waited for his bag at the Lyon Airport, he wondered how far he should go in making changes with regard to the sales force. Whatever he did would be controversial, but he was convinced some changes were necessary.

Richardson Manufacturing Company Inc.
A Domestic Company Considers International Marketing Opportunities

In 1907 Emmit D. Richardson, father of Bob and Ray Richardson, began serving agriculture in Glen Elder, Kansas. In February 1922 he purchased a blacksmith shop in Cawker City, Kansas, a farming community in the North Central part of the state, which at that time had a population of 1,064. By 1992 the population of Cawker City had declined to 686, but net sales of the successor to Richardson's original blacksmith shop, the Richardson Manufacturing Company, Inc., were $1,730,000 and net profit was $158,000. Richardson's 1988–1992 profit and loss statement and balance sheet are shown in Tables 1 and 2. The Richardson brothers, both of whom were graduates of Kansas State University, divided responsibilities for company operations. Bob, with the title of President, concentrated upon the financial side of the company, and Ray took responsibility for design, engineering, and manufacturing. As sales of the company expanded, the two brothers decided to expand the executive staff of the company by hiring a director of sales. The man selected for this position was George "Jiggs" Taylor. Before coming to Richardson, Jiggs had been for 15 years the personal pilot to E. C. Riley, Cawker City's most famous entrepreneur whose widespread operations included a 5,000-acre Mexican cotton ranch, apartment buildings and office buildings in widely scattered locations, distributorships for farm implements, domestic and foreign automobiles, cattle feed lots, and, finally, a construction company whose operations consumed the liquid funds of Mr. Riley's operations and forced him into bankruptcy.

PRODUCTS AND U.S. MARKETS

Richardson 1992 sales were accounted for by three principal products.

313 units

① Products 40 and 45: The Richardson AD-Flex Treader and Mulch Treader, 45 Percent of Sales ($814,000)

This implement, which had been invented by James Van Sickle, a son-in-law of E. D. Richardson, was priced at $200 per foot at retail and sold mainly in 11- to 15-foot lengths. It was designed for the ground tillage and follows the initial ground breaking either by the traditional moldboard plow or by one of the more recent approaches to ground breaking, such as the undercutter plow.[1] The treader enabled a farmer to practice what was known as stubble mulch farming, a system of farming including harvesting, tillage, and planting operations that maintains much of the crop residue anchored on the soil surface. The main purpose of this system of farming is to keep enough residue on the surface to protect both the soil and the young crop from damage by water and wind erosion.[2]

---

[1] The moldboard plow was a device that cut a furrow into the earth and with a curved board or metal plate turned over the earth from the furrow. The undercutter plow simply cuts under the earth to form a furrow without turning over the earth.
[2] "Use of Stubble Mulch Tillage Tools," by Walter E. Selby, Extension Agricultural Engineer (duplicated) (no date).

TABLE 1 Profit and Loss Statement, 1988–1992

	1988	1989	1990	1991	1992
Sales	1,202,617.46	1,227,057.54	1,467,471.96	1,696,081.00	1,820,324.24
Less: Cash discount given	60,109.76	59,659.20	77,803.64	88,834.86	90,815.60
Net sales	1,142,507.70	1,167,398.34	1,389,668.32	1,607,246.14	1,729,508.72
Beginning inventory	11,915.00	156,321.76	156,763.76	131,263.76	140,277.96
Purchases	567,504.80	553,042.46	593,512.00	679,339.18	622,761.76
Direct Mfg labor	118,160.88	112,184.38	138,751.10	157,330.64	163,144.16
Subtotal	804,860.68	821,548.60	889,032.86	967,933.44	926,183.88
Ending inventory	156,321.76	156,769.76	131,263.62	140,277.96	100,738.84
Cost of goods sold	648,538.92	664,778.84	757,769.24	827,655.48	825,445.04
Gross profit (loss) on manufacturing	493,968.78	502,619.50	631,899.08	779,590.66	904,063.68
Indirect manufacturing expense	124,864.74	122,107.46	162,860.22	186,951.74	205,888.34
Production control expense	4,438.22	3,004.44	6,812.34	5,679.80	7,351.92
Engineering expense	27,200.22	34,797.06	34,477.20	45,294.74	44,037.90
Sales expense	172,033.26	170,457.02	210,453.76	287,673.86	308,465.48
Advertising expense	49,558.02	55,893.22	53,795.98	63,648.92	66,629.50
Administrative and office expense	93,520.38	93,563.76	123,747.92	149,533.68	159,317.82
Net profit (loss) on manufacturing	22,353.94	22,796.54	39,751.66	40,807.92	112,372.72
Other income					
Sales tax collections	749.02	935.32	558.34	635.90	704.12
Parcel post charged tax	23,903.24	26,944.30	32,150.36	31,038.98	33,043.10
Interest income	2,679.72	3,005.36	4,288.88	2,719.74	2,548.28
Rental income	1,912.00	2,666.84	2,226.00	1,884.00	1,824.00
Cash discount on purchases	4,111.50	4,718.76	3,353.96	5,423.92	5,851.04
Salvage scrap sales	2,355.52	575.26	1,517.64	9,000.26	1,514.08
CO-OP patronage dividend	332.04	351.14	252.40	288.18	286.92
Other expenses					
Rental expenses	1,095.80	1,957.48	1,847.12	9,067.92	1,072.36
Net profit (loss) on operations	57,301.18	59,916.08	82,292.12	82,730.98	157,071.90

(handwritten: (under cutter plow))

(a) Product 46: The Richardson AD-Flex Stubble Mulch Plow, 40 Percent of Sales ($728,000) *(handwritten: 243 units)*

This plow, which was pulled by a tractor, was priced at $200 per foot of length, retail. The average length sold was 15 feet. It was especially designed to prepare a seed in ground that received limited annual rainfall. It was an undercutter plow that literally cut a straight furrow under the soil instead of turning the soil over as the tra-

ditional plow did. Richardson's principal markets for this plow were wheat farmers in the three-state area of Kansas, Colorado, and Nebraska. The total potential U.S. market for this type of plow was estimated by Bob Richardson to be $30–50 million. The competition in the undercutter plow market was described by Mr. Taylor as "extreme." There were five major competitors, all of them small specialized manufacturers like Richardson. Deere and Oliver, two full-line implement manufacturers, had entered this market and withdrawn ac-

TABLE 2 Balance Sheet, 1988–1992

	1988	1989	1990	1991	1992
Current assets					
Cash in register	300.00	300.00	300.00	300.00	300.00
Farmers & Merchants State Bank	(36,177.86)	(37,139.04)	(46,256.20)	(49,562.78)	(54,591.66)
Exchange National Bank	2,000.00	2,318.80	2,613.86	1,991.78	2,006.58
Accounts receivable	37,270.26	28,599.80	48,973.60	31,022.10	77,717.20
Investments					
Treasury bills			50,000.00		
Note participation	50,638.50	50,000.00			
Saving and loan	41,943.52	44,535.26	51,940.40	51,272.00	50,200.00
Stamps	123.22	118.86	5.32	5.32	
Inventory	156,321.76	156,769.76	131,263.62	140,277.96	100,738.84
Total current assets	252,419.40	245,503.44	239,040.60	175,306.38	176,370.96
Fixed assets					
Depreciable assets cost less accumulated depreciation investment in Cawker	109,571.40	114,039.32	133,288.96	141,549.64	135,742.08
City Clinic	160.00				
Deposits	332.82	479.30	731.70	762.20	903.36
Land special assessment improvements	14,433.86	15,331.48	18,569.16	18,866.78	19,164.40
Total fixed assets	124,499.08	129,850.10	152,589.82	161,178.62	155,809.84
Total assets	376,918.48	375,353.54	391,630.42	336,485.00	332,180.80
Current liabilities					
Accounts payable	4,446.64	8,784.10	28,663.46	8,485.00	4,180.80
Accrued property taxes					
Notes payable					
Cash with order	4,973.72	1,894.60			
Total current liabilities	9,420.36	10,678.70	28,663.46	8,485.00	4,180.80
Net Worth					
Capital	328,000.00	328,000.00	328,000.00	328,000.00	328,000.00
Paid-in surplus	2,196.94	2,196.94	2,196.94	2,196.94	
Shareholders undistributed taxable income	20,087.00	20,087.00	20,087.00	20,087.00	
Net income (loss) year to date	57,301.18	59,916.08			
Net income paid to shareholders	40,087.00	59,916.08	82,292.12	117,697.94	157,071.90
Total net worth	367,498.12	364,674.84	362,966.96	328,000.00	328,000.00
Total liabilities and net worth	376,918.48	375,353.54	391,630.42	336,485.00	332,180.80

good dealership customer service good prod top perf.

cording to Mr. Taylor apparently due to production problems and the small size of the market. Richardson's success in this market was attributed by Mr. Taylor to "our dealer organization, service, a good product, and top performance." The main competitive weakness, in Mr. Taylor's view, was the relatively high average price of the Richardson product.

The AD-Flex Picker Treader and the Mulch Treader were identical in performance and were both tractor-drawn farm implements. The only difference between them was in construction. The AD-Flex Picker Treader was a modular design and was used in tandem with the AD-Flex Stubble mulch plow. The only direct competitor in this product line was by the Williston Co. of Albany, Georgia, who began production of a product in 1991. The treader was a substitute for the spring tooth harrow, a traditional farm implement with large steel teeth, that was used to break up the soil after plowing. The advantage of a mulch treader was best realized in geographical areas that were semiarid where the soil was subject to erosion by wind and water. The treader inverted the soil, thus conserving moisture while the spring tooth harrow broke the soil up and exposed moisture in the soil to the air which resulted in evaporation and moisture loss. The retail price of a mulch treader was $200 per foot, and sold mainly in 11- to 18-foot lengths. This was approximately double the retail price of a quality spring tooth harrow. Richardson estimated that the 1992 market for spring tooth harrows was about $40 million.

The Richardson brothers considered the treaders to be the main hope for the company's continued expansion. They held patents on the treaders and were encouraged by their growth in popularity. The treader was first used in 1983 by Kansas wheat farmers and then spread to wheat farmers in Nebraska and Colorado. More recently, its use had spread to corn, soybean, and alfalfa growers in Illinois, Southern Louisiana, Indiana, Utah, California, and to Canada as well.

③ Product 442: The Richardson Flexo Guard, 15 Percent of Sales ($220,000)

The Flexo Guard was an attachment for combines that extended ahead of the cutting sickle to retrieve and deliver grain heads that would otherwise fall back onto the ground. This device was sold at retail for $90 to $100 all over the Middle West, in California and Arizona, and to a limited extent in the East. Richardson faced one competitor in the Flexo Guard market, another small company located in

Clay Center, Kansas, a town of 4,613 people only 77 miles east of Cawker City. Richardson, which had manufactured the Flexo Guard for almost 15 years, had a majority of the available market. The complete 1992 product line and the sales of each product are shown in Table 3.

competitive adv over competitors

CUSTOMERS

What kind of farmer bought the Richardson Stubble Mulch Plow and Mulch Treader? According to Mr. Taylor, the farmer who buys our product is interested in change as a means of increasing his profitability. The person who will switch from the traditional implement to our new design is a farmer who is aggressive and who understands costs and performance. We can make a strong impression on this kind of farmer. We offer 25 percent less power consumption when our tools are used, and our method leaves the seedbed in much better condition for retaining moisture and therefore in much better condition to produce high crop yields. We're selling lower-cost ground preparation, better crop yields, and a soil erosion prevention method of farming. (KSF)

U.S. Channels of Distribution _dealers_

Richardson employed a two-phase distribution program. Roughly 75 percent of the company's sales were realized by 88 contract dealers located in the company's three principal territories: Kansas, 38 dealers; Oklahoma and the Texas Panhandle, 32 dealers; and Colorado and Nebraska, 18 dealers. A sales representative was assigned to each of these territories and called upon the dealers in the territory. Each of the contract dealers was located in a geographical trading area, and almost all the dealers were contract dealers for one of the major implement manufactur-

3 # sales reps

Product	Product Description	1992 Jan–Dec	1992 Percentage
40	Ad-flex Treader	589,828.12	32.4%
41	Dual Hitch	526.96	
42	Flexo Guard	220,359.08	12.1%
43	Simflex	4,543.60	0.2%
44	Sta-Kleen	6,122.96	0.3%
45	Mulch Treader	224,528.18	12.3%
46	Ad-flex Plow	727,111.74	39.9%
47	Furrow Opener Wire Winder	35,508.28	2.0%
48	Cylinder and Concave Rasp		
49	Miscellaneous	15,015.96	0.8%

TABLE 3 Product Sales, 1992

ers such as John Deere or International Harvester.

The remaining 25 percent of the company's sales were through seven distributors, located in Kansas City, Missouri; Dallas and Amarillo, Texas; Evansville, Indiana; Fargo, North Dakota; Raleigh, North Carolina; and Stockton, California. The geographical distribution of Richardson sales is shown in Table 4. The discount schedule was 40 percent off list for distributors, and for dealers, 20 percent plus 5 percent 10 days, net 30 days.[3] In addition, dealers could earn up to an additional 7 percent of list through volume discounts which were paid in the form of rebates at the end of the year.

U.S. Advertising and Promotion

Richardson spent $66,628 on advertising in 1992, or roughly 7.5 percent of sales. The entire program was print, and magazines were the principal media, with newspapers and mailed circulars filling out the program. A partial list of the farm trade magazines used was as follows:

Colorado Rancher & Farmer

Dakota Farmer

Farmer Stockman (Oklahoma, Kansas, Texas)

Farm Journal (Montana, Wyoming, North and South Dakota and other midwest states)

High Plain Journal (Colorado, Kansas)

Irrigation Age (Montana, Wyoming, South Dakota, Nebraska, Kansas, Colorado)

Kansas Farmer

Nebraska Farmer

Western Farm Life

The production and placement of company advertising was handled by the George Eschbaugh Agency in Wilson, Kansas, a town 64 miles south of Cawker City. In addition to print advertising, Richardson also supported a promotional program at a cost of about $8,000 to $10,000 per year. This program, which was implemented by the three territory managers responsible for direct sales to dealers and for distributors in their areas, consisted mainly of facilitating and arranging demonstrations and making necessary arrangements to rent space and transport equipment to fairs in the area. Mr. Taylor thought that field demonstrations arranged by county agricultural

---

[3] That is, 25 percent off list if the bill was paid in 10 days, net about (20 percent off list) due in 20 days.

TABLE 4   Geographical Distribution Richardson's Sales 1991–1992

	No. of Farms Growing Wheat	Acres of Wheat Harvested 1991	Annual Rainfall	Richardson's 1992 Sales
Kansas	84,171	11,081,000	19–35″	591,444.00
North Dakota	N.A.	7,962,000	14–18″	0.00
Oklahoma	31,200	5,217,000	18–37″	775,594.00
Montana	15,513	4,734,000	12–18″	0.00
Texas	29,172	3,326,000	18–33″	96,908.00
Nebraska	39,712	3,325,000	16–29″	95,896.00
Colorado	9,600	1,961,000	10–14″	0.00
Washington	8,755	2,922,000	9–20″	0.00
Other U.S. and Canadian	—	—	—	260.48
Total U.S.	366,598	59,004,000		1,820,324.00

N.A.—Not available.

Source: Company records.

agents were particularly effective because they attracted, as he put it, "people who are really interested, not just the curiosity viewers that you get at the fairs."

EXPORTS

In the late 1970s Richardson had shipped a small order to a company in South America that had seen an advertisement for a Richardson product and placed an order. Since then, Richardson had not made any efforts to achieve foreign sales, and none had materialized. Finally, on June 8, 1991, Richardson received an unsolicited letter from Napier Bros. Limited, an Australian manufacturer and distributor of agricultural implements requesting "your best price C.I.F. Port of Brisbane for the supply of a Mulch Treader equipped with Zero Angle Attachment and 15″ Dual Wheels less tyres and tubes and less hydraulics." (See Figure 1.) With the press of business, Richardson did not get around to answering the letter immediately, and

on the first of July he received a second letter from Napier requesting a reply to the first letter. Meanwhile, Mr. Taylor had requested a freight forwarder in Kansas City to provide him with a quotation on charges for ocean shipment of equipment to Australia. He received a quotation on July 20 and discovered, to his surprise, that an implement that sold for $1,891.68 in Cawker City would incur shipping and insurance costs of $1,285 just to the port of Brisbane, for a total C.I.F. price of $3,176.68. This did not, of course, include inland transportation in Australia, or the 23 percent F.O.B. ad valorum Australian duty on imported implements.[4] He was somewhat taken aback by the cost of shipping abroad, particularly as he recalled having just made a shipment weighing 3,000 lb (the same weight as the Australian quotation) to Fresno, California, by truck at a cost of $508.00.

The realization that the Richardson Mulch Treader would cost roughly twice as much in Australia as it did in Kansas dampened considerably Mr. Taylor's hopes that an Australian market for the treader might be opened up. Nevertheless, he forwarded the quotation to Napier Bros. To his surprise, a month later he received an

---

[4] This duty could be reduced to 7.5 percent if it was shown that no Australian manufacturer was offering for sale a "suitably equivalent good." If neither an Australian nor a U.K. company were supplying the item, the duty could be eliminated.

NAPIER BROS. LIMITED
(INCORPORATED IN QUEENSLAND)
Manufacturers of Agricultural Implements and General Engineers.
Registered Office: Bunya Street, Dalby, Queensland.

1370/02   8th June, 1991.

Request for Pricing Quotation

Richardson Manufacturing Co., Inc.
Cawker City,
KANSAS. . . . . .U.S.A.

Dear Sir,

    We refer to correspondence which we had with you some two years ago in regard to the possibility of importation of one of your Mulch Treaders. At that time, we were unable to raise sufficient interest in the machine to warrant its importation but we have now received very definite enquiries and we would appreciate your quoting us your best price C.I.F. Port of Brisbane for the supply of a Mulch Treader equipped with Zero Angle Attachment and 15″ Dual Wheels less tyres and tubes and less hydraulics in the following sizes—

10′3″
12′3″
14′3″
15′3″

    With your quotation, which we would appreciate in seven <u>copies for customs</u> purposes, we shall be obliged if you could also forward us <u>twenty copies</u> of your descriptive leaflets.

    We would appreciate your forwarding the above information as early as possible and at the same time would you please advise the best delivery available from time of receipt of order.

Yours faithfully,

<u>NAPIER BROS. LIMITED</u>

(N. Coldham-Fussell)

<u>SECRETARY</u>

FIGURE 1

order for the MTBCD-153L (Dual Wheel Unit) Mulch Treader with a C.I.F. Port of Brisbane price of $3,665.10.

By October 5, the Mulch Treader for Napier Bros. was crated and ready to be shipped. Everything seemed to be in order until October 17 when Richardson learned from its forwarding agent in Kansas City that it would be unable to get the Mulch Treader on an ocean vessel until November. As a result, Richardson wrote to Napier Bros. requesting an extension on the letter of credit and also an adjustment on price as the ocean freight turned out to be $60.00 higher than was anticipated. Napier increased and extended its letter of credit as requested and also expressed concern that the delay in shipment might make it impossible to test the Mulch Treader on stubble after the conclusion of the 1991 wheat harvest in mid- to late December. When Mr. Taylor learned that the shipment would arrive in Brisbane on December 19, he was hopeful that this would enable Napier to arrange for a test following the December 1991 harvest. If this were not done, the next harvest was a year away, and Richardson would lose an entire year in its efforts to penetrate the Australian market.

In the ensuing months, Taylor heard nothing from Napier. In May 1992, at the suggestion of Ray Richardson, he attended a regional export expansion conference sponsored jointly by Drake University and Iowa export expansion council. Attending the conference reminded Mr. Taylor again of the potential of export markets, and he resolved to follow up the Richardson lead as soon as he returned to Cawker City. The letter he wrote is reproduced in Figure 2.

Mr. Taylor received an immediate reply from Napier. (See Figure 3.) Six weeks later he received another letter that enclosed the results of a field test of the Richardson treader by an Australian government agricultural extension agent by the name of Tod. The following are excerpts from the agent's report, dated June 6, 1992:

> In general this machine has exceeded our expectations in its ability to handle heavy straw and weeds, and to prepare soil for conventional planting equipment and we are very pleased with its performance.

> It would be a tremendous help in saving our soil from erosion, which in this state is a problem of some magnitude. Most of the 5 million acres of cultivated land in this state has a subtropical summer rainfall, most of which falls in high density rainstorms, which, allied with the winter cropping programs, makes it imperative that crop residues be kept standing as long as possible to help conserve this rain and prevent soil erosion. Most of our machinery is designed for the gentle winter rainfall areas of the southern states where this type of erosion is not a problem. Therefore it is unsuitable for our conditions.

> To sum up, your mulch treader could solve one of our two main problems in the search for suitable stubble mulching machinery, that is, preparing a standing stubble quickly for planting. However, our other pressing need is for a more efficient subsurface tillage implement, with enough tyres to give soil disturbance for weed killing. Neither the present scarifier nor the chisel plough have enough clearance for heavy stubble, and the latter is not an efficient weed killer. We would be interested to hear if your company makes an implement of this type.

May 27, 1992

Napier Brothers Limited
Bunya Street
Dalby,
Queensland, Australia
Attention: N. Coldham-Fussell

Dear Sir:

We thank you for putting one of our Mulch Treaders to work in your country. We have not to date received any word of its success, therefore we are very interested to know many things such as: types of soil the machine was used in, when and where it was used, what crops used on, annual rainfall amounts, whether it satisfied your expectations and any other pertinent information regarding the machine you have available.

Assuming the answers are favorable, can you suggest a preferred way to introduce this tool into general use? Do you distribute your own agricultural implements or work through other distributors? Also do you feel we have a market for our Mulch Treader in your country?

May we hear from you by return airmail.

If we may be of any assistance at any time, please do not hesitate to call on us.

Sincerely yours,

RICHARDSON MANUFACTURING CO., INC.

George A. Taylor
Director of Sales

GAT/mm

FIGURE 2

Napier Bros. Limited
Bunya Street
Dalby
Queensland, Australia

31st May, 1992

Richardson Mfg. Co. Inc.
P.O. Box 5
Cawker City
Kansas, 64730, U.S.A.

Attention: Mr. G. A. Taylor, Director of Sales

Dear Sir:

We thank your for your letter of the 27th May, 1992.

In connection with the second paragraph of your letter, I have asked our Design Staff to prepare for you a report to answer the matters which you raised in the second paragraph of your letter. As soon as this is in hand we will forward it to you. We are also endeavoring to obtain a report from the Government Department of Primary Industries who have been particularly interested in this project and we will also forward this to you.

We advise that our Company manufactures and distributes a wide range of agricultural tillage and general purpose equipment. The company has its own subsidiary marketing organisation, i.e., Napier Machinery Sales Pty. Limited which markets through distributors and dealers in the Eastern States of Australia. In addition we manufacture equipment for tractor companies and number amongst our clients, Ford, Fiat, Case, Massey-Ferguson and Chamberlain. In addition we have a substantial export operation working mainly in South America, South-East Asia and East Africa.

As the Mulch Treader only arrived towards the end of the mulching season, it was not possible for a complete testing to be carried out and we had it in mind to wait for the results after this year's harvest in approximately October/December before taking the matter up further with you. If there is sufficient interest in this item we feel that there may be an opportunity to develop substantial business by the following steps:

FIGURE 3

(a) Initially importing the units,
(b) As volume grows, entering into part manufacture of the implements, and
(c) When volume is sufficient enter into some arrangement to manufacture the units under license.

licensing

We would appreciate your thoughts on these types of arrangements and will forward you the reports on the operations of the machine as soon as they come to hand.

Yours faithfully,

NAPIER BROS. LIMITED (N. Coldham-Fussell, Export Manager)

FIGURE 3 *CONTINUED*

July 22, 1992

Napier Brothers Limited
Bunya Street
Dalby
Queensland, Australia 4405
Attention: Mr. N. Coldham-Fussell

Dear Sir:

We have read with much interest your letter and Mr. Tod's report regarding the use of the Mulch Treader. We are enclosing some literature on our AD-Flex Plow which is a highly successful implement for undercutting stubble and the AD-Flex Picker Treader may be attached for a more effective weed kill.

The undercutting plow is made in five foot sections and may be used by itself leaving the stubble standing or by adding the Picker Treader which somewhat mixes the stubble and mulches the soil, also tearing out the growing vegetation. It would appear to be a highly suitable implement for your stubble mulching program with the Mulch Treader following up to do a more complete job of chopping up the straw and finishing up the seed bed.

We do have a new model plow but the literature and instruction books are not available as yet, although the picker treader is shown mounted on the new model plow.

In Mr. Tod's report, he asked for more information on adjusting the treader so we are enclosing an operators manual which explains adjustments under the heading of OPERATING INSTRUCTIONS.

The middle buster tyne sells for $20.41. This includes bracket, bolts and curved shank. A chisel point or small shovel may be attached. We cannot furnish this point.

The steps you outlined in your letter of May 31st certainly look feasible in regards to the distribution of our implements.

I certainly wish it were possible to visit with you personally regarding the operations of the plows and to see the conditions you are confronted with as the farmers in the arid and semi-arid regions of this country have and are adopting these practices and implements. Their farming expenses are being reduced approximately one-third and are conserving more moisture along with eliminating soil erosion by water and wind and many are claiming higher yields per acre over previous practices.

FIGURE 4

In Mr. Tod's report, he mentions a slasher which we are not sure of. Possibly what we call a stalk cutter or rotary mower. Perhaps you could enlighten us more on this implement.

I presume you will pass along this information to Mr. Tod and if we can be of further assistance, please do not hesitate to let us know.

Twenty sheets of mulch treader literature will be forwarded under separate cover.
Sincerely,

RICHARDSON MANUFACTURING CO., INC.

George A. Taylor
Director of Sales

GAT/mm

Enc. 210.09 81-1-77 Mulch Treader
      210.6 5M/6-1-77 AD-Flex Plow
      410.09 6-10-77 Instruction Booklet

FIGURE 4 *CONTINUED*

We would also be grateful for more information on the adjustment of the treader to get a level surface when using the machine as a cultivator only.

H. H. Tod, Agricultural Extension Agent

Growers RepresentativeSoil Conservation Committee

Mr. Taylor replied to the two letters and report from Australia. (See Figure 4.) After signing this letter, Mr. Taylor wondered if Richardson was following the right approach to international marketing. One possibility he considered was to sign on with an export merchant. He had recently attended an export expansion conference in Iowa where he had been approached by a Kansas City export manager who offered to take on the Richardson line of equipment, for export markets if Richardson would give him the distributor discount of 40 percent plus an additional "export bonus" of 15 percent off list. The problem with this offer, according to Mr. Richardson, was that 55 percent off list cut too deeply into Richardson's operating margin. (See Table 5 for company operating ratios.) Also, he wondered how much push an export merchant would give to the Richardson line.

Tables 6, 7 and 8 and Figures 5 and 6 contain data Mr. Taylor kept in a file labeled "International Markets." As he opened this file his thoughts were focused on the question of whether Richardson should take the plunge and go international. It seemed clear that there was a market overseas for Richardson's products, but the question in Taylor's mind was how to approach these markets. Also, he wondered how much attention and effort he should give to international as opposed to domestic markets.

NEGOTIATION ASSIGNMENT

Richardson teams: Negotiate an agreement with Napier for penetrating the Australian market with Richardson products. Napier teams: Negotiate an agreement with Richardson for penetrating the Australian market.

Issues (partial list)

Sourcing: location and responsibility

Marketing: responsibility, plans, budgets

Product adaptation

Pricing

Distribution

Selling, advertising, promotion

Service

Design: export licensingl, joint venture, split ownership

Timing

Plan

Key assumptions

[handwritten: ↦ operating margin]

TABLE 5 True Operating Ratios, 1992		
	1992	
(1) Cost of goods sold	825,445.04	
Less: Salvage scrap sales	1,514.08	Cr
Cash discount on purchases	5,851.92	
(2) 500's engineering expenses	818,079.04	
Add: 50% Ray's salary from 602	44,037.90	
(3) 600's sales expenses	25,000.00	
Less: 50% Ray's salary to 500's	69,037.90	
Parcel post and freight charged for patronage dividend	308,465.48	
Add: Out freight from 800's (parcel post)	25,000.00	Cr
(4) 800's administrative and office expenses	33,043.10	Cr
Less: Out freight to 600's	286.92	Cr
Sales tax collections	5,340.80	
Interest income	255,476.26	
	159,317.82	
	5,340.80	Cr
	704.12	
	2,548.28	
	150,724.62	

True Operating Ratios for	1992	1991
Cash discount/total sales	4.99%	5.23%
Cost of goods sold/total sales	44.95	47.94
Indirect manufacturing expense and production control expense/total sales	11.71	11.82
Engineering expense/total sales	3.79	4.14
Selling expense/total sales	14.00 *16.9l.*	13.64
Advertising expense/total sales	3.66 ✓	3.75
Administrative and office expense/total sales	8.28	8.62
Net profit on operations/total sales	8.62	4.86
	100.00%	100.00%

[handwritten: 22.3]

[handwritten: total 1992 sales 1820 324]

TABLE 6 Acres of Wheat Harvested in Selected Geographical Areas

Area	Acres Harvested (in millions)	Yield Per Acre (in bushels)
European Economic Community	48.2	33.9
United States	49.9	26.3
Canada	29.7	27.9
Mexico	1.7	35.0
Argentina	12.9	17.8
India	31.3	12.2
Australia	20.3	23.0

TABLE 7 Wheat Farm Investments

	U.S.	Australia	Canada	Argentina
No. of Farms	366,593	51,000	77,395	
Farm value				
Land			40,716–83,358	
Building	132,794.00	152,000–186,000	33,548–52,720	
Livestock			5,598–9,120	
Total	132,794.00	152,000–186,000	79,862–145,198	
No. of acres/farm	456.00	1,800.00	802–1,434	
Value/acres	244.00	84–104	100–102	
No. of tractors/farm	2.10	1.62	1.48	0.29
Annual rainfall	17–30″	11–20″	20–30″	12–22″

▼ DISCUSSION QUESTIONS

1. Identify the strengths and weaknesses of Richardson in the North American Market. Should Richardson go international? Why? Why not?

2. If Richardson decides to go international, what alternative strategies should it consider?

3. Recommend a strategy for Richardson. Identify objectives and develop a marketing, sourcing, staffing, and financial plan for years 1 and 5.

TABLE 8

File Note: Canada

The climate in the Canadian wheat belt in the province of Saskatchewan is similar to that here in Kansas. All farm implements and equipment manufactured in the United States can be imported into Canada duty free.

File Note: Argentina

The taxes in Argentina are 90 percent ad valorem on C.I.F. value, a 5 percent statistic tax on C.I.F. value and a charge of 20 Argentine pesos per gross kilo. Also, there is a 10 percent sales tax on retail value in Argentina levied at the time of importation.

File Note: Australia

Australia's wheat belt follows the eastern coast, plus a small section in the west. The particular states and their 1966–67 acreages are

New South Wales	7,135*	15,300†
Victoria	3,138	6,400
Queensland	1,227	3,400
South Australia	2,960	5,100
Western Australia	6,347	8,100
Total Australia	20,823	31,900
Total U.S.	159,000	145,600

The wheat belt is typified by a 10–20″ rainfall, somewhat less than the 17–30″ annual rainfall in the United States. The Department of the Interior mentioned in its April 1967 publication, "The Northern New South Wales and Queensland wheats rely heavily on the conservation of summer rain moisture in the soil, while spring rains are important for the growth of wheat in Victoria." The Bulletin states more explicitly later that rains in all the regions are very unreliable and that the threat of a serious drought is omnipresent. The soil is also less rich than in the United States and Canada and is particularly deficient in nitrogen and phosphate.

It is difficult to draw conclusions based on the number of farms. In the United States there are 3,400,000 farms, but they differ from the 252,000 Australian farms; many of the Australian farms are devoted to sheep grazing, making the average acres per farm considerably higher than in the United States, which considers livestock farms a separate category. Over 51,000 farms grow wheat in Australia, but few grow solely this crop.

The tractor sales in 1964 were a record 25,000 units, whereas the U.S. sales were 143,000 units. Tillage implements sold about 9,000–11,000 units in Australia, 83,000 in the United States. Nearly 87 percent of all tractors owned in Australia belong to farmers in the wheat belt states named above.

The farmer has a supported pricing structure for export wheat. The wholesale wheat price in 1966–67 was $1.75 compared with $1.41 in the United States. The government offers the wheat farmer rural credits and preferential interest rates and guarantees to marketing groups for prepayments. Favorable depreciation allowances plus investment credits aid the farmer. Also, farm items that are not available in the country may be imported duty-free.

Australia has a climate and soil that are suitable to stubble mulch farming. Both the mulch treader and the AD-Flex Plow could be used to advantage here. It appears from the tractor sales figures that the Australian farmer does tend to be a capital-expenditure-oriented businessmanager. Figure 6 substantiates this by demonstrating a consistently high, for the size of the country, tractor sales pattern.

---

* Acres of wheat, in thousands.
† Acres of total grains, in thousands.

Source: Commonwealth Bureau of Statistics, Canberra.

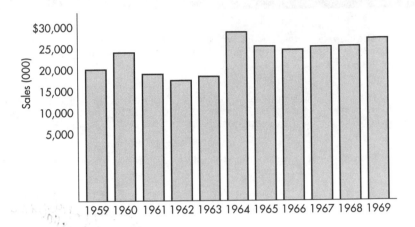

FIGURE 5
New Tractor (Wheels) Sales in Australia, 1959–1969

FIGURE 6
Map of Australia

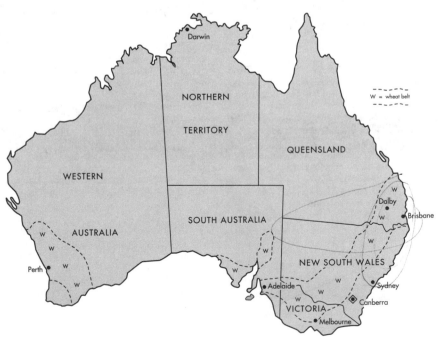

Parker Pen Co. (A): International Marketing Strategy Review[1]

It is circumstance and proper timing that give an action its character and make it either good or bad.—Agesilaus

INTRODUCTION

The meeting at sunny Palm Beach concluded with nary a whimper of dissent from its participants. After years of being run as a completely decentralized company whose managers in all corners of the world enjoyed a high degree of flexibility, Parker Pen Co., of Janesville, Wisconsin, was forced to reexamine itself. The company had enjoyed decade after decade of success until the early 1980s. By this time, Parker faced strong competitive threats and a deteriorating internal situation. A new management team was brought in from outside the company—an unprecedented step for what had been until then an essentially family-run business. At the March, 1984 Palm Beach meeting, this new group of decision makers would outline a course of action that would hopefully set Parker back on a path to success.

The men behind the new strategy were supremely confident of its chances for success—and with good reason. Each was recognized as a highly skilled practitioner of international business and their combined extensive experience gave them an air of invincibility. They had been recruited from larger companies, had left high-paying, rewarding jobs and each had come to Janesville with a grand sense of purpose. For decades, Parker had been a dominant player in the pen industry. In the early 1980s, however, the company had seen its market share dwindle to a mere 6 percent and, in 1982, net income plunged a whopping 60 percent.

To reverse this decline, Parker recruited James Peterson, an executive vice president at R.J. Reynolds, as the new president and CEO. Peterson hired Manville Smith as president of the writing instruments group at Parker. Smith, who was born in Ecuador and had a broad international background, came from 3M where he had been appointed division president at the tender age of 30. Richard Swart was vice president/marketing of the writing instruments group. He spent 11 years at the advertising agency BBDO and was an expert on marketing planning and theory. Jack Marks was head of writing instruments advertising. Marks came to Parker from Gillette, where, among other things, he assisted in the worldwide marketing of Paper Mate pens. Rounding out the team was Carlos Del Nero, manager of global marketing planning, who brought with him considerable international experience at Fisher-Price. Each of these men was convinced that Parker would right itself by following the plan they unveiled at Palm Beach.

[1] Cases (A), (B), and (C) were prepared by Charles J. Anderer, research associate, under the supervision of Warren J. Keegan, Professor of International Business and Marketing, as part of the International Business Case Study Project, Center for International Business Studies, Pace University. This project was funded in part by a grant from the United States Department of Education. Copyright © 1986 by the Board of Trustees, Pace University.

A BRIEF HISTORY OF PARKER PEN

The "Rolls Royce" of the Pen Industry

The Parker name has been identified with pens since 1888 when George S. Parker delighted ink-splotched pen-users everywhere by introducing a leakproof fountain model called the Parker Lucky Curve. Parker Pen would eventually blossom into America's, if not the world's, largest and best-known pen maker. Parker's products, which would eventually include ballpoint pens, felt-tip pens, desk sets, mechanical pencils, inks, leads, erasers, and, of course, the fountain pen, were also known for their high price tags. In 1921, for example, Parker introduced the Duofold pen. The Duofold, even though it was comparable to other $3 pens on the market, was extravagantly priced at $7. Parker was able to charge a premium price because of its reputation for quality and style, and its skill in positioning products in the top price segment.

Parker's position as America's leading pen maker was solidified during the years when the pen was mainly viewed as a gift item. High school and college graduates in the forties and fifties, for example, were quite likely to receive a Parker "51" fountain pen (priced at $12.50) commemorating their achievement. Indeed, it was with a "51" that General Douglas MacArthur signed the Japanese Peace Treaty in 1945. Parker's stylish products and high profile name would keep it at the top of the pen market until the late sixties when American competitors A.T. Cross and Sheaffer, as well as a few foreign brands, knocked them out of first place once and for all.

Of course, Parker would not have lost its hold on the market had it not made some oversights along the way. In addition to a more competitive environment, Parker failed to come to terms with a fundamental change in the pen market—the development of the disposable, ballpoint market. When Parker unveiled the $25 "75" pen in 1963, it showed that it remained committed to supplying high-priced pens to the upper end of the market. As the sixties wore on, a clear trend toward cheap ballpoint and soft-tip pens developed. Meanwhile, Parker's only ultimately successful addition to its product range in the late sixties was the "75" Classic line, yet another high-priced pen.

A Brief Flirtation with Low-Priced Pens

Parker did, however, make an effort to compete in the lower price segment of the market in the late sixties only to see it fail. In an attempt to capitalize on the trend toward inexpensive pens, Parker introduced the T-Ball Jotter, priced at $1.98. The success of the Jotter led it to move even further down the price ladder when it acquired Eversharp. Whereas the Jotter had given Parker reason to believe it could make the shift from pricy pens to cheap pens with little or no difficulty, the Eversharp experience proved to be different. George Parker, a grandnephew of the company's founder and president of Parker at the time, stated the reasons for the Eversharp failure, as well as its consequences:

> All the market research surveys said go lower, go lower, go lower, that's where the business is. So I said, 'Go lower? Fine. But we don't know how.' We bought Eversharp and tried to run it ourselves, and we couldn't do it. Our people just couldn't think in terms of big units, and they didn't know how to sell people on the lower-priced end of the business—grocers, supermarkets, rack jobbers. The result was,

Bic and Paper Mate were cleaning up in the lower-priced end, Cross in the high, and Parker was getting squeezed in the middle. Volume was going up, but our costs went up faster, and our profits were squeezed. (*Forbes*, 10/1/73)

The 1970s: The Illusion of Success

Despite the difficulties Parker encountered when it left its niche in the upper end of the pen market, the company experienced a healthy period of growth and profitability for most of the 1970s. Demand for its products remained strong, and its worldwide markets expanded significantly due to a rise in consumer income and increasing literacy rates in much of the Third World. Parker also chose to diversify during this decade, and its most noteworthy acquisition, Manpower, Inc., proved to be a very strong asset. In 1975, when it acquired Manpower, a temporary-help firm, Parker was the slightly more profitable of the two. With the boom in temporary services in the late seventies and early eighties, however, Manpower eclipsed Parker in sales and earnings and eventually subsidized its parent company during down periods.

Why did Parker fall from its position of leadership in the writing instrument market? There were many reasons, and one of the most important was the weakening of the U.S. dollar. At its peak, Parker accounted for half of all U.S. exports of writing instruments and 80 percent of its total sales came from 154 foreign countries. Parker was especially strong in Europe, most particularly in the United Kingdom. When sales in the strong European currencies were translated into dollars, Parker earned huge profits.

The downside of a weak dollar, however, was that it gave Parker the illusion that it was a well-run company. In fact, throughout the seventies, Parker was a model of inefficiency. Manufacturing facilities were dated and inefficient. Production was so erratic that the marketing department often had no idea what type of pens they would be selling from year to year or even month to month. Under the leadership of George Parker, nothing was done by company headquarters to update these facilities or to develop new products. As a result, subsidiaries and distributors around the world saw fit to develop their own products. By the end of George Parker's reign, the company's product line included 500 writing instruments.

That distant subsidiaries would have the leeway to make such decisions was not at all unusual at Parker, for it had long been known as one of the most globally decentralized companies in the world. Decentralization, in fact, was something that Parker took pride in and considered to be vital to its success as a multinational. Yet it was this very concept that Peterson and his new management team would hold to be responsible for much of what ailed Parker Pen.

PARKER'S GLOBAL OPERATIONS BEFORE PETERSON

In addition to having a hand in manufacturing and product line decisions, Parker's subsidiaries developed their own marketing strategies. More than 40 different advertising agencies promoted Parker pens in all the corners of the globe. When Peterson came to Parker, he was proudly informed that the company was a "federation" of autonomous geographical units. The downside to the "federation" concept, Peterson thought, was that home country management often lacked the information needed to make and coordinate basic business decisions. Control was so completely decentralized that Parker didn't even know how many pens it was selling by the time Peterson and his group arrived.

On the other hand, decentralization obviously had its positive aspects, most noticeably in the field of advertising. Pens mean different things to different people. Whereas Europeans are more likely to choose a pen based on its style and feel, a consumer from a lesser developed country in the seventies viewed the pen as nothing less than a badge of literacy. In addition, tastes varied widely from country to country. The French, for example, remained attached to the fountain pen. Scandinavians, for their part, showed a marked preference for the ballpoint. The logic behind having so many different advertising agencies was that, even if it appeared to be somewhat inefficient, in the end the company was better off from a sales standpoint.

Some of the individual advertising agencies were able to devise excellent, imaginative campaigns that struck a responsive chord among their local audiences. One example was the Lowe Howard-Spink agency in London. The Parker U.K. division became the company's most profitable during the tenure of the Lowe agency. An example of its creativity is an ad entitled "Rediscover the lost art of the insult." Gracing the ad is a picture of a dead plumber, on his back, with a giant Parker pen protruding from his heart. Part of the text is as follows:

Do you know plumbers who never turn up?

Hairdressers who missed their vocations as butchers?

Drycleaners who make your stains disappear—and your clothes with them?

Today, we at Parker give you the chance to get your own back.

Not only are we offering a beautiful new pen called the Laque which owes its deep lustre to a Chinese technique 2000 years old, but we are attempting to revive something that went out when the telephone came in.

The well-armed, witty, malicious dart. (*Ad Age*, 6/2/86)

While the Parker U.K. division was a success, however, the company's general inefficiencies, loss of market share, and lack of strategic direction were finally revealed in the early eighties with the rise of the U.S. dollar. Parker's financial decline was even more precipitous than the dollar's increase. When the huge 1982 losses were registered, Peterson was brought in from R.J. Reynolds to try and turn things around for Parker. He decided that every aspect of the company needed to be closely examined, not the least of which was Parker's decentralization of global operations.

▼ DISCUSSION QUESTIONS (A)

1. What would you do if you were in James Peterson's shoes in January of 1982?

2. What changes, if any, would you make in Parker's marketing strategy?

3. Which aspects of Parker's structure would you discard? Which would you keep?

4. Assume that you are James Peterson and you have just hired a new management team composed of highly qualified executives from outside companies. You and your new team are convinced that you have the solution to Parker's problems but there are many holdovers who disagree with you. How would you implement your plan? To what extent would you incorporate the views of Parker management into your plan?

Parker Pen Co. (B): Parker Goes Global

We will be creating more news in the next two years than we have in the past ten.—James Peterson, July 1982.

James Peterson relished the chance to be the top man at Parker Pen. He spent 24 years at Pillsbury and had a taste of what it was like to be at the helm of a corporation when he rose to the rank of president, the number two power spot in the company. At R.J. Reynolds, he was an executive vice president—an influential position, to be sure, but not one that afforded him the freedom of movement that he would have liked. When he was brought to Parker in January of 1982, Peterson, then 54, had finally had the chance to run a company. All the theories he held to be true would be tested. All the lessons he had learned after some 30 years of practical business experience—much of it in international operations—would now be applied.

His years at R.J. Reynolds had convinced him of the superiority of global marketing, which he understood to mean standardized product and promotion strategies the whole world over. This view made him unalterably opposed to the loose structure that had characterized Parker Pen before his arrival. In the opinion of Peterson, there was absolutely no way that any company operating in the modern world would be able to survive such disarray. That a subsidiary thousands of miles away could decide not only what products it would manufacture but also how they would market them ran counter to everything Peterson believed.

Peterson quickly moved to remold Parker Pen in his own image. In addition to too much decentralization, Peterson thought Parker lacked "a good enunciation of business philosophy." According to Peterson, "every good company has to have one." In order to correct this problem, Peterson devised an eight-point state-ment of his management philosophy and had it translated into more than 40 languages and sent in letter form to Parker managers all over the world. The statement contained such phrases as, "There is no substitute for quality," and, "Like most managers, I don't like surprises." The letters concluded by saying: "As I get to meet each of you in the months ahead, I will be discussing this business philosophy with you and asking you how you have used it." (*Ad Age*, 7/26/82)

THE DISMANTLING OF DECENTRALIZATION: FROM 40 AGENCIES TO 1

The core of Peterson's revitalization efforts would be directed at dismantling the geographical organization that Parker had evolved into over the years. He slashed the product line from 500 to the 100 most profitable items. The manufacturing function was consolidated, greatly reducing the number of units produced overseas. As for what products would be manufactured, that was to be strictly decided by the management team at the Janesville headquarters. Of course, the manufacturing facilities themselves would have to be updated, for no longer could the production department be allowed to dictate to marketing executives exactly what kind of products it would be selling. None of these measures in and of themselves was startling—each addressed problems that needed to be corrected. However, when Peterson decided to get rid of Parker's 40-odd advertising agencies in favor of one "world-class agency," more than a few eyebrows were raised.

The logic behind the decision to go with one advertising agency (Ogilvy & Mather) was consistent with Peterson's desire to make Parker Pen a global marketing corporation. With one agency instead of 40, not only could money be saved, but strategies could be coordinated on a global scale. One problem, however, was that formerly productive agencies such as Lowe Howard-Spink in London were fired. This had a devastating effect on morale at Parker U.K., the company's most profitable subsidiary which had in effect been subsidizing the same American division that was now telling it how to advertise.

"THE WORLD'S NO. 1 PEN COMPANY"

Even though Parker had experienced many problems before Peterson arrived, the company was still very proud of its tradition as a leading producer of "quality writing instruments." Of course, this pride was sometimes translated into overblown statements such as, "Parker is the world's No. 1 pen company." This indeed was the party line at Parker even though it was paid little more than lip service. When Manville Smith arrived in 1982, he commissioned a study to see just how important Parker was. His findings shocked him: Parker had only a 6 percent share of the global pen market and it didn't even attempt to participate in a segment that was responsible for 65 percent of all sales of pens in the world—that is pens that sold for less than $3.

The new management team wanted to make Parker more than just a fictitious No. 1 company. In order to recapture market share, Parker would have to participate in the lower end of the market—the same area that George Parker himself had so hastily abandoned in the late sixties. A new $15 million state-of-the-art plant would be built whose main function would be to manufacture the Vector, a

roller-ball pen selling for $2.98. The Vector was Manville Smith's pet project. Using a new automated line at Parker's new plant, Smith calculated that the Vector could be produced for 27 cents per unit and therefore generate huge profits for the company. After the Vector, Smith planned to plunge even deeper into the low-price market with the Itala, an even cheaper model that would be Parker's first disposable pen.

THE FIRST RUMBLINGS OF DISSENT: GEORGE PARKER

Although George Parker was still formally the chairman of Parker Pen, he was expected to lead a quiet, charmed life in Marco Island, Florida and never to be heard from again. In fact, George Parker was paying very close attention to the new developments in the company that bore his name, and he was none too happy. As his above remarks might suggest, he was scornful of a strict market research approach to the pen business. He also took pride in Parker Pen's autonomous federation system that provided a high degree of flexibility to the company's many subsidiaries. Even more disturbing to him was the planned foray into the lower depths of the marketplace, as he might put it. Cheap pens were beneath Parker Pen, in his opinion, and nothing could be more disgraceful than a disposable pen bearing his name. What were they manufacturing anyway, garbage bags?

Compounding George Parker's displeasure was his sincere dislike for James Peterson, whom he dubbed "motormouth." To him, Peterson was the embodiment of everything that was wrong with the new Parker Pen. The grandnephew of the company's founder still had many well-placed friends in the company, and his constant criticism of the new management team probably did little to aid their cause.

PROBLEMS: FINANCIAL LOSSES, SMITH GETS FIRED, ONE WORLD MARKETING FAILS

Despite all the complaints from George Parker, Peterson's major problems lay elsewhere. The strong dollar that had exposed so many of his company's weaknesses got even stronger. Recession was a worldwide plague. The costs of new plant development were not absorbed by profits and the company lost $13.6 million in fiscal 1983. Still, Peterson had the luxury of time on his side, since he had little more than one full year under his belt. One more year like 1983, however, and he was gone.

In Peterson's opinion, only a full-fledged global marketing effort could save Parker. At the March, 1984 Palm Beach meeting, it was decided that Parker would participate "in every viable segment of the writing instrument business." In addition, it was declared that, "The concept of marketing by centralized direction has been discussed and consensus was reached." The management team, filled with a sense of purpose, then set out to achieve its lofty goals.

There remained one major problem: Parker's new plant was proving to be a failure. The plant was not functional for the 1983 Christmas season, costing the company millions of dollars in sales. Even as Peterson and his group were working round-the-clock to see its strategy through, the computer-automated plant which was supposed to spearhead Parker's drive into the lower end of the market, broke down repeatedly. With automation having failed, the company was forced to hire labor again and its costs skyrocketed. Manville Smith, who had placed his name next to the fully automated Vector project, was fired by Peterson as a result.

Smith's departure was important because he was the only member of the management team that held out for local advertising flexibility. Smith had worked closely with Ogilvy & Mather (O & M) on Parker's first worldwide advertising campaign. At Smith's urging O & M devised a campaign that allowed for some degree of local flexibility. When Smith left, however, Peterson took over the advertising reins and pushed very hard for "one-look" advertising and the results were disastrous.

The fashion in which Peterson pro-

Year Ended Feb. 28	Revenues (Millions)	Net Income	Earnings	Dividends (Per Share)	Range
1985	$843.7	$5.4	$0.32	$0.52	21–13
1984	708.8	11.8	0.70	0.52	21–12
1983	635.3	d13.6	d0.80	0.52	17–11
1982	679.1	15.7	0.92	0.50	24–14
1981	723.2	37.7	2.23	0.44	26–14

TABLE 1 Parker Pen Co. Selected Operating Results

d-Deficit
Balance sheet as of June 30, 1985:
  Current assets: $284.5 million
  Current liabilities: $239.5 million
  Current ratio: 1.1–to–1
  Long-term debt: $27.1 million
  Common shares: 17,635,000
  Book value: $7.65
Source: Annual reports.

moted his advertising policy was enough to alienate once and for all those remaining managers that supported his efforts. A proclamation issued from the Janesville office and sent across the globe headquarters stated that: "Advertising for Parker pens [no matter model or mode] will be based on a common creative strategy and positioning. . . . The worldwide advertising theme, 'Make your mark with a Parker,' has been adopted. . . . [It] will utilize similar graphic layout and photography. It will utilize an agreed-upon typeface. It will utilize the approved Parker logo/graphic design. It will be adapted from centrally supplied materials. . . ."

The new advertising campaign was indeed rigidly controlled. Subsidiaries were sent their materials and told to get on with it. Managers abroad were seen as simple implementers of the global marketing strategy with little or no input. The problem was that many of them realized right away that the new advertising campaign wouldn't work in their markets. In fact, the campaign really didn't work anywhere. Jack Marks would later qualify it as "lowest-common denominator-advertising," that "tried to say something to everybody, and didn't say anything to anybody."

The last to admit failure was Peterson himself, who ignored all evidence and tried to move forward with a second wave of global advertising in January of 1985, this time for the Vector, which had finally made it off the production line. By this time, however, Peterson's position was terminally weakened. Production problems persisted, morale was low, resentment of the management team was high and re-action to yet another generic campaign was so negative that Peterson felt compelled to resign.

POSTSCRIPT: "GLOBAL MARKETING IS DEAD"

The successor to Peterson as CEO was Mitchell Fromstein, president of what once was Parker's Manpower subsidiary. Since it was purchased in 1975 by Parker, Manpower continued to grow to the point where it was far more profitable than its parent and, indeed, subsidized it for several years. Manpower would wind up taking over Parker, finally selling it to a group of British investors in 1986.

Fromstein was an implacable foe of Peterson's. Manpower was as international as Parker Pen, and Fromstein had his own views as to how an international business should be run. When he assumed control of Parker in January 1985, he gathered the company's country managers in Janesville and told them: "Global marketing is dead. You're free again." (*Ad Age*, 6/2/86)

▼ DISCUSSION QUESTIONS (B)

1. Why did Peterson's global strategy fail?
2. What lessons can be drawn from the decline and fall of Parker Pen?

Parker Pen Co. (C): Global Marketing Strategy: An Interview with Dr. Dennis Thomas

President, The Berol Corporation,[1] Danbury, Conn. 06810

Charles Anderer[2]: I would first like to thank you for taking the time to share your views on global marketing and Parker Pen in this interview.

Dennis Thomas[3]: It's my pleasure.

CA: I would like to start out by asking you a question about an article that we both have read.[4] Do you agree with the notion that the big issue today is not whether to go global but how to tailor the global marketing concept to each business?

DT: If it's an either or proposition, I am broadly in agreement with the proposition. I believe that there are relatively few major markets where the local conditions are so self-contained, so capable of being kept self-contained, and so different, either for cultural or other kinds of reasons, that the underlying, increasing level of similarity that is coming into most major marketplaces, as opposed to the nuances of necessary local difference, cannot form the bedrock of acceptable product offerings, positionings and what you have. Also, the economies of scale and the relative size of self-contained markets, in and of themselves, are of decreasing appeal other than for a small business which chooses to remain small. But in many industries and many marketplaces, the products which adequately serve market needs

increasingly have within them either outright commodities or commodity-like ingredients if they are likely to be products that are positioned in a marketplace over a period of decades rather than over a few fashion cycles of a few months or a few years. . . . The real question is: What is the appropriate international scale for the business and what is the appropriate international scale for the underlying marketplace?

CA: What forces do you see behind the increasing similarities of markets? Telecommunications is one that comes to mind. . . .

DT: Sure. We are much more aware, whether we are conscious of it or not, of what other parts of the world look like. . . . Broadly speaking, people behave as consumers who may be appealed to in the same kinds of ways. Whether they are at level two or level four of a Maslow hierarchy or any kind of structure you would like to adopt, we are becoming more steadily accepting of the fact that they are likely to go through the same kinds of progressions. The form that a status need may take in one society as opposed to another may be somewhat different, but status needs exist in both. How well developed they are, whether people may exercise them, how many people, in what kinds of ways, and what they will be looking for—those are all to my mind subsidiary kinds of questions, but you know it's going to be there.

You do, also, have the fact of increasing international communities. People travel, they go from one culture and from one history to another. The world is becoming more interrelated, either directly through people transfer or indirectly

---

[1] The Berol Corporation manufactures a variety of office products including a wide range of writing instruments.
[2] Case writer and researcher, the Leading Edge Case Study Project, Lubin Graduate School of Business, Pace University.
[3] President, The Berol Corporation, Danbury, Conn.
[4] J. A. Quelch and E. J. Hoff, "Customizing Global Marketing," *Harvard Business Review*, May–June 1986, pp. 59–68.

through visual transfer, on a much more regular basis. Something that has already happened in Tokyo will be there for you to see on the six o'clock news. It sounds as though it's a long way between that phenomenon and whether or not you can sell the same pen in Japan and the United States. But I don't think it's as far-fetched as many have historically supposed when you stop and think about it.

There is no reason why the intervention of water should be a cutoff point between groups of people and their often similar characteristics.

CA: When you look at recent developments in the global business arena such as Rupert Murdoch's bid to establish a global communications empire and the growing concentration of the world's advertising agencies as evidenced by the rash of mergers and acquisitions which culminated with Saatchi & Saatchi's purchase of Ted Bates Worldwide, do you see an irreversible trend toward the globalization of business and, if so, what do you make of it?

DT: There probably is a trend and, certainly, the existence of a large number of international unifiers in various forms of communication is going to make it more possible for companies to entertain the notion of doing business internationally. Whether, however, businesses will look for over-homogenization and try to bring it about to make their own lives easier or simply to see a reflection of their own set of values cast on a worldwide stage remains to be seen. That's an area where I'm a little puzzled and, perhaps, a little concerned at this point in time. There are important shades, colors, and nuances in individual countries or regions or cultures whether those cultures happen to coincide or not with international boundaries. I am also not so sure that there won't be an encouragement or an enticement to make Parker pen type mistakes.

The economic incentive to homogenize the world is indeed very strong. It is also probably the natural route for the northern hemisphere in particular to counter demographics and broad scale cultural differences. There is more appeal to continue to do as you have done particularly if [the firm] has evolved to a "higher level." To look to do the same thing somewhere else is somehow more appealing than to go back two or three paces and start over in an emerging country or society and be successful doing the things you did ten or fifteen years ago.

Pure volume and demographic growth is likely to be much more concentrated in the southern hemisphere and the far east over the next twenty years or so. However, there are more concerns about political and societal stability in those kinds of arenas. They are more prone to political and economic volatility than they once were and they are no longer easy to colonize in the economic sense. They're more likely to pinch whatever technology they need, start their own businesses, and kick you out than used to be the case. You can't sit back and control the world from New York or London or Frankfurt as once you could. It's a more unruly place, therefore, we prefer to deal with safer and more secure boundaries which are spread across the northern hemisphere with digressions into the south when we consider it relatively safe. The trend that you've identified is partly a response to this way of thinking and that's how you can make the economic case for continuing to do what you are doing.

CA: In addition to making developing nations more technologically sophisticated, what are the broader implications of worldwide availability of and easy access to advanced technologies?

DT: Since there is more access to technology and much less in the way of protection and security around technologies and, because of the sheer length of life of many technologies and many basic product categories, the opportunity for capital substitution in place of human substitution has to a large extent already taken place. Therefore, there is a more even access to the various forms of production advantage—whether it be economies of scale, optimum size of plant and configuration, or an optimum form of technology. Quite simply, the thresholds for entry into many kinds of industries are not that great. And, certainly, the ability to maintain exclusivity or erect boundaries is nowhere near what it used to be. You cannot keep people out.

CA: Static demographics and markets, worldwide technological parity and converging product quality make it more important than ever to have a handle on your costs and to be efficient. Are we moving toward the day when only the largest and most highly efficient firms can afford to compete internationally?

DT: Yes. Unless you set out to be, and deliberately restrain your ambitions to very clearly identified and defensible niches of one kind or another. It's a very, I think, competent strategist and manager who can make a success of a totally niche-based strategy. Not many people can do that. Most companies simply cannot afford to.

I think you can afford to internationally extend some of the segmentation that you have already domestically achieved. For example, if you've got a particular product portfolio that has appeal in a certain market segment that you've historically concentrated on within your domestic base, it is sometimes easier to transfer that segmentation geographically than to add other segments to it domestically. By the same token, it is perhaps easier to extend yourself horizontally than to move vertically. Certainly to move up. It may not be easier to move down, as many people point out when evaluating Parker Pen's strategy.

I don't think that many people operating in product fields where differenti-

ation is possible yet not, for very long, sustainable either in terms of an individual product or a product category could follow a niche-based strategy. It's only the real late arrival to a market that, by default, has to pursue such a strategy. For the other players, I think there has to be a combination of capability to operate at the low-cost end and forms of niche-differentiation either in terms of market boundaries (segmentation) or in terms of product characteristics. Although the latter, as I say, are more difficult to sustain over time.

CA: Besides the problem of moving down the product line in the case of Parker Pen, many observers felt that the company's drastic shift from a largely decentralized organization to the more tightly controlled version that is necessary when implementing a classic global marketing strategy automatically ruled out the strategy's chances for success because it resulted in too much loss of employee morale on the local level. Do you see this as a problem in any company undergoing that same shift from a decentralized to a centralized organization?

DT: A lot depends on how you do it. The time scale that you negotiate to achieve [the strategic shift] with, either with your board or with your stockholders as opposed to with your managers, goes a long way toward determining success or failure. To achieve some of those things in terms of internal human scale often requires a longer commitment than might be available in terms of an external financial scale. There is probably an underlying sentiment that says, satisfy those external audiences and see if you can't sit on top of the internal ones . . . and, yes, if these guys don't like it, presumably there are others that are prepared to operate within that kind of a changed culture.

But I believe that, in Parker's instance, they probably put an impossible time scale on themselves to achieve the desired degree of change in acceptable human terms without precipitating unnecessary turnover. You see, a certain amount of turnover is not only to be expected but is probably necessary because the kinds of values and skills that you've looked for and rewarded in the truly decentralized operation may not be as valid or as useful in the more integrated approach. Particularly if you give the pendulum a big yank and a swing towards the other end you can expect the sheer momentum to throw people off from side to side. It's really a question of how many people did you lose that you didn't want to or that, at the end of the day, you couldn't afford to? This is more the measure of success or failure in implementing that kind of strategy.

And, finally, by what audacity do you believe that your insights, analytical abilities, creative talents, administrative skills and business acumen combine to make such a decision failure-proof? For the decision to come from an individual or a very small group of individuals, some of whom might be very new to that industry and to that marketplace . . . you've got to have a lot of reasons to justify having self-confidence in that small a pool of talent than what might have been available out of a goodly proportion of your previously successful decentralized managers. But if you have a French operation, for example, that had been losing money for quite a period of time or about whose management you have questions concerning their capability, you would have those questions whether the company was centralized or decentralized. The question is: How flexible are some of those domestic managers? They may learn, grow, and develop in some extraordinary ways by being exposed to the international world. So it's not that they're always right and the center is always wrong either.

CA: It seems as if Parker not only gave itself very little time to accomplish its transition from decentralization to centralization but that it also engaged in draconian measures on the operational side. I speak here of dropping all 40 of its advertising agencies in favor of a single "world class" agency. Can a single agency hope to be all things to all people or, in the case of Parker, do the job more effectively than a multitude of agencies?

DT: It depends on the advertising program that they come up with, which in turn depends on the degree of internationalism within the agency. I think one of the difficulties is that, historically at least, some of the worldwide agencies have been strongly oriented to their home countries—that is, wherever they started—be it the United States or Japan. There is a substantial difference between an American agency operating in France and a French agency, that has been fused to an American agency through acquisition, operating in France. Some advertising agencies, just like some multinationals, are unmistakably ethnocentric.

It's also a question of the extent to which certain appeals in relation to a product themselves are international. Some products lend themselves to a high degree of uniformity in terms of what it is that they will do and in terms of what it is that will appeal in relation to what they do. From one country to the next, you may well be able to have very easy local adaptation as long as you avoid some of the major cultural pitfalls. If, for example, there are visual symbols that are somewhat obscene in certain cultures and perfectly O.K. in others and you screen for those adequately, you may be able to get away with a high degree of uniformity. If you can, then I would think that the proportional level of local resistance would be that much lower. The question is whether local management thinks the program will work in terms of its market segment.

CA: Can a pen in the Parker price range which was generally moderate to expensive, be successfully marketed in uniform fashion from country to country?

DT: Let's try and pick it apart a little bit. You might have some elements of appeal in terms of a relatively uniform visual configuration. Whether that product performs as a fountain pen or a ballpoint or a felt-tip or a roller ball—that's easily variable from the inside out. You can have a common external configuration with a fair variety of tip, and therefore, performance variation coming out of it. So you could have an element of design uniformity that, given a fair degree of demand in whatever geographically international market segment you are targeting, should not compromise the product's appeal to different people.

The higher up you go in terms of price, the closer you get to a piece of personal jewelry or adornment, and the easier it is to market the product uniformly. In the higher segments it is purely an issue of cosmetics—whether the product, which you would want to be slim and elegant no matter the country, would be better in silver for that market or in gold for this market—these are second order questions. The real question is: Do people regard personal adornment with writing instruments as a way of expressing a level of achievement and status in their local community? If the answer is yes, then you can very easily market that product on an international scale. An interesting example might be Dunhill. Admittedly, their success has been on a limited international scale. Still, it is interesting to think how a tobacco seller gets into writing instruments and the fact that the same Dunhill pens are available in world-class cosmopolitan cities. This is a good example of a totally uniform product and presentation on an international scale in a particularly narrow market segment.

At the other end of the scale, you go right down to the commodity product and the same argument prevails for slightly different reasons. If what you are interested in is a very basic writing instrument to make a mark on paper you have two choices: Do you want to be able to make that mark and subsequently to change it, in which case you go predominantly for a wood-case pencil, or, do you want to be able to make it and have a certain amount of longevity associated with it, in which case you go for a ballpoint pen? These products are fairly basic, straightforward, and, I would say, uniform. As long as you take into account the lower, if not the lowest, common denominator in terms of writing surface and your ballpoint is able to operate on lower-quality paper as opposed to the finest bond, you can probably make, sell, and present the same product in India as you can in Ghana or in Peru because the basic consumer's need is uniform on a worldwide basis.

CA: Let's switch from marketing the product to producing it. As you know, Parker was beset by production woes before and after it marketed its products globally. How important is the production process in the pen industry in general and how far do you think faulty production went toward the undermining of its global marketing plan?

DT: Reliable consistency is important in that industry as in most. In Parker's instance, I think the very marked contrast between the new Parker and the old Parker in terms of production had as much of a disruptive effect as anything else. Secondly, I believe that very often people coming into any industry new, or relatively new, tend to shortchange the need to understanding manufacturing and technological processes. Such understanding enables managers to know with confidence what kinds of future commitments they can make and expect to meet. Historically, company takeover or turnaround specialists don't usually have strong personal background or interest in the manufacturing function. They tend to have spent their time in either marketing or finance rather than in manufacturing, so that function gets shortchanged.

I would suspect that the new Parker management didn't have the ability to look at the projections for the rationalization and re-equipment program and say: "Come on guys, you say you can do that in 15 months. Where is your Kentucky Windage Factor? Where are the critical delivery bottlenecks? How reliable are those suppliers? What has been their track record in terms of on-time delivery? What allowance has been made for de-bugging? Do we have people experienced with that kind of equipment? Are we getting equipment that's new to the suppliers as well as new to our own production people? In which case, you should probably build a safety factor into the de-bugging period rather than just the shortest possible time to get it done." I'm probably beginning to sound like a cracked record, but it points out the need to know what is realistic and achieveable. This is never going to be satisfactory, but at least you know how much time things should be taking and then how much you're compromising, as opposed to how much you don't know you're overpromising to yourself or to other people.

NAME INDEX

Harper, Earl, 202n
Harrigan, Kathryn Rudie, 294
Harrigan, Richard, 379n
Harris, Philip R., 134, 269n
Hartz, C. Scott, 347
Hassan, Salah S., 233n, 235n, 272
Hayes, Michael, 693n
Heath, Daniel, 230
Heenan, David A., 294, 327n,
      328n, 349
Hendon, Donold W., 116
Hendon, Robert Augelea, 116n
Henzler, Herbert A., 320
Herbig, Paul A., 135
Herrera, Julio, 294
Hertzfeld, Jeffrey M., 349
Heslop, Louise A., 364, 366n, 382
Heston, Alan, 74n, 230
Hicks, Jonathan P., 285n
Hiebing, Roman G., Jr., 62
Higashi, Chikara, 265n
Hildebrand, Terry, 368n
Hill, Charles W.L., 294
Hill, David, 135
Hill, John S., 103n, 119n, 134,
      222n, 382
Hill, Julie Skur, 447n
Hills, W. Daniel, 320
Hoff, F.J., 57n, 729
Hoffman, Peter, 439
Holbein, James R., 174
Hollander, Stanley C., 417n
Holtzmann, Howard, 174
Honeycutt, Earl D., Jr., 135
Honnold, John, 174
Hotchkiss, Carolyn, 138n
Hotstede, Geert, 119n
Hoy, Harold J., 62
Huang Yunxian, 681, 682
Huey, John, 281n
Hulbert, James M., 59-60
Hultoy, Mary Ann, 643n
Hunter, Brian, 257n
Hunter, Donald, 242n
Huszagh, Sandra, 488n, 489
Hwang, Peter, 294

I

Imgruth, Max, 579-80, 584, 589
Inamori, Kazuo, 420
Ingrassia, Paul, 195n
Issak, Robert A., 100

J

Jackson, 139n
Jacobs, Laurence W., 135
Jacquemin, Alexis, 321
Jaffe, Eugene D., 230, 365
Jaikumar, Jay, 135
James, Harvey S., 293
James, William L., 382
Janzen, 275n
Jarillo, J. Carlos, 349
Jatusripitak, Sol'Kid, 294
Javagli, Rajshekhar G., 443n
Jenkins, John R.G., 677n
Joachimsthaler, Erich, 262n
Johansson, Johnny K., 366n, 382
Johnson, Gerald A., 349
Johnson, Thomas E., 472n
Johnston, C.B., 616n
Jones, Daniel T., 320
Jones, Kevin K., 331n
Jordan, Ann, 134
Jorde, Thomas M., 349
Joyce, Romy, 537n, 538n
Joynt, Pat, 134
Jung, Carl, 106
Justis, Robert T., 293

K

Kang Qiushun, 681
Kang, T.W., 134
Kanso, Ali, 438
Karinch, Maryann, 655
Katsanis, Prevel, 233n
Katzenbach, Jon R., 502n
Kaufman, Colin, 143n, 174
Kaynak, Erdener, 275n, 413n, 414,
      420n
Keegan, Warren J., 202n, 207n,
      366, 382, 557n, 564n, 579n,
      721n
Kelly, John M., 230
Kendall, Suan, 263n
Kenessey, Zoltan, 230
Kennedy, Carol, 538n, 539n
Kennedy, Paul, 100
Keown, Charles F., 135
Kernan, Jerome B., 434
Ketelhorn, Werner, 349
Keynes, John Maynard, 178, 179
Kim, W.C., 294
Kindleberger, Charles P., 204

Kiplinger, Austin H., 230
Kiplinger, Knight A., 230
Kishii,, 443
Kissin, Warren D., 294
Kobrin, Stephen J., 129n
Kodama, Fumio, 349
Koepfler, Edward R., 294
Kogut, Bruce, 294
Kollat, D.T., 134
Kopp, Hermann, 671
Korth, Christopher M., 469n
Kotabe, Masaaki, 382
Kramer, Hugh E., 135
Kravis, Irving B., 100, 230
Kreiger, Abba M., 272
Kreiger, Andrew, 179n
Krugman, Paul R., 230
Kruybosch, Carla, 349
Kuczmarski, Thomas D., 373, 382
Kuhn, Thomas, 548
Kuznets, S.S., 79
Kvint, Vladimir, 135

L

Lafili, Louis, 293
Lambert, Daniel, 646n, 647n
Lane, Henry, 242n, 368n
Langeard, Eric, 230
Lardner, James, 306n, 390n
Lauritano, Paul, 320
Lavidge, Robert J., 689n
Lawrence, Paul, 341n, 349
Lee, Chong S., 294
Lee, James, 109
Lee, Thomas H., 320
Lei, David, 333n, 349
Lessard, Donald, 197
Lester, Richard K., 320
Levin, Doron P., 279n
Levin, Gary, 440n
Levitt, Ted, 437
Levitt, Theodore H., 14, 104-5,
      234, 353, 438
Lewis, Arthur W., 100
Lewis, Jordan D., 349
Li Dali, 677, 680, 681, 682, 684
Li Jiatao, 321
Lin, Carolyn, A., 135
Lindberg, Bertil C., 230
Lindsey, Jennifer, 348
Liotard-Vogt, Pierre, 437
Lipman, Joanne, 436n

Vogel, R.H., 231
Volcker, Paul, 178n
Voss, Bristol, 350

W

Walmsley, Jane, 134
Walter, Ingo, 197
Walters, Peter G.P., 383
Walton, Richard, 349
Wang Huan, 681
Wang Xin, 677n
Warner, Malcolm, 134
Wasilewski, Nikolai, 231
Wayne, Leslie, 362n
Webster, Frederick E, Jr., 6n
Weekly, James K., 230
Weichmann, Ulrich, 56n
Weidenbaum, Murray L., 293, 320
Weinberger, Marc G., 444n
Weitz, Richarn N., 442n
Wells, Ken, 431n, 433n

Wells, Louis T, Jr., 37n, 504n, 519, 521
Werner, Steve, 320
Westney, D.E., 320
Wever, Kirsten S., 350
Wheelwright, Steven C., 321
White, Robert M., 320
Whitwam, David, 504
Wigle, Randy, 395n
Wilemon, David, 383
Williams, Jeffrey R., 321
Wilson, Gary, 559
Wind, Yoram, 62, 295
Witmeger, D., 117n
Wolfe, Bonnie Heineman, 272
Womack, James P., 320
Wortel, Shari Ann, 616n
Worthley, Reginal, 135
Wright, Richard W., 40n
Wright, W., 284n
Wysocki, Bernard, Jr., 335n

Y

Yablonsky, Dennis, 350
Yamada, Haru, 134
Yang Decong, 686
Yang, Yoo S., 293, 295, 503n
Yellin, Susan, 355n
Yoder, Stephen Kreider, 326n
Yoshida, Kosaku, 350
Yoshino, Michael Y., 295
Yu Bingqing, 681, 682

Z

Zachary, G. Pascal, 326n
Zappacosta, Pierluigi, 649, 651, 654, 660-61, 652. 664
Zhou Hongyou, 681

SUBJECT INDEX

ence system, 248-49
Broker, as indirect sales agent, 413
Brown Boveri, 537
Brussels tariff nomenclature (BTN), 474-75
Budgets, influences on marketing, 525-27

C

C.I.F. (cost, insurance, freight), 392-93
Cadbury Beberages Ltd., 126
Cadbury-Schweppes, 618, 619
Call option, 193
Calvin Klein, 246
Camel, 15
Campbell Soup, 125, 367
Canada
  advertising expenditures, 444, 451
  aerospace industry, 647-48
  export support services, 469-71
  export-dependent economy, 463
  exporters, 463-65
  trade commissioner, 468, 470
Canada Life Styles Inc., 236
Canada-U.S. Auto Pact, 279
Canada-U.S. Memorandum of Understanding, 164
Canadair Inc., 647
Canadian Foremost, 304, 390
Canadian high-tech companies, 466
Canadian Institute of Chartered Accountants (CICA), 190
Canadian International Trade Tribunal (CITT), 576
Canadian softwood lumber, 394-95, 472
Canadian Tire Corp., 368, 418
CANCON Corp., Ltd., 621
Canon, 301, 308, 375
CanWest Communications Corp., 335
Capital resources factors, 313
Caribbean Community and Common Market (CARICOM), 252-53
Carrefour, 418
Carrefours, 206
Cascades Inc., 335-36
Cases
  A.S. Norlight, 671-74
  aerospace industry, 646-48

Choufont-Salva, Inc., 591-606
Club Med, Inc., 546-74
Curtis Automotive Hoist, 607-16
Euro Disney, 557-64
Fortron International Inc., 664-70
Grasse Fragrances S.A., 693-703
I.M.P. Group Limited, 643-45
Logitech, 649-64
Metro Corporation, 627-32
Neilson International, 616-26
Odysseus, Inc., 633-42
Parker Pen Co., 721-34
Special Import Measures Act, 574-79
Swatch Watch U.S.A., 579-89
transnational companies, 555-56
Wuhan Art and Advertising Company, 677-92
Cash in advance, 487, 603
Casio, 587
Casti Connubii, 605
Caterpillar, 46, 305, 306
Central American Common Market (CACM), 253
Champion Road Machinery, 398
Chance, competitive advantage and, 317
Chanel, 234, 245
Channel agents, 410, 423-24
Channel structure, 393, 415-20
  consumer products, 415-17
  global retail channels, 417-19
  industrial products, 419-20
Channels, distribution, 408-428
  channel utility, 408
  constraints, 410-15
  defined, 408
  environmental characteristics and, 414-15
  indirect sales agents, 412-14
  innovation in retail channels, 422-23
  intermediaries in, 411-12, 421
  in Japan, 424-26
  in less developed countries, 420-22
  new market entry strategy, 423-26
  objectives, 409-410
  rationalization of structure, 393
Charybdis Metallfabrik GmbH (CMF), 637-38
China, 140, 467, 621
  advertising in, 667-679
  direct selling in, 415

China International Advertising Corporation, 679
Choufont-Salva, Inc., 591-606
Chrysanthemum and the Sword, The (Benedict), 105
Chrysler, 48, 195
Chrysler Canada, 463
Ciba-Geigy, 152, 400
Clearing account barter, 489
Closed-end barter, 489
Club Med, 439, 546-74
Club of Rome, 504
Cluster analysis, 223
Clustering, 31-32
Coca-Cola, 25, 57, 58, 104, 281, 300, 400, 432, 434, 439, 557
Cold war, end of, 66
Colgate, 433-34
Palmolive Co., 46-47, 152, 207
Collaboration
  competitive advantage through, 308
  See also Global strategic partnerships (GSPs)
Combustion Engineering (CE), 16, 537
Command allocation system, 67
Commercial Fan Moteur (CFM) International, 335
Communicability of innovation, 112
Communication(s)
  as driving force, 15
  intercultural, 116
Communications media in selected countries, 210
Communism, collapse of, 65, 66, 542
Companie Nationale de Pharmacie, S.A., 598
Company-owned outlets, 410
Compaq, 375
Comparative advantage, theory of, 11-13
Comparative analysis, 380-81
Comparative analysis in market research, 222
Compatibility
  of innovation, 112
  product design and, 362-63
  targeting based on, 245
Compensatory import taxes, 477
Competence centers, 60
Competition, forces influencing, 297-301
Competition Law

In-house export organizations, 484-85
Incipient demand, 212, 213, 214
Income elasticity, 84
    measurements, 219-20
Incoterms, 167, 168, 169
Independent marketing adit, 532
Indicative planning method, 526-27
Indirect sales agents, 412-14
Individual Export Permit (IEP), 471
Indonesia, 154
Industrialized countries, 70-72, 80
Industrializing countries, 70-72
Inflation, and pricing, 395-96
Information acquisition, 46
Information, sources of, 203-205
Information subject agenda, 199-201
Infrastructure, resource, 313
Innovation
    characteristics of, 111-12
    diffusion of, 110-13
Instrument equivalence, 216
Intellectual property laws, 151-52, 153
Intellectual property piracy, 165
Interaction effect, 113
Interest stage in adoption process, 111
Internal (self-) audit, 532
International business law
    international rules, 139-45
    legal issues, 149-63
    market entry, 147-49
    national rules, 137-38
    obstacles to the international trade in intangibleservices, 171-73
    product, 145-47
    services, 170-73
    strategic importance, 145-63
International business, underlying forces of, 18-23
International Centre for the Settlement of Investment Disputes, 140, 141, 143, 155
International Chamber of Commerce (ICC), 143
International commercial law, 143-45
    major instruments, 144
International Comparison Project (ICP), 74
International Construction and Engineering (ICE), 627,

628, 631-32
International corporations, 42-43
International divisional structure, 505, 506
International economic law, 139
International Institute for the Unification of Private Law (UNIDROIT), 143
International Marketing (Samli, Still and Hill), 119n
International Monetary Fund (IMF), 20, 139, 141, 149, 150, 172, 179, 180
International products, 355
International rules, 139-45
    capital and investment values, 142-43
    instrument and scope, 140-41
    international monetary rules, 142
    nature and enforceability, 139
    public law of international business, 139-43
    trade rules, 141-42
Invention, product, 371
Invention/geocentric pricing policy, 404-405
Investment
    productivity and, 150
    standards, 125, 361
Ireland, 613
Italy, 613, 614

J

J. Sainsbury, 126
J. Walter Thompson, 447
J.C. Penney, 584
J.P. Morgan, 29
Jacob Suchard, 618
Japan, 433, 467, 620
    advertising style, 442-43
    agricultural goods, 468
    business behavior, 120
    Canada, differences, 265
    company organizations, 521-22
    global advertising agencies, 447
    "Large Scale Retail Store Law," 418
    manufacturer-owned stores, 417
    MITI, 467
    motorcycle industry, 214
    pricing strategy, 388
    revaluation of yen, 397
    7-eleven stores, 423
    trading company, 425-26

John Deere, 398
Joint ventures, 157, 283-84, 402-403
Jolly Green Giant, 112

K

Keiretsu, 264, 336-39
Kellogg's, 367, 380
Kennedy round. See GATT
Kentucky Fried Chicken, 442
Knowledge
    as asset, 227
    interaction with information, 199
    international marketing skill, 225
    trading house and, 278
Knowledge resources factors, 313
Komatsu, 305, 306
Korea, 467, 581, 620
    global advertising agencies, 447
KPMG Corporate Finance, 326
Kraft, 440
KYE (Genius), 649, 656, 658
Kyocera Corporation, 419-20

L

La Societe Franco-Canadien des Papiers, 336
Landor Associates, 432
Latent demand, 212, 213, 214
Latin America
    business behavior, 120
    nations, 118-19
Latin America Free Trade Area (LAFTA), 75
Laura Ashley, 236, 418
Laura Biagiotti, 246
Layers of competitive advantage, 306-307
Leadership, 501-502
Legal Guide to International Business Transactions (Raworth),137n
Lenwest, 283
Less developed countries, 270-71
Letters of credit, 486
Leverage as driving force, 15-16
Levi Strauss & Co., 104, 374, 432
Licensing, 281-82
    case study on, 627-32
    problems with, 155-57
Lifestyle groups among Euroconsumers, 239-40
LIFO (last-in, first-out) costing method, 396

global strategies, 387-95
and government controls and subsidies, 397-98
and internal organizational considerations, 386-87
Japanese approach, 388
and market demand, 398
market-holding strategy, 390-91
market-skimming (price-skimming) strategy, 389-90
objectives, 388-93
penetration pricing, 390
problems with, 160-61
sourcing as strategic tool, 393
transfer, 161, 399-403
Print, advertising, 444, 445, 450
Private law of international business, 143-45
    instrument and scope, 143, 145
    nature and enforceability, 143
Privitization, 67
Pro Set, 621
Procter & Gamble, 246, 309, 370, 386, 395, 430
Procurement policies, 473
Product cultures, 431
Product diversification, 477
Product fit, 482
Product life cycle, 36-38
Product trade-cycle model, 37-41
Product-market profile, 478
Products, 353-81
    attitude toward foreign, 363-66
    classifications, 354-55
    complementary, 359
    defined, 353
    design, 359-63
    global brands, 357-58
    international business law, 145-47
    saturation levels, 89, 359
    strategic alternatives for geographical expansion, 366-72, 376
    See also New products
Psychographic segmentation, 236-40
Public law of international business, 139-43
Publicity, 430
Purchasing, 49
Purchasing agent, 497
Purchasing power parity (PPP), 184-87, 386

Q

Quality as driving force, 15
Questionnaires, 216-17
Quotas, and trade control, 472

R

Radio, advertising, 444, 445
Ralston Purina, 285
Raytheon, 328
RCA, 306
Regional Free Trade Agreement (RFTA), 21-22
Regional management centers, 508-512
Regional market characteristics, 248-70
    Africa, 269-70
    Asia/Pacific, 263-66
    Eastern Europe, 261-62
    Latin America, 267-68
    Middle East, 268-69
    North America, 262-63
    Oceania, 266
    Western Europe, 259-60
    world statistics by region, 258-59
Regional trade agreements, 21-22
Regression analysis, 223-25
Relative advantage of innovation, 111-12
Renault, 374
Rent-A-Wreck, 108
Resource utilization, 16
Restraining forces, 16-18
Restrictive administrative and technical regulations, 473
Restrictive customs procedures, 473
Revaluation, 396-97
Revenue Canada. *See* Department of National Revenue
Revlon International, 245, 246
RJR-Nabisco, 15, 48
Roche, 400
Rolex, 234a
Rome Convention, 140, 151
Russia, 140
    direct selling in, 415
    distribution of bread, 411
    PepsiCo barter deals, 488-89

S

S.C. Johnson Son, 426
Sabritas, 616, 622-23
Safety needs, 107, 108n
Saks Fifth Avenue, 584

Salamander AG, 283
Sale of Goods Act, 138
Sales promotions, 430
Sampling, 217-18
Sandoz, 29
Sanwa, 337
Saudi Arabia, 444, 445-46
Scale, economies of, 16
Scales, 211
Scanning, 46, 201
Scanning modes, 201-202
Schick, 439
Scylla A.A., 637-38
Seagrams, 334, 439
Search scanning mode for marketing research, 201, 202, 208
Sears, 584
Secretariat for Central American Economic Integration (SIECA), 253
Segmentation, global market, 31-32, 233-43
    behavior, 240-43
    benefit, 243
    defined, 233
    demographic, 234-36
    psychographic, 236-40
Segmentation, subcultural
    American consumers, 242
    China's potential consumers, 244
    differences between Canadians and Americans, 239, 242-43
Selective monetary controls, 473
Self-actualization meeds, 108
self-reference criterion, 109-110, 115, 131
Service trade, 170, 171-73
7-Eleven, 418, 423
Share-of-market data, 527
Sharp, 391
Sheaffer, 722
Shipping Cost, 481
Shop America in-store catalog, 423
Siemens AG, 328, 345
Singapore, 467, 581, 621
Single-column tariff, 475
Siren Ltd., 636
Societe Suisse pour l'Industrie Horiogere (SSIH), 580, 583
Softwood lumber. *See* Canadian softwood lumber
Soga-sosha (general trading company), 426